Kilo Uniform Sierra 3rd Substitute 9

MARINER'S GUIDE TO NAUTICAL INFORMATION

Priscilla Travis

CORNELL MARITIME PRESS
A Division of Schiffer Publishing, Ltd.
4880 Lower Valley Road, Atglen, PA 19310

DEDICATION

The *Mariner's Guide* is dedicated to
Hal and Margaret Roth
who inspired me and countless other sailors for more than 30 years, and to **Ted Brewer** who designed a wonderful sailboat that takes me across the seas. I'm also grateful to family, friends, and students who have sailed with me, sharing their skills and knowledge and asking the many questions that formed the idea for this book.

Photo credits: All photos and illustrations are by the author, with the exception of the two photos of U.S. Coast Guard 47-ft. motor lifeboats. These were taken by U.S. Coast Guard Petty Officer 3rd Class Erik Swenson, and are used by permission of the U.S. Coast Guard.

Library of Congress Control Number: 2011930978

Designed by Mark David Bowyer
Type set in Trajan Pro / Zurich BT

ISBN: 978-0-87033-625-6
Printed in China

Schiffer Books are available at special discounts for bulk purchases for sales promotions or premiums. Special editions, including personalized covers, corporate imprints, and excerpts can be created in large quantities for special needs. For more information contact the publisher:

Published by Schiffer Publishing Ltd.
4880 Lower Valley Road
Atglen, PA 19310
Phone: (610) 593-1777; Fax: (610) 593-2002
E-mail: Info@schifferbooks.com

For the largest selection of fine reference books on this and related subjects, please visit our website at **www.schifferbooks.com**
We are always looking for people to write books on new and related subjects. If you have an idea for a book please contact us at the above address.

This book may be purchased from the publisher.
Include $5.00 for shipping.
Please try your bookstore first.
You may write for a free catalog.

In Europe, Schiffer books are distributed by
Bushwood Books
6 Marksbury Ave.
Kew Gardens
Surrey TW9 4JF England
Phone: 44 (0) 20 8392 8585; Fax: 44 (0) 20 8392 9876
E-mail: info@bushwoodbooks.co.uk
Website: www.bushwoodbooks.co.uk

CONTENTS

ACKNOWLEDGMENTS

My sincere thanks go to the following people who assisted in the development and preparation of this book with their advice, expertise, and support.

John Adey, Director, Technical Department, American Boat and Yacht Council

Ted Brewer, Naval Architect, Brewer Yacht Designs, Ltd. *Permission to quote and paraphrase from his books and website.*

Skip Burdon, President and CEO, American Boat and Yacht Council

Jerry Cardarelli, Vice-President, BoatU.S Towing Services. *Permission to quote salvage contract information from the BoatU.S. website.*

Vincent Duke, Oceanireland. *Permission to use the compass pivot wear quotation.*

Captain Mary Ann DeGraw

Al Golden, President and Agent, International Marine Insurance Services, Inc.®

PA2 Brandyn Hill, U.S. Coast Guard Public Affairs Detachment Baltimore. *Permission to use U.S. Coast Guard photographs of 47-foot motor lifeboats.*

Pat Kearns, Owner, Recreational Marine Experts Group, Inc.

Dave McKone, G4DRX. *UK radio licensing information.*

Dan Nowlan, Offshore Director, US Sailing. *Permission to use the Safety at Sea Seminar material from the website.*

CDR Brian Roche, Deputy Commander, U.S. Coast Guard Sector Baltimore

Hal and Margaret Roth

Steve K4CJX. *Permission to quote from the Winlink website.*

Fred and Marilyn Sirasky

Gregory Zinga, M.D

INTRODUCTION

This modern nautical reference is intended for the complete novice and for those who are already enjoying time afloat. There are no presumptions about the reader's familiarity with nautical matters. If you don't know the pointy end from the square end or what an anchor is, the really basic things are in here. People with some experience on the water will find new things to learn and discover new aspects of the familiar. The book is arranged alphabetically to give easy access to words and topics. The reader will detect a bias toward cruising under sail because that's been my experience. However, cruising isn't defined by the type of boat, its size or where you go. You can have a great cruise around a lake, explore a bay, venture along the coast or go offshore under sail and power. It's an activity for all who take pleasure afloat.

Use the book for browsing or for studying a particular topic area. Keep it handy when reading nautical books or articles that may not explain enough; it will help fill in the blanks. As a self-test, choose a topic area from the *Topic Index* and see how many words and concepts you already know. Spoken language and slang is infrequently explained, unless you ask the speaker, so you'll also find examples and explanations of spoken language. There are many cross-references, which are indicated by words in small capitals.

The book has basic, commonly-understood definitions. There may be several ways to define or explain some nautical words and concepts. Sailors are an opinionated lot and understandings vary among mariners. As you learn you'll be able to comprehend the subtle differences. Not everything you encounter will be used correctly, as you'll discover, and sailors in different countries may have variations of these definitions. If you sail with an international crew, check that the words mean the same to everyone aboard.

The Navigation Rules figure prominently in the book. Learning the Rules is one of the most important steps toward becoming a safe and competent mariner. Memory aids are included to help you learn. Reading only the Navigation Rules entries in this book is *definitely not a substitute* for a thorough mastery of the Rules themselves.

Safety is emphasized throughout. We all want to have a good time on the water and return home with all the fingers we started with, nothing in a sling or a cast, and memories that don't include a visit to the hospital. The emphasis on safety isn't intended to discourage you from enjoying being on the water but the fact remains. There are factors that create inherent risk, and thinking about ways to prevent and deal with dangerous situations will help you take control and manage emergencies that do arise.

Governments issue safety regulations and many organizations worldwide work to develop safety standards for recreational and commercial vessels and equipment. So many variables affect safety afloat that just having all the required and recommended equipment does not ensure safety. If you're a DIY person, safety is important in many types of repair, upgrade, and renovation activities. Regulations and standards don't prevent accidents; they're guidelines, not guarantees. The ultimate responsibility rests with the vessel operator and crew.

The technical entries give a summary of a topic or technique; consult books and articles for detailed and sometimes different instructions. Not all technical information is applicable to all vessels or situations. The explanations of these topics are intended for a general reader, rather than a specialist, who may have a different or more comprehensive perspective. The bibliography has a selection of technical reference books, articles, and websites that provide thorough discussions of these topics. If you're in doubt about technical matters, consult a marine professional.

If you're a fan of 18th century naval matters, the square-rigger days, wooden vessels, or commercial or naval ships, there are specialized reference works devoted to these topics. If you're a racing sailor, you'll have some different terms and definitions; that vocabulary is rich and ever-changing.

Why learn the nautical lingo? You can say "pull that rope" or "tie it to that metal thing on the dock" or "turn to the right." Using the correct language and having a general understanding of concepts is important because in many circumstances quick, accurate communication is essential. There may not be time to explain in detail. Nautical language can be very precise or annoyingly imprecise. That's what makes it interesting to learn.

Whether you're just starting out in boating activities, enjoying weekends afloat, contemplating extended cruising or planning to cross an ocean there are many things in here that will help you become more competent, confident, and comfortable afloat. Fair winds and smooth seas deliver boundless pleasure, but when things get blustery and bumpy, you'll be glad you read the book and have it on your shelf.

Mariner's Guide

A

Abbreviations:

ft = foot or feet
GHz = gigahertz
GPS = global positioning system or receiver
in = inches
kHz = kilohertz
kn = knot or knots
m = meter or meters
mb = millibar or millibars
MHz = megahertz
NM = nautical mile or miles

Note: Quotation marks denote spoken language.
Cross references are indicated by words in SMALL CAPITALS.

24-hour time, military time – clock time expressed in four digits, without using a.m. or p.m. 0815, 1142, 1435, 2210. Noon is 1200, one minute after noon is 1201. Exact midnight is 0000. One minute after midnight is 0001. It's standard practice to use 24-hour time in the ship's log and when speaking on a radiotelephone.

200-mile limit – indicates an exclusive economic zone (EEZ), which is a protected area of the ocean under the control of a country. The zone extends from the coast out 200NM, with some variations. A state controls the rights to fishing and mineral exploitation in its EEZ. The 200-mile EEZ was established under the United Nations Convention on the LAW OF THE SEA in 1982. The Law of the Sea Convention also established the concept of the TERRITORIAL SEA.

500mb chart, constant pressure chart – a weather chart based on measurements taken in the upper atmosphere where the average barometric pressure is 500mb. The 500mb level is the location of the JET STREAM. Winds at this level drive the surface weather, and thus the 500mb chart is an important predictor of what will happen at sea level. The height of this constant pressure area averages approximately 5,600m/18,000ft, but it can be lower or higher, depending on the temperature of the atmosphere. It's higher in a warm atmosphere and lower in a cold one. Small numbers on the *contour lines* indicate the heights above the earth in meters; these lines are not ISOBARS. See the bibliography under "Weather" for resources with explanations of the 500mb chart and how to use it.

"A" suffix, VHF radio channel – in the U.S. some VHF channels have the letter "A" after the number (e.g., 22A) which indicates SIMPLEX use of the *ship station* transmit side of an international DUPLEX channel. The operations on an A channel are different than international operations on the channel. Newer VHF radios have a "U.S.-Canadian-International" (or U.S./Int'l) button/switch to change the radio for the country. "A" channels are generally used only in the U.S., and their use is normally not recognized or allowed outside the U.S. The letter "B" indicates simplex use of the *coast station* transmit side of an international duplex channel. The U.S. does not currently use "B" channels for simplex communications in this band. *See* "B" SUFFIX.

aback – when the wind comes from the "back side" of a sail (the side opposite to where the wind was coming from at first) the sail is aback or taken aback, or the vessel is taken aback.

abaft – behind a particular object or part of the vessel and toward the STERN. "Abaft the MAST." (the word "of" is not used with abaft).

abaft the beam – a RELATIVE BEARING of more than 90° to the CENTERLINE of the vessel.

abandon ship – to leave the vessel in an extreme emergency, and take to a LIFE RAFT, lifeboat, or to go into the water in FLOTATION CLOTHING or lifejacket. Consider abandoning ship only after very careful analysis of the circumstances. Of course, an uncontrolled fire, an explosion or rapid sinking requires immediate action. Stay with or near the vessel, if at all possible, because search-and-rescue will be able to find you more easily, and staying aboard the vessel (even if she's awash) is more comfortable (in relative terms) than being tossed around in a life raft. There are a number of stories about abandoned yachts being found days, weeks or months later, still afloat. Abandon ship only when you have to step up into the life raft, unless the danger is immediate! Have an ABANDON SHIP KIT and an ABANDON SHIP PROCEDURE. If you sail only near land the kit can be basic.

abandon ship kit, ditch kit – a bag, usually made of flotation material, that contains items necessary for survival in a LIFE RAFT. Some commercial bags have supplies and others are empty. An offshore kit is more extensive than a kit for an inshore vessel. Put a rope on the handles so it can be tied on deck and in the life raft. A raft comes with some survival gear packed inside, but it's usually not very comprehensive, even if it's called the "offshore package." There are lists of recommended contents for the ditch bag in yacht cruising books, marine equipment catalogs, and on websites. Make sure the bag isn't too heavy to lift or float: commercial bags suggest a weight limit. It may never be used, except in an ABANDON SHIP DRILL, but outfit the kit properly and check its contents every season. See the next entry.

abandon ship procedure – the very last resort. Assign everyone a task for abandoning ship when doing the SAFETY CHECKOUT. Have a written EMERGENCY PROCEDURE CARD. The general procedure is:

• Account for all crew. Everyone put on lifejackets or FLOTATION CLOTHING, if available. Put on extra clothing, if there's time. Even if you're in the tropics it will be cold in the water or in the life raft.

• Broadcast MAYDAY on all appropriate transmitting devices: EPIRB, VHF/DSC radio, SINGLE-SIDEBAND, satellite phone, etc.

• If in sight of land or another vessel, use DISTRESS SIGNALS appropriate for day or night.

• Put the SHIP'S PAPERS into the ABANDON SHIP KIT (keep all papers in a waterproof envelope).

• Put the abandon ship kit on deck. Tie it on until it's put into the life raft.

• Put the supply of FLARES on deck (keep them in one container).

• Put the EMERGENCY WATER SUPPLY on deck and tie it on.

• If there is time, gather extra water, food, and clothing and put in a bag. Put the bag on deck.

• Prepare the life raft for deployment; tie the raft's PAINTER securely to a strong point on deck before throwing it overboard.

• Launch the life raft. Put abandon ship kit, spare water, food, flares, and clothing into raft.

• Keep the raft painter tied to the boat until she starts to go down; have a knife ready to cut the rope. A raft tied to a vessel is easier to spot from the air or from another vessel, and the boat may float awash for a long time or not sink at all.

• Distribute seasickness medication to everyone, whether they feel ill or not.

• Do not drink water for the first 24 hours.

• Inventory the contents of the raft's survival kit and the abandon ship kit.

• Stay occupied; post a rotating lookout, give everyone a task.

In some rescue circumstances the crew may participate in a HELICOPTER ASSIST.

abeam, broad on the beam, on the beam – at a right angle (90°) to the CENTERLINE of the vessel. "Turn onto the new course when the lighthouse is abeam."

ablative paint, copolymer paint – a soft ANTI-FOULING paint that renews its protection by wearing away in the water and releasing fresh biocide. Good for vessels that don't need a super-smooth bottom.

aboard – on a vessel. *See* CLOSE ABOARD.

ABS – abbreviation for the AMERICAN BUREAU OF SHIPPING, a marine CLASSIFICATION SOCIETY.

ABYC® – abbreviation for the AMERICAN BOAT AND YACHT COUNCIL, a marine safety standards organization.

AC, alternating current – electrical current that flows first in one direction in a circuit and then reverses and flows in the other direction. One complete change is one HERTZ (Hz). The number of changes per second is the frequency.

In North America and some other countries AC is 120 VOLTS/60Hz. In many parts of the world AC is 220 or 230 volts/50Hz. 230 volts is the EU standard. AC is supplied by shore power, a GENERATOR, or an INVERTER. The abbreviation AC is usually used instead of the words. The relevant ABYC standard is E-11 AC and DC Electrical Systems on Boats.

AC panel – an electrical panel on a boat where the switches (or CIRCUIT BREAKERS) that control various AC circuits are located. Some switches might include a BATTERY CHARGER, refrigerator, air conditioner, cabin lights, etc. An electric cable from shore is connected to a SHORE POWER INLET on the boat. Not all boats have AC power aboard.

AC wiring – all wiring for AC power should be installed, replaced, or repaired to meet the standards and accepted safe practices for marine wiring. The relevant ABYC Standard is E-11 AC and DC Electrical Systems on Boat. *See* WIRE, ELECTRICAL, MARINE USE.

accident reporting – in the U.S., if there's an accident on the water, under the following circumstances the operator of the vessel or vessels must file a boating accident report with the state boating authority:

- A person dies.
- A person disappears from the vessel under circumstances that indicate death or injury.
- A person is injured and requires medical treatment beyond first aid.
- Damage to vessels or property of $2,000 or more (lower limits in some states).
- A boat is destroyed.

If the vessel operator dies or is unable to report the accident, the owner is responsible for making the report (unless the owner was the operator). See the bibliography under "Safety" for a link to a blank copy of an accident reporting form that's accepted by most states. The report should be filed within 48 hours for a fatal accident or 10 days for a non-fatal accident. In some accidents the Coast Guard or police will be involved and may give additional instructions.

accommodation, the – (used in the singular) the cabin area; the living space below decks.

accumulator tank – a plastic or metal tank used in a pressure water system. Its purpose is to maintain pressure in the water lines and reduce the cycling of the water pump. Commercial accumulator tanks are available, or there are DIY instructions to make one. An accumulator tank is also used in some refrigeration systems.

accuracy of charts – *see* CHART ACCURACY.

accuracy of electronic navigation – *see* GPS ACCURACY and ELECTRONIC NAVIGATION ACCURACY.

accuracy of GPS – *see* GPS ACCURACY.

active metal – *see* METAL, ACTIVE.

adjustment, compass – *see* COMPASS ADJUSTMENT.

Admiralty Law, maritime law – the body of law that deals with maritime legal issues and cases on the seas, which include bays, rivers, and lakes connected to the seas. The term is derived from The Admiralty, the department of the British government formerly in charge of the Royal Navy.

adrift – (1) not at anchor, moored or attached to the shore. The word implies being not under control. However, a vessel adrift or drifting is UNDERWAY, according to the definition in Rule 3(i) of the NAVIGATION RULES. (2) something that is loose, not tied down. "The sailbag came adrift when we took GREEN WATER over the FOREDECK."

advance and transfer – terms applied to the movement of a ship, but it's useful for a small vessel operator to understand the concepts when navigating near moving ships. Advance is the distance a ship travels on her initial course from the time the HELM is put over until she settles on her new course. Transfer is the distance a ship travels perpendicular to her initial course when she makes a turn. In practical terms, this means that when a ship turns she takes up more room than just the turn itself. Stay well clear of a moving ship.

advection fog – *see* FOG, ADVECTION.

aft – toward the STERN.

afterguy, guy – a control line used on a SPINNAKER POLE to adjust the FORE-AND-AFT angle of the pole, and thus the shape and effectiveness of the SPINNAKER. The line runs from the WINDWARD CLEW of the spinnaker, through the jaws on the outboard end of the pole, and back to the COCKPIT.

aground, grounding – when a vessel's keel is touching or resting on the bottom she is aground. There are degrees of being aground: hard aground (FAST aground) means that the boat is firmly aground or stuck. When a vessel goes aground (takes the ground) she has suffered a grounding. If a boat goes aground in tidal waters, sometimes waiting for the tide to rise is enough to free the boat (assuming no damage has occurred), unless you're unfortunate enough to have gone aground at high tide. There are various techniques used to free a vessel from being aground. *See* GROUNDING, SOFT; GROUNDING, HARD; NEAPS; SPRINGS, STRAND, and EQUINOCTIAL TIDES.

aground, lights and shapes – when aground a vessel over 12m/39.4ft in length displays at night an ANCHOR LIGHT and two ALL-AROUND red lights in a vertical line. A vessel over 50m/164ft also displays a white all-around light forward, and a white all-around light AFT that is lower than the forward light. A vessel over 100m/328ft also illuminates her decks with work lights. The DAYSHAPE is three black balls in a vertical line. How often have you seen a recreational vessel show these lights or shapes when aground? They are prescribed in NAVIGATION RULES 30(a,b,d).

Ah – abbreviation for AMPERE HOUR.

ahead – (1) forward of the BOW. Directly ahead is DEAD ahead. (2) direction of forward motion.

"ahoy" – verbal call to attract attention. Although an old term, it's still in use.

a-hull, lying a-hull – a vessel lying broadside to the waves. Lying a-hull is a technique for riding out a storm with no sails set and the HELM lashed or locked to LEEWARD. It is one of several STORM TACTICS.

aid to navigation (ATON, AtoN), mark – a fixed structure or buoy located to help mariners determine their position, locate a channel, avoid an obstruction or danger, or to provide navigation information. A LIGHT LIST has detailed information about all the aids to navigation, lighted or unlighted, in a particular area. Use caution when relying on any aid to navigation, especially floating aids. If you see a navigation aid operating improperly or note that it's damaged or missing entirely, report it to the Coast Guard. Government agencies install and service most aids to navigation, but private companies or individuals may install aids related to their business, as for a channel to a marina or a fuel dock. The placement and maintenance of private aids depends on the skill and budget of the company that services the aids, and thus the reliability of a private aid may be uncertain. *See* BUOYAGE, SYSTEMS OF; BUOYS, NAVIGATION; CARDINAL SYSTEM OF BUOYAGE, and the next entry.

aids to navigation, cautions – "But the chart says there's a red buoy here." "I can't see any lights that flash what we're looking for." Because most aids to navigation are not observed continually by the Coast Guard you can't be 100% certain of their proper operation or the location of floating aids. **A prudent mariner doesn't rely on a single source of navigational information; always use a second method to determine the position of the vessel.**

- Aids may have been moved, changed or removed since the chart was published, and you may not have seen the NOTICES TO MARINERS that report the change.
- Aids to navigation can be damaged or moved by storms or by being hit by a ship; their power can go out; failure of aids in remote areas may go unnoticed for a long time.
- Positively identify an aid to navigation that you're relying on; buoys look alike at a distance, and what you see may not be the buoy you assume it is. Never assume! Go over and take a close look at its number, name, and/or color.
- Buoys and lighthouses may not show their proper CHARACTERISTICS; lights can be extinguished, sound signals may be inoperative or may have been permanently discontinued. In calm seas, bell and whistle buoys may be silent. Fouling by birds, marine growth, or ice cover can alter the color of a buoy.
- Buoy positions are approximate positions. In tidal areas buoys drift around their charted positions at low tide because of the length of their mooring chains. Don't go too close to one that marks a hazard.
- The symbol on a chart for a buoy located near or on a navigational hazard (such as a shoal, isolated danger, reef, etc.) may be offset slightly on the chart in the direction of the preferred navigable water, so that the hazard will not be obscured by the buoy symbol. Avoid passing too closely to buoys.
- Lights may have solar sensors that turn them off in daylight. In some HIGH LATITUDE areas, where there's almost 24 hours of daylight in the summer, some lights are routinely turned off.

• Lighthouses and large lighted aids to navigation may have an EMERGENCY LIGHT that turns on if the main light fails. This light may have a different characteristic and intensity than the regular light. A LIGHT LIST indicates the aids to navigation that have emergency lights, and it's also noted on some charts.

• Atmospheric conditions and RESTRICTED VISIBILITY can affect the color and visibility of lights. The color or colors and the characteristics of the light may appear to be different from what the chart or light list indicates. The distance from the light also affects what you see: colored lights may not be visible as soon as a white light, and the phases of alternating lights may not appear to be correct until you are closer.

air, airs – synonym for wind or winds. "The race was very slow because of the light airs."

air cushion vehicle – a HOVERCRAFT.

air draft, draught (pronounced draft) – the height above the waterline of the highest point on a vessel, including any lights or antennas on the MASTHEAD. Knowing the air draft is essential when planning to go under a fixed bridge or under overhead cables that cross a navigable area. In tidal waters consider the state of the tide when figuring the air draft.

air terminal – also called a STATIC DISSIPATER, it may be used in a LIGHTNING PROTECTION system.

AIS – abbreviation for Automatic Identification System. AIS is a system that broadcasts information about a vessel, aid to navigation, offshore structure, rescue aircraft or AIS shore station to vessels equipped for AIS reception. One very useful capability of AIS is that it allows the Coast Guard to electronically "ghost in" AIS signals for missing or new navigation aids, hazards, or boundary areas. With the increasing use of AIS, it will soon become as important as a compass on all vessels. Install inexpensive AIS receive-only equipment, or select AIS TRANSPONDER equipment (more expensive). There are two types of AIS transponders:

AIS Class A is required by international maritime regulations on many large vessels (except warships), and increasingly on smaller commercial vessels. It transmits at 12.5 watts, range 20-60 miles. Data sent includes the LATITUDE and LONGITUDE of the vessel, MMSI number, NAVIGATION STATUS, SPEED OVER THE GROUND, HEADING, a UTC time stamp, and other data applicable to ship operations. While the vessel is UNDERWAY critical data is sent every 2-10 seconds, depending on vessel speed; while at anchor every three minutes. Some less-critical data, such as vessel name, CALL SIGN, type and size of vessel, DRAFT, destination, and ETA, is sent every six minutes. AIS A also transmits safety text messages.

Class B AIS may be installed voluntarily on small vessels, including yachts. It transmits at two watts, range 5-12 miles. These units transmit most of the Class A data *except* navigation status, DRAFT, destination, and ETA, or safety text messages. The transmission interval is every 30 seconds to six minutes, depending on boat speed and type of data. A Class B unit needs an MMSI number (from the FCC or your national radio authority) with proof of issuance, and a completed *Class B Static Data Information Form* (available from the AIS vendor; see the bibliography under "Electronics" for a sample). FCC regulations require that for units shipped to customers in the U.S. the vendor or a qualified technician must pre-program the unit with the vessel's MMSI number and identification information. The user cannot do it, and pre-programmed units are usually not returnable. AIS-*receive only* equipment does not need an MMSI number.

For a number of reasons the transmission or reception of AIS data may be subject to inaccuracies or interruption. However, unlike radar, AIS is not affected by rain or sea CLUTTER. AIS can be integrated with a CHART PLOTTER or radar. For a discussion of this technology see www.navcen.uscg.gov/enav/AIS. An interesting website with live tracking of AIS-equipped vessels and aids to navigation worldwide is at www.marinetraffic.com. See the next entry.

AIS capabilities and limitations – don't overestimate the capability of AIS as a collision-avoidance tool: (1) "We have an AIS TRANSPONDER; the ships will see us." A ship may see you, but she may not be able to maneuver to avoid you, or she may have the right of way. (2) You must have the skills to evaluate accurately the CLOSEST POINT OF APPROACH and the TIME TO THE CPA. You must know how to navigate in RESTRICTED VISIBILITY. Ship watch standers are more highly-trained and experienced than most recreational AIS users. (3) not all large vessels are required to transmit AIS, and their transmitting and receiving equipment may fail or operate incorrectly. Maintain a visual lookout.

AIS radio – a VHF/DSC radio that has an integral AIS receiver to permit direct contact on the radio with AIS vessels.

alee – to LEEWARD. Used in the command when TACKING: "HARD ALEE."

Aleutian Low – a semi-permanent, subpolar area of LOW PRESSURE located in the Gulf of Alaska near the Aleutian Islands. It's a generating area for storms, and lows often reach maximum intensity in this area. The low is most active from late fall to late spring. During the summer, it's weaker, and retreats towards the North Pole, becoming almost nonexistent, and the North Pacific HIGH PRESSURE SYSTEM dominates.

alignment, shaft – *see* SHAFT ALIGNMENT.

alignment error – if a compass isn't perfectly aligned with the CENTERLINE of the vessel alignment error will be present, and HEADINGS indicated by the LUBBER'S LINE will be inaccurate. The compass on a new vessel and a newly-installed compass should be checked for alignment error as part of the COMPASS ADJUSTMENT process.

all-around light – defined in Rule 21(e) of the NAVIGATION RULES, an all-around light is visible through 360°. All-around lights include the ANCHOR LIGHT and the special red, white, or green lights displayed to identify particular types of vessels. *See* NAVIGATION LIGHTS, SPECIAL.

"all hands on deck" – words to get all the crew on deck. Crew should pay attention to this sentence; sometimes it's an urgent command and sometimes it's said to get everyone TOPSIDE for a special event, such as a pod of dolphins leaping around the boat.

alloy – a metal composed of two or more different metals. Examples include ALUMINUM, BRASS, BRONZE, steel, cast iron and many other metals. Different metals are combined in an alloy to improve some property of the metal, such as strength or corrosion-resistance.

aloft – above the deck level; in the rigging or on the MAST.

aloft, going – *see* MAST CLIMBING.

alow (rhymes with ago) – the opposite of aloft; on deck. It's an older term, used in the phrase "aloft and alow," the nautical equivalent of "high and low."

alter, altering – used with "course" to indicate a change of direction. "I am altering course to STARBOARD." "Alter course to PORT and stay clear of me. I have a diver down."

altering course to avoid collision – *see* COLLISION, ACTION TO AVOID.

alternating current – *see* AC.

alternator – equipment mounted on or near an engine or generator, driven by one or two V-BELTS (same as on a vehicle engine), that charges the batteries when the engine's running. An alternator can have a single or a dual output. A dual output alternator is like having two alternators: each output can be directed to a specific battery, such as the engine start battery and the HOUSE BATTERY. Alternators for marine use should meet U. S. Coast Guard, ABYC, or other marine electrical equipment standards. The output of an alternator is controlled by a REGULATOR, so it doesn't overcharge the batteries. The regulator may be internal to the alternator or a separate item. A separate regulator offers more options for the control of the alternator's charging output.

aluminum, aluminium – a frequently-used marine metal because of its light weight, good strength, and corrosion resistance. A protective oxide forms on the surface of bare aluminum to protect it from further corrosion; if this oxide is scratched it self-repairs. Some boats have unpainted aluminum hulls above the waterline. Different alloys are used in the marine environment: in general, 5000-series aluminum is used for boat hulls and tanks; 6000-series is used in EXTRUSIONS for MASTS, SPARS, and tubes. Cast aluminum is used for a variety of fittings, from WINCH handles to deck CLEATS. Aluminum is ANODIC to everything except magnesium and zinc; therefore, galvanic action will cause it to corrode faster than the metal it's in contact with, either directly or via fasteners. To prevent GALVANIC CORROSION, all non-aluminum fittings should be electrically-isolated from an aluminum surface with plastic isolators, waterproof BEDDING COMPOUND, and corrosion inhibiting chemicals on fasteners. The bottom of an aluminum boat or other underwater aluminum parts should never be painted with an ANTIFOULING paint that contains copper; use a paint that's designed for aluminum. ABYC Standard T-1 deals with aluminum applications for boats and yachts. *See* GALVANIC SERIES.

American Boat and Yacht Council, ABYC® – a not-for-profit membership organization that develops and promotes technical and safety standards for small craft, marine equipment and installation, and offers professional certification training for the marine industry. Projects and repairs should follow ABYC standards, especially where safety is concerned, which is important for the DIY-inclined person. ABYC works with U.S. government agencies, other marine industry organizations, ISO, and European organizations to harmonize standards. The U.S. Coast Guard, NMMA®, TRANSPORT CANADA, and marine technical and safety authorities in a number of countries incorporate ABYC standards into their regulations. The organization issues safety standards and technical guidance; it *does not certify* the products themselves. Worldwide members include boat builders and repairers, MARINE SURVEYORS, law firms, insurance companies, vessel owners, trade associations, government agencies, and equipment manufacturers. The ABYC website has a searchable database of global companies that have self-certified that their products and services meet one or more criteria of marine standards organizations. The WESTLAWN Institute of Marine Technology is an ABYC educational affiliate. ABYC headquarters are in Annapolis, Maryland. The website has a number of excellent, open-access technical publications and downloads for the general public, including a free trial of the ABYC Standards. www.abycinc.org.

American Boat and Yacht Council Standards – the references to ABYC Standards and documents in this book are to alert the reader to areas where U.S. standards have been developed. A serious DIY person should become familiar with the standards, and, even if you don't do your own work, it's a good idea to understand the basics to communicate with the professionals who will do the work. Most technical reference books cite appropriate standards where applicable. The Standards have clear definitions for the technical terms. Standards are not the same as regulations, but government regulations may incorporate standards.

American Bureau of Shipping, ABS – a marine CLASSIFICATION SOCIETY.

American Practical Navigator, The – the formal name for BOWDITCH.

American Sailing Association, ASA – an authority on sailing instruction, sailing schools, and certification programs in the U.S. Sailing schools may choose to affiliate with ASA and offer recognized certification courses, which enable students to learn sailing, improve their skills, qualify for CHARTERING a sailboat, or become ASA instructors. Many sailing schools across the U.S. and in a number of other countries offer ASA courses. www.asa.com.

American Wire Gauge – *see* AWG.

amidships (*n.*), midship (*adj.*) – (1) at or toward the CENTERLINE of the boat. "Put the sail bag more amidships, so it doesn't fall overboard." (2) at or near the middle of the vessel, partway between the BOW and the STERN. "I'm going to add midship CLEATS PORT and STARBOARD."

ammeter – an analog or digital meter that measures AMPS. It may be portable, mounted on the engine instrument panel, and/or on the boat's AC or DC electrical panel. An ammeter on an AC or DC panel indicates if the BATTERY CHARGER or ALTERNATOR is charging and how much charging current it's supplying. If the needle on a gauge or numbers on a digital meter haven't moved above zero or stay at a low reading the charger or alternator isn't working properly.

amp, ampere (A), amperage – a measure of the rate of flow of AC or DC electric current. The number of amps being supplied by an ALTERNATOR or being used by equipment may be displayed on an AMMETER on an electrical panel. A hand-held MULTIMETER can also be used to measure amperage. In practical terms, knowing the amperage of an electrical device or group of devices on a particular circuit indicates how much electrical current must be supplied. Use amperage information to select the appropriate WIRE GAUGE for a circuit, the size of the CIRCUIT BREAKER/FUSE, and the rating (in amps) for any switches or other devices used in the circuit. Knowing the amperage of all the DC devices aboard helps you calculate the potential load on the batteries, and select a battery with an appropriate AMP-HOUR rating. Find amperage information for equipment or light bulbs in the equipment manual, on a label on the equipment, in a marine supply catalog, or marked on the packaging of the item. Use the WATTAGE FORMULA to do calculations involving WATTS, VOLTS, and amps.

amp-hour, ampere hour, Ah – a measure of battery capacity; of how long power can be drawn from a battery before it becomes discharged. Select batteries with reserve capacity. A BATTERY MONITOR shows how much a battery is being discharged and how many amp-hours remain. Fully discharging a battery shortens its life. Consult technical references when selecting a battery and associated equipment. See previous entry.

AMVER – acronym for Automated Mutual-Assistance Vessel Rescue System, established in 1958. Sponsored by the U.S. Coast Guard, AMVER is a computer-based, voluntary global ship reporting system used worldwide by search-and-rescue authorities. Rescue coordination centers (RCCs) can identify participating ships in an area and divert the appropriate vessels to respond to a DISTRESS call. AMVER has saved people on ships and yachts worldwide. Commercial vessels and private yachts may volunteer to participate in the AMVER system: see the fact sheet at www.amver.com.

anabatic wind – *see* WIND, ANABATIC.

anchor – (1) a metal device used to secure a vessel to the seabed. A wide variety of ANCHOR TYPES and ANCHOR WEIGHTS are available. (2) to deploy an anchor.

anchor alarm, anchor watch (electronic) – a feature on a GPS, CHART PLOTTER, or radar that allows a pre-determined radius to be set around an anchor position. If the boat moves outside of this circle a warning alarm is triggered. Read the equipment manual, and learn how to set the alarm. An ANCHOR WATCH is also a procedure done by the crew.

anchor ball – a black ball DAYSHAPE required by Rule 30 of the NAVIGATION RULES to be displayed near the BOW of a vessel at anchor during daylight hours. If anchored in a designated special anchorage area (noted on a chart) an anchor ball is not required, but may be displayed.

anchor bearings – BEARINGS taken on objects on shore when at anchor, used to determine if the boat is DRAGGING. Use at least three objects. Take visual or RADAR BEARINGS and write them down; they are important for an effective ANCHOR WATCH.

Anchor Buddy™, buddy – another name for a SENTINEL.

anchor buoy – a small buoy used with a TRIP LINE (buoy rope) to mark the position of an anchor or to retrieve the anchor if it gets FOULED on the bottom. An anchor buoy isn't always necessary. In a crowded harbor another boat may run over the trip line or someone may pick it up, thinking it's a mooring buoy.

anchor cable – same as ANCHOR RODE.

anchor chain – several different types are available; see the CHAIN entries. The BITTER END of an all-chain anchor RODE should be secured in the CHAIN LOCKER with a length of rope that comes up on deck, where it can be cut, if necessary to free the chain in an emergency. Attach a FENDER to the chain as a buoy, cut the rope and throw the fender over, so you can get away from a dangerous situation, and later retrieve the anchor.

anchoring system equipment – the following are basic components of an anchoring system: anchor(s), chain or rope rode, anchor roller(s), chocks, cleats, chain spring, chain stopper, capstan or windlass, Samson post, and chafing gear (all of these terms are discussed elsewhere in the book. Not all boats will have all these items). ABYC Standard H-40 Anchoring, Mooring and Strong Points is a guide for the design, construction, selection, and installation of fittings and equipment for anchoring and mooring. It includes a table of design loads for sizing deck hardware and a table of working load limits for rope and chain anchor rodes. The operator of a vessel is responsible for equipping the boat with GROUND TACKLE and mooring lines appropriate to the size of the vessel, her intended use, and area of operation.

anchor light, riding light – a white ALL-AROUND light displayed by a vessel at anchor from sunset to sunrise; Rule 30 of the NAVIGATION RULES. A vessel less than 50m/164ft in length at anchor displays one anchor light. A vessel over 50m at anchor displays an anchor light at the BOW and a white all-around light at the STERN that is *lower* than the bow light. A vessel over 100m/328ft also illuminates her decks with work lights. The DAYSHAPE for all anchored vessels is a black ball.

anchor locker – a compartment on deck at the BOW where the RODE and anchor is stowed, if it's not mounted on an ANCHOR ROLLER. If there's no compartment the rode may be stowed belowdecks in a rope or CHAIN LOCKER.

anchor, parts of – the parts of an anchor are the crown, the stock, the shank, and the flukes. The crown is the part at the end where the flukes are. A TRIP LINE may be attached to the crown, if there's a chance that the anchor could become fouled (caught) on an obstruction on the bottom. The flukes are the flat, hook-shaped, or plow-shaped parts that dig into the bottom. The stock is a bar that projects laterally out from the sides of the flukes. It prevents the anchor from landing on its side, rather than with the flukes down when it hits the bottom. Danforth® and Danforth-type anchors have a stock. Some anchors are stockless (e.g., a CQR™). The shank is the long, central part to which the anchor RODE is attached at one end.

anchor rode, anchor cable, rode – the chain and/or rope attached to an anchor. A rode can be all chain, all rope, or a combination of both. Some yachts use a rode made of strong, flat webbing, mounted on a reel for easy deployment. A webbing rode is suitable for small vessels and for a STERN anchor. When rope is used, connect a minimum of 20ft/7m of chain (the length of the boat is a good guide) between the rope and the anchor. Mark the rode in feet or meters at intervals so that you can determine the proper SCOPE when anchoring. ABYC Standard H-40 Anchoring, Mooring and Strong Points has a table of working load limits for rope and chain anchor rodes.

A custom bow fitting and anchor roller, with a stainless steel Bruce® anchor and a windlass for chain and line. This is the bow of the 63ft/19.2m beautifully restored 1936 double-ended ocean racing yawl, *Bloodhound*. She was owned by Queen Elizabeth II and Prince Philip in the 1960s. As an accurate restoration she doesn't have lifelines.

anchor roller, bow roller – one or more rollers at the BOW of the boat on which an anchor is stowed, ready for deployment. A roller can be mounted directly on the STEM of the boat or on a projection designed for it. Boats with a BOWSPRIT may have the roller(s) on the bowsprit. See BOBSTAY for a photo. Not all boats have a roller, in which case the anchor is stowed in an ANCHOR LOCKER on the FOREDECK or in CHOCKS on the deck.

anchor, sea – *see* SEA ANCHOR.

anchor setting – when an anchor sets, it buries into the seabed. For a good, secure grip on the bottom: (1) pay out the proper SCOPE. (2) allow the boat to settle back on the RODE, stretching it out. (3) back down *slowly* on the rode to pull the anchor gently into the bottom. (4) once the anchor seems to be holding increase the engine RPMS in reverse to make sure it will dig in and hold with more strain on it. If anchoring under sail, BACK the MAIN to go ASTERN. Take a BEARING on an object ashore to see if the boat is dragging as you increase the rpms. If the anchor doesn't hold try increasing the scope and repeating steps 2-4. If it still doesn't hold, try a different location in the anchorage. Take time setting the anchor and you'll sleep more soundly when the wind pipes up. If you're in tropical waters take a swim and check how the anchor is buried in the sand. *See also* ANCHOR WATCH TECHNIQUES.

anchor shackle – *see* SHACKLE.

anchor, to sail at – some sailboats and powerboats actually TACK back and forth on their anchor RODES, taking up quite a bit of room in the anchorage. The shape of the boat's underbody and the amount of WINDAGE influence whether a boat will sail at anchor. Hoist a RIDING SAIL, a MIZZEN sail (on a KETCH or YAWL), or deploy a second anchor (on shorter SCOPE than the first) to help limit the swing. Be a good neighbor to others in the anchorage.

anchor types – no single anchor is right for all types of seabeds. Select anchors according to the size of the boat and for the characteristics of the bottom most commonly encountered where the boat operates. A cruising boat usually carries several different types and weights of anchors to meet different conditions. Marketing literature is not necessarily a good guide. Claims may be made that a newer type of anchor is much better than the old standbys, such as the CQR™ or Danforth®, so read comparative studies, done by *unbiased* and competent sources, comparing the effectiveness of different anchors. Decide for yourself.

anchor, to swallow – *see* "SWALLOW THE ANCHOR."

anchor watch – (1) having a crew member keep an eye on the position of the boat while at anchor to ascertain if the boat is DRAGGING. It's a good idea to check the position occasionally, even in light winds. Post an anchor watch if other boats are anchored too close or when strong winds are occurring or expected. (2) an anchor alarm feature on a GPS, CHART PLOTTER, or radar that can be set to warn if the boat drags outside a pre-determined area. Don't rely completely on electronics – have a person on visual watch, too, because someone may drag into you. See the next entry.

anchor watch techniques – for an effective anchor watch, especially when strong winds are expected or occurring:

- Take visual bearings and/or RADAR BEARINGS on shore features when first anchoring. Write them down.
- Have fenders and lines ready, in case your boat drags or another vessel drags onto you.
- Have a horn and searchlight ready to alert other boats.
- Turn on the VHF, in case someone calls to alert other boats.
- Turn on the DEPTH SOUNDER, and watch the depths (take the state of the tide into account).
- If the GPS, CHART PLOTTER or radar has an ANCHOR ALARM/WATCH feature learn how to set and use it.
- Use CHAFING GEAR on a rope rode.

anchor weight – technical articles, ABYC tables, books, marine supply catalogs, and anchor manufacturers' websites have tables of recommended weights for anchors, based on boat length or weight (DISPLACEMENT). The tables usually assume winds under 30 knots in a protected anchorage, with good holding. If the boat is heavier than typical boats of a particular length or has more WINDAGE, select the next size larger. Bigger is better, unless you're saving weight on a racing boat, the ANCHOR ROLLER limits the size of an anchor, or the boat doesn't have an ANCHOR WINDLASS. A heavier anchor digs in more quickly and may be able to penetrate kelp or marine grass better than a lighter anchor. If you cruise to remote areas the anchoring conditions may not be ideal, and you'll be glad for a heavier anchor. A SENTINEL can be used to help increase the holding power of any anchor.

anchor, weighing – raising the anchor from the bottom and bringing it aboard. When the anchor's off the bottom it's AWEIGH, and the rode is said to be UP AND DOWN. Learn how to retrieve an anchor under sail and power. Use agreed-upon hand signals or wireless communicator headsets for COMMUNICATION BETWEEN BOW AND STERN.

anchor windlass – a WINDLASS or CAPSTAN mounted on the FOREDECK, used to raise the anchor or to adjust mooring lines.

anchorage – a location that's suitable for anchoring a boat. A good anchorage has the following general characteristics:

- Anchoring is permitted in the area. Prohibited areas are indicated on the chart.
- Protection from the present wind and the expected wind.
- Protection from waves and/or SWELL at all STATES OF THE TIDE.
- Suitable water depth (not too deep).
- Bottom characteristics that provide good HOLDING, with no obstructions to FOUL the anchor.
- Sufficient swinging room (not too small or crowded with other boats or moorings).
- An easy exit, if you have to leave at night or in an emergency.

Some areas are designated as SPECIAL ANCHORAGE AREAS on a chart; other anchorages are described in COAST PILOTS and CRUISING GUIDES, or you may discover a good one on your own.

anchorage area, special – *see* SPECIAL ANCHORAGE AREA.

anchorage, untenable – somewhere you don't want to be. Even if you've carefully selected an anchorage, conditions may change unexpectedly making the anchorage unsafe. Leave at the first sign of trouble; don't wait to see if conditions will improve (they rarely do). Pre-plan an escape route when you arrive, using WAYPOINTS if necessary, so you can move safely, even at night or in poor visibility. You may have to free the BITTER END of the anchor RODE and buoy it with a FENDER, rather than take the time to WEIGH anchor. Return later to get it.

anchoring etiquette – be a good neighbor and:

- Choose a spot away from vessels already anchored.
- Use appropriate SCOPE. Extra, unnecessary scope makes the boat take up too much room, and she may swing into another boat.
- Tie off the HALYARDS so they don't slap against the MAST!
- Keep the noise down (generator, loud music, late-night party, etc.).
- Hoist the ANCHOR BALL in the daytime and use an ANCHOR LIGHT at night.
- If the boat SAILS AT ANCHOR, hoist a RIDING SAIL or drop a second anchor on short scope to limit the swing.
- Ask permission before picking up an unused mooring, unless it's clearly a rental or public mooring. Don't trust an unknown mooring if it will be even a little windy.
- Re-anchor elsewhere if your boat swings too close to someone who was there first.

You're responsible if your vessel causes damage by dragging into another boat or a shore installation.

anemometer – an instrument that measures wind speed, usually with small rotating cups that catch the wind. Anemometers are used at the MASTHEAD, and small hand-held units are available.

aneroid barometer – a type of BAROMETER.

angel – another name for a SENTINEL.

anhydrous lanolin – a natural lanolin paste that prevents moisture from getting in between metals. It lubricates, inhibits corrosion, and prevents GALLING. Use it on STAINLESS STEEL fasteners and on TURNBUCKLE threads. Marine supply stores sell the brand name LANOCOTE® or, for economy, buy a large jar from a pharmacy.

anode – (1) a zinc anode. (2) the positive (+) terminal on a battery. The CATHODE is the negative(-) terminal. See the next entry.

anode, sacrificial zinc, zinc – an anode is designed to protect underwater metals from damage from GALVANIC or STRAY CURRENT CORROSION in saltwater. The anode protects by sacrificing itself to corrosion, rather than the metal it's mounted on or near. Anodes are made of zinc because zinc is one of the least-NOBLE metals in the GALVANIC SERIES. Zincs are mounted on the hull and on underwater metal fittings. Do not paint zinc anodes (they don't work under paint). There may be one or more anodes (a ZINC PENCIL) in an engine, generator, or seawater-cooled refrigeration condenser to protect the cooling system (check equipment manuals for location). How anodes work, how many are needed, and their placement on the hull underwater is a complex subject discussed in technical books. In general, there may be one or more anodes mounted on the hull, one or more on the rudder, one or more on the propeller shaft or propeller, and possibly others. Having the right number of anodes and the correct placement is important: too many or too few can be a problem. If it seems that the zincs are wasting away too quickly (there is no hard and fast rule), read technical material on the subject of anodic protection, and consult a qualified professional. A CORROSION METER can be used to diagnose and correct problems before damage is done to underwater metal. Just adding more zincs isn't a good way to attempt to correct what could be a serious problem. A CATHODIC PROTECTION system may also be an option.

anodic – acting like an ANODE, i.e. corroding in the presence of more-NOBLE metals in seawater. Less-noble metals are anodic on the GALVANIC SCALE.

anodizing – an electrochemical or chemical process that hardens the natural oxide on ALUMINUM and on non-FERROUS metals; it's usually done in a factory. The term refers to the process and to the surface produced by the process. Anodizing increases corrosion resistance, and it's also is done to add color to the metal, instead of painting. Gold-anodized spars are sometimes seen on sailboats. When HALYARDS are allowed to drum against the MAST not only does this annoy (enrage?) persons nearby, but it damages the anodizing.

answer the helm – to respond to the HELM; to steer. A boat must be moving for the rudder to steer the boat. "She won't answer the helm" means "I can't steer."

"answer up" – the practice of repeating what the skipper or another crew member says to you, when it's important information, such as the compass course, a direction to turn or on which side of the boat to leave an aid to navigation or hazard. Verbal confirmation tells the other person that you've heard correctly.

Antarctic Circle – the parallel of LATITUDE at approximately 66°33'S. The area south of this parallel has a period of 24-hour daylight and 24-hour darkness that coincide approximately with the December and June solstices in the Southern Hemisphere. The ARCTIC CIRCLE is the northern equivalent.

anticyclone – a HIGH PRESSURE SYSTEM.

anti-exposure suit, anti-exposure coverall – *see* EXPOSURE SUIT and IMMERSION SUIT.

antifouling paint, antifouling – special marine paint applied below the waterline to repel the growth of organisms, such as barnacles, marine grass, and slime. There are paints designed for saltwater and freshwater environments. Traditional bottom paints repel marine growth through the action of copper oxides in the paint. New paints are being developed that are less toxic to the environment, including paints that have no metals in them (good news to owners of aluminum boats). Antifouling paints are produced for specific conditions encountered in different geographical areas. They may be ABLATIVE (soft paint that wears away in normal use, exposing new protective paint), or hard paints (designed for boats that stay in the water all of the time or that are scrubbed regularly). Read manufacturer's literature, product labels, product evaluation reports, and follow safety precautions when applying, sanding, or removing this paint.

anti-seizing compound – a gel or paste applied to threaded parts to prevent SEIZING or GALLING, and to lubricate the threads. ANHYDROUS LANOLIN and special thread lubricants are available: Lanocote® and Tef-Gel™ are two brands. Don't use an anti-seizing compound that contains copper on aluminum.

anti-siphon valve, siphon break, vented loop – a special device inserted in a hose that prevents water from siphoning into the boat through a hose that's connected to a THROUGH-HULL below the waterline or below the HEELED waterline. There's a small hole in the valve that lets air in, which prevents a vacuum from forming and causing siphoning. If this hole clogs the valve won't work, so cleaning it is part of a maintenance schedule. Anti-siphon valves are used on engine water intake lines, fuel tank vent lines, and toilet intake and discharge hoses (a vented loop). If a toilet located below the waterline doesn't have a vented loop it's possible that water could siphon back into the toilet and flood the boat if the SEACOCK isn't kept closed when not in use. Someone always forgets to close it, so it's safer to have a loop in the line.

aperture – the space between the hull and a KEEL-HUNG RUDDER or between a SKEG and the rudder. The aperture may be cut into a rudder (see the photo with KEEL, FULL). The propeller is located in the aperture.

A three-blade propeller in an aperture and an unbalanced keel-hung rudder. The small gray rectangle is a zinc anode and the larger rectangle is a radio ground plate.

A large aperture for the three-blade propeller on a motorsailer.

apparent wind – the direction and speed of the wind that a moving boat "feels," which is the result of the true wind and the wind created by the motion of the boat.

apparent wind angle – the angle of the apparent wind to the CENTERLINE of the boat, expressed in degrees to PORT or STARBOARD.

apparent wind indicator, AWI – a mechanical or electronic WIND INDICATOR that indicates the apparent wind angle. Usually mounted at the MASTHEAD, it's a useful visual aid when under sail.

ARC – acronym for the Atlantic Rally for Cruisers, an OCEAN-CROSSING RALLY sponsored by the WORLD CRUISING CLUB. There are various rallies, such as the ARC Europe, ARC Portugal, and World ARC, a round the world voyage. www.worldcruising.com.

arc of visibility – the area over which the light on an aid to navigation (usually a lighthouse or fixed structure) is visible when looking *toward* the light *from* the sea. The arc of visibility is indicated on charts and in a LIGHT LIST.

Arctic Circle – the parallel of LATITUDE at approximately 66°33′N. The area north of this parallel is the Arctic. In the summer some areas of the Arctic can be quite mild, compared to the Antarctic. It has periods of 24-hour daylight (the midnight sun) and 24-hour darkness that coincide approximately with the December and June solstices in the Northern Hemisphere. The ANTARCTIC CIRCLE is the southern equivalent.

area of uncertainty – *see* UNCERTAINTY, AREA OF.

arming the lead (pronounced led) – putting grease, shortening, margarine, butter, or peanut butter (it works) into the hollow recess in the bottom of a SOUNDING LEAD to pick up a sample of the bottom where you're planning to anchor. Although the characteristics of the bottom are indicated on some charts, you may want to anchor in an area where these notations are lacking or you're unsure of what's down there. Carry a container of old grease.

ARPA, MARPA – acronym for Automatic Radar Plotting Aid and "mini-ARPA." ARPA is a feature of modern radars that analyses radar TARGETS and provides information about course, speed, CLOSEST POINT OF APPROACH, time to CPA, and other navigational information. For full functionality, ARPA radars must be interfaced with other instruments on a vessel. The ARPA required for ships under IMO regulations meets higher standards than the mini-ARPA found on most recreational vessel radars. For ARPA to be effective it requires a stable vessel; when a sailboat HEELS to the wind or seas, ARPA can lose targets and take time to reacquire them. If there is ARPA on the radar, carefully read the manual about this feature and its limitations.

array – the rotating SCANNER on a radar that sends out the radar beam. With an open array the scanner is not covered; the scanner of a closed array is covered with a RADOME. An open array radar is usually used on large vessels; it requires more power, but has a longer range and more features than smaller radars. Sailboats usually use a closed array to protect the scanner from damage by lines or sails, unless the boat is large.

ASA – abbreviation for the AMERICAN SAILING ASSOCIATION.

ashore – on the shore or to the shore.

aspect ratio – the relationship of width to height, expressed as a ratio such as 3:7. A sailboat's design has an aspect ratio, defined by the length of the boat and the height of the MAST; a sail's aspect ratio is defined by the length of the FOOT and the height of the sail.

assistance at sea, duty to provide – the NAVIGATION RULES cite 46 U.S. CODE§2304: "a master or individual in charge of a vessel shall render assistance to any individual found at sea in danger of being lost, so far as the master or individual in charge can do so without serious danger to the master's or individual's vessel or individuals on board." There are civil and criminal penalties for violating this rule. Even without the rule, by centuries-old maritime tradition, mariners have a moral duty to provide assistance at sea, within their capabilities. Assistance can be as basic as standing by a vessel in distress until rescue services arrive. The GOOD SAMARITAN CLAUSE is the second part of the duty to provide assistance, as expressed in U.S. Code §2303. These sections of the U.S. Code are at the end of the U.S. Navigation Rules.

asymmetric spinnaker – *see* SPINNAKER, ASYMMETRIC.

astern – toward the STERN of the boat, or referring to something that's behind the boat. To go backwards; to go astern.

astro-navigation – same as CELESTIAL NAVIGATION.

athwart – across a vessel at right angles to the CENTERLINE; from BEAM to beam. "There's enough room to put the DINGHY athwart the boat AMIDSHIPS."

athwartships – at a right angle (90°) to the CENTERLINE of the boat. A rowboat seat is mounted athwartships.

ATIS – acronym for Automatic Transmitter Identification System, which is used on several major European inland waterways, such the Rhine, Danube, and Rhone. While the system was developed for ships, if you plan to take a yacht to waters where ATIS equipment is required, check with the authorities of the particular country or countries where you will sail to see what is required of yachts. See the bibliography under "Radio" for relevant websites. The requirements come from an international agreement called RAINWAT (**R**egional **A**rrangement concerning the Radiotelephone Service on **In**land **Wat**erways). The signatory countries are Austria, Belgium, Bulgaria, Croatia, the Czech Republic, France, Germany, Hungary, Luxembourg, Moldova, Montenegro, The Netherlands, Poland, The Slovak Republic, Switzerland, and Serbia. It is not the same as system as AIS.

atoll (pronounced **a** tall or a **tall**; "a" as in cat) – a ring-shaped coral reef or island enclosing a lagoon. Some atolls have a navigable entrance into the lagoon. A chain of small islands may be part of an atoll.

ATON, AToN – acronym for aid or aids to navigation.

Aurora Australis, Southern Lights – the same as the Aurora Borealis (Northern Lights), but in the Southern Hemisphere. It's a feature of winter nights in the middle and HIGH LATITUDES that fascinates us with shifting shapes and colors.

Aurora Borealis, Northern Lights – a phenomenon of middle and HIGH LATITUDES in the Northern Hemisphere, it features shifting shapes and colors in the winter night sky (and occasionally in the summer).

austenitic steel – a type of STAINLESS STEEL that doesn't have magnetic properties. Take a magnet when visiting a CHANDLERY or hardware store; some stainless steel fasteners are slightly magnetic, but plain steel fasteners and fittings "jump" onto a magnet.

Automatic Identification System – *see* AIS.

Automatic Radar Plotting Aid – *see* ARPA.

Automatic Transmitter Identification System – *see* ATIS.

automation of the distress system – *see* DISTRESS SYSTEM, AUTOMATION OF.

automation of navigation functions – as the sophistication of marine electronics continues to develop, recreational vessels as well as ships rely increasingly on electronics to provide all navigation information. With a MULTIFUNCTION DISPLAY (or INTEGRATED BRIDGE SYSTEM) and a number of alarms enabled, the skipper comes to assume that the vessel is safe with the electronics keeping navigation watch. Numerous examples of yacht and ship groundings have demonstrated that this false confidence is misplaced, with over-reliance on GPS, in particular, being a prime factor in marine accidents. Therefore, it's essential that mariners learn traditional (non-electronic) navigation and PILOTING skills, and monitor the electronics with proper visual observations. Adopt the adage "trust but verify," and LOOK OUT THE WINDOW.

autopilot – electronically-controlled mechanical equipment for steering the vessel without having someone at the HELM. An autopilot cannot "see" so someone must be on WATCH when underway on autopilot. More than one yacht (or ship) has come to grief when the autopilot was set to automatically follow the WAYPOINTS in a route, and no one kept a careful visual lookout. SELF-STEERING is a non-electric autopilot, and it also doesn't see.

auxiliary – (1) a sailing vessel with an engine. (2) the main engine in a sailboat, or another engine, such as a generator, that's not the propulsion engine.

awash – a rock, boat or object that is so low that the water washes over it; partly or mostly submerged.

aweigh – when an anchor is no longer attached to the bottom, it is aweigh, and the rode is UP AND DOWN. When the anchor is off the bottom the vessel is UNDERWAY, according to the NAVIGATION RULES.

AWG – abbreviation for American Wire Gauge, a measure of the diameter of electrical wires. *See* WIRE GAUGE, AWG.

AWI – abbreviation for APPARENT WIND INDICATOR.

azimuth – another name for a BEARING. The term is usually used in CELESTIAL NAVIGATION.

Azores High – in the North Atlantic, the Bermuda High develops in the summer and fall near Bermuda; in the winter and early spring this high moves eastward and is called the Azores High. It's a semi-permanent HIGH PRESSURE SYSTEM.

B

"B" suffix, VHF radio channel – the letter "B" after a VHF radio channel indicates SIMPLEX use of the *coast station* transmit side of an international DUPLEX channel. The U.S. does not currently use B channels for simplex communications in this band. Newer VHF radios have a "U.S.-Canadian-International" (or U.S./Int'l) button/switch to change the radio for the country. *See* **"A" SUFFIX.**

baby stay, jackstay – another name for an **INNER FORESTAY. JACKSTAYS** are not the same thing.

back, to – (1) to bring the wind on the opposite side of a sail. To back a **JIB**, pull the **CLEW** to **WINDWARD**, and to back the **MAIN** pull or push the **BOOM WINDWARD.** Backing a sail causes the **BOW** of the boat to fall away from the wind, and the boat to move **ASTERN.** *See* **ABACK.** (2) when the direction of the wind changes in a counterclockwise (anticlockwise) direction it backs or hauls. "The wind will back (haul) to the east later today." The opposite is **VEER (1).**

back splice, backsplice – *see* **SPLICES, TYPES OF.**

backstay – a long wire or metal rod that runs from the top of the **MAST** to the **STERN.** It's the outermost piece of **STANDING RIGGING** at the stern. A boat may have a single backstay, two full-length backstays, or a split backstay, which looks like an inverted Y, with two legs coming off the upper part of the backstay that go to each side of the **TRANSOM** on **PORT** and **STARBOARD.** *See* **BACKSTAYS, RUNNING.**

backstay, hydraulic – on racing sailboats and some cruising boats the tension of the backstay or backstays is adjusted with a hydraulic tension device, instead of **TURNBUCKLES** or a **TACKLE.** The powerful hydraulic device easily changes the tension so the skipper can bend the **MAST** in response to particular sailing conditions.

backstays, running – adjustable **BACKSTAYS** on either side of the boat that go part way up the **MAST**, used to support the mast when sailing with the wind **ABAFT** the beam and/or with a **STAYSAIL.** They're also used with a **FRACTIONAL RIG,** to counteract the pull of the **HEADSTAY.** They're deployed as needed. Not all sailboats have running backstays.

backwash – waves reflected back to sea from a steep shore or a **BREAKWATER.** Backwash may combine with the incoming waves to create a confused and sometimes dangerous sea.

baggywrinkle – brush-like soft material attached to **SHROUDS, STAYS,** and sometimes the **SPREADERS** to prevent the **MAINSAIL** from chafing on the rigging when sailing **DOWNWIND.** Found on some **TRADITIONAL** boats, baggywrinkle is rarely seen on modern vessels, even though it's effective chafe protection (and a conversation starter). It's easily made from short pieces of old **THREE-STRAND** rope. **MANILA** rope makes better baggywrinkle than synthetic rope, because it stays stiff, while synthetic rope becomes soft and matted. See the bibliography under "Lines" for an instructional website and **MARLINSPIKE SEAMANSHIP** books. It's very easy to make. For another photo see **BOWSPRIT**.

Baggywrinkle. The upper one is made from manila rope strands; the lower one is made of synthetic rope strands.

bail – (1) to remove water from a boat with a bucket or other container. (2) a U-shaped metal rod on the underside of a BOOM or other spar to which BLOCKS or other hardware are attached.

Baja fuel filter – *see* FUEL FILTER, BAJA.

balanced rudder – *see* RUDDER, BALANCED.

ball valve – a valve used to control the flow of a liquid or a gas. It has a ball inside with a large hole in it; when the valve handle is in line with the valve body the hole is open through the valve. When the handle is at right-angles to the valve the ball rotates so the hole isn't open (valve is closed). A ball valve is usually a full-flow device, which means that the opening isn't restricted as in a GATE VALVE. Check for ABYC compliance or UL listing on ball valves for use as a SEACOCK or with fuel or a gas.

ballast – extra weight low in a boat that adds STABILITY. The ballast in a sailboat is in the KEEL or a CENTERBOARD. Ballast may be internal or external to the hull. A MULTIHULL has very little ballast compared to a MONOHULL; the widely-spaced hulls help provide stability.

ballast, water – some high-tech racing sailboats and cruising yachts have water ballast, which is stored in tanks and pumped to the WINDWARD side to reduce heeling.

ballast/displacement ratio – the percentage of ballast compared to the DISPLACEMENT of the vessel. A high ballast ratio adds to the STABILITY and STIFFNESS of the yacht, but there's no magic number, and other design factors are important to overall stability. Some approximate examples:

- 70-80% ballast – high-performance racing yacht.
- 45-65% ballast – ocean racing yacht.
- 30-45% ballast – cruising sailboat.
- 20-30% ballast – motorsailer.

bank, the banks – (1) a plateau under the sea that rises from the ocean floor, creating relatively shallow areas compared to the surrounding depths. Because of the dramatic change in depth, wave conditions in strong winds and storms are frequently more severe on the banks than in nearby deeper water. Banks provide fishing grounds because the UPWELLING of the sea brings fish food toward the surface. Well-known banks and fishing areas include Georges Bank (between Cape Cod and Cape Sable, Nova Scotia), the Grand Banks of Newfoundland, the Flemish Cap (in the north Atlantic, about 350 miles east of Newfoundland), Dogger Bank (northeast England in the North Sea), the Bahama Banks, and the Agulhas Bank (off the southeast coast of Africa). (2) a shallow area made up of shifting sand, gravel, or other loose material such as a sandbank. (3) the edge of a channel.

bank cushion – a term relevant to a ship navigating a narrow channel, but it's useful for a small vessel operator to understand the concept when passing a ship in a channel. In a channel with steep banks, the BOW wave of the ship tends to force her bow away from the near bank. Although the ship's helmsman counteracts bank cushion, a small vessel should not get too close to the ship. When passing a ship in a narrow channel, even though she's traveling at reduced speed, her bow wave may push your boat off course and her bow may move slightly toward you. See the next entry.

bank suction – a term relevant to a ship navigating a narrow channel, but it's useful for a small vessel operator to understand the concept when passing a ship in a channel. Bank suction causes the ship to tend to be drawn toward the near bank. Obviously, a small vessel should never pass between a ship and the near bank, even if looks like there's lots of room. See previous entry.

bar – an area of sand, mud, or other loose material that has formed across the mouth of a river, an INLET, or a harbor entrance, reducing the depth of water in the entrance. Under certain conditions crossing a bar can be dangerous or impossible, even if there's sufficient depth of water for a vessel. PILOT BOOKS and CRUISING GUIDES warn of known hazards at bars. The Columbia River bar on the Oregon-Washington border is an area with exceptionally rough conditions because of the combination of the bar, the river current, and ocean waves or SWELLS. U.S. Coast Guard vessels are tested and lifeboat crews trained at the nearby National Motor Lifeboat School. Columbia River bar PILOTS (2) are among the most-skilled in the world.

Barber hauler – a line attached to a HEADSAIL CLEW, or its SHEET that adjusts the angle of the sail by pulling the clew toward the CENTERLINE of the boat. It was invented in the 1960s by California racing sailors Manning and Merrit Barber.

bareboat charter – *see* CHARTER.

bare poles, under bare poles – a sailing vessel with no sails set, particularly in a storm. It's one of several STORM TACTICS.

barometer – an instrument used to measure atmospheric pressure. (1) an aneroid barometer has a round dial and a needle that indicates the pressure. There is a mechanical device inside that responds to changes in pressure and moves the needle. A second pointer with a knob on it is used to mark the position of the barometer's needle, so you can see the change up or down. Aneroid barometers range in price from approximately $125 to $350 and much more; very precise aneroids are expensive. The dial may have two or three scales: an inch scale (represents inches of mercury), a MILLIBAR scale, and perhaps a centimeter scale. Before taking a reading, tap the glass face to settle the needle. (2) Electronic, battery-operated barometers are available from a variety of sources, and they are less expensive than aneroids. These barometers present pressure readings in digital form; the instrument can be set to read in millibars or inches. An electronic barometer may also have a BAROGRAPH feature that saves the pressure changes over time, and displays them in graphic form. Both types of barometer should be calibrated. See the next entry and BAROMETER, MERCURY.

barometer calibration – for best results, adjust an aneroid or electronic barometer to agree with a current reading at a nearby weather office, such as an airport or Coast Guard station. You need to know the altitude of the station's barometer to correct its reading for sea level (assuming your barometer is at sea level). The barometer may have a table or formula in its instructions to correct for sea level, or find instructions with an Internet search (many websites available).

Barometer Instructions, Fitzroy's – detailed instructions for using a barometer to forecast the weather were published by British Rear-Admiral Robert Fitzroy in 1858 in his *Barometer and Weather Guide*. His instructions are valid and very useful today. The complete instructions are reproduced in the appendix to Hal Roth's *Handling Storms at Sea*, and a condensed version is included in the annual *Eldridge Tide and Pilot Book*. See the bibliography under "Sailing" and "Publications" for the complete citations.

barometer log – even if you have a BAROGRAPH, it's good to keep a written log, especially as bad weather is approaching. Take readings hourly or more frequently (even every 30 minutes when a storm approaches). Knowing the rate of fall will help you gauge the severity of the low and its proximity to your location, so you can prepare yourself and the boat. *See* LOW, RAPIDLY INTENSIFYING.

barometer, mercury – a barometer that uses the level of mercury in a glass tube to indicate the atmospheric pressure. "Inches" in a barometer weather report means inches of mercury (abbreviated "inHg").

barometric pressure at sea level – the average barometric pressure at sea level is 1013.25 mb/29.92 inches. The normal pressure range at sea level is 940 to 1050mb/ 27.76 to 31.01 inches.

barometric pressure, lowest recorded – the lowest barometric pressure ever recorded on earth (not in a tornado) was 869.9 mb/25.69 inches in TYPHOON "TIP." The lowest pressure recorded in the Atlantic BASIN was 882mb in Hurricane Wilma (2005).

barometric pressure, units of – millibars (mb) or inches (inHg) are two common units used to designate barometric pressure. In the U.S., weather reports for the general public usually use inches; marine forecasts use inches, millibars, or both. Some weather services use hectopascals (hPa), which are the same as millibars. One hPa = one mb.

barograph – an instrument that records and displays the changes in barometric pressure over time. A traditional barograph uses a mechanical stylus to trace the pressure readings on graph paper affixed to a rotating drum. An electronic barograph displays the information in graphic form on its screen. Most electronic barometers have this function. Having a record of changes in pressure over time is important for predicting the weather. With or without a barograph, when bad weather is approaching, keep a written BAROMETER LOG.

basic boating course – usually refers to a classroom or online course, but some courses include on the water training. The websites of the U.S. COAST GUARD AUXILIARY, the U.S. POWER SQUADRON, and the CANADIAN POWER AND SAIL SQUADRONS have information about SAFE BOATING COURSES. Organizations in other countries offer similar training for new boaters. Completion of a basic course is sometimes required for operator licensing.

basic knots – *see* KNOTS, BASIC,

basin – (1) an area of water, usually enclosed with walls, with water deep enough for the vessels that use it. A basin can be a marina, a docking area, a turning basin for ships, or a TIDAL or a NON-TIDAL BASIN. (2) a basin in the ocean is an area where the sea floor is lower than surrounding areas. The north and south Atlantic oceans have a number of basins, created by the division of the ocean floor by the mid-Atlantic Ridge and numerous east-west RIDGES. (3) an almost landlocked area of water leading off a larger body of water.

batten – (1) thin and narrow strips of fiberglass, wood, or light-weight metal inserted into BATTEN POCKETS in the LEECH of a sail to hold its shape. Battens can be short or run the full width of the MAINSAIL (fully-battened main). (2) a strip or bar of wood or metal. Large vessels may use battens to fasten down the hatch covers on cargo holds. See the next entry.

batten down, "batten down the hatches" – to prepare a vessel for HEAVY WEATHER by making sure gear on deck and below is stowed properly and tied securely with extra LASHINGS.

batten pockets – the pockets sewn on the LEECH of a sail or across the whole width of the sail (fully-battened main), into which BATTENS are inserted. *See* SAIL, PARTS OF.

battenless main – *see* MAIN, BATTENLESS.

battery, battery bank – many boats use batteries like those in a vehicle (same size and larger sizes). A boat can have one battery dedicated to starting the engine (engine-start battery) and another for all other DC uses (the HOUSE BATTERY). A battery bank is two or more batteries joined together by cables (large wires) to form a larger single battery. A BATTERY SELECTOR SWITCH selects the battery to be used. An ALTERNATOR charges the batteries when the engine is running. Batteries should be secured firmly in an acid-proof box, which is ventilated to allow the escape of explosive hydrogen gas produced by the charging process. ABYC Standard E-10 Storage Batteries deals with batteries and their installation, and Standard A-31 is Battery Chargers and Inverters.

battery cables – large wires attached to the BATTERY TERMINAL STUDS. Usually, but not always, they go from the positive (+) terminal to a BATTERY SELECTOR SWITCH, and from the negative (-) terminal to the ENGINE GROUND or SHIP'S GROUND. Cable sizes go from small diameter (AWG 6) to large diameter (4/0 - called "four-ought"). *See* WIRE GAUGE, AWG.

battery charger – permanently-mounted electrical equipment powered by shore power used to charge the boat's batteries. Battery chargers and marine installations must meet ABYC Standard A-31 and TA-27. Portable automotive battery chargers are not approved for marine use. Because there are so many different types of battery chargers and charging options available, consult a professional or good technical references before purchasing or replacing a marine battery charger. See the next entry.

battery charger-inverter – an INVERTER and a BATTERY CHARGER combined in a single unit. For marine use, this equipment should be approved by UL or ABYC, and be properly-installed to meet ABYC Standard A-31.

battery, house – the battery dedicated to uses other than starting the engine, such as the ELECTRONICS, cabin lights, electric bilge pump, pressure water pump, etc. It's usually larger in capacity than the ENGINE START BATTERY because it supplies more electrical needs.

battery isolator – a device in a BATTERY SWITCH or in a circuit that electrically isolates multiple batteries to prevent them from draining into each other.

battery jump-starter – a portable, rechargeable battery that can be used with a weak battery to jump start the engine, or as a portable 12-VOLT power supply. It can be used to provide emergency power to specific electronic equipment if the boat's electrical system fails, and it's very useful for checking the MAST lights when the mast is in storage off the boat. Buy one at an automotive supply store.

battery, lead-acid – *see* BATTERY TYPES.

battery maintenance – regular maintenance is important to the life of a boat's batteries. Neglected batteries don't last long. Keep the tops of batteries clean and dry, remove corrosion from the terminals with an inexpensive battery cleaning tool, use a chemical corrosion-preventative on the terminals, and make sure that the terminals and the cable connections are tight. For lead-acid batteries check the water level in the cells regularly, and use only distilled (de-ionized) water to top up. For batteries other than the standard lead-acid type, check the manufacturer's maintenance recommendations or other technical resources. When working around batteries, wear eye protection and waterproof gloves (battery acid burns skin and clothes). For long battery life don't discharge a battery below 50% of its AMP HOUR capacity. A BATTERY MONITOR indicates how many amp hours are remaining in a battery.

battery monitor – a display instrument connected to the batteries that provides accurate measurements of VOLTS, AMPS, and AMP HOURS remaining or being used for each battery. There are various types available. This instrument provides continual information about the state of charge of the batteries.

battery selector switch, battery isolation switch – a large, high-capacity switch used to choose between one or two batteries (or BATTERY BANKS). The switch has multiple positions, such as Battery 1, Battery 2, Both, and Off. A battery switch may also incorporate a battery isolation feature, which prevents batteries from draining into each other. Never turn off a battery switch or move it to another switch position while the engine is running, to prevent damage to the ALTERNATOR DIODES. Some switches are designed to permit moving the switch when the engine's running, but it's always safer to turn off the engine before changing the position of the battery switch.

battery terminals, posts – batteries have a positive (+) and a negative (-) terminal (post). Protect both terminals with insulating covers; red on positive and black on negative. Some batteries have integral STUDS on their posts for the cables; others have plain posts that require separate bolt-on terminals. The battery posts aren't the same size; buy a positive and a negative terminal. When working on a battery take care that a metal tool doesn't bridge the two terminals or contact bare wires or metal parts of the boat or the engine. It creates a dramatic spark! See the next entry.

battery terminal studs – the standard studs to which battery cables are attached are not the same size: the stud on a positive terminal is 3/8″(10mm) in diameter, and the stud on the negative terminal is 5/16″(8mm) in diameter. The end fittings (terminals) on battery cables should be sized to fit both the cable and the studs. Pre-made battery cables, red for positive and black for negative, have end fittings of the proper size.

battery testing – a lead-acid battery can be tested with a HYDROMETER, a load test, or a MULTIMETER (open-circuit test). Do the test after the battery hasn't been charged or discharged for at least six hours, preferably overnight.

Hydrometer test: a hydrometer is a device for measuring the specific gravity of the electrolyte (acid solution) in a lead-acid battery. It consists of a glass or plastic tube with small colored balls inside and a suction bulb on top. When a sample of electrolyte is drawn into the tube the balls float to a level that indicates the state of the charge of the particular cell on a scale marked on the tube or instruction sheet. Test all the cells; there can be one dead cell while the others are OK. Auto supply stores sell several sizes of this inexpensive test device. Sealed, maintenance-free batteries may have a built-in hydrometer.

Load testing (testing under load) reveals more about the condition of the battery than the voltage readings from a multimeter test. There are two methods of load testing, explained in technical references. Battery types other than lead-acid (including sealed batteries) may have different testing procedures; consult a technical reference.

Multimeter test (open circuit test): use a *digital* multimeter (an analog meter isn't accurate enough). Even a good meter is not a perfect diagnostic instrument. Before testing, allow the battery to rest overnight with the battery charger turned off, and nothing turned on to draw current. To test, set the meter to read DC volts. Connect the meter's red probe to the positive (+) battery terminal and the black probe to the negative (-) terminal. Various tables give slightly different readings and percent of charge. This is one guide:

100% charged	12.7 V or greater
80%	12.5 V
60%	12.3 V
40%	11.9 V
20%	11.6 V
fully-discharged	11.4 V

Even though a battery's voltage may read in an acceptable range, the battery may still be on its last legs. The measurement of the AMP-HOUR CAPACITY, with a BATTERY MONITOR, is a better guide to the actual health of batteries.

battery types – batteries used aboard usually supply 12-volt DC, but large vessels may have a 24-volt system. A variety of adjectives are used to describe battery types (primarily for marketing purposes), such as starting, deep-cycle, dual-purpose, golf-cart, traction, marine, and other terms. Types of batteries (internal constructions) include lead-acid (the most common), gel-cell, AGM (absorbed glass mat), and some new high-tech developments such as lithium-ion. Don't mix different battery constructions because they have different charging requirements. Old batteries shouldn't be used with new batteries in a battery bank. Many considerations go into selecting batteries for a boat; consult technical references or a marine electrician.

battery voltage – may be displayed on an analog or digital meter on a boat's DC panel or on a BATTERY MONITOR as a general guide to the state of charge of the batteries. Measure battery voltage directly on the battery with a MULTIMETER, as part of a BATTERY TESTING process. It is more accurate than a reading on an electrical panel.

beacon –(1) a general term for a lighted or unlighted structure affixed to the seabed or to the shore as a aid to navigation. Lights and DAYBEACONS are types of beacons. (2) an emergency beacon such as an EPIRB or a PERSONAL LOCATOR BEACON.

beacon, emergency – *see* EPIRB and PERSONAL LOCATOR BEACON.

beacon, personal locator – *see* PERSONAL LOCATOR BEACON.

beam – (1) the width of a vessel, usually at the widest point. (2) a transverse (ATHWARTSHIPS) support for the deck; deck beams. (3) a narrow band of electromagnetic energy transmitted by some electronic equipment, such as radar or a DEPTH SOUNDER TRANSDUCER.

beam ends, on her beam ends – describes a vessel that's HEELED so far over that there's danger of suffering a KNOCKDOWN. "That squall put *Elwing* on her beam ends."

beam reach – sailing with the APPARENT WIND on the BEAM between a CLOSE REACH and a BROAD REACH. *See* POINTS OF SAIL.

beam sea – seas that approach a vessel on the BEAM. Beam seas can cause the boat to roll.

bear, bears – verb used when referring to a BEARING: "When we're clear of the danger area the water tower will bear 70°." "The harbor entrance bears 125°."

bear away, bear off – turning the boat away from the wind. Same as FALL OFF and HEAD DOWN.

bearing or azimuth – the horizontal angular direction of an object expressed in degrees as (1) a true bearing with reference to TRUE NORTH. (2) a magnetic bearing with reference to MAGNETIC NORTH. (3) a relative bearing with reference to the HEADING of the vessel. A bearing is always measured *from* one point *to* another. For example, the bearing of a RANGE is given as seen from seaward to the range markers. Use bearings to help determine the boat's position, a course to steer, to check the accuracy of a compass, or to assess the risk of collision.

bearing, collision – *see* COLLISION BEARING.

bearing, cutless – the bearing at the AFT end of the STERN TUBE or in a SHAFT STRUT, which the propeller shaft goes through. Often called just "the cutless," it's a sleeve (shell) of metal or plastic lined with a rubber bearing material that has longitudinal grooves in it. The grooves allow water into the bearing to lubricate the shaft as it turns. Over time, the cutless bearing becomes worn; when there's more than approximately 1/16-in/1.8mm free movement in the bearing, it's time to replace it. It is sometimes incorrectly spelled "cutlass," which bothers the spelling police.

bearing, mechanical – a part in mechanical equipment that helps other parts move smoothly, reduces friction, and provides a site for lubrication. Bearings are sealed or open; some can be maintained, and others are maintenance-free. They wear over time. There are bearings all over a boat: the prop shaft CUTLESS BEARING, RUDDER STOCK bearings, ball bearings in BLOCKS and TRAVELER CARS; roller bearings in WINCHES and WINDLASSES, in ROLLER FURLERS, in ALTERNATORS, and in many other types of equipment. The pivot in a magnetic compass is usually a jeweled bearing. Some bearings are replaceable by a boat owner or a shop technician; others are not. Consult the instructions or parts diagram for a particular piece of equipment to locate bearings, and see if they're replaceable, or if there is recommended maintenance.

bearing, radar – a BEARING taken with radar. This is a RELATIVE BEARING, unless there's a vessel HEADING sensor connected to the radar. With a heading sensor the bearing can be read as a TRUE or a MAGNETIC bearing.

bearing, relative – the horizontal angular direction of an object relative to the HEADING of a vessel, measured in degrees from the BOW in a clockwise direction. A relative bearing is measured *from* the vessel *to* the object. The bearing may also be expressed verbally (1) in degrees with reference to the PORT or STARBOARD bow of the vessel, as in "45 degrees off the port bow." (2) in POINTS, with reference to the bow, BEAM, and QUARTERS of a vessel, as in "two points off the starboard bow," or "one point off the port quarter." Use a HAND-BEARING COMPASS, COMPASS BINOCULARS or a PELORUS to measure relative bearings.

bearing steady, range decreasing – indicates a collision course. See COLLISION BEARING and other COLLISION entries.

beat, beating – (1) to sail approximately 45° (or closer) to the wind; CLOSE-HAULED. Also called sailing upwind. "We were beating all morning to get here." (2) a beat is a course sailed close to the wind. "We were on a beat all the way." See POINTS OF SAIL.

Beaufort wind force, Beaufort scale, Beaufort numbers (pronounced **bo**-furt) – a table of graduated wind strengths with a Beaufort Force (F) number, wind speed in knots, a descriptive wind name, a description of the effects observed on the water, and the theoretical height of waves in the *open sea*. U.S. marine weather forecasts give wind speeds in KNOTS with a descriptive term somewhat related to the Beaufort scale. Many international marine forecasts use the Beaufort numbers and terms. The scale was developed in 1805 by Sir Francis Beaufort, a British geographer and HYDROGRAPHER.

Beaufort Wind Force Scale

FORCE	KNOTS	WIND	SEA CONDITIONS	WAVE HT. (ft/m) *
0	0	calm	like a mirror	no waves
1	1-3	light air	ripples like scales, no foam crests	¼ ft / 0.1m
2	4-6	light breeze	small wavelets, glassy crests don't break	½-1ft / 0.2-0.3m
3	7-10	gentle breeze	large wavelets, glassy crests, some breaking; scattered whitecaps	2-3ft / 0.6-1m
4	11-16	moderate breeze	small waves become longer, numerous whitecaps	3.5-5ft / 1-1.5m
5	17-21	fresh breeze	moderate waves become longer, many whitecaps, some spray	6-8 ft / 2-2.5m
6	22-27	strong breeze	larger waves form, whitecaps everywhere, more spray	9.5-13 ft / 3-4m
7	28-33	near gale	sea heaps up, foam crests begin to be blown into streaks	13.5-19 ft / 4-5.5m
8	34-40	gale	moderately high waves of greater length, crests break into spindrift, foam blown into well-defined streaks	18-25 ft / 5.5-7.5m
9	41-47	severe gale	high waves, seas begin to roll, crests topple, dense foam streaks, spray affects visibility	23-32 ft / 7-10m
10	48-55	storm	very high waves, overhanging crests, sea is white with blown foam crests, heavy shock-like seas, reduced visibility	29-41 ft / 9-12.5m
11	56-63	violent storm	exceptionally high waves, sea covered with long foam patches, wave crests blown into foam, poor visibility	37-52 ft / 11.5-16m
12	+64	hurricane	air filled with foam and spray, sea completely white, visibility seriously impaired	+52 ft / +16m
				*in the open sea

becalmed – to lose the wind completely, as a result of being in an area with no wind or in the LEE of a mountain or a very large vessel. "They were becalmed for two days in the DODRUMS."

becket – (1) an attachment point, like a loop, on the bottom of a BLOCK. (2) a short rope intended for a specific purpose; a becket rope.

becket bend – a SHEET BEND tied around an EYE SPLICE or a BOWLINE. *See* KNOTS. BASIC for a photo.

bed(s) – (1) a foundation for something heavy, such as an engine (engine beds), a generator, or tanks. (2) to affix a fitting to the hull, deck, or SPAR using an adhesive or waterproof BEDDING COMPOUND, along with the fasteners. See the next entry.

bedding compound – an waterproof adhesive or putty designed for bedding fittings or structural parts of a vessel. Bedding compound prevents water from getting under a fitting or between structural parts. To bed a fitting, spread bedding compound on the underside of the fitting and on the surface where the fitting goes. Then tighten down the securing bolts or screws. Read the instructions with the bedding compound; some instructions recommend tightening the fasteners after the compound has set up a little. Consult a marine supply catalogue for types of bedding compounds suitable for different uses.

belay – (1) to make fast; to wrap a line securely around a CLEAT or other fitting. (2) As a spoken command, belay means to stop doing a particular action or to cancel a previously-given instruction. "Belay hoisting the main."

below, below decks – beneath the deck or in the cabin. "Please go below and get the binoculars."

bend – (1) a bend usually refers to a knot used to join two ropes or to tie a line to something, such as an anchor bend or a SHEET BEND. *See* KNOTS, BASIC for a photo. (2) to tie a line onto something, to put a flag on a HALYARD, or to put sails on a SPAR or STAY. "Bend this line on the CLEW of the JIB."

bergy bit (pronounced **ber** gee, "g" as in give) – a piece of floating glacier ice that's smaller than an ICEBERG and larger than a GROWLER. Bergy bits float above the surface. A typical bergy bit can be as large as a small house. See ICEBERG for a photo.

Bermuda High – in the North Atlantic, the Bermuda High develops in the summer and fall near Bermuda; in the winter and early spring it moves eastward and is called the Azores High. It's a semi-permanent HIGH PRESSURE SYSTEM.

Bermudan, Bermuda rig, Marconi rig – the triangular MAINSAIL on modern sailboats. See SAIL, PARTS OF for a drawing.

berth – (1) the mooring location for a vessel when she's not at sea: "My boat is in berth C-8." When used as a verb berth refers to a mooring location. "Berth your vessel on that pier." (2) a place for sleeping, also called a bunk. (3) when used with "wide" it means a safe distance: "Give the BREAKWATER a wide berth when you enter the harbor."

beset, nipped – caught in the ice when navigating in polar regions. "When we were trying to navigate the Northwest Passage in 2005, we were beset near Banks Island for three weeks."

best bower – the heaviest BOWER anchor on a vessel.

bight – (1) the part of a rope away from the ends; a loop in the middle of a rope. The word is used in knot-tying instructions. (2) a bay or indentation in the shoreline. "There's a good ANCHORAGE in that bight."

bilge, bilges – the interior of the hull below the cabin SOLE.

bilge alarm, high water alarm – an electronic device that senses the level of water in the bilge and sounds an audible and/or visual alarm. Some are operated by the boat's battery power, and some by an internal battery.

bilge blower, blower – an electric fan used to ventilate the engine compartment or engine room and the bilge. The fan draws air and (fumes, if any) from the engine room and bilge, and discharges them above the waterline through vent(s) in the hull near the deck level at or near the STERN.

bilge, firm – a term applied to the shape of a hull. A boat with a relatively sharp curve where the bottom meets the waterline has firm or hard bilges. A boat with a relatively gentle curve from the bottom to the waterline has slack bilges. *See* BILGE, TURN OF.

bilged – holed below the waterline; to have a hole in the bilge. "The boat had been bilged on the rocks by the time the Coast Guard arrived."

bilge keel – *see* KEEL, BILGE.

bilge pump – a manual or electric pump that removes water from the bilge or BILGE SUMP. The pump can be mounted directly in the bilge, or have a pickup hose in the bilge. It discharges overboard above the waterline through an outlet hose. All boats should have a good manual pump permanently installed, in addition to electric pumps. An electric pump has an automatic FLOAT SWITCH to turn it on when the water reaches a certain level. If a boat has bilges divided into separate compartments, several pumps will be needed. See ABYC Standard H-22 Electric Bilge Pump Systems. See the following bilge pump entries.

bilge pump capacity – manual and electric bilge pumps are rated in how many gallons per minute (gpm) or per hour (gph) they discharge. These figures are theoretical, measured in a lab, and don't take into account important factors such as the type or length of the hoses, the number of bends in the hoses, or the level to which the water must be pumped to discharge overboard (the pump's head). An electric pump may not have a full 12-volts of power available, and if it pumps for a long time, without the battery being charged simultaneously, the voltage will drop and the capacity decrease. Select an electric bilge pump with the largest capacity that will fit in the available space in the bilge. *See* BILGE PUMP INSTALLATION, below.

bilge pump cycle counter – is there a leak you don't know about? If you're not aboard, you don't hear the pump, and even if you are aboard you may not hear it running. A bilge pump cycle counter counts the number of times an electric pump turns on, and displays the number on a small meter. It's a useful addition to a bilge pump system.

bilge pump float switch – a switch that turns on an electric bilge pump when the water rises to a certain level. Float switches are mechanical, with a float that rises with the water, or electronic, with no moving parts. Some mechanical floats can be jammed in the open or closed position by debris in the bilge. Both types of switches require a little maintenance: check that the float operates properly and keep the switch clean.

bilge pump installation or modification – for a manual or electric bilge pump the following practices will help to maximize pumping efficiency:

- Use smooth-bore hoses (corrugated hoses restrict the flow of water).
- Use hoses and fittings of the largest diameter possible. Reducer fittings restrict the pump output.
- Keep the same diameter of hose and fittings from the pump to the overboard discharge, if possible.
- Minimize the number of sharp bends in the hoses.
- Consider the use of a CHECK VALVE in a long discharge line, to prevent water from flowing back to the pump when it stops pumping. However, a check valve somewhat restricts the flow.
- Locate the overboard discharge above the typical HEELED waterline on a sailboat, or about 8"/20cm above the loaded waterline on a powerboat. If the overboard discharge isn't above the heeled or loaded waterline, install an ANTI-SIPHON VALVE in the hose to prevent water from siphoning back into the boat through the discharge hose. However, this valve will reduce the output of the pump.
- Use a THROUGH-HULL discharge fitting that's as large as possible. A through-hull smaller than the hose restricts the flow.
- Keep the boat's battery charged with a marine battery charger or SOLAR PANELS when you're not aboard. Leaks may develop mysteriously, and an electric pump's output capacity is affected by low battery voltage. If you suspect a secret leak, install a BILGE PUMP CYCLE COUNTER.
- If there's any chance that oily pollutants can get into the bilge, put an oil-absorbent cloth or "bilge sock" in the bilge. It's illegal everywhere to allow oily water to go overboard.

The relevant ABYC Standard is H-22 Electric Bilge Pump Systems.

bilge pump, manual – many manual pumps (except tubular DINGHY pumps) have a rubber DIAPHRAGM that moves up and down to create suction and discharge forces in the hoses as the handle is moved. Locate a manual pump within reach of the helmsman. Secure the handle with a LANYARD or in a clip when it's not in use, so it can't be lost overboard. Test the pump regularly by pouring clean water into the bilge and pumping it out. Carry a spare pump diaphragm. When replacing an old pump, install the next size larger, if possible. A manual pump is tiring to work for a long time, so choose one with a large capacity. Large-capacity portable bilge pumps mounted on a board are available, and they're a good piece of emergency equipment. A big manual pump may help save the boat.

bilge pump selection – *see* BILGE PUMP CAPACITY.

bilge, slack – a term related to the design of a hull. A boat with a gentle curve from the bottom to the TOPSIDES (rather than a sharp curve) has slack bilges. A sharper curve at the bilge is a firm or hard bilge.

"bilge sniffer" – slang name for a FUME DETECTOR.

bilge sump, sump – a recess in the bilge into which water drains and collects so it can be pumped overboard. Some boats have more than one sump.

bilge, turn of the – where the bottom of the hull curves up toward the TOPSIDES, or the area of the CHINES in a hard-chined boat. *See* BILGE, FIRM and BILGE, SLACK.

Bimini (top) – a fabric cover over the COCKPIT area for sun and weather protection, usually mounted on a collapsible metal frame. A DODGER/SPRAY HOOD helps protect the cockpit from spray.

binnacle – the place where the main steering compass is mounted. On many yachts the binnacle is part of the steering PEDESTAL.

binoculars, image-stabilized – these binoculars have higher magnifications than typical marine 7-power binoculars, because they're stabilized. Two common specifications are 15x50 and 18x50. The first number is the magnification power; the second number is the size in millimeters of the objective lenses (the large lenses). The field of view of stabilized binoculars is not as wide as on non-stabilized. Read the specifications and consult a knowledgeable dealer. If possible, test before buying. See the next entry.

binoculars, marine – electronics can't "see" everything, and if the electronics go out, binoculars are only visual aid you have. They're an important safety item. If your activities on the water keep you close to home and you don't sail at night, then selecting binoculars is a relatively simple task. However, if you cruise away from home or sail at night, good marine binoculars are very important. Any manufacturer can claim to have "marine" binoculars; the term is non-specific. A standard type of non-stabilized marine binocular is the 7x50. The first number is the magnification power; the second is the size in millimeters of the objective lenses (the large lenses). Here are some basic guidelines for selecting marine binoculars:

- Magnification – above seven-power it's hard to hold binoculars steady, the field-of-view is narrower, so it's not easy to keep objects centered as the boat moves, and the image is less-bright at higher magnifications. Stabilized binoculars have higher magnifications.
- Light transmission efficiency – binoculars with large objective lenses gather more light and give a brighter image than those with smaller objective lenses. This is especially important at night. 50mm is a common objective lens on marine binoculars. A good binocular transmits 93-97% of the light it gathers to your eyes. Read the specifications.

• Field of view – a common field of view specification for marine binoculars is approximately 385 ft/120m at a range of 1,000 yds/1000m. It's important to have good image quality (no distortion) across the whole field of view.

• Waterproof – the best marine binoculars are truly waterproof, even when submerged. Look for specifications that say "nitrogen-purged" or "fog proof." Condensation can occur in binoculars that are not waterproof, which destroys the optical quality. Make sure the binoculars are guaranteed in writing to be waterproof (not just "water-resistant," whatever that means).

• Individual focus eye pieces – individual focus helps ensure watertight integrity. The eye pieces have a small reference scale so they can be set to each person's eyes.

• Strong construction, rubber armored – no binocular is shockproof; it's a precision instrument and should be protected, but a thick rubber coating makes it easy to grip, stops it from sliding around, and offers some shock protection. Good marine binoculars will be heavier than lower quality ones. However, the weight helps you hold it steady, and usually you don't wear binoculars around your neck for a long period of time.

• Integral compass – some models have an built-in compass for taking BEARINGS, especially important for sighting on distant objects.

• Purchase a brand from a company that has a good reputation for making quality marine binoculars. Buy the best you can afford. Knowledgeable staff in a store can help you make the right choice. Good binoculars last for generations. Test them outside the store, if possible, and read the specifications carefully when comparing models by price. You get what you pay for. Image-stabilized and NIGHT VISION DEVICES are expensive; try to test them in actual conditions on a moving vessel, if at all possible.

• Buy a foam floater strap for the binoculars and test it in seawater (or fresh water if you operate on lakes). The strap is comfortable around your neck, and if the binoculars go overboard (gasp!) you have a chance to retrieve them.

binoculars, night vision – *see* NIGHT VISION DEVICES.

biodiesel – *see* DIESEL FUEL, BIODIESEL.

bite, bites – the anchor bites when it grabs hold of the bottom; when it bites, it begins to SET, digging itself into the seabed. "There was so much kelp we couldn't get the anchor to bite."

bitt, bitts (either word may refer to a single bitt) – a strong vertical post or pair of posts mounted on the BOW and/or STERN for mooring and anchor lines. A bitt may have a horizontal bar or pin through it to help hold a line. Bitts are also used on piers and docks, and on towing vessels for the towlines. A single bitt on the bow may be called a SAMSON POST. For other photos see BULWARK, the dock photo with DROGUE, CANOE STERN and HORSE.

A large mooring bitt (lower center) on the stern of *Wilhelmina Maria*, an 1895 Hollandaise sailing barge.

A double bitt on the foredeck of a restored 1895 sailing fishing vessel. The bitt holds the inboard end of the retractable bowsprit. The chain pipe leads the anchor chain into the chain locker below the deck.

bitter end – (1) the tail end of a rope or chain. (2) the end of the anchor RODE that is attached to the boat.

black box – a descriptive term for any device whose workings are not understood by or accessible to its user. In electronics, a black box is a sealed piece of equipment, such as black box AIS. Aircraft have a black box flight data recorder. Almost anything could be referred to as a black box if we don't understand (or need to understand) how it works.

Black Box Theory – every mariner should read John Vigor's thoughtful essay. It will make you think differently about SEAMANSHIP, and help limit the operation of MURPHY'S LAW. www.johnvigor.com/Black_Box_Theory.html.

black water – term for sewage on a boat; the discharge from the HEAD (toilet) is black water. *See* GRAY WATER and NO DISCHARGE AREA.

blade(s) – (1) the parts of a propeller that move the boat. (2) the end of an oar that's in the water. (3) a JIB that doesn't overlap the MAST, or a STORM JIB.

bleeding the engine, bleeding the fuel system – bleeding gets rid of air in the fuel system. If air gets in, especially with a diesel engine, it won't be possible to start the engine, or the engine will stop running. Air can get into the system when a FUEL FILTER is changed, if a leak develops, or when work is done on any part of the fuel system. The engine manual describes how to bleed the engine; the procedure differs with engines. It's not especially difficult, and anyone who operates a diesel should know how to do it. Running the engine for five or more minutes before departure helps ensure that air hasn't gotten into the system since the last time the engine was run.

blind piloting – *see* PILOTING, BLIND.

"blip" – slang for a RADAR RETURN.

block – the nautical term for "pulley." Blocks have one or more SHEAVES (pronounced shivs) over which ropes run. The BOOM has blocks on it for the MAINSHEET, and there are blocks for the JIB SHEETS, among many types of blocks on a sailboat. Several blocks with line make up a TACKLE.

block and tackle, purchase – other names for a TACKLE.

block, cheek – a block designed to be mounted on a flat surface or a SPAR.

block, fiddle – a block with two SHEAVES (pronounced shivs), one mounted above the other, rather than side-by-side.

block, foot – a block mounted on a plate, intended to be attached to a SPAR or the deck.

block, loads on – the loads exerted on a block from a SHEET, HALYARD, or other line vary with the angle the rope makes going through the block, as well as the load from whatever the line is attached to. The sharper the angle, the higher the load on a block. Examples (approximate): 30° angle through the block equals 50% more load; 60% angle equals 100% more load. If a line makes a 180° turn through a block, it has 200% more load. Take this into account when purchasing blocks. SHEET LOADS and the potential for shock loads should also be considered when selecting blocks.

block size – the size of the block and the diameter of the rope used in it should match. Marine equipment catalogues give the recommended size range for lines for each block. A too-small block will chafe the line or it may not be strong enough.

block, snatch – a block with a hinged SHELL on one side that can be opened to put the middle (the BIGHT) of a line in it, rather than having to REEVE the line through the block from the end. Snatch blocks have a SNAP SHACKLE on one end so they can be moved easily to where they're needed.

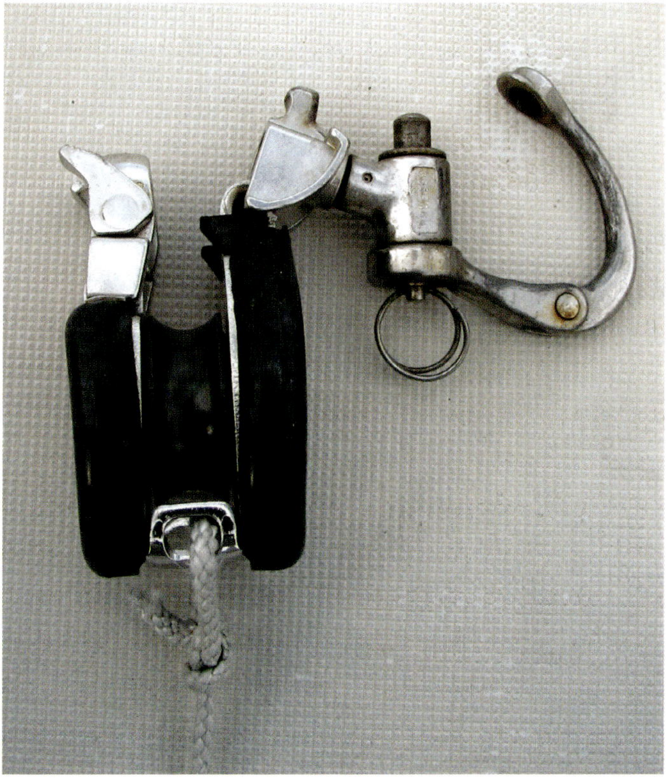

A snatch block in the open position. The snap shackle is to the right.

block, turning – a block used to change the direction of a line. Turning blocks of various types are used for HEADSAIL SHEETS, HALYARDS, and CONTROL LINES that are led back to the COCKPIT.

blood knot, double overhand knot – a basic STOPPER KNOT in the end of a rope, to prevent it from escaping through a BLOCK, FAIRLEAD, LINE STOPPER, or other small opening. It's larger than a FIGURE-EIGHT KNOT. It's called a blood knot because it was used at the end of the whip lashes on a cat-o'-nine tails, used to flog unfortunate sailors. *See* KNOTS, BASIC for a photo.

blower – same as BILGE BLOWER.

"blow-me-down" – a name for a very strong gust or KATABATIC WIND.

bluewater, blue water – offshore or ocean-going; a blue water passage or a bluewater yacht.

BMEA – abbreviation for the BRITISH MARINE ELECTRONICS ASSOCIATION.

board – (1) to go backwards is to make a STERNBOARD. (2) a name for a LEG when tacking: a long board is a long TACK and a short board is a short tack. "If we make a couple of short boards here that'll be enough to clear the SHOAL area." (3) to go aboard a vessel. Before boarding it's polite to ask the skipper or other crewmember for "PERMISSION TO COME ABOARD"

boarding ladder – a metal, wood, plastic, or rope ladder deployed over the side or STERN of a boat to assist climbing aboard. Some boarding ladders are permanently mounted; others are portable. See KEEL, BILGE for a photo of a stern boarding ladder.

boarding ladder, emergency – a portable folding ladder designed to be deployed easily and quickly when recovering a person in the water. Several types are available, including some that can be deployed by someone in the water by pulling a short rope attached to the folded ladder. Even if the boat has a boarding ladder on the STERN, carry a separate emergency ladder, because sometimes it's too rough to climb aboard at the stern.

boat, ship, yacht – loosely-used terms referring to vessels. A boat is a vessel smaller than a ship. Ship refers to a medium-sized or larger vessel that can carry one or more boats, such as life boats or workboats. Ship also refers to particular types of SQUARE-RIGGED sailing vessels. Yacht is a general term for a vessel used for pleasure (as opposed to a COMMERCIAL VESSEL); a motor yacht or a sailing yacht. The term yacht may be used in some cases to refer specifically to a sailboat.

boat builder regulation and standards – in the U.S. the Coast Guard issues regulations for boat builders and importers of recreational boats. The regulations incorporate standards developed by ABYC, UL, and other safety standards organizations. In general, the regulations define standards for electrical and fuel system installation and ventilation for boats with inboard gasoline engines, and safe loading, vessel capacity, and flotation requirements for small boats. In most cases compliance with the regulations is the boat manufacturers' responsibility. The Coast Guard has a voluntary factory inspection program for powerboats under 21ft in length, which is designed to help manufacturers comply with regulations before marketing the boat. See www.safeafloat.com. The USCG issues safety and recall notices if defects are found in recreational marine products after manufacture. The notices are available at www.uscgboating.org (recalls and safety defects tab), and at www.boatus.com (boating safety tab). In Canada, Transport Canada regulates small vessel construction. In the EU standards are promulgated in the RECREATIONAL CRAFT DIRECTIVE (RCD). Canadian, EU, and U.S. consumer affairs groups, manufacturers, and boating magazines publish defective product notices and recalls. The best way to be certain that your boat complies with mandated safety standards is to have a VESSEL SAFETY CHECK.

boat designs – *see* DESIGNS, YACHT.

boathook, boat hook – several types are available, with fixed or telescoping handles. If you buy a telescoping aluminum boathook, get the longest and strongest one available. Watching someone flailing at a mooring buoy line or PICK-UP FLOAT with a short boathook while standing on a high BOW is entertaining for spectators on other boats, and possibly dangerous for the struggling crew member on the bow. There are many other uses for a long boathook, and it can be closed down for stowage. For obvious reasons, never FEND OFF with a telescoping boathook in its extended position. Wooden and some aluminum boathooks float, which is handy when it gets caught on a mooring buoy's line or chain, and it gets pulled out of your hand. Certainly, don't tie a boathook to your wrist; imagine the possibilities. See MOORING, PICKING-UP for a photo of a proper boathook.

boating license – *see* LICENSE, BOATING.

boat manual or boat information book – a book that gives the specifications of the vessel and its systems, and describes details of the operation of the vessel. The manual may also include inventories of gear aboard, a stowage plan, a diagram of the location of all THROUGH HULLS, and other necessary or useful information. The book can be created by the owner and/or the boat manufacturer. Keep the book updated with changes. ABYC report T-24 Owner/Operator's Manuals is a basic guide. *See also* MANUAL, OWNER-OPERATOR.

boat names – should be short and simple. Remember that you may be asked to spell the name in the PHONETIC ALPHABET on the radio. Do you want to spell *Unidentified Floating Object* in phonetics? Also, choose a name that cannot be mistaken for DISTRESS or urgent communication on the radio: a name that sounds anything like "Mayday" (such as "Mahdee" or "Pay Day") is a poor choice. As I write this I'm looking at a sailboat named "Call The Cops."

Boat Owners Association of The United States, BoatU.S. – a member organization with a magazine, member benefits, and a comprehensive, open-access website for recreational mariners at www.boatus.com. Check the links at the top of the webpage. For the DIY person, see the technical guides, which discuss marine products, equipment installation, maintenance, safety, and operation. The BoatU.S. Foundation (www.boatus.org) has an online learning center, with information about the requirements for boater licensing in the U.S., and online courses that meet the requirements.

BoatU.S. – usual identification of the BOAT OWNERS ASSOCIATION OF THE UNITED STATES.

BoatU.S. Foundation – *see* BOAT OWNERS ASSOCIATION OF THE UNITED STATES.

bobstay – a metal rod, wire or chain extending from underneath the front of a BOWSPRIT down to the STEM near the waterline. The bobstay counteracts the tension of the HEADSTAY on the top of the bowsprit, but it's not used on all bowsprits. For other photos, see BOWSPRIT, CATBOAT, and JIB, YANKEE.

A two-part rod bobstay, with a dolphin striker extending down from the bowsprit. The anchors are CQRs™.

bollard – a strong vertical post or two attached posts, made of metal, strong wood, or sometimes concrete found on a pier or a wharf, used for mooring lines. Also used on towing vessels for towlines and WARPS (may be called a towing BITT).

bolt cutters – bolt cutters are for use on MILD STEEL (such as non-hardened steel bolts and chain).They are ineffective for cutting STAINLESS STEEL RIGGING and hardened chain. A RIGGING CUTTER is needed with these metals.

bolt rope – a rope or thinner line sewn along the LUFF (also called a luff rope) and/or FOOT of a sail to strengthen the edge or to feed it into a groove on a SPAR.

bonding, bonding system – bonding is connecting all metal, non-current carrying parts of a vessel, such as the engine, propeller shaft and propeller, SEACOCKS, metal equipment housings, and any metals that come into contact with seawater (either externally or in bilge water) to a common ground point (the SHIP'S GROUND). The purpose of a bonding system is to protect underwater metals from STRAY CURRENT CORROSION, to ground the electrical system, and to provide lightning-strike protection. The connections at all bonded items should be kept tight and free of corrosion for the system to be effective. Bonding is a complex subject discussed in technical literature, but it's an important topic to understand.

bomb (meteorological) – *see* LOW, RAPIDLY-INTENSIFYING.

boom – (1) a horizontal SPAR attached to a MAST that holds the FOOT of a FORE-AND-AFT sail. The boom is affixed to the mast by a device called the GOOSENECK. (2) a floating barrier to contain pollution or prevent entry into an area.

A containment boom around a sunken fishing vessel in a marina.

boom brake – a BOOM control device that consists of the control unit, which is attached to the boom near mid-point (where a VANG would normally be located), and one or two control lines which are led back to the COCKPIT. One of the benefits of a boom brake is that it slows down the force of an accidental JIBE; however, it may not be as effective in preventing a jibe as a true PREVENTER. There are several brands available.

boom crutch, boom crotch, boom gallows – a support for the BOOM when the MAINSAIL is furled or to hold the boom steady when REEFING the main. A crutch is single vertical support, in contrast to a GALLOWS, which is an ATHWARTSHIPS frame for the boom to rest on.

boomkin – a short SPAR or frame extending horizontally from the STERN of a boat. A boomkin may be used as an attachment point for a BACKSTAY or for SHEET BLOCKS on a KETCH, SCHOONER, or YAWL.

boom, main – *see* MAIN BOOM.

boom vang, "kicking strap," "go fast" – other names for a VANG.

boom, wishbone – *see* WISHBONE BOOM.

boot, mast – *see* MAST BOOT.

boot, turnbuckle – *see* TURNBUCKLE BOOT.

boot top – a decorative stripe or stripes along the waterline, usually of a contrasting color to the hull and the bottom paint.

bosun's chair – a wooden or cloth seat or a climbing harness that's attached to a HALYARD for hoisting a person up the MAST to perform some task. A bosun's chair should be designed so that the user will not fall out of it. *See* MAST CLIMBING.

bottom – (1) the seabed; the "ground." (2) the part of a boat below the waterline.

bottom, characteristics of – identified on charts with different abbreviations. Check the characteristics of the bottom where you plan to anchor. If there's no notation on a chart or if you're unsure of what's down there, take a sample of the bottom with a LEADLINE (the boat should have one of these). *See* HOLDING GROUND.

bow (rhymes with now) – the front part of a boat; the "pointy end." (except on a PRAM).

bow and beam bearings – a simple PILOTING technique using BEARINGS on a single object ashore to determine two LINES OF POSITION, which can be crossed to produce a FIX. A number of books explain how to take and PLOT these bearings.

Bowditch (rhymes with **now** ditch) – the informal and usual name for *The American Practical Navigator*, a comprehensive navigation reference book. It was first published in 1802 by its original author, Nathaniel Bowditch. Through numerous revisions it's remained a basic reference for professional and serious recreational mariners. There are detailed chapters on PILOTING, ELECTRONIC NAVIGATION, CELESTIAL NAVIGATION, navigation mathematics, safety, oceanography, ice navigation, and marine meteorology. It is available in paper, as a searchable CD-ROM or for free download. See *Bowditch* in the bibliography under "Navigation and Piloting."

bow, doubling the angle on – *see* DOUBLING THE ANGLE ON THE BOW.

bow, down at the – *see* DOWN AT THE BOW.

bower, bower anchor (rhymes with tower) – the main anchor on a vessel, usually the heaviest one. "With the storm coming you'd better use your best bower."

bow line (rhymes with now line) – a line that leads from the BOW of the boat to the dock or mooring buoy. See MOORING LINE for a diagram.

bowline (pronounced **bo**-lin) – a basic knot made in the end of a rope to create a loop. Use a bowline to attach the SHEETS to the CLEW of a HEADSAIL or to form a loop in the end of a mooring line. See KNOTS, BASIC for a photo.

bow, plumb – a bow with a straight STEM from deck to the waterline, with no curve or angle.

A plumb bow on a BOC 50 racing sailboat.

bow pulpit – another name for BOW RAIL(S) .

bow rail(s), bow pulpit – the safety rails around the BOW of a boat to which the LIFELINES are attached. Some bow rails are split, to make it easier to climb on and off the boat when she's MED MOORED. Logically, STERN RAILS are at the other end of the boat.

A split bow rail. A Bruce® anchor is on the starboard bow roller. Note the small ventilator in the forehatch. The mast is deck-stepped.

bow roller – another name for an ANCHOR ROLLER.

bowsprit – a SPAR projecting from the BOW, with the HEADSTAY attached to the outer end on top and a BOBSTAY attached underneath. Short bowsprits don't need a bobstay. For other photos see BOW, PLUMB; BOBSTAY; CATBOAT; CLASSIC VESSEL; CUTTER; DOUBLE-ENDED; JIB, YANKEE; KEEL, LIFTING; KETCH, and YARDARM.

A sail-training schooner, with students standing on the bowsprit. There are ratlines on the shrouds and baggywrinkle on the rigging.

bow thruster – a propeller-like device or a water-jet mounted ATHWARTSHIPS in the hull (in a tube or tunnel) underwater near the BOW to help maneuver a vessel at slow speeds. Some thrusters are external to the hull. It's controlled from the HELM position. There may be a thermal overload protection device in the electrical circuit, and if it overheats from continuous use or from encountering an obstruction, the thruster may not be able to be operated until the heat dissipates. A bow thruster is especially useful in CLOSE QUARTERS or when a vessel must MED MOOR. Ships may have bow and stern thrusters.

A small bow thruster on a powerboat.

brackish – water that has less salt than seawater but more salt than fresh water. There's brackish water in the northern Chesapeake Bay, Delaware Bay, and the Hudson River on the U.S. east coast; San Francisco Bay on the west coast; parts of the St. Lawrence River in Canada; the Thames estuary, the Baltic Sea, and the Black Sea in Europe.

braid – *see* ROPE, BRAIDED.

brash, brash ice – small pieces of ice, approximately six ft/2m in size.

brass – a soft metal ALLOY of copper, zinc, tin, and other metals (in varying proportions depending on the type of brass). It's yellow-gold in color or may be chrome plated. Brass is used for interior fittings, plumbing fittings, and marine hardware. Brass fittings should not be used with seawater systems below the waterline; use BRONZE or STAINLESS STEEL. There are many different types of brass, such as naval brass, red brass, Admiralty brass, and manganese bronze (a brass). Each type has specific properties that make it more suited to some marine applications than others. All "brass" is not the same. *See* GALVANIC SERIES.

breaking out an anchor – when an anchor has dug itself firmly into the seabed or become stuck on something on the bottom, the power of a crew member or a WINDLASS may not be enough to break it out (free it). Books and articles describe techniques for breaking out a stuck anchor; some involve the use of the engine, sail power, or a TRIPPING LINE.

breaking strength – the breaking strength of rope or chain as expressed in reference tables is the optimum strength observed in lab tests on new rope or chain. It's only a rough indication of the breaking strength of a rope or chain under conditions of use. Shock loads, angular pulls, twisting, and other forces exert heavier loads than those in lab tests. Use tabulated breaking strengths as a comparative or general guide. *See* CHAIN, SAFE WORKING LOAD and ROPE, SAFE WORKING LOAD.

breaking wave – *see* WAVE, BREAKING.

breakwater, mole – a structure, either natural or man-made, that deflects or repels waves, thus protecting a marina, harbor, or coastal area from wave action and damage. A jetty or pier may also be a breakwater. Some breakwaters are submerged at some stage of the tide; this is indicated on a chart. A breakwater AWASH is hard to see, unless a boat has run up on it and is sitting there as a warning.

breast line – a line from the vessel to the dock, extending at right angles to the CENTERLINE of the vessel. It holds the boat close to the dock. More than one breast line can be used. See MOORING LINE for a diagram.

bridge – on a ship the bridge is the location from which the vessel is controlled and navigated. Bridge may also be applied to the navigation and steering location aboard smaller vessels.

bridge deck – the raised area at the COMPANIONWAY that separates the COCKPIT from the companionway LADDER, and helps prevent water in the cockpit from going below into the cabin. Some boats don't have a bridge deck, so the cabin doors or companionway DROP BOARDS must be closed underway in anything but calm conditions.

bridge-to-bridge radiotelephone regulations – these regulations apply in waters subject to the INLAND WATERS NAVIGATION RULES, out to the three-mile limit. Small boat operators should know which vessels are subject to these regulations in case they need to contact a vessel. The following vessels must monitor designated VHF channels while navigating Inland Waters:

- Every power-driven vessel of 20m/65.6ft or greater in length.
- Every vessel of 100 gross tons and upward carrying one or more PASSENGERS FOR HIRE.
- Every towing vessel of 26ft/8m or more in length.
- Every dredge and floating plant in or near a channel or FAIRWAY engaged in operations that are likely to restrict or affect the navigation of other vessels, except for an unmanned or intermittently-manned floating plant under the control of a dredge.

In the U.S. the channels are 13, 16, 22A, (67 for some specific areas on the Mississippi River), and any applicable VTS frequencies where the vessel is operating.

bridge, fixed – the clearance height of a bridge printed on a chart is measured from high water. You must know the vessel's AIR DRAFT to be sure she can pass under the bridge at high water. If there's a large tide RANGE you may be able to wait until low water if the MAST is too high. Some bridges have a clearance gauge on or near a bridge PIER; the gauge indicates the distance from the lowest part of the bridge to the water (not the depth of the water under the bridge.) A fixed bridge may have a painted mark or green or white lights to indicate the preferred channel or span and the center of the highest part of the span.

bridge, opening, lifting or swing – this type of bridge may have lights to indicate whether it's open (green) or closed (red); at a distance it may not be easy to tell if it's open. A NAUTICAL ALMANAC, COAST PILOT, or CRUISING GUIDE may have information about the VHF channels and SOUND SIGNALS to use to contact bridges, and the operating hours. When approaching this type of bridge don't get too close in anticipation of its opening; something may delay or prevent opening, and current or wind may force the boat into the bridge. Even if you think the bridge tender can easily see you waiting, call the bridge, give your boat name and which side of the bridge you're on, and say you want to come through on the next opening. You definitely don't want the tender to lower or swing the bridge as you approach or go through (it happens).

bridle – a length of rope (or two lines tied together at one end) with the other ends attached to the boat or another object, and with an attachment point in the middle for another line. Some uses for a bridle include for a STERN DROGUE or a SEA ANCHOR, as a TRAVELER on a small sailboat, to lift a DINGHY, with a SPINNAKER POLE control line, for towing, for securing to a mooring buoy, or in certain anchoring conditions, such as when TIDE RODE, to help position the boat.

brightwork, bright-finished – varnished wood above or below decks. See the photo with KEEL, FULL for a bright-finished yacht.

British Marine Electronics Association, BMEA – a trade association for the leisure marine electronics industry, similar in function to the U.S. NMMA®.

British Waterways Marinas, Ltd., BWML – 18 BWML marinas are located on navigable inland rivers, the Thames, and the Humber. Yachts seeking a long-term berth at a British Waterways Marina must comply with BWML regulations for berthing. These regulations include having a Boat Safety Certificate and a British Waterways craft license. The Boat Safety Certificate requires an inspection of the vessel for compliance with specific safety rules. Because of differences in standards and requirements for yacht safety equipment and installations in North America and some other countries outside the EU, it is unlikely that a yacht from those areas will pass the Boat Safety Scheme (BSS) examination. In some cases, expensive modifications and/or the purchase of new, approved equipment may be required for the vessel to pass inspection and obtain a certificate. See www.bwml.co.uk. and the bibliography under "Design" for a link to the BSS requirements.

broach, broach-to – under some sea conditions or in strong or gusty winds a sailboat may HEEL suddenly, turn sharply and lose control, resulting in a broach. The ability to release SHEETS quickly is essential to recovering. When a boat surfs down the face of a wave the wave speed may exceed that of the boat, resulting in little or no water moving past the rudder. The rudder cannot steer, and thus the boat can be turned broadside to the waves in a broach. The phrase broach-to is also used. "The big waves ASTERN made us broach-to, even though we were paying attention at the helm."

broadband radar – *see* RADAR, BROADBAND.

broad on the beam – same as ABEAM.

broad on the bow – a bearing of approximately 45° measured from the BOW AFT to either STARBOARD or PORT.

broad on the quarter – a bearing of approximately 135° measured from the bow AFT to the STARBOARD or PORT QUARTER.

broad reach – sailing with the APPARENT WIND on the QUARTER; between a BEAM REACH AND DOWNWIND. *See* POINTS OF SAIL.

bronze – a metal with copper alloyed with a variety of other metals, depending on type of bronze. It's yellow-gold in color, and looks somewhat like BRASS, but it's a harder metal. Sometimes the names brass and bronze are used interchangeably, but they are different metals. Bronze has decorative and functional uses above and below the water; it may be chrome-plated. In general, bronze is more resistant to salt-water corrosion than brass. Types include phosphorus bronze, aluminum bronze (salt-water uses such as fasteners, pumps and valves, pipe fittings, heat exchangers, bearings in machinery); silicon bronze (marine fasteners, TURNBUCKLES, WINCHES). Manganese bronze is actually a brass. *See* GALVANIC SERIES.

buddy – another name for a SENTINEL.

buddy boat – (1) a vessel that you're traveling with. (2) on a radar screen, a buddy boat is a vessel that follows the same course and moves at the same speed as your vessel.

building or renovating a boat – these words scare some mariners to death and make the eyes of others gleam with anticipation. There are articles, magazines, and books devoted to this topic. It's the ultimate DIY challenge. Before committing your life to building or renovating read as much as you can and talk to people who have tackled what you're contemplating.

Hmmmm. Which one should I buy to fix up?

Well, dear, what about this one?

It'll take much longer than you expect and cost more than you imagine. Too many partially-completed projects sit abandoned or wait to be saved by someone who sees a bargain boat. Here are some thoughts:

• Research and compare the cost of building new or properly renovating a good-quality older boat with the cost of buying a similar-quality well-equipped new or relatively new yacht.

• Research what older boats are worth the time and money; consult a **MARINE SURVEYOR** before deciding on boats to consider.

• You must have considerable technical skill and/or competent assistance to tackle a new build or a major renovation. Do an honest self-assessment.

• It's necessary to have lots of time, a proper work location, access to professional assistance (if needed), and many tools, some specialized and expensive.

• Take some professional technical skills and certification courses, unless you're already very experienced in electrical system design and installation, engines and associated systems, woodworking, fiberglass or metal work, plumbing, refrigeration, rigging, painting, and the many skills necessary to do a proper job. You may subcontract some of the work, and you'll need a good understanding of all areas to deal with the professionals.

• Learn the **ABYC** or relevant European technical standards for recreational vessels and follow them. Join ABYC for the years of the project and call upon their resources, including their certification courses. Make sure subcontracted work is done in accordance with accepted marine standards and practices in your country.

• A careful project plan and work schedule and adequate funding is essential to success.

• If you have a sailing partner make sure the partner is involved in the project as much as possible. If your partner isn't engaged with your "life's work" you may be sailing off alone.

bulb keel – *see* **KEEL, BULB.**

bulkhead – (1) a vertical partition (wall) below decks. Bulkheads may be **TRANSVERSE** or **FORE-AND-AFT**. (2) a seawall of metal, wood, concrete, or stone used to prevent erosion of the shoreline.

bulkhead, watertight or collision bulkhead – a bulkhead that prevents water in one part of a boat from moving through the vessel. A common feature on ships, yacht designers may incorporate watertight bulkheads in some designs. A watertight collision bulkhead is located in the forward (and sometimes **AFT**) part of a vessel, and completely encloses an area near the **BOW** or **STERN**, extending from **BILGE** to deck level. If a watertight bulkhead has an access opening, that opening must also be watertight.

"bulletproof" – really strong and indestructible. Nothing is bulletproof on a boat, but having good quality, well-maintained equipment helps to approach this goal.

bullseye – a type of rope **FAIRLEAD** with a smooth hole in it; made of plastic or wood.

bulwark – the part of a vessel's hull that extends above the deck at the outboard edge of the deck; higher than a **TOE RAIL**. Bulwarks usually have holes (scuppers or freeing ports) in them to allow water to run off the deck.

A sturdy ketch motorsailer with high bulwarks. The bow line leads to a Samson post.

The wooden slats serve as freeing ports on this canoe-stern motorsailer. The stern lines are tied to bitts by the bulwarks on port and starboard. The small white mushroom over the stern light is a GPS antenna.

bumper – the LANDLUBBER's name for a FENDER.

bunk – a sleeping place aboard a vessel; also called a berth.

bunk board – a long, vertical piece of wood along the outer edge of a BUNK that's high enough to keep a person secure in the berth. The bunk board is removed or hinged to fold down under the cushion when not in use. A LEE CLOTH serves the same function as a bunk board.

bunt – yes, a baseball term, but on a boat it's the loose or excess part of a conventionally-reefed sail. REEF PENDANTS (reef points) tie up the bunt when the sail is reefed.

buoy – (1) a floating object used as an aid to navigation, to mark the location of something on the bottom, or for mooring a vessel. (2) to attach a buoy to something on the bottom to mark its location or to aid in retrieving it. "Buoy the anchor in case it FOULS on the bottom."

buoyage, direction of – indicated by the color, shape, and/or markings of buoys to show the PORT or STARBOARD side of channels when a vessel is *returning from sea*. In areas where channels intersect or a river meets the sea the direction of buoyage may change, so it's essential to refer to the chart.

buoyage, systems of – the placement of buoys and other aids to navigation used in a particular region of the world. There are two regions: IALA A and IALA B. The U.S. and Canada are in Region B; Europe is in Region A. In both regions buoyage has LATERAL SIGNIFICANCE. The two areas are generally the same, with one *very important* difference: in Region A *green* MARKS are kept to STARBOARD when returning from the sea. In Region B *red* marks are kept to starboard when returning from the sea ("red right returning"). The CARDINAL SYSTEM OF BUOYAGE is used in some areas. In the U.S., different systems of buoyage are used on the Mississippi and Western Rivers and on the INTRACOASTAL WATERWAY.

buoy, navigation – a floating aid to navigation, lighted or unlighted, and painted in colors which indicate the purpose of the buoy and/or which side to pass it on. A BUOY SHAPE and a TOPMARK (if any) may have LATERAL SIGNIFICNCE. Basic shapes include can (flat top), nun (tapered at the top), spherical, and spar (a vertical pole). In general, buoys with pointed tops indicate the STARBOARD side of a channel, and those with flat tops indicate the PORT side. CARDINAL BUOYS are painted in specific combinations of yellow and black, and they have one of four different triangular topmarks that indicate the safe side to pass a danger. Buoys may also be numbered, lettered, or named. Consult a NAUTICAL ALMANAC or other reference for the details of the buoyage system in use where you're operating. Many buoys have radar reflectors, and some have a RACON or AIS. The distance at which radar picks up a buoy varies with the radar itself and its settings, the size of the buoy, whether the buoy has a radar reflector, the height of the seas, and atmospheric conditions such as rain or snow. Some buoys are seasonal, removed in the winter; this is indicated on the chart and in a LIGHT LIST.

buoy reports – include wind speed and direction, and WAVE HEIGHT and PERIOD. They are sometimes given in VHF marine forecasts and WEATHER REPORTS.

buoy rope – another name for a TRIP LINE.

buoy shape – the shape of some buoys has significance to navigation, while other shapes do not. Consult a reference for the country or area of operation. *See* BUOYS, NAVIGATION.

buoy, special purpose – some buoys don't have LATERAL SIGNIFICANCE. Examples include sewer outfall or pipeline buoys, research or weather buoys, fish farm buoys, anchorage area buoys, and restricted area buoys. The size, shape, color, and other markings varies greatly. A NAUTICAL ALMANAC usually has a chart of the special purpose buoys used in an area.

burdened vessel – older term for the GIVE-AWAY VESSEL.

Bureau Veritas, BV – a marine CLASSIFICATION SOCIETY.

burgee (pronounced **bur**-jee) – a flag for a yacht club, organization, or the vessel's private flag. Burgees are displayed afloat or ashore at a club or other facility. According to FLAG ETIQUETTE a burgee should be flown at the MASTHEAD or on a flag HALYARD, not at the STERN (which is reserved for the ENSIGN).

bury, the – the part of a KEEL-STEPPED MAST that extends beneath the deck.

buttonhook turn – a WILLIAMSON TURN used in a MAN OVERBOARD RECOVERY.

Buys Ballot's Law – a rule of thumb for locating a LOW PRESSURE SYSTEM. In the Northern Hemisphere, stand with your back to the wind and put your left arm out to the side – that's the direction of the low. High pressure will be on your right hand. In the Southern Hemisphere, face *into the wind*, and the low is to your left side and the high to your right. This rule was defined by Dutch meteorologist Christophorus Buys-Ballot in 1857.

BV – abbreviation for BUREAU VERITAS, a marine CLASSIFICATION SOCIETY.

BWML – abbreviation for the BRITISH WATERWAYS MARINAS, LTD.

by the head – same as DOWN BY THE HEAD.

by the lee – when sailing with the wind ASTERN (DEAD DOWNWIND) if the wind comes from the same side that the BOOM is out on, the vessel is sailing by the lee. Sailing by the lee can cause an accidental JIBE if the MAINSAIL is taken ABACK. An accidental jibe can break gear or injure a crew member. For this reason, a careful crew uses a PREVENTER or a BOOM BRAKE. A by the lee situation can be created by a wind shift, by the boat's motion in the seas, or by the inattention of the helmsman.

by the stern – same as DOWN BY THE STERN.

C

CA – abbreviation for the CRUISING ASSOCIATION.

cabin – the living areas below the deck; the ACCOMMODATION. The main cabin is called the SALOON, and the table in this cabin is the saloon table.

cabin sole, cockpit sole – the "floor" of the cabin or COCKPIT.

cable – five basic definitions:

1. A large-diameter electrical wire as used on batteries or in a high current circuit, such as for an electric WINDLASS.
2. A term used to describe wire used in a steering system; "steering cables."
3. Co-axial cable, used with antennas.
4. Rope or chain used for anchoring (the anchor cable), or for towing (a towing cable).
5. A cable is a measurement of distance equal to one-tenth of a nautical mile (0.1NM) or approximately 600ft/183m.

cable, co-axial or coax – co-axial cable has a single center CONDUCTOR surrounded by an insulating material, with an outer metal braid shield around that, and all covered with an outer plastic sheath. Coax is used with antennas. Buy the best quality (Belden is one maker of high-quality coax). It's foolish to pay hundreds of dollars for a good marine radio and antenna, and then use cheap, ineffective coax with it. The longer the run from the equipment to the antenna, the better quality the coax must be to minimize signal loss. Choose coax with 98% braid (braid helps minimize interference; cheap coax skimps on the braid). Coax is identified with numbers and letters printed on the cable: RG-58 and RG 8X have an outer diameter of about ¼-inch/6mm. These types are suitable for runs of under 30 feet/9m. RG 8A/U is about 0.5in/12mm in diameter, suitable for runs of over 30 feet. RG-213U is the best quality coax, especially for MASTHEAD antennas. TV antenna coax shouldn't be used; it looks the same, but it's not suitable for radio antennas.

cable, shielded – an electrical cable with two or more CONDUCTORS surrounded by a metal shield (either a metal braid or thin, flexible metal foil). Shielded cables prevent the radiation of electrical interference from AC or DC current in the wires.

cable ties, wire ties – strong, thin plastic strips with a gripper on one end, used to tie up electrical wires and cables, SEIZE the screw pin of a SHACKLE, attach things on deck and below, and many other tying jobs where a strong and quick fastener is needed. These are as useful as DUCT TAPE and WD-40® They come in various widths, lengths, and colors. Buy black cable ties with UV resistance for fastening things on deck. They don't last forever, so check them for sun damage. When the unneeded end of a cable tie is clipped, it can create a sharp edge, unless it's trimmed flat at the gripper part. If the ends don't have to be cut for appearance, leave them on; otherwise, beware. Regular cable ties can't be reused, but there are ties that can be opened and used again. Put 25 strong cable ties in the DAMAGE CONTROL KIT.

calibrated chain – *see* CHAIN, CALIBRATED.

call sign – letters and numbers assigned by a government to a licensed RADIOTELEPHONE. When giving a call sign speak the letters in the PHONETIC ALPHABET. In the U.S. if a radio is not required to be licensed, there's no call sign. Some U.S. vessels are required to have a radio license, and some older U.S. vessels have a license from when it was formerly required for all vessels; thus call signs are still used by some recreational vessels. The ITU governs which letters are used in the call signs of each country. *See* LICENSE, SHIP STATION.

calling and distress channels – Channel 16 on the VHF radiotelephone is assigned by international maritime agreement to calling (initial contact) and DISTRESS communication. There are multiple SINGLE-SIDEBAND DISTRESS FREQUENCIES. In the U.S. CHANNEL 9 has been designated as the calling channel for recreational vessels; its use is voluntary and varies in regions of the country.

calve, calving – the release of a mass of ice from a glacier or ICEBERG. The waves produced by calving can be large and dangerous to both small and large vessels, if they're close to the glacier or iceberg.

camber – (1) the ATHWARTSHIPS upward curve or arch of a vessel's decks above the deck edge. Deck camber makes it easier to stand when the vessel is HEELED, if you're on the WINDWARD side. (2) the curve built into a sail.

cam cleat – a device that grips a rope to hold it in place. One type has two rotating parts (the cams); lead the line through the cams to hold it, and lift it up and out to free it. JAM CLEATS and LINE STOPPERS perform a similar function.

Canadian Coast Guard – performs many of the same functions as the U.S. Coast Guard. The website has information for recreational and commercial mariners. Explore the links at www.ccg-gcc.gc.ca.

Canadian Coast Guard Auxiliary – a volunteer organization with a membership of 5,000 recreational mariners and commercial fishermen who are trained to assist the Coast Guard with safe boating activities and search-and-rescue (SAR) duties. The Auxiliary works on the seacoasts and on major inland waterways, and responds to approximately 25% of the marine SAR incidents. www.ccga-gcac.com.

Canadian Power and Sail Squadrons – an organization for Canadian boaters that provides boating education, safety resources, and activities for its members and the general boating public. In addition to many classroom courses, the Squadrons offer a basic boating course, leading to the required Pleasure Craft Operator Card (PCOC). Working cooperatively with TRANSPORT CANADA, Squadrons also offer a free Recreational Vessel Courtesy Check, during which a trained examiner will go over the safety equipment and discuss safety issues. There are *no* government reports involved. www.cps-ecp.ca.

Canadian Safe Boating Council, CSBC – an organization that promotes boating safety through activities such as the Safe Boating Awareness Week, an annual safe boating symposium, and safety-related awards. Organizations and individuals dedicated to improving safety on the water comprise the membership. www.csbc.ca.

Canadian Standards Association, CSA – a trade organization that promulgates standards for public safety, health, and the environment, some of which affect the marine industry.

Canadian Yachting Association™, CYA – the national governing body for the sport of sailing and powerboating. The CYA offers a variety of educational programs, works with the Canadian National Sailing Team, and sponsors and supervises racing events. Many yacht clubs and sailing schools are members of the CYA. www.sailing.ca.

canoe stern – a pointed end at the STERN like a canoe, rather than a flat or curved TRANSOM. A vessel with a pointed BOW and a canoe stern is called a double-ender. Southern Cross, Valiant, Westsail, and Colin Archer designs are examples of double-enders. For other photos see BULWARK, DORADE BOX, DOUBLE-ENDED, and RUDDER, OUTBOARD.

A canoe stern on a restored older sailboat. There are two bitts at the stern, and a small pram mounted in chocks on the cabin top.

canvas – general term for the sails (even though they aren't made of canvas). "We set every bit of canvas when the wind died and we still couldn't get above two knots."

cap shrouds – SHROUDS that extend from the deck to the MASTHEAD; also called upper shrouds.

capacity, current-carrying (electrical wire) – *see* WIRE, CURRENT-CARRYING CAPACITY.

cape – a headland or prominent land area projecting into the ocean. To circumnavigate the world passing south of the "Five Great Capes" is an achievement. The five are:

- Cape Agulhas or the Cape of Good Hope (both at the southern extremity of Africa).
- Cape Leeuwin (the southwest corner of Australia).
- Southeast Cape of Tasmania.
- Southwest Cape at the end of Stewart Island/Rakiura (south of New Zealand).
- Cape Horn (the southern extremity of South America).

capsize – to overturn. Keelboats are much less-likely to capsize than boats without a KEEL, because the BALLAST is located low in the keel. Ballast is designed to right the vessel if it capsizes. A KNOCKDOWN is a partial capsize.

capstan – a vertical WINDLASS, usually at the BOW, for handling anchor and MOORING LINES or chain. The rotating part of a capstan that takes a chain is called the chain GYPSY or chainwheel. Some capstans are only for rope. A capstan isn't designed to hold the weight of a boat at anchor: a CHAIN SPRING and a CHAIN STOPPER (if fitted) should be used on a chain rode, or a rope rode should be secured to strong bow fittings. A capstan can be manual, electric, or hydraulic. The terms windlass and capstan are sometimes used interchangeably.

car – deck or sail hardware that slides along a track. SHEET BLOCKS are mounted on cars, a TRAVELER has a car for the MAINSHEET blocks, and a FULLY-BATTENED MAINSAIL has cars at each batten to ride in or on the MAST track. Harken® calls its mast cars "battcars" and Schaefer's are "battslides."

carabiner, safety carabiner – a snap hook used on the boat end of a safety HARNESS TETHER. This carabiner should be a locking type so it can't open accidentally. Some safety carabiners include Wichard® #2454 or 4237 and Gibb #77. If the carabiner has both aluminum and stainless steel parts rinse it regularly in fresh water and spray it with a corrosion-preventative spray.

carbon monoxide (CO) detector/alarm – a very important safety item aboard a boat that has an engine and/or a non-electric heating device (kerosene, propane or other gas, or a solid fuel heater). Carbon monoxide is deadly. Choose a *marine* CO detector/alarm. Relevant ABYC Standards are A-1 Marine Liquefied Petroleum Gas (LPG) Systems, A-3 Galley Stoves, A-7 Liquid and Solid Fueled Boat Heating Systems, H-2 Ventilation of Boats Using Gasoline, H-4 Cockpit Drainage Systems, and P-1 Installation of Exhaust Systems for Propulsion and Auxiliary Engines. See also Standard A-24 Carbon Monoxide Detection Systems, TH-22 Educational Information About Carbon Monoxide, and TH-23 Design, Construction and Testing of Boats in Consideration of Carbon Monoxide.

card – usually means the COMPASS CARD.

cardinal buoy, cardinal mark – a buoy used in the CARDINAL SYSTEM OF BUOYAGE.

cardinal directions, cardinal points, cardinals – the four main compass directions: north, east, south, west. The intercardinal directions are northeast, southeast, southwest, and northwest.

Cardinal marks awaiting deployment at sea. Their triangular topmarks are not yet in place. From left to right they are north, south, east, and west marks.

cardinal system of buoyage – a system of navigation aids placed to indicate the *safe side* on which to pass a hazard to navigation, such as an isolated danger. Cardinal buoys (marks) have horizontal bands of yellow and black, different triangular TOPMARKS, and light patterns that indicate whether the buoy is located north, east, south, or west of the danger. The safe water

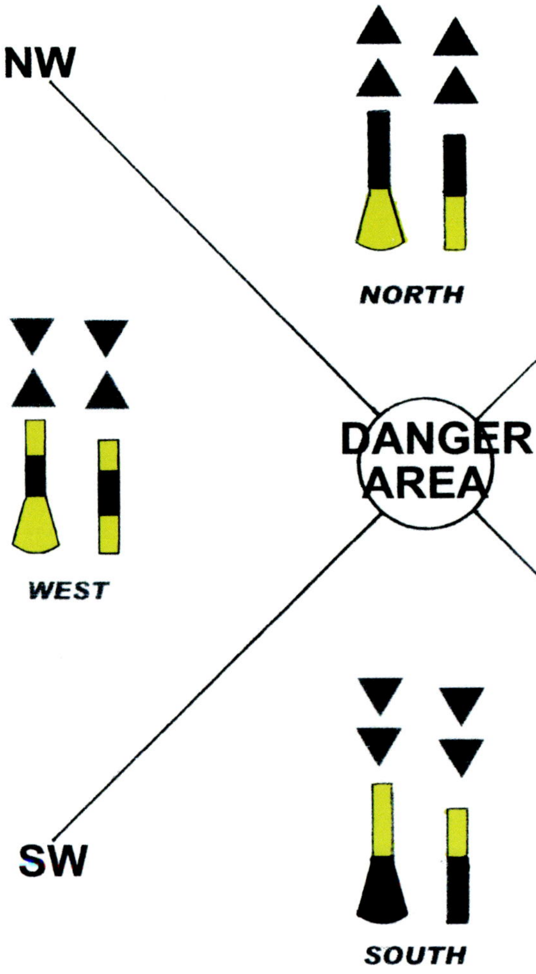

Cardinal Marks

is on the named side of the buoy: if it's a north cardinal mark, the safe water is to the north of the buoy. When navigating at night in an area with cardinal marks, consult a NAUTICAL ALMANAC for the light patterns used on these buoys. There are few cardinal marks in U.S. waters, but they're used in Canada and other countries.

careen (rhymes with marine) – to lay a boat over on her side on a sloping beach to expose one side of the bottom for cleaning, painting, or repair. Turn the boat around when the tide comes back in to work on the other side. Not all types of boats can be successfully and safely careened; it's not an operation to be taken lightly. The shape of the vessel's UNDERBODY is an important consideration; a yacht with a narrow FIN KEEL isn't a good candidate for this operation. A gently-sloping beach, with no rocks, is required. There must be sufficient TIDE RANGE, and careening shouldn't be attempted at or near the highest tides of the month or there may not be enough water to re-float the yacht. It's not seen very often these days, but it's a useful technique if done carefully and correctly. It may be a good idea to notify the Coast Guard (if you're not in a remote area) to let them know you're careening, otherwise people may call them and report the vessel as distressed. Some CRUISING GUIDES identify a careenage. Careening is not the same as DRYING OUT alongside, which is done along a wall or on a SCRUBBING GRID.

Caribbean 1500 – an offshore OCEAN CROSSING RALLY conducted by the CRUISING RALLY ASSOCIATION.

carry – (1) having sails set, carrying sail. "Joan's boat can carry a lot of sail in these winds." (2) refers indirectly to the depth of the water to reach a particular location. "You can carry seven feet all the way to the fuel dock."

carry away – to go overboard. Gear, SPARS, or sails can carry away in HEAVY WEATHER or when a vessel takes GREEN WATER over the deck.

cartography, cartographer – the art and science of making maps and charts; the person who does this work.

cast off – to completely let go or free a rope; to SLIP. Not the same as EASE, PAY OUT, SURGE, or VEER.

casting the lead – taking SOUNDINGS with a LEADLINE.

catamaran, cat – a vessel with two hulls connected by a central main structure. In a cruising catamaran the main accommodation is in the center, with smaller cabins in the hulls (in a large cat). There's much more living space than on a similar-sized MONOHULL. The interior can be quite luxurious and there's lots of deck space. They're especially popular for cruising in tropical waters. Catamarans are sail or power vessels. Large cats have an engine in each hull. They sail upright, HEELING very little (four or five degrees is a typical maximum even in strong winds), and attain high speeds under sail. The loads on the rigging can be quite high.

The motion of a cat in a **SEAWAY** is different from a monohull and on some **POINTS OF SAIL**, such as **DOWNWIND**, more comfortable. Cats don't go to **WINDWARD** especially well, and they can be uncomfortable on a **BEAT** or with rough seas on the **BEAM**. Because they don't have a **KEEL**, **LEEWAY** is greater with a cat than a monohull. Their speed is adversely affected by the weight of excess gear and supplies, but a large cat can carry extra weight. Some people say that "too much weight turns a cat into a dog." Some marinas charge extra because the wide beam takes up more space. A number of designers and builders in the U.S., France, Australia, and other countries

A small cruising catamaran with a cockpit enclosure, two horseshoe buoys with orange floating strobes attached, and a stern boarding ladder on the starboard hull. She's listing a bit to starboard.

offer a wide range of custom and production cruising catamarans. Even diehard monohull sailors have been converted to cat cruising. Some catamaran brands/builders include: Admiral, Antares, Broadblue, Chantier Marine, Dean, Discovery, Dolphin, Fountaine Pajot, Gemini, Lagoon, Leopard, Maine Cat, Manta, Majestic, Moxie Yachts, Nautitech Yachts, Outremer, Perry, Prout, Royal Cape, Seawind USA, TomCat Boats, and Voyage Yachts. See the photo with TONNAGE YIELDS TO TONNAGE for a big power catamaran.

Definitely a catboat. She has a small headsail furled on the short bowsprit. The American flag is properly displayed two-thirds of the way up the leech of the mainsail.

catboat, cat – a sailing vessel with one MAST located forward near the BOW. Some cats have a small HEADSAIL and some have just a MAINSAIL. Nonsuch and some Freedom yachts are large catboats; they have an UNSTAYED MAST. *See also* the photo with WISHBONE BOOM.

catenary – the curve made by the anchor RODE as it goes from the BOW of the boat to the anchor on the bottom. Proper SCOPE creates a catenary that allows the pull on the anchor to be from a low angle, thus helping it to stay dug into the bottom. An all-chain rode provides a better catenary because of the weight of the chain. Add a SENTINEL (extra weight) to the anchor rode to increase the catenary and the holding power.

cathode – (1) the negative TERMINAL on a battery. (2) when dissimilar metals are immersed in seawater, the metal that resists corrosion better is the cathode. *See* GALVANIC SERIES.

cathode ray tube, CRT – a type of display screen used on some radars. The screen is like an old TV (before flat screens).

cathodic – functioning as a CATHODE.

cathodic protection – a technique to control the corrosion of dissimilar metals immersed in salt water by making the less-NOBLE (more easily corroded) metal function as a CATHODE. This is done by putting ANODES (zincs) on the metal to be protected. The zinc corrodes instead of the other metal. Cathodic protection may also be created by an IMPRESSED CURRENT SYSTEM (a system that uses electrical current to control corrosion). ABYC Standard E-2 Cathodic Protection deals with anodes and other aspects of cathodic protection. *See* GALVANIC SERIES.

cat's paw – (1) a ruffle or ripple on the surface of the water caused by a very light puff of wind. When becalmed a sailor looks for cat's paws and hopes. (2) a HITCH made of two loops in the BIGHT of a rope, to put over a hook.

A cat's paw hitch made by twisting two loops in the bight of the line. It's used with a lifting sling. The hitch is secure under a strain.

cavitation – cavitation can occur when a propeller comes out of the water while the engine is running in rough seas. The engine races because there's no water for the prop to grab. There's a more technical definition of cavitation used in propeller theory.

cay (pronounced key) – alternate spelling of KEY(3).

CCA – abbreviation for the CRUISING CLUB OF AMERICA.

CE mark – the CE mark is a manufacturer's certification that a product has met EUROPEAN UNION (EU) safety, health, and environmental requirements for the consumer market. There are standards for marine equipment, which are similar in intent to UL or other marine equipment and installation standards promulgated in North America.

ceiling – on a boat, the ceiling refers to the interior sides of the boat along the hull. In a fiberglass boat it's called the hull liner. A ceiling may be made of wood, plastic-covered material, or fiberglass. Look for it inside LOCKERS and in other places where the cabin is open to the hull. In some places the inside of the hull may be bare, not covered with a ceiling. The OVERHEAD is the term for what is over your head when you're below decks.

celestial navigation, astro-navigation – determining the geographic position of a vessel with SEXTANT observations (sights) of the sun, moon, planets, and stars. The navigator converts the sextant readings into information from which a position can be calculated. Accurate time, a NAUTICAL ALMANAC (2), and SIGHT REDUCTION tables or a NAVIGATION COMPUTER are used to determine the LATITUDE and LONGITUDE at the time the sight was taken. There are a number of methods of SIGHT REDUCTION. Consult a celestial navigation textbook for full explanations of this navigation method. The U.S. POWER SQUADRON and the CANADIAN POWER AND SAIL SQUADRONS, nautical training schools, the RYA, and other organizations teach celestial navigation. You don't have to be a mathematics genius to learn how to do it. Offshore sailors are encouraged to learn celestial.

Celsius, C – a temperature scale used in many countries outside the U.S and by scientists. On this scale the freezing point of water is 0° and the boiling point is 100°. Two useful equivalents: 10°C = 50°F and 20°C = 68°F. FAHRENHEIT is the temperature scale generally used in the U.S.

centerboard – a retractable KEEL-like appendage, hinged on a pivot so it can be lowered and raised. The centerboard goes up into a watertight construction in the hull called the centerboard trunk, or it retracts into the keel. A centerboard is usually found on small sailboats, but larger yachts may have a combination keel and centerboard, or have a centerboard with internal BALLAST. Some Irwin, Endeavor, and Shannon yachts (and others) have a keel-centerboard configuration. A DAGGERBOARD is like a centerboard but it slides up and down in its trunk, rather than pivoting. See the next entry.

centerboard boat with internal ballast – sailboats of this type can be large or small; they're popular in shallow or tidal water areas because of their limited DRAFT. A basic amount of internal BALLAST provides initial stability and the centerboard provides LATERAL RESISTANCE. This design doesn't have the overall stability of conventional KEEL designs, nor can it POINT as high. It may not be easy to HEAVE TO. The centerboard mechanism requires careful maintenance. Because there's no keel, the rudder is relatively unprotected in the case of a grounding, and it can catch errant nets and ropes. The hull form is relatively flat and wide, with shallow bilges (limited storage space). A centerboard boat can safely DRY OUT in a tidal harbor, and she's easy to store on land. Some boats will PLANE in good winds.

centerboard trunk – the housing for a CENTERBOARD or a DAGGERBOARD.

centering the rudder – *see* RUDDER, CENTERING.

centerline – an imaginary line drawn down the center of a vessel from the BOW to the center of the STERN. It's used as a reference point. Away from the centerline is outboard; toward the centerline is inboard.

Central North Pacific Basin – the region north of the equator between 140°W and the INTERNATIONAL DATE LINE. The Central Pacific Hurricane Center (CPHC) in Honolulu, Hawaii is responsible for tracking TROPICAL CYCLONES in this region.

central pressure – the barometric pressure at sea level in a LOW or HIGH PRESSURE SYSTEM. On a SYNOPTIC CHART the pressure, in MILLIBARS, may be written in the center of the system.

certificate of competence – a general term for a boating license that indicates the person has passed a written or on-the-water test. *See* LICENSE, BOATING: CEVNI and the next entry.

Certificate of Competence, International, ICC – an ICC is required by many European countries (except the UK) as evidence of basic operator competence. A number of sailing organizations and private companies in the UK and Europe offer ICC training. Obtaining the ICC requires a practical, on-the-water test. The certificate specifies whether it is valid for power or sail or both types of vessels and for inland or coastal waters. The ICC is accepted as proof of operator competence where it is required or for chartering a boat. The RYA offers courses for U.S. and Canadian citizens; see www.rya.org.uk, ICC link.

certified, certification – for marine equipment this implies testing by an appropriate agency or the manufacturer's compliance with specific rules. Certification organizations, such as UL, CSA, ISO, and CE monitor the use of their logos on products and in marketing literature. For vessels, certification involves the approval of design and construction according to the requirements of a marine CLASSIFICATION SOCIETY.

cetane number, CN – a numerical performance rating for diesel fuel, indicating how well it ignites in the cylinders; it's similar to octane number for gasoline. The higher the number, the better the performance rating. Cetane is a chemical added to improve diesel fuel ignition. Some DIESEL FUEL ADDITIVES boost cetane.

CEVNI – skippers intending to take a boat through the European Inland Waterways system, i.e. canals, rivers, lakes, etc. *outside* the waters of the UK, must pass a test called the CEVNI, which deals with European Inland Waterways Regulations. Most people take the CEVNI test in conjunction with the INTERNATIONAL CERTIFICATE OF COMPETENCE (ICC) exam. European authorities will accept a certification of operator competence from your state or a U.S Coast Guard merchant mariner's license in lieu of an ICC, but you'll still need to pass the written CEVNI test if you're going to operate a boat (your own or a CHARTER vessel) on European canals. Persons of any nationality may take this test at a UK training school or in France.

CFR – abbreviation for the U.S. Code of Federal Regulations, the general and permanent rules published in the U.S. Federal Register by executive departments and agencies of the Federal Government. Sections of the CFR apply to vessels, and are embodied in the U.S. NAVIGATION RULES.

CG66 – abbreviation for the UK Maritime and Coastguard Agency's "voluntary safety identification scheme" for recreational vessels and small craft. It's a free vessel-registration database that assists search-and-rescue activities should a boat require assistance. See the bibliography under "Safety" for a link to CG66.

chafing gear – protective rubber, leather or cloth materials on mooring or anchor lines where they rub on the boat, pier or any other surface. See WORM for the procedure for making permanent chafing gear.

chain – steel chain for an anchor RODE is available in a variety of sizes and grades. Many yachts will use some grade of regular chain, rather than large, heavy-duty STUD-LINK CHAIN. Chain used in the marine environment should be GALVANIZED, or it won't last long. STAINLESS STEEL chain is available but it's very expensive. Use CALIBRATED chain with a chain GYPSY and match the link size to the gypsy. The strength of chain needed for an all-chain anchor rode depends on the DISPLACEMENT of the vessel, its WINDAGE, and a safety factor for the maximum winds likely to be encountered. There are tables in reference book, on websites, and some marine equipment catalogues for estimating the windage of a vessel and anchor loads in various wind strengths. Research this topic before making a decision to buy or replace chain. Select CHAIN SHACKLES for use with anchor chain that match or exceed the strength of the chain. A larger link at the anchor end of the chain is required to accommodate the pin diameter of a proper-strength shackle. ABYC Standard H-40 Anchoring, Mooring and Strong Points has a table of working load limits for rope and chain anchor rodes. See types of chain, below.

chain, BBB – *see* CHAIN, PROOF COIL.

chain, calibrated – chain that has all links exactly the same size. Use calibrated chain with a WINDLASS or CAPSTAN so the links fit properly into the pockets on the chain GYPSY.

chain, high tensile – the strongest regular GALVANIZED chain is high tensile, G70 (G7) grade (called transport chain in the U.S.). Some authorities recommend that this grade chain *not* be used in an anchoring system because it's more brittle (less forgiving of shock loads) than lower grade steel chain.

chain, high test – after PROOF COIL, the next strongest GALVANIZED chain is high test chain, G40 or 43 (G4) grade. Because it's stronger than proof chain, a smaller size may be able to be used to save weight. To match the chain strength use a CHAIN SHACKLE *two* sizes larger than the chain; this requires an end link larger than the other chain links. For example, a 5/16in/8mm chain should have a 0.5in/12mm shackle. High test chain can be re-galvanized once without losing too much strength.

chain gypsy – *see* GYPSY.

chain hook – a strong metal hook with a slot that fits between two links of chain. Attach the hook to a length of stretchy rope to make up a CHAIN SPRING. Chain hooks are sized for a particular size of chain, and they're available in GALVANIZED or STAINLESS STEEL A chain hook with two claw-like hooks at the front of it is called a devil's claw, which does the same thing as a chain hook.

chain locker – a compartment at or near the BOW, usually below decks, designed for the stowage of an all-chain RODE. A well-designed chain locker allows the chain to self-stow, so a person doesn't have to go below to move a heap of chain from under the CHAIN PIPE so all of it can come down from the deck.

chain pipe – a large-diameter pipe or tube that leads from the deck to a below-decks CHAIN LOCKER. The pipe guides the anchor chain into the locker. It may be located directly under a CAPSTAN or WINDLASS or be a separate, capped fitting in the deck. For an offshore trip seal the chain pipe so water can't get in. Use a foam plug shaped to the pipe opening, and seal around the foam with plastic modeling clay (Play Doh) or plasticine. DUCT TAPE a loose chain pipe cover. See the photo of the bow deck BITT for an example of an open chain pipe.

chainplates – strong metal plates or straps bolted or welded (to a metal hull) or other structural parts of a sailboat. The lower ends of the SHROUDS, some STAYS, and BACKSTAYS are attached to chainplates, usually with TURNBUCKLES or other adjusting mechanisms. For another photo see CHARLIE NOBLE.

Three chainplates amidships. On many boats the chainplates are not visible. The turnbuckles are covered with white plastic boots.. Note the high mast safety rail.

chain, proof coil or common chain – the lowest strength regular steel GALVANIZED chain is proof coil, G30 (G3) grade. BBB proof coil is short link chain for use with a WINDLASS. This chain is the least expensive, but the size of the chain will have to be large enough to get the strength required, which means more weight for a given length of chain, compared to HIGH TEST chain. To match the chain strength use a CHAIN SHACKLE one size larger than the chain, which requires an end link larger than the other chain links. For example, a 5/16"/8mm chain should have a 3/8in/10mm shackle, and 3/8in/10mm chain requires a 7/16in/12mm shackle. Proof coil chain can be re-galvanized.

chain, safe working load (SWL) – to estimate the safe working load for a particular chain, apply a safety factor to its breaking strength. Technical books, some marine supply catalogs, and websites have tables of chain strength, which indicate either the breaking strength or the safe working load. Use information specifically for the type of chain (PROOF COIL, HIGH TEST,

STAINLESS STEEL, or STUD-LINK). A safety factor of 6:1 (one-sixth of the breaking strength) is usually used for ordinary applications. If the chain will be subject to shock loads or extreme strain, use a higher safety factor. In contrast to nylon rope, chain has no elasticity and it can't absorb shock loads, so a CHAIN SPRING should be used with an all-chain RODE. Chain loses strength over time in the marine environment, and from re-GALVANIZING; thus the safety factor decreases as chain ages. ABYC STANDARD **H-40** ANCHORING, MOORING AND STRONG POINTS has a table of working load limits for rope and chain anchor rodes.

chain shackle – shackles for use with anchor chains must be one or two sizes larger than the chain to have the required strength, depending on the type of chain. This means that the chain must have a larger end link than the other links to accommodate the shackle pin diameter. Look for the working load limit (WLL) or safe working load (SWL) stamped on the shackle. In the U.S. this is usually measured in tons (2000lbs). Some low-cost domestic and imported shackles are not tested and don't have the SWL or WLL mark. Use GALVANIZED shackles with galvanized chain and STAINLESS STEEL shackles with stainless chain. *See* CHAIN, HIGH TEST and CHAIN, PROOF COIL for shackle size recommendations.

chain spring – with an all-chain anchor RODE, it's a good idea to take the strain of the chain onto a rope chain spring. Make the spring from one or two strong lines (stretchy, THREE-STRAND nylon is best). Secure the line(s) to CLEATS or a BITT at the BOW. Attach the outer end of the spring to the chain with a CHAIN HOOK or a ROLLING HITCH. Let the spring out until there's slack in the chain and the spring is holding the weight of the boat. The spring should have chafe protection where it passes through bow CHOCKS. Using a chain spring prevents it from making loud noises on the ANCHOR ROLLER, and dampens jerking and shock loads caused by wind or wave action. A chain spring can also be used with a MOORING EYE.

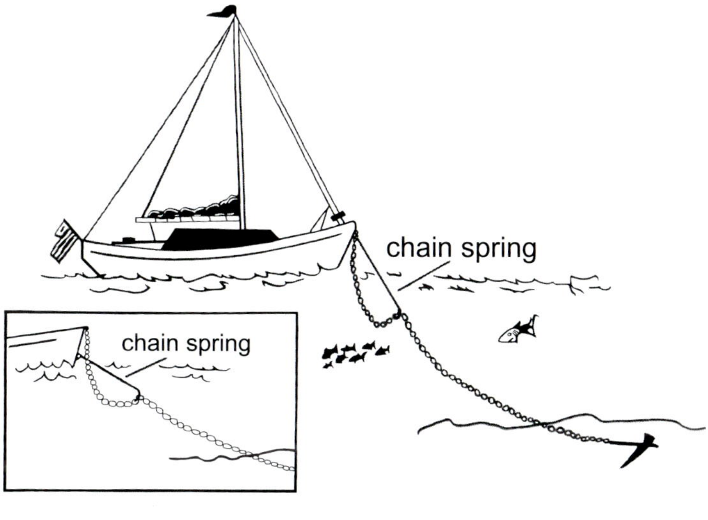

A chain spring leads from the bow to the anchor chain. The inset shows a chain spring leading from a mooring eye low on the stem.

chain, stainless steel – very expensive, doesn't rust and its strength is similar to HIGH TEST steel chain. Grade 316L STAINLESS STEEL is typically used. Use only stainless steel shackles with a strength that meets or exceeds the chain strength.

chain stopper – on a boat with an all-chain anchor RODE install a chain stopper in front of an anchor WINDLASS or CAPSTAN or as a separate item if there's no windlass. A windlass or capstan is not designed to take the weight of a boat at anchor. The stopper has a locking latch that prevents the chain from going out accidentally and the stopper takes the strain when the boat is anchored. Disengage the latch to let the chain out and re-engage it when the necessary amount has been VEERED. Stoppers are designed for specific sizes of chain. Use a CHAIN SPRING with a chain stopper.

A chain stopper in the closed position. The latch at the front of the stopper lifts up to allow the chain to run out. It's time to end-for-end this chain.

chain, stud-link – this heavy-duty chain has a bar (stud) across the middle of each link that prevents the link from deforming under strain. Available in sizes starting at 0.5in/12.5mm, stud-link chain is very strong, but 90ft/27.5m of this size chain weighs 242lbs/110kg, which makes it suited to large vessels where extra weight in the CHAIN LOCKER is acceptable.

Stud-link chain on an old ship's anchor. The masts of *HMS Trincomalee*, 1817, stand tall over the museum buildings at Hartlepool Historic Quay, on England's east coast.

chain swivel, anchor swivel – a swivel is sometimes used in a permanent mooring system, but it's not recommended for use in a yacht's all-chain RODE. The strength of a swivel is *lower* than the same size CHAIN SHACKLE, so to have the required strength for the whole permanent mooring system the size of the larger swivel may not fit with the other parts. Also, the GALVANIZING wears off and the swivel rusts. A STAINLESS STEEL swivel can be used, but research its strength; it may have to be quite large to be as strong as the rest of the system.

chain tensioner – a device with a hook on one end and a lever on the other end, that's installed on the BOW deck ABAFT the ANCHOR ROLLER. It pulls the anchor chain tight to keep the anchor snugly seated against the roller. A tensioner isn't designed to hold the weight of the boat when at anchor like a CHAIN STOPPER or a CHAIN SPRING.

chainwheel, chain wheel – another name for a chain GYPSY.

chandler, chandlery – a chandler is a person or company that sells boat equipment in a store called a chandlery.

channel – (1) a VHF or SINGLE SIDEBAND radiotelephone channel. (2) an area leading to a harbor where the water depth is deeper than the surrounding areas; a FAIRWAY. A channel may be unmarked, have navigation aids delineating its boundaries or a RANGE or SECTOR LIGHT indicating the centerline. Channels are natural or dredged. A chart may indicate a date for dredging, but the depths even in recently-dredged channels can change. Because ships need to stay in the channel, a yacht following a ship channel should stay outside or wait for a ship to pass before entering a channel. When navigating in a channel with ships, if necessary call them on VHF CHANNEL 13 and make sure you know each others intentions. In RESTRICTED VISIBILITY small vessels may run buoy-to-buoy just outside the channel, but be aware that other boats may be doing the same thing. *See also* CHANNEL, NARROW.

Channel 6 – the VHF channel designated as the international channel for Intership Safety, used for ship-to-ship safety messages and for search-and-rescue communication with Coast Guard ships and aircraft. It's a WORKING CHANNEL, but it shouldn't be used for ordinary conversation.

Channel 9 – the VHF channel designated in the U.S. as the calling channel for recreational vessels. Use it for the initial call to another boat, a marina, or for a radio check. Because this designation is not a law, the use of Channel 9 varies in different regions of the country. Once contact is made on Channel 9 both stations should switch to a WORKING CHANNEL for the communication itself. FCC regulations require boaters with VHF radios to maintain a watch on either Channel 9 or Channel 16, whenever the radio is turned on and not communicating with another station. Because important announcements are made on Channel 16, it's better to keep radio watch on this channel. If the radio has a DUAL WATCH or PRIORITY SCAN feature, channels 9 and 16 can be monitored.

Channel 13 – the VHF channel designated as the international channel for BRIDGE-TO-BRIDGE communication of *navigational* information between vessels on INLAND WATERS. It's a WORKING CHANNEL. Ships and power-driven vessels over 20m/65.6ft use 13. In an area with shipping, monitor this channel to learn about the movement of large vessels. Channel 13 and 67 are also used to contact some opening bridges. The radio automatically switches to LOW POWER on 13 and 67, as required by FCC regulations.

Channel 16 – the VHF channel designated as the international calling and distress channel. Coast Guards and large vessels monitor Channel 16, so it's the channel to use for contacting them. *See also* CHANNEL 9.

Channel 70 – the VHF channel authorized *exclusively* for distress, safety, and calling purposes using DIGITAL SELECTIVE CALLING (DSC). No other uses are permitted.

channel, duplex – a VHF or SINGLE SIDEBAND (SSB) radiotelephone channel that has different frequencies for transmitting and receiving. On all VHF radiotelephones and many SSBs you don't have to know the frequencies; selecting a particular channel number does it automatically. On older SSB radios both frequencies for a duplex channel must be entered. The SSB radio manual explains the procedure. *See* CHANNEL, SIMPLEX; "A" SUFFIX and "B" SUFFIX.

channeled wind – *see* WIND, CHANNELED, FUNNELED, AND GAP.

channel, narrow – navigating in a narrow channel or FAIRWAY has special rules, which are given in Rule 9 of the NAVIGATION RULES. The Rules are slightly different for INLAND and INTERNATIONAL waters; read both carefully. The following rules for navigating in narrow channels are relatively the same in both Inland and International waters:

- Keep to the STARBOARD side of the channel. Under the Inland Rules, when navigating on the Great Lakes, Western Rivers and other designated waterways a vessel proceeding *with* the current has the right of way over a vessel proceeding against the current.
- A vessel less than 20m/65.6ft in length or a sailing vessel shall not impede the passage of a vessel that can safely navigate only in the channel.
- A fishing vessel shall not impede the passage of any other vessel in the channel.
- Don't cross the FAIRWAY if crossing will impede a vessel which can only navigate within the channel.
- When OVERTAKING in a narrow channel, if the vessel to be overtaken must take an action to let you pass safely, use the appropriate SOUND SIGNALS (which are different under Inland and International Rules). The other vessel responds with her whistle signal (which are different in Inland and International). *See* SOUND SIGNALS, MANEUVERING.
- When nearing a bend or area in a channel where the view of another vessel may be obstructed, navigate with caution and sound the appropriate whistle signal.
- Avoid anchoring in a narrow channel (unless an emergency arises).

channel, simplex – a VHF or SINGLE-SIDEBAND radiotelephone channel that uses the same transmitting and receiving frequency. *See* CHANNEL, DUPLEX; "A" SUFFIX and "B" SUFFIX.

channel, single-sideband radio – the ITU has assigned channel numbers to **single-sideband** (SSB) frequencies, thus permitting the entry of a channel number for frequency selection, rather than the longer frequency numbers. A SSB manual usually lists all the channels and their corresponding frequencies. *See* SINGLE-SIDEBAND DISTRESS FREQUENCIES for examples.

channel, VHF radiotelephone – numbered channels on the radio which are selected according to the type of communication. The channels numbers are related to specific transmit and receive radio frequencies, which you don't have to know; selecting the channel number does this automatically. Channels are designated for calling (to make the initial contact) and as working channels (to talk on once contact has been made). A VHF radio manual, boating reference book, NAUTICAL ALMANAC, or the U.S. Coast Guard website have tables of the channel designations for the U.S. Recreational mariners should normally use channels listed as "Non-Commercial." For VHF channels used locally, as for bridges, marinas, etc. consult an up-to-date CRUISING GUIDE or a nautical almanac for the area. Use the proper channels for the purpose of the communication. Users may be fined by the FCC or government authority in other countries for improper use of the channels. *See* individual channel number entries, and "A" SUFFIX and "B" SUFFIX, DUAL WATCH, PRIORITY SCAN and the next entry.

channel, working or working frequency – the VHF radio channels/ frequencies designated for communication between vessels and shore stations, after initial contact has been made on CHANNEL 9 (in the U.S.) or Channel 16. If you know the working channel of a shore station or vessel make the call directly on that channel. A NAUTICAL ALMANAC usually has the working frequencies for a particular country; some are not the same as in the U.S. or Canada (especially with reference to "A" SUFFIX and "B" SUFFIX channels). *See also* CHANNEL 6 and CHANNEL 13.

Chapman* or *Chapman's – common name for Maloney's *Chapman Piloting and Seamanship*, "the bible of boating." This large, comprehensive reference book has almost everything you need to know about boating under sail and power. It's kept up-to-date with frequent editions. It should be the first book in a boating library; it'll take you from basic to advanced levels. See the bibliography under "Sailing" for the complete citation.

characteristic of a light – the description of a navigation light as fixed (not flashing), or the number flashes, the time (in seconds) for a cycle of flashes, and the color or colors of the light. Characteristics are printed on a CHART near the light and in a LIGHT LIST.

charger-inverter, inverter-charger – a marine battery charger and an INVERTER combined in a single unit. Consult technical references and a marine electrician before purchasing.

Charlie (Charley) Noble – the nautical name for a stovepipe chimney from a GALLEY stove or cabin heater. Sailors who like traditional language still use this name. The name is said to derive from 19th century merchant ship captain Charles Noble, who kept his crew busy polishing the ship's copper smokestack, which they affectionately named after their captain.

This ketch motorsailer sports a large Charlie Noble. The mast is in a tabernacle. The two chainplates are attached to timbers behind the bulwark and to frames below the deck.

chart – proper name for a map used for marine navigation. Charts are paper and electronic. Both types should be kept up-to-date (corrected) by using the NOTICES TO MARINERS and the electronic chart updates supplied by chart software suppliers. Using out-of-date and uncorrected charts can be dangerous. Charts are large-scale (showing a small area in detail) or small-scale (showing a large area in less detail). Government agencies and private chart publishers issue charts. See the following chart entries.

chart accuracy – paper and electronic charts are only as accurate as the surveys upon which they're based. Some charts rely on surveys done years ago, when very precise surveying methods weren't available. Significant changes may have occurred to the land or underwater features since a recent survey. A new EDITION of a chart doesn't necessarily mean that a new survey's been done; it is issued when enough changes have accumulated to warrant a new chart. In confined waters, the accuracy of chart data may be less than that of the position-fixing system in use. GPS positions are often more precise than the charts. Give a wide berth to charted hazards. *See* CHART DATUM, HORIZONTAL.

chart, constant pressure – another name for an ISOBARIC CHART.

chart corrections – the changes affecting navigation that have occurred since the chart edition was published in paper or electronic form. They are disseminated in print and online in notices to mariners. U.S. chart corrections are posted weekly on the Internet in the LOCAL NOTICE TO MARINERS (LNM) and in NOTICES TO MARINERS (NM). In other countries government and private chart publishers issue corrections, many on websites. There is a legal obligation to carry up-to-date, corrected paper or electronic charts aboard. If an accident occurs or an insurance claim is made questions may be asked about the charts used aboard the vessel. For an excellent, informative website see www.allianceforsafenavigation.org. In addition to important resources about paper and electronic charts, there's a link that allows you to check if your NOAA charts are updated.

chart datum, horizontal – the horizontal geographical datum to which positions on a chart are referenced. Datum information is written near the title of a chart. Various datums are used; some are new and some are old. New charts use WGS84 or NAD83, which are considered equivalent. Charts that use a different datum specify if it's equivalent to WGS84. If a chart with an older datum is compared to a WGS84 chart, a single geographic position will have a slightly different LATITUDE and LONGITUDE. This is called DATUM SHIFT. A navigator may decide to set the datum on the vessel's GPS to the datum of the chart. However, for a chart with a datum other than WGS84 or its equivalent, the most accurate positions are obtained by setting the GPS to WGS84 and applying the DATUM ADJUSTMENT factor indicated on the chart. Of course, if the GPS can't be set to a particular datum, the datum adjustment factor will have to be applied when plotting positions derived from the GPS. Despite care in selecting datums, inaccuracies can still occur. A **prudent mariner doesn't rely on a single source of navigational information; always use a second method to determine the position of the vessel.**

chart datum, vertical – the vertical reference datum (plane) for the level of water from which depths and heights above water indicated on a chart are measured. For depths, the sounding datum is some level of low water, such as mean low water (MLW), mean lower low water (MLLW), lowest astronomical tide (LAT), or extreme low water. For heights above the water some level of high water is the reference level; for example, mean high water (MHW). There's a notation on the chart about what vertical datum is used.

chart edition – a new edition of a paper or electronic chart is issued when enough changes to a previous edition have occurred to warrant a new chart, or when a new survey has been done. Minor changes between editions are disseminated in NOTICES TO MARINERS or by the electronic chart publisher. The edition date is on the lower left corner of a paper chart, outside the border. Some paper charts are hand corrected by chart agents, and the date of the corrections may be noted near the edition information. *See* **CHARTS, PRINT-ON-DEMAND.**

chart, electronic – a chart displayed on a CHART PLOTTER or a computer with navigation software. It's an electronic reproduction of a paper chart, in either RASTER or VECTOR form. There are many different data formats, most of which are not compatible with each other. As electronic charting evolves, the industry will address compatibility issues. Using electronic charts makes it easier to navigate, and frees crew to keep a proper visual lookout and check the boat's position, using traditional PILOTING skills. It's often assumed that having electronic charts eliminates the need to learn "old-fashioned" paper chart plotting and navigating skills; just turn on the chart plotter and watch the little boat icon sail along the course. Learning paper chart piloting will allow you to determine if the chart plotter is giving incorrect information (which can happen). Verify navigation with visual, non-electronic observations. For safe navigation it's important to understand the limitations of electronic charts:

- Electronic charts are reproductions of a paper chart, and any inaccuracies on the paper chart will be on the electronic chart.
- The accuracy of chart data on electronic or paper charts may be less than that of the position-fixing system (GPS) in use.
- It may be necessary to change to another chart view to look at the whole course, identify a distant object or to determine the BEARING and RANGE to the object. Changing to another view may be confusing, and important details may be lost or overlooked.
- Overlays from radar and/or AIS on the screen can obscure important chart details. Turn off unnecessary layers, but be aware that some of these layers may be needed on another chart view.
- The navigator must understand all the features and capabilities of a chart plotter to use it effectively: read the manual and practice, before relying on the chart plotter in critical navigation situations.
- The electronic chart may not have been updated with changes. Updates are issued by the software supplier at regular intervals, but changes between those intervals will have to be researched using NOTICES TO MARINERS.

• In areas where channel locations and depths change frequently, buoys may be moved before the changes are posted in a notice to mariners. Use your eyes and follow the buoys.

• Standards for the accuracy of electronic charts and the intervals for updating are not regulated for the recreational marine market as they are for ships.

• Electronics may provide inaccurate information or fail altogether.

• The small screen of some chart plotters may not be easy to read. Some navigators prefer the larger display of a computer for the electronic charts.

A prudent mariner doesn't rely solely on the information provided by electronic charts and chart plotters. For an excellent, informative website see www.allianceforsafenavigation.org. *See also* AUTOMATION OF NAVIGATION FUNCTIONS.

charter, chartering – nautical term for renting a boat. Sail and power yachts may be chartered all around the world, which is a good way to see different places, or to help you decide what kind of boat you like, if you're thinking about buying one. A bareboat charter is taking the boat without a captain; you do the driving. A captained charter includes a captain and sometimes a crew (for a large yacht). To qualify for a bareboat charter you'll fill out an application, give your boating experience, and the charter company will decide what kind of charter you can have. Sometimes you'll have almost enough experience to qualify for a bareboat, but the company will put a captain aboard for a day or two to evaluate your skills. If you're OK, the captain departs. Some sailing areas are better for beginners, and some are for more-experienced sailors. Read articles in sailing magazines, talk to charter companies and to people who've chartered about where they went and what company they used.

chart, gnomonic (pronounced noh **monick**) **or great circle chart** – this CHART PROJECTION is used for ocean passage planning charts, polar region charts, and some LARGE SCALE harbor plans. Chart features: (1) GREAT CIRCLE routes are straight lines. (2) lines of LATITUDE are curved (not parallel), and the MERIDIANS converge. (3) small scale gnomonic charts are used to plan great circle routes for an ocean passage; for some voyages of over 600 miles a great circle route is shorter than a RHUMB LINE route.

chart, international, INT – a SMALL-SCALE chart that is published by various countries, using the same specifications. An international chart has the chart number used in the particular country and the international number with the suffix "INT."

chartlet – a small chart or chart sketch that shows a detailed plan of a particular anchorage, harbor, or part of a harbor. Chartlets are found in CRUISING GUIDES, NAUTICAL ALMANACS, COAST PILOTS, and printed in a section of some large-scale charts.

Chart No. 1 – the standard symbols and abbreviations used on charts are shown in Chart No.1, *Nautical Chart Symbols and Abbreviations*, which is an essential reference aboard a boat that uses either paper or electronic charts. Other countries may also have a similar Chart No.1 for their charts, which is useful for the terms and words in a foreign language and for differences in chart symbols. U.S. Chart No.1 is no longer printed, but it's available for free download at the NOAA website: www.nauticalcharts.noaa.gov (click on "nautical charts and publications" and follow the links). Some nautical bookstores/CHANDLERS may still have printed copies. *See also* Calder's *How to Read a Nautical Chart* in the bibliography under "Charts."

chart, online – an online chart viewer for all U.S. NOAA charts is available at www.nauticalcharts.noaa.gov/mcd/OnLineViewer.html. See the bibliography under "Charts" for more information about this website.

chart, pilot – pilot charts are ocean charts, not to be used for navigation, that show prevailing winds, currents, air and sea temperatures, wave heights, ice limits, visibility, barometric pressure, and weather conditions on a SMALL SCALE CHART for each month in a year. The navigator uses pilot charts to select ocean routes with regard to the expected weather and ocean conditions. The information used to compile the pilot charts was obtained from oceanographic and meteorological observations made over many decades. Pilot charts are available as single charts for a particular month and area and in books of charts.

chart plotter – (1) an electronic instrument that stores charts in electronic form and displays them on a dedicated screen. An integral GPS or a GPS connected to the chart plotter allows the position of the boat to be displayed on the electronic chart, along with the course line and WAYPOINTS (if used). (2) a COMPUTER with navigation software and electronic charts interfaced with a GPS can be used as a chart plotter. A prudent navigator doesn't rely solely on a chart plotter; use visual navigation and PILOTING techniques. A chart plotter can't see. Read articles about chart plotters before purchasing, and study the manual to learn to use this aid effectively and safely. *See* AUTOMATION OF NAVIGATION FUNCTIONS; CHART, ELECTRONIC; CHART, RASTER; and CHART, VECTOR. (3) another name for a COURSE PLOTTER.

chart, print-on-demand – paper charts printed by private companies using data from a government chart agency; they're up-to-date on the day they're printed. NOAA nautical charts are available in print-on-demand form from www.oceangrafix.com.

chart projection – a chart projection transfers the geographic features on the sphere of the earth to the flat plane of a paper chart. Most charts use either the MERCATOR or the GNOMONIC projection. The Mercator is most often used for nautical charts.

chart protractor – same as COURSE PLOTTER.

chart publishers – charts are published in paper and electronic forms by governments and by private publishers. Government charts for U.S. waters are issued by NOAA. Canadian government charts are available from chart agents for the Canadian Hydrographic Service (www.charts.gc.ca); UK government charts from chart agents for the UK Hydrographic Office (www.ukho.gov.uk). Some private publishers reproduce government charts; others produce their own based on government charts. The same cautions about CHART ACCURACY apply to all charts, no matter who produces them.

chart, raster (raster navigation chart, RNC) – an electronic chart that's a visual scan of a paper chart. It cannot provide any information that was not on the paper chart.

- Horizontal datums and CHART PROJECTIONS may differ between various brands of raster charts and even within a series of raster charts.
- Chart features can't be simplified or removed. It's just like the paper chart. This could affect the readability of radar or AIS information superimposed on the chart.
- It's usually not possible to get additional information about charted objects from a raster chart.
- It may be necessary to change to another chart view to look at the whole course, identify a distant object or to determine the BEARING and RANGE to the object. Changing to another view may be confusing, and important details may be lost or overlooked.
- If the chart is rotated to a view other than NORTH-UP, this can affect the readability of chart text and symbols because everything on the chart rotates.
- When zooming in or out on a raster chart everything on it grows larger or smaller.
- Depending on the source of the chart, different colors may be used to show similar chart information, and different colors may be used for daytime and nighttime viewing.

In confined waters, the accuracy of chart data on electronic or paper charts may be less than that of the position-fixing system (GPS) in use. *See* CHART DATUMS; CHART, VECTOR; and CHART, ELECTRONIC.

chart scales – a small scale chart shows a large area in less detail; a large scale chart shows a small area in greater detail. There are four basic categories; the scales are approximate in each category:

Sailing charts – (smallest scales). 1:10,000,000 (and smaller) to 1:600,000. Passage planning over a large area, crossing an ocean.

General charts – 1:600,000 to 1:150,000. Coastwise navigation outside off-lying dangers, usually in sight of land.

Coastal charts – 1:150,000 to 1:50,000. Navigation near shore, entering harbors. Scales near 1:50,000 are the most frequently used.

Harbor charts – (largest scales) 1:50,000 to 1:5,000. Details of harbors. CHARTLETS may have even larger scales.

chart, small craft or **leisure chart** – in the U.S. and other countries, chart publishers offer paper charts for the recreational mariner. They are supplied in a smaller format than regular charts, in a booklet or folio, or as single pages. Small craft charts are usually LARGE SCALE charts. They may have helpful information on them specifically of interest to recreational vessel operators.

chart, synoptic – *see* SYNOPTIC CHART.

chart, vector (electronic navigation chart, ENC) – a vector chart is more complex than a RASTER chart. Each point on the paper chart is digitally mapped and transferred to the vector chart. This allows chart information to be manipulated.

•Click on a feature (such as a lighthouse) to display the details of that feature.

•Turn various layers or details on or off.

•Monitor depths to warn before GROUNDING.

•Zooming in and out on a vector chart changes the view only of the geographical features, while the text keeps it's same size and orientation. You can zoom in to large magnifications without distortion.

•It may be necessary to change to another chart view to look at the whole course, identify a distant object, or to determine the BEARING and RANGE to the object.

•Vector charts look computer-generated.

•Vector charts lack most TOPOGRAPHIC features that are on some paper charts.

•Vector charts cost more than similar raster charts.

In confined waters, the accuracy of chart data on electronic or paper charts may be less than that of the position-fixing system (GPS) in use. *See* CHART, RASTER and CHART, ELECTRONIC.

checklist, pre-departure – just as aircraft pilots have a pre-flight checklist, it's a good idea for a skipper to have one. A basic checklist for daily operation includes: engine (oil level, cooling water, fuel), navigation lights, horn, radar reflector, lifejackets, JACKLINES, HARNESSES and TETHERS, FLARES, and other emergency signaling equipment, bilge pump operation, operation and preparation of electronics, selection of charts for the trip, PASSAGE PLAN preparation, stowage on deck and below, rigging check, weather, and additional items if embarking on a long or offshore passage. See Mapes's *Ready to Sail* and Burke's *Bluewater Checklist* in the bibliography under "Sailing" for two examples of books with checklists.

checklists – useful for regular procedures on a boat, such as departure, arrival in port, closing up the boat, and maintenance tasks, such as winterizing. Having checklists specific to the boat helps not only the skipper, but allows other crew members to participate in the process and learn about the boat. EMERGENCY PROCEDURE CARDS are checklists for effective action in an emergency.

check valve – a valve inserted in a fluid line that prevents the liquid from flowing in two directions (stops backflow). Check valves are used in potable water lines and bilge pump discharge lines, as well as other locations. A check valve can malfunction and allow backflow. Some valves can be opened and repaired; others have to be replaced. A check valve restricts the flow to some degree.

cheeks – the sides of a BLOCK; the shell or the plates on either side of the SHEAVE (pronounced shiv).

chest, sea – *see* SEA CHEST.

chine, hard chine, radius chine – a chine or hard chine is the sharp angle between the **TOPSIDES** and the bottom on a flat or vee-bottom boat. Hard chines and radius chines are used on some metal and wooden boats. A radius chine approximates a curved hull by using multiple sections of flat material formed around a radius. For another photo see the blue sailboat with **KEEL, BILGE**.

This strong metal cutter is designed for high latitude adventures, with an enclosed, heated pilothouse. One chine is visible above the waterline. The headsail is roller-furling and the hanked-on staysail is furled on deck. The white line just below the deck level is a strong, welded rub rail.

Lady Salope, a 45ft /13.7m aluminum Ovni cutter. The headsail is roller-furling and the hanked-on staysail is in the blue bag. Two chines are visible. She has a large reverse transom and a stern arch for various antennas and a wind generator.

chock – (1) a metal fitting mounted on the deck or **TOE RAIL** that holds a mooring or anchor line in place as it leads away from the boat. Chocks are located near the **BOW** and **STERN** and sometimes **AMIDSHIPS**. Some chocks are open and others are closed (HAWSE HOLE). Use CHAFING GEAR on ropes in a chock. (2) metal or wood hardware that holds deck equipment in place, such as a LIFE RAFT, a DINGHY or an anchor.

chop, lop – short, irregular steep seas, of varying degrees of roughness. A chop can be slight or heavy. A chop on the BOW is a head chop or head sea.

chrome – a thin coat of chromium applied by ELECTROPLATING to metals and plastics to create a very shiny surface. "Hard" or engineering chrome (not harder, just thicker) is used on precision machinery, like hydraulic cylinder rods where wear is a factor. Hard chrome is applied over steel, so if the chrome surface is damaged the steel will rust through the damaged area, and the protective value of the chrome lost. Decorative chrome (or nickel-chrome) plating is a very thin coating. On well-made marine equipment, such as WINCHES, the manufacturer carefully applies the chrome to increase resistance to wear. However, chrome can wear off over time; some objects can be re-chromed in a factory, but it's expensive. If chrome *peels* it's a manufacturing defect, not the result of environmental factors.

chronometer – a very accurate timepiece, to which other clocks can be compared. A ship's chronometer may be set to UTC. Some watches are accurate enough to be a chronometer. Precise time, to the second, is important for CELESTIAL NAVIGATION.

CHU – radio station of the Canadian National Research Council (NRC). It broadcasts UTC time signals, with voice announcements in English and French, on three frequencies: 3330, 7850, and 14,670 kHz. WWV/WWVH in the U.S. also broadcasts UTC time signals.

chum, anchor chum – another name for a SENTINEL.

chute – slang for a SPINNAKER. The term comes from the old name, parachute spinnaker.

Chutescoop® – a SPINNAKER SOCK, used when setting or furling the sail. Chutescoop® is the registered trade mark of the V.F. Shaw Co., Inc.

cill (pronounced sill) – alternate spelling of SILL.

circle of uncertainty – *see* UNCERTAINTY, AREA OF.

circuit breaker – a switch that trips (turns itself off) if there's an unsafe electrical condition in the equipment or the circuit attached to it. Unlike a fuse that must be replaced, a circuit breaker can be reset after the electrical fault is corrected. The switches on many AC and DC electrical panels are also circuit breakers. Circuit breakers are rated in AMPS, and should be selected to correspond to the amperage draw of a piece of equipment or all the equipment on a circuit. Use the WATTAGE FORMULA to make the calculation.

CIRM – acronym for the INTERNATIONAL ASSOCIATION FOR MARINE ELECTRONICS COMPANIES.

classic vessel – get any group of mariners together and ask them for a definition of classic and you'll have as many answers as people in the group. The adjective is applied to both sailboats and powerboats. In the early 21st century classic generally applies to handsome and elegant vessels built before the 1950s or modern replicas. In the next century perhaps classic will be applied to yachts designed after 2050. Taste changes. A classic yacht has aesthetically-pleasing lines and a relatively narrow beam, a good deal of BRIGHTWORK and polished or chromed brass, perhaps LONG ENDS, and a hull form with deep bilges (for a sailboat). Traditional is sometimes used as a synonym, although a vessel may be traditional and not be described as classic. For photos see CANOE STERN, DORADE BOX, AND FRACTIONAL RIG.

This beautiful old sailboat is worth a second glance. The roller furling headsails don't detract from her classic lines.

classification society, marine – an organization that sets standards and issues rules for the design and construction of ships and large yachts. A yacht or ship built to a society's classification standards has her design approved by the society's engineers, and the vessel is surveyed periodically by society SURVEYORS during construction and SEA TRIALS. After launch, periodic inspections are conducted by society surveyors to confirm that the vessel still meets the classification standards. A yacht may be advertised as being constructed to the standards of a classification society, but she doesn't have a classification certificate unless she has undergone the full certification process. A builder may voluntarily follow the standards, but not seek certification. Some well-known classification societies are the American Bureau of Shipping (ABS), Bureau Veritas (BV), Det Norske Veritas (DNV), Germanischer Lloyds (GL), Lloyd's Register of Shipping (LR), and Registro Italiano Navale (RINA).

claw, devil's – *see* DEVIL'S CLAW.

"claw off" – to drive a vessel under sail or power away from a LEE SHORE in HEAVY WEATHER.

clear – to make sure a rope is not tangled. "Clear the HALYARD before you DOUSE the sail." "The SHEET's clear now."

clear, clearance – to pass through Customs when entering or departing a foreign country. A clearance is permission to enter or depart the country. See PORT OF ENTRY, PRATIQUE, and the next two entries.

clearing in, inward clearance, entering – the process followed by a vessel and her crew when arriving at a foreign port. Specific requirements for individual countries are available from a variety of sources, including government and CRUISING WEBSITES. Websites (rather than printed documents) may be a better source of up-to-date regulations, as rules can change frequently. It's very important to follow all regulations carefully to avoid legal problems abroad. A skipper may choose to hire a SHIP'S AGENT to facilitate clearance procedures, if the bureaucracy or regulations are complicated, or if there's a language barrier. In some countries foreign vessels are required to clear into and out of each port; in other countries a single clearance serves for all ports in the country. Clearing in involves one or more government officials: Customs and Immigration officers, a health authority, and perhaps an agricultural authority. Some officials perform multiple functions. In general, to clear into a country:

• Fly the **Q FLAG** at the **STARBOARD SPREADER** upon entering the **TERRITORIAL** waters of the country. The **COURTESY FLAG** may be flown below the Q flag.

• Contact Customs and Immigration immediately upon arrival in port. Only the captain may go ashore before a vessel has been cleared, unless a Customs officer or representative advises otherwise.

• Welcome the officers: they will either come aboard or direct you to go to the relevant offices ashore. At a minimum, the officials will request boat documents and passports for each crewmember, and in some countries a clearance from the vessel's last port of call (a **ZARPE**) is also required when entering. The importation of certain foods, plant products, pets, or firearms (including **FLARE** guns) may be restricted or prohibited.

• Complete the paperwork and pay any fees (if required). When everything is complete the officials will grant **PRATIQUE.** The authorities may issue a cruising permit that specifies how long the vessel may stay in the country. The time crewmembers can stay may be different from the time of the cruising permit; check regulations carefully. Enquire about the **CLEARING OUT** procedures necessary when departing.

• Remove the Q flag and replace it with the **COURTESY FLAG**, unless it's already flying.

clearing out, outward clearance – the process of departing a port or a country by vessel. In some countries foreign vessels are required to clear into and out of each port; in other countries a single inward clearance serves for all ports in the country. Obtain the necessary permissions from officials before departure. A required outward clearance is in the form of a document (a **ZARPE**, in Spanish-speaking countries) or stamps on a clearance document.

cleat – (1) a metal or wood fitting with "horns" around which lines are secured. See the next entry for a photo. *See* also **CAM CLEAT** and **JAM CLEAT**. (2) wooden strips across a gangplank or ramp to prevent feet from slipping when the ramp is at an angle. (3) wood or metal strips used to join two pieces of wood or metal. (4) to attach a line to a cleat, **BITT** or other attachment point.

A proper cleat hitch with the locking turn parallel to the other turns. The line to the left leads to the boat.

cleat hitch – the basic hitch used to secure the end of a line to a cleat. Wrap the rope three-quarters of the way around the base, put a figure-eight turn over each horn, and lock a final turn over one horn with a twisted loop locking turn. Make the locking turn parallel to the figure eight for a **SEAMANLIKE** appearance. Slippery rope may need one more figure eight turn before the locking turn. A number of multiple turns aren't necessary. Some people do many figure eights without a locking turn, but this hitch can come loose, and if a cleated line must be released quickly lots of unnecessary turns take time to untangle. Putting the eye splice at the end of a line (or a **BOWLINE**) through the base of an open cleat and back over the horns is very secure, but the only way to release the loop from the cleat is to take the strain off the line, which may not be easy in some cases.

How long would it take to free these dock lines?

clevis pin – a smooth metal pin with a flat head larger than the diameter of the pin, and a hole near the opposite end for a **COTTER PIN**. There are no threads on a clevis pin. It's used in **SHACKLES**, rigging **TOGGLES**, and with other hardware, such as **BLOCKS**. Don't replace a missing clevis pin with a bolt; it isn't as strong, and bolt threads can abrade the metal it contacts.

clew – the lower **AFT** corner of a triangular sail, at the corner opposite the **TACK**. On a **MAINSAIL** the clew is the corner of the sail that goes to the aft end of the **BOOM**. On a **JIB** the clew is where the jib **SHEETS** attach. *See* **SAIL, PARTS OF.**

clinometer – a device for indicating the angle of HEEL of the vessel. It may have a swinging pendulum that points to a scale on an arc, or have a bubble in a curved tube that moves along a measured arc as the boat heels.

close aboard – near the vessel. "When you pass the green buoy keep it close aboard to **PORT**."

close-hauled – sailing at approximately 45° to the **APPARENT WIND; BEATING.** *See* **POINTS OF SAIL.**

close quarters, close quarters situation – (1) an area where maneuvering room is limited because of other vessels, docks, land, etc. (2) a close quarters situation under Rule 7 of the **NAVIGATION RULES** is when the risk of collision may exist. The Rules do not define distances or what constitutes a risk of collision. Each captain must judge the speed of the vessels, assess prevailing conditions, and determine how much room should be maintained between vessels *to avoid* a close quarters situation. *See* **COLLISION, RISK OF.**

close reach – sailing between approximately 45° and 90° to the **APPARENT WIND**; between **CLOSE-HAULED** and a **BEAM REACH.** *See* **POINTS OF SAIL.**

closed cell foam – a synthetic foam material that doesn't absorb water. It's used in flotation clothing, lifejackets, and boat cushions.

closed cooling system, closed system cooling – a type of engine COOLING SYSTEM.

closest point of approach (CPA) – the closest distance at which two vessels will pass if they both maintain their courses and speeds. It's important to determine both the CPA and the TIME TO CLOSEST POINT OF APPROACH (TCPA) to maintain a safe distance between vessels and alter course, if necessary, in a timely manner. Modern radars with ARPA can calculate the CPA and TCPA (only if the radar is properly interfaced with other instruments on the boat), some AIS receivers can calculate it, or it can be calculated by hand on a MANEUVERING BOARD or RADAR TRANSFER PLOTTING SHEET. It takes skill and practice to plot the CPA and calculate the TCPA quickly on paper.

clouds, types of – we know that clouds are associated with various types of weather and the ability to read the clouds is important for understanding and predicting the weather. A weather book or cloud picture chart gives the basics about weather associated with cloud formations. Below is a list of the general types of clouds, from the highest to the lowest (the heights are for clouds in the mid-LATITUDES), with general comments on the associated weather. Cloud heights are lower in polar regions and higher in tropical regions. See the bibliography under "Weather" for book recommendations.

The *highest clouds* are noctilucent ("night-shining") clouds, seen just after sunset in HIGH LATITUDES, and increasingly in lower latitudes. They're streaky clouds glowing with an electric blue-white color. They form in the mesosphere, the layer of the atmosphere above the stratosphere, approximately 50 miles/80km above the earth. Noctilucent clouds have no connection with the weather.

High clouds: cirrus, cirrocumulus, cirrostratus (16,5000-42,600ft/5,000-13,000m), composed mostly of ice crystals. A few cirrus clouds are seen in fair weather. Increasing cirrus indicates the approach of a WARM FRONT and a change in the weather within 24 hours. Cirrocumulus (a MACKEREL SKY) may warn of the approach of a storm. Cirrostratus are thin, translucent, sheet-like clouds, through which the sun or moon may sometimes be visible. They usually indicate rain or snow within 24 hours.

Middle level: altocumulus and altostratus (6,500-20,000ft/2000-7,000m), usually made of water droplets, but may have ice crystals where the atmosphere is cold enough. Altocumulus clouds are small puffy clouds (like a mackerel sky). In the summer on a humid, warm day they may signal thunderstorms later in the day. Altostratus are thick sheet-like clouds that cover the sky, blocking out the sun. They form a few hours ahead of a warm front, which is likely to bring rain or snow.

Low level: cumulus, cumulonimbus, nimbostratus, stratocumulus, stratus (surface to 6,500ft/2,000m), usually composed of water droplets. Fair weather cumulus are puffy, cotton ball clouds. Cumulus clouds can become cumulonimbus (see the next paragraph). Nimbostratus are thick, dark, wet clouds that produce rain or snow that can last a long time. Stratocumulus are low, puffy gray clouds in rows, with sky visible between the rows. They usually mean fair weather or perhaps light rain, but if they group together blocking out the sky they become nimbostratus. Stratus clouds are gray sheets completely covering the sky; they're like fog that doesn't reach the ground. Light drizzle may come from these clouds, or it can remain dry.

Vertical clouds: cumulus and cumulonimbus clouds may extend from the surface to 42,600 ft/13,000m). Cumulus can build in height as air is convected upward, becoming cumulonimbus (thunderheads). Strong winds aloft can blow the top of these clouds into an anvil shape; the point of the anvil indicates the direction the storm is moving. Thunderheads are dark on the bottom and whiter above. These clouds warn of dangerous, severe weather and they shouldn't be ignored.

Unusual cloud formations: (1) mammatus are stormy-looking, puffy clouds that hang downward in groups, usually seen with cumulonimbus clouds. They're created by air moving downward, which usually means that a storm is dissipating or moving away. (2) lenticular clouds look like a lens or flying saucer; they form on the downwind side of mountains. (3) nacreous clouds occur at very high altitudes (13 to 19 miles/21 to 30 kilometers). Just after sunset they glow with vivid colors (like mother-of-pearl or nacre, from which the name is derived). They don't predict the weather. (4) contrails are streak-like clouds created by jet aircraft exhaust. They form at 16,400-42,600ft/5,000-13,000m and can become cirrus clouds.

clove hitch – a type of knot used for tying a rope on a round or square object, such as a piling or a rail. A clove hitch is frequently used to tie FENDERS on LIFELINES. *See* KNOTS, BASIC for a photo.

club, club boom, jib boom – a short BOOM on the FOOT of a JIB or STAYSAIL.

clutter – unwanted echoes produced on a radar screen by rain, snow, or waves that can obscure real TARGETS. A radar has anti-clutter controls to reduce this problem. However, if the controls aren't adjusted properly small targets may be suppressed. Read the radar manual and practice adjusting the controls.

CMG – abbreviation for COURSE MADE GOOD; same as COURSE OVER THE GROUND.

coachroof, coach roof – a part of the deck that's raised to increase headroom in the cabin.

coaming – raised areas around a COCKPIT, HATCH, or COMPANIONWAY to help keep water out.

coastal navigation – same as PILOTING or INSHORE NAVIGATION.

coastal waters – a general term, the usage of which varies in different countries. Coastal waters usually include the area from the shore of the mainland or island, the bays, harbors, and the sounds, extending as far out as 60 to 100NM. Weather forecasts for coastal waters have more limited areas, as defined in the forecast or on the weather service website. *See* FORECAST, SEA AREA.

Coast Guard Rescue Service, UK – an organization of volunteers that provides coastal search-and-rescue assistance to the Maritime and Coast Guard Agency (MCA). For information about volunteering see the bibliography under "Safety." *See also* ROYAL NATIONAL LIFEBOAT INSTITUTION.

coast pilot, sailing directions – interchangeable names for a book or series of books published by government agencies, with detailed information for a specific geographic area. Sailing directions supplement nautical charts, and although they are written for large vessels they're an excellent resource for the recreational mariner. In some cases a pilot may have the only information if a CRUISING GUIDE or NAUTICAL ALMANAC isn't available for a particular area. Sailing directions include information essential to safe navigation, such as anchorages, bridge and cable clearances, channel descriptions, harbor photographs, general tides and currents (not TIDE TABLES), dangers to navigation, LARGE-SCALE CHARTLETS, facilities for ships and yachts, prominent land features, TRAFFIC SEPARATION SCHEMES, weather information, and much more. The NGA publishes worldwide sailing directions for free download at http://msi.nga.mil/NGAPortal/MSI.portal; click on "Publications." The Canadian Hydrographic Service issues sailing directions for Canadian waters in paper form (www.charts.gc.ca). The UK Hydrographic Office issues worldwide sailing directions in paper form, available from a network of dealers (www.ukho.gov.uk). Update pilots and sailing directions using NOTICES TO MARINERS.

Coast Pilot®, U.S. – the United States Coast Pilot® series consists of nine volumes covering each of the Coast Guard Districts and the Great Lakes. They're available in paper and PDF form. See the bibliography under "Navigation and Piloting."

coax – *see* CABLE, COAXIAL.

cockpit – the central area on a boat where the crew sits, and where the HELM is located. If the cockpit is near the STERN it's an AFT cockpit; if it's more toward the BOW it's a center cockpit. Some boats have two cockpits, one with the helm and the other for the crew.

cockpit drains – water that comes into the cockpit from rain, snow, or waves should drain quickly overboard so that excess weight won't stay aboard and cause a dangerous condition. This is especially important to a boat that ventures offshore, and when the boat is in storage. If the boat has an open TRANSOM there may be no drains, but if there are drains you can test how well they work. ABYC Standard H-4 Cockpit Drainage Systems gives details for testing drainage on land and in the water.

cockpit sole – the floor of the COCKPIT.

code, color (electric wires) – *see* WIRE, ELECTRICAL, MARINE COLOR CODE.

code flags, signal flags – a set of single-color and multi-colored flags used to communicate with the INTERNATIONAL CODE OF SIGNALS. A complete set includes 26 alphabetical flags, one each for the numbers zero to nine, three repeaters/substitutes, and the answering pennant. Flags may be easier to interpret than light or sound signals over a distance, and flags are sometimes used in conjunction with light or sound signals. There are specific meanings assigned by international maritime agreement to single-letter flags (urgent, important, or commonly-used signals), two-letter FLAG HOISTS (general messages), and three-letter hoists beginning with the letter M for the medical signal code. For example, the A flag indicates "diver down, keep clear;" the B flag indicates the vessel is carrying dangerous cargo (such as fuel); the O flag indicates Man Overboard; the Q flag is displayed when a vessel enters the waters of a foreign country; flag hoist N and C is a DISTRESS SIGNAL. The full set of code flags is also used when DRESSING SHIP.

The flags of the International Code of Signals.

It's useful to have a chart of the meaning of commonly-used flags. Plastic reference cards and some NAUTICAL ALMANACS have these charts. Ships carry *The International Code of Signals* book to allow communication across language barriers without the need for words. See the bibliography under "Miscellaneous" for information about a free download.

code zero – a large GENOA used for sailing on a CLOSE REACH in light winds. The area of a code zero is larger than a genoa but not as large as an ASYMMETRICAL SPINNAKER. It was created to meet the requirements of a racing rule, but has found favor on some cruising yachts.

"coffee grinder" – the slang name for a PEDESTAL WINCH.

coiling rope – BRAIDED ROPE can usually be coiled in either direction, but THREE-STRAND rope should be coiled in a clockwise direction. Alternatively, lay the rope out in figure-eight coils (FLAKE it) to avoid putting kinks in it. Don't "elbow wrap" rope or electrical cable.

cold front – *see* FRONT, COLD.

cold molded – a type of wooden hull construction that uses thin layers of wood laminated with epoxy resin. A lightweight, strong hull results from proper cold molding techniques.

cold water survival – *see* SURVIVAL IN COLD WATER.

collision, avoiding (restricted visibility) – Rule 19 of the NAVIGATION RULES contains the actions for vessels that are *not* IN SIGHT of one another when navigating *in or near* an area of restricted visibility. In summary:

- Proceed at a safe speed adapted to the conditions and RESTRICTED VISIBILITY.
- Maintain a visual lookout.
- Consider the circumstances and the reduced visibility when determining your SAFE SPEED, assessing the RISK OF COLLISION, or deciding on an action to take to avoid a collision.
- Consider the circumstances and the reduced visibility when observing the Rules for operating in or near a TRAFFIC SEPARATION SCHEME or in a NARROW CHANNEL.
- If you see another vessel on radar alone, determine if a CLOSE-QUARTERS SITUATION is developing or if the risk of collision exists. *If so, take avoiding action in ample time*. Two important stipulations: (1) if possible, do not alter course to PORT for a vessel forward of your BEAM, except if you're overtaking a vessel. (2) if possible, do not alter course towards a vessel ABEAM or ABAFT your beam.
- If you have determined that a risk of collision does *not* exist, but you hear the fog signal of another vessel forward of your BEAM, or if you cannot avoid a close-quarters situation with another vessel forward of your beam, reduce steerageway to the bare minimum, or take all way off, and navigate with extreme caution until danger of collision is over.

collision, avoiding (unrestricted visibility) – Rules 8 and 14-17 of the NAVIGATION RULES contain the actions for *power-driven* vessels to take to avoid a CLOSE-QUARTERS SITUATION or a collision in unrestricted visibility. These rules apply only when vessels are visually IN SIGHT of each other (Rule 3(k).

Navigating in RESTRICTED VISIBILITY and with radar when you can't see the other vessel does *not* apply in this case. The rules apply to *two* vessels meeting HEAD ON, CROSSING, or OVERTAKING, not to MULTIPLE VESSELS converging. In summary:

- When taking action to avoid collision, take action early and maneuver in accordance with the Rules; Rule 8(a).
- Make a course change and/or speed change that will be clearly evident to the other vessel visually or on radar. Avoid a succession of small changes; Rule 8(b).
- Take action to avoid collision that is sufficient to give a safe passing distance between vessels; Rule 8(d).
- The PORT-hand vessel in a CROSSING SITUATION shall avoid (if possible) crossing ahead of the vessel on her STARBOARD side; Rule 15.
- The STAND-ON vessel shall take action if the GIVE-WAY vessel is not taking appropriate action in compliance with the Rules; Rule 17(a, b).
- If the stand-on vessel must maneuver to avoid a collision, she shall avoid (if possible) turning to port toward a vessel on her port side; Rule 17(c).
- Either vessel shall slow down, stop, or go ASTERN to avoid a collision, or to get more time to assess the situation; Rule 8(e).

The Rules are designed to prevent vessels from getting into a close-quarters situation where the risk of collision exists. In unrestricted visibility, if a collision occurs it's usually the result of one or both vessels violating the Rules.

collision bearing or collision course – in a CROSSING SITUATION, if the BEARING of another vessel doesn't change and the RANGE (distance) between vessels is decreasing, you're on a collision course. As soon as you become aware that a crossing situation exists, take a visual bearing on the other vessel. Sight over a fixed position on the boat, such as a STANCHION, or use a HAND-BEARING COMPASS or COMPASS-BINOCULARS. In one minute (or less) take another bearing, looking at the vessel from the same point on your boat, to see if the bearing has changed. If the bearing is the same or has changed very little, take action as appropriate under the NAVIGATION RULES. Even if the bearing changes, risk may exist, particularly when approaching a large vessel, a tow, a vessel at close range or if the speeds of the vessels are high. See COLLISION, AVOIDING (two entries) and COLLISION, RISK OF.

collision bulkhead – *see* BULKHEAD, WATERTIGHT.

collision mat – a large square, rectangular, or triangular piece of canvas or heavy cloth, with GROMMETS and ropes along the edges, used to put a temporary patch over a hole or damaged area in the hull. (This is called fothering, a good, old-time word). If you don't have a mat, use an easily-accessible sail. Use ropes to maneuver the mat over the damaged area, and tie it tightly in place around the hull. Water pressure helps hold the patch on and somewhat reduces the inflow of water, so there's some time to try a stronger repair. Order a ready-made mat, have a sailmaker/canvas shop make one or you can make your own. The overall size should be approximately 6ft/2.5m by 4ft/2m, with strong grommets inserted into a hem around all sides.

collision, risk of, determining – Rule 7 of the NAVIGATION RULES says that you "shall use all available means appropriate to the prevailing circumstances and conditions to determine if risk of collision exists." If there is any doubt, assume that there is risk of collision. Take systematic visual COLLISION BEARINGS:

- If the bearing doesn't change, risk of collision exists.
- Even if the bearing changes risk may exist, particularly when approaching a large vessel, a tow, a vessel at close range, or when vessel speeds are high.
- Use radar, if available, and plot the CPAS manually, or use ARPA, AIS, and all other means to assess the risk of collision.

color blindness – if a person is color blind this may affect safety if he/she is not able to discern the colors of navigation buoys and lights. Ask the crew. See also NIGHT VISION, HUMAN.

color code, electrical wire and cable – *see* WIRE, ELECTRICAL, MARINE COLOR CODE.

colors, evening – *see* MAKING COLORS.

colors, making – *see* MAKING COLORS.

COLREGS – another name for the NAVIGATION RULES.

"come about, coming about" – same as "GO ABOUT, GOING ABOUT."

comfort at sea – it's related to the DISPLACEMENT of a boat and her hull form. In general, light boats bounce around more and are less-comfortable for the crew than heavier boats of a similar size. Some yachts manage to combine light weight and a reasonable degree of comfort. Naval architect Ted Brewer devised a practical "Comfort Ratio (CR):"

> This is a ratio that I dreamed up, tongue-in-cheek, as a measure of motion comfort but it has been widely accepted and, indeed, does provide a reasonable comparison between yachts of similar type. It is based on the fact that the faster the motion the more upsetting it is to the average person. Given a wave of X height, the speed of the upward motion depends on the displacement of the yacht and the amount of waterline area that is acted upon. Greater displacement, or lesser WL area, gives a slower motion and more comfort for any given sea state.
>
> Beam does enter into it as a wider beam increases stability, increases WL area, and generates a faster reaction. The formula takes into account the displacement, the WL area, and adds a beam factor. The intention is to provide a means to compare the motion comfort of vessels of similar type and size, not to compare that of a Lightning class sloop with that of a husky 50 foot ketch.
>
> The CR is : Displacement in pounds divided by (.65 x (.7 LWL + .3 LOA) x $B^{1.333}$). Ratios will vary from 5.0 for a light daysailer to the high 60s for a super heavy vessel, such as a Colin Archer ketch. Moderate and successful ocean cruisers, such as the Valiant 40 and Whitby 42, will fall into the low-middle 30s range.
>
> Do consider, though, that a sailing yacht heeled by a good breeze will have a much steadier motion than one bobbing up and down in light airs on left over swells from yesterday's blow; also that the

typical summertime coastal cruiser will rarely encounter the wind and seas that an ocean going yacht will meet. Nor will one human stomach keep down what another stomach will handle with relish, or with mustard and pickles for that matter! It is all relative.

commercial vessel – the definition is important to understand if you are thinking about earning some money with your recreational vessel. In general, a commercial vessel is one that's operated for profit in activities such as fishing, carrying cargo or paying passengers, full-time or part-time. The U.S. Coast Guard defines a commercial vessel as any vessel engaged in commercial trade or that carries passengers for hire. In general terms, "passenger" means a person on the vessel who is not the captain, a crewmember, the owner, a representative of the owner, or a representative of a CHARTER company. "Passengers for hire" are persons aboard who have "contributed consideration as condition of carriage on the vessel." The full legal definitions is in 46U.S. Code §2102(21)(A). For example, if a boat takes one or more persons out to fish who have paid money or contributed anything of value *as a condition of going on the trip*, she is a commercial vessel under the definition. The voluntary sharing of expenses for food, fuel or supplies for a trip does not make the vessel a commercial vessel under the definition. Warships are not commercial vessels.

In the U.S. the Coast Guard is responsible for the safety of commercial vessels and has specific rules for the inspection, certification, equipping, and licensing of operators for various classes of these vessels. TRANSPORT CANADA (www.tc.gc.ca) monitors and inspects Canadian-registered small commercial vessels (two classes: under 12m and 12 to 24m in length). In the UK the MCA issues the regulations for small commercial vessels (under 24m in length), which include skippered and bareboat CHARTER vessels, sport fishing and dive boats, vessels carrying fewer than 12 passengers, commercially-operated RIBs, workboats, and pilot boats. Inspections and certifications are carried out by MCA-approved organizations. See the bibliography under "Design," and the RYA website (www.rya.org.uk) for summaries and links to the MCA requirements. *See also* INSPECTED VESSEL and STABILITY TEST.

commission, commissioned – (1) to commission a vessel is to prepare her for operation, particularly after the boat has been laid up or newly-built. (2) a vessel is commissioned or in commission when she's ready for use and able to be operated. The opposite is DECOMMISSION, DECOMMISSIONED.

communication between bow and stern – instead of hand signals between a person on the BOW and the helmsman, try a wireless communication system. A number of low-cost, small units are available. FCC regulations prohibit the use of handheld VHF radios as an intercom. If you don't use a wireless device or hand signals and need to communicate with words, the person on the bow must *face the helmsman* when speaking or yelling.

companionway – the main entrance to a boat's cabin. The steps leading into the cabin are called the ladder. The companionway is usually closed on top with a sliding hatch, and the AFT opening may be closed by hinged doors or removable DROP BOARDS/WASHBOARDS. A DODGER/SPRAY HOOD can be used to protect the companionway from rain and spray.

companionway slide – the sliding hatch that covers the top opening of a companionway. If it has a solid cover that it slides into when it's open, that's called the TURTLE.

compass – (1) a magnetic, electronic, or GYRO**compass**. This is the most important instrument aboard a boat. If purchasing or replacing a compass, buy the best you can afford. (2) a drawing instrument with two legs, used to draw arcs and circles. It has a pointed tip on one leg and a pencil holder or pencil lead on the other leg. It's a useful tool for navigating with paper charts.

compass accuracy – a large compass is more accurate and easier to read than a small, inexpensive one. However, the accuracy of any magnetic compass is affected by VARIATION and DEVIATION. See the next entry.

compass adjustment, compass correction, compass compensation – the process of removing DEVIATION from a magnetic compass. To begin, prepare a DEVIATION TABLE. If deviation exceeds five degrees on any heading the compass should be adjusted. Some compasses are sealed and can't be adjusted. A professional compass adjuster can be hired or try it yourself. CHAPMAN describes several methods for determining deviation and adjusting a compass. Here's one method. On a good compass the adjustment magnets are accessible under the compass shell or housing. Some compasses have external adjusting magnets in tubes near the base of the compass. The magnets are attached to small rods, one set mounted ATHWARTSHIPS, and the other aligned FORE-AND-AFT. There's a screwdriver slot in one or both ends of the rods. Read the compass manual for specific instructions. A non-magnetic screwdriver (supplied with some compasses) is needed. The procedure should be done on a calm day in an area with little or no current and minimal vessel traffic.

1. Loosen the compass slightly from its base, so the whole instrument can be rotated, if necessary to correct ALIGNMENT ERROR.

2. Use the RANGES or GPS WAYPOINT BEARINGS that were selected when the deviation table was made. Stay steady on each course for about two minutes, so there's time to do the adjustments.

3. Run the boat first along the northerly range and turn the *athwartships* corrector until the compass reads the same as the *magnetic* bearing of the range or waypoint.

4. Turn the boat onto the exact RECIPROCAL (the southerly course), and see if the compass displays the correct reading. If it doesn't, there is alignment error; i.e. the compass itself is not aligned precisely with the CENTERLINE of the vessel. Note how many degrees the reading is off.

5. To correct alignment error rotate the whole compass slightly to remove *one-half* of the error. Tighten the compass base fasteners just enough to hold it in position.

6. Repeat steps 3 and 4, and perhaps step 5 until the deviation on the north and south headings is minimal or removed.

7. Run the east-west ranges or waypoints, as you did for the north-south courses. Repeat steps 3 and 4, and adjust the *fore-and-*

aft corrector to remove the deviation. Usually alignment error was removed in step 5.

8. When the deviations have been corrected on the CARDINAL headings, firmly tighten the compass on its base.

9. Run the ranges or waypoint bearings on the INTERCARDINAL headings (or every 30° around the compass to be more precise), and write down the deviation on each heading, if any.

If a satisfactory adjustment can't be accomplished, and deviations of more than a few degrees remain, write out a deviation table for the cardinal, intercardinal (or every 30°) headings, and use it to determine compass courses. If deviations greater than five degrees persist it may be necessary to hire a professional compass adjuster. ABYC document T-17 Compass Installation deals with installation and adjustment.

compass adjustment, steel boat – a magnetic compass on a small steel vessel (not a ship, which usually has a GYROCOMPASS) must have a DEVIATION TABLE prepared and the compass adjusted more often than on a wood, fiberglass or aluminum vessel. A steel boat takes on the earth's magnetism when she stays in one orientation, as when stored on land or in a berth for a long time or when the vessel moves to a new area of operation some distance away from its usual location. Some skippers of steel yachts prepare a deviation table and don't adjust the compass; others may install QUADRANTAL CORRECTORS along with preparing a deviation table and adjusting the compass.

compass bearing – a BEARING made with reference to a magnetic compass. It's measured *from* the boat *to* the object. A compass bearing taken from a vessel is a RELATIVE bearing. The label for a compass bearing is a capital C (285°C), which is used when writing in the log. The local VARIATION and the deviation on the boat's HEADING at the time the bearing was taken must be applied to the compass bearing to get a TRUE BEARING to plot on the chart.

compass-binoculars – binoculars with an integral compass, excellent for taking RELATIVE BEARINGS.

compass bowl – the housing for the COMPASS CARD. The bowl is filled with COMPASS FLUID.

compass bubble – see COMPASS FLUID for causes and correction.

compass card – the circular disk inside a compass that has the degrees marked on it. A card may be flat or curved. It's mounted on a special, sensitive pivot so it can turn freely. *See* COMPASS PIVOT WEAR.

compass compensation – same as COMPASS ADJUSTMENT.

compass correction – *see* CORRECTING (1) , (2) and COMPASS ADJUSTMENT.

compass correctors – the adjustment magnets under a compass, used in the process of COMPASS ADJUSTMENT, or QUADRANTAL CORRECTORS.

compass course – (1) the course to steer, CORRECTED for VARIATION and DEVIATION. (2) the course being steered. The label for a compass course is a capital C (325°C), which is used when writing in the log. *See also* HEADING.

compass, electronic or fluxgate compass – a type of magnetic compass that operates with a somewhat different internal mechanism than a traditional compass. This compass indicates MAGNETIC directions, which are usually presented as a digital readout. Electronic compasses are used on a boat either as a stand-alone instrument or as part of an AUTOPILOT or other electronic equipment. They require a simple COMPENSATION process, which is explained in the instrument manual.

compass error – the angle in degrees by which a compass reading differs from TRUE NORTH; it's the algebraic sum of VARIATION and DEVIATION. It's not really an "error." *See* CORRECTING (1).

compass fluid – the fluid (usually a special oil) in a compass that serves to dampen (slow down) the movement of the COMPASS CARD when the boat moves, and it also magnifies the card. The fluid can become cloudy with age or contaminants, and a bubble may develop in it. The bubble is caused by the loss of fluid, which can go unnoticed. Normally there's enough fluid in a compass so that it responds to temperature changes without a bubble forming. In a good compass there's a flexible rubber diaphragm inside which stretches or contracts as the fluid responds to temperature changes. This type of compass can be re-filled with fluid from the compass manufacturer. You may be able to do this yourself (check the compass instructions or contact the manufacturer). Carry a quart/liter of the proper fluid in case a bubble develops, or fluid escapes if the diaphragm fails. To add fluid to correct a bubble:

- Chill the compass for an hour or two in a freezer, or three or four hours in a refrigerator.
- Take it out of the freezer, and use a very small funnel or an eye dropper to put fluid into the fill hole (usually a screw fitting).
- Add fluid slowly to the fill hole and rotate the compass gently from side to side to allow air to escape from the hole.
- Hold your finger over the fill hole and rotate the compass upright to see if the bubble is gone. If not, add more fluid until the bubble goes away.
- Reinstall and tighten the fill hole screw.

If the diaphragm develops a leak, contact the manufacturer and see if the diaphragm is replaceable. If it is, you may be able to do this yourself and refill the compass; ask the manufacturer or check the website for instructions and a diagram of the compass construction. Alternatively, send it to the manufacturer for repair.

compass, fluxgate – *see* COMPASS, ELECTRONIC.

compass, hand-bearing – *see* HAND-BEARING COMPASS.

compass, magnetic – an instrument that reacts to the magnetic field of the earth. It points to MAGNETIC NORTH and indicates magnetic directions. The direction of magnetic north varies with geographic location. The LUBBER LINE indicates the HEADING of the boat. A compass can be affected by DEVIATION, which may be removed by the process of COMPASS ADJUSTMENT. ABYC document T-17 Compass Installation discusses installation and adjustment.

compass pivot wear – in a good quality compass, the compass card rests on a precision-jeweled pivot so it can move freely. Over time this pivot can become worn, causing the compass card to stick or act erratically. Vincent Duke of Oceanireland advises: If these symptoms develop, check the pivot by bringing a magnetic object such as a small magnet or a screwdriver close enough to the compass to deflect it about five or ten degrees. When the magnetic object is removed the compass should return quickly to the original bearing. Repeat this procedure several times, deflecting the card in opposite directions by changing the location of the magnetic object relative to the compass. If the compass doesn't return to exactly the same bearing, the pivot is either worn or defective, and the compass is due for overhaul or replacement. An overhaul can return a compass to new condition, so don't discard an expensive piece of equipment without first getting a professional evaluation. Just because you rarely use your boat doesn't mean that the pivot can't wear. A boat kept on a mooring is constantly changing direction 24 hours a day, wearing away at the pivot jewel.

compass, points of – the points of a compass are 32 divisions of a circle, in 11-1/4° increments. In the old days a sailor had to know how to "box the compass" and recite the 32 points in the correct order. POINTS are used for the specifications of navigation lights in the NAVIGATION RULES and to describe RELATIVE BEARINGS.

compass rose – a graduated circle marked in degrees, printed in various locations on nautical charts. On most charts there are two concentric circles: the outer circle indicates TRUE NORTH; the inner circle indicates MAGNETIC NORTH. The difference between true north and magnetic north, expressed in degrees east or west, is VARIATION. Inside the compass rose is a notation of the degrees and minutes of variation in the area, and the amount of yearly increase or decrease in degrees. Check the date of the chart to see how many years have elapsed since it was printed, and apply the correction if it's a degree or more. A navigator uses a compass rose to determine COURSES and BEARINGS. Select the rose nearest to where you're operating.

compass, telltale – a compass mounted upside down over the skipper's berth so he or she can check the approximate HEADING of the boat without going on deck. A small compass that works upside down is an inexpensive choice.

compass, zone balancing – the dip in the earth's magnetic field is different in the Northern and Southern Hemispheres. In the Northern Hemisphere the earth's magnetic field is directed downward, and in the Southern Hemisphere the field is directed upward. Dip causes a compass card to tilt, and a tilted card doesn't align correctly with MAGNETIC NORTH. This affects the accuracy of the instrument. Compasses are usually "balanced" for use in one hemisphere. Some Danforth GLOBALBalance® Card System compasses are advertised to remain level in all six zones. If the boat will sail in the other hemisphere determine if her compass is balanced for all zones or can be modified, or if a different compass is required.

compressed natural gas, CNG – a stove fuel, which is lighter than air, but not as readily available as PROPANE. Relevant ABYC Standards are A-22 Marine Compressed Natural Gas (CNG) Systems, and A-26 LPG and CNG Fueled Appliances.

compression post – a vertical support extending from the KEEL in the BILGE to under the deck below a deck-stepped MAST. It helps reduce the downward compression force of the mast on the deck or cabin top.

compulsory-equipped – vessels required by USCG, GMDSS, SOLAS, or IMO regulations to have certain radio and other equipment aboard. A compulsory-equipped vessel is any one of the following:

- A vessel of more than 300 GROSS TONS navigating in the open sea.
- A vessel certified by the U.S. Coast Guard to carry more than six PASSENGERS FOR HIRE in the open sea or tidal waters of the U.S.
- A vessel of more than 100 gross tons certified by the U.S. Coast Guard to carry at least one passenger on navigable waterways.
- A power-driven vessel over 20m/ 65.6ft in length operated on navigable waterways.
- A tow boat of more than 7.8m/25.6ft in length operated on navigable waterways.
- An un-inspected commercial fishing vessel otherwise required to carry a VHF radio.
- A vessel required to carry an AIS TRANSCEIVER.

A vessel that is not required to comply with equipment regulations is VOLUNTARY-EQUIPPED.

computers – many boats routinely carry one or more computers aboard, either a laptop or a specially-designed system. Some professional and recreational navigators prefer a computer because of the wide variety of software available for navigation and vessel management. In addition to running navigation programs and serving as a CHART PLOTTER, a computer can be interfaced with a variety of on-board electronics and serve as a MULTIFUNCTION DISPLAY, as well as take care of other typical computer tasks. A laptop can be taken home to plan passages, update WAYPOINTS, review LOGS, plan maintenance schedules, etc. The decision about buying a ruggedized laptop or system (designed for harsh environments) or having several lower-cost laptops (as back ups) is an individual one, depending on budget, and where and how the computer system will be used. There are companies that specialize in the design and installation of on-board computer systems. To get a fully functional system that meets all your expectations, consult with professionals.

conductor, conductive – (1) a material that transmits electrical current, heat, or sound. "Conductor" is frequently used to mean metal or electrical wire. Grease containing graphite and carbon fiber (as used in SPARS, RUDDERS, and other marine components) are also conductive.

constant pressure chart – an ISOBARIC CHART.

constant velocity joint, CVJ – a specialized SHAFT COUPLING that reduces vibrations transmitted to the hull by the propeller shaft, and permits some degree of misalignment at the coupling. *See* SHAFT ALIGNMENT and COUPLING, FLEXIBLE.

constrained by draft, CBD – Rule 3(h) of the NAVIGATION RULES says, a "vessel constrained by her DRAFT means a power-driven vessel which, because of her draft in relation to the available depth and width of the navigable water is severely restricted in her ability to deviate from the course she is following." This definition applies to *power-driven* vessels in INTERNATIONAL waters only. Rule 28 prescribes the lights and DAYSHAPE:

• At night a CBD vessel shows three ALL-AROUND red lights in a vertical line ("three reds in a row, no room below").

• She also displays SIDELIGHTS, a STERN LIGHT, and the MASTHEAD lights appropriate to a power-driven vessel of her size.

• The dayshape for a CBD vessel is a black cylinder.

AIS-A messages indicates CBD status.

contiguous zone – a band of water extending outside the TERRITORIAL SEA for as much as 24NM over which a coastal nation exercises legal control to enforce Customs or other regulations. In the U.S. this zone extends out to12NM from the coastline.

continental shelf – the zone bordering a continent and extending to a depth from which there is a steep descent toward greater depths. At the edge of a continental shelf the depths are usually between 300ft/90m and 600ft/180m. The exact definition varies with countries, and the purpose of the definition. For example, it may be defined differently in connection with oil and gas exploration.

continuous wave FM radar – *see* RADAR, BROADBAND.

contour lines – lines on a CHART, TOPOGRAPHIC map, or a 500MB CHART that connect equal depths or heights.

control lines – lines other than SHEETS and HALYARDS that perform various sail control functions. Examples include reefing lines, roller furling lines, Cunningham lines, outhauls, downhauls, topping lifts, guys, vang tackles, spinnaker pole lines, and Barber haulers. These controls are defined elsewhere in this book.

controlled-access area – another name for a SAFETY ZONE.

convection – the vertical movement of air in an UNSTABLE atmosphere. When air is convected (drawn upward), cumulus and perhaps cumulonimbus CLOUDS are created, leading to rain or thunderstorms.

convergence and divergence, coastal – localized wind effects that occur when winds blow parallel or almost parallel to a coastline. (1) Convergence: when sailing along a coastline with the wind ASTERN (or almost astern) and the land is to STARBOARD, the angle of the wind over the land is different from that over the sea. Because of friction over land, the land wind is deflected toward the sea, while the wind over the sea angles toward the coast (less friction over water). This convergence usually results in a band of water a few miles out from the coast that has winds perhaps 25% stronger than the sea wind. Close to the shore there may be an area with light winds. (2) Divergence: when sailing along a coast with the wind astern (or almost astern), and the land is to PORT the effect is the opposite of convergence. The land wind is deflected toward the land and the sea wind angles away from the shore. This divergence usually results in a band of lighter winds near the shore. Coastal convergence and divergence are also influenced by the heating or cooling of the land, the formation of a sea breeze, and the topography of the land along the coast. If there are mountains or HEADLANDS, the winds may be CHANNELED or FUNNELED. If there are open spaces between high terrain there may be GAP WIND effects. A COAST PILOT or CRUISING GUIDE may note areas where these effects are likely to occur, and under what conditions. Looking at the

TOPOGRAPHIC FEATURES on a chart, if any, may also help you predict the influence of coastal land on the wind.

conversion of directions – to convert between TRUE, MAGNETIC, and COMPASS directions this is an easy memory aid: write the first letters of "**T**imid **V**irgins **M**ake **D**ull **C**ompany" in a vertical line. To convert going *down* the list add west (subtract east) VARIATION and DEVIATION. When converting *up* from the bottom of the list subtract west (add east). The letters represent: True, Variation, Magnetic, Deviation, Compass.

T
V down
M add
D west
C

A mariner should know how to perform these simple calculations, even when relying upon electronic navigation.

coolant – the antifreeze solution in a FRESH WATER-COOLED ENGINE. Check the engine manual to see if a specific type of coolant is recommended. As with a vehicle, coolant should be drained and replaced from time to time, according to recommended intervals in the engine manual or a technical reference. Check the level of the coolant by looking at the EXPANSION TANK. See the next entry.

cooling system, engine – there are two basic types of cooling systems on recreational vessel marine engines and generators: raw water-cooled and fresh water-cooled (also called two-stage or closed system cooling). In a raw water system the water the boat operates in (salt or fresh water) is pumped through the entire engine to keep it cool. This type of engine does not have an EXPANSION TANK. There are advantages to a fresh water cooling system, and some raw water cooled engines may be able to be retrofitted with fresh water cooling. In a fresh water-cooled engine, sea or lake water is pumped through a heat exchanger to cool an antifreeze solution (the coolant) that runs through the engine. Sea or lake water cools the exhaust in both types of engines. The raw water and fresh water pumps in an engine have IMPELLERS. If the engine overheats or water stops coming out the exhaust outlet, check the RAW WATER STRAINER and the raw water pump impeller. The raw water impeller is relatively easy to change, if it's accessible. A SPEEDSEAL pump cover makes this task easier. *See also* ENGINE, AIR-COOLED.

Coordinated Universal Time, UTC – the international basis for standard time. UTC time is referenced to the PRIME MERIDIAN at the LONGITUDE (0° 00'00") of Greenwich, England. Precise UTC time signals are broadcast continually on SINGLE- SIDEBAND radio by WWV and CHU. Meteorologists use UTC as the time for taking observations and for forecast times, the Coast Guard uses it for the time of announcements and other messages, it's the time stamp for AIS transmissions, mariners write it in the ship's log, and use it for CELESTIAL NAVIGATION. UTC is also known as Zulu time or Z-time. Although a GPS shows UTC, it may not be precisely accurate, due to the time interval between updates from the GPS satellites. In 1972, UTC replaced GREENWICH MEAN TIME (GMT) in official usage, but many people still say GMT.

coordinates – the LATITUDE and LONGITUDE of a position.

copper – a soft metal used in plumbing pipes, electrical wires and cables, wire TERMINALS, and electrical equipment because of its good conductivity. It's also used for fastenings in the construction of small wooden craft (copper ROVES) and for rust-proof tacks.

cordage – the general term for ROPE and LINE.

Coriolis effect, Coriolis force – the rotation of the earth causes worldwide winds and ocean currents to be deflected from a straight line to either the right or the left; this is the Coriolis effect. In the Northern Hemisphere winds and currents are deflected to the right, and in the Southern Hemisphere they're deflected the left. The deflection is strongest near the Poles and least near the equator. It's named after a 19th century French engineer, Gaspard-Gustave de Coriolis, who discussed rotational effects, although not specifically in reference to the earth's rotation.

cornering winds – *see* WINDS, CORNERING.

corposant – another name for ST. ELMO'S FIRE.

correcting, to correct – (1) the process of converting a MAGNETIC or COMPASS direction to a TRUE direction. To go from compass to magnetic or magnetic to true, *subtract* westerly VARIATION or DEVIATION (*add* easterly variation or deviation) to the initial direction. Use the algebraic sum of variation and deviation (west is plus and east is minus) when converting directly from compass to true. The process of converting from true to magnetic or compass is called UNCORRECTING. In casual use "correcting" is used to indicate either correcting or un-correcting. For an easy method of converting directions, see CONVERSION OF DIRECTIONS. (2) the process of removing deviation from a magnetic compass is correcting or COMPASS ADJUSTMENT. (3) the process of updating a paper or electronic chart with the relevant changes since the last edition of the chart; CHART CORRECTION.

correctors – magnets used in the COMPASS ADJUSTMENT procedure.

corrosion – deterioration of metals exposed to a marine environment or from electrical problems. Corrosion that goes unnoticed can have serious consequences for the metals involved and for safety. Corrosion in metals on a wooden boat can also affect and weaken the wood near the metals. Salt water hastens corrosion more than fresh water. Corrosion may be localized (pitting of dissimilar metals, CREVICE CORROSION in fittings) or more widespread. There are three types of corrosion: ELECTROCHEMICAL (metal exposed to the air or an ELECTROLYTE), GALVANIC, which occurs between dissimilar metals, and STRAY-CURRENT CORROSION, caused by electrical faults. More than one type of corrosion can occur at the same time. Read *The Boatowner's Guide to Corrosion* by Everett Collier for a comprehensive, readable discussion of all aspects of corrosion and its control. See the bibliography under "Corrosion" for the full citation.

corrosion control – a somewhat complex technical subject, with differing theories about techniques. In general, corrosion control involves protecting metals, isolating dissimilar metals from contact with each other, and taking specific measures to prevent corrosion above and under the water. The best book on the subject for boat owners and marine professionals is *The*

Boatowner's Guide to Corrosion by Everett Collier. ABYC Standard E-2 Cathodic Protection discuss practices designed to minimize the effects of GALVANIC and STRAY-CURRENT CORROSION.

corrosion, crevice – corrosion in the marine environment that can occur when metals are in contact with each other, either directly or through fastenings, and where *oxygen is excluded*. Crevice corrosion may occur inside SWAGED or MECHANICAL terminals, at contact points between rigging TOGGLES and TANGS or CHAINPLATES, under tape used on TURNBUCKLES, as well as other places. Because crevice corrosion occurs in hidden areas it may go unnoticed until it's too late and something bad happens. A DYE PENETRANT TEST and thorough RIGGING INSPECTION will reveal signs of crevice corrosion.

corrosion, electrochemical – occurs on a metal exposed to the atmosphere or an ELECTROLYTE. Rusting of FERROUS metal is one type, as is corrosion of a single metal in seawater. It's a relatively slow process, in contrast to GALVANIC and ELECTROLYTIC corrosion, which may be very rapid.

corrosion, electrolytic – *see* CORROSION, STRAY CURRENT.

corrosion, erosion – caused by water moving rapidly across a metal. It can occur in pipes, pipe joints, pumps, valves, heat exchangers, and exhaust systems (particularly at the exhaust discharge elbow), as well as other locations. Erosion corrosion is hidden, and it may go unnoticed until a part fails. Make regular inspections of areas where it's likely to occur.

corrosion, galvanic – corrosion between dissimilar metals that occurs in an ELECTROLYTE. The metals must be connected by a CONDUCTOR or be in contact with each other and also in contact with the electrolyte. In general, galvanic corrosion may be reduced or prevented by:

- Electrically isolating dissimilar metals and their fasteners with plastic insulating materials and waterproof BEDDING COMPOUNDS.
- Keeping metals dry with paints and other waterproof coatings.
- Using metals that are near each other on the GALVANIC SERIES.
- Using an ANODIC or CATHODIC PROTECTION system.

corrosion meter, corrosion test meter – a specialized VOLTMETER that's able to measure very small voltages, to check a boat's BONDING SYSTEM and the corrosion potential of metal-hulled vessels. Corrosion meters are available for use by the boat owner (approximately $300). They have informative instructions. A digital MULTIMETER with a silver/silver chloride test lead may also be used. A CORROSION MONITOR can be installed for continuous monitoring of galvanic activity. See the next entry.

corrosion monitor – a permanently-installed electrical device, with a meter, that continually checks the condition of the boat's BONDING SYSTEM to detect a change in the potential for corrosion. Professional advice and installation is recommended.

corrosion, stray current or electrolytic corrosion – occurs with two or more metals exposed to the same ELECTROLYTE. It's caused by faults in DC and AC electrical systems. It can cause very rapid corrosion and destruction of the metal, and damage wood to which the metals are attached. (1) DC stray current corrosion is caused by DC currents leaking from faulty wire insulation, improper wiring and equipment installation, electrical shorts, "hot" wires in a damp or wet bilge, poor GROUNDS (loose, corroded), or from similar electrical problems on nearby boats in a marina. (2) Some causes of AC stray current corrosion are incorrect AC wiring on the boat or in the shore power supply, automotive battery chargers improperly used aboard, a live electric extension cord dropped into a wet bilge, some POLARITY INDICATORS, and some other electrical equipment. Stray current corrosion causes less-NOBLE metals in contact with seawater to become ANODIC and corrode. ANODES (zincs) and BONDING are two methods of preventing stray current corrosion from causing damage. Stray current corrosion and the proper installation of AC and DC electrical systems and equipment aboard a boat is a complex subject. Read *The Boatowner's Guide to Corrosion* by Everett Collier for a thorough, readable discussion of all aspects of corrosion and its control. (See the bibliography under "Corrosion" for the complete citation). Consult a qualified expert, and have a CORROSION SURVEY performed, if you suspect a problem.

corrosion survey – an examination of a vessel and its equipment to determine the level of CATHODIC PROTECTION, test for AC and DC STRAY CURRENTS, test BONDING and galvanic isolation, and check for AC stray current sources aboard. The survey is typically done by a qualified marine expert or a technician who has completed an ABYC Corrosion Certificate course.

COSPAS_SARSAT– the international satellite-based search-and-rescue (SAR) system with global coverage that processes emergency signals from any 406MHZ EPIRB or PERSONAL LOCATOR BEACON, and initiates and coordinates SAR response. The system was created in 1979 as a joint effort between the U.S., Canada, France, and the former Soviet Union. SARSAT is an acronym for Search-and-Rescue Satellite-Aided Tracking and COSPAS is the Russian-language acronym. See www.cospas-sarsat.org. and click on "Beacon" for information about approved beacons (EPIRBs), registering a beacon in various countries, and other user information. The DASS (Distress Alerting Satellite System) is under development to enhance the capabilities of the COSPAS-SARSAT system. See http://searchandrescue.gsfc.nasa.gov/dass/index.html for more information.

cotter pin, cotter ring, split ring – small split pins and rings inserted in TURNBUCKLE STUDS (to keep the turnbuckle from rotating) and in CLEVIS PINS (to keep them from falling out). Cotter pins should be spread only about 10° (rather than bent back or around in a loop). A small bend is enough. In an emergency, such as a dismasting, cotters will have to be removed, and a sharp bend makes it difficult. A cotter ring is a split ring that can be removed fairly easily and reused. One use is for the clevis pins on BLOCKS, so there aren't sharp ends sticking out. As an alternative to cotters on turnbuckle studs, tap screw threads into the holes in studs, and use short, round-head machine screws in place of the cotters. Screws are easy to remove in an emergency, and they don't have sharp ends sticking out, so the turnbuckles don't have to be taped, which invites CREVICE CORROSION under the tape.

counter – the part of the STERN on a yacht that's out of the water ABAFT the waterline. Some yachts have a long counter and others a short one. If the hull rests on the water all the way to the stern, the boat doesn't have a counter. If the boat is docked where small waves approach her from astern, the waves may make a slapping noise under the counter. *See* ENDS.

coupling, flexible – a shaft coupling that reduces the vibrations transmitted to the hull by the propeller shaft, and permits a slight degree of misalignment between the coupling and the shaft. See the next entry.

coupling, shaft – the device at the end of the engine TRANSMISSION that connects the propeller shaft to the engine. Shaft couplings are rigid or have a degree of flexibility. A rigid coupling transmits engine vibrations to the hull, and shaft alignment is critical. A flexible coupling absorbs some engine vibrations, and it can accept a small degree of misalignment. A CONSTANT-VELOCITY JOINT reduces vibration even more than a flexible coupling, and also allows for a greater degree of misalignment. Equipment catalogues and manufacturers' websites discuss the acceptable degree of misalignment for a particular flexible coupling.

course, altering to avoid collision – *see* COLLISION entries.

course – (1) the actual path the vessel is traveling; the track; the COURSE OVER THE GROUND. (2) the intended direction of travel; the course the helmsman is steering. Course and HEADING are often used interchangeably, although, strictly speaking, they aren't the same. The notation of a course in a log should have the letters T, M or C written after the degrees, to indicate if it's a true course, a magnetic course, or a compass course. (3) a series of courses laid out to be followed by racing boats; a race course.

course, collision – *see* COLLISION COURSE and COLLISION entries.

course made good, CMG – same as COURSE OVER THE GROUND (COG).

course, magnetic – *see* MAGNETIC COURSE.

course over the ground (COG), course made good (CMG), track – the boat's actual course over the ground, as it's affected by current, wind, and LEEWAY. The COG may not be the same as the vessel's HEADING. A GPS displays the COG.

course plotter, chart protractor, chart plotter – a transparent, flat plastic navigation tool for use on paper charts. It has a protractor on it that's aligned with lines of LATITUDE (or LONGITUDE in some cases) to draw or read courses on the chart. It's easier to use than a PARALLEL RULER, especially on a small chart table or in the COCKPIT, because you don't have to use a COMPASS ROSE, as is necessary with a parallel ruler. There are several types of plotters available; some are known as Breton or Portland plotters. Examples are the Blundel-Harling Portland Course Plotter, used by professional navigators, and Weems and Plath® #133 and #255. The UNITED STATES POWER SQUADRON uses a simple 4"x15" plotter for its boating courses. Mine is over 40 years old and it's still going strong.

course to steer, CTS – the course to steer as determined from plotting on the chart or from a GPS or CHART PLOTTER calculation. The CTS takes into account the SET of a current and the LEEWAY of the vessel. The CTS changes as the current and leeway change. The CTS may not be the same as the COURSE OVER THE GROUND or the HEADING because of the effects of current, wind and leeway.

course-up display – an orientation for a stabilized radar that is interfaced with other electronics to show the course at the top of the screen. A course-up display may be the same as a HEAD-UP display, if the course and the vessel's heading are the same, which is not always the case. *See also* NORTH UP DISPLAY.

courtesy examination – another name for a VESSEL SAFETY CHECK.

courtesy flag – *see* FLAG, COURTESY.

courtesy lights – small, low-intensity lights used below decks to illuminate various areas at night. They are usually installed near the sole, rather than overhead. Red courtesy lights allow the crew to move about without having to turn on night vision-destroying white lights.

cowl vent – a high or low-profile, vertical ventilation device made of metal or flexible plastic with a large opening on top that directs the air below decks. A cowl vent may be mounted on a DORADE BOX or directly on a hole through the deck. It's a more efficient ventilation device than a flat air vent mounted low to the deck.

CPA – abbreviation for CLOSEST POINT OF APPROACH.

crab, crabbing – crossing a current by adjusting the vessel's HEADING to counteract the effects of a current on the BEAM.

crab angle – the angle away from the intended course that must be steered to counteract the effect of a current setting across the BEAM. For example, you may have to steer 10° to PORT of your intended course to counteract a strong current pushing on the port side of the boat. That's the crab angle.

crevice corrosion – *see* CORROSION, CREVICE.

crew comfort – is both physical and psychological. Involve them as much as possible; show them the written-out PASSAGE PLAN. Find useful tasks for inexperienced people and give responsibility to experienced crew. Teach those who want to learn. The skipper is ultimately responsible for crew comfort and attitude. A busy crew is less-prone to SEASICKNESS. See the bibliography under "Crew."

crew list – required by Customs and Immigration when entering a foreign country. The crew list includes the names, passport numbers, and nationality of everyone on board. Other information may be required by a particular country. Some countries may require multiple copies of this list.

crew information, crew briefing – if there are new or inexperienced crew coming aboard, explain your expectations to them a number of days before they join the boat. This is important for both a day sail and a longer trip. First-time or beginning sailors are understandably nervous about what the experience will be like; they worry that they'll make mistakes and may be asked to do things on the boat they don't understand. To ease their anxiety describe what the trip will involve (protected or open waters, sailing, motoring, likely weather conditions, sightseeing ashore, etc.).

Estimate how long the trip may take. Make sure they understand that delays are possible.

Tell all crew when they should arrive at the boat; if being late will be a problem, explain why. Make sure they know how to find the boat. Get them there early enough so you don't have to rush off as soon as they arrive. If the skipper feels time pressure, this adds to the crew's anxiety.

Describe what is aboard for their comfort and safety.

Explain what they should and should not bring with them; for example, the type and amount of clothing, boat shoes, seaboots or ordinary rubber-soled shoes, food or water, no hard luggage, etc.

Explain the things you are likely to ask them to do, in general terms.

The more the crew feels that they are involved, within their capabilities, the more they're likely to come aboard as happy participants rather than worried passengers. When the crew arrives review what you told them as you show them around the boat and help them stow their gear. *See also* CREW SELECTION.

crew medical information – it's a good idea to have appropriate medical information about all crew members for use in an emergency, if a person becomes unconscious or can't communicate. To keep the information confidential, ask each person to write out his/her health status details, medical conditions, allergies, and medications, and put the information in a sealed envelope, to be opened only in an emergency. Write the crew member's emergency contact person on the front of the envelope. Return the envelopes when they're no longer needed. Medical information about family members and friends who don't care about confidentiality should be written down for accurate communication; in an emergency important details may be overlooked. If a person goes to a hospital send the information with the patient.

crew overboard, COB – same as MAN OVERBOARD.

crew safety checkout – *see* SAFETY CHECKOUT.

crew selection – sometimes there's no choice, but whether you choose the crew or take what you can get, they should be trained to be as effective as they can be within their limitations and the time available. Consider the following crew factors:

Experience: different for a daysail in good conditions, a BEAT across the bay, or an open-water passage.

Skills: if possible, the crewmembers should have varied skills, so that one or more can take over when other crewmembers or the skipper need a break or if they're unable to function.

Attitude: crew who work well together and truly enjoy being on the water may be more valuable than a crew of highly-skilled but contentious, competitive crewmembers.

Health: if you're near medical assistance, it may not be a concern, but if you'll be a day or more away from assistance, having a reasonably healthy crew is important. The stress of sailing and rough weather can trigger unknown or unrevealed health problems. *See* CREW MEDICAL INFORMATION.

Personal issues: heavy alcohol intake, hidden drinking, drug use, significant fears, phobias, interpersonal communication problems, poor hygiene habits, snoring louder than the engine, etc. Add your favorite "issue."

The attitude of the skipper can go a long way to shaping a harmonious crew, whether it's family members, friends or strangers. Explain your expectations for the crew so they can ask questions or tell you if they feel uncomfortable with what they may be asked to do.

crew, two-person – ideally, both persons should be able to do all the essential jobs aboard the vessel while underway and when docking or anchoring. Having one person entirely responsible for doing or supervising everything all the time places an undue burden on that person. The more-competent person should take care to train the other crew member so that he/she will be able to take over routinely, not just in an emergency. Attending an on-the-water school may be a good way to learn independent of the skipper. Practice is important so that both people maintain their skills. A task requiring a degree of strength may have to be done differently or more slowly by a less-strong person. When possible, the strongest individual should do the tasks requiring strength and/or agility. On a long trip one person is essentially SINGLE-HANDING so the other can rest.

crimped terminals – (1) end fittings for electrical wire and cable, attached with a HAND CRIMPER tool. Crimped terminals are preferable to SOLDERING. See the next entry. (2) fittings used to form an eye in wire or for end fittings on wire rigging or LIFELINES. Special tools are used: one is like a large bolt cutter and another is a bolt-together tool that clamps over the terminal and compresses it onto the wire as the bolts are tightened. Read about the recommended uses for each. Crimped terminals may not hold the rated strength of the wire, as do MECHANICAL or machine-SWAGED terminals, so hand-crimping may not be suitable for high-load applications. Two brands of hand-crimp terminals are Nicopress™ and Talurit™. C. Sherman Johnson Co. (http://csjohnson.com) offers hand-crimp lifeline terminals.

crimper, hand – (1) a tool used to attach fittings to rigging or LIFELINE wire. See previous entry. (2) a tool used to attach end fittings to electrical wire and cable. These crimpers should be the ratchet-type, to get a secure, proper crimp. A double-crimper that crimps both the metal terminal and the insulation over the wire is a good choice. Yes, they cost more, but an inexpensive wire stripper/crimper tool doesn't do a proper job. Crimping, rather than SOLDERING, is the standard for marine wiring.

cringle – a metal reinforcing ring set into a sail; a large GROMMET. Cringles are used at the TACK for attachment hardware, the HEAD for a HALYARD, and the CLEW for JIB SHEETS or an OUTHAUL on a MAINSAIL. Reef cringles are used on a SLAB-REEFED MAINSAIL at the LUFF and LEECH for the reefing control lines. See the drawing with SAIL, PARTS OF.

crossing – a general term that refers to a voyage, frequently across an ocean or large body of water. "How long will the crossing take?"

crossing situation – Rule 15 of the NAVIGATION RULES gives the rules for *power-driven* vessels in a crossing situation where risk of collision exists. This Rule applies to two vessels IN SIGHT of each other, not in RESTRICTED VISIBILITY. In a crossing situation you see some part of the side of the other vessel, and at night *either* the red *or* the green navigation light.

- If the vessel is on your STARBOARD side, you are the GIVE-WAY vessel, and should keep out of the way of the other vessel.

• Avoid crossing in front of the other vessel, if at all possible.

• If either vessel is in doubt as to the other's intentions she shall sound the DANGER SIGNAL.

• Under INLAND Rules, on the Great Lakes, Western Rivers, or specially-designated waters a power-driven vessel crossing a river shall keep out of the way of a vessel ascending or descending the river.

• The vessels shall use SOUND SIGNALS as prescribed in Rule 34.

The rules are slightly different for INTERNATIONAL and INLAND WATERS.

If you see the BOW of the vessel or the MASTHEAD (RANGE) lights and both the red and green NAVIGATION LIGHTS, it's a HEAD-ON SITUATION, which has different rules.

crossing the line ceremony – a naval tradition conducted when a vessel crosses the equator from north to south. By tradition the Southern Ocean is the realm of King Neptune. "Pollywogs" (those who have never crossed equator) are expected to pay homage to Neptune and his court. The ceremony consists of a variety of humorous initiation activities, directed by the "shellbacks" (those who have crossed the equator before, playing the roles of Neptune and his court). Some cruise ships and yachts devise their own method of celebrating this event.

cross sea(s), cross swell – jumbled seas that result from waves created by a wind from one direction meeting waves or SWELLS coming from a different direction.

cross-set, cross-setting – a current that sets across the vessel's course.

cross-track error, CTE, XTE – the distance a vessel has strayed from her intended COURSE or TRACK. Cross-track error is automatically computed by a GPS or CHART PLOTTER that is navigating toward a WAYPOINT. CTE can also be computed manually on paper between FIXES.

crosstrees – another name for SPREADERS.

cross wind – a wind that blows across the BEAM; a beam wind.

crown – *see* ANCHOR, PARTS OF.

CRT – abbreviation for CATHODE RAY TUBE, used in some radars and old TVs.

cruiser, cruising yacht – a yacht designed primarily or totally for cruising, with the crew living aboard while traveling on short or long trips. Coastal and offshore designs differ and there's a lot of variety in cruisers. In some, performance under sail is emphasized and these yachts have features of CRUISER-RACERS. Other designs emphasize comfort over speed.

A cruiser usually has more creature comforts and simpler rigging than a racing boat.

A cruiser may be heavier than designs that emphasize speed because of stronger construction. LONG-KEELED yachts and MOTORSAILERS are at the heavy end of the DISPLACEMENT spectrum.

Designers use a variety of KEEL configurations and RUDDER types, but the overall design of cruising boats tends to be somewhat conservative. Technology from racing yachts is becoming more common on some cruising designs.

Cruising boats intended for long voyages to remote areas require a design and gear that is robust enough to stand the rigors of extended cruising and not be so high-tech that it's difficult to find repair services.

Cruisers are generally more SEA-KINDLY than racing boats.

Many monohull designs fall into this category, among them are yachts and designs by Amel, Ted Brewer, Bowman, Cabo Rico, Contest, Contessa, Bruce Farr, Dufour, Gozzard, Halberg-Rassy, Hans Christian, Hinckley, Hylas, Island Packet, Kaufman, Malö, Moody, Morris, Najad, Nicholson, Oyster, Passport, Rival, Rustler, Sadler, Swan, Tartan, Taswell, Trintella, Vancouver, van de Stadt, Waquiez, Westerly, Vagabond, Valiant, and Vindo. *See* CATAMARAN for some cruising cats. *See also* COMFORT AT SEA and DISPLACEMENT, TYPES OF. For modern cruiser photos see CHINE; ENDS; MAST, UNSTAYED; ROLLER FURLING; SPINNAKER, ASYMMETRIC; TIDE RIPS, and TRANSOM, TRADITIONAL.

cruiser-racer, racer-cruiser – a sailing yacht designed to serve a dual purpose, depending on which design and rigging characteristics are emphasized. Performance yachts (a marketing term) fall into the cruiser-racer category; they're designed for speed and comfort. Saving weight in the construction and equipping of this type of boat is important.

A performance yacht has a tall, powerful rig and a large sail plan.

The hull form is U or V-shaped forward, with a wide BEAM that continues toward the STERN.

The STEM is relatively straight and the hull usually has a REVERSE TRANSOM, giving a long waterline length for increased speed.

The BILGES are usually quite shallow, with limited storage, and a small amount of bilge water seems like a lot.

A cruiser-racer has some type of FIN KEEL, a BULB keel, a WINGED keel, or a LIFTING keel, making her relatively STIFF. A deep or narrow fin keel may prevent the boat from being able to DRY OUT safely along a wall in a tidal harbor. A deep fin-keeled boat may have to be hauled with a crane or MARINE HOIST (not a MARINE RAILWAY), and she may require a special storage cradle and extra supports when on land.

A SPADE RUDDER is common on these boats, which gives good maneuverability, including when going ASTERN under engine.

The propeller shaft exits the boat to an external STRUT. Because both the rudder and the prop are exposed they may be damaged in a grounding or from floating or submerged debris. Some vessels have SAILDRIVE propulsion.

A racer-cruiser may be difficult to HEAVE TO.

Accommodations for the crew range from Spartan to luxurious.

A few examples of MONOHULL designs in this category include: Arcona, Beneteau, Bavaria, Dehler, Frers, Hanse, Hunter, J-Boats, Jeanneau, and Swan. See the photos with KEEL, LIFTING for an example of a custom cruiser-racer and MARINE RAILWAY for an older racer-cruiser.

Cruising Association, CA – membership is open to all applicants. The CA has publications (including an excellent annual *Cruising Almanac* for northwest Europe, covering the Faeroes to Gibraltar), member activities, port representatives, a large reference library, cruising area reports, and pilot updates for the waters of the UK, the Baltic, the Mediterranean, and European Inland waterways. Headquarters in London. Open-access and members-only information on the website at www.cruising.org.uk.

cruising club, yacht club – there are two general types of clubs: one is open to all applicants, with minimal specified qualifications, and the other requires specific qualifications as well as nomination and approval by members of the club. Benefits of membership in a cruising club include access to cruising information from members, port representatives, publications, meetings and social activities, seminars, instruction, and cruises in company.

Cruising Club of America, CCA – qualification, nomination and approval are required for membership. The mission of the CCA is to promote long distance cruising by amateurs and high standards for vessels and seamanship. The Club has activities for members worldwide and members-only and open-access information on the website. CCA members have written books and cruising guides, which are available to the general public through nautical booksellers. See the bibliography under "Publications." The CCA headquarters are in Massachusetts. www.cruisingclub.org.

cruising chute – another name for a CRUISING SPINNAKER.

cruising guide, pilot, sailing directions – a book with information relevant to cruising in a particular area, aimed at recreational mariners, and written by persons who know an area well. It has details about harbors, anchorages, navigation, marinas, shore facilities, local weather, history, and other useful information, which supplements a government COAST PILOT or NAUTICAL ALMANAC. A cruising guide usually isn't published annually and it may not have TIDE TABLES, but it may have good local knowledge tidal CURRENT DIAGRAMS. See the bibliography under "Publications" for a sample of cruising guides.

cruising information websites – a number of websites offer information about countries and areas, new regulations, and links to other websites. Some websites offer open-access and others have sections for members only. Among many, these stand out (in alphabetical order):

www.cruisingclub.org: the website of the CRUISING CLUB OF AMERICA (CCA). Open-access and members-only sections.

www.cruising.org.uk: the website of the CRUISING ASSOCIATION (CA). Open-access and members-only sections.

www.noonsite.com ("The global site for cruisers"): global and up-to-date. Open-access.

www.oceancruisingclub.org: the website of the OCEAN CRUISING CLUB (OCC). Open-access and members-only sections.

www.onpassage.com ("The global site for cruising sailors"): global, with some different information than on Noonsite. Open-access.

www.ssca.org: the website of the SEVEN SEAS CRUISING ASSOCIATION (SSCA). Open-access and members-only sections.

See the bibliography under "Sailing" for general sailing and cruising websites.

cruising permit – in many countries foreign vessels are issued a permit by the authorities which indicates how long the vessel may stay in the country's waters. The time of the cruising permit may be different from the time allowed for the crew to remain in the country. *See* CLEARING IN.

Cruising Rally Association – sponsors OCEAN CROSSING RALLIES, including the Caribbean 1500, the Atlantic Cup, and other offshore sailing experiences. www.carib1500.com.

CSA – abbreviation for the CANADIAN STANDARDS ASSOCIATION.

CSBC – abbreviation for the CANADIAN SAFE BOATING COUNCIL.

CTE – abbreviation for CROSS-TRACK ERROR.

CTS – abbreviation for COURSE TO STEER.

cuddy, cuddy cabin – the cabin on a small boat. It usually doesn't have standing headroom.

Cunningham – a type of DOWNHAUL on a MAINSAIL, used to adjust the tension of the LUFF. It's used on racing sailboats and some cruising boats. Named after the inventor, Briggs Cunningham, a well-known American racing skipper.

current – (1) the horizontal flow of water. The direction *toward which* a current flows is its SET. A current that flows towards the east is an easterly current; it sets easterly. The speed of the current is its drift. Currents are caused by wind, flow from a river, the changing of the tides (a TIDAL CURRENT), and other natural forces. (2) the flow of electrons in an AC or DC electrical circuit.

current diagrams – indicate the strength and direction of currents. They are found in a TIDAL ATLAS, a NAUTICAL ALMANAC, and some CRUISING GUIDES.

current, hydraulic – in an open waterway that connects two bodies of water, differences in the time of high and low water at either end of the waterway causes the current to flow back and forth. Examples of waterways with hydraulic currents are the East River in New York city, the Chesapeake and Delaware Canal, and the Cape Cod Canal on the U.S. east coast.

current, mixed – a TIDAL CURRENT that has noticeably different speeds on the EBB and the FLOOD.

current, ocean – a horizontal flow of water in the sea that isn't caused by the tides or weather. Ocean currents are relatively constant in strength and direction, as they're created by prevailing winds, such as TRADE WINDS. Seasonal factors or localized weather phenomena may create variations in the direction and strength of the current. Major ocean currents include the GULF STREAM, the California Current, the North Atlantic and North Pacific Currents, the North Atlantic and the Labrador Currents, equatorial currents, the Agulhas Current in the southwest Indian Ocean, and the Southern Ocean Current.

current table – a table showing the time and direction of the current at the start of the FLOOD and the EBB. There are tables for main reference stations and correction factors for subordinate stations.

cut – (1) the cut of a sail refers to how it's designed and the way the sailcloth panels are laid out. Some terms include cross-cut, miter cut, radial cut, high cut (the FOOT has an upward curve away from the deck), deck sweeper (low foot near the deck). A sailing vessel can be recognized by the "cut of her JIB," to use the old phrase. (2) a narrow passage or channel from the coast to the sea, either natural or man-made, such as Town Cut at St. George's, Bermuda and Government Cut in Miami, Florida.

cutlass or cutless bearing – *see* BEARING CUTLESS.

cutter – a sailboat with two JIBS forward of the MAST: a jib and a STAYSAIL. Some SLOOPS have twin headsails and are not technically a cutter. The mast on a cutter may be slightly further AFT than the mast on a similar sloop. See JIB, YANKEE for another photo.

A gaff cutter with a reefed main beats in 25 knots.

cutter, rope or line – *see* LINE CUTTER.

CYA – abbreviation for the CANADIAN YACHTING ASSOCIATION.

cycle – one cycle is the period of time in which one action is completed. In electricity, one cycle per second is one HERTZ (HZ). Hertz is both singular and plural, and the words "per second" are not used with Hz. The number of cycles in a given period is the FREQUENCY. The frequencies of ALTERNATING CURRENT and radio waves are expressed in Hertz.

cyclone, cyclonic – a cyclone is the meteorologist's name for a LOW PRESSURE SYSTEM; cyclonic is an adjective applied to wind or weather associated with a low. The air circulation around a low pressure system is counter-clockwise (anticlockwise) in the Northern Hemisphere and clockwise in the Southern Hemisphere. In casual speech some people use cyclone as a synonym for a tornado.

cyclone, extra-tropical – a term used in advisories and tropical summaries to indicate that a CYCLONE has lost its tropical characteristics, usually by moving into cooler waters. An extra-tropical cyclone can still have winds of HURRICANE or TROPICAL STORM force.

cyclone, subtropical – a CYCLONE that forms in the area between the equator and approximately 50°N. It has characteristics of both tropical and extra-tropical cyclones (see the previous and the following entries). It's usually an upper-level cold LOW PRESSURE SYSTEM. The radius of maximum sustained winds extends approximately 100NM or more from the center.

cyclone, tropical – a warm-core CYCLONE that originates over tropical or subtropical waters. It has a well-defined center and circulation. Warm waters sustain a tropical cyclone; if it moves out of tropical areas it becomes EXTRA-TROPICAL.

- D -

daggerboard – a type of small boat CENTERBOARD, that is raised or lowered vertically by hand in a centerboard trunk (a watertight slot through the boat), rather than with a pivoting hinge.

damage control kit – materials and tools stored for easy access. Commercial kits are available or you can assemble your own. Suggested supplies include:

good-quality DUCT TAPE (of course)
self-amalgamating tape
water-activated pipe wrap tape
underwater epoxy sealant
can of spray foam insulation
tapered wood plugs
wooden wedges, various sizes
pieces of 0.5in/12mm plywood
4in x10in/10cm x 25 cm copper flashing
rubber patching material (tire inner tube)
stainless steel wire
12in/30cm plastic CABLE TIES (25-30)
hose clamps, small to very large
nut driver that fits hose clamp screws
RIGGING CUTTER
curved-jaw Vise-Grips (mole grips)
regular pliers
wire cutter
claw hammer
small hand axe
pry bar (approximately 18in/45cm long)
sharp knife
hacksaw
metal snips (cut copper flashing
folding wood saw (camping tool)
rags, old towels
pair of leather work gloves
LED headlamp

Keep everything in one box, tool bag or LOCKER for quick access in an emergency. Check the kit yearly for expiration dates on water-activated pipe wrap, epoxies or other materials that have a limited shelf life.

damp, to and dampened – to lessen or smooth out the movement of a device such as a compass, wind instrument, or the boat itself. A compass and an electronic wind instrument is dampened by an internal mechanism to smooth out the readings, so the compass readings or the wind speed numbers don't change too rapidly. Stabilizers on a yacht or ship dampen the roll of the sea.

dan buoy – another name for a MAN OVERBOARD POLE. Fishers also use dan buoys to mark positions of fishing gear.

danger angle, horizontal – the horizontal angle between two charted objects that indicates safe water when passing a navigation hazard. On the chart, the navigator measures the angle between the two objects and notes the maximum or minimum angle necessary to avoid the hazard. Take frequent measurements as the boat proceeds past the danger. A SEXTANT held on its side is a very accurate way of measuring the angle. CHAPMAN and navigation books describe how to do this technique.

danger angle, vertical – the maximum or minimum angle on a charted object of known height that should be maintained to safely pass a hazard. If you know the height of an object above sea level, measure the angle from the sea to the top of the object with a SEXTANT, to determine the distance you must stay out to avoid the hazard. Enter the height of the object and the observed sextant angle into Table 16 in BOWDITCH (or other reference table) or use a NAVIGATION CALCULATOR to determine the distance off. Heights of shore-based aids to navigation are given in a LIGHT LIST and on charts. Take into account the state of the tide when measuring the height and the angle. CHAPMAN and navigation books describe how to do this technique.

danger bearing, danger circle – the BEARINGS on a single charted object that indicate safe water when passing a navigation hazard. Draw bearings from the object that safely pass the hazard, and measure those angles on the chart. As the vessel proceeds on her course the navigator takes frequent bearings on the object to stay in safe water. Select a prominent object beyond the danger area that's on the side of the boat that will pass the danger. Use visual or RADAR BEARINGS. CHAPMAN and navigation books describe how to do this technique. *See also* SEXTANT ANGLE, HORIZONTAL.

dangerous semicircle – *see* SEMICIRCLE, DANGEROUS.

danger signal – a whistle signal given by a vessel to indicate *uncertainty or doubt*. Rule 34(d) of the NAVIGATION RULES specifies that if a vessel is in doubt as to the actions of another vessel, "the vessel in doubt shall immediately indicate such doubt by giving at least five short and rapid blasts on the whistle." This signal is *not* a DISTRESS SIGNAL.

danger zone – informal term for the area around the vessel from DEAD AHEAD to just ABAFT the STARBOARD BEAM (the area covered by the boat's green NAVIGATION LIGHT). If another vessel moves into this zone, presenting a risk of collision, under the NAVIGATION RULES you are the GIVE-WAY vessel and must keep clear of the other vessel.

DASS (Distress Alerting Satellite System - a new system under development to enhance the capabilities of the COSPAS-SARSAT system. For more information see http://searchandrescue.gsfc.nasa/gov/dass/index.html.

date line – the short name for the INTERNATIONAL DATE LINE.

datum – *see* CHART DATUM.

datum adjustment factor – see the next entry.

datum shift, datum adjustment factor – a datum shift is the difference between the position displayed on a GPS and the position on a chart. The amount of the difference, in tenths of a minute north or south and east or west, is the datum adjustment factor. A datum shift occurs when a GPS is set to a different datum than that of the chart. Charts *not* based on WGS84 (or an equivalent datum) indicate the amount of datum shift in a note in the information block or elsewhere in the chart. It reads: "Satellite-derived positions cannot be plotted directly on this chart. Satellite-derived positions must be moved *x* tenths of a minute east (or west) and *x* tenths of a minute north (or south) to agree with this chart." For a chart with a datum other than WGS84 or its equivalent, the most accurate position is obtained by having the GPS receiver set to WGS84, and then applying the datum adjustment indicated on the chart. Always keep a safety margin near navigational hazards. **A prudent mariner doesn't rely on a single source of navigational information; always use a second method to determine the position of the vessel.**

davit(s) –stationary or mechanical "arms" that are used for raising and lowering a DINGHY on a yacht or a lifeboat or workboat on a larger vessel. Davits with TACKLES are used in a pair on the STERN (or the side of a large yacht). Lifeboat davits are used along the sides of a ship. A large vessel may have a single davit at the BOW to handle a heavy anchor.

A RIB dinghy on strong davits. The crossbar limits lateral movement.

The RIB dinghy is secured tightly under the davits.

daybeacon, daymark – general name for an unlighted aid to navigation on a piling or free-standing on shore. Some have a DAYBOARD with colors, numbers, shapes, or information to guide navigation. If a daybeacon is lighted it's called a light.

dayboard – a square, rectangular, or triangular board, painted in various colors, and/or with letters or numbers, used on a DAYBEACON. The dayboards on a RANGE are vertical and have vertical bands in contrasting colors to help you line up the range markers more easily.

dayshape, shape – the black shapes (ball, diamond, cone, cylinder) displayed ALOFT on vessel during daylight to indicate the nature of the vessel, her operation restrictions or what the vessel is doing. The rules for displaying shapes are specified in Rule 20 and 25-30 of the NAVIGATION RULES. *See* FISHING VESSEL and STEADYING SAIL for photos.

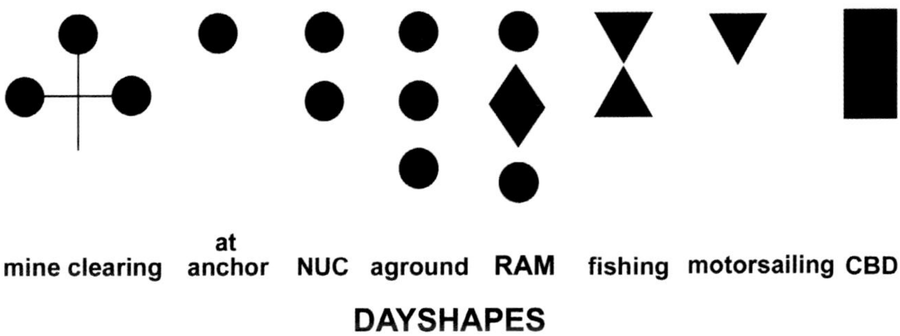

The dayshapes prescribed in the Navigation Rules. NUC = not under command; RAM = restricted in ability to maneuver; CBD = constrained by draft.

day's run – the distance traveled by a vessel in 24 hours, traditionally measured from noon to noon.

DC, direct current – electrical current that comes from the boat's battery, usually 12 VOLTS. Many boat electronics (such as a DEPTH SOUNDER, VHF RADIO, GPS, RADAR, CHART PLOTTER) operate on 12V. The cigarette lighter outlet aboard a boat (or in a vehicle) supplies 12V. Large vessels may have 24V systems. The abbreviation DC is usually used instead of "direct current." DC is supplied by color-coded (red) positive (+) wires and (black) negative (-) wires. If the POLARITY is reversed (for example, connecting a positive wire to a negative wire) a short circuit results, there may be a spark, and equipment can be damaged. *See* WIRE, ELECTRICAL, MARINE COLOR CODE.

DC electrical panel – an electrical panel on the boat where the switches (and FUSES or CIRCUIT BREAKERS) that control the DC equipment and circuits aboard are located. Some switches might include VHF radio, DEPTH SOUNDER, cabin lights, navigation lights, bilge pump, GPS, refrigeration, radar, CHART PLOTTER, etc.

DC polarity – *see* POLARITY.

dead – "directly," as in dead ahead, dead AFT, dead on the BEAM, dead DOWNWIND, and dead RUN.

dead ahead – directly in front of the vessel. A wind coming from dead ahead is "on the nose."

dead downwind, dead run – sailing with the wind directly on the STERN. *See* BY THE LEE and TACKING DOWNWIND.

deadhead – (1) a log, piling, or other large timber that floats vertically in the water with the top just at the surface or a little below it. A deadhead is hard to see because very little sticks up, but if the boat hits one it could be very dangerous. A SECURITÉ CALL may be used to warn of a deadhead. (2) a large wooden BOLLARD.

deadlight, storm shutter – a fixed (permanently-closed) PORT, or a solid piece of wood, metal or heavy plastic used to close off a vessel's PORTS for an ocean passage or in a storm.

dead reckoning, DR – calculation of a vessel's position along an actual or proposed COURSE line, using the time underway and the speed of the vessel to determine the distance traveled from the last known accurate position (a FIX). A DR calculation does *not* take into account the effects of current, wind, or LEEWAY. The formula is **D**istance = **S**peed x **T**ime (in hours). It's called the time, speed, and distance formula. To use minutes for the time, multiply the distance by 60. The formula is 60D=ST. Some people can calculate any one of the factors mentally; for others the memory aid shown in the photo may be helpful. The term "dead" comes from "deduced reckoning." An ESTIMATED POSITION is more accurate than a DR position, because it takes into account the effects of current, wind, and leeway.

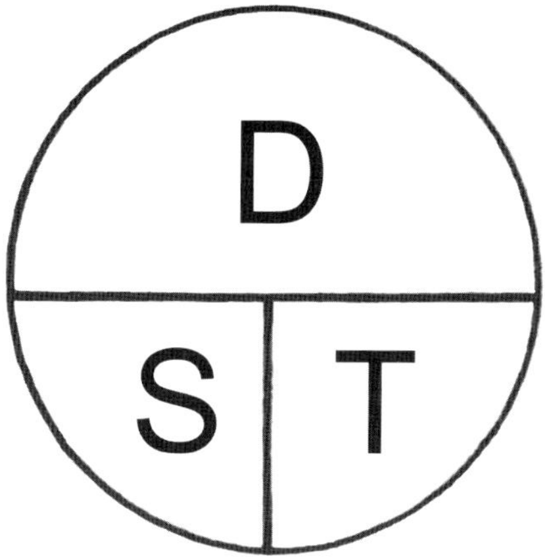

time, speed, and distance formula

To determine one of the numbers, put your finger over the one you want, and do the mathematical operation indicated by the position of the other two factors.

debrief – after emergency drills and after mastering a new sailing, anchoring or navigational challenge, review what the crew did well and what might have been done better. It's good for learning and for crew cohesiveness. It's even good to debrief yourself if you're SINGLE-HANDING.

decibel, dB – a numerical expression of the relative strength or loudness of an electronic signal or an audible sound. *See* GAIN and SIGNAL TO NOISE RATIO.

decimal – a decimal in a number is spoken as "decimal," not "point."

decimal minutes and seconds – some chart scales and LIGHT LISTS use minutes and seconds as divisions of degrees. Navigation instruments, such as GPS and CHART PLOTTERS, use tenths or hundredths of minutes. If the instrument doesn't do the conversions, you'll have to use a NAVIGATION COMPUTER, do the calculation with a math formula or print out a table of the equivalents. There's a convenient conversion chart for seconds to tenths and hundredths of a minute included in the *Eldridge Tide and Pilot Book* (see the bibliography under "Publications").

deck – the exterior walking surfaces on a vessel. In the COCKPIT and below decks in the cabin what you walk on is called the sole. On a boat the FLOORS are not under your feet.

deck fill, deck plate – a round plate with a screw-in cap located on deck (or on the TRANSOM) for taking on fuel or water. On many boats there is also a deck plate marked "Waste," to pump out the HOLDING TANK at a pump-out station or offshore by the crew. All deck plates should have clear, permanent markings on them or on a permanent label near each fill. You definitely don't want to put water into the fuel tank or vice-versa.

deck, flush – *see* FLUSH DECK.

deckhouse – a cabin or raised structure built on the deck of a vessel. If it has a steering wheel it's a wheelhouse or a PILOTHOUSE.

deck light(s) – (1) lights mounted on a MAST or on the SPREADERS that illuminate the deck. When these lights are used at night, deck crewmembers lose their NIGHT VISION for about 20 minutes after the lights are turned off. (2) deck light is sometimes used to refer to flat pieces of glass (usually a prism) set into a deck to provide light below decks.

deck plate – (1) logically, a plate in the deck, with a removable cover. Among many uses, deck plates are used to cover ventilation holes in the deck, or to allow access to the RUDDER POST to fit an EMERGENCY TILLER. (2) another name for a DECK FILL.

deck-stepped mast – *see* MAST, DECK-STEPPED.

deck sweeper – slang for a GENOA or other HEADSAIL with a low FOOT. The low foot increases sail area, but it reduces visibility ahead to LEEWARD, and it may scoop waves when the boat is HEELED in rough weather, possibly damaging the sail.

deck wash – a system that pumps lake or seawater to clean the anchor chain and the decks. If a vessel has a large fresh water capacity or a WATERMAKER, a deck wash may use fresh water.

decommission, decommissioned, lay up, laid up – (1) to remove gear, sails, and otherwise make the boat no longer ready to be operated; to lay up. Decommissioning is done at the end of a sailing season or when the vessel won't be used for a long time. (2) a vessel that is no longer ready to be operated is decommissioned, out of commission, or laid up. The opposite is COMMISSION, COMMISSIONED.

decompression lever(s) – some small diesel engines have levers on each cylinder which can be raised to release some of the compression pressure in the cylinders when trying to start it, either by hand-cranking (a fun experience) or with a weak battery. Crank the engine, and when it gets turning over fairly rapidly, put down one lever at a time, and, with luck, the engine starts.

deep draft – *see* DRAFT, DEEP.

deepening – adjective applied to a LOW PRESSURE SYSTEM in which the barometric pressure is decreasing. Deepening indicates that the low is intensifying, foretelling bad weather See the next two entries.

deepening, explosive – a decrease in the minimum sea-level pressure of a TROPICAL CYCLONE of 2.5mb per hour for at least 12 hours, or 5mb per hour for at least six hours. *See also* LOW, RAPIDLY-INTENSIFYING.

deepening, rapid – a decrease in the minimum sea-level pressure of a TROPICAL CYCLONE of 1.75mb per hour, or 42mb during 24 hours. *See also* LOW, RAPIDLY-INTENSIFYING.

Defense Mapping Agency, DMA – a U.S. government agency that produced nautical charts for waters outside the U.S. DMA's functions were taken over by the NATIONAL IMAGERY AND MAPPING AGENCY (NIMA), which have been taken over by the NATIONAL GEOSPATIAL AND INTELLIENCE AGENCY (NGA). Some charts have DMA or NIMA designations or numbers.

DGPS – acronym for DIFFERENTIAL GPS.

degree – (1) one degree is 1/360th of a circle. There are 60 minutes in a degree, and 60 seconds in a minute. For navigational purposes degrees are expressed verbally and in writing using three digits: 004°, 030°, 210°, etc. DUE north is 000° (not 360°). The zeros in a number are pronounced "zero" when speaking, as in "zero zero four." (2) a measurement of temperature, in degrees CELSIUS (C) or FAHRENHEIT (F).

de-ionized (de-ionised) water – same as DISTILLED WATER.

delivery, yacht – taking a vessel from one location to another under the command of a captain who is not the yacht owner. A professional captain may be hired; this may be required by a MARINE INSURANCE underwriter or a boat dealer, and some deliveries are done by experienced friends of the owner. The owner may choose to be aboard with a professional skipper to gain experience. Not all delivery captains are competent just because they have a professional mariner's license; do your homework and check references before hiring someone.

demarcation line(s) – printed lines on a chart that indicate the boundaries between INLAND and INTERNATIONAL waters, for the application of the NAVIGATION RULES. The location of demarcation lines in U.S. waters are also specified in the *Navigation Rules* book, and in U.S. COAST PILOTS®.

departure – (1) the point at which the DEAD RECKONING and course calculations begin as a voyage commences. "We took departure from Cape Spear." See the next entry. (2) the distance in nautical miles between two MERIDIANS at a given LATITUDE is the departure.

departure, to take – when beginning an offshore passage take departure by accurately fixing your position before leaving sight of land. It's the last known, accurate position as you embark. It's where the DEAD RECKONING and all other course calculations start. Note the departure LATITUDE and LONGITUDE in the written log.

depression – a LOW PRESSURE SYSTEM, which is usually accompanied by low CLOUDS and precipitation. The term is sometimes used mean a TROPICAL DEPRESSION.

depression, tropical – *see* TROPICAL DEPRESSION.

depth contour(s) – curved lines on a chart indicating equal depths along the line; small numbers written in the lines indicate the depth represented by the line. Contour lines are important to help determine the boat's position, and to locate safe water for the vessel. In RESTRICTED VISIBILITY or at night with few or no lighted aids to navigation you may be able to follow a depth contour to help navigate toward your destination and stay in safe water. Consider the state of the tide when using depth contours.

depth finder – same as DEPTH SOUNDER.

depth sounder, echo sounder, fathometer, sonar – an electronic instrument used to measure the depth of the water, by sending out a signal from a TRANSDUCER, usually located forward of the keel on the hull below the waterline. The sounder indicates *one* of three depths, depending on how it's calibrated: (1) the depth under the transducer. (2) the depth under the KEEL. (3) the depth at the boat's waterline (the actual depth of the water). It's essential to know how the instrument is calibrated. If the calibration isn't noted in the vessel's information notebook, calibrate it. See the next entry and FORWARD-LOOKING SONAR.

depth sounder calibrating – unless there's a notation in the boat's notebook (or a note on the instrument) you don't know what depth a DEPTH SOUNDER indicates on its readout. Is it the depth under the KEEL? The actual depth of the water? The depth under the TRANSDUCER? To determine what it reads, use a LEADLINE, and check the depth of the water at the area where the transducer is located. Compare the depth on the leadline to the depth shown on the instrument. The depth reading will be approximate because the leadline isn't at the actual position of the transducer, and the depth may be different where the leadline was dropped. Most depth sounders can be set to read either the actual depth of the water or the depth under the keel; that most useful reading is the actual depth of the water. Read the instructions in the manual. If the factory setting is not changed it will read the depth under the transducer. To make sure the crew knows what depth the sounder indicates, put a note on the instrument.

depth-sounder, forward-looking – *see* FORWARD-LOOKING SONAR.

depth soundings, soundings – the depth of the water is indicated on a chart by small numbers printed in various places where measurements (soundings) have been taken. The chart indicates whether the depths are in feet, FATHOMS, or METERS. The chart also indicates the level of the tide (CHART DATUM) to which the depths refer, which is some stage of low water. In shallow water take into account the state of the tide. Under some conditions there may be less depth than indicated by the printed soundings. However, *all depths are approximate*. Always leave a margin for safety. *See* DEPTH-SOUNDER CALIBRATING.

de-power – to spill the wind from a sail to slow down or prevent excessive HEELING.

desalinator – another name for a WATERMAKER.

Det Norske Veritas, DNV – a marine CLASSIFICATION SOCIETY.

developing gale or storm – a term used in U.S. HIGH SEAS and OFFSHORE forecasts and on SYNOPTIC FORECAST CHARTS to indicate that gale or storm force winds are not occurring now, but are expected to occur before the end of the forecast period.

deviation – the difference in degrees between a MAGNETIC COURSE (as shown on a chart or determined by a GPS) and the reading on the boat's compass when steering the course. Deviation varies with the HEADING of the vessel; it's expressed in degrees east or west. It may be an inherent characteristic of the vessel, or deviation can be created or changed if iron or steel objects (such as tools), audio speakers, batteries, current-carrying wires, or magnetic items are placed near the compass. The only way to determine if there is significant deviation affecting a boat's compass is by preparing a DEVIATION TABLE (see the next entry). On small vessels, for practical purposes deviations of one to three degrees may be ignored. It's good SEAMANSHIP to prepare a deviation table to check the accuracy of the compass.

deviation table – indicates the amount of DEVIATION on the CARDINAL and INTERCARDINAL HEADINGS, or every 30° around the compass. Before preparing the table, make sure the compass is free of alignment error (see COMPASS ADJUSTMENT). To make a deviation table select a calm day in an area with little or no current or vessel traffic. You won't get accurate results if waves, current, or LEEWAY affect the boat. The process takes about an hour. Under power, maintain each heading for at least two minutes to allow the compass to settle on its reading. There are three basic methods: (1) steering the vessel on RANGES. (2) using the vessel's GPS. (3) SWINGING SHIP. The first two methods are described below.

Using a chart of the area, select charted, fixed objects (not buoys) that can be used to form ranges, covering the cardinal and intercardinal directions (or every 30° around the compass) within ten degrees. Select ranges that can be run in both directions, i.e. north and south, east and west, etc. Note the MAGNETIC BEARINGS of these ranges.

Steer the boat on the ranges and their exact RECIPROCALS, noting the compass readings for each heading. The difference between the magnetic bearing and the compass reading is the deviation. See CONVERSION OF DIRECTIONS to determine the deviation (east or west) on each heading. Running ranges gives the most accurate results.

Alternatively, a GPS can be used instead of ranges. For best results, set the GPS set to display TRUE directions. The instrument default may be magnetic, and the automatic magnetic VARIATION assigned by the GPS may be inaccurate by a few degrees.

Steer either toward charted, fixed (not floating) features that are within 10° of the cardinal or intercardinal directions, or enter WAYPOINTS located in the cardinal and intercardinal directions (or every 30°).

Steer on the true bearings (as indicated on the GPS) to each charted feature or waypoint. Stay on each course for at least two minutes. Do the same with the reciprocals of these bearings. Note the compass reading on each heading and compare it with the GPS true bearing.

Apply the local variation (from the COMPASS ROSE nearest where you're operating) to the true bearings get the magnetic bearings. The difference between the magnetic bearing and the compass reading is the deviation.

If a vessel has more than one steering compass create a table for each compass.

If the deviation is less than three degrees on any heading, for practical purposes these can be ignored. If deviation exceeds three degrees on any heading do COMPASS ADJUSTMENT. Check a compass for deviation by preparing a deviation table under any of the following circumstances:

- If deviations change more than a few degrees from the boat's deviation table.

• If the compass seems to be inaccurate or unreliable.

• When a new or repaired compass is installed.

• If the environment near the compass has been changed, as when adding or removing electrical equipment or magnetic items.

• After periods time afloat or ashore when the vessel hasn't moved for more than a few months.

• When the vessel travels to a new area of operation, particularly with changes of more than approximately five degrees in LATITUDE or LONGITUDE.

• After a lightning strike, a severe grounding or a fire.

• If welding has been done aboard the vessel, especially on a metal boat. Remove all compasses from the boat before welding.

• After a new engine or a generator has been installed.

See also COMPASS ADJUSTMENT, STEEL BOAT.

devil's claw – a CHAIN HOOK with two claw-like fingers at one end that grip a chain link. It may be used with a CHAIN SPRING.

de-zincification – the loss of zinc from a zinc ALLOY (such as BRASS or BRONZE) when immersed in or exposed to salt water. The evidence of de-zincification is visible in the pink color of the metal. De-zincification causes fastenings, parts, or hardware to become weak or break.

diaphragm – (1) a flexible membrane used in pumps to create suction and discharge pressure. Oil-resistant rubber or neoprene diaphragms are used in manual bilge pumps and foot pumps. (2) in a compass the diaphragm is located at the bottom of the bowl. It allows the compass fluid to expand and contract with temperature changes.(3) there's a diaphragm in a mechanical FUEL LIFT PUMP. If the fuel pump on an engine has a small priming lever on it, it may be a mechanical pump with a diaphragm. A diaphragm may be a replaceable part.

dielectric – a substance used to isolate dissimilar metals from each other to prevent GALVANIC CORROSION. (1) plastic material or tape. (2) a dielectric gel or paste used to protect splices, connections in electrical wires, and to isolate fasteners in dissimilar metals. Tef-Gel™ is one brand of dielectric paste.

"diesel bugs" – slang term for microbes, bacteria, fungus, mold, or yeast in the fuel whose activity produces contamination that will clog filters and in extreme cases damage an engine. DIESEL FUEL ADDITIVES are available to prevent or eliminate contamination.

diesel engine – diesel engines are used on boats because they are more suited to the marine environment, they're efficient, and the fuel is safer than gasoline. Diesels don't have spark plugs or require electricity to keep running; the heat produced by compression in the cylinders ignites the fuel. Essentially, all a diesel requires is clean fuel and a good air supply. Relevant ABYC Standards are P-1 Installation of Exhaust Systems for Propulsion and Auxiliary Engines, and P-4 Marine Inboard Engines and Transmissions. See the next entry and also DECOMPRESSION LEVER, and GLOW PLUG. If there's a GASOLINE ENGINE on a boat learn the safety precautions necessary when operating and fueling gasoline engines.

diesel fuel – with the advent of increasingly-stringent exhaust emission standards from the U.S. EPA and environmental authorities in other countries, diesel fuel is being produced with lower sulfur content. There is an implementation timetable in the U.S. for low sulfur (LSD) and ultra-low sulfur (ULSD) diesel for marine use, but after 2014 *all* diesel fuel will be ULSD. What this means to the boat owner is that ULSD fuel has less lubricity than previous fuels, which will require research to determine the requirements, if any, for DIESEL FUEL ADDITIVES for a particular engine. Older engines may need a lubricity additive, while newer engines are being produced that will work satisfactorily with ULSD. Read articles and consult with the engine manufacturer or a knowledgeable diesel mechanic. See the bibliography under "Engines" for a study on the efficacy of lubricity additives. Relevant ABYC Standards are H-32 Ventilation of Boats Using Diesel Fuel and H-33 Diesel Fuel Systems.

diesel fuel additives – chemicals may be added to diesel fuel to boost CETANE, increase fuel economy, disperse water, clean the injectors, improve cold-weather starting, prevent or eliminate microbial contamination ("DIESEL BUGS"), or improve lubricity. Some additives are specifically formulated to eliminate "bugs" (e.g., BioBor JF®, Bioguard, and Pri-Ocide), while other additives are multi-purpose, such as products from ValvTect and Racor. Check the engine manual or contact the engine manufacturer for recommendations about additives appropriate for a particular engine.

diesel fuel, bio-diesel – biodiesel fuel is a non-petroleum based fuel that can be used in any diesel engine without modification. It also has a beneficial effect, helping to clean the fuel tank and cutting down on carbon formation in the engine cylinders. In addition to pure biodiesel, there are several types available, depending on the percentage of biodiesel blended with regular diesel.

diesel, runaway – *see* RUNAWAY DIESEL.

differential GPS, DGPS – GPS to which additional electronic correction factors have been added to make the signals and positions obtained more accurate than regular GPS. The position accuracy is approximately 7-23ft/2-7m.

digital selective calling – *see* DSC RADIO.

dinghy, "dink," tender – a small boat used to ferry crew and supplies to and from a larger boat when it's not moored at a shore location. It may be an INFLATABLE or a rigid dinghy. The line at its bow that ties it up is the painter. You may decide not to put the name of the big boat on it ("tender to *Audacious*"), because when the dinghy is ashore it signals potential thieves that there may be no one aboard.

dinghy, stowing and towing – where to put the dinghy is often a challenge. For a dinghy stowed at the STERN care must be taken that it doesn't block the stern navigation light from any angle. There are limited choices for a rigid dinghy or a RIB and more options for an inflatable. For coastwise trips:

- On DAVITS at the stern. Not all davits are strong enough to hold the weight of the dinghy with an outboard motor attached.

The dinghy must be secured tightly enough to prevent motion in a seaway. Cross-lashings help control lateral movement.

• On deck where there's room. On a large yacht the dinghy may fit between the MAST and the deckhouse, on the cabin top ABAFT the mast, on the BOW deck, or perhaps ATHWARTSHIPS. A rigid dinghy or a RIB will need special CHOCKS to hold it securely. An inflatable can be stowed partially or fully-deflated on deck. If it's on the FOREDECK, make sure crew can get around it to work at the bow.

• On yachts with a REVERSE TRANSOM (swim platform) an inflatable can be stowed on its side or stern, leaning back against the transom. However, it may block the stern light, and it must be removed if you need to use the stern platform.

• Semi-towed, attached to the stern of the yacht with the bow pulled up onto the boat and the stern trailing in the water. Perhaps OK for short trips in calm water.

• Towed. OK for short trips in calm water, but towing can be a good way to lose a dinghy if the weather deteriorates. Use several attachment points on the dinghy for the towline, not just its bow eye. On a dinghy with a solid TRANSOM, install through-bolted PAD EYES port and starboard inside the transom (facing forward), attach a BRIDLE to the eyes, and lead the towline from the bridle through the dinghy's bow eye to the yacht. This puts the towing strain on the strongest part of the dinghy.

For an offshore passage, the ideal stowage for an inflatable is deflated in a locker or deflated and securely lashed on deck. A RIB or rigid dinghy must be securely lashed in chocks or on deck. A dinghy in davits offshore risks being damaged or lost.

"dink" – slang for DINGHY.

diode – an electrical component in a circuit or electrical equipment that allows current to flow only in one direction. A diode can be "blown" if reverse POLARITY is applied; for example, if DC wires are connected incorrectly, or if a BATTERY SWITCH is turned off when the engine is running.

dipping a light – a simple technique for determining the distance from a lighthouse (not a light buoy) when you *first observe* the light over the horizon. At this point, you're at the extreme GEOGRAPHIC RANGE of the light, where the ocean SWELL or lowering your height of eye by bending your knees will make the light appear and disappear. You need

Your height of eye measured from your observation point on the boat to the water.

The height of the light above sea level, from a LIGHT LIST or the chart.

A geographic range table, found in NAUTICAL ALMANACS, a light list, and BOWDITCH.

Using your height of eye and the height of the light, look up the distance off in the table. If you take a BEARING on the light with a HAND-BEARING COMPASS or COMPASS-BINOCULARS, this gives you a LINE OF POSITION to go with the distance off, thus creating a FIX, independent of electronics.

dipping the colors, dipping the ensign – a naval tradition rarely observed today, except when returning a salute from another vessel. U.S. Navy Regulations, Chapter 12, Article 1263: "When any vessel, under United States registry or the registry of a nation formally recognized by the Government of the United States, salutes a ship of the Navy by dipping her ensign, it shall be answered dip for dip. If not already being displayed, the national ensign shall be hoisted for the purpose of answering the dip." U.S. Navy and Coast Guard vessels are entitled to receive this salute, and they dip their ensigns in return, which is the only time that the U.S. flag is dipped in salute. To dip the ENSIGN to a Navy or Coast Guard vessel, lower it quickly and smoothly and immediately raise it to its former position. If the flag is on a flagstaff at the stern it's not easy to dip it; a dip requires that the flag on a staff be lowered to about 45° from the vertical position, and most flagstaffs on small vessels are already angled downwards. Naval vessels will return the salute if they aren't busy or on maneuvers.

direct current, DC – *see* DC.

directional light – a lighted aid to navigation that projects a narrow beam of white light, sometimes with red or green sectors on either side of the central white beam. The white light indicates the center of a channel or harbor approach. If the light isn't visible, the boat is too far to the right or left in the channel (or too far away). The cut off between sectors may not be sharp, depending upon your distance from the light. Also called a SECTOR LIGHT.

directional stability – *see* STABILITY, DIRECTIONAL.

dismast, dismasted – to lose the MAST, as a result of a variety of causes: the failure of one or more parts of the rigging, a severe GROUNDING, the force of the wind (not necessarily a strong wind), or a ROLLOVER in extreme conditions. It can definitely spoil your day. *See also* RIGGING CUTTER, RIGGING INSPECTION, and DAMAGE CONTROL KIT.

displacement – the usual way to indicate the weight of a vessel. A vessel's displacement is equal to the weight of water displaced when the vessel is floating. It's expressed either in pounds or TONS (TONNES). "What does your boat displace?" "What's her displacement?" asks for her weight.

displacement hull – a hull that rests in the water and is not designed to PLANE. However, under some conditions of strong winds and large waves a displacement hull may plane.

displacement/length ratio, d/l ratio – the d/l ratio is a general way to compare types of boats. It's calculated by taking the displacement in long tons (2,240 lbs.) and dividing it by 0.01 times the LENGTH ON THE WATERLINE (LWL) cubed; $[Dt/(.01\ LWL)^3]$. Low displacement/length ratio yachts are light and fast, but less comfortable at sea; higher d/l ratio yachts are slower and more comfortable. Of course, these terms are relative. When racing, the crew endures discomfort in rough seas to win. When equipment and supplies are added to a vessel the d/l ratio is changed; that's why adding weight to a light displacement yacht is detrimental. When weight is added to a heavier yacht the ratio isn't affected as much.

In general, boats fall into broad categories, based on their displacement/length ratios:

Boat type	D/L ratio
light racing multihull	40-50
ultra-light ocean racing sailboat	60-100
very light ocean racing sailboat	100-150
light ocean racing sailboat	150-200
light cruising AUXILIARY	200-250
average cruising auxiliary	250-300
moderately-heavy cruising auxiliary	300-350
heavy cruising auxiliary	350-400

displacement mode, non-displacement mode – when a vessel is operating with its hull or hulls in the water she is in the displacement mode. A WING-IN-GROUND EFFECT CRAFT, a HYDROFOIL, or a HOVERCRAFT operating *above* the water is in the non-displacement mode. The distinction is used in the NAVIGATION RULES for NAVIGATION LIGHTS and other rules applicable to these types of vessels.

Distance Between Ports, Pub. 151 – a reference book from the NGA of tabulated distances between worldwide departure ports, junction points, and arrival ports. Although designed for ships, the information is useful for voyaging yachts and as a general reference. See the bibliography under "Miscellaneous."

distance log, trip log – (1) an electronic instrument that measures the distance traveled through the water, which may or may not be the same as the distance traveled over the ground, because of the effects of current, wind, or LEEWAY acting on the vessel. A distance log may be combined with a speed log in one instrument. (2) a feature on a GPS that accurately measures the distance over the ground the vessel has traveled.

distance by vertical angle – if the height of a vertical object, such as a lighthouse, is known, the distance off can be calculated from a vertical SEXTANT angle. Heights of objects are on charts, in a LIGHT LIST, and in a COAST PILOT Consider the state of the tide when calculating the heights. Determine the distance with a table (found in some NAUTICAL ALMANACS, a light list or BOWDITCH Table 16), or with a NAVIGATION CALCULATOR. To stay a safe distance away from a danger, set the sextant to the angle necessary to keep the vessel a safe distance off, and observe the angle as you pass the object. CHAPMAN and navigation books discuss this technique.

distilled (de-ionized) water – the only type of water to use to top up a lead-acid battery. Carry an extra supply; it may not be easy to find in some places. If the boat has maintenance free, sealed batteries water is not needed.

distress – a distress situation is when human life is in danger or the vessel is in danger of being destroyed. *See* MAYDAY and DSC RADIOTELEPHONE.

distress, false or accidental – in most countries there are civil and/or criminal penalties for issuing a false distress alert. If a voice MAYDAY, DSC

MAYDAY, a PAN PAN, or an EPIRB alert is made *accidentally* you *must* cancel it by immediately calling the Coast Guard. If you have a PERSONAL LOCATOR BEACON, read the manual for how to cancel an accidental activation.

distress frequencies, radio – VHF CHANNEL 16 and designated SINGLE-SIDEBAND DISTRESS FREQUENCIES.

distress light, electric – an electric DISTRESS light for night use. For U.S. Coast Guard approval it must *automatically* flash the international MORSE CODE SOS distress signal (three short flashes, three long flashes, and three short flashes). Check a distress light by shielding it from view. Of course, lacking an automatic distress light, flash SOS repeatedly on any available light.

distress signals – the following DISTRESS signals are permitted under Rule 37 of the NAVIGATION RULES: red star shell (FLARE), red parachute flare; orange smoke flare; continuous sounding of a horn; flames on the vessel (in a metal container); a gun fired at intervals of one minute; an orange flag with a black ball and black square on it; a square flag with a black ball under it; sending Morse code SOS by light or sound signals; a spoken MAYDAY call by radiotelephone; waving both arms slowly up and down; DSC alarm; signals from an activated EPIRB; any color dye marker in the water; the CODE FLAGS N over C. Under the INLAND RULES a strobe light may also be used as a distress signal. In addition to the signals in the Rules, anything that doesn't conflict with any other prescribed light or sound signal under the Rules may be used to attract attention in the event of distress. More than one distress signal can be used at a time. By tradition the American flag flown upside down is a distress signal, but it's not official; someone may think the flag has just fallen down. SIGNALS TO ATTRACT ATTENTION can be used when it's not a distress situation.

distress signals, visual – U.S. Coast Guard regulations require that all recreational vessels carry USCG-approved visual distress signals. Vessels less than 16ft/4.9m must have visual signals if they operate at night. Vessels over 16 ft must have signals for day and night use. Daytime signals are red handheld flares, red parachute flares, red meteor flares, combination flare and smoke signal, orange smoke, and a distress flag (a black square and a black ball on an orange flag). Night signals include an electric SOS DISTRESS LIGHT, and all the day signals except orange smoke. CHAPMAN and the Coast Guard website has the specific requirements. If the boat ventures offshore have more than the minimum and consider SOLAS equipment. To see if you have the required signals aboard, have a VESSEL SAFETY CHECK.

distress system, automation of – DIGITAL-SELECTIVE CALLING (DSC) and the GMDSS system are the main parts of the international efforts to fully automate the maritime distress system. The goal is to have distress messages sent and received without the need for humans to constantly monitor radio frequencies.

disturbance, tropical – *see* TROPICAL DISTURBANCE.

ditch bag, ditch kit – same as ABANDON SHIP KIT.

ditty bag – a small bag containing miscellaneous useful items, small tools, or one's personal items. The name comes from "ditto bag" because it was supposed to have at least two of everything; you can't run out to the corner store at sea.

diurnal – a period or cycle of one day. *See* SEMI-DIURNAL and TIDE, DIURNAL.

diurnal inequality – a difference between events in a day, such as unequal heights of high or low water, or the unequal flow of tidal currents. *See* TIDE, MIXED.

divergence, coastal – *see* CONVERGENCE AND DIVERGENCE, COASTAL.

diver's flag – a red flag with a diagonal white stripe across it. A vessel with a diver down should display this flag. A diver working away from a vessel should have a float moving along with him/her with the flag attached to a flagstaff. Fly the flag even if you're swimming to clean the bottom or clearing a PROP WRAP. Some state regulations require it to be flown when divers are down, but for safety use the flag even if it's not required. The blue-and-white "Alpha" CODE FLAG ("diver down") is only displayed by a vessel that is RESTRICTED IN ABILITY TO MANEUVER because the divers or equipment are attached to the vessel with hoses and/or cables. No matter which flag is flown, give vessels displaying these flags a wide berth and pass at reduced speed.

diverter valve, three-way valve – a Y-valve used in some waste systems to allow toilet waste to be directed overboard (where permitted) or into a HOLDING TANK. In seawater this valve will salt-up over time and not be able to be operated, so it's a maintenance item.

dividers – a small hand-held instrument with two adjustable "legs" used by a navigator to measure distances on a chart. There are several types available: a "one-hand" divider requires only one hand to use it (obviously). Dividers with a center wheel hold the setting between the legs.

DIY – well-known acronym to some boat owners. We do DIY either because we enjoy it (?) and/or because of economic considerations. Equipment and installations that involve safety, such as electrical, fuel, and propane systems should follow ABYC recommendations or the recommendations of a particular country's boating technical authority. In some countries DIY is not permitted on PROPANE or other gas systems. Read technical books and articles, and also the instructions with the products. The BOATU.S. website has a number of technical guides: see www.boatus.com/boattech. If you're BUILDING OR RENOVATING A BOAT in the U.S., consider joining ABYC to have access to their technical resources. Even if you decide not to tackle a project yourself, learn the vocabulary and read about how to do it so you can speak knowledgably with the technicians who'll do the work. Ask questions and make sure the work will be done to your expectations.

d/l ratio – abbreviation for DISPLACEMENT/LENGTH RATIO.

DMA – abbreviation for the DEFENSE MAPPING AGENCY.

DNV – abbreviation for DET NORSKE VERITAS, a marine CLASSIFICATION SOCIETY.

dock – (1) a general term for a place to tie up a vessel at a shore-based berth. A dock may be floating (also called a PONTOON) or fixed, either to the shore or to pilings. (2) to put a vessel in a berth or alongside a dock or pier.

docking is a contact and spectator sport – a humorous? adage that reminds us of the facts of docking no matter how careful we are. Some guidelines:

• Before approaching the dock review what the crew should do.

• Give the crew enough time to deploy FENDERS and the dock lines before making the final approach.

• When coming alongside, make "No Leaping" a rule. No matter how fit or agile a crew person is, if he/she falls between the boat and the dock an injury can result. Get close enough for the crew to step or jump easily onto the dock; if the boat is too far away, try again.

• No person aboard or on the dock should attempt to fend off with arms, legs, or a BOATHOOK unless the vessel is *very* small. Even a boat of moderate size exerts a heavy force when coming alongside, no matter what the speed is. Let the boat hit rather than have a person get injured.

• If possible, in addition to the fenders tied on the LIFELINES, have a crewmember ready with a moveable fender to stick in between the boat and the dock or a nearby boat, wherever it's needed.

• Approach slowly and in control; don't rely on a strong reverse thrust of the engine to stop forward progress. Try to avoid docking with the wind or current ASTERN.

• Spectators, including marina staff, on a dock may not know how to take the lines. Give very clear, simple, and specific instructions to them about what they should do with each dock line. Make sure the crew handling the lines knows what to say.

• Give a person on the dock the MIDSHIP SPRING line *first* because he/she can't do as much damage as when you give the person a BOW or STERN line. If the bow is pulled in with the bow line (it's almost inevitable that this happens) you can't control the boat, and the bow hits. With the midship spring all someone can do is pull the middle of the boat toward the dock, which is a good thing. Once the middle of the boat is secure, deploy the bow and stern lines, and any other SPRINGS that may be needed.

• When docking single-handed or with only one other crewmember and you aren't sure which side of the boat will be next to the dock, before approaching put fenders and a midship spring on each side of the boat. Have a bow and stern line ready to deploy to the proper side as soon as the midships spring is secured. Usually the helmsman or a single-hander can toss a stern line from the COCKPIT to the dock (perhaps attach it temporarily to a cockpit WINCH or CLEAT so it's close to the helm position), and then have time to handle the bow line.

dock line, mooring line, warp – interchangeable terms for the ropes used to secure a vessel. Tie off dock lines on the dock or pier, and bring the WORKING ENDS back aboard so they can be adjusted from on board. Alternatively, lead the ropes around the fittings on the dock and bring both ends back on the boat. This allows easy adjustment of the lines from aboard, and when you depart it's easy to SLIP the lines, without crew having to be on the dock. If you don't know whether you'll be able to go PORT side to or STARBOARD side to at a dock, put a MIDSHIPS SPRING on each side. It can be used to hold the vessel while the BOW and STERN lines are shifted.

documents, boat – *see* SHIP'S PAPERS.

documentation – if a U.S. vessel isn't registered with a state, she can be documented with the federal government (if at least five net tons, about 26ft/7.6m). Federal documentation establishes the vessel's nationality, ownership, permission for specific use (recreational or COMMERCIAL), and her eligibility for a preferred ship's mortgage (boat loan). A boat mortgage company usually requires documentation. The process can be done by an owner, but many people hire a documentation company to navigate the federal requirements. If a vessel travels to a foreign country a documentation certificate is preferable as proof of vessel ownership and her status as a U.S. vessel. CHAPMAN has a good discussion of the why and how of documentation.

dodger, spray hood – a cloth cover, usually with clear plastic windows, mounted on a frame over the COMPANIONWAY to protect it and the forward part of the COCKPIT from rain or spray coming from forward of the BEAM. Dodger frames usually can be hinged to fold down. A permanent dodger made of solid materials is called a rigid dodger. WEATHER CLOTHS may also be called dodgers. See the photo with DUCT TAPE for a creative example of a dodger/spray hood.

dog(s), to dog, "dog down" – (1) metal or plastic screw-type or friction closers for hatches and watertight doors. (2) to dog or dog down is to close tightly. "Did you dog the FOREHATCH?"

dog house – a small cabin on the deck.

do it yourself – *see* DIY.

Doldrums, the – the sailor's name for the INTERTROPICAL CONVERGENCE ZONE (ITCZ).

dolphin – (1) a group of pilings or heavy poles driven into the seabed or riverbed, joined together in a group, to which aids to navigation may be affixed, or intended as a mooring for a large vessel. (2) a marine mammal (3) another name for a dorado or mahi-mahi fish.

dolphin striker – a short SPAR or STRUT projecting down from under a BOWSPRIT and attached near the middle of the BOBSTAY. The dolphin striker improves the angle between the bobstay and the bowsprit to help counteract the upward pull from the HEADSTAY. Not all bowsprits have a dolphin striker; it's used on a fairly long bowsprit. See the photo with BOBSTAY.

Dorade box, Dorade vent – a water-trap device mounted on deck, with a COWL VENT on top. The construction of the box (it may

A Dorade box with chromed cowl vent (forward of the deckhouse) on the 63ft/19.2m beautifully-restored 1936 double-ended ocean racing yawl, *Bloodhound*. She was owned by Queen Elizabeth II and Prince Philip in the 1960s. As an accurate restoration she doesn't have lifelines.

be round or rectangular) prevents water that enters the vent from getting below decks, while allowing air to flow through the vent. The box is named after the yacht, *Dorade*, which first used these simple devices.

double, to – to travel around a HEADLAND or CAPE and proceed on approximately the RECIPROCAL course on the other side. "We doubled Cape Horn at midnight."

double-ended, double-ender – a boat with a CANOE STERN and a pointed BOW. Sailboats, powerboats, and some rowing boats may be double-enders. Considered a SEAWORTHY design, double enders are favored by some long-distance sailors. Southern Cross, Valiant, Westsail, and Colin Archer designs are examples of double-enders.

A double-ended gaff sloop with an outboard rudder.

double overhand knot – another name for a BLOOD KNOT, a STOPPER KNOT.

doubling the angle on the bow – a PILOTING technique to determine a FIX using a single object on shore and two BEARINGS, the second of which is double the angle of the first. Accurate bearing measurement is necessary. CHAPMAN and navigation books explain how to do this technique.

doubtful – expressed on a chart as "ED" (existence doubtful) or "PD" (position doubtful), which means that the charted feature was reported but hasn't been confirmed. This isn't the same as POSITION APPROXIMATE (PA).

douse (rhymes with mouse) – to lower or furl a sail very quickly. "We'll have to douse the MAIN as soon as we enter the harbor."

"douser" (rhymes with mouser) – slang for a SPINNAKER SOCK.

down – a direction away from the wind; head down means to turn away from the wind. UP and "HEAD UP" indicate a direction toward the wind.

downbound – traveling with the current. DOWNSTREAM and DOWNTIDE are synonyms. A vessel traveling against the current is UPBOUND. The terms are used in the NAVIGATION RULES.

downburst – a strong downward current of air from a cumulonimbus CLOUD, often associated with an intense thunderstorm. Damaging winds can occur under a downburst. *See* DOWNDRAFT.

down by the head, by the head – phrase that describes a boat that has her BOW below the designed waterline.

down by the stern, by the stern – a phrase that describes a boat that has her STERN below the designed waterline.

downdraft – (1) a small-scale downward current of air, usually accompanied by a rain shower or a thunderstorm. Like a DOWNBURST, a downdraft can produce damaging surface winds. *See* WINDS, KATABATIC and WIND SHADOW. (2) the strong blast of air felt below a hovering helicopter; the wind speed can reach 75 knots.

downhaul – a line or a TACKLE used to pull a sail down, or to hold down the end of a SPAR or SPINNAKER POLE.

downslope winds – *see* WINDS, KATABATIC.

downstream – in the same direction as a the current. Down tide and downbound are synonyms. The opposite is up tide, UPBOUND, and upstream.

down tide – the direction in which the current is flowing. When traveling with the current you are going down tide or downstream. "The current is so strong here, let's pass that buoy down tide so we don't hit it." The opposite of down tide is up tide or upstream, a direction toward the flow of the current.

downwind, running before the wind – (1) in the same direction as the wind or away from the wind. The opposite is upwind. (2) sailing with the APPARENT WIND between a BROAD REACH and ASTERN (DEAD DOWNWIND). Also called sailing off the wind. *See* POINTS OF SAIL and WING-AND-WING.

downwind poles – two SPINNAKER or WHISKER POLES used to hold out the CLEWS of two JIBS when a yacht is sailing DOWNWIND.

downwind tacking – *see* TACKING DOWNWIND.

DR – abbreviation for DEAD RECKONING.

draft, draught (pronounced draft) – (1) the vertical distance from the boat's waterline to the lowest point of the vessel (usually, but not always, the bottom of the KEEL). The draft indicates the minimum amount of water needed to float the vessel without touching the bottom. Keep a safety margin when navigating in shallow water in case the actual draft is not the same as indicated in the vessel's specifications. The draft may be greater when the boat is loaded with full tanks and all supplies and gear. A vessel in fresh water floats approximately four inches/10cm lower than in salt water. "How much does your boat draw?" asks for her draft. (2) the curvature built into a sail by the sailmaker is the draft. (3) The AIR DRAFT is the height of the tallest point on the boat above the waterline.

draft, deep – The phrase "deep draft vessel" is used in COAST PILOTS and on some charts to distinguish a ship from smaller vessels. It may be used in a general way in casual speech to refer to a boat with a deep KEEL.

draft, shallow or shoal draft – describes a vessel that can navigate in shallow water. It's a relative term, with no specific measurement implied. A MULTIHULL has a very shoal draft.

drag, dragging – (1) any force that slows the speed of a boat. Drag is a result of the design of the boat's UNDERBODY, a fixed-blade propeller when it's not turning, FOULING on the bottom, and other causes. (2) when a boat's anchor doesn't hold fast to the bottom it drags. The owner of a boat that drags and causes damage may be held responsible. (3) a wire drag is used by survey vessels to locate or clear obstructions on the bottom. A vessel pulling the wire is dragging or sweeping. There's a chart symbol to indicate that an area has been swept by a drag.

drag device – general term referring to a DROGUE, a SEA ANCHOR, or anything towed behind a boat to slow her down in storm conditions.

dragging, preventing and stopping – the best insurance against dragging is selecting a good ANCHORAGE, having the right anchor (proper weight for the boat and proper type for the bottom characteristics), on enough SCOPE, and firmly SET into good HOLDING GROUND. Despite care in anchoring, one day you'll probably drag (even two anchors can drag). If a boat at anchor lies broadside to the wind she may be dragging, but a strong current can make a vessel lie across the wind. When an anchor grabs it pulls the BOW of the boat into the wind. Some suggestions for stopping dragging:

- Let out more scope if there's enough room in the anchorage, and there's enough RODE.
- Use the engine to ease the strain on the rode, if it's a temporary strain. Be careful to not run over the rode; have crew at the bow to watch and signal the helmsman.
- Set a second anchor, but if the boat is dragging fast there's no time to do this.
- Re-anchor elsewhere, if there's room.
- Leave the anchorage.

drainage winds – *see* WINDS, KATABATIC.

draw – *see* DRAFT.

drawing – describes a sail when it's trimmed properly and filled with wind, rather than flapping or fluttering. "Now that Jackie's trimmed the JIB it's drawing better."

dredge (vessel) – lights and DAYSHAPES for vessels conducting dredging operations are prescribed in the Annex to the NAVIGATION RULES. Even though you understand the lights and shapes, call a dredge to confirm where and how to pass the vessel. When passing, operate at a slow speed.

dress, dressing – to make electrical wires and cables neat and orderly, using CABLE TIES, WIRE LOOM, or SPIRAL WRAP. Dressing wires makes things shipshape, prevents strains or damage to the wires, and organizes them into groups, so it's easier to work on the system at a later time.

dressing ship – decorating a vessel with flags on national holidays and on special occasions such as a launching, a regatta, or a vessel's first or final trip. With a full set of CODE FLAGS, arrange them in a series FORE-AND-AFT over the boat, extending from the BOW to the STERN. The first flags go over the STEM or the BOWSPRIT to near the water, and then up and across the MASTHEAD or mastheads, and back down to the stern, with the last flag almost touching the water. A string of small decorative flags can be used instead of code flags, but don't use a collection of COURTESY FLAGS to dress ship (according to FLAG ETIQUETTE it's disrespectful to use national flags as decorations). To dress ship with a set of code flags:

Yachts dress ship at the Yarmouth (England) Old Gaffers Festival.

• Hoist the national **ENSIGN** at the stern staff.

• Connect the full set of code flags together in this recommended sequence, starting from the bow: AB2, UJ1, KE3, GH6, IV5, FL4, DM7, PO Third Repeater, RN First Repeater, ST Zero, CX9, WQ8, ZY Second Repeater. This gives a pleasing visual effect.

• Hoist the string of flags to the masthead on one or two **HALYARDS.** Arrange the ends of the string so they drape over the bow and stern.

• Dress ship at 0800, and leave the flags up until sunset (**EVENING COLORS**).

• Dress ship only at anchor or at a dock, except when participating in a marine parade, a regatta, or other unique situation.

drift, drifting – (1) the speed of a current is its drift. (2) a vessel moving without the aid of the sails or engine is drifting or adrift, but is **UNDERWAY,** according to Rule 3(i) of the **NAVIGATION RULES.**

drifter – (1) a sail used in light airs; a very large **JIB** made of light-weight sailcloth. (2) a type of inshore fishing vessel.

drogue, stern or series (rhymes with rogue) – a **DRAG DEVICE** deployed from the **STERN** of a vessel on a long, heavy line, while **RUNNING** before the wind in **HEAVY WEATHER** or storm conditions. The drogue lies near the surface of the water and helps to keep the stern toward the waves, slowing the speed of the vessel so she doesn't surf out of control. When using a drogue neither the engine nor the sails are used. Drogues are made in various configurations. A series drogue (Jordan series drogue) is a number of small fabric cones on a long line, attached to a stern **BRIDLE.** The Galerider™ is a webbing basket, also deployed on stern bridle and a long line. A drogue may be improvised by towing long lengths of heavy lines and old tires, if you have them. Before embarking on an ocean passage stow the drogue and its related equipment in an accessible location; digging around in the bottom of a deep **LOCKER** isn't a good thing when a storm approaches. Read about deploying a drogue and techniques to get the drogue back aboard when the storm's over. Try it in moderate winds. *See also* SURFING, YACHT and **SEA ANCHOR.**

Two series drogue cones on a 1-1/8"/28mm braid line. The cones are approximately 8"/20cm long.

The complete series drogue for a 42ft/12.8m, 32,000lb/16ton offshore yacht. Two bitts are visible on the dock near the bow and amidships.

drop boards, washboards – removable boards that close the COMPANIONWAY.

dry-dock – industrial-scale equipment for removing a vessel from the water and to work on the hull without putting her on land. It's normally used for large vessels. One type of dry-dock is a floating, barge-like vessel that submerges to allow a ship to be floated into one end through a door or doors. The doors are closed and the water's pumped out. Inside the dry-dock work can be done as if the ship were on land. "Dry-dock" is sometimes used to mean putting a vessel on land.

A large fishing vessel awaits repair in the dry-dock as the water is being pumped out.

The dry-dock is now dry and work begins.

dry exhaust – *see* ENGINE, AIR-COOLED.

drying harbor – a harbor in which little or no water remains when the tide goes out.

The tide range here is 18ft/5.5m.

drying-out grid – another name for a **SCRUBBING GRID**.

dry out – to intentionally take the ground in a harbor, usually alongside a wall or on a SCRUBBING GRID. A boat with a **LONG KEEL**, a **KEEL-CENTERBOARD**, a wide **FIN KEEL**, or **BILGE KEELS** is suited to drying out. With a sufficient range of tide, cleaning, painting, or repairs can be done on the bottom. Research the techniques for drying out, so the yacht will stay upright as the tide goes out. It's not difficult, and it's done regularly in some parts of the world. *See also* **LEGS (2)** and **CAREEN**.

A group of boats sit in their mud berths. In addition to the powerboats and small sailboats, there are two bilge-keelers and a fin-keeled boat on legs (at right). At high water there's 7-23ft/2-7m in this harbor.

A fin keeled sailboat has been skillfully dried out along the harbor wall, using six mooring lines. Behind the mast on the wall there are two large timbers that the boat slides up and down along; she's not touching the stone wall. The tide mark on the gauge astern of the boat show that there's almost 16ft/5 at high water.

DSC – abbreviation for **DIGITAL SELECTIVE CALLING**.

DSC Mayday call – for the position of the vessel to be transmitted with a **DSC MAYDAY CALL**, you must have a VHF radio *with integral* **GPS** or have an operating GPS connected to the radio. The speed of rescue is entirely dependent on people being able to find you. In addition to the Coast Guard, DSC-equipped vessels nearby will hear your distress call and may be able to assist before the Coast Guard arrives. See the next two entries for details.

DSC radio – a **VHF** radio or **SINGLE-SIDEBAND** radiotelephone that has digital selective calling capability. Many VHF radios manufactured after 1999 have DSC. A DSC radio operates the same as a regular VHF radio for non-DSC calls, but the procedure for making a DSC call is different; it's explained in the radio manual. Using DSC you can contact other vessels directly, if you know their **MMSI** number, issue an "all ships" call, find the locations of friends on the water who have a DSC radio, among other easy-to-use functions. The radio manual explains the features. One of the purposes of establishing the DSC system is to free up Channel 16. However, the most important feature is the DSC distress calling function; see the next entry.

DSC radio distress call – the semi-automated distress (MAYDAY) call button on a DSC radio is its *most important feature*. When the emergency button is activated, the radio sends out a distress signal that includes the vessel's MMSI number and position (*only if the radio has integral GPS or is connected to an operating GPS*). Once activated, the radio automatically transmits the distress message even if no one's at the radio. This frees everyone to attend to the distress condition. When the Coast Guard responds, the distress call is automatically cancelled, and you communicate directly by voice with them. The emergency feature is very simple to use; explain its use to all crewmembers. Read the radio manual carefully to know how to use it before an emergency arises. If you have a DSC radio, obtain the MMSI number and program it into the radio. *This number is necessary for the distress feature to work*. A U.S.-registered vessel needs only one MMSI number, no matter how many DSC devices she has. Prior to obtaining the number, you will be asked to provide certain information about the boat. The Coast Guard uses this information to help speed search-and-rescue. See the MMSI entries for information about obtaining a number in the U.S., Canada, and the UK.

dual voltage – *see* VOLTAGE, DUAL.

dual watch – a feature on many VHF radios that allows two channels to be monitored at the same time. With the radio set to dual watch, it listens on one channel, and gives priority to Channel 16. This is important in areas with shipping, because ships communicate navigation information on CHANNEL 13 (*see* BRIDGE TO BRIDGE). Use dual watch on Channel 13 and 16 to stay aware of ship movements. PRIORITY SCAN monitors more than two channels.

duct tape, Duck Tape®, gaffer tape – the sailor's friend. All duct tape is not created equal; some is good only for temporary use where strength or durability isn't important. Do some research, pay a little extra, and get good, strong tape for critical uses. Sometimes a duct tape repair is forever. To remove duct tape sticky residue try WD-40®.

The whole dodger/ spray hood is made of blue duct tape, and a nice job it is, too.

due – used with compass directions means "exactly," as in due east (090°), due south (180°), due west (270°), and due north (000°).

duplex channel – *see* CHANNEL, DUPLEX.

Dutchman sail – a sail furling and reefing system designed by Doyle Sailmakers.

Dutchman's log – an old technique for measuring the speed of a boat, but it can be used today. If you know the length of the vessel from BOW to STERN (in feet), drop a floating object, such as a ball of paper, off the bow, and time the number of seconds it takes for the object to reach the stern. Divide the length of the boat (in feet) by the time in seconds to get the approximate speed. A good math exercise for the children.

Dyform® wire rope – a special type of STAINLESS STEEL WIRE ROPE for rigging. It's 30% stronger than regular 1x19 stainless steel wire rope. End fittings designed for use with Dyform wire are available for mechanical attachment or for machine SWAGING.

dye marker – a distress or emergency locating signal for search-and-rescue aircraft or ships. Throw the dye canister into the water, and it's highly-visible from the air or a ship's bridge.

dye penetrant test – a system of chemicals applied to welds, rigging, fittings, or other non-porous surfaces to reveal defects and cracks in the material. This test is part of a comprehensive RIGGING INSPECTION. Dye penetrant kits contain a cleaner, a dye penetrant, and a developer. The general procedure for performing the test is:

1. Thoroughly clean the surface of the metal with a soft wire brush and a clean rag.
2. Apply the metal cleaner to remove oil and grease, and wipe the surface dry.
3. Spray the penetrant (a red dye) onto the surface to be tested. Leave it on for about five minutes so it can seep into any defects.
4. Wipe off the excess penetrant with a rag.
5. Spray the metal with the cleaner once again to remove the excess red dye, and wipe dry.
6. Spray the surface evenly with the developer solution. The developer absorbs penetrant from cracks or defects, and red lines or spots will appear on the surface, revealing flaws. Sometimes flaws are so small that this test doesn't reveal them.

Two sources for dye penetrant kits are Magnaflux (Spotcheck) or Promtech Aerosol. Welding supply stores usually have dye penetrant supplies in stock, and some marine supply catalogues carry the kits. Instructions may vary from this basic list; read the product labels.

Dynaplate™ – a porous BRONZE plate mounted underwater for the SHIP'S GROUND in a BONDING SYSTEM, an RF GROUND, or as part of a lightning protection system on non-metallic boats.

E

ear plugs – yes, ear plugs. These can be very important aboard a boat. Whether it's a snoring crewmember or other annoying sounds when you're trying to sleep, ear plugs may help you get some rest. When the boat is very noisy, as when it's rough, the many sounds all blend together in one cacophony, but when it's not very noisy one or two sounds may stand out. If you can't stop the rolling can, the banging BLOCK, or the clicking bottles, put the ear plugs in. You will still be able to hear someone call you, and loud sounds that need your attention won't be blocked out. Add an eye mask (or a bandanna) to block out the light, and you may sleep like a baby.

earth, earth connection – another name for a GROUND (2).

ease or "start" – to let out a line slowly under full control, as with a SHEET or mooring line, until it's in the desired position. Easing or starting means letting out a relatively small amount of line at a time while maintaining control. "Start the sheet." "Ease the BOW line." PAY OUT or VEER means letting out more line.

Eastern North Pacific Basin – the portion of the North Pacific ocean east of 140W. The National Hurricane Center in Miami, Florida is responsible for tracking TROPICAL CYCLONES in this region.

easting – to make good a distance in an easterly direction. "We were running down our easting when the SWELLS increased." Northing, southing, and westing may also be used in this sense.

ebb – the outgoing tide. An ebb tide is a falling tide. The flood is the incoming tide.

ECDIS – acronym for Electronic Chart and Display Information System, certified by the IMO for use on ships. ECDIS charts are VECTOR charts based on government charts. They may have extensive overlays of other information such as AIS and radar information provided by other instruments on the BRIDGE. IMO standards permit the use of RASTER charts in some circumstances. Charts used on recreational vessels usually do not meet ECDIS standards.

echo – a radar TARGET.

echo sounder – another name for a DEPTH SOUNDER.

ECS – abbreviation for electronic charting system. An ECS uses RASTER or VECTOR CHARTS.

ED – abbreviation for existence DOUBTFUL.

eddy, eddies – swirling currents of water or air that flow in different directions around a main current. Learning where the eddies are along the coast and in the ocean can help avoid a HEAD TIDE or find a FAIR one. COAST PILOTS, some CRUISING GUIDES, satellite forecasts, and WEATHER ROUTERS provide information about significant eddies around a main current.

"elbow wrap" – wrapping a rope or electrical cable between elbow and hand isn't SEAMANLIKE; it puts twists in the rope or wire, and marks a person as a LANDLUBBER. *See* COILING ROPE.

ELCI – see EQUIPMENT LEAKAGE CIRCUIT INTRRUPTER.

electric, electrics, electrical – terms usually applied to the AC system or equipment, but it may be applied in a general sense to both AC and DC systems and equipment.

electric propulsion, hybrid-electric propulsion – silent power for yachts and commercial vessels supplied by low-speed, high-torque electric motors, powered by large BATTERY BANKS. The powerful electric motor replaces a diesel or gasoline engine. The battery bank is recharged by shore power, power from a freewheeling propeller while under sail, a DC generator installed in the system, SOLAR PANELS, a WIND GENERATOR, or a combination of these methods. An all-electric propulsion system is suited to boats that make short trips and don't need to motor long distances. A cruising sailboat that needs a longer range may use a hybrid-electric system, which has a small diesel generator to recharge the batteries and supply other onboard power needs. As this technology evolves electric power may become the choice for environmentally-conscious mariners.

electrical standards worldwide – AC supplied in different countries varies in both VOLTAGE and FREQUENCY. Consult www.kropla.com/electric2.htm for worldwide standards, which include the types of plugs used in each country. An excellent resource for travelers.

electrical systems, marine – the applicable ABYC Standard is E-11 AC and DC Electrical Systems on Boats. U.S. Coast Guard requirements incorporate many of these standards. The complete E-11 Standard is available with a free trial of ABYC Standards at www.abycinc.org. For a summary see www.marinco.com/page/abyc-standards. The European RECREATIONAL CRAFT DIRECTIVE (RCD) has standards for pleasure vessels built or sold in the EU.

electrode – another name for a TERMINAL on a battery. The positive electrode is the ANODE and the negative electrode is the CATHODE.

electrolysis – often used incorrectly to mean corrosion. The correct definition of electrolysis is the breakdown of an ELECTROLYTE caused by current passing through it.

electrolyte – a solution that conducts an electrical current. The acid and water solution in a lead-acid battery is an electrolyte, and seawater is an electrolyte with respect to ELECTROLYTIC or GALVANIC CORROSION.

electrolytic corrosion – *see* CORROSION, ELECTROLYTIC.

electronic barometer – *see* BAROMETER.

electronic chart – *see* CHART, ELECTRONIC.

Electronic Chart and Display Information System – *see* ECDIS.

electronic navigation – using electronics such as GPS, CHART PLOTTER, DEPTH SOUNDER, radar, AIS, and other navigational electronics. All electronics have limitations, as do the users. The complexity of some electronic navigation systems require that we read the manual and practice regularly using the equipment. Navigating with electronics is *not* a "set it and forget it" activity. Using electronics should free the crew to keep a good lookout and practice visual PILOTING and position-determining skills. Even ships with an array of modern, expensive electronics and a full bridge crew of professional officers go AGROUND or suffer collisions with navigation aids or other vessels.

A prudent mariner doesn't rely on a single source of navigational information; always use a second method to determine the position of the vessel. *See* CHART, ELECTRONIC; GPS ACCURACY, and the next entry.

electronic navigation accuracy – GPS positions are often more precise than the charts. In confined waters, the accuracy of the chart data may be less than that of the position-fixing system in use. Leave a margin of safety near dangers.

electronics – (1) general term referring to navigation equipment that runs on 12V DC, such as a DEPTH SOUNDER, VHF or SINGLE-SIDEBAND RADIO, AUTOPILOT, radar, AIS and other instruments. (2) collective noun for all the electronic instruments. "The electronics package on Dave's boat is really great."

electroplating – the process of coating one metal with a thin layer of a different metal through an electrochemical process. Electroplating is used to increase resistance to wear or corrosion and for appearance, among many uses.

electropolishing – an electrochemical process that removes impurities from the surface of metals, leaving them clean and bright. Marine hardware is frequently electropolished. PASSIVATION is a form of electropolishing.

eLoran – a new system under development in the U.S., the UK, and western Europe, intended as a backup for GPS, especially critical since the U.S. discontinued Loran-C in 2010. As the system develops more equipment will become available and the price will decrease. Until the system is fully-operational there's no backup for a GPS system failure or outage. That's only one reason why knowing visual navigation and PILOTING techniques is very important.

embayed – unable to put to sea because of wind, seas or currents that trap the vessel in a harbor or bay. When the vessel's embayed she may also be on a LEE SHORE.

emergency boarding ladder – *see* BOARDING LADDER, EMERGENCY.

emergency drill – OK, let's admit it, all of us probably neglect this responsibility to some degree. COMMERCIAL VESSELS are required to practice emergency drills. Make this "serious fun" aboard a recreational boat. Regularly having serious fun can and does save lives. Most drills can be accomplished in less than 30 minutes. After a proper SAFETY CHECKOUT, which includes assigning each person a task to do in an emergency, surprise them, day or night. Even (or especially) a two-person crew should practice. Emphasize safety: everyone should be careful during practice. Some suggestions:

- Write the words "Fire Drill" or "Flooding Drill" on a piece of paper. When the crew can't see you, put it in a location where fire or flooding is likely to occur. Then send someone below on a errand to near where the sign is placed. The crew member goes below, finds the sign and calls out "Fire Drill or "Flooding Drill" to initiate the practice. Be creative.
- Call out "man overboard drill" and throw a floating object like a FENDER or a cushion overboard. Do it at night with a floating strobe light attached.
- Call out "abandon ship drill."

• After the drill review how it went (DEBRIEF), to see if the crew can improve the basic procedures. Revise the EMERGENCY PROCEDURE CARDS based on practice.

Drills are also a good way to check the condition of emergency equipment. *Turn off the radio* when you simulate making a MAYDAY call, so it doesn't accidentally transmit. Use a drill to test the EPIRB with its *test* function. Research with fishing vessel crews shows that frequent practice of emergency drills saves lives.

emergency drill, fire – where are the extinguishers? Can crew get to one or more extinguishers no matter where a fire occurs? How can you get out of a forward cabin if the fire is AFT? Can you get out of an aft cabin if the fire is forward? Is it easy to release an extinguisher from its bracket? A fire is the most frightening emergency afloat, and knowing what to do can save your life. When doing a fire drill check the gauges on the fire extinguishers to see if they need service. Practice an abandon ship drill as part of a fire drill.

emergency drill, man-overboard – practice all the man OVERBOARD RECOVERY TECHNIQUES appropriate to the vessel and crew. On a short trip in protected conditions and good weather, you may choose not to practice, but everyone should know where the man-overboard equipment is located and how to deploy it. At the very least, explain "SHOUT, THROW SPOT, STEER, RECOVER."

emergency light – a secondary light on some aids to navigation that can be activated if the main light fails. It usually doesn't have the same intensity or RANGE as the main light, and it may have different CHARACTERISTICS. If a navigation aid has an emergency light this is indicated in a LIGHT LIST, and it may be may be written on a chart.

emergency procedure cards – on brightly-colored paper, print and laminate concise lists of the tasks to be done in event of fire, FLOODING or major damage, and ABANDONING SHIP. Write a priority list for each emergency. Read emergency at sea books and articles and make each list specific to the boat and typical number of crew. Review the cards with the crew during the SAFETY CHECKOUT. Put the cards in an accessible place. Create the cards even if you normally sail with just two aboard, and if you single-hand, procedure cards will help you remember in a time of stress. Having an organized procedure, which the crew has practiced, helps to calm anxiety and fear, and increases the chance of conquering the emergency. See Meisel's *On-board Emergency Handbook* under "Emergencies" in the bibliography.

emergency pump – *see* FLOODING.

emergency pump and helicopter drop – although a scared crewmember with a bucket can move a lot of water, in the case of major FLOODING, the vessel's normal pumps and the crew won't be able to keep up. A MAYDAY or PAN PAN call is in order. The yacht may be able to be saved if a helicopter or rescue vessel can get a gasoline-powered high capacity dewatering pump to the boat in time. Of course, while waiting for the pump do everything possible to lessen inflow of water: that's why the vessel should have a DAMAGE CONTROL KIT and a COLLISION MAT. If a rescue vessel is bringing a pump, the following instructions for a helicopter drop aren't needed; the crew on the vessel will get the pump going. If a helicopter will be involved, prepare for its arrival by following the instructions in the HELICOPTER ASSIST entry in this book. In general, here's what to expect when the aircraft lowers a pump:

- The pump is in a floating container with easy instructions inside.
- After lowering the pump the helicopter will move away from the vessel.
- Try to keep the pump container upright when it arrives on deck.
- Take the pump out of the box and follow the instructions.
- Usually there are two fuel containers, giving about six hours of pumping.
- If it looks like everything is under control, the helicopter will depart.
- Keep the pump and container aboard and return it when back in port.

If the helicopter can't lower the pump onto the deck it can drop it into the water, and send a retrieval line to you, so you can pull the pump aboard. *See* FLOODING.

emergency tiller – *see* TILLER, EMERGENCY.

emergency water supply – it's a good idea to have a supply of water independent of the water in the boat's tanks. If tank water goes bad, runs out, or it's necessary to abandon ship, extra water could save your life. For a cruising yacht, have at least two 6gal/25liter jerry jugs of fresh water (or the equivalent in smaller containers); put rope handles on jerry jugs, and stow in an accessible place.

e-Navigation, e-Nav – an initiative of the IMO involving electronic systems for ships and shore facilities to automate safety, improve security and vessel monitoring, and encourage global standardization of systems and operations. Worldwide, Coast Guards will be implementing e-Nav technology as it's developed, which will indirectly affect small vessel operators. One aspect of the technology is "virtual aids to navigation," which uses AIS or other electronic means to GHOST IN an aid to navigation without physically placing a buoy or structure.

ENC – abbreviation for Electronic Navigational Charts® produced by NOAA, which are VECTOR charts that conform to international standards.

end for end – to turn a rope or chain so that the wear is equalized. End for end HALYARDS, SHEETS, and the ANCHOR RODE, as well as other lines.

ends – (1) the overhangs at the BOW and STERN. A vessel with LONG ENDS has a bow that curves upward and outward from the waterline and a stern with a long COUNTER. If the bow goes straight down to the water (plumb bow) and the stern rests on the water the boat doesn't have ends. (2) *See also* BEAM ENDS.

This modern yacht has no ends (except for a slight overhang at the bow). The mast is deck-stepped on the cabin top.

engine, air-cooled – some fishing vessels, workboats, and other vessels have engines that are cooled by air, rather than water. Because there's no water to cool the exhaust gases, these engines have a dry exhaust system which must be insulated to protect the surrounding materials and crew from the high heat.

engine alarms – devices that beep or buzz when a pre-set threshold is exceeded. The basic engine alarms are for low oil pressure and too-high cooling water temperature. There may be other alarms indicated in the engine manual or boat information notebook.

engine beds – the structural members mounted on or near the hull that support an engine or generator.

engine controls – control systems for shift and throttle control should be installed and maintained to meet relevant marine standards. Relevant ABYC Standards are P-14 Mechanical Propulsion Control Systems and P-24 Electric/Electronic Propulsion Control Systems. You and a crewmember should know how to operate the shift and throttle directly on the engine in case the control system fails.

engine cranking – don't crank a marine engine for longer than about 30 seconds at a time. There's a chance that exhaust water may back up into the engine (because it's not being discharged out of the boat), or that air may get sucked into the engine if there's an air leak in the fuel system. Consult a diesel engine reference book and/or a mechanic for starting problems.

engine, fresh water cooled – an engine that uses coolant (an anti-freeze solution like in a vehicle) to cool the engine rather than sea or lake water (raw water). *See* COOLING SYSTEM, ENGINE and ENGINE, RAW WATER COOLED.

engine ground – a common ground point on the engine that's part of the vessel's BONDING SYSTEM. The SHIP'S GROUND is the main system ground.

engine hour meter – one of the ENGINE INSTRUMENTS.

engine installation and exhaust systems – for efficient and safe operation all components of the engine installation and exhaust system should comply with ABYC Standard P-1 Installation of Exhaust Systems for Propulsion and Auxiliary Engines, and P-4 Marine Inboard Engines and Transmissions. *See also* ABYC P-6 Propeller Shafting Systems.

engine instruments – the basic instruments on an engine or generator instrument panel are a tachometer, an oil pressure gauge, an engine cooling water temperature gauge, and an engine hour meter. Some instrument panels may have other monitors, such as an exhaust temperature alarm. Many gauges are analog, with a needle, but some have digital readouts.

Tachometer, tach (rhymes with thermometer, tack): a dial or digital readout that indicates the revolutions per minute (rpms) of the engine. Check the ENGINE MANUAL for the top rpm that should not be exceeded.

Oil pressure gauge: check the engine manual for the oil pressure range. When the engine key is first turned on (before the engine starts) a loud beeping or buzzer should sound: this is the oil pressure alarm. The alarm goes off because the engine isn't running so there's no oil pressure. If the alarm doesn't sound, it may be broken. When the engine is running, the first hint of trouble may be a decrease in oil pressure on the gauge, well before the alarm goes off. If the gauge on the panel isn't working check the OIL PRESSURE SENDER first.

Water temperature gauge: check the engine manual for the proper cooling water temperature range. An increase in temperature may indicate a clogged water intake strainer or other problems. If the temperature gauge doesn't work at all check the WATER TEMPERATURE SENDER first.

Engine hour meter: a small meter with numbers that counts the hours of engine operation; every time the start key is turned on, the meter starts counting. The meter may be incorporated into the tachometer or be a separate item. Engine hours are important to note so that refueling, oil changes, and other engine service tasks can be performed at the proper intervals. If there's no engine hour meter you have to keep track of the clock hours of engine operation, so it's worth installing one to simplify this chore.

Exhaust temperature (raw water failure) alarm: if the cooling water flow becomes blocked exhaust gas temperature will rise and the alarm sounds, preventing damage, if the engine is quickly shut down. The usual engine water temperature gauge may not reveal a blockage until damage has been done. An exhaust temperature alarm can be relatively easily added to the exhaust system.

engine maintenance log – a written record of all the work done on the engine, whether by you or someone else. The log should include the dates, the engine hours, the tasks performed, the parts and supplies used (if any), and notes about the process, including any modifications or repairs. This log is important for making sure the required maintenance is done, and for diagnosing problems in the future. A buyer may request this log when you sell the boat.

engine manuals – the engine should have several manuals, some of which may be aboard, and some of which can be purchased or downloaded from the manufacturer's website.

The *operator's manual* is the most basic: it explains the operation of the engine, describes the controls and gauges, outlines the maintenance schedule, and gives the engine specifications.

A *shop manual* gives detailed, technical instructions for repairing the engine and replacing parts. It's designed for use by a skilled mechanic. Even if you aren't in this category, if you venture away from home waters have this manual aboard for a professional to use.

A *comprehensive parts manual* is essential for ordering parts and for locating where things are on the engine. It's very useful for the exploded diagrams that show how the parts fit together. After taking something apart, it's good to know how to put it back together correctly, with no parts left over.

Some engines have an *installation manual*, which is useful for checking for installation problems, and if the engine has to be pulled for repair.

engine, raw water cooled – an engine that is cooled entirely by sea or lake water running through it. *See* COOLING SYSTEM, ENGINE and ENGINE, FRESH WATER COOLED.

engine room automatic fire extinguishing system – an excellent safety feature. There are many types available, some suitable for owner installation (follow the directions carefully), and others for professional installation. With an automatic system in a diesel engine room or compartment, there must also be an automatic engine stop control installed in the system, so the engine is immediately shut down when the extinguishing system activates. If the engine continues to run after the extinguishing agent is discharged, it will suck up the material into its air intake, and the extinguishing benefits will be lost, and the engine possibly damaged.

engine start battery – a battery or BATTERY BANK dedicated to starting the engine.

engine stop control – (applies to diesel engines). Some diesels are stopped by turning off the key, and on some engines there's a separate stop control. Move the control to the stop position (it works by cutting off the flow of fuel). Remember to reset the stop or the engine won't be able to be restarted (it happens). A RUNAWAY DIESEL is an emergency situation.

English language – the worldwide language of professional communication for ships and aircraft. Use PROWORDS on the radio because they are generally understood and facilitate accurate communication. For ships' officers and crew the IMO has standardized many English words and phrases in a book of *Standard Marine Communication Phrases*.

ensign – (1) a country's national flag. The national ensign flown by a vessel must be the flag of her registry, which may not be the same as the country of her owner. According to FLAG ETIQUETTE the national ensign is displayed on a flagstaff at the STERN of the boat, or on the LEECH of the aftermost sail. In this case, the flag should be located about two-thirds of the length of the leech above the BOOM.(See the photo with CABOAT). The ensign is normally flown UNDERWAY, when entering and leaving a port, and in harbor from 0800 to sunset, or in accordance with local customs. While in port, if you leave the boat and will not return before sunset, lower and stow the ensign before departing. The vessel's ensign as well as flags of other countries should be treated with respect. Replace a tattered, faded ensign or COURTESY FLAG. (2) the official flag of an organization. *See also* DIPPING THE COLORS, MAKING COLORS, UNION JACK, and YACHT ENSIGN.

entering – another term for CLEARING IN.

entry, entrance – the BOW of the vessel just above the waterline. A "fine entry" is a slim bow.

Environment Canada, EC – the Canadian federal government department responsible for issuing land and marine weather forecasts and warnings in Canada. EC maintains an informative website, not just for Canadian weather, at. www.weatheroffice.gc.ca/canada_e.html. *See also* TRANSPORT CANADA.

Environmental Protection Agency – see the next entry.

EPA – abbreviation for the U.S. Environmental Protection Agency, charged with regulating air and water quality standards. Standards affecting the maritime environment relate to discharge of water and pollution from vessels, diesel fuel, and engine exhaust emissions, as well as number of other environmental standards. In 2012 "clean diesel" fuel regulations took effect, and in 2014 requirements for the after-treatment of engine exhaust will begin to affect small craft diesels. See http://epa.gov/otaq/marine.htm for a summary of EPA marine regulation issues.

EPIRB (pronounced **ee-**perb) – acronym for an Emergency Position Indicating Radio Beacon, which is a battery-operated, satellite-based DISTRESS (MAYDAY) alerting device. It operates on a frequency of 406MHz for the satellites, and it also transmits a 121.5MHz homing signal that's used when a rescue service arrives near the scene. When an EPIRB is activated, its signals go to a satellite system, monitored worldwide by COSPAS/SARSAT,which coordinates rescue efforts. An EPIRB with an integral GPS can reduce the time it takes for rescue services to locate a distressed vessel by as much as 40 minutes compared to a non-GPS EPIRB. The unit should be tested once a month, or as specified in the instructions: carefully read the EPIRB manual or label to see how to perform the test procedure. If the beacon is *accidentally* activated, a canceling voice message *must* be sent immediately to the Coast Guard; *see* MAYDAY, FALSE OR ACCIDENTAL.

Two types of EPIRBs are available: Type I, which has a HYDROSTATIC RELEASE so it can float free and self-activate if submerged, and Type II, which must be manually-released and activated. Each EPIRB has a unique number that identifies the beacon and the vessel to which it belongs. It's *required by law* that the boat's EPIRB be registered with the appropriate government agency and the registration renewed every two years. Registration informs search-and-rescue about the boat sending the signal, which helps in the rescue effort. See the bibliography under "Emergencies" for beacon registration information. A PERSONAL LOCATOR BEACON is *not* a substitute for a full-size EPIRB (and it's registered to a person, not a vessel).

The battery expiration date is indicated on the unit, usually five or six years. In operation, an EPIRB's battery life is rated for 48 hours at -40°C/F (longer when it's warmer). The EPIRB battery should be replaced only by a service center authorized by the beacon manufacturer. Improper replacement batteries or parts can quickly lead to the failure of an EPIRB when it's needed. EPIRB batteries have a long life, even after their replacement date. There have been numerous cases of the Coast Guard responding to beacon signals that were traced to a landfill. When discarding an old EPIRB, if possible return the old beacon to its manufacturer (check the website). Otherwise, remove the EPIRB's battery and recycle it according to local regulations; don't throw those lithium batteries in the trash. Note: in 2009 the satellite system stopped receiving signals from old EPIRBs that operated on 212.5/243 MHZ. If you have one of these old units lying around, dispose of it properly.

equinoctial gales – logically, gales that occur around the time of the EQUINOXES.

equinoctial tide – the highest SPRING TIDES occur on or near the dates of the equinoxes. Don't go hard aground or STRAND on these days or the boat may be stuck for six months until another equinoctial tide occurs, unless you can hire a crane or a heavy-lift helicopter.

equinox – the vernal equinox is approximately March 21; the autumnal is approximately September 23. The equinoxes are defined by the positions of the sun and moon in relation to each other. At the time of the equinoxes the length of the day and night are equal: sunrise occurs at 0600 local time and sets at 1800. Changes in the weather may occur around the time of the equinoxes.

Equipment Leakage Circuit Interrupter, ELCI – this is similar to a GROUND FAULT CIRCUIT INTERRUPTER, but it's a device that protects the whole boat from shock hazards. ABYC Standard E-11 AC and DC Electrical Systems on Boats says an ELCI "shall be installed with or in addition to the main shore power disconnect circuit breaker(s)."

estimated position, EP – calculation of a vessel's position along an actual or proposed COURSE line, using the course steered, DEAD RECKONING (DR), and also taking into account the effects of wind, LEEWAY, and current on the vessel. An EP may also be calculated using DR information and depth measurements. Mark the EP on a paper chart with a small square, the letters EP with the time, and write it in the log. A new DR starts from an EP. When navigating near shore or other hazards, EPs should have a circle of uncertainty drawn around them to help avoid hazards. *See* UNCERTAINTY, AREA OF. Always leave a margin for safety.

estimated time of arrival, ETA – the estimated time for a trip is calculated by dividing the distance to be covered by the estimated speed. A GPS calculates the ETA as you travel, if a destination WAYPOINT or route has been entered into the instrument.

etiquette, anchoring – *see* ANCHORING ETIQUETTE.

etiquette, flag – *see* FLAG ETIQUETTE.

European Union, EU – European states linked together politically and legally. The EU has harmonized common standards for the construction and marketing of recreational vessels and marine equipment in the RECREATIONAL CRAFT DIRECTIVE (RCD). Products that meet EU standards display the CE MARK. See INTERNATIONAL MARINE CERTIFICATION INSTITUTE. There are also other regulations that affect foreign RECREATIONAL VESSELS visiting EU countries, such as Customs and importation regulations. As of 2010, member states included Austria, Belgium, Bulgaria, Cyprus, Denmark, Estonia, Finland, France, Germany, Greece, Hungary, Republic of Ireland, Italy, Latvia, Lithuania, Luxembourg, Malta, The Netherlands, Poland, Portugal, Romania, Slovakia, Slovenia, Spain, Sweden, and the United Kingdom. Candidate countries: Croatia, Macedonia, Iceland, Turkey.

evening colors – *see* MAKING COLORS.

exclusion zone – another name for a SAFETY ZONE.

existence doubtful, ED – *see* DOUBTFUL.

expansion tank – a translucent plastic tank near a FRESH WATER COOLED engine that allows for the expansion and contraction of engine COOLANT as its temperature changes. The tank usually has a minimum and maximum fluid level line (like on a vehicle). Check the level of coolant by looking at the tank. A RAW WATER COOLED engine doesn't have an expansion tank.

explosive deepening – *see* DEEPENING.

exposure suit, exposure coverall, anti-exposure suit – a one-piece work suit with built-in soft foam flotation, worn by rescue service personnel, oil rig workers, and recreational boaters. It floats you and offers protection from the cold if you fall in, but it doesn't exclude water like an IMMERSION SUIT. FLOTATION CLOTHING is a good choice for cool weather boating activities.

extra-tropical cyclone – *see* CYCLONE, EXTRA-TROPICAL.

extrusion – metal that is shaped by forcing it through dies. MASTS, BOOMS, and other SPARS may be made of extruded aluminum.

eye, eye of the storm – other names for a HURRICANE EYE.

eye bolt, eyebolt – a bolt with a fixed ring on one end. It's used on the BOW of small boats for the bow line or PAINTER, and for a variety of uses elsewhere on a boat.

eye of the wind – the eye of the wind is the exact direction where the wind comes from. When TACKING, the BOW of the boat goes through the eye of the wind.

eye splice – a permanent loop made in the end of a rope. *See* SPLICES, TYPES OF.

F

F, F-number – (1) abbreviation for FAHRENHEIT. (2) abbreviation for Force, used in the BEAUFORT WIND FORCE SCALE.

Fahrenheit, F – the standard scale used to measure temperature in the U.S. On this scale, the freezing point of water is 32°F and the boiling point is 212°F. Two useful equivalents: 50°F = 10°C and 68°F = 20°C. CELSIUS is used by scientists and in many other countries.

fair – (1) said of a line (or other rigging) that runs directly to its destination without encountering an obstruction or chafe points. "Make sure the STERN line leads fair to the dock." (2) describes a favorable wind or a current that assists the boat's progress. "If we leave now we'll have a fair TIDE all the way." (3) smooth, as in a fair hull (no visible defects), or a fair curve (a smooth curve). (4) to make something smooth is to fair it.

fair current, fair tide – a current that's flowing in the same direction that a boat is traveling, thus helping the boat go faster.

fairlead – a device that controls the direction of a line so it won't tangle or chafe, and leads it FAIR to its destination. ROLLER FURLING lines, HALYARDS, and other CONTROL LINES may have fairleads to lead the lines back to the COCKPIT.

fairway – a navigable channel leading to a harbor or port, usually marked with aids to navigation and/or a RANGE or SECTOR LIGHT. *See also* CHANNEL, NARROW.

fairway buoy – a buoy that marks the entrance to a FAIRWAY and another name for a SAFE WATER MARK.

fair wind – a wind that aids a sailboat's progress, usually applied to a wind from ABEAM to ASTERN.

fake – another term for FLAKE.

fall, falls - the hauling part (the lines) of a TACKLE; used in the singular or plural. "The VANG tackle's fall is damaged and the whole line has to be replaced." "Grab the falls and haul really hard."

fall off – to turn the vessel's BOW away from the wind. Same as BEAR AWAY, BEAR OFF, and HEAD DOWN.

Farwell's Rules of the Nautical Road – a fascinating (yes, really) discussion of the legal aspects of the NAVIGATION RULES. The book is a gold-mine of information about the application of the rules of the road as they have been interpreted in collision cases by courts and administrative tribunals. Written by Craig H. Allen (a lawyer, former U.S. Coast Guard officer and licensed master mariner), *Farwell's* is a comprehensive reference for anyone who attempts understand what the terse and sometimes cryptic Navigation Rules really mean. You'll also get a sense of why the interpretation of the Rules is so difficult for mariners and the courts alike. Don't tackle *Farwell's* until you've mastered the Navigation Rules on your own. See the bibliography under "Navigation Rules" for the complete citation.

fast – held firmly or tie securely, as in fast aground or "make fast."

fast aground – really stuck when AGROUND.

fathom – six ft/1.83m. A measurement of depths on some nautical charts.

fathometer – another name for a DEPTH SOUNDER.

fatigue – metals, plastics, and other rigid or semi-rigid materials that are subjected to repeated stress, flexing, and bending eventually may develop cracks and fail. Rigging and fittings, TANGS, CHAINPLATES, SHACKLES, TOGGLES, TURNBUCKLES, hulls, bulkheads, engine beds, pipes, wire and cable, and *many* other items aboard a vessel can develop fatigue cracks. The normal stresses of life aboard a boat causes them, but some fatigue occurs because of preventable causes. A thorough RIGGING INSPECTION looks for signs of metal fatigue; a comprehensive MARINE SURVEY looks for signs of fatigue in stressed areas.

FCC – abbreviation for the U.S. FEDERAL COMMUNICATIONS COMMISSION.

feathering propeller – *see* PROPELLER, FEATHERING.

Federal Boat Safety Act of 1971, FBSA/71 – it establishes minimum safety standards for U.S. boats and equipment, procedures for registering (numbering) undocumented vessels that have propulsion machinery, and administers other responsibilities related to non-commercial and some small COMMERCIAL VESSEL activities. *See also* DOCUMENTATION.

Federal Communications Commission, FCC – the U.S. government agency that regulates all wireless communication, including maritime communications in the U.S. Among many responsibilities, the FCC approves types of wireless communication equipment, including those on RECREATIONAL VESSELS, U.S.-registered COMMERCIAL vessels, and foreign ships in U.S. territorial waters. FCC regulations incorporate rules made under international agreements and U.S. Coast Guard rules. *See* IMO, ITU, and LICENSE, RADIOTELEPHONE.

"feel the bottom, smell the bottom" – when a vessel is in water that's very close to her DRAFT, you can sense that the water is shallow without looking at the DEPTH SOUNDER. The boat slows down almost imperceptibly, and the motion through the water seems different. This effect is more noticeable at slow speeds, which should be used in very shallow water. Waves also "feel the bottom" and grow steeper and break as they move into shallow water.

fender – a soft, cushioning device to protect a boat's TOPSIDES when alongside a dock or another vessel. They are cylindrical, round or flat pads. All types are useful. With fenders bigger is better, despite stowage problems. You'll appreciate having big fenders the first time the boat is tossed against a dock by waves or pressed by a BEAM wind. In addition to fenders tied on the LIFELINES, have a loose fender available so crew can move where it might be needed to FEND OFF. Fenders shouldn't hang over the side when the boat is underway, except in preparation for coming alongside. Called a bumper by LANDLUBBERS.

fender board – a strong board or plank that's hung horizontally across two or more cylindrical FENDERS on the outside of the boat, usually AMIDSHIPS. There are lines at each end of the board to tie it on the LIFELINES or deck fittings. The fender board protects the TOPSIDES of the boat and the fenders from abrading on pilings or rough walls. It's essential gear when mooring next to pilings or piers with vertical slats, because fenders don't stay in place. Deploy the fender board *after* the boat is secured, not before, because the board may become caught when coming alongside.

fend off, fending off – to push a boat away from a dock or another vessel or to slow her progress when coming alongside. Everyone worries about the boat hitting something. A natural reaction is to fend off with arms or legs, but unless the boat is very small and moving very slowly this can be dangerous. Approach at a slow speed so that if she bumps it won't cause damage. If the boat's going to hit, move a FENDER to where the impact will occur. Keep a movable fender handy on deck. To push a boat away use the SHROUDS, BOW or STERN RAILS or the boat itself. LIFELINES and STANCHIONS are usually not strong enough to take a vigorous push. Fending off with a boathook (especially a telescoping one) can be dangerous.

The men struggle to fend off a large yacht forced onto the dock by a strong beam wind.

ferrous – *see* METAL, FERROUS

ferry glide – to use a current to advantage when it's across the BEAM. Ferry-gliding can be done under power, sail, or oars. Steer the vessel across the current at an angle toward the current (UPSTREAM), and let it push the boat sideways toward the destination. *See* CRAB.

fetch – (1) the distance from land across the water that the wind travels to reach a location. The longer the fetch, the higher the theoretical WAVE HEIGHT. (2) to reach a location or navigation mark without having to TACK. "If we sail as close to the wind as possible we'll fetch the entrance buoy at the channel." LAY (1) is a synonym for fetch.

fetch and wave height – *see* WAVE HEIGHT for a table.

fiberglass, glassfibre – the most common hull construction material for yachts and some commercial vessels. Abbreviations include FRP (fiberglass reinforced plastic) and GRP (glass reinforced plastic).

fid – a tapered wood or wood-and-metal hand tool used to splice rope. A MARLINSPIKE is a metal fid. The terms are used interchangeably.

fiddle(s) – a raised vertical "lip" (wood or molded plastic) along the edges of flat surfaces (such as on the GALLEY counter, the chart table, and the cabin table) used to help prevent things from sliding off. Fiddles are also strips of wood placed across open shelves, such as bookshelves, to keep items in place.

fiddle block – *see* BLOCK, FIDDLE.

figure eight knot – a basic STOPPER KNOT in the end of a rope, to prevent it from escaping through a BLOCK, FAIRLEAD, LINE STOPPER, or other small opening. See BLOOD KNOT and KNOTS, BASIC for a photo.

fill(s) – when the pressure rises in a LOW PRESSURE area the low fills.

fire aboard – a MAYDAY situation, unless it's a *very* small fire that you are certain can be extinguished quickly. If the fire is large or involves fuel don't waste time with a Mayday or an extinguisher – *get off the boat*. *See* EMERGENCY DRILL and EMERGENCY DRILL, FIRE.

fire blanket – a special fire-resistant fabric used to smother *small* fires, such as burning clothing or a fire on a GALLEY stove. Locate one near the galley, but not near the stove.

fire drill – *see* EMERGENCY DRILL, FIRE.

fire extinguishers – in the U.S. the Coast Guard specifies the minimum number and type of extinguishers required according to the length of the vessel, and whether it's a RECREATIONAL or COMMERCIAL vessel. A number of websites and marine supply catalogues give the requirements. In general:

- Have more than the minimum required number of extinguishers.
- Make sure crew can get to one or more extinguishers no matter where a fire occurs.
- Check the extinguisher gauges regularly; have refillable extinguishers serviced at an approved service facility.
- Learn how to use different types of extinguishers before they are needed.
- Shake dry-chemical extinguishers once a month so the powder doesn't cake inside.
- Consider installing an ENGINE ROOM AUTOMATIC FIRE EXTINGUISHING SYSTEM.

ABYC Standard A-4 Firefighting Equipment includes the U.S. Coast Guard requirements.

fire port – a small opening into the engine room or engine compartment through which the hose of a fire extinguisher can be introduced, and the extinguisher discharged without opening a hatch or door. The engine should not be running when an extinguisher is to be used. An ENGINE ROOM AUTOMATIC FIRE EXTINGUISHING SYSTEM is also important, even if there's a fire port.

fire, re-flash – after a fire appears to be out it may smolder and break out again (re-flash). Maintain a watch over a fire area for at least an hour after the fire is out.

Fire Triangle – the three things needed to support combustion are heat, oxygen, and fuel (combustible material). Take away any one of the three and the fire is extinguished.

first aid kit – many types are available commercially or assemble your own kit. Select items appropriate to the type of cruising, and whether you'll be close to medical aid or farther away from assistance. Take a First Aid and CPR course, and have a first aid manual aboard. The Red Cross and St. John Ambulance conduct excellent first aid courses, and publish good basic manuals.

first mate – the second person in command of a vessel, not just an assistant to the skipper. If it says "First Mate" on your coffee mug, shirt, or hat there are high expectations for you.

fisherman's staysail, "gollywobbler" – a light air, four-sided sail flown between the FOREMAST and MAIN MAST on a SCHOONER.

fishing vessel, F/V – the NAVIGATION RULES, 3(c) define a "vessel engaged in fishing [as] any vessel fishing with nets, lines, trawls or other fishing apparatus which restricts maneuverability, but does not include a vessel fishing with trolling lines or other fishing apparatus which do not restrict maneuverability." Fishing vessels move in unpredictable directions when fishing.

This fishing vessel's dayshape is made of solid materials. The white object on the mast of the sailboat to the right is a radar reflector.

This fishing vessel's dayshape is made of netting.

• Under the Rules sailboats, POWER-DRIVEN VESSELS, and sea planes are obligated to stay out of their way when they are actually fishing. When they stop fishing, they are power-driven vessels.

• The required DAYSHAPE for a F/V is two black cones apex-to-apex; (Rule 26). Some vessels display solid cones, and some use a netting tube, pinched in the middle to create two cones. The net isn't as easy to see as two solid cone shapes. Fishers rarely remove the dayshape, even when they stop fishing.

• There are several different combinations of NAVIGATION LIGHTS prescribed in the Rules for fishing vessels, depending on the size of the vessel, whether the boat is trawling (using nets) or fishing (using lines), and whether she's UNDERWAY and making way (see Rule 26 and Annex II).

• When a vessel stops fishing, her lights should be those of a power-driven vessel, but sometimes the captain doesn't make the change.

• A F/V at anchor does *not* display an ANCHOR LIGHT.

Fishing vessels may have deck lights and gear that interfere with the visibility of their navigation lights, or they may be improperly lit; for example, not changing navigation lights when their operations change. Learn the lights and dayshape for fishing vessels so you can give them a WIDE BERTH.

fishing vessels fishing as a fleet – under Rule 1(c) of the NAVIGATION RULES warships, vessels under convoy, and fishing vessels fishing as a fleet may display additional lights, DAYSHAPES, or use additional whistle signals which, as far as possible, don't conflict with those authorized elsewhere in the Rules.

Five Great Capes, the – *see* CAPE.

fix – the accurate position of a vessel, as determined by careful visual observations and/or electronic means. Some methods of obtaining a fix are:

• Passing close by an aid to navigation.

• With a BEARING and an accurate distance off, as determined by radar, by SEXTANT VERTICAL ANGLE, or by DIPPING A LIGHT.

• Crossing two or more simultaneous bearing LINES OF POSITION (visual or radar bearings).

• Reading the position from a GPS.

Use more than one method to determine a fix. A DEAD RECKONING position and an ESTIMATED POITION are not as precise as a fix.

fix, running, R Fix – a LINE OF POSITION obtained from a BEARING on a single object advanced to a later time to give an ESTIMATED POSITION along a course line. Apply the DEVIATION (if any) of the boat's HEADING at the time of the bearing. CHAPMAN and navigation books discuss this technique.

fixed light – a light on an aid to navigation that is continually on (not flashing). The abbreviation on a chart is "F." A fixed light may be combined with a FLASHING LIGHT.

fixed-mount – term applied to electronic equipment that is permanently installed on the vessel, rather than portable equipment.

fixed propeller – *see* PROPELLER, FIXED.

flag, courtesy – a vessel visiting a foreign country flies the civil ENSIGN (national flag) of that country at the STARBOARD SPREADER. The courtesy flag is a mark of respect, and it identifies the vessel as foreign (of interest to government authorities and residents alike). Some officials and residents take offense if the flag is flown incorrectly, not displayed at all, or if it's tattered or faded. After the boat is granted PRATIQUE, replace the Q-flag with the courtesy flag. Research the correct procedure for the country. For example, in some countries it's customary to fly the courtesy flag only after the Q- flag is lowered, while in other countries you're expected to fly it above the Q-flag before arrival. According to FLAG ETIQUETTE, no other flag should be flown above the courtesy flag, and a foreign courtesy flag or string of courtesy flags shouldn't be displayed as a decoration, or for DRESSING SHIP.

flag etiquette – rules and guidelines for the proper display of flags aboard a vessel and ashore. Following etiquette is a mark of respect for your national ENSIGN and the flags of other countries. The UNITED STATES POWER SQUADRONS® website (www.usps.org) has guidelines for the proper display of flags aboard U.S.-registered recreational vessels, and the websites of national yachting groups (such as the RYA in the UK), explain the proper etiquette to be observed in a particular country.

What does this flag hoist spell? Check the code flags entry to discover what it says.

flag halyard, signal halyard – a light line, usually attached to one or both SPREADERS on a sailboat, used to hoist flags. The ENSIGN of the vessel's own country is never flown at a spreader. A COURTESY FLAG is hoisted on the STARBOARD spreader halyard.

flag hoist – two or more CODE FLAGS on one HALYARD, used when signaling with the INTERNATIONAL CODE OF SIGNALS.

flag, private or private signal – a BURGEE or other flag designed for a particular vessel; the owner's flag. The private signal is usually flown from the head of the MAIN MAST on a short flagstaff, called a "pig stick."

flake – a method of COILING ROPE by making loose figure-eight coils on deck. Flaking is a good way to lay out a rope so it will run freely.

flap gate – another name for a TIDAL GATE (2).

flare, distress – a DISTRESS SIGNAL for use at night or in RESTRICTED VISIBILITY. Flares are dated, but having an in-date flare is no guarantee that it will operate when needed. SOLAS flares are more reliable than non-SOLAS. Make sure that all flares have either Coast Guard or SOLAS approval. Flares are pyrotechnic devices and are hazardous to use. Some are hand-held and some are shot from a flare gun. Read instructions carefully before flares are needed, and, if possible, wear eye protection and gloves when firing them. Attend a flare shoot if a local yacht club or boating organization sponsors one. Firing a SOLAS parachute flare from your hand is an exciting experience! In some states and countries a flare gun may be considered a firearm, requiring that you declare it to officials and possibly surrender it for the period the vessel is in the country. Many countries have specific regulations for the disposal of old flares. Check with the Coast Guard or other boating organization for disposal instructions; never put them in the trash. Under development are non-pyrotechnic flares, such as special lasers, to address safety concerns.

flare, hull – the outward curvature of the hull from the waterline to the deck level. *See* TUMBLEHOME.

flashing light – a navigation aid light that flashes a certain number of times in a specified time period. The abbreviation on a chart is "Fl;" for example Fl5s, which means a white light flashing once in five seconds. If the light has a color, red, green, or yellow will be indicated; for example, FlG 4s (a green light flashing once every four seconds).

Flemish coil, Flemish flake – a flat spiral coil of rope, like a mat, seen on decks and docks. The coil looks nautical, but don't leave it down for a long time, because the rope doesn't dry underneath and the deck stays damp.

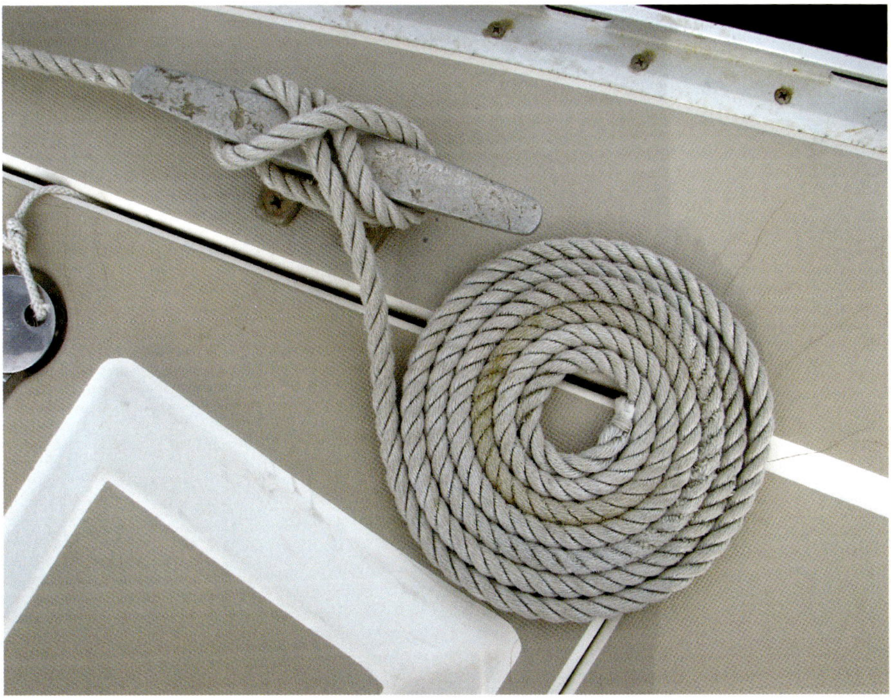

A Flemish coil and a proper cleat hitch.

flexible coupling – *see* COUPLING, FLEXIBLE.

FLIR – acronym for forward-looking infrared (thermal) imaging, NIGHT VISION DEVICE technology.

float plan, trip plan – this is different from a PASSAGE PLAN. A float plan or trip plan is a description of your intended trip that's given to a responsible adult who isn't aboard the vessel. The float plan includes details about the boat, its safety equipment, the number of people aboard, the departure point and the destination, the approximate time of departure, and the estimated time of arrival. If you don't notify the person with the float plan of your arrival or a change in plans, that person may make inquires as to your whereabouts, and notify the Coast Guard if it seems necessary. Float plans are not required, and they're usually not taken by the U.S. Coast Guard, but may be accepted by Coast Guards in other countries. See www.uscgboating.org (safety tab) for a good discussion of float plans.

float switch – short name for a BILGE PUMP FLOAT SWITCH.

flood – the incoming tide; a rising tide. An ebb tide is a falling tide.

flooded battery – another name for a lead-acid battery. *See* BATTERY TYPES.

flooding – almost as serious as a fire aboard, uncontrolled flooding can sink a boat in a very short time. A 2.5in/64mm hole 1ft/0.3m below the waterline lets in 120gallons per minute (gpm). A 3in/75mm hole 2ft/0.6m below the waterline lets in 250gpm. Flooding can result from a number of causes, such as a broken SEACOCK, a hose that comes off below the waterline, siphoning through a hose near the waterline, or a collision with an object or another vessel. If you go below and find lots of water in the bilge or above the cabin SOLE, taste it on your finger to see if it's salt water (obviously, if the boat's in fresh water this won't tell you anything). The basic procedure for dealing with a major flooding emergency includes:

- Issue a MAYDAY or PAN PAN call, as circumstances indicate.
- Operate all available pumps, including buckets.
- Locate the source of the leak. Having a THROUGH HULL DIAGRAM helps crew quickly check them, if they can't immediately determine where the leak is.
- Try to minimize the inflow of water; use a COLLISION MAT if there's damage to the hull.
- Use the DAMAGE CONTROL KIT.
- Prepare the ABANDON SHIP KIT, in case it's needed.

Normal electric and manual bilge pumps can't deal with a large quantity of water. For this reason, some skippers increase pumping capacity by (1) installing a SAFETY SEACOCK or a valve system on the engine water intake so the engine can draw from the bilge or bilge sump, and/or (2) installing a very high capacity pump belted to the engine or generator. With thoughtful engineering, this pump may also be used as a deck washdown pump, so it performs two functions. While these two additional pumps may not keep up with major flooding, they may give time until a rescue vessel or helicopter can bring a really big pump. *See* EMERGENCY PUMP, HELICOPTER DROP.

floors – the ATHWARTSHIPS structural members in the BILGE to which a boat's frames are attached. The floors are under the CABIN SOLE. LIMBER HOLES are drilled or molded through the floors to allow water to drain between the floors to a BILGE SUMP.

flotation clothing, float coat, float suit – comfortable outerwear with built-in soft foam flotation that both insulates from the cold and floats a person if he/she falls overboard. Some flotation clothing is U.S. Coast Guard-approved as a Type V lifejacket (check the label). *See* EXPOSURE SUIT and IMMERSION SUIT.

flotsam – the wreckage of a vessel, its cargo, or gear floating on the water. Frequently used as the name for any floating trash. JETSAM is sometimes used as a synonym.

fluid, compass – *see* COMPASS, FLUID.

fluid, transmission – *see* TRANSMISSION FLUID.

fluke(s) – *see* ANCHOR, PARTS OF.

fluky – adjective applied to light winds that unpredictably and frequently change direction. "It was so fluky out there today that we came in early."

flush deck, flush-decked – a vessel with no cabin or other structure on the deck, or with only a small cabin (DOGHOUSE) located well AFT and a large expanse of flat deck forward.

fluxgate compass – *see* COMPASS, ELECTRONIC.

fly, flying – (1) to use a SPINNAKER or other sail. "This is a perfect time to fly the spinnaker." (2) a sail set flying is not on a SPAR or STAY; it's attached only at the TACK, HEAD, and CLEW. (3) to let fly is to free completely, particularly applied to SHEETS. (4) the fly is the horizontal part of a flag, from the HOIST to the flapping end.

FM continuous wave radar – *see* RADAR, BROADBAND.

foc's'le (pronounced **folk** s'l) – the usual spelling and pronunciation of forecastle, the forward part of a vessel where the crew's quarters are located. On a yacht the foc's'le is usually called the forward cabin or the BOW cabin.

fog – caused by tiny water droplets suspended in the air near the ground; it's basically a stratus CLOUD that reaches the sea or ground. Visibility in fog varies from almost zero (it's never really zero) to about three miles. Marine forecasts and reports indicate the visibility either with actual numbers ("visibility less than one-half mile in fog"), or by a term with a specific meaning ("very poor" or "dense"). A glossary on a marine weather service's website has the exact meaning of adjectives used in the reports and forecasts. The most common types are ADVECTION, ARCTIC (SEA SMOKE), PRECIPITATION, and RADIATION fog.

fog, advection or sea fog – advection fog forms when warm wind blows over cold land or water. It forms day or night when conditions are favorable, and it can last for days. The sun doesn't help dissipate this type of fog. Coastal fog is the form of advection fog most encountered by boaters and residents of coastal areas. When the water warms up later in the summer advection fog may be less-likely to form. On the North American east coast warm winds follow the GULF STREAM northward to New England and onward toward

Newfoundland, forming extensive fog, particularly over the cold water of Maine and the Atlantic coast of Canada. The Grand Banks of Newfoundland, where the cold Labrador Current meets the warm Gulf Stream, has the highest number of foggy days in the world. On the west coast, warm Pacific ocean winds encounter colder water along the Pacific coast and fog forms. See the other forms of fog (Arctic, precipitation, and radiation), below.

fog, Arctic or sea smoke – evaporation fog that forms when very cold air drifts across comparatively warm water. It can freeze, creating freezing fog. It's a HIGH LATITUDE phenomenon.

fog bank – a well-defined mass of fog seen at a distance.

fogbound – the fog is so thick that vessels stay in harbor, anchor or drift, keeping a careful lookout.

fog, dense –in U.S. marine forecasts dense fog means visibility less than one-half nautical mile.

fog navigation – just because all the modern electronics are aboard don't go charging off into the fog. Do you know the required SOUND SIGNALS for RESTRICTED VISIBILITY for your boat and for all other vessels? Do you know the capabilities and the limitations of the electronics, and have skill in using them? Are you prepared to navigate safely if the electronics fail? Does the boat have an effective radar reflector? Does your trip go through waters with hazards to navigation, or is it in relatively open water? Will there be suitable anchorages along the way if you need to anchor and wait? Lots of things to consider before taking off – sometimes it's best to wait in a safe harbor. When navigating in RESTRICTED VISIBILITY:

- Turn on the NAVIGATION LIGHTS.
- Sound the proper fog signals for your vessel if there's a chance other vessels may be nearby or if you see something on radar or AIS at less than four miles. Note that the sound signals for a sailing vessel are different from a power vessel's. *See* SOUND SIGNALS, RESTRICTED VISIBILITY.
- Post a lookout forward on the vessel.
- Proceed under sail, if possible, so you can hear. If under power, stop or idle the engine from time to time.
- Find a navigation aid to fix the boat's position visually before continuing to rely on the electronics, and use DEAD RECKONING (DR) , along with electronic navigation.
- Use the DEPTH CONTOURS on the chart to stay in safe water and to help confirm the boat's position.
- Be aware that any WAYPOINT you select may have been chosen by others. Use extra caution when approaching navigation buoys, channels, and harbor entrances in fog.
- Stay out of channels used by ships (if possible). When running the buoys just outside a channel be vigilant, as other vessels may be doing the same thing.
- If you have doubts about your position or hazards in an area, find a nearby safe area to anchor, and sound the proper signal for a vessel at anchor.

fog, precipitation or rain fog – precipitation or rain fog occurs when rain from a warm layer of air falls through a colder layer of air near the surface.

fog, radiation or ground fog – this type of fog forms when the land cools after sunset, radiating its heat back into the sky. The skies must be clear and the winds calm for it to develop. This fog is stationary because there's no wind, in contrast to ADVECTION FOG, which moves. Ground fog is usually very dense, and it has a depth of from approximately 3ft/1m to 1,000ft/300m. It forms in the evening and lasts until near sunrise, when the heat of the day burns it off.

fog, sea – another name for ADVECTION FOG.

fog signals – NAVIGATION RULE 35 prescribes the SOUND SIGNALS for RESTRICTED VISIBILITY. Mariners must know the signals for their own vessels and for all other vessels.

fog signals, automatic – some VHF radios and LOUD HAILERS have pre-programmed fog signals that can be automatically sounded at the proper intervals. Make sure to select the correct signal for your vessel and type of operation. *See* SOUND SIGNALS, RESTRICTED VISIBILITY

fogbow – a rainbow in fog that has a white band with red on the outside and blue on the inside.

folding propeller – *see* PROPELLER, FOLDING.

following seas – waves from ASTERN. We all wish for FAIR winds and following seas.

foot – (1) the bottom edge of a sail. *See* SAIL, PARTS OF. (2) the base of a MAST. (3) to sail fast. "If we foot along at this speed we'll get there an hour early." "I bet we can outfoot *Rebel* if we trim the GENOA better."

foot block – *see* BLOCK, FOOT.

Force – *see* BEAUFORT WIND FORCE SCALE.

fore-and-aft – oriented parallel to the CENTERLINE of the vessel; longitudinal (does not refer to geographic LONGITUDE).

forecastle (pronounced **folk** s'l) – *see* FO'C'SLE.

foredeck – the deck of a vessel forward of the MAIN MAST, or forward of the HELM or wheelhouse on a powerboat.

forefoot – the area of the hull underwater where the STEM meets the KEEL.

foreguy – a line leading to the BOW from the OUTBOARD end of a SPINNAKER POLE, to hold the pole out; it may be called a PREVENTER when used with a BOOM.

forehatch – a hatch located forward of the MAST or near the BOW.

foreign, go – to sail to another country. Every time you go foreign it's a special experience that takes planning and preparation. Before departing, research the procedures for CLEARING IN and CLEARING OUT and make sure you have the necessary SHIP'S PAPERS.

foreign waters – for a U.S.-registered vessel, foreign waters are waters outside U.S. jurisdiction. In addition to more distant waters, the waters of Canada, Mexico, the Bahamas, and the British Virgin Islands are foreign waters for U.S. vessels. With respect to *radio licensing*, sailing in international waters (as when crossing DEMARCATION LINES or when on the HIGH SEAS) is permitted, as long as the vessel doesn't visit a foreign port. *See* LICENSE, RADIOTELEPHONE OPERATOR, and LICENSE, SHIP STATION.

foreland – another name for a HEADLAND.

foremast – the forward MAST on a SCHOONER, it's usually shorter than the MAIN MAST.

forepeak – a stowage area below deck at the BOW of the vessel; sometimes used to mean FOC'S'LE.

fore reach – to move slowly ahead when HOVE TO; to maintain headway when coming about; or drifting forward after taking in the sails or stopping the engine.

foresail (pronounced **fore** s'l) **–** general term for any sail set forward of the MAIN MAST; a HEADSAIL

forestay – another name for the HEADSTAY.

forestaysail (pronounced fore **stay** s'l), **staysail** – a JIB set on a STAY located between the HEADSTAY and the mast.

foretriangle – the forward vertical area of a sailboat that's defined by the forward edge of the MAST, the HEADSTAY, and the deck. The word is commonly used when talking about the size of a JIB. For example, a 90% jib is 90% of the foretriangle and a 135% jib is larger than the foretriangle, with the CLEW extending AFT past the mast.

forward – a direction on the boat toward the BOW or ahead of the boat.

forward-looking sonar – a DEPTH SOUNDER that can look ahead and, to some degree, to the sides below the vessel. It's a relatively new technology for the yacht market, although ships and research vessels have used commercial versions for years. This type of sonar has limitations, and the crew must learn to use it properly. Forward-looking sonar can generally see ahead only about six times the water depth, because echoes from the surface and the bottom interfere with its readings. Use it while navigating very slowly; at higher speeds the sounder can't see far enough ahead to warn of an obstacle. See the bibliography under "Electronics" for websites.

fothering, to fother – using a COLLISION MAT over a hole in the hull. A still-valid old-time word.

fouled, foul – (1) tangled, caught, or unable to run freely. A line is fouled when it's tangled; an anchor is fouled when it's caught on an obstruction on the bottom. (2) unfavorable, as in a foul tide, current, or wind. (3) applied to the bottom of the vessel, foul indicates a cover of marine growth or organisms. "This boat is so slow because of her foul bottom."

foul ground – description of the bottom when it has obstructions on it that are a hazard to anchoring.

fouling – marine organisms, grass, and slime that grows on the bottom of a vessel. Fouling creates DRAG, which slows the boat. "The fouling is bad here this year." Logically, ANTIFOULING paints are designed to prevent fouling.

foul tide – a current (whether tidal or not) that flows toward the boat and thus impedes her progress. A FAIR TIDE assists the vessel's progress.

foul weather gear, oilskins, waterproofs – waterproof clothing worn by sailors and landlubbers. Sometimes the most fashionable gear is not the most waterproof or the most visible if the person falls overboard. Read unbiased evaluations of gear before you spend a lot of money. A **SOU'WESTER** (2) is waterproof fisherman's gear. It may not be fashionable on a yacht, but it keeps you dry and it's available in bright yellow and orange.

founder – to fill with water and sink. A boat that's **SWAMPED** may founder, unless it has flotation material.

fractional rig – a sailboat on which the **HEADSTAY** is attached to the **MAST** at some point below the **MASTHEAD**. The attachment point on the mast is called the **HOUNDS**. A fractional rig may have **RUNNING BACKSTAYS**. One concern with a fractional rig is that there may be only one **HALYARD** that reaches the masthead, which could present a problem if someone needs to go to the **TRUCK** and the main halyard is unavailable. For another photo see **MAST, UNSTAYED**.

A classic sloop with a fractional rig displays beautifully-trimmed sails.

frap, frapping – to pass turns of rope or wire around two or more objects to bind them tightly together or to strengthen them. The turns are called frapping turns. Frapping implies using heavier, larger rope or wire than when **SEIZING**.

free, to free – (1) not secured, tied or tangled. "Make sure the **HALYARD** can run free." (2) to let go a line completely; to cast off, or to untangle it. "Free the **SHEET**." (3) running free is sailing on a **BROAD REACH** or **RUN**. *See* **POINTS OF SAIL**.

freeboard – the vertical distance from the boat's waterline to the deck. The freeboard may be different from **BOW** to **STERN** or the same on a boat with a straight **SHEER**. A boat with high freeboard has more **WINDAGE** than one with a lower profile.

freeing ports – another name for **SCUPPERS**.

freewheel, freewheeling – refers to a propeller that turns while the boat is moving under sail. A freewheeling prop may be used to generate electricity (with a special device attached to the propeller shaft), but the shaft turning all the time wears the **CUTLESS BEARING** and may cause a little noise. If freewheeling is undesirable a shaft brake of some kind can be fitted to stop rotation. A **FOLDING** or **FEATHERING PROP** doesn't freewheel.

French hitching – decorative and practical ropework on an item, such as a steering wheel rim or a **BOATHOOK**. It's easily done with a single light line, or with three lines (called St. Mary's hitching). This type of hitching looks nice and gives a secure hand grip. Some **MARLINSPIKE SEAMANSHIP** books show how to do this easy technique.

frequency – the number of times an action or a complete cycle of actions is repeated in a specific time period. (1) the frequency of **ALTERNATING CURRENT** and radio waves is expressed in **HERTZ**, which means cycles per second. (2) the **PERIOD** of a wave (the time from crest to crest) is the frequency of the wave, usually measured in seconds.

frequency, dual – equipment that can operate on either 50 HERTZ or 60 Hz ALTERNATING CURRENT. A typical label on dual VOLTAGE, dual frequency equipment reads: "Input 100-240VAC 50-60Hz." See the next entry.

frequency-sensitive – electrical equipment that can operate only on one frequency of AC. Even if VOLTAGE is the same, a 60Hz device may not work properly on 50Hz power. Check the label on the equipment or the equipment manual.

frequency, radio, RF – the radio SPECTRUM includes frequencies from 9kHz to 300GHz. Worldwide spectrum use is regulated by the ITU and the communications authorities in each country.

frequency, working – same as WORKING CHANNEL.

"freshen the nip" – *see* NIP.

fresh-water cooled engine – *see* COOLING SYSTEM.

front, frontal system – a transition zone between two air masses of different densities, and usually of different temperatures. The advancing air mass gives the name to the front; for example, with a cold front the colder air is advancing. Fronts are identified on SYNOPTIC charts and weather maps by symbols that indicate if it's a COLD front, a WARM front, a STATIONARY front, or an OCCLUDED front. The weather associated with a front is called a frontal system. See the next four entries.

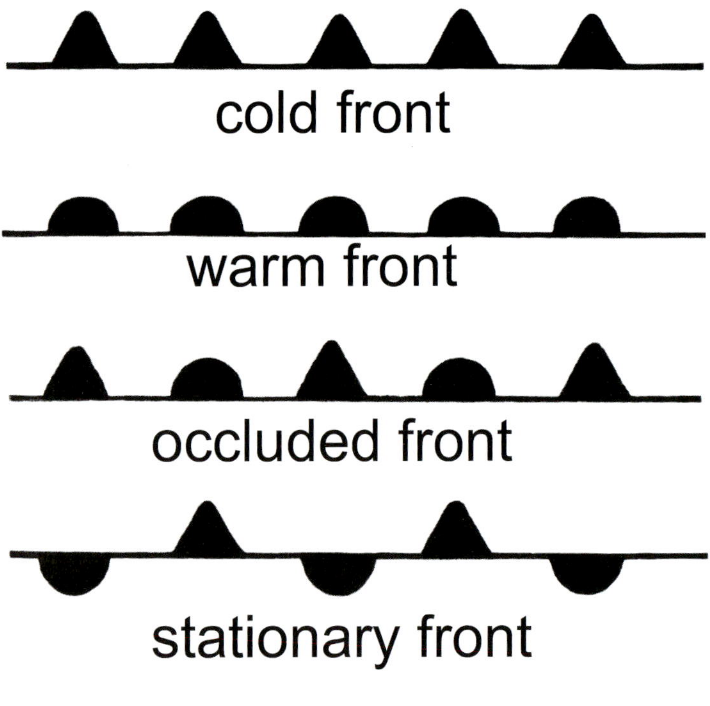

These symbols are used on synoptic charts.

front, cold – the transition zone between a cooler air mass that is moving forward to replace a warmer air mass. Usually after a cold front passes the temperature and the humidity decrease, the barometric pressure rises (sometimes quickly), and the wind shifts from southwest to northwest (in the Northern Hemisphere), or from northwest to southwest (in the Southern Hemisphere).

front, occluded – a combination of a warm and a cold front. It forms when a cold front overtakes a warm or stationary front. A cold occlusion results when the coldest air is behind the cold front, and a warm occlusion results when the coldest air is ahead of the warm front.

front, stationary – a transition zone between warm and cold air masses that is moving very slowly or not at all.

front, warm – the transition zone between a warmer air mass that is moving forward to replace a colder air mass. Usually when a warm front passes the temperature and humidity increase, the barometric pressure rises, and the wind shifts from southeast to southwest in the Northern Hemisphere, and from northeast to northwest in the Southern Hemisphere.

FRP – abbreviation for fiberglass reinforced plastic, commonly used in boat building.

fuel – (1) term usually meaning diesel fuel but may be used in a general sense for either diesel or gasoline. (2) to take on fuel; "fuel up."

fuel consumption – the number of GALLONS/LITERS PER HOUR varies with RPMS. A vessel should have a chart of fuel consumption at various rpms. Fuel gauges, if any, can be inaccurate. Some vessels have a "fuel range gauge" which can be set to either nautical miles or statute miles. Make sure it's set to the same miles as the GPS. The capacity of the tank indicated in the boat manufacturer's specifications may be incorrect, definitely a problem if the tank is actually smaller. Measure capacity when filling an empty or almost empty tank. It may be possible to create a measured tank "sounding stick" as a backup to gauges. Leave a margin for error, make a fuel consumption chart, and carry spare fuel in cans.

fuel filter – a device with a replaceable filter element that removes solid contaminants from fuel before they reach the engine. A filter that removes both solids and water is a fuel/water separator. Filters are used on diesel and gasoline engines and generators, and are specific to the type of fuel. Many boats have two or more filters: one in the line between the fuel tank(s) and the engine (the primary filter), and one or more mounted on the engine (secondary filters). The engine manual shows where the on-engine fuel filters are located. Carry spare filter elements. The major cause of engine stoppage is a fuel or filter problem. Signs that a filter is becoming clogged include a loss of power, a change in the engine RPMS while running, an increase in the vacuum reading on a VACUUM GAUGE, or the engine stops. Oops, now what? *See also* FUEL FILTER MANIFOLD, MICRON RATING, and FUEL POLISHING.

fuel filter, Baja (pronounced **Ba** hah) – a brand-name filter funnel used on deck to pre-filter diesel or gasoline before it goes into the tank. Skippers who cruise to remote areas where fuel quality may be poor can take one of these water trap/sediment filter units to keep contaminants out of the tank.

fuel filter, primary – a filter installed between the fuel tank(s) and the engine.

fuel filter, secondary – a filter installed on the engine.

fuel filter manifold – two PRIMARY FUEL FILTERS connected together with a valve system that allows filters to be changed while the engine's running. Commercial filter manifolds are available, or a skilled individual can fabricate one. Observe the ABYC safety standards for fuel system installations; see next entry.

fuel hose, fuel system – in the U.S. the hoses used in a fuel system must meet specific requirements for safety. The best way to ensure that a boat has the proper fuel hoses is to have a free VESSEL SAFETY CHECK. Newer boats should be in compliance, but older boats may not, or work may have been done on a fuel system by an unqualified individual. *See also* PROPANE HOSE.

fuel lift pump, feed pump – a small pump mounted on or near a diesel engine between the PRIMARY fuel filter and the secondary (on-engine) fuel filter. The lift pump may have a replaceable filter element. It can be a mechanical pump (may have a small priming lever on it), or an electrical pump.

fuel polishing – running diesel fuel from the boat's tank(s) through a special filtering system, separate from the PRIMARY and SECONDARY filters, to remove contaminants such as water, sediment, bacteria, and algae ("DIESEL BUGS"). The clean fuel is returned to the tanks. Contamination can be a major problem. It affects the performance of an engine, clogs the fuel filters and, in the worst case, damages the engine. Use a fuel polishing service, which comes to the boat and pumps the fuel through its filtering system, or install a permanent polishing device in the boat's system. If you take on a load of bad fuel (it can happen), or if the fuel in the tanks becomes contaminated, fuel polishing may save you from having to discard the fuel. FUEL ADDITIVES may not be able to clean badly contaminated fuel.

fuel-water separator – a filter that removes both solid contaminants and water from fuel.

"full and by" – older phrase, still used today, that means sailing close to the wind with all sails DRAWING. "We were full and by all the way down the coast."

full-flow – a valve, SEACOCK or other device in a fluid line that doesn't restrict the flow of liquid when it's open. The opening inside is the same diameter as the intake and output end of the valve.

fully-battened main – *see* MAIN, FULLY-BATTENED.

fume detector, "bilge sniffer" – a sensitive instrument that can detect small concentrations of explosive vapors (gasoline, PROPANE) in the bilge before a dangerous level is reached. The instrument has warning lights and an audible alarm. Xintex® is one manufacturer of fume detectors. The relevant ABYC Standard is A-14 Gasoline and Propane Gas Detection Systems.

funneled wind – *see* WIND, CHANNELED, FUNNELED, AND GAP.

furl – to lower and fold a conventional MAINSAIL or JIB, or to roll a sail around a STAY or into the MAST or BOOM. The equipment that rolls up a sail is a ROLLER FURLING device.

furling line – the line that goes to a ROLLER FURLING device.

fuse – a AC or DC safety device that protects equipment and circuits from an electrical fault. Unlike a CIRCUIT BREAKER, which can be reset after it blows, a fuse must be replaced. Fuses are found on electrical panels, inserted in the positive (+) wire to DC equipment, and sometimes on or inside electronic equipment. If something doesn't turn on and you've checked the power to the equipment and the fuse or circuit breaker in the power line, check the manual to see if there's a fuse on or inside the equipment.

F/V – abbreviation for fishing vessel. F/V *Hopeful*.

- G -

gaff rig, gaff sail – the gaff rig, with a four-sided MAINSAIL, was used on sailboats prior to the development of the triangular MARCONI mainsail, and it's seen on classic vessels and modern reproductions. *See* SAIL, PARTS OF for a drawing, and STEADYING SAIL and JIB, YANKEE for a photo.

gain – (1) a control on an electronic instrument (such as a radar or a radio) that adjusts the ability of the device to receive and process signals. A volume control is one type of gain control. (2) Gain is also applied to radio antennas to indicate their ability to receive signals; it's expressed in DECIBELS (dB) in the specifications.

gale – winds of 34 to 47 kn (BEAUFORT FORCE 8-9). In some forecasts "gale" is used for F8 (34-40 kn), and "severe gale" for F9 (41-47 kn) winds.

gale warning – issued by government weather services when sustained surface winds or frequent gusts of 34 to 47 kn (BEAUFORT FORCE 8-9) are forecast or occurring in a particular area. See previous entry and SMALL CRAFT WARNING, STORM WARNING, HURRICANE WARNING.

gales, equinoctial – *see* EQUINOCTIAL GALES.

galley – the kitchen on a boat.

"galley slave" – the cook. Take proper care of a good galley slave or you'll be sorry.

galley stove fuel – a number of fuels are available. PROPANE (LPG) is the most common, but stoves are made for butane, kerosene (paraffin), camping gaz (butane/propane mix, sold in Europe), COMPRESSED NATURAL GAS (CNG), and AC electric power. If the boat will travel to foreign waters, check that the stove fuel is readily available in the countries you'll be visiting. The relevant ABYC Standards are A-1 Marine Liquefied Petroleum Gas (LPG) Systems, A-3 Galley Stoves, A-14 Gasoline and Propane Gas Detection Systems, A-22 Marine Compressed Natural Gas (CNG) Systems, A-26 LPG and CNG Fueled Appliances, and A-30 Cooking Appliances with Integral LPG Cylinders.

gall, galling, galled – applied to metals, to gall means to become stuck or SEIZED. When threaded parts are in contact under pressure, they may become stuck together and be difficult to turn. One place where this can occur is between the threads of a TURNBUCKLE screw and the turnbuckle body. To reduce the potential for galling, some sailors specify that the threads of the turnbuckle and the body be of different metals, i.e. a BRONZE body and a STAINLESS STEEL threaded STUD, or vice-versa. Dissimilar metals are less likely to gall. Use an ANTI-SEIZING COMPOUND to lubricate threads and help prevent galling.

gallon to liters – one U.S. gallon is equal to 3.79 liters. One British(Imperial) gallon equals 1.2 U.S. gallons or 4.55 liters. One liter is equal to 0.26 U.S. gallons and to 0.22 British (Imperial) gallons. Have a conversion table or formula if the boat travels to countries where different measures are used.

gallon or liters, weight of –one U.S. gallon/3.8 liters: (1) water weighs 8.35lbs./3.8kg. (2) diesel fuel weighs 7.15lbs./3.2kg. (3) gasoline averages 6.2 lbs./2.8kg. A British (Imperial) gallon weighs about 12% more. Use this information to decide if you really want to hand-carry two six-gallon/25 liter JERRY JUGS of liquid more than a short distance.

gallons or liters per hour, gph, lph –a measure of the FUEL CONSUMPTION by an engine or generator in each hour of operation. The higher the RPMS or when pushing into the wind or against a head current, the more fuel is used. An operator needs to know the approximate gph/lph used by the engine or generator in order to calculate when refueling will be needed. Not all boats have a fuel gauge, nor is it accurate. Prepare a fuel consumption chart for the boat.

gallows, boom gallows – a permanent frame for the BOOM to rest on while FURLING or REEFING a conventional MAINSAIL, or when using a STORM TRYSAIL It consists of two upright posts of metal or wood and an ATHWARTSHIPS crosspiece, usually with notches or vertical tabs to hold the boom positioned in the center and/or off to PORT or STARBOARD. A BOOM CRUTCH is a single vertical support for the boom.

galvanic corrosion – *see* CORROSION, GALVANIC.

galvanic isolator – *see* ISOLATOR, GALVANIC.

galvanic series – in practical terms, the galvanic series indicates how different metals corrode in seawater. The least noble metals at the top of list corrode more than the more noble metals lower on the list. For metals close to each other in the list, the least noble one corrodes less when it's in contact with the more noble metal. The further apart two metals are on the list, the more the least noble one will corrode when it's in contact with the more noble metal. Consult an expanded list, such as the table in ABYC Standard E-2 Cathodic Protection, for more specific types of metals. A general list for the galvanic series:

Least noble, anodic, corrode more
magnesium and magnesium alloys
zinc
galvanized steel
aluminum alloys
mild steel and iron
cast iron
type 410 stainless steel (ACTIVE)

type 304 (18-8) stainless steel (active)
various brasses
tin
copper
various brasses and bronzes
bronzes
cupronickel alloys
lead
Monel®
nickel (PASSIVE)
Type 304 (18-8) stainless steel (passive)
Type 316 (18-8), austenitic SS (passive)
silver
titanium
gold
platinum
graphite
Most noble, cathodic, corrode less

See individual entries for many of these metals.

galvanize, re-galvanize – (1) usually refers to hot-dip galvanizing, a process used to coat steel or iron with zinc, to prevent rusting or GALVANIC CORROSION. Anchors, chain, dock BOLLARDS and CLEATS, and iron or steel equipment can be galvanized. Untreated FERROUS metals rust quickly in a saltwater environment; less-so in fresh water. (2) re-galvanizing may be done when the original galvanizing wears off. When anchor chain begins to rust it's sometimes economical to have the chain commercially re-galvanized. This process weakens it slightly because of the high heat involved. It's suitable for PROOF COIL and BBB (G30), and for HIGH TEST CHAIN (G40). Re-galvanizing isn't recommended for HIGH TENSILE (G70), because the high heat significantly reduces the strength of this chain.

galvanized wire rope – *see* WIRE ROPE, GALVANIZED.

gam – a social gathering of sailors, on land or on ships that get together at sea. It's an old word, still in use.

gangway – a plank or ramp on the side of a vessel used for boarding and disembarking. A passerelle is a gangway deployed off the BOW or STERN.

gap winds – *see* WIND, CHANNELED, FUNNELED AND GAP.

garboard, garboard strake, garboard drain – on a wooden vessel the garboard strake is the LONGITUDINAL plank fastened along each side of the keel, PORT and STARBOARD. The term garboard refers to that area of the hull along the keel, whether the boat is wood or made of other materials. A garboard drain allows bilge water to drain when the vessel is on land. If the boat has a garboard drain make sure it's reinstalled before launch.

gasoline – used only in gasoline engines (obviously), but it's important to check the fuel hose from the pump when filling a DIESEL tank to make sure it is, in fact, the diesel hose.

gasoline engine – some boats have an inboard gasoline engine or generator, which require that stringent safety practices be followed for installation, maintenance, and re-fuelling. Gasoline is much more flammable than DIESEL FUEL, and the fumes are heavier than air and may collect in the bilge, causing an explosion hazard. The relevant ABYC Standards are A-14 Gasoline and Propane Gas Detection Systems, E-11 AC and DC Electrical Systems on Boats, H-2 Ventilation of Boats Using Gasoline, H-24 Gasoline Fuel Systems, and P-1 Installation of Exhaust Systems for Propulsion and Auxiliary Engines.

gate, lifeline – *see* LIFELINE GATE.

gate valve – a valve with a hand wheel commonly seen in home plumbing. Gate valves are not approved for marine use as SEACOCKS, but they may be used in interior plumbing systems. The internal mechanism for closing and opening the valve is a small gate that goes up or down when the hand wheel is turned. Most gate valves are not FULL-FLOW devices, because the gate restricts the size of the opening even when it's open. A BALL VALVE with a quarter-turn handle is easier to operate, and the handle position clearly indicates if the valve is open or closed.

gear, gears, in gear – (1) general term to refer to equipment on a boat: boat gear, personal gear, safety gear, galley gear, etc. (2) gears: forward and reverse power to the propeller shaft, supplied by the TRANSMISSION. (3) in gear: when the transmission is engaged in forward or reverse. When the engine is in gear the propeller is turning. "Don't put the engine in gear until we've drifted away from the mooring buoy."

gearbox – another name for the TRANSMISSION on an engine.

General Prudential Rule – the General Prudential Rule is expressed in the Rule 2(b) of the NAVIGATION RULES :

> In construing and complying with these rules, due regard shall be had to all dangers of navigation and collision, and to any special circumstances, including the limitations of the vessels involved, which may make a departure from the above rules necessary to avoid immediate danger.

In general, this means that a vessel may depart from the Navigation Rules when *two* conditions are met: (1) the circumstances must be special, and (2) the danger must be immediate. The Rules don't define "special" or "immediate." The interpretation is complicated, and it keeps lawyers and judges busy when dealing with marine accident cases. The RULE OF GOOD SEAMANSHIP is related to the GPR.

generator, gen set – equipment that supplies AC power, independent of a shore power supply. A generator has its own engine; it may be small and portable or larger and permanently mounted aboard a vessel. The relevant ABYC Standard is A-27 Alternating Current Generator Sets. There are also DC generators. *See also* ALTERNATOR.

generator, water – a towed or permanently-mounted device that supplies DC current to charge the batteries while under sail. Both types have a small propeller that spins by the force of the water to create the charging current. They start producing current at approximately five knots of boat speed. Some water generators have a REGULATOR, while others don't, and they must be monitored so that they don't overcharge the batteries.

generator, wind – a small wind turbine with propeller blades that supplies DC current to charge the batteries. There are a number of types available. Many wind generators are permanently-mounted on a pole at the STERN or another location away from sails and rigging. Some are hung in the rigging while at anchor. They start producing charging current in 8-10 knots of wind. A generator may have a REGULATOR so it won't overcharge the batteries, but some don't and must be monitored so they don't overcharge. Most wind generators have a wind speed limit, and must be stopped (or they have an automatic cut-out) when it gets too windy. For photos see the Ovni sailboat with CHINE and TRANSOM, TRADITIONAL.

genoa, genny (pronounced **jen**-o-ah, jenny) – a large HEADSAIL that overlaps the MAIN MAST, coming AFT to the main SHROUDS or further aft, if it's a large genoa.

Gennaker™ – a CRUISING SPINNAKER made by North Sails. The name is a combination of genoa and spinnaker.

geographic range – the theoretical distance at which a light is visible in normal atmospheric conditions, and taking into account the curvature of the earth. The geographic range is determined by the height of the light and the HEIGHT OF EYE of the observer. Some LIGHT LISTS or charts indicate the geographic range based on the height of the light and a "standard" height of eye of 15ft/4.5m. DIPPING A LIGHT is a technique used to estimate the distance from a light when the observer is at its extreme geographic range. The U.S. Light Lists give the NOMINAL RANGE of lights.

geostrophic wind – *see* WIND, GEOSTROPHIC.

Germanischer Lloyd, GL – a marine CLASSIFICATION SOCIETY.

GFI, GFCI – acronym for GROUND FAULT INTERRUPTER, or ground fault circuit interrupter.

ghost, "ghost in" – (1) to sail slowly in very light wind. "We ghosted into the anchorage just as it got dark." (2) unwanted images on a radar screen. (3) to put an AIS signal electronically in a specific place to warn of a new hazard to navigation, a boundary area, or to replace a missing aid to navigation. The Coast Guard can "ghost in" an AIS signal (a virtual aid to navigation) where necessary, a great safety feature. *See also* E-NAVIGATION.

"ghoster" – a light weather sail.

GHz – abbreviation for GIGAHERTZ.

gibe, gibing – alternate spelling of JIBE, JIBING, and pronounced with a "j" sound.

gigahertz, GHz – one billion HERTZ. (1,000,000,000 cycles per second).

gimbals, *n.*, gimbaled, *adj.* (pronounced **gim** buls, "g" as in give) – a mechanism that allows a piece of equipment to remain level aboard a boat at most angles of HEEL. A compass has internal gimbals so the COMPASS CARD stays level; a galley stove, a cabin table, some kerosene cabin lights, and some radar SCANNER mounts are gimbaled.

gipsy (pronounced **jip**-sea) – alternate spelling of GYPSY.

give-way vessel, burdened vessel – in a right of way situation, under Rule 16 of the NAVIGATION RULES, the give-way vessel shall "insofar as possible take early and substantial action to keep well clear" of the STAND-ON VESSEL. Burdened vessel is an older term still in use.

GL – abbreviation for GERMANISCHER LLOYD, a marine CLASSIFICATION SOCIETY.

glass or the glass – old-time name for a BAROMETER. "At sea with a low and falling glass, soundly sleeps the careless ass." *See* WEATHER RHYMES.

"glasses" – informal name for BINOCULARS. "Please give Chuck the glasses."

Globalstar – a private company, with a constellation of satellites, that provides satellite voice and data services and satellite phones. Globalstar's marine service areas currently extend over 200 miles or more off coastal areas of North and South America, Europe, Australia, and East Asia, with coverage over almost all of the entire North Atlantic and the northeast Pacific. www.globalstar.com/en.

glow plugs – some small or medium-sized diesel engines or generators may have a glow plug for each cylinder. These help preheat the cylinders so that the engine starts more easily. There's a button or switch on the engine instrument panel (usually labeled "Pre-heat"). Depress and hold it in for the number of seconds specified in the engine operator's manual. After the appropriate number of seconds, start the engine and hold the button down for a few more seconds, or as specified in the manual. Glow plugs take power from the ENGINE START BATTERY, and if the battery's low there may not be enough power to turn the engine over rapidly enough for it to start. Long preheat times with difficult starting may signal that one or one or more glow plugs have failed, or that FUEL FILTERS are clogged. Carry spare plugs if you cruise far away from home. It's relatively easy to test and replace them; refer to a diesel engine technical reference book. Not all diesels have glow plugs.

GMDSS – acronym for the Global Maritime Distress and Safety System. GMDSS regulations apply to all commercial vessels over 300 GROSS TONS, and to various classes of PASSENGER and fishing vessels. Vessels not subject to the regulations may install GMDSS equipment on a voluntary basis. All systems and equipment must meet international standards for reliability. GMDSS provides emergency and safety communications and information worldwide. GMDSS equipment automates a ship's radio distress channel monitoring and alerting functions. Safety information broadcast under GMDSS includes such things as navigation and weather warnings, weather forecasts, and urgent safety messages. NAVTEX is one part of the GMDSS system.

GMDSS Sea Areas – all GMDSS ships must be capable of communicating with the shore and transmitting a distress alert by two different means. The required equipment for a GMDSS vessel is determined by its area of operation and the availability of shore-based communication services. Sea Area A1 is an area within VHF range of a DSC coast station (about 30 - 40 miles). Sea Area A2 is an area within MEDIUM-FREQUENCY range of a DSC coast station (about 150 miles). Sea Area A3 is an area covered by the INMARSAT Satellite System (excluding A1 and A2 areas). Sea Area A4 is basically the polar regions that aren't covered by the other areas.

GMDSS weather forecasts – forecasts provided by NAVTEX and *some* Internet sources are GMDSS-compliant, meeting GMDSS standards for dissemination (not *accuracy* of forecast, however). A website with worldwide weather information, including links to forecasts issued within GMDSS is at www.users.zetnet.co.uk/tempusfugit/marine/gmdss.htm.

GMT – abbreviation for GREENWICH MEAN TIME, the worldwide time reference standard, otherwise known as UTC or COORDINATED UNIVERSAL TIME.

gnomonic chart – *see* CHART, GNOMONIC.

"go about, going about" – steering the BOW of the boat through the wind to put the wind on the other side of the sails; TACKING. Same as "come about, coming about."

"go fast" – a slang term for a BOOM VANG.

go foreign, going foreign – *see* FOREIGN, TO GO.

goggles – secure goggles can be an important thing to have if crew needs to go on deck in driving rain and wind, or to participate in a HELICOPTER ASSIST. Diver's or ski goggles are more comfortable than a diver's face mask.

going aloft – *see* MAST CLIMBING for safety tips.

"gollywobbler," – slang name for a FISHERMAN'S STAYSAIL.

Good Samaritan clause – the NAVIGATION RULES cite 46 U.S.CODE.§2303(c) in relation to ASSISTANCE AT SEA:

> An individual complying with [the rules of this section] or gratuitously and in good faith rendering assistance at the scene of a maritime casualty without objection by an individual assisted, is not liable for damages as a result of rendering assistance or for an act or omission in providing or arranging salvage, towage, medical treatment, or other assistance when the individual acts as an ordinary, reasonable, and prudent individual would have acted under the circumstances.

This legal language might help you feel better about rendering assistance.

good seamanship – *see* SEAMANSHIP.

Good Seamanship, Rule of – *see* RULE OF GOOD SEAMANSHIP.

gooseneck – (1) the fitting that holds the forward end of a BOOM to the MAST. It allows the boom to move from side to side, as well as up and down. (2) a type of marine muffler that prevents seawater from entering the exhaust system, usually used at the STERN. May also be called a swan neck muffler. (3) a curved tube at the base of a DECK-STEPPED mast through which mast wires are led through the deck.

goose-winged – same as WING-ON-WING.

gph – abbreviation for gallons per hour. *See* FUEL CONSUMPTION and GALLONS OR LITERS PER HOUR.

GPS, DGPS – (1) abbreviation for a global positioning system that uses satellites; coverage is worldwide. DGPS is DIFFERENTIAL GPS, a more accurate system. (2) the electronic instrument for determining the position of a vessel (or a vehicle). A GPS is relatively simple to use, and it's a good aid for determining the accurate position of a vessel, her speed, and course over the ground. A GPS may be included in a CHART PLOTTER or other electronic instruments such as a VHF radio, AIS, or a DEPTH SOUNDER. See the next entry and WAAS.

GPS accuracy – the repeatable accuracy (return to the same position 95% of the time) for GPS is approximately 50ft/15m; for DGPS it's approximately 7-23ft/2-7m. Many factors affect the precision of a GPS position, including a temporary outage, the failure of one or more satellites in the system, or SOLAR ACTIVITY, as well as problems on the vessel itself. If the GPS is set to apply VARIATION automatically when it displays MAGNETIC directions (see the setup menu), check that the variation it uses is the same as that shown on the COMPASS ROSE nearest your area of operation. There can be differences of several degrees, even between different brands of GPS. In some cases a few degrees can be significant. The precise solution to this problem is to set the GPS to give TRUE directions and then apply the variation from the chart to get magnetic directions for steering. Always leave a margin for safety when relying on electronic positions, especially when PILOTING in confined waters. GPS positions are often more precise than the charts. See the brochure *Using Nautical Charts with GPS* at http://msi.nga.mil/NGAPortal/MSI.portal; click on "miscellaneous products." **A prudent mariner doesn't rely on a single source of navigational information; always use a second method to determine the position of the vessel.** *See also* AUTOMATION OF NAVIGATION FUNCTIONS, CONVERSION OF DIRECTIONS and WAAS.

grab rails – handrails mounted below decks and above deck on the cabin top, along the deck, or anywhere a good handhold is needed. A well-planned boat has strong, through-bolted grab rails strategically-placed for safety.

"granny rails" –safety rails mounted on either side of the mast or around three sides of the MAST, where a crew member can stand securely or attach a HARNESS TETHER while working at the mast. The formal name is mast safety rails, but many people say "granny rails" (even some "grannies").

gray water – waste water from sinks and showers is gray water; it's usually discharged overboard, unless specifically prohibited by law. Some jurisdictions prohibit the discharge of both gray and BLACK WATER; this will require the holding tank to be pumped out more frequently than if just black water is going into it.

Great Capes, the – *see* CAPE.

great circle, great circle route or course – a great circle is a line that passes through two points the earth's surface; it's the shortest distance between these two points. Radio waves, WIND WAVES, and ocean SWELLS follow great circle paths. A straight line drawn on a GNOMONIC CHART is a great circle course. East to west, west to east courses, routes of over approximately 600 miles, and routes that go closer to the poles (rather than nearer the equator) may be shorter if the vessel takes a great circle course rather than a RHUMB LINE. A GPS or NAVIGATION COMPUTER can calculate the difference in distance for a great circle course or a rhumb line course between two WAYPOINTS. To choose between the two, in addition to the distance, consider the prevailing winds, ocean currents, and weather systems on both routes. A PILOT CHART helps make routing decisions.

green flash – a brief, bright green edge or rays on the top of the rising or setting sun, which may be seen when the atmosphere is very clear and there's a good view of the horizon.

"green to green, red to red" – lines from a longer 19th century rhyme that serves as a memory aid for remembering navigation rules for vessels approaching each other. The relevant lines are "green to green, red to red/ perfect safety, go ahead." For the complete rhyme, see NAVIGATION RULES MEMORY AID.

green water – a whole sea breaking over something, rather than just the crest of the wave. It's something you'd like to avoid, but a WELL-FOUND vessel usually can cope with some green water.

Greenwich Mean Time – *see* GMT.

Greenwich meridian, prime meridian – the MERIDIAN from which LONGITUDE is measured east or west, and from which world TIME ZONES are calculated. It's the longitude of Greenwich, England, 0° 00.00′.

GRIBs, GRIB file (Gridded Binary Format data) – a format used for meteorological data, so it's easy to transmit over the Internet and by wireless means. GRIBs are typically used for computer-generated weather and wind models (there's no guarantee that the data is accurate), but in the future GRIBs will be used also for human forecaster-interpreted data. Learn the limitations of GRIBs. When used alone they're of limited accuracy; always compare GRIB forecasts with NAVTEX, other GMDSS forecasts, or SYNOPTIC CHARTS, along with your own assessments. Commercial services that market GRIB forecasts to the recreational boating community may make overstated claims for their products – user beware! For an excellent discussion of GRIBs and their use see Frank Singleton's comprehensive weather website at http://weather.mailasail.com/Franks-Weather/Home.

grommet – (1) a round metal reinforcing ring used on cloth, such as sails and flags. REEF PENDANTS (reef points) go through grommets on a sail. Large grommets on the TACK, CLEW, and the HEAD of sails are called CRINGLES. (2) A rope spliced into a round shape is a rope grommet.

gross tons (GT) – *see* TONS, GROSS.

ground – (1) the bottom of the seabed or lake. (2) an electrical ground to the earth or water; the SHIP'S GROUND. Another name for an electrical ground is an "earth" or "earth connection." A ground is part of the BONDING SYSTEM on a vessel.

ground, engine – *see* ENGINE GROUND.

ground fault circuit interrupter, GFCI – a ground fault circuit interrupter is a device that protects people from AC shock hazards, particularly in damp or wet areas. You probably have GFIs at home in the kitchen, bath, on outdoor electrical outlets, or as a portable device to be used with electrical extension cords. The detector senses an electrical fault and switches off in hundredths of a second, before you receive a dangerous shock. After the hazardous condition is corrected the GFI can be reset. ABYC Standard E-11 AC and DC Electrical Systems on Boats requires whole boat protection in the form of an EQUIPMENT LEAKAGE CIRCUIT INTERRUPTER (ELCI), which "shall be installed with or in addition to the main shore power disconnect circuit breaker(s)." In addition to an ELCI, individual GFCIs may be used on single-phase AC circuits to provide additional protection.

ground, hull – the SHIP'S GROUND. On non-metallic boats some sort of external plate is used on the hull to achieve a ground. DYNAPLATE® is one type of hull ground.

ground, radio – *see* RF GROUND.

ground swell – a long and deep ocean SWELL caused by a distant storm. When an ocean swell reaches water shallower than the deep ocean, it increases in height and becomes a ground swell. When a ground swell gets bigger, it may signal the approach of a storm.

ground tackle – inclusive term for all the components of a boat's anchoring system: the anchor, chain, rope, SHACKLES, and other attachment hardware. "Al's boat has excellent ground tackle."

ground, to take – to take the ground means that the boat's KEEL is on the bottom. It can be an intentional act, as when taking the ground in a DRYING HARBOR. The phrase also refers to a GROUNDING.

ground waves – *see* PROPAGATION.

grounding, go aground – when a vessel touches the bottom and gets stuck she's suffered a grounding. A serious grounding is a STRANDING, where the boat's left high and dry when the tide goes out. See the next two entries.

grounding, hard or severe – when a boat grounds on rocks, coral, or a very hard bottom she stops suddenly, even if you're going slowly, or she may bounce over the obstacles before coming to rest. In addition to KEEL, RUDDER or hull damage from hitting something, a sudden stop may dismast the boat, break rigging, displace interior BULKHEADS, shear engine motor mounts, and cause other damage not immediately evident. Crewmembers can be thrown overboard or fall and injure themselves. After you've determined that everyone is OK:

- Get the sails down or shut down the engine.
- Make sure there are no holes in the boat, and then deal with any visible damage, in a priority order.
- If the boat is holed it may be safer to be stuck on the rocks so she doesn't sink, unless the tide is rising and present or expected future weather conditions dictate otherwise.
- Get the pumps and buckets going if a leak is present.
- If the situation is serious and life is in danger, issue a MAYDAY call. If it's not life-threatening, issue a PAN PAN call.
- If holes can be patched well enough to be fairly watertight, perhaps the vessel can be re-floated. Use the DAMAGE CONTROL KIT and perhaps a COLLISION MAT.
- If there are holes and the tide is rising, act quickly to patch holes.
- Reduce DRAFT by taking heavy things off the boat (in the DINGHY or with assistance from another boat), and emptying water tanks. Remove as much weight as possible if there is time, and there's a potential to re-float the vessel.

If the boat won't float free when the tide rises (or she's aground at high tide), it may be possible to get a tow into deeper water. However, towing can cause more damage, and the situation is likely to become SALVAGE. A MARINE SURVEY should be performed after a hard grounding.

grounding, soft – going gently aground in calm conditions on a soft bottom may not be a calamity, but merely an inconvenience. No matter how careful you are, one day you'll go aground. As soon as you feel the boat touch bottom, take quick action (if possible): under sail, TACK or JIBE as appropriate. Under power try to back off and steer away from the shoal. You must know where the deep water is. If these quick actions don't free the boat and she's stuck:

- If under sail, lower the sails, or free the SHEETS to spill wind from the sails.
- Immediately assess the state of the tide, the nature of the bottom, and the effects of wind and waves. Is there time to try several techniques, or must you act quickly because of the tide or weather conditions?
- If you don't know where deeper water is, take soundings around the boat with a LEADLINE.
- If there's a chance that the boat will be driven further aground set an anchor in deeper water (using the DINGHY or an assisting boat) You may be able to use this anchor as a KEDGE to pull the boat off the shoal.

Some basic techniques to free a boat from a soft grounding, depending on how stuck she is, include:

- Use power in reverse and/or forward to move off the shoal. If the bottom is very soft, watch out for mud or sand getting into the engine water intake.
- SALLY (rock) the boat, if the weight of the crew is enough to have an effect, along with engine power.
- Use the wake of passing powerboats to lift the boat as you try to power off the shoal. Call them on the radio and ask them to provide a wake (they'll be surprised at the request).
- Reduce DRAFT by HEELING: use a sail sheeted in flat (if the wind is right and the boat will not be driven further onto the shoal). Try a HALYARD attached to a KEDGE set in deep water, or attached to another boat that is strong enough to pull the MAST down at an angle. Put the BOOM out to one side with weight on the end (crew members, anchors). If the boat has a WINGED KEEL heeling increases draft, but sometimes it works.
- Reduce draft by taking heavy things off the boat (in the dinghy or with assistance from another boat), and emptying water tanks. Remove as much weight as possible.
- Set a kedge out in deeper water (using a dinghy or an assisting boat), and winch the boat toward the kedge.
- Wait for the tide to rise, if conditions are safe, and you didn't run aground at high tide or in non-tidal waters.
- Accept an offer of a tow from a another boat, but use your own rope as a towline, and make sure to discuss money up front.

If it's a commercial tow boat the captain will give instructions, and explain the costs.

• If you're aground at high tide or in a non-tidal area and/or conditions are not good, call for towing assistance (if you're not in a remote area).

It may be effective to use several techniques in combination. See previous entry, SALVAGE, and EQUINOCTIAL TIDE.

growler – a piece of ice smaller than a BERGY BIT floating low in the sea. Growlers are not visible on radar, and their size (about 20ft/6m) long makes them a hazard to ships and smaller vessels.

guard rails, guard wires – other names for LIFELINES.

gudgeon – *see* PINTLE, GUDGEON.

Gulf Stream – a strong, warm water current that extends northward from the Gulf of Mexico and Florida along the U.S. east coast. Near Cape Hatteras it turns east. The general rate of flow varies from approximately six or seven knots in the Straits of Florida, to three or four knots as it continues up the coast.

In addition to the main flow of the current, the Gulf Stream develops EDDIES, which can hinder or help a vessel transiting the stream. Warm eddies, with a clockwise rotation, form north of the stream, and they may persist for up to six months. Cold eddies form south of the stream; they rotate counterclockwise (anticlockwise), and may persist up to two years. On the outside of some of the eddies the currents may reach six or seven knots. Gulf Stream eddies keep the climate on southwest coast of Ireland, the coasts of England, and the west coast of Norway warmer than the LATITUDE would suggest.

As the stream flows eastward it develops meanders, and the Stream can vary greatly, as much as 500 miles in a year.

The boundaries of the Gulf Stream are identified as the North Wall and the West Wall. The North Wall is the north boundary that extends northeast from Cape Hatteras. The West Wall is the boundary near the U.S. east coast, typically south of Cape Hatteras.

Conditions in the Gulf Stream can be treacherous, especially with wind against the current. Ships as well as yachts have been lost or severely damaged in storms.

After the stream heads eastward off the U.S. coast, it continues northeast to Iceland, across to Ireland and the UK, and eventually to the west coast of Norway. Find the location of the Gulf Stream at http://polar.ncep.noaa.gov/gsf. Detailed custom forecasts specifically for mariners transiting the Gulf Stream are provided by private forecasters, Jenifer and Dane Clark, at http://users.erols.com/gulfstrm/. General forecasts are available at www.wunderground.com and www.weatherbylee.com. NOAA does not issue Gulf Stream forecasts.

"Gumby suit" – slang name for an IMMERSION SUIT, because the wearer looks like the Gumby cartoon character.

gunkhole, gunkholing – (1) a gunkhole is a shallow, protected anchorage. (2) gunkholing is exploring shallow waters.

gunwale (pronounced gunn'l) – the upper edges along the hull of an open boat. The oars of a rowboat rest on the gunwales.

gut, pass – a narrow passage between two bodies of water bordered by land. It may be man-made or a natural feature. If there's a large tide range, the current can be strong in a gut. Plum Gut, at the eastern end of Long Island Sound in New York, is one example.

guy – a line used to control a SPAR, such as a SPINNAKER POLE. Guys are named by their function, such as AFTERGUY or FOREGUY.

gybe, gybing – alternate spelling of JIBE, JIBING, and pronounced with a "j" sound.

gypsy (pronounced **jip**-sea) – a vertical or horizontal WINCH used for handling an anchor RODE and mooring lines. Three types: (1) a chain gypsy (also called a chainwheel or wildcat) is a wheel on an anchor WINDLASS that has indentations (pockets) into which individual chain links fit. The pockets hold the chain as it's pulled in. The size of the chain links and a gypsy must be matched; use CALIBRATED CHAIN with a chain gypsy. (2) a rope gypsy has a round drum, with no chain pockets. (3) a combination gypsy has pockets for the chain links and a smooth portion for rope. See WINDLASS for a photo.

gyrocompass, gyro (pronounced **jai** row) – an electrically-operated compass used on ships and large vessels. The gyro indicates TRUE NORTH, and it's not affected by FERROUS metal in the ship's hull. Because it's not a magnetic compass it doesn't require COMPASS ADJUSTMENT

H

hail, hailing – to call, calling.

hailing port – informal term for the vessel's home port or port of registry, as painted on the STERN.

half tide – describes the state of the tide between high and low water. The adjective half-tide is applied to an underwater feature, such as a rock or ledge, that's visible at half tide, or to a LOCK or BASIN (a half-tide basin) where vessels can enter at half tide to wait until there's enough water to enter an inner harbor.

halliard – alternate, older spelling of HALYARD.

halo – a bright circle or arc around the sun or moon, caused by the reflection or refraction of light by ice crystals in high cirrus or cirrostratus CLOUDS. In warm months, a halo may indicate that there's a WARM FRONT nearby, which brings rain.

halyard – a line used to hoist a sail, a SPAR, or a flag. Halyards take the name of the sail they hoist along with the word halyard: MAIN halyard, JIB halyard, SPINNAKER halyard, etc. See the next two entries.

halyard, external – a halyard that's exposed for its whole length, from the deck to the MASTHEAD or other attachment point and back down; none of it runs inside the mast. External halyards are easy to inspect and replace. However, externals have more WINDAGE, they can foul on MAST STEPS, SPREADERS, or rigging, the whole length of the line is exposed to the sun and dirt in the air, and, unless the ends are kept secure at all times, either end can go up the mast. Oops! Tie them securely away from the mast when they're not in use, to prevent slapping on the mast, damaging the ANODIZING and infuriating the neighbors.

halyard, internal – a halyard that runs inside the mast for approximately half of its total length. The end that attaches to a sail is external, but the rest is inside the mast, exiting via a slot lower down on the mast. The advantage of internal halyards is that they cause less WINDAGE, and part of the halyard is protected from sun and dirt. If there's a STOPPER KNOT in the end that comes out of the mast that end won't disappear into the mast. However, the other end can escape, so keep it secure. The part of an internal halyard that isn't inside the mast should be tied away from the mast when not in use so it doesn't slap. Some disadvantages of internals are that in some wind conditions they can drum or slat inside the mast (difficult to correct), they may get stuck in the mast, and it's harder to REEVE internals when they are removed for inspection or replacement.

hammerhead – a dock or pier that's at a right angle to another dock at the seaward end; a "T" dock or pier. A hammerhead is sometimes reserved for visiting yachts to moor temporarily at a marina, while the skipper checks in at the office for a berth assignment.

hand – (1) to furl a sail. "It's time to hand the sails." (2) a crewmember is a hand; the whole crew comprise the hands; "ALL HANDS ON DECK." (3) used with PORT or STARBOARD (port-hand, starboard-hand) hand means "on that side." "In North America the starboard-hand marks are red when you come in from the sea."

"hand, reef, and steer" – phrase applied to a crewmember who is able to do the basic tasks on a sailing vessel; an old phrase still in use. "Be sure to get someone to come with us who can hand, reef and steer!"

hand-bearing compass – a small compass intended for use in one's hand to take BEARINGS on objects. These bearings are RELATIVE BEARINGS. A hand-bearing compass may be in the shape of a large hockey puck or have a handle with the compass on top. COMPASS-BINOCULARS are also an excellent hand-bearing compass Use it at a location on the boat that's free from undue magnetic influence, and that has appropriate visibility for the bearings you want to take.

handheld radio – a small, portable VHF radio; usually referred to as "the handheld." It has lower power and less range than a FIXED-MOUNT radio. A handheld is only for communication from a vessel to a shore station or between vessels; it's illegal in the U.S. to use it ashore like a walkie-talkie, or as an intercom aboard a vessel. Use the same RADIO PROCEDURE with a handheld as a fixed-mount radio. A waterproof handheld is an important item in an ABANDON SHIP KIT, as well as in a wet COCKPIT. *See also* LICENSE, SHIP STATION.

hand lead (pronounced led) – another name for a LEADLINE.

hand-swaged wire fittings – *see* TERMINALS, HAND CRIMPED.

handy billy – general name for a small TACKLE used for a variety of purposes. A VANG made of BLOCKS and line can be used as a handy billy.

hanks – small snap hooks used on the LUFF of a non-ROLLER FURLING HEADSAIL to attach it to its STAY. Two types are piston hanks and snap-on hanks. A sail with hanks is called a hanked-on sail.

harbor, drying – *see* DRYING HARBOR.

harbor dues, port fees – fees charged to use a harbor. Dues may be levied for anchoring, for using a mooring buoy (in addition to the mooring rental fee), or for using a marina (in addition to the marina fee). CRUISING GUIDES and NAUTICAL ALMANACS indicate if yachts are charged harbor dues.

"harbor fever" – a slang term for "PORT FEVER."

"hard alee" "helm's alee" "lee-ho" – words spoken by the helmsman to alert the crew when the wheel or tiller is put over to begin a TACK. The helmsman says "READY ABOUT" first to alert the crew to get ready.

hard aground, fast aground – the vessel is firmly aground.

hard chine – a sharply-angled CHINE.

hard dinghy – a DINGHY made of rigid material, in contrast to an INFLATABLE.

"harden up," "head up" – to turn the boat more toward the wind. Usually spoken as a command.

hard lay – a type of rope construction. The other type is soft lay. *See* LAY (4).

hard, on the – on the shore. "I stored my boat on the hard this year."

"hard over" – said of the steering wheel, tiller, or rudder when it's as far as it can go in one direction. "I've got the wheel hard over. Now what?"

harness, safety – an arrangement of strong webbing straps worn on the shoulders and chest by crewmembers, especially at night and in rough weather. It's an important piece of personal safety gear, and it should be properly constructed and maintained.

Safety harnesses should be available for all crew members, and be pre-adjusted to their sizes.

Purchase harnesses that meet the standards of the ISAF or other offshore racing organizations. SNAP SHACKLES and safety CARABINERS should have a minimum breaking strength of 5,000lbs/2,300kg.

A harness can have a single or double tether, which should be no longer than 6 ft/2m. Some crew prefer a short tether, under about 3ft/1m. Attach it at the wearer's chest with a snap shackle that has a strong, easily-grasped pull LANYARD. This allows the person to release the tether if he/she becomes entangled or falls overboard and is dragged along by the boat. Use a safety carabiner hook on the deck end of the tether to attach it to JACKLINES or other strong points on deck.

Try to clip on to something well inboard (toward the CENTERLINE) so if you fall you don't go over the side. Don't clip onto to LIFELINES, STANCHIONS, or the steering PEDESTAL guard; they aren't strong enough to take the weight of a falling crewmember.

Install strong PAD EYES in the COCKPIT, so the crew can stay clipped on while sitting. Put two near the COMPANIONWAY to clip onto before getting into the cockpit, and two at the HELM position.

A safety harness may be part of an inflatable lifejacket. Use one or two crotch straps with an inflatable lifejacket and harness, to prevent it from riding up over the wearer's head in the water when it's inflated.

harness tether – the rope or web strap used with a SAFETY HARNESS to keep the crewmember attached to the JACKLINES or strong attachment points on deck. It should have a minimum breaking strength of 5,000lbs/2,300kg. See previous entry.

hatch, hatchway – an opening in a vessel's deck, closed with a cover. The relevant ABYC Standard is H-3 Exterior Windows, Windshields, Hatches, Doors, Port Lights and Glazing Materials.

haul, haul out, "**haul up**" – (1) to pull strongly on a line. (2) to take a boat out of the water. (3) applied to wind, to shift in a counterclockwise (anticlockwise) direction; to back. "I think the wind will haul to the west later today." (4) to "haul up" is to head toward the wind.

hauling part – the hauling part of a TACKLE is, logically, the end of the rope that you pull on.

haul-out facility – a boatyard, marina, or other location that has equipment for getting a boat out of the water, such as a MARINE HOIST, crane, MARINE RAILWAY, or boat trailer. ABYC report T-28 deals with boat lifting and storage ashore. Because standards are not mandated, there are significant differences in haul-out facilities, techniques, and equipment everywhere.

have way on – *see* WAY.

hawse hole, hawse pipe – an opening in a high TOE RAIL or the BULWARKS of a vessel through which mooring lines or an anchor RODE are led. It's a type of fully-enclosed CHOCK.

hawser – a large rope used for towing, or any large rope.

head – (1) the upper corner of a triangular sail, where the HALYARD is attached. *See* SAIL, PARTS OF. (2) the BOW or the bow area of the vessel. (3) a MARINE TOILET or the entire toilet compartment. (4) the vertical distance above a pump intake to which a liquid must be raised when the pump is discharging. (5) a HEADLAND.

headboard – a fitting at the head of some MAINSAILS, consisting of flat plates of thin metal, other strong material, or layers of reinforced cloth with one or two holes in it, to which the main HALYARD is attached.

headboard shackle – a SHACKLE at the end of the HALYARD that attaches to the HEADBOARD on a MAINSAIL. Several types are available. A screw-pin shackle is the most secure.

"head down" – turn more away from the wind; fall off, bear away, bear off.

head, down by the – *see* DOWN BY THE HEAD.

heading – the direction the BOW is pointing. The heading may not be the same as the COURSE OVER THE GROUND because of the effects of current, wind, or LEEWAY. Course and heading are often used interchangeably, although, strictly speaking, they aren't the same.

headlamp – an LED headlamp is indispensable aboard a boat. Have a number of them, one for each crewmember. Wear it when working on deck at night, for working on the engine, for inspecting those inaccessible places below decks, or when reading in your bunk. Hold it in your hand to shine its bright light close-up in a confined space. Some have a red light for use at night. It's the best thing on a boat since DUCT TAPE and WD-40®.

headland, head, foreland – a relatively high cliff or mountain with a steep face near the sea. Some CAPES have high headlands. Winds can CORNER around a headland or have DOWNDRAFTS, and a TIDE RACE may form around headlands. A COAST PILOT, CRUISING GUIDE, or NAUTICAL ALMANAC may discuss conditions around headlands. Some well-known headlands include Cape Race (Newfoundland), Bloody Foreland (Northern Ireland), Cape Wrath (northern Scotland), Cape Finisterre (Spain), Gibraltar, the Cape of Good Hope, and Cape Horn.

head of navigation – as far inland as a vessel can navigate up a river or a bay.

head-on situation – applies to two *power-driven* vessels. Under the NAVIGATION RULES a head-on situation exists when you meet a vessel on a RECIPROCAL or nearly reciprocal course. This is when the other vessel is ahead or nearly ahead, and you see mostly her BOW, or at night when you see both sidelights, and the two MASTHEAD (RANGE) lights (on a large vessel) in line or almost in line. If you see mostly the side of the other vessel or only a red or green NAVIGATION LIGHT you are in a CROSSING SITUATION. Rule 14 of the Navigation Rules says:

- When two power-driven vessels are meeting, so as to involve risk of collision, *both* vessels should turn to STARBOARD, and the vessels should pass at a SAFE DISTANCE PORT to port.
- "When a vessel is in any doubt as to whether [a head-on] situation exists she shall assume that it does exist and act accordingly."
- Under INLAND Rules, "a vessel traveling with the current [DOWNBOUND] has the right of way, she "shall propose the manner of passage, and shall initiate the MANEUVERING SIGNALS prescribed by Rule 34(a), as appropriate."
- Vessels shall sound the appropriate maneuvering signals prescribed by Rules 9 and 34.
- If either vessel is in doubt as to the other's intentions she shall sound the DANGER SIGNAL.

head rules – (1) don't put anything into the HEAD unless you've eaten it first. (2) he/she who clogs the head unclogs it (no previous experience necessary). (3) in general, men should refrain from urinating over the side. An unfortunate number of drowned male victims are found with their zippers down.

headsail (pronounced **head** s'l) – a sail at the BOW, or any of the sails forward of the MAST.

head sea – waves coming from the direction toward which the boat is heading; waves on the BOW. Head seas may cause the boat to PITCH.

headstay, forestay, jibstay – interchangeable terms for the wire or rod running from the MASTHEAD (or lower on a FRACTIONAL RIG) to the BOW of the boat or to a BOWSPRIT. It's the outermost piece of STANDING RIGGING at the bow.

head tide – a current that flows toward the BOW, in opposition to the intended direction of travel, impeding progress.

head to wind – the BOW of the boat is pointing directly into the wind. This occurs when TACKING, and if the tack is unable to be completed the vessel is IN IRONS.

"head up," "harden up" – to turn the boat more toward the wind.

head-up display – a head-up display shows the direction the BOW (the vessel's head) is pointing at the top of the screen. It displays what you see in front of the boat. As the boat's heading changes the screen display moves with it. Head-up is usually the default mode on recreational vessel radars, because it's the easiest to interpret. A course-up display may be the same as a head-up display, if the course and the vessel's heading are the same, which is not always the case. Some electronics, such as AIS or a CHARTER-PLOTTER, require that a HEADING sensor be interfaced with the equipment to provide a head-up display; their default mode may be NORTH-UP.

headway – the forward progress of the boat; moving ahead. The opposite is STERNWAY.

headwind – wind coming from ahead toward the boat.

heat exchanger – part of the cooling system on a FRESH WATER COOLED engine, generator, or some refrigeration systems. Sea or lake water is pumped through the heat exchanger to cool the COOLANT that circulates through the exchanger. The coolant then goes through the system. A heat exchanger may have a ZINC PENCIL in it to reduce corrosion; check it regularly. If it corrodes too much, zinc flakes can block the tubes and passages in the heat exchanger. Inspect and maintain a heat exchanger according to instructions in the engine or refrigeration manual, or a technical resource.

heat exhaustion – heat exhaustion may occur suddenly after exercise, physical activity causing excessive sweating, or being out in the hot sun too long, without adequate fluid intake, and especially when the humidity is high. The body's ability to regulate temperature may be affected by certain medical conditions (such as hypothyroidism or cardiac disease), and by certain medications, including OTC seasickness preventatives (Dramamine, Bonine/meclizine), and prescription scopolamine, as well a some other prescription drugs.

General symptoms include: heavy sweating; cool, moist, and pale skin; feeling faint, dizzy or fatigued; headache; rapid and weak heartbeat; heat cramps; dark-colored urine.

First aid for mild heat exhaustion includes: get the person out of the sun, elevate the feet and legs slightly, loosen or remove most clothing; cool the head and body by sponging or spraying with cool water. Have the person sip cool water or a non-caffeine, non-alcoholic beverage. Monitor the person carefully. If the person faints, shows signs of confusion, has a seizure, or doesn't seem to be recovering, call for emergency medical help. Heat exhaustion can quickly become HEATSTROKE.

heat stroke – heatstroke is a medical emergency; issue a MAYDAY call. Heatstroke is caused by exercise or strenuous activity in hot weather, without adequate fluid intake. As with heat exhaustion, the body's ability to regulate temperature may be affected by certain medical conditions (such as hypothyroidism or cardiac disease), and by certain medications, including OTC seasickness preventatives (Dramamine, Bonine/meclizine), and prescription scopolamine, as well a some other prescription drugs.

General symptoms may include those of heat exhaustion, but the skin may be hot and dry. However, if exertion is the cause, the skin may be moist. Other symptoms: rapid heartbeat and rapid shallow breathing; cessation of sweating; irritability, confusion or unconsciousness; fainting, which may be the first sign in older adults. The main symptom of heatstroke is a highly-elevated body temperature, generally greater than 104°F/40°C,which you may be able to detect with your hand on the forehead (the person will feel very hot).

First aid while awaiting medical assistance: get the person into a cool environment; drape the victim with damp sheets or cloths, or spray cool water on the body and head; fan the person with an electric or paper fan. Give sips of cool water or a non-caffeine, non-alcoholic beverage if the person is alert enough to drink and swallow.

heating systems – in addition to electric heating, boats use liquid and solid fuel heating devices. Venting for these devices is extremely important to avoid CARBON MONOXIDE poisoning. The relevant ABYC Standard is A-7 Liquid and Solid-Fueled Boat Heating Systems.

heave to, heaving to, hove to ***(adj.)*** – stopping the boat at sea under sail, with the JIB ABACK, so that most forward progress is halted. The basic procedure is:

TACK the boat without freeing the jib SHEET. The jib will be aback after the BOW goes through the wind.

Adjust the helm: on a tiller-steered sailboat push the tiller down (to LEEWARD) and LASH it in that position. On a wheel-steered boat turn the wheel toward the wind and lash it in that position (a wheel brake on the PEDESTAL may not be strong enough to hold the wheel).

Adjust the helm and the position of the sails to get the boat to lie quietly. Heaving to with a HEADSAIL larger than about 95% of the FORETRIANGLE may be difficult; it may be necessary to ROLLER-REEF the sail or change to a smaller headsail.

Practice in light winds and in rough conditions.

Different boats heave to differently. Some very lightweight boats with FIN KEELS will not heave to at all; typical cruising boats usually do.

Heaving to is done in good weather as well as in HEAVY WEATHER or as a storm tactic, so the crew can rest. "We'll heave to outside the harbor until dawn." "Let's heave to while we eat lunch."

heaving line, messenger – a light line, usually with a MONKEY'S FIST or other weight at the end, that can be thrown some distance. When the heaving line reaches its destination (a dock, another vessel or a person) a heavier line is attached to the BITTER END of the heaving line, and the heavy line is pulled across. Some heaving lines are specifically-designed to be thrown to a person in the water (a throwing or rescue line).

heavy seas – *see* SEAS, HEAVY.

heavy weather – a non-specific term that refers to a combination of strong winds and large waves. When the wind increases to gale force (over

33 knots) in unprotected waters, conditions may be heavy weather for small craft, but lesser winds can create heavy weather, particularly with WIND AGAINST TIDE. Heavy weather is not necessarily dangerous to a WELL-FOUND boat with an experienced crew and enough SEA ROOM to stay safe. *See* STORM TACTICS.

heavy weather in harbor – see HURRICANE STRATEGIES IN HARBOR.

heavy weather preparation – a WELL-FOUND, SEAWORTHY vessel with a competent crew can cope with heavy weather, and having a plan specific to the boat is important. In general, to prepare for expected heavy weather:

Update the weather forecast from all available sources.
Start a written BAROMETER log.
Update the vessel's position and write it in the log. Record the position at least hourly.
Make a sailing plan to deal with the expected weather; discuss with crew.
REEF sails, get STORM SAILS ready, change to TRYSAIL (as needed if available).
Prepare DROGUE or SEA ANCHOR, in case it's needed.
Secure all deck gear, including WINCH handles, with extra LASHINGS.
Secure lines on deck that could become loose.
Check the navigation lights.
Crew don appropriate clothing, lifejackets, HARNESSES and TETHERS.
Crew take seasickness medication, as appropriate, before feeling ill.
Pump the bilges, and check during the heavy weather.
Charge the batteries.
Fill fuel tank, if you have extra fuel in cans, and the tank is below half full.
Close unneeded SEACOCKS.
Secure COCKPIT LOCKER lids.
Stow all loose cabin gear.
Rig LEECLOTHS for the bunks.
Eat a hot meal before it gets really rough.
Put hot food and water in insulated containers.
Keep snacks in a handy location.
Have the crew get some rest, if possible, before it gets rough.

hectopascal, hPa – a unit of barometric pressure equal to one MILLIBAR (1hPa = 1mb).

heel, heeling – (1) to lean to one side as a result of the wind on one side of the sails. Heeling too much slows the boat down; REEFING the sails helps the boat sail more upright and faster. LISTING is caused by the uneven loading of the vessel. (2) the bottom end of the MAST is the heel.

Even though the mainsail is reefed, this sloop heels over in a 30 knot gust.

height above water – the height above the water for lights, bridges, and power lines that cross the water is measured from some level of high water. The height of a light includes the light and the elevation of the land it's located on: for example, a 40ft/12m light on a 100ft/30m cliff is 140ft/43m above the high water level, which is the height noted on a chart and in a LIGHT LIST.

height of eye – the distance from the waterline of the vessel to the eye of an observer on deck. Knowing your height of eye from a typical observation point is important for calculating the distance to the horizon, the GEOGRAPHIC RANGE of a light, or when DIPPING A LIGHT.

helicopter assist or rescue – all over the world, helicopter crews assist and rescue mariners from ships and yachts You've probably seen exciting videos of the experience, and were glad it wasn't you in the video. A helicopter may be dispatched in emergency circumstances such as a MAYDAY or PAN PAN call for sinking, fire, or a serious medical emergency. A helicopter assist involves lowering a "trail line" to the vessel, and then sending down whatever is needed, such as an EMERGENCY PUMP, a lifting basket, or a rescue crewmember. *Follow the instructions of the aircraft crew to the letter, and confirm your understanding.* The following are general instructions:

A Norwegian rescue helicopter practicing. The white water on the vessel's port side is created by the helicopter's downdraft.

- Before the helicopter arrives, review the general procedures with the crew. You will not be able to hear when it's overhead.
- Everyone put on lifejackets. Don IMMERSION SUITS or EXPOSURE SUITS (if they're aboard) if there's a chance that you will ABANDON SHIP.
- Clear all loose equipment off the decks or tie it down very securely, including extra lines around furled sails. Don't furl the MAINSAIL if the engine's inoperative; the boat needs to be steered.
- If possible, at least one person on deck should put on goggles or a diver's face mask, because the hurricane-force DOWNDRAFT from the rotor will make it impossible to look up. Crew without goggles should turn their faces away from the downdraft. Have the crew put on gloves (to handle the TRAIL LINE, winch cable, or equipment from the helicopter).
- Have a hand flare or smoke flare ready; the pilot will tell you if or when to light it. At night turn on deck lights (but don't shine any light at the helicopter).
- Monitor the VHF radio, but do not transmit, unless you need to tell the coast guard or helicopter of an important *change* to your circumstances, such as the deterioration of on-scene weather or

a medical condition. The crew will call when they need to give you instructions. The person at the boat's radio must be able to communicate with the crew on deck. You will not be able to hear if you try to use a handheld radio on deck.

• The pilot will tell you how to maneuver the boat. You may be asked to motor at a particular angle to the wind with the sails down, or sail CLOSE-HAULED on a particular TACK. The helmsman must concentrate on steering a straight course, which may be difficult if it's rough.

• When the trail line or cable is down, let it touch the deck or water *first* to discharge static, before a person touches it.

• *Never* attach any line from the helicopter to your vessel or let it snag on anything. Keep the trail line from tangling when you've pulled it in.

• Follow hand and verbal signals from the helicopter or rescue crew.

If the sea state is too rough for a rescuer to be lowered to the boat, the helicopter may lift a person or the crew from a LIFE RAFT or DINGHY, or directly from the water. Do not abandon ship until you're instructed to do it. Small rescue helicopters generally have a round-trip range of about 160 miles, including time at the rescue site. The round-trip range of long-range helicopters varies from 250NM to 950NM, depending on the type of aircraft. Proper preparation on your vessel minimizes the time the helicopter must stay on station, which can be critical for a successful rescue. In the UK and some other countries it may be possible to participate in a training exercise. Around England and Scotland helicopter crews train regularly, and they may be willing to use your vessel for practice. The exercise is done in good weather, and it's the best way to prepare, should you ever need the real thing. *See* MEDEVAC; AMVER, and the bibliography under "Emergencies" for a Coast Guard instructional video.

helm – (1) the TILLER or the wheel on a boat. (2) the position on the boat where the wheel or tiller is located. A vessel may have more than one helm position or steering station. (3) to steer the boat; to helm.

helmsman – the person steering the vessel, whether female or male.

"helm's alee" – same as "HARD ALEE."

HELP position – acronym for "Heat Escape Lessening Position." If you fall into cool or cold water wearing a lifejacket, fold your arms over your chest and raise your knees toward your chest. This position lessens the escape of heat from your body, and wearing a lifejacket allows you to float upright while curled up. The HUDDLE POSITION is sometimes used with two or more persons in the water. See also SURVIVAL IN COLD WATER.

her, she – traditional pronoun used to refer to a vessel, instead of "it," with many speculations about how this term came to be used. One explanation is that a good boat takes care of us like a good mother, and we should speak of her with respect.

herd mentality – all we, like sheep, go astray: "Those boats are anchored over there. It must be good HOLDING, so let's anchor there." "All the other boats are leaving, so the weather must be OK for us to go." One of the things we like about being on the water is the feeling of freedom, and then, without really thinking about it, we may fall in step with the crowd. Sometimes it's very important that you make your own careful decisions and stick to them, despite what other sailors are doing. You're the best judge of the boat's capabilities and the crew's skills. Avoid letting SCHEDULES shape your judgment. Choosing an anchoring or mooring location and assessing if the weather is right to embark are just two of many decisions that should be made independently. Develop skills and rely on them. Consult with others, but decide for yourself.

Hertz, Hz – one cycle per second. The old phrase was "cycles per second." "Per second" is not used with Hertz. The word is both singular and plural. "In the U.S. the AC frequency is 60 Hertz." The cycle was renamed in honor of Heinrich Hertz, who discovered radio waves in the 1880s.

HF – abbreviation for HIGH FREQUENCY.

HF Fax – another name for WEATHERFAX.

high – short name for a HIGH PRESSURE SYSTEM.

high, higher – close to the wind; closer to the wind. "We're sailing too high on this heading." The opposite of high and higher with respect to the wind is LOW and LOWER.

high-cut – a HEADSAIL with the FOOT raised upward in a curve; the CLEW is higher than the TACK. A high cut JIB is less likely to scoop water in rough seas when the boat is HEELED. The opposite of high-cut is, not surprisingly, LOW-CUT.

high-frequency, HF – frequencies from 3MHz to 30MHz are in the HF portion of the SPECTRUM. *See* MEDIUM FREQUENCY and the next entry.

high-frequency, HF, radio – a receiver or TRANSCEIVER that operates on frequencies from 3MHz to 30MHz. Frequencies in this range are good for medium to long-distance communication. A SINGLE-SIDEBAND radio is an HF radio.

high latitude – an non-specific term applied to waters north or south of approximately 60°. High latitude cruising means sailing in far northern or southern waters. See the bibliography under "Sailing" for high latitude sailing resources.

high power, low power (radiotelephone) – a VHF or SINGLE-SIDEBAND radiotelephone contact can be made on most channels using either high or low power (VHF Channels 13 and 67 automatically default to low power, and that can't be changed). Select low power first if the other station is relatively near. High and low power only affect transmission, not reception. If you can't hear another station, changing to high power has no effect.

high pressure system, high, anticyclone – an area where the barometric pressure is higher than the surrounding areas. The air circulation around a high pressure system is clockwise in the Northern Hemisphere and counterclockwise (anti-clockwise) in the Southern Hemisphere. This rotation is a result of the CORIOLIS EFFECT. In a high, air is converged and being forced downward. Wind flows from an area of high pressure to an area of lower pressure. When the pressure rises in a LOW it "fills." If the pressure rises rapidly, strong winds result. High pressure systems generally mean good weather, possibly with light winds. Some highs are residents of an area. In the North Atlantic, the Bermuda High develops in the summer and fall near Bermuda; in the winter and early spring this high moves eastward and is called the Azores High. In the winter, the Canadian High or Arctic Air Mass brings cold weather to North America. In the Pacific, the North Pacific high influences weather on the west coast of North America, as well as in the Pacific. The Pacific High hangs around in the central Pacific near the Hawaiian Islands. There's also an Antarctic High that lives over central Antarctica.

high seas – (1) the high seas are ocean waters not under the jurisdiction of a country or state that has a seacoast; i.e., waters outside the TERRITORIAL SEAS. *See* 200-MILE LIMIT. (2) In U.S. marine weather forecasts, the high seas are that portion of the Atlantic and Pacific Oceans which extend off the east and west coasts out to 35°W in the Atlantic and to 160°E in the Pacific. This area includes both coastal and offshore waters.

high water – high tide; the level at which the water rises no higher before it starts to go down. The STAND may or may not occur at the time of high tide.

high water alarm – another name for a BILGE ALARM.

hike out – to put the crews' weight on the WINDWARD side of a sailboat to reduce HEELING. Racing boats may send all unnecessary crew out to perch on the windward RAIL.

"hip-towing," "on the hip" – a tug with a barge or barges attached to the tug at her STERN QUARTER. The NAVIGATION LIGHTS on this vessel and the barges will depend on the size of the tug and whether she is in INLAND or INTERNATIONAL waters. For example, a tug captain might say on Channel 13: "This is *Rosemary McAllister* headed south off The Battery with two barges on the hip."

hitch – a name applied to some knots that are constructed around something. Examples are a HALF-HITCH, a ROUND TURN AND TWO HALF HITCHES, and a CLOVE HITCH. *See* KNOTS, BASIC for photos.

hockle – a kink in a rope that occurs when a THREE-STRAND rope is twisted against its LAY and the strands open up at the point of stress. The kink can't be removed or corrected, and the rope is permanently damaged at that point. A hockle can be created when one end of the rope is tied to something, and the rope is twisted strongly against the lay. It can also occur in wire rope.

A hockle in 0.75in/20mm line. It took a lot of force to create it, and the rope is seriously damaged at this point. It will have to be cut into two shorter ropes.

hogged, hogged sheer – (1) a vessel is hogged when the BOW and STERN ends of the boat have dropped lower than the middle of the boat, resulting in a upward curve at the SHEER (reverse sheer). The term usually applies to a wooden boat whose KEEL has sagged over the years, but a vessel made of other materials with a broken internal keel structure can have a hogged sheer. (2) the term may be applied to a vessel designed with a sheer that is convex (a reverse sheer).

hoist – (1) to raise a sail, a flag, or other object. (2) the forward vertical edge of a flag. (3) a flag hoist is a group of flags, such as CODE FLAGS, raised together on one HALYARD.

holding, holding ground – a general term referring to the nature of the bottom in an anchorage. Good holding is firm sand, thick mud, or clay; poor holding is a thin layer of sand over flat rock or coral, soft or soupy mud, weeds and kelp, large rocks, stones, SHINGLE, and shells. Rocks and coral are marginal, even for a short-term anchorage, because the anchor can get stuck and also damage coral. Other sailors' evaluation of the holding in a location may not be accurate: some don't anchor properly, so they'll say the holding is poor. But sometimes they're right.

holding tank – a tank fitted on many boats into which the waste from the HEAD is discharged and retained for disposal at a PUMP-OUT STATION or offshore. Some boats have a DIVERTER VALVE which allows waste to be pumped overboard, instead of into the holding tank, when the boat is in waters where overboard discharge is legal. *See* GRAY WATER and the next entry.

"honey wagon" – slang for a vessel that travels a harbor to pump out holding tanks. It's a mobile PUMP-OUT STATION.

hood – another name for the TURTLE.

"hook, the" – an informal expression that refers to an anchor. "We dropped the hook in the cove overnight."

"hook, lunch" – a lunch hook is an anchor lighter than the boat's main or BOWER anchor, used for anchoring temporarily in calm conditions.

horizon, distance to – how far away is the horizon or something barely visible on the horizon? The distance depends on the height of the eye of the observer. Use a NAVIGATION CALCULATOR, refer to a table in a LIGHT LIST, or see Table 12 in BOWDITCH for a height of eye and distance to the horizon table.

horizontal sextant angle – *see* SEXTANT, HORIZONTAL ANGLE.

horn, ship's horn – another term for a vessel's WHISTLE, used to make the prescribed SOUND SIGNALS under Rules 32-35 of the NAVIGATION RULES.

horse – a metal rod mounted ATHWARTSHIPS on deck that functions as a TRAVELER.

horse latitudes – LATITUDES between approximately 30° and 35° north and south of the equator, noted for calms and light winds.

horseshoe buoy – a buoyancy aid in the shape of a U or horseshoe, used as part of MAN-OVERBOARD EQUIPMENT. The horseshoe should have the name of the vessel on it For a photo see CATAMARAN.

A horse made of metal rod to which the mainsheet tackle is attached. The rudder post is abaft the horse, and the pipe tiller is attached directly to the post. The tire is around a stern bitt. This restored 1895 sailing fishing vessel was built at Ramsey, Isle of Man, England.

hose – there are so many types available that the user should research the types of hose for a particular application. Consult a good marine supply catalog or a knowledgeable salesperson to get the correct type for the intended use. Some hoses are designed or approved for use in an exhaust system, a hot water system, pressurized systems, with gasoline or diesel fuel, oil, PROPANE, potable water, sewage, etc. Using the proper hose is important – all hoses are not equal just because they look alike.

hose clamp, Jubilee® clip (in the UK) – there are a lot of hose clamps on a boat. For critical applications, such as hoses on SEACOCKS, exhaust systems, RUDDER STOCK bearings, and other hoses below the waterline, use two clamps for safety, and select high quality clamps with stainless steel screws. Less-expensive clamps have mild steel screws that rust. Check the screws with a magnet. The ends of hose clamp bands are very sharp. Look for "Tail Tips" on the Internet or in a marine supply catalogue. They're small red (or other color) plastic caps that fit snugly over the ends of 0.5in/12.5mm clamp bands, preventing cuts and blood stains on the boat, as well as telltale scars. See the bibliography under "Maintenance." Hose clamps have many other uses, including for emergency repairs. Put an assortment of clamps in a DAMAGE CONTROL KIT.

hose installation and removal – installing and removing hoses is sometimes a challenge. Even when the inner diameter of the hose and the fitting to which it attaches are perfectly matched it can be a struggle. Put a little liquid dish detergent on the inside of the hose and on the fitting to which it attaches to help it slide on more easily. Sometimes the *careful* use of a heat gun on the hose can be very helpful to get it to slide on or off its fitting. Be careful not to melt plastic hoses or soften them so much that they become too large.

hot knife – an electric knife or an attachment for a soldering iron used to cut sailcloth or synthetic rope. Cutting with a hot knife seals the edges of the cloth, and melts the strands of a cut rope together. WHIP the ends of a rope cut with a hot knife.

hounds – (1) the attachment point on the MAST, some distance below the MASTHEAD, for the HEADSTAY on a FRACTIONAL RIG. (2) the area where the SPREADERS meet the mast.

house battery – *see* BATTERY, HOUSE.

The hovercraft ferry speeds through a misty morning.

hovercraft, air cushion vehicle – a vessel that operates above the surface of the water on a cushion of air that is produced by a powerful fan under the vessel. When the hovercraft is above the water it's operating in the non-displacement mode; when the fan stops, the vessel settles onto the water and it operates in the DISPLACEMENT MODE. Small hovercraft are used as rescue vessels in shallow water areas; large hovercraft are used for a variety of purposes, including as ferries. Rule 23(b) of the NAVIGATION RULES specify the lights for an air-cushion vessel operating in the non-displacement mode.

hPa – abbreviation for Hectopascal, a unit of pressure equal to one MILLIBAR (1hPa = 1mb).

huddle position – when several persons are in the water awaiting rescue, it is sometimes recommended that they move close together, face-to-face, and put their arms around each other to help conserve body heat and keep the group together. At least one person must be wearing a lifejacket for the group to remain afloat in the upright position. However, some experts note that the huddle position requires that the persons raise their arms to hug each other, thus releasing body heat from the armpits. If everyone is wearing a lifejacket a preferable alternative would be for each person to assume the HELP position (thus conserving individual body heat) and tie themselves together so they don't drift apart.

hull – the main body of a vessel, from the deck level down to where the KEEL joins the hull.

hull down – describing a vessel when only her SUPERSTRUCTURE or MASTS are visible because the hull is obscured by waves, SWELLS, the curvature of the earth, or intervening land. "By the time we tried to see her name she was hull down."

hull form or hull shape – see KEEL entries.

hull ground – *see* GROUND, HULL.

hull speed, theoretical – is calculated using the SPEED/LENGTH RATIO formula.

hurricane – a TROPICAL CYCLONE that has maximum sustained surface winds of 64 knots or greater, occurring in the Northern Hemisphere east of the INTERNATIONAL DATELINE to the GREENWICH MERIDIAN. TYPHOON is used for storms in the Pacific. The stages of development of a hurricane are TROPICAL DISTURBANCE, TROPICAL DEPRESSION, TROPICAL STORM, hurricane. Warm water sustains it. When it moves out of tropical waters or makes landfall it usually weakens because there is no longer warm water to feed it. See the bibliography under "Weather" for publications related to hurricanes.

hurricane categories – in the U.S., hurricane winds are categorized using the Saffir-Simpson Hurricane Wind Scale. This scale has five categories, based on the wind strength at a particular observation time. The category of a hurricane may change over time, and intensification can occur rapidly. As the scale number increases, the potential for damage from the winds and STORM SURGE increases. In general, potential damage rises by about a factor of four for every category increase.

Category 1 – winds of 64-82 kn (74-95 mph)
Category 2 – winds of 83-95 kn (96-110 mph)
Category 3 – winds of 96-113 kn (111-130 mph)
Category 4 – winds of 114-135 kn (131-155 mph)
Category 5 – winds over 135 kn (155 mph)

hurricane, Category 5 – the Atlantic Basin and its neighboring countries have experienced a number of hurricanes that were Category 5 at their strongest or when they made landfall. The first Category 5 hurricane on record to hit the U.S. was the Labor Day Hurricane (1935). The strongest Category 5 storms on record (so far) are: Camille (1969) had a record storm surge of 24.3ft/7.4m; Allen (1980), one of the strongest storms ever recorded in the Atlantic; Gilbert (1988), the most powerful storm ever recorded in the Atlantic, with 200 mph winds and a central pressure of 889.9mb; Andrew (1992); Mitch (1999); Isabel (2003); Ivan (2004); Emily (2005); Katrina (2005); Rita (2005), the eye experienced a 77mb drop in just 39 hours; Wilma (2005), the central pressure of 882mb is the record for the lowest pressure recorded in the Atlantic basin; Felix (2007) had a pressure drop of 83mb in 12 hours; Dean (2007).

hurricane eye – the center of a TROPICAL CYCLONE where the winds may be light and the sky clear, but with confused seas and very low barometric pressure. The eye of a storm can be seen on satellite images.

hurricane force winds – hurricane force winds are winds above 64 kn (BEAUFORT FORCE 12). The word "force" is used when talking about the winds, to distinguish them from the hurricane itself. In the U.S. hurricane winds are identified by categories from 1 to 5, with 5 the most severe. *See* HURRICANE CATEGORIES.

hurricane hole – a small, presumably-safe anchorage for use in a major storm. It has all the characteristics of a good ANCHORAGE. It's good if lines can be run to the shore. Hurricane holes are identified in CRUISING GUIDES or by LOCAL KNOWLEDGE. Get there early – 48 hours ahead of a storm's predicted landfall is usually much too late to find room. *See* HURRICANE STRATEGIES.

hurricane, major – in the U.S. a major hurricane is defined as one with winds over 96 kn/111mph; a Category 3 or 4.

hurricane season – logically, the portion of the year that has most of the hurricanes. The hurricane season in the Atlantic, Caribbean, Gulf of Mexico, and the Central Pacific basin is from June 1 to November 30. In the Eastern Pacific basin the season is from May 15 to November 30. Hurricanes don't pay attention to these dates, and they may form before or after the season. TROPICAL CYCLONES can occur year-round in any basin.

hurricane strategy at sea – a complex subject analyzed by many writers. Before going offshore when there might be the remote possibility of encountering a hurricane, study weather textbooks, STORM TACTIC books (see the bibliography under "Sailing"), and the *Mariners Guide to Hurricane Awareness in the Atlantic Basin*, available for download at ww.nhc.noaa.gov/marinersguide.pdf.

hurricane strategy in harbor – many articles have been written about strategies. These techniques apply to any strong storm, not just a hurricane. No matter what strategy you choose remove all sails, flags, other cloth items on deck, deck gear; deflate an inflatable and stow it safely below or take it to a safe place ashore. Secure HALYARDS away from the mast. The basic choices are:

- Haul out on land if safe and protected land storage facilities are available. Schedule a haul out early because boatyard schedules fill up when a storm approaches.

• Stay at a dock: rarely a good idea, but it may be the only choice. Deploy all the FENDERS and get some old tires for fenders. Triple mooring lines and add heavy chafe protection. If possible, set a good anchor (or two) ABEAM to hold the boat off the dock, or run lines to another pier or the shore. Running lines to another floating dock is not a good option because in a storm floating docks move all over the place.

• Stay on a mooring in a well-protected harbor. You must be absolutely certain that the mooring is in good condition and of sufficient weight for the vessel. The STORM SURGE and high tide can cover a mooring, if the chain isn't long enough. In addition to multiple strong, chafe-protected mooring lines, SHACKLE a length of strong chain to the mooring's chain, and run it over the ANCHOR ROLLER, making sure it can't jump out of the roller. Use a CHAIN SPRING. If there's no anchor roller, rig a chain spring to the extra chain, along with the mooring lines.

• Stay on a system of your own anchors: lay out an anchoring system with three heavy anchors set 120° apart, each on long SCOPE, allowing for the expected storm tide. Put the heaviest anchor in the direction of the expected strongest winds. There must be enough room in the anchorage to use this system. Add heavy chafe protection on all lines and a chain spring on a chain rode.

Whether to stay aboard the boat is a difficult decision. Most articles advise getting off the boat well before the storm, but if you decide to stay analyze the risks and be prepared. Read the excellent BoatU.S. guide for hurricane preparedness for boats, marinas, and yacht clubs at www.boatus.com/hurricanes/hurr_prep_guide.pdf. Scary photos and a full discussion of strategies.

hurricane warning – issued by government weather services when sustained surface wind of 64 kn (BEAUFORT FORCE 12) or greater are expected to hit a coastal area within 24 hours or less. Even though winds may drop below 64 knots, a hurricane warning may remain in force when dangerously high seas or storm tides are possible.

HW, HWN, HWS – abbreviations for high water, high water NEAPS, high water SPRINGS. *See* LW, LWN, LWS.

hybrid-electric propulsion – *see* ELECTRIC PROPULSION.

hydraulic current – *see* CURRENT, HYDRAULIC.

hydraulic systems – these are generally reliable, as long as leaks don't develop. Check hose and piping connections, hydraulic rams, and other inspection points; carry spare hydraulic fluid of the proper type for the system. Hydraulic fluid is usually red or red-brown; if you see stains, there's a problem. The relevant ABYC Standard is H-30 Hydraulic Systems. *See also* STEERING SYSTEMS.

hydrofoil – some vessels, including high speed ferries, operate on foils, which are wing-like structures mounted on STRUTS under the hull that lift the vessel above the water. Hydrofoils can attain speeds of 45 or 50 knots. When the vessel is operating above the water she's in the non-displacement mode;

when she slows down and the hull is in the water, she's in the DISPLACEMENT MODE. The NAVIGATION RULES makes this distinction for NAVIGATION LIGHTS and other rules applicable to hydrofoil vessels.

hydrography, hydrographer – the study of the physical features of the seabed, the tides, currents, waves, and nearby land; a person who performs hydrographic studies. A hydrographic survey is conducted to make or update a chart, or for other scientific purposes.

hydrometer (rhymes with thermometer) – a device for measuring the specific gravity of the ELECTROLYTE (acid and water) in a lead-acid battery to determine the state of charge of the battery. *See* BATTERY TESTING.

hydrostatic release – a safety device used on LIFE RAFTS and EPIRBS. A hydrostatic release operates by water pressure; when it's submerged to 5-15 ft/1.5-4m the release opens, freeing the equipment attached to it. A hydrostatic release unit must be properly installed, inspected, and maintained according to the manufacturer's instructions. Some devices can be serviced, others are approved for a limited number of years. All crewmembers must understand how the device works, and the procedures for launching life rafts and EPIRBs. That's part of a good SAFETY CHECKOUT.

hygrometer (rhymes with thermometer) – an instrument that measures relative humidity. A "humidity meter." Some electronic barometers have a hygrometer feature.

hypothermia – occurs when a person gets cold and loses heat faster than the body can make it. It can occur when a person is exposed to cool or cold air, water, wind, or rain. Children and older adults are more susceptible to hypothermia than younger, healthy adults. Even when the air temperature is above 50° or the water temperature is above 60° someone can become hypothermic in as little as an hour, and much sooner when it's colder or windy. When a person is immersed in water the body loses heat faster than when not in the water. Hypothermia is an emergency condition that can quickly lead to unconsciousness or death if heat loss continues.

Early symptoms of hypothermia include:

Shivering, apathy, poor judgment, numb hands or fingers, slow reaction time, slurred speech, unsteadiness or loss of balance, and cold, pale or bluish skin.

Late symptoms include:

Weakness, sleepiness, confusion, abnormal behavior, stiffening of the muscles, slow pulse, shallow and slow breathing, shivering (may stop if body temperature drops below 90°F/32.2°C), the trunk of the body feels cold to the touch, and eventual loss of consciousness.

Medical treatment for hypothermia depends upon how severe it is. If the person is unconscious, having severe breathing difficulties or does not have a pulse, issue a MAYDAY call. Check for breathing and a pulse, start CPR if necessary. Handle the victim slowly and gently, as rough handling can affect the heartbeat.

- If hypothermia seems severe but not life-threatening, call for medical assistance.

• Put the person in a bunk and elevate the feet.

• Remove all wet clothing and get the victim into warm, dry clothes. Use warm blankets, warm, wet towels, hot water bottles, if available. Apply gentle warmth to the head, neck, chest, and groin areas, not the arms and legs. Do not rub the person's skin.

• Keep the victim warm for several hours or more. Once a victim has stopped shivering, using blankets does nothing to warm the person; gentle external heat is required.

• Give the person warm fluids if he/she is able to drink, but do not give alcohol. A beverage with sugar in it helps replace calories lost from hypothermia.

• If hypothermia is severe do not give fluids or food.

• Do not allow the person to move around, even if he/she says "I'm OK." Keep the person lying down in a comfortable position until medical help takes over or mild hypothermia is controlled.

Lifejackets, EXPOSURE SUITS, and IMMERSION SUITS can help prevent hypothermia and increase the time of SURVIVAL IN COLD WATER. If you're in the water use the HELP POSITION. If boating activities take you into cool or cold climates and waters be prepared to prevent and treat hypothermia.

Hz – abbreviation for HERTZ, a unit of frequency equal to one cycle per second. "Per second" is not used with Hz.

- I -

IALA–AISM – abbreviation for the International Association of Marine Aids to Navigation and Lighthouse Authorities, which is a non-governmental technical association based in France. IALA works to "harmonize aids to navigation worldwide, and to ensure that the movements of vessels are safe." The website has links and informative articles, including a comprehensive *International Dictionary of Aids to Marine Navigation.* www.iala-aism.org. Click on "Publications."

IALA A or Region A – specific areas in the world where *green* buoys mark the STARBOARD side of channels when returning from sea (*green right returning*). Region A includes the Atlantic coasts of Europe and Africa, the Mediterranean, the Indian Ocean, and the areas in the western Pacific that aren't in IALA B.

IALA B or Region B – specific areas in the world where *red* buoys mark the STARBOARD side of channels when returning from sea (*red right returning)*. Region B includes the Atlantic and Pacific coasts of North and South America, the Great Lakes, the Caribbean, Japan, the Philippines, South Korea, and the Arctic to Greenland.

IALA buoyage system – *see* IALA A and IALA B.

IBS – abbreviation for INTEGRATED BRIDGE SYSTEM.

iceberg – ice broken off from a glacier; it's harder than SEA ICE. Ice reports define many types of icebergs.

This bergy bit is over 60ft/18m high.

A 35ft/10.6m sloop approaches a berg under power.

ice cover – in ice reports, the amount of the sea in an area that's covered with ice is expressed in tenths.

ice navigation – many skills are required, in addition to an appropriate vessel. A basic reference is the Canadian Coast Guard's *Ice Navigation in Canadian Waters*, along with information on Canadian Coast Guard websites. See the bibliography under "Navigation and Piloting" for a PDF download of an ice navigation document from the NGA. Ice Navigation is the subject of Chapter 33 in BOWDITCH. With the increasing interest in HIGH LATITUDE voyaging, books and articles aimed at recreational mariners discuss ice navigation.

ICW – abbreviation for the INTRACOASTAL WATERWAY.

idle, idle speed – the lowest RPMS when an engine is running. Idle speed is moving under power at the lowest rpms possible.

IHO – abbreviation for the INTERNATIONAL HYDROGRAPHIC ORGANIZATION.

"I'll see you on one" or "I'll see you on two" – these informal phrases are used on the radio by some professional captains of *power-driven* vessels operating on INLAND WATERS in the U.S. Under the Inland NAVIGATION RULES, VHF radio confirmation between vessels may be used instead of whistle signals. The words "one" and "two" refer to the SOUND SIGNALS that would normally be exchanged between two power-driven vessels in a HEAD-ON or OVERTAKING situation. "I'll see you on one" means "I intend to leave you on my PORT side." "I'll see you on two" means "I intend to leave you on my STARBOARD side." The proper response, if the other captain agrees, is "Roger, port to port" or "starboard to starboard." Even with agreement on the VHF, the vessels may also use sound signals, if they wish. If a recreational mariner uses radio contact when meeting or overtaking he/she should use the formal phrases "I intend to leave you on my starboard (or port) side."

immersion suit, survival suit – a watertight, full body flotation suit with hood and gloves that floats and protects the wearer in an ABANDON SHIP situation. Fishing and commercial vessels carry immersion suits, and recreational vessels operating in offshore or cold waters may also want to have them aboard. If you have a suit, practice putting it on, and try to do it in less than a minute. Sitting down and slithering into the suit works best. Put plastic grocery bags on your feet so they slide down the legs more easily. Store the plastic bags in the suit. The slang name is "Gumby suit" because the wearer looks like the Gumby cartoon character.

IMO – abbreviation for the INTERNATIONAL MARITIME ORGANIZATION.

impeller – a rubber or metal wheel with blades or vanes on it that moves liquids through a pump. Impellers are used in the RAW WATER and FRESH WATER pumps on an engine, electric bilge pumps, and other types of electric pumps. An impeller can wear out and blades or vanes can break off. If a broken piece gets into the engine cooling system it can cause a blockage. Check the engine raw water impeller once a season or if the engine starts to overheat. *See also* SPEEDSEAL.

impeller puller – a special tool used to remove an IMPELLER from a pump, such as the RAW WATER pump on the engine. They're available in several sizes. You may have removed an impeller with screwdrivers, but an impeller puller makes it easier, and it doesn't damage the pump.

impressed current system – a type of CATHODIC PROTECTION that uses electronic equipment to automatically control DC current to limit GALVANIC CORROSION. This equipment is expensive, and must be chosen carefully and installed properly. Seek competent professional advice. ABYC Standard E-2 Cathodic Protection discusses impressed current systems.

inboard – (1) a direction toward the CENTERLINE of the boat. OUTBOARD is away from the centerline. (2) an engine mounted inside a vessel.

inches of mercury, inHg – the reading of a MERCURY BAROMETER is expressed in inches of mercury. In the U.S., weather reports for the general public usually use inches. One inch of mercury is equivalent to 33.86mb. The average sea level barometric pressure is 29.92in/1013.25mb. *See also* HECTOPASCALS.

in extremis – when two vessels approach each other and the situation arises where *both* must maneuver to avoid a collision, the situation is described as *in extremis*. No matter whether the vessel is the STAND-ON VESSEL or the GIVE-WAY VESSEL, if a collision is imminent both vessels are obligated to take action to avoid collision. Rule 17(b) of the NAVIGATION RULES says:

> When, from any cause, the vessel required to keep her course and speed [the stand-on vessel] finds herself so close that collision cannot be avoided by the action of the give-way vessel alone, she shall take such action as will best aid to avoid collision.

In general, if vessels observe the Rules, *in extremis* situations may be avoided.

inflatable – a DINGHY, TENDER, or other boat made of rubberized fabric and filled with air. It can carry fairly heavy loads for its size. An inflatable is easy to stow when deflated, but it's not easy to row when it's breezy, and it can be

Time to take Fido, with his lifejacket, ashore.

damaged more easily than a boat made of solid material. An inflatable with a solid lower hull (and inflatable tubes above the hull) is a RIB (rigid inflatable boat). The military, rescue services, law enforcement agencies, and private companies use large, seaworthy RIBs. The relevant ABYC Standard is H-28 Inflatable Boats.

in irons, in stays – when a sailboat tries to TACK and loses forward momentum (WAY), the BOW may not pass through the wind. The boat won't fall off onto either tack and she's in irons or in stays. BACKING the jib may help bring the bow around. When a boat gets in irons she is said to have "missed stays."

injector – injectors deliver fuel to the engine's cylinders. They're precision devices that require clean fuel to operate properly; maintain the PRIMARY and SECONDARY fuel filters. Carry a spare injector in case one becomes inoperative. Check the ENGINE MANUAL or a technical resource for the recommended injector service interval.

Inland Navigation Rules: NAVIGATION RULES applied to U.S. waters which are inside (shoreward of) the DEMARCATION LINES. *See* INLAND WATERS.

inland waters – may be used to refer to lakes and bodies of water away from the seacoast. See the next entry.

Inland Waters – as defined in the U.S. NAVIGATION RULES, Inland Waters are the waters between the DEMARCATION LINES and the shore, and on the Canadian waters of the Great Lakes, where there is no conflict with Canadian law. "Inland" in this sense does *not* mean waters away from the sea, such as a lake or river. Some of the navigation rules for Inland Waters differ slightly from INTERNATIONAL RULES. Mariners operating in U.S. waters must know the International and Inland Rules, unless the vessel never ventures outside a demarcation line. If you don't operate in U.S. waters you don't need to study the Inland Rules (lucky you).

inlet – (1) an opening from the sea into a smaller body of water. Inlets may be natural features or man-made. Under some conditions entering or leaving an inlet can be difficult or dangerous. Strong currents may occur in inlets, and an onshore wind, especially against an outgoing current, can create dangerous conditions. In a storm it's safer, even if it's very uncomfortable, to stay at sea, away from the hazards of land, than to run into an inlet, seeking shelter. Looking into the inlet from the sea you may not be able to judge the conditions because you're seeing the backs of the waves. You can't see how high they really are or what happens as they are forced into the inlet. The troughs of the waves may be very close to the bottom, even if the depth on the chart looks adequate for your draft. Boats and lives have been lost when mariners decided to try and run an inlet. If in doubt, stay out. Don't let "PORT FEVER" influence your judgment. COAST PILOTS, NAUTICAL ALMANACS, and CRUISING GUIDES describe inlets and their known dangers. (2) an intake opening in a boat or equipment, such as a THROUGH-HULL inlet, a POWER INLET, a hose inlet on a pump, etc.

The ebbing tide meets 35 knots coming in, raising a short, breaking sea.

inlet, power – *see* POWER INLET.

Inmarsat, INMARSAT – acronym for the International Maritime Satellite Organization. This satellite communications company is part of the GMDSS system, providing distress and commercial communication services. It's a Broadband Global Area Network (BGAN). IRIDIUM satellite phones use these satellites. *See* the next entry.

Inmarsat-C SafetyNet – an internationally-adopted, automated satellite system that provides weather forecasts and warnings, navigation warnings, and other safety-related information to all types of vessels. It's part of GMDSS. There are no user fees for receiving SafetyNET broadcasts; you just have to have the equipment, which is somewhat expensive. National Weather Service SafetyNET broadcasts are disseminated using Inmarsat. For additional information about this system, including broadcast schedules see www.nws.noaa.gov/om/marine/inmarsat.htm. As the size and cost of Inmarsat-C equipment decreases, voyaging yachts are adding this equipment.

in-mast furling – a MAINSAIL that's FURLED or REEFED by rolling it up into the MAST.

inner forestay, staysail stay, baby stay – a STAY located between the HEADSTAY and the MAST. This stay goes part way up the mast. It's used as extra support for the mast, or a STAYSAIL or STORM JIB can be hoisted on it.

inoperative – term used in local NOTICES TO MARINERS and VHF radio navigation warnings to indicate that a navigation aid light or sound signal is not working at all. When the aid to navigation is fixed, the VHF radio announcement will say it's WATCHING PROPERLY.

inshore, inshore waters – a non-specific term used in general speech and in marine forecasts. The exact number of miles out from shore varies with a country. Many forecasts use the 12NM TERRITORIAL SEA limit. Check the website of the marine weather service for the definition, or the voice broadcast may specify the forecast distance.

inshore navigation – same as PILOTING.

in sight – Rule 3(k) of the NAVIGATION RULES says "vessels shall be deemed to be in sight of one another only when one can be observed *visually* from the other." If you can see another vessel only on radar or AIS, she's not in sight under the Rules.

inspected vessel – under U.S. Coast Guard regulations, COMMERCIAL VESSELS that carry more than six PASSENGERS FOR HIRE must be approved and inspected by the U.S. Coast Guard. A commercial vessel that does not carry more than six passengers doesn't have to be inspected. Small-vessel inspection rules apply to commercial vessels under 100 GROSS TONS. If you're thinking about part-time or full-time commercial activity with your power or sailboat contact the Coast Guard sector office in your area of operation. They have an informative "initial inspection checklist" for what must be done to qualify. Certifications for the number of passengers and area of operation vary based on the findings during the inspection process. The essential parts of the process involves:

Review of vessel design and drawings. This is the first step.

Compliance with specifications for construction and internal arrangement of the vessel.

Evaluation of stability and seaworthiness, including STABILITY TESTS.

Compliance with specifications for lifesaving and firefighting equipment.

Compliance with bilge pumping system requirements.

Having the required navigation aids aboard: paper charts, publications, electronic aids depending on area of operation.

DRY-DOCK inspections at specified intervals after certification.

Regular maintenance of safety equipment, as per the labels.

Having a captain (and crew, if required) that hold the appropriate USCG mariner license.

Permanently-moored commercial vessels, such as casinos and restaurant-barges, are not inspected.

inspection mirror – a small mirror mounted on a long handle that can be used to look into, around, and under things you can't easily see. It's especially useful for examining an engine to check for leaks in hidden areas.

inspection port – a hole in a tank or other part of the vessel, sealed with a cover, which can be removed to check the area behind the port. An inspection port in a tank has a liquid-tight cover. Inspection ports are used in fuel, water, or holding tanks, and for other inaccessible areas that require maintenance.

in stays – same as IN IRONS.

insurance, insurance agent, insurance broker – *see* MARINE INSURANCE.

integrated bridge system, IBS – an integrated bridge system is a combination of interconnected electronic systems, allowing a ship's bridge officers centralized access to multiple sources of data from the vessel's instruments. With improvements in small vessel electronics and the interconnection of navigation instruments, the concept of the IBS is becoming more prevalent aboard recreational vessels, where it may be called a MULTIFUNCTION DISPLAY. The performance standards for integrated bridge systems aboard ships are regulated by the IMO, which require, among many things, that if one part of the system fails the other parts will continue to operate. Standards for recreational vessels are not regulated.

intended track – *see* COURSE.

intercardinal points, intercardinal directions – northeast, southeast, southwest, northwest, which are between the cardinal points of north, east, south, and west.

intermediates – *see* SHROUDS.

intermediate stay, baby stay, inner forestay, staysail stay – a STAY ABAFT the HEADSTAY. It goes part way up the MAST.

internal ballast – ballast carried inside a vessel, rather than outside in a KEEL. Sailboats with internal ballast have a CENTERBOARD to perform the ballast function of a keel, improving LATERAL RESISTANCE and stability.

International Association of Lighthouse Authorities – *see* IALA.

International Association for Marine Electronics Companies, CIRM – represents the marine electronics industry worldwide, by developing standards and regulations, and providing technical resources for the industry. www.cirm.org.

international chart – *see* CHART, INTERNATIONAL.

International Code of Signals – a system of one, two, and three-letter signals for communicating visually, with sound or with radio communication. Each letter and combination of letters has a specific meaning, which is understood internationally by ships' officers and government agencies, such as rescue services. The letters are communicated by one or more of the following techniques:

With flag signals using CODE FLAGS.

With a flashing light or sound signals, using MORSE CODE.

With voice over a radiotelephone or a LOUD HAILER. The letters, spoken in the PHONETIC ALPHABET, can be used if there is a language barrier or excessive noise.

With signals made manually or with flags (SEMAPHORE SIGNALING).

Some NAUTICAL ALMANACS have a list of common one and two-flag signals. Having the complete code reference book aboard can be both useful and important on a yacht that travels across oceans. See the bibliography under "Miscellaneous" for a download and the book form of the publication.

International Date Line – 180° LONGITUDE, where the calendar day begins. Crossing the Date Line heading west, advance the date one day; when crossing on an easterly course put the date back one day. The Date Line is the boundary between the +12 and the -12 TIME ZONES, but the time is the same in these two zones.

International Hydrographic Organization, IHO – an intergovernmental organization, headquartered in Monaco, that supports navigation safety and protection of the marine environment. It has over 80 member countries. The objectives of the IHO are "to coordinate of the activities of national hydrographic offices to facilitate uniformity in nautical charts and documents, to encourage the adoption of reliable and efficient methods of performing hydrographic surveys and to encourage the development of the sciences of hydrography and descriptive oceanography." www.iho-ohi.net/english/home.

International Marine Certification Institute, IMCI – an EU-based organization for marine manufacturers, that assesses their compliance with relevant RECREATIONAL CRAFT DIRECTIVE (RCD) safety and quality standards. Manufacturers who enlist the services of IMCI can display the CE mark on products that are covered by the RCD. The IMCI has inspectors in North America (as well as many other countries) for manufacturers who market their products in EU countries. www.imci.org.

International Maritime Organization, IMO – a specialized agency of the United Nations with 169 Member States and three Associate Members. The IMO is based in London. Its mission is to ensure "safe, secure and efficient shipping on clean oceans." It regulates the outfitting and operation of most commercial vessels (except warships) engaged on international voyages. International standards and regulations adopted by the IMO affect recreational vessels in a variety of ways: GMDSS, SOLAS, changes to the NAVIGATION RULES, VTS, AIS, E-NAV, and other areas related to navigation and safety may apply to all vessels, large and small. www.imo.org.

International Navigation Rules – another name for the NAVIGATION RULES.

International Organization for Standardization, ISO – "the world's largest developer and publisher of International Standards." 162 countries are members of ISO. The headquarters are in Geneva, Switzerland. ISO has standards applicable to the marine industry. www.iso.org/iso/home.htm.

international port traffic signals – *see* PORT TRAFFIC SIGNALS, INTERNATIONAL.

International Sailing Federation, ISAF – the worldwide controlling authority for organized sailing in all its forms, racing and cruising, with 128 member organizations. It's based in Southampton, England. The primary goal of the ISAF is "to ensure that as many people as possible go sailing." As one of its functions, the ISAF issues rules and guidelines for offshore racing safety, which are also excellent guides for cruising sailboats venturing offshore. See www.sailing.org. *See also* OFFSHORE SAFETY.

International Telecommunications Union, ITU – the ITU regulates the worldwide use of the entire radio SPECTRUM to prevent interference and facilitate effective communication. There are three ITU Regions, which may have different SPECTRUM frequency allocations for various radio services. The ITU has established three VHF radiotelephone channels recognized worldwide for maritime safety purposes:

Channel 13 (156.650 MHz) - Intership navigation (BRIDGE-TO-BRIDGE).
Channel 16 (156.800 MHz) - Distress, safety, and calling.
Channel 70 (156.525 MHz) - DIGITAL SELECTIVE CALLING (DSC).

The ITU has designated five SINGLE-SIDEBAND DISTRESS FREQUENCIES for worldwide maritime distress communications.

International Waters – as defined in the U.S. NAVIGATION RULES, International waters are the waters to seaward of the DEMARCATION LINES on a chart. You can be in sight of land and be in International waters. Some of the U.S. waters to which the International Navigation Rules apply include the ocean waters off all of Cape Cod Bay, Vineyard Sound, Nantucket Sound, the rivers and bays of most of Maine, and the rivers and bays of Alaska and Puget Sound. Some navigation rules for International waters differ slightly from INLAND Rules. When operating in U.S. waters a mariner must know both the International and Inland Rules, unless the vessel never ventures outside a demarcation line or into waters which fall under the International Rules.

Internet weather forecasts – *see* WEATHER WEBSITES.

intertidal zone – the area of the shore that's underwater at high water and dries out at low water. Perfect for beachcombing and looking for creatures who inhabit the intertidal zone.

Intertropical Convergence Zone, ITCZ – the region near the equator where the northeasterly and southeasterly TRADE WINDS converge, forming an often continuous band of clouds or thunderstorms. The zone exists all year. The weather can be cloudy and squally, with thunderstorms and gusty winds. TROPICAL DEPRESSIONS may form here. Mariners call this area the DOLDRUMS because of its unpredictable weather patterns. Sailing vessels try to cross the ITCZ quickly so they aren't delayed by extensive calms. In the summer the ITCZ moves northward or southward some 270NM away from the equator. It is visible on satellite imagery or on a SYNOPTIC CHART surface analysis. See the next entry and SOUTH PACIFIC CONVERGENCE ZONE.

Intertropical Convergence Zone, Southern, SITCZ – The southern intertropical convergence zone is located between approximately 10°S to 3°S and 130°W to 90°W. It occurs only from March to May.

Intracoastal Waterway, ICW – a mostly inland waterway used by recreational and commercial vessels that runs along the U.S. east coast from New Jersey to Brownsville, Texas. Some parts of the ICW have open water and some are very shallow. There are CRUISING GUIDES specifically for the ICW. STATUTE MILES are used on the ICW.

inventory, vessel – *see* STOWAGE PLAN.

inverter – electrical equipment that changes the DC current from the batteries into ALTERNATING CURRENT so AC-powered equipment can be used aboard. There are small inverters that plug into a cigarette lighter to power small AC items or large inverters that are permanently mounted. For marine use, this equipment should be properly installed and meet ABYC Standard A-31 Battery Chargers and Inverters.

inverter-charger or charger-inverter – *see* BATTERY CHARGER-INVERTER.

Iridium® satellite communication – Iridium Communications, Inc. operates the world's largest commercial satellite constellation, with 66 satellites and a ground network. The company also provides equipment for worldwide maritime and land communication. Iridium telephones can be rented or purchased. Satellite telephones, while expensive, have few limitations compared with other forms of worldwide communication. www.iridium.com.

"Irish pennant"– refers to frayed strands on the end of a rope or loose, flapping lines. Heat-sealing and WHIPPING the ends of synthetic rope prevents fraying, and securing loose lines keeps things shipshape. Politically-incorrect term still in use, but probably not by the Irish.

Irish Sailing Association, ISA – the national governing body for recreational and competitive sail and power boating activities. The ISA promotes education and training for operators of all watercraft. The website has links to courses and course providers. www.sailing.ie.

ISAF – abbreviation for the INTERNATIONAL SAILING FEDERATION.

ISO – abbreviation for INTERNATIONAL ORGANIZATION FOR STANDARDIZATION.

isobar(s) – lines of equal atmospheric pressure drawn on a SYNOPTIC chart. Small numbers on the lines indicate pressures in MILLIBARS at 4mb intervals. The central pressure of a HIGH or a LOW can be estimated (within plus or minus 4mb) from the nearest isobar. More-curved isobars indicate an acceleration of wind. Straight isobars indicate relatively less wind than a curved isobar. Kinks in an isobar point away from the center of a low. A sharp kink indicates a sharp change in wind direction. In general, closely-spaced isobars indicate stronger winds because of the steep PRESSURE GRADIENT; however, wide spacing can also have strong winds. Learning how to interpret isobars and other features of synoptic charts is essential to become a proficient weather forecaster. *See also* GEOSTROPHIC WIND.

isobaric chart, constant pressure chart – a weather map (SYNOPTIC) that depicts conditions at a level where there is equal atmospheric pressure. For example, a 500-MB CHART shows conditions at the level of the atmosphere where the atmospheric pressure is 500mb.

isolation, electrical – not in contact with the vessel's BONDING SYSTEM or other metal parts of the vessel that are connected to the SHIP'S GROUND.

isolation transformer – *see* TRANSFORMER, ISOLATION.

isolator, battery – *see* BATTERY ISOLATOR.

isolator, galvanic – a device installed in the SHORE POWER GROUND conductor that permits AC to pass but blocks DC current to help prevent STRAY CURRENT CORROSION. The relevant ABYC Standard is A-28 Galvanic Isolators.

ITCZ – abbreviation for INTERTROPICAL CONVERGENCE ZONE.

ITU – abbreviation for the INTERNATIONAL TELECOMMUNICATIONS UNION.

- J -

jacklines – strong webbing, rope, or wire, affixed to strong attachment points, that runs along the deck from the BOW to near the STERN on PORT and STARBOARD. Clip a safety HARNESS TETHER to the jacklines, so that you're attached to the boat while moving on deck. If possible, run the jacklines inside the SHROUDS, rather than nearer the deck edge, to lessen the chance of going overboard with the tether attached to the jackline and you in the water. If you make jacklines use materials (webbing, rope or wire, SNAP SHACKLES, CARABINERS, and attachment hardware) that have a minimum 5,000lb/2,300kg breaking strength. UV rays damage webbing and stitching over time; cover the stitching with tape and replace jacklines if they're out in the sun a lot. There's no way to tell if a jackline has been weakened until it breaks.

jackstay – another name for a BABYSTAY or INNER FORESTAY. JACKLINES are not the same. See previous entry.

Jacob's ladder – a portable rope ladder used to board or disembark from a vessel.

jam cleat – a type of cleat with an open channel that has ridges in it to grip the rope, or a cleat with one horn that is lower than the other, into which the line is jammed to hold it. *See also* CAM CLEAT.

"jenny" – slang for GENOA.

jerry jugs – containers for water, fuel, or other liquids. They're available in metal or plastic. Jugs may be colored to identify a particular type of liquid, such as red for gasoline, yellow for diesel fuel, blue for water or kerosene (paraffin). Label the containers with permanent markings. Typical capacities range from one gallon/3.75 liters to approximately 6.5 gallons/25 liters. See GALLON/LITER, WEIGHT OF to determine how much a full jerry jug weighs, depending on what's inside.

jerry rig – incorrect usage of JURY RIG.

jetsam – anything thrown off a vessel or that washes up on the shore. FLOTSAM is sometimes used as a synonym.

jet stream, JSTR – an area in the upper atmosphere where strong winds blow in a narrow band. The position of the jet stream varies day-by-day, and terrestrial weather is related to the position and strength of the stream. TV weather reports often show the jet stream, especially when it is causing changes to the weather. You can also see it on 500-MB CHARTS.

jetty – a structure on wood, metal, or concrete pilings or made of stones or concrete that projects out from the shore. A jetty may serve as a BREAKWATER or a pier, and some INLETS have jetties at the entrance.

jib – a general term for a triangular sail set on the HEADSTAY or other stay forward of the MAST. A jib can roll up around the stay (a ROLLER-FURLING jib), or it may be attached to the stay with HANKS (snapped around the stay and hoisted with a HALYARD). If a boat has three jibs in her sail inventory, they may be numbered 1 (the largest), 2 (the middle size), and 3 (the smallest). There's no specific size indicated by the numbers. Jibs have different names, which vary somewhat between racing and cruising sailors. Some of the names include genoa, staysail, Yankee, blade, Solent, code zero, working jib, jib, storm or spitfire jib, and new names yet to be invented. See individual entries.

jib, 100%, 130%, etc. – the percentages indicate the area of the sail as a percentage of the FORETRIANGLE. Other numbers are used. A 100% jib extends AFT to the MAST; higher percentages overlap the mast. A 150% comes very far aft on the boat, to almost AMIDSHIPS in some cases. See the racing sloop photo with WEATHERCLOTHS.

jib, blade – a small jib that doesn't overlap the MAST. Some blade jibs are STORM JIBS.

jib boom – a small BOOM used on the FOOT of a jib, especially on a SELF-TACKING JIB.

jib, flying – a jib affixed only at the HEAD, TACK, and CLEW, and not attached to a STAY.

jib halyard – the line that hoists a jib.

jib, overlapping or "lapper" – a jib with an area larger than the FORETRIANGLE. It extends AFT, overlapping the MAST to some degree.

jib, self-tacking – a jib or STAYSAIL, usually with a short BOOM along its FOOT, that can be TACKED without tending the SHEETS. It may have a small TRAVELER or HORSE for its sheet.

jib sheets – the lines that control the angle of the jib to the wind. There are two sheets on most jibs, one for use on each TACK.

jib, Solent – a non-overlapping jib.

jib, spitfire – another name for a STORM JIB.

jib, staysail – a small jib set on a STAY between the HEADSTAY and the MAST. Usually just called a staysail (pronounced **stay** s'l). A CUTTER has a staysail.

jib, storm – a very small jib used in **HEAVY WEATHER** or storm conditions. Some storm jibs are made of red or orange sailcloth to enhance visibility at sea.

jib, working – the basic jib used in most conditions on a vessel that has more than one **HEADSAIL**. Yachts with a large sail inventory have names or numbers for types of working jibs.

jib, Yankee – a **HEADSAIL** that's set above and forward of a **STAYSAIL**. May be used on a boat with a **BOWSPRIT**. Sometimes used to refer to a **HIGH-CUT** non-overlapping jib.

A sturdy gaff-rigged Yarmouth 23 cutter with a Yankee jib. The roller-furling staysail isn't being used. Note the short bowsprit and bobstay.

jibe, jibing ("j" as in jump, rhymes with scribe, scribing) – (1) to change **TACKS** by bringing the **STERN** of the boat through the wind, to put the wind on the other side of the sails. The commands for jibing are "ready to jibe" (to the crew), and "jibe-ho" from the helmsman when he/she begins to turn into the jibe. **WEAR, WEARING** are older terms for jibe, jibing. (2) jibe is also used as a synonym for a **TACK (2)**: "We were on the port jibe all the way to Bermuda." (Also spelled gybe or gibe, and pronounced like jibe).

"jibe ho" – spoken when the helmsman begins to turn the boat into a **JIBE**.

Jubilee® clip – the name of a brand of HOSE CLAMP made in England, and used generically.

jumper struts, jumper stays, "jumpers" – short SPARS, STRUTS, or STAYS on the front of a MAST, located a short distance down from the masthead The struts hold the jumper stays out from the mast, to support the upper portion of the mast. Not all sailboats have these.

jury rig, jury-rigged – making a temporary repair with improvised materials and techniques. DUCT TAPE is frequently a component of a jury rig.

K

katabatic wind – *see* WIND, KATABATIC.

kedge, kedging – (1) to kedge or kedging is the process of moving a vessel with an anchor. Try kedging to free a boat that isn't too firmly aground. (2) a kedge is an anchor used for kedging; it's usually lighter in weight than the main anchor. *See* GROUNDING, SOFT.

keel – (1) the main structure on the CENTERLINE of a vessel, located at the bottom of the hull. It extends from the STEM to the STERN. (2) the FORE-AND-AFT BALLAST structure protruding beneath the hull that provides stability and reduces LEEWAY. Lead is used in many keels because of its weight. See the following entries for types of keels.

keel, bilge or twin keel – a SHALLOW keel located away from the CENTERLINE, toward the TURN OF THE BILGE. They're used in pairs: one to PORT and one to STARBOARD, and they're usually angled (canted) outward, so that they are somewhat vertical when the boat is HEELED on either TACK. Some small boats have three keels: a central one and two short ones on the port and starboard bilges. Because the keels are shorter than a regular keel, a bilge keeler can go into shallow or tidal areas, and she'll sit upright on her keels when the water goes out, and thus safely take the ground. For another photo see DRY OUT.

The bilge keels on this sailboat are canted outward and she has a spade rudder. The keels protect the rudder to some extent.

The bilge keels on this sailboat are vertical. The large skeg at the stern gives her three-point support.

keel bolts – the bolts that secure an EXTERNAL or ENCAPSULATED keel to the hull. Because the keel is an absolutely essential structural component of a MONOHULL sailboat, it's good if it doesn't fall off. On some yachts it's relatively easy to inspect the tops of the keel bolts and see if the nuts have loosened, if they're rusty, or if there's water seeping in around them. On some yachts getting to the tops of the bolts may involve removing structural items. If inspection indicates a potential problem, it's a big job to inspect the bolts themselves, but it must be done. Keel bolts can fail without warning, so regular inspection is essential. For an older vessel or after a hard GROUNDING a MARINE SURVEYOR may recommend a full inspection of the keel bolts. On a metal vessel the keel is usually welded onto the hull. If the keel falls off it can ruin your day.

keel, bulb – a streamlined BALLAST bulb mounted on the bottom of a relatively deep FIN KEEL. This keeps the ballast low and makes the boat STIFFER. Bulb keels are used on both racing and cruising sailboats.

The side view of a streamlined bulb keel.

The end view of a bulb keel.

keel, canting – a high-tech, movable keel found on some racing yachts and some cruising designs. The keel can be moved (canted) outward to counteract HEELING. Canting keels were developed for maxi ocean racing sailboats, where money is usually not a problem.

keel-centerboard – this design has two basic configurations: a LONG keel or a FIN KEEL with a CENTERBOARD. The keel houses the retractable board. The mechanism must be well-engineered and regularly serviced. The centerboard helps reduce LEEWAY, improving performance on the wind, and when retracted it allows access to shallow waters. This type of boat can DRY OUT in a tidal harbor (perhaps using short LEGS), and she's easy to store on land. The hull form is usually V-shaped, with a moderate beam. Because of the hull shape, a keel-centerboard boat has a more comfortable motion at sea than a boat with a flat hull form, and she'll HEAVE TO. The bilges are relatively deep, giving good storage. The keel protects the RUDDER if a grounding occurs, and lessens the chance of catching underwater ropes, nets, and debris. Some designs by Hinckley, Hood, and Shannon yachts, as well as other designers, are keel-centerboarders.

keel, deep or shallow – the adjectives deep and shallow refer to the vertical length of the keel (how much the keel projects downward from the hull). The deeper the keel, the STIFFER the boat, and the less LEEWAY she makes. Obviously, a deep keel restricts the depth of water the boat can navigate. Hauling and land storage may require special trailers and cradles if the keel is really deep.

A very narrow and deep bulb keel on *Pindar*, an Open 60 class ocean racer.

keel, encapsulated – a lead or iron keel (of any shape) that's secured to the hull with KEEL BOLTS and covered with fiberglass bonded to the keel material and to the hull. The goal is to prevent water from reaching the keel bolts via the hull-keel joint. An encapsulated keel is easy to maintain, but over time or if damaged, water can get in under the fiberglass and create problems. After a GROUNDING, inspect the keel and repair any damage to the fiberglass to prevent water entry. A **MARINE SURVEYOR** may recommend the inspection of the **KEEL BOLTS** after a severe grounding. See the next entry.

keel, external – a lead or iron keel (of any shape) that's secured to the hull with **KEEL BOLTS** and not encapsulated with a fiberglass covering. The joint between the keel and the hull must be kept waterproof to prevent water from reaching the keel bolts and corroding them. An external keel is relatively easy to maintain because all of it is visible for inspection. See previous entry.

keel, fin – fin keels come in many types: fairly wide or narrow, **DEEP** or **SHALLOW**, or with a **BULB** or **WINGS**. Many modern yachts have some type of fin keel. This type of keel facilitates easy maneuverability, but gives less **DIRECTIONAL STABILITY** than a **FULL** keel. A free-standing, unprotected **SPADE** rudder is usual with a fin. Some keels have a long or a short **SKEG** attached to the **AFT** edge of the fin, with the rudder attached to the skeg, which helps protect the rudder. The propeller shaft exits the hull **ABAFT** the keel, supported by a **SHAFT STRUT** near the end. The prop is unprotected, and underwater debris or lines can catch on it. The propeller stream acts directly on the rudder, so a fin-keeler is relatively easy to steer when going **ASTERN**. Some fin keel boats have **SAILDRIVE** propulsion, so there's no prop shaft. A boat with a narrow fin may be too unstable to **DRY OUT** against a wall in a tidal harbor. A deep fin keel boat requires a special cradle, trailer, or extra blocking when stored on land. See the photo with **KEEL, DEEP**.

A spade rudder and a narrow fin keel on a racing yacht. Note the prop shaft, shaft strut, and two-blade folding propeller forward of the rudder.

keel, full or long keel – this type of keel is a favorite of some long-distance sailors, because of **DIRECTIONAL STABILITY** in the seas. The keel extends from well forward to well **AFT**, and it may be **DEEP** or **SHALLOW**. The hull is V-shaped with a moderate beam. Older full-keel yachts have narrow beams. These hull forms make for a **SEAKINDLY** motion. The bilges are deep, with good storage. Full-keel yachts are usually, but not always, heavier than other similar-sized boats. The rudder attaches directly to the aft end of the keel, or to a **SKEG** at the aft end of the keel. The propeller shaft goes through the keel, which protects the shaft, prop, and rudder. This type of yacht is less-maneuverable than a **FIN KEEL** boat, and she's not easy to maneuver when going **ASTERN** under engine. A long-keeled boat easily **HEAVES TO**. The long keel allows the boat to stand firmly when **DRYING OUT** against a wall in a

A full-keeled yacht on the marine railway. The outboard rudder has an aperture cut into it for the propeller.

tidal harbor, or when stored on land. Some examples of full-keeled yachts include designs by Camper and Nicholson, Cheoy Lee, Colin Archer, Island Packet, Pacific Seacraft, Rustler, Tayana, Valiant, as well as many others.

keel, lifting or swing keel – depending on the type, a lifting keel may either be raised up into the boat or swung back. These boats don't have a regular keel; most or all of the ballast is in the deep, lifting keel. An electric or hydraulic mechanism raises and lowers the keel. It must be well-designed, engineered, and carefully maintained. The deep keel gives good performance on the wind, while allowing access to shallow water when the keel is up. With the keel raised, this boat can easily dry out in a harbor and be stored on land. A lifting keel boat may have two short rudders; or kick-up rudders. The basic hull form of a lifting keel boat is relatively flat, with shallow bilges. In addition to custom designs, some models of Alubat, Beneteau, Delphia, Jeanneau, Ovni, and Southerly yachts have lifting keels. As the technology improves and becomes more affordable this type of keel may be seen more frequently on cruising yachts that visit shallow waters.

A 75ft/23m luxury ocean cruiser/racer with a lifting keel. In the raised position (as shown here) she draws 9.5ft/4.4m. With the keel lowered her draft is 14ft/4.9m. The yacht is *Bella Pita*, designed by Bill Tripp Associates.

keel, long – *see* KEEL, FULL.

keel, long or short – the adjectives long and short usually refer to the FORE-AND-AFT length of the keel, but also may refer to the vertical length of the keel. Context should show which is intended.

keel, shallow – *see* KEEL, DEEP OR SHALLOW.

keel-stepped mast – *see* MAST, KEEL-STEPPED.

keel, twin – *see* KEEL, BILGE.

keel, winged – a FIN keel with short horizontal wings on the bottom. There may be extra ballast in the wings, similar to a BULB keel. The wings help counteract LEEWAY when sailing UPWIND, and allow for a shallower DRAFT. This keel can take the ground in a DRYING HARBOR, but if it gets stuck in a GROUNDING it

A ballast bulb winged keel, viewed from astern.

A ballast bulb with small wings at the aft end.

The aft end of a winged ballast bulb.

may be difficult to free. Winged keels are used on some **PERFORMANCE CRUISERS** and racing sailboats.

keeping station – same as **STATION-KEEPING.**

kellet – another name for a **SENTINEL.**

ketch – a type of sailing vessel that has two masts, with the **AFT** mast (the **MIZZEN** mast) shorter than the **MAIN MAST**. The mizzen mast is located forward of the **RUDDER POST**. A **YAWL** has a mizzen, but it's located **ABAFT** the rudder post. It's not always easy to tell where the rudder post is; the definition reflects a technical distinction.

A gaff cutter ketch (a former fishing vessel) overtakes a small sloop.
The mizzen is sheeted to a boomkin projecting from the stern.

key – (1) the button on a radiotelephone microphone that is depressed and held to speak. It must be released to hear the other station (people forget!). When the key is depressed static is heard by other stations; release the key while you're thinking. (2) to key or keying is the act of pressing the button on a microphone. (3) alternate spelling of cay, a low flat tropical island or series of islands; such as Deadman's Cay.

"kicking strap," "kicker" – slang names for a **VANG.**

kilo – (1) prefix for 1,000. (2) short form of kilogram (2.2 lbs.).

kilogram, kg – the metric weight of 2.2 lbs.

kilohertz, kHz – 1,000 Hz. *See also* **MEGAHERTZ** and **GIGAHERTZ.**

king plank – on a yacht with a planked wooden deck (or a real or simulated teak overlay) the king plank is the plank along the CENTERLINE into which the other planks are fitted.

A varnished king plank on a bare teak deck.

king spoke – the spoke of a steering wheel that's at the top of the wheel when the RUDDER is centered. It's usually marked in some way, with tape, string, or a decorative knot, such as a TURK'S HEAD. A hydraulic STEERING SYSTEM wheel doesn't have a king spoke, but the vessel may have a RUDDER POSITION INDICATOR. *See* RUDDER, CENTERING.

"kite" – slang for a SPINNAKER or other light air sails. "Ken was flying the kite when the HALYARD broke."

knees, hanging knees – structural features used between the deck frames and the hull to strengthen the joint between the hull and deck.

knockdown – (1) refers to a vessel being tipped onto her side by the action of strong winds and/or waves so that the deck edge almost touches the water. A 90° knockdown puts the MAST in the water. A 360° knockdown is a ROLLOVER (eek!). A minor knockdown can cause damage, and injure crewmembers. A 360° may dismast the vessel, along with other serious consequences. Fortunately a severe knockdown is rare, and extreme conditions are usually required to produce it. If you dare, see PITCHPOLE. (2) name for an very strong gust or KATABATIC WIND.

knot(s), kn (singular and plural)– (1) a unit of speed that equals one nautical mile per hour (approximately 1.15 statute miles per hour). The words "per hour" are never used with the word knot. "Our speed is eight knots." (2) a general term for a knot, BEND, or HITCH used when working with ropes. *See* KNOTS, BASIC.

knot meter, knotmeter – another name for a SPEED LOG.

knots, basic – the basic knots a mariner should know how to tie quickly, correctly, and in the dark include the **BOWLINE, BLOOD KNOT, CLEAT HITCH, CLOVE HITCH, FIGURE EIGHT KNOT, ROLLING HITCH, ROUND TURN AND TWO HALF HITCHES, SHEET BEND**, and **SQUARE KNOT**. *See also* **KNOT TYING**.

A bowline. Note that the tail is inside the loop. If it's outside the loop, the knot is incorrectly tied.

A blood knot, one type of stopper knot.

A figure eight knot, another stopper knot.

A cleat hitch.

A clove hitch (L) and a slipped clove hitch (R). Both types are commonly used to tie fenders to the lifelines, and they can be used to tie a line to any round object.

The blue line is tied on the white line with a rolling hitch. The blue line should be pulled to the right, *parallel* to the white rope. The hitch is used to pull laterally on a rope or round object, for example, when clearing a winch override.

A round turn and two half-hitches. Take the line twice around the object and finish with two half hitches. This hitch is good for tying dock lines to pilings or a line to a round or square object.

A sheet bend. It's used for tying two lines of different diameters, as well as ropes of the same diameter. It's more secure than a square knot. A sheet bend can also be tied around an eye splice or a bowline; in which case it's called a becket bend.

A square knot (bottom) and a slipped square knot. Both types are used with reef pendants or for joining two lines of the same diameter.

knots, decorative – these knots have occupied sailors' free time for centuries. Many decorative knots are also useful: use a Turk's head to mark the KING SPOKE on a steering wheel or to make a nautical bracelet; add gripping power to a TILLER, steering wheel, or BOATHOOK, with FRENCH HITCHING or COACHWHIPPING; use a decorative pattern for the rope on a bell clapper. Basic books on MARLINSPIKE SEAMANSHIP usually have some decorative knots. If you get really hooked on knots, check out the classic *Ashley Book of Knots* (see the bibliography under "Lines" for the complete citation).

knots, sailors' – many different types. The common attributes of these knots are (1) they should be easy to tie. (2) they should suit the intended uses. (3) they should be secure. (4) they should be able to be untied relatively easily after being subjected to a strain. *See* KNOTS, BASIC.

knot strength – any knot in a rope decreases the overall strength of the rope because a knot distorts the rope fibers, and they may cut into each other. Ropes can break at a knot, unless some other area of the rope is weak. A knot reduces the BREAKING STRENGTH of a rope, and in critical applications this may be an important consideration. For example, a BOWLINE reduces the strength of the rope to approximately 60% of the breaking strength, and a SHEET BEND to approximately 50%. *See* ROPE, SAFE WORKING LOAD; SPLICES, TYPES OF and KNOTS, BASIC.

knot tying – (1) learn basic knots. (2) when tying a knot "dress" it by keeping its shape until it's drawn up tight. (3) learn knots beyond basic ones that are useful on your boat. (4) practice: unless you use a knot frequently you'll forget how to tie it.

knot tying websites – one of the best is www.animatedknots.com. It's very comprehensive, has animations that show how to tie the knots, and offers downloads and a CD. There are knots for all sorts of non-nautical applications as well. There's even a phone app!

A bell rope on a fishing vessel. Perhaps the fish will jump aboard to see this fine example of marlinspike seamanship.

L

labor, laboring – to PITCH and roll heavily in rough seas, making little HEADWAY. When a vessel labors she also WORKS. "We were making slow progress, laboring in the CROSS SEAS and strong wind."

ladder – term for any type of stairs aboard a vessel; the COMPANIONWAY ladder.

ladder, boarding – *see* BOARDING LADDER.

lagoon – a body of water separated from the sea by land or an ATOLL. It may have an entrance (a PASS) or be completely enclosed.

laid rope – *see* ROPE, LAID.

laid up – synonym for DECOMMISSIONED.

LANBY – acronym for LARGE NAVIGATIONAL BUOY.

land breeze, offshore breeze – a breeze that blows from the land toward the sea. A land breeze generally occurs at night when the land cools and the sea is warmer than the land.

landfall – the first sight of land after an offshore passage. The PASSAGE PLAN should include details about the expected landfall and nearby alternate ports or harbors. A landfall is always a special event. Yes, you can shout "Land ho!"

landlubber – a person who isn't SEAMANLIKE aboard a vessel, either through lack of experience afloat or not making an effort to learn how to do things properly. Examples of some landlubberly actions are "elbow wrapping" rope or electrical cable, tying a line to a CLEAT with a heap of wraps, leaving loose ropes lying around on deck, not stowing things properly and securely below decks, and not bothering to learn any nautical vocabulary.

Lanocote® – brand name of ANHYDROUS LANOLIN, used as a water-excluding lubricant and ANTI-SEIZING product on fasteners and threaded parts.

lanyard – a short, light line for tying or holding something. Tie a hat on with a lanyard, or use one to a attach a knife or small tool to your wrist or belt.

lanyard, neck – any neck lanyard worn aboard, including hat lanyards, should be made of very low-strength string (not cloth webbing or line) so it will break easily if it gets caught on something. Breakaway lanyards (with a "weak link") are available. Better yet, use a collar clip on a short line for a hat lanyard.

"lapper" – slang term for a large JIB that overlaps the MAST.

large navigational buoy, LNB, LANBY – a buoy much larger than a typical navigation buoy, located in open water near major ports. It's approximately

A large navigational buoy awaits repair.

40ft/12m in diameter and height, and, in addition to a powerful light, it has other aids such as sound signals, AIS, or RACON. LNBs have replaced LIGHTSHIPS.

large-scale chart – a chart that shows a small area in more detail. *See* CHART SCALES.

lash, lashings – (1) to tie tightly with light or heavy line. "Lash the extra fuel containers to the STERN rail." (2) lashings are, logically, the lines used to lash. See the photo with SEIZE.

LAT – abbreviation for lowest astronomical tide. *See* CHART DATUM.

lateral mark – a navigation aid that indicates the PORT or STARBOARD side of a channel or the safe side for passing a hazard. The meaning of lateral marks is different in the two IALA REGIONS.

lateral plane – *see* STABILITY, DIRECTIONAL.

lateral resistance – resistance to sliding sideways while sailing; resistance to making LEEWAY.

lateral significance – term applied to buoys that indicate a particular side of a channel or the safe side for passing a hazard. If a buoy has safe water all around, it has no lateral significance.

lateral stability – *see* STABILITY, LATERAL.

lateral system of buoyage – a system where the shape, color, and/or numbers on a buoy indicate the preferred side of a channel or the safe side to pass a danger. *See also* CARDINAL SYSTEM OF BUOYAGE.

latitude – the distance from the equator measured in degrees, minutes, and seconds north or south from the equator. Latitude lines are called parallels. Latitude is measured on the scales at the sides of a nautical chart. One minute of latitude equals one NAUTICAL MILE. On a SMALL-SCALE CHART, use the part of the latitude scale nearest your area of operation to measure distances. *See* LONGITUDE.

Law of the Sea – short name for the United Nations Convention on the Law of the Sea, also called the Law of the Sea Convention, or the Law of the Sea Treaty. It's an international agreement that defines the rights and responsibilities of nations in their use of the world's oceans. The Law of the Sea also establishes guidelines for protecting the environment and managing marine natural resources.

lay, to lay – (1) to achieve a desired course and pass a location or aid to navigation without having to TACK. A synonym for FETCH (2). "We can lay that course if the wind doesn't VEER any more to the east." (2) to plan or follow a course. "Let's lay a course for St. Michael's." (3) command to the crew to go somewhere: "lay forward" or "lay aloft." (4) the lay is the direction the strands are twisted in THREE-STRAND rope (or other laid rope): right-hand lay and left-hand lay. All the laid rope in the photos in this book is right-hand lay. A rope is un-laid when the strands of rope are separated for splicing. There are two types of lay: hard and soft. A hard-laid rope is firm to the touch, and it resists snagging and holds knots and splices better than a soft-laid rope.

lay up, layup –(1) to lay up is to store the boat ashore or to DECOMMISION. (2) layup refers to the methods used by boat manufacturers to build a fiberglass hull.

lazarette – a storage LOCKER at or near the STERN of a vessel.

lazyjacks – a system of light lines running from the MAST to the BOOM, designed to catch and control a conventional MAINSAIL as it's lowered, so it doesn't fall off the boom See the photo with TRANSOM, TRADITIONAL.

lazy sheet – for a sail with two SHEETS, such as a HEADSAIL, the lazy sheet is the one that's not in use on a particular TACK.

LCD – abbreviation for liquid crystal display, used for some radar screens, and for many flat-screen TVs.

leach – incorrect spelling of LEECH, when used to refer to that part of a sail.

lead (rhymes with need) – a fracture or passage through ice that's navigable by a vessel. A shore lead is a passage between the shore and pack ice, or between pack ice and an ice cliff or ice wall.

lead, leadline, hand lead (pronounced led) – a small-diameter rope, marked in feet, meters, or FATHOMS, with a lead or bronze weight (the sounding lead) on one end, used to measure the depth of the water. A rock or other object of approximately two pounds tied to a marked line can be used as a substitute, lacking a proper leadline. A real sounding lead has a cavity in the bottom that can be filled with grease or other sticky substance (a process called ARMING THE LEAD) to bring up a sample of the bottom. Taking soundings with a leadline is "swinging the lead" or "casting the lead." The person swinging the lead is the leadsman. When exploring a shallow area, tie a light leadline of perhaps 10-15ft/3-5m to a long BOATHOOK and have a crew member stand on the BOW, taking soundings ahead of the boat, as you move very, very slowly; an economical alternative to FORWARD-LOOKING SONAR.

A simple leadline with cloth markers. Note the cavity in the bottom of the weight for arming the lead. The rope is 3/8"/10mm, which is easier to grip than a smaller-diameter line.

leading lights – another name for a RANGE. The term applies to any range, lighted or unlighted. "There are leading lights at that harbor."

leading line – a RANGE line printed or drawn on a chart.

leak test, leak check – test all connections in a PROPANE or other gas system with a commercial leak test solution or a solution of soapy water. Apply the solution to all connections; if bubbles appear, there's a leak.

learning to operate a boat – you can learn to do this at any age. Children as young as four participate in junior sailing programs, and people in their 80s take learn-to-sail courses. Whether you're interested in sailboats or powerboats there are many ways to learn. Certainly, a knowledgeable friend or family member can teach you, but many people learn best if they take a basic course on the water, and continue with more courses if they like it. There are programs for all levels: for someone who's never been on a boat to experienced sailors who want to learn new skills. There is on-the-water training, Internet and classroom instruction, courses for women, for couples, and instruction offered on your own boat. Some instruction is free. As you gain experience you may decide to take a cruising course, which combines cruising, living aboard, and learning, usually in an interesting location. Check sailing and powerboat magazines, a local yacht or boat club, and research on the Internet. If you're brand new to the water, take a basic course first. See SAFE BOATING COURSE, U.S. COAST GUARD AUXILIARY, U.S. POWER SQUADRON, and www.boaterexam.com for U.S. and Canadian basic courses. *See also* LICENSE, BOATING.

"leave it to port" or "leave it to starboard" – phrase used to tell someone how to pass an aid to navigation, a hazard, or another vessel. These phrases are more accurate than "pass it on port" or "pass it to starboard," because of the implication of the port side of a vessel or the aid to navigation (which doesn't have a PORT or STARBOARD side). "Leave it to port" and "leave it to starboard" is more precise.

LED – abbreviation for light-emitting diode. An LED light doesn't have a filament; electric current makes the diode light up. LEDs are used for small indicator lights, flashlights, headlamps, cabin lights, and increasingly in NAVIGATION LIGHTS. LEDs use much less power and have a significantly longer life than a filament bulb. LED navigation lights and substitutes for filament bulbs are available, but they're more expensive. To replace a filament bulb in a navigation light, make sure the LED meets the technical specifications for visibility as stated in the NAVIGATION RULES. The LED manufacturer should specify in the advertising material if the LED complies. Research this technology to see if it's right for your boat.

ledge – flat, rocky underwater areas with deeper water to seaward of the ledge An anchor may not hold on a ledge, or if it holds temporarily the anchor may later drag off the ledge into deeper water.

lee, in the lee – away from the wind, DOWNWIND, or sheltered from the wind. The side of the boat opposite the wind is the lee side. However, the wind blows *toward* a LEE SHORE.

leeboards – large, hinged external flaps mounted PORT and STARBOARD AMIDSHIPS along the hull of a sailing vessel to serve as a substitute for a KEEL. The leeboard is lowered into the water as the boat sails. They're used on boats designed for shallow waters, such as the traditional Dutch barge boat or the Thames sailing barge. A few modern TRADITIONAL yacht designs have leeboards.

A leeboard amidships on the port side of a modern ketch with raked masts.

A leeboard on the starboard side of a traditional Dutch Lemsteraak. Her draft with the leeboards up is approximately 20in/0.5m; with the boards down it's between 3.2ft/1m and 6.2ft/1.8m. These former fishing vessels have good sailing qualities and are built today for cruising and racing.

lee bowing (bowing rhymes with **now-**ing) – sailing CLOSE-HAULED with the current on the LEE BOW, to gain a little extra distance to WINDWARD. The effect is most noticeable with a strong current. See the bibliography under "Sailing" for a contrary opinion. Lee bowing is not the same as "lee bow," which is a sailboat racing tactic, where a TACK is executed ahead and to LEEWARD of an oncoming boat, when the boat can't cross legally under the racing rules.

leech – the AFT or trailing edge of a triangular or GAFF sail; the side of a sail opposite the LUFF. *See* SAIL, PARTS OF. Sometimes spelled incorrectly as "leach," which bothers the spelling police.

leech line – some sails have a light line sewn in a cloth seam along the LEECH that's used to adjust the curvature of the leech or to stop it from flapping.

lee cloths – pieces of fabric (approximately 6ft/2m long by 3ft/1m wide) used on the BUNKS to prevent a crewmember from falling out when HEELED or in rough weather. One long edge of the lee cloth is permanently attached to the wood or fiberglass under the outer edge of the bunk cushion, and the other edge has GROMMETS and lines to tie it up to a BULKHEAD or the OVERHEAD. Some boats have BUNK BOARDS instead of lee cloths.

lee helm – the tendency of a sailboat to turn away from the wind (fall off) when the wind is gusty or when the HELM is released for a moment. Lee helm may be a natural tendency of the boat or it can be created by the sail trim. Lee helm is more of a concern than WEATHER HELM, because when the boat falls off in a gust the boat may heel more sharply; with weather helm the boat ROUNDS UP and spills wind from the sails.

"lee-ho" – same as "HARD LEE." Some people say "lee-oh," which is OK unless there's a crewmember named Leo.

lee side, lee rail – the side of the boat away from the wind; the outer edge of the deck (the rail) on the lee side.

lee shore – the DOWNWIND or LEEWARD shore. The wind blows *toward* a lee shore. Being close to a lee shore when at anchor or underway may be dangerous. For example, if the wind or waves increase, a vessel can be driven aground or onto the shore, if sail or engine power are unable to move the boat away from the shore ("claw off") into safer waters. A prudent skipper keeps this in mind when approaching a lee shore. A WEATHER SHORE is the opposite of a lee shore. *See* EMBAYED.

lee tide – a current that is flowing in the same direction as the wind.

leeward (pronounced **loo**'urd) – the direction away from the wind. The opposite of WINDWARD. *See* WEATHER, TO.

leeway – the amount a boat slides sideways along an intended COURSE due to the effect of wind, current, or waves.

leg, legs – (1) a single TACK, COURSE, or a portion of a PASSAGE. (2) wood or metal supports LASHED or bolted to a boat at the TOE RAIL area near AMIDSHIPS to support her when she DRIES OUT (takes the ground intentionally in a tidal harbor). The legs are long enough to reach from the bottom of the KEEL to the deck level or above. Boats that cruise in areas where harbors dry out may carry a special set of legs created for the vessel. (3) "long legs" is slang for having a DEEP KEEL. "Andrew's boat has long legs."

Legs port and starboard allow this fin-keeled sailboat to take the ground in a drying harbor. The legs attach to special fittings on the hull.

leisure chart, small craft chart – charts designed for recreational mariners. *See* CHART, SMALL CRAFT

length on deck, LOD – the length of a vessel measured along the CENTERLINE of the deck from the tip of the BOW to the end of the STERN, *excluding* any projections at the bow or stern. See the next entry.

length overall, LOA – the length of a vessel measured along the CENTERLINE *including* any structural projections at the bow and stern (such as a BOWSPRIT, stern platform, or DAVITS). The length of a vessel with bow and stern projections is described by two measurements: the LOA, which includes the projections, and the length on deck. A marina asks for the LOA of a vessel to assign a proper-length berth.

length on the waterline, LWL – the length of a vessel along the CENTERLINE, from BOW to STERN, as measured at the waterline level. LWL may also mean LOAD WATERLINE. The speed of a vessel is related to the length of the waterline: *see* SPEED/LENGTH RATIO FORMULA.

license – in many countries a license issued by a government authority may be required for (1) a vessel operator. (2) a radiotelephone operator. (3) a ship's radio station. Outside U.S. waters operator license requirements may apply to all boaters on specific waters, such as canals, or ocean waters. There is a trend toward governments requiring operator licensing or certificates of competence. *See* CERTIFICATE OF COMPETENCE, INTERNATIONAL, CEVNI and the individual entries under LICENSE.

license, boating, Canada – all Canadian operators of powered recreational vessels (including those with electric motors) must have a Pleasure Craft Operator Card (PCOC), and there are fines for not having the card with the operator. The CANADIAN POWER AND SAIL SQUADRONS offers a certification course, which may be taken online: see www.boaterexam.com/canada.

license, boating, U.S. – the states may require some or all operators of recreational power, sail, or PERSONAL WATERCRAFT to have a boating license or certificate. Check with your state's boating authorities or the U.S. POWER SQUADRON website (www.usps.org) for license laws and boating safety certification requirements. Another website that has the requirements for all U.S. states and Canada, and several ways to learn and get certified is www.boaterexam.com. For a free online course that may meet your state's requirements also check www.boatus.org. State requirements do not apply to boat operators who are not residents of the U.S.

license fees, U.S. – in the U.S. the FCC charges a fee for a Restricted Radiotelephone Operators Permit, and for renewing or applying for a SHIP STATION license. A ship station license is valid for ten years. The RRO Permit is good for your lifetime. *See* LICENSE, RADIOTELEPHONE OPERATOR, U.S. and the other license entries, below.

license, radar – a license is not required for radar on U.S. vessels that navigate only in U.S. waters. *See* LICENSE, SHIP STATION, U.S. VESSELS.

license, radio operator, Canada – the Canadian government requires that Canadians who use a marine radio have a Restricted Operator Certificate (Maritime). Everyone who uses a VHF or other marine radio must have an ROC(M). There are fines for operating without the card. If you have a card issued before DSC radios became universally available, the CANADIAN POWER AND SAIL SQUADRONS encourages you to get a DSC endorsement for your certificate. For a summary of Canadian radio operator licenses, see the Canadian Power and Sail Squadrons website at www.cps-ecp.ca, and the bibliography under "Radio."

license, radio operator, Ireland – any operator of a shipboard radiotelephone must hold a Restricted Operator Certificate (VHF only), or if the vessel has a VHF-DSC radio the operator must have a Short-Range Certificate, which includes exam modules 1 and 2.

license, radio operator, UK – licensing of UK marine radiotelephone operators is handled by Ofcom. The minimum required operator's license is the Short Range Certificate (SRC), which may be obtained by taking an approved course. This certificate covers the operation of VHF and VHF-DSC radios in GMDSS SEA AREA 1 (areas within range of VHF shore stations).The license is valid for a lifetime (unless it's revoked because of an actionable violation of communication laws and procedures.) Different requirements may apply to operators on COMPULSORY-EQUIPPED vessels or vessels that travel outside VHF range (Long Range Certificate required). See the bibliography under "Radio" for Ofcom licensing websites.

license, radio operator, U.S. – the FCC requires a Restricted Radiotelephone Operator (RRO) Permit for U.S. boaters who have a SINGLE-SIDEBAND TRANSCEIVER, and for boaters with a VHF radio who will visit FOREIGN WATERS. This permit is also necessary when a vessel is required by law to have a marine radio (vessels 20m/65.6ft or larger and other categories) There is no test to obtain the permit, but there is an FCC fee. The permit is authorized for the holder's lifetime. See the following entries.

license renewal, ship station, U.S. vessels – in the U.S. if you operate a vessel that is *not* required by law to license transmitting equipment (VOLUNTARY COMPLIANCE), and you have a current license for the equipment, you aren't required to renew this license when it expires, but you *may* renew the license and keep your call sign. If your U.S.-registered vessel will visit FOREIGN WATERS you *must* renew it.

license, ship station, Canadian vessels – Canadian vessels don't need a station license in Canadian waters, but if the vessel will travel to another country, including the U.S., a station license is required. The license is renewable annually. For a summary of Canadian ship station and operator licenses, see the CANADIAN POWER AND SAIL SQUADRONS website at www.cps-ecp.ca, and the bibliography under "Radio."

license, ship station, Irish vessels – an Irish-registered vessel with radio transmitting equipment must have a ship station license. This license is also required to register an EPIRB or PLB. Ship radio licenses are issues by the Department of Transport's Marine Radio Affairs Unit (MRAU).

license, ship station, UK vessels – Ofcom regulates the licensing of UK marine radio communication equipment, which includes MF, HF, VHF, and UHF radio, satellite communication equipment, radar, EPIRB, and SART. A ship station license does not expire (validate it every ten years), and it must be kept on the vessel. It's free if ordered online. A Ship *Portable* License is required for each hand-held DSC radio (because each DSC radio has a unique MMSI number). Failure to hold a valid license is a criminal offence, and the rules are enforced by Ofcom officers. See the bibliography under "Radio" for Ofcom licensing websites.

license, ship station, U.S. vessels – the FCC regulates the licensing of all wireless *transmitting* equipment in the U.S. Equipment that does not transmit (receive-only) doesn't require a license. U.S. recreational boaters who navigate *only* in U.S. waters can use a VHF radio (FIXED-MOUNT or handheld), AIS, an EPIRB, and marine radar without having an FCC ship station license. A license is not needed for an AIS *transmitter*, but an MMSI number is required. The following U.S.-registered vessels *must* have a ship station license:

- Vessels over 20m/65.6ft.
- Any vessel required by law to have a radio TRANSCEIVER.
- Any vessel that has a SINGLE-SIDED TRANSCEIVER or a marine satellite terminal.
- Any vessel that visits FOREIGN WATERS.
- If you travel to a foreign port, you are also required to have a radiotelephone operator's license, in addition to a ship station license. *See* LICENSE, RADIO OPERATOR, U.S.

• If you transmit radio communications *to* foreign stations from your vessel a ship station license is required.

The license is valid for ten years and is renewable. A ship station license cannot be transferred to another person or vessel; the license is specific to the vessel *and* the vessel's owner. A new owner can't modify your license, but must apply for a new license.

license, U.S. Coast Guard merchant mariner – captains and some crewmembers on certain U.S. vessels are required to hold a Coast Guard merchant mariner's license. Captains of passenger-carrying vessels (of any size or number of passengers), COMMERCIAL VESSELS, and towboats are examples of required operator licensing. A captain operating a vessel carrying six or fewer PASSENGERS FOR HIRE, must hold at least a "SIX-PACK" license. A yacht dealer or a sailing school may require USCG licenses for vessel operators and instructors. A MARINE INSURANCE company may require that a DELIVERY captain be licensed. Applicants for all classes of license must: (1) pass a government background check. (2) pass a physical exam. (3) pass a drug test. (4) have a prescribed amount of sea time, depending on the license desired. (5) pass a comprehensive written examination for the particular class of license. Non-U.S. citizens may apply for a merchant mariner license, but they must have a valid I.N.S. Alien Registration number. Some recreational mariners choose to obtain a USCG license for the learning experience, personal satisfaction, and because some marine insurance companies offer a discount to licensed mariners. For information about merchant mariner licenses see www.uscg.mil/nmc.

lie a-hull, lying a-hull – *see* A-HULL.

A heavy weather coxswain and boat crew from U.S. Coast Guard Station Monterey operate a 47-foot motor lifeboat in 10 to 13-foot swells. *U.S. Coast Guard photo by Petty Officer 3rd Class Erik Swanson*.

A motor lifeboat of the Norwegian rescue service, the Redningsselskapet.

lifeboat – (1) one or more specially-designed motorized boats carried by ships, intended for use when abandoning ship. (2) a specially-designed motorized rescue vessel, used by coast guards and rescue services. See ROYAL NATIONAL LIFEBOAT INSTITUTION for an RNLI motor lifeboat.

lifejacket – the U.S. and other countries have requirements for the number and types of lifejackets aboard a vessel, and who must wear them. When operating outside home waters observe the local requirements for wearing lifejackets. The U.S. Coast Guard requires U.S.-registered vessel to have a USCG-approved lifejacket for each person aboard, plus at least one approved throwable flotation device (float cushion, LIFE RING, etc.) on all vessels 16ft/5m or longer. There are many types of lifejackets available; select them carefully to meet your particular needs. If it isn't comfortable you won't wear it, so try it on in the store. Children and small adults require lifejackets sized for their body weight. Read labels on lifejackets, product literature, or marine equipment catalogs. Foam jackets are bulky but don't require much maintenance. Inflatable lifejackets are more comfortable, but they aren't suitable for non-swimmers, and they require periodic inspection and maintenance. Some general guidelines for lifejacket selection (the types are U.S. designations, but the usage descriptions apply to non-U.S. products):

Type I for offshore or rough, open water use. These jackets have more flotation than inshore jackets, and generally will turn an unconscious person face-up. They are bulky. For adults and children.

Type II for near-shore use in calm or inland waters. Some models will turn an unconscious person face-up in the water and some will not. For adults and children.

Type III for calm water activities; uses indicated on labels. Adult models only.

Type IV is a throwable device such as a float cushion, a life ring, or HORSESHOE BUOY.

Type V are special-use lifejackets and FLOTATION CLOTHING, which include boardsailing vests, EXPOSURE SUITS, float coats, work vests, INFLATABLE LIFE JACKETS with or without an integral HARNESS, and others. For use by persons at least 16 years of age.

If possible, test a lifejacket in shallow water or a pool. It should fit snugly and not ride up. Use crotch straps with some lifejackets, especially inflatables, and with children's lifejackets. A lifejacket may not support a person the same in rough water as in calm. If a jacket doesn't keep your mouth well above the water, you need one with more buoyancy. Follow the manufacturer's care instructions. A lifejacket won't help anyone if it's falling apart or it's stuck in the bottom of a locker. See the bibliography under "Safety" for websites.

lifejacket regulations – in addition to Coast Guard requirements, some states have specific regulations for who must wear a lifejacket and on what size vessel. If a state doesn't have rules, the Coast Guard rules apply. Some countries have strict lifejacket regulations for adults as well as children, including for riding in a DINGHY. Observe local regulations when visiting another country.

lifeline gate – a short section of LIFELINE, PORT and STARBOARD, that can be opened to allow easier access to the deck when coming aboard from a dock or DINGHY. Gates are usually locked closed with a PELICAN HOOK (or other secure safety hook). Lifeline gates should be closed when the crew no longer needs them for access, even at anchor, and certainly when underway. *See* the next entry.

lifelines, life rails, guard rails, guardwires – wires attached to STANCHIONS, or solid wood or metal rails that extend from BOW to STERN along the edge of the deck. TURNBUCKLES or LASHINGS keep wire lifelines tight. Many stanchions are quite short, and low lifelines aren't very effective in preventing someone from falling overboard. Also, stanchion bases may not be strong enough to take the weight of someone using the lifelines to help climb aboard or falling against them, or the base may pull out of the deck. Use caution when relying on lifelines and stanchions. Don't attach a safety HARNESS TETHER to lifelines or stanchions. The relevant ABYC Standard is H-41 Reboarding Means, Ladders, Handholds, Rails and Lifelines.

life raft – a safety device specifically designed for ABANDONING SHIP. Commercial and recreational vessels carry life rafts. They're made of coated, rubberized fabric, they inflate automatically when thrown into the water (or have a HYDROSTATIC RELEASE), and they must be inspected at regular intervals by a certified inspection station. Models are available for near-coastal use, offshore use, and for various numbers of persons. Rafts for use on COMMERCIAL VESSELS have different specifications. If stowage space on a yacht is limited consider a life raft packed in a soft case (a valise), but it's preferable to have a raft in a protective hard-shell case, mounted in CHOCKS where it can easily be deployed. Research brands, types, and unbiased evaluations of life rafts before renting or buying one. If properly cared for and regularly inspected a good life raft will last many years. As long as the raft passes the certification process, its age doesn't matter. Some life raft inspection companies will allow you to watch your raft being repacked; it's very instructive. Rafts come with a package of survival gear, but it's rather basic, even if it's called the "offshore package." Make up your own ABANDON SHIP KIT to supplement the raft's kit. An ocean-crossing yacht should have a comprehensive kit.

life ring, ring buoy – a circular flotation device to throw to a person in the water. The name of the vessel should be painted on it. It should be Coast Guard approved.

Lifesling® – equipment for use in a man-overboard incident, to recover and bring the victim aboard. It's used with one of the MAN OVERBOARD RECOVERY TECHNIQUES. There are several other brand names of this type of towed device.

light air – general term describing little or no wind, perhaps three to five knots. Light airs can be FLUKY.

light, anchor – *see* ANCHOR LIGHT.

light characteristic – *see* CHARACTERISTIC OF A LIGHT.

light float – a DOUBLE-ENDED boat-shaped navigation buoy occasionally used in areas with a strong current.

light, geographic range – *see* GEOGRAPHIC RANGE.

light list – a navigational publication which gives details about all the aids to navigation, lighted or unlighted, in a particular area or country. Government agencies publish light lists at various intervals, but not necessarily annually. The list includes additional important information which is too detailed to be written on a chart. In the U.S., light lists are the responsibility of the Coast Guard. They're available in seven regional volumes in paper and online at www.navcen.uscg.gov. Scroll down to "Maritime Information," click on "Nav Pubs and Documents" and follow the links. The Canadian List of Lights, Buoys, and Fog signals are available in four regional volumes, in paper and online at www.notmar.gc.ca. The UK Hydrographic Office (www.ukho.gov.uk) publishes worldwide light lists (paper only).

light list number – the aids to navigation in a LIGHT LIST are numbered sequentially. The first number of a light is the number used in the country that issues the light list. A second number, printed in italics, may also be given: this is the international number for the navigation aid as assigned by the IHO. Major aids to navigation may have two numbers.

light, nominal range – *see* NOMINAL RANGE.

lighthouses – these aids to navigation are generally considered to be the most reliable guides for the mariner, compared to floating aids, which may be damaged or missing from their locations. In some countries, the government agencies responsible for the maintenance of navigation aids have specific websites just for lighthouses. Historic information about U.S. lighthouses is available at www.uscg.mil/history/h_lhindex.asp. England, Scotland, and Ireland maintain websites with current specifications, photos, and historical information for all the lighthouses in each country or area.

Smeaton's Tower, 1749. Eroded over time by storm waves, in the 1880s it was moved stone by stone, from Eddystone Reef in the English Channel to stand on the shore at Plymouth Hoe, England. It was designed by civil engineer John Smeaton.

The Old Head of Kinsale lighthouse in Ireland, established in 1853, to replace a previous light established in 1814. *RMS Lusitania*, a Cunard ocean liner, was torpedoed 11 miles off this light in 1915, with the loss of almost 1,200 lives.

For England and Wales, including the Channel Island see www.trinityhouse.co.uk; Scotland and the Isle of Man: www.nlb.org.uk; Ireland and Northern Ireland: www.commissionersofirishlights.com. These websites are not a substitute for the information in a LIGHT LIST, but they are very interesting. Because most lighthouses are automated, many are are available for rent as vacation accomodations, usually with spectacular views.

The lighthouse on the breakwater at Whitby in England. It no longer has a light, but serves as conspicuous landmark for the harbor entrance.

The top of Sumburgh Head lighthouse, Shetland Isles, northern Scotland. Established in 1821, the engineer was Robert Stevenson, grandfather of Robert Louis Stevenson.

A lighthouse on the west coast of Norway. It's available for a vacation rental and comes with a boat because it's on a small island.

The red cap used on many Norwegian lighthouses and fixed navigation lights.

The lighthouse at The Needles chalk cliffs, established in 1859 on the south coast of England. The original lighthouse was built in 1786.

Auskerry Light in Orkney, northern Scotland. Engineered by David and Thomas Stevenson, it was established in 1866.

Beachy Head lighthouse on the south coast of England, established in 1904. The previous lighthouse was built in 1828.

lightning protection – in general, lightning protection is achieved by having a lightning rod (air terminal) or a STATIC DISSIPATER at the top of the mast, connected directly to an underwater GROUND plate. The protection system doesn't prevent a lightning strike, but is intended to conduct the strike current into the water, so it has less chance of damaging the vessel, her equipment and, most importantly, her crew. No lightning protection system can be considered 100% effective; if a boat is struck there can be serious consequences. Consult technical references for details about lightning protection systems. The relevant ABYC report is TE-4 Lightning Protection. It's a complex subject, with areas of disagreement among experts.

lightship, light vessel – an unmanned ship moored in an important location as an aid to navigation. It has strong lights, sound signals, AIS, weather observation equipment, and other automated aids to navigation. Most lightships have been replaced by LARGE NAVIGATIONAL BUOYS, but there are a few ships remaining at sea. Decommissioned lightships have become floating museums around the world.

A decommissioned lightship.

lights, navigation – *see* NAVIGATION LIGHTS.

lights, running – another name for NAVIGATION LIGHTS.

limber holes – holes in the FLOORS of a vessel that allow bilge water to drain to a central sump, thus preventing water from being trapped between the floors. Keep limber holes open.

line – the correct term for most cordage used aboard a boat. Lines have specific names that indicate their function, such as HALYARD, SPRING LINE, mooring or dock line, SHEET, etc. It's called "rope" when it hasn't been put to use, and "line" once it has a job. *See* ROPE, and ROPE, CARE OF.

A newly-installed scissors-type line cutter.

line cutter, rope cutter – a device installed on or near the prop shaft that cuts rope if it comes near the propeller, helping to prevent a **PROPELLER WRAP**. It's not a fool-proof device: it may not cut plastic sheeting or nets, and sometimes it doesn't cut the rope. However, most of the time it does its job. Rope cutters are used on yachts, commercial boats, and rescue vessels. There are three general types available:

One or more blades on the shaft or prop that cut against a fixed blade, like a scissors, such as Spurs ®, The Stripper™, and Gators. Tests have shown that a scissors-type cutter is more effective than a single blade cutter.

A single, round cutter blade mounted on the prop shaft, such as the PropProtector™ or Shaft Shark.

A device affixed to the propeller, between the prop and the **CUTLESS** bearing, with a cutter mounted on the hull or **SHAFT STRUT**. The device on the prop is intended to prevent the rope from wrapping around the shaft, and it feeds the rope into the cutter before it becomes entangled. QuickKutter™.

Most cutters can be installed on land without removing the prop. Many mariners consider a rope cutter to be an important safety device.

This scissors-type line cutter has been on the boat long enough for a few barnacles to grow.

line of position, LOP – a line PLOTTED on the chart along which a vessel is located. A RANGE or a BEARING establishes a line of position. Crossing a second line of position with the first, or applying a distance off to a LOP gives a FIX. An ESTIMATED POSITION may be determined by relating a line of position to depth SOUNDINGS.

line, parts of – the basic names for the parts of a line are the bight (any part of a line between the ends, or a loop in the line); the bitter end (the end attached to something); the standing part (the part of a line that's *not* used in making the knot, or the part around which a knot is made); and the working end (the part of the line that's used to make the knot). The words are used in knot-tying instructions.

line, roller furling – the line used on a ROLLER FURLING HEADSAIL must be strong enough to withstand the strain placed on it when the sail is REEFED by partially rolling it in, or when it's furled in strong winds. Inspect it, END-FOR-END it, and replace if damaged or old. Have a spare.

lines – the shape of a vessel's hull. A marine architect's drawing shows the lines. "*Pride of Baltimore* has beautiful lines."

line safety – *see* ROPE SAFETY.

lines, on her – describes a vessel that is floating evenly on her designed lines. "Now that we've moved all that extra chain out of the LAZARETTE she's on her lines."

lines, squeaking – some people say they like the sound of a squeaking dock line; to them it's "so nautical." But to others the sound can be quite annoying. To keep lines quiet put some dish-washing detergent on the line where it's rubbing on a cleat or CHOCK. Fill an old dish detergent bottle with 1/3 water and 2/3 detergent, and keep it handy to squirt on noisy lines. Rubber or cloth chafe guards may also stop the noise. Old, dry lines under strain squeak the most.

line stopper, stopper, rope clutch – a piece of deck hardware used to secure a line, but that's easily opened to release the line when necessary. Feed the rope through the hole in the front of the stopper and close the lever (a clamp) to hold it. Lift the lever handle to free it. Most line stoppers allow the line to be pulled in with the lever down. They're sized for a particular diameter of line. Put a STOPPER KNOT in the end of the line so it can't slip out. These handy items are used for HALYARDS and other CONTROL LINES on the MAST, and for lines led to the COCKPIT.

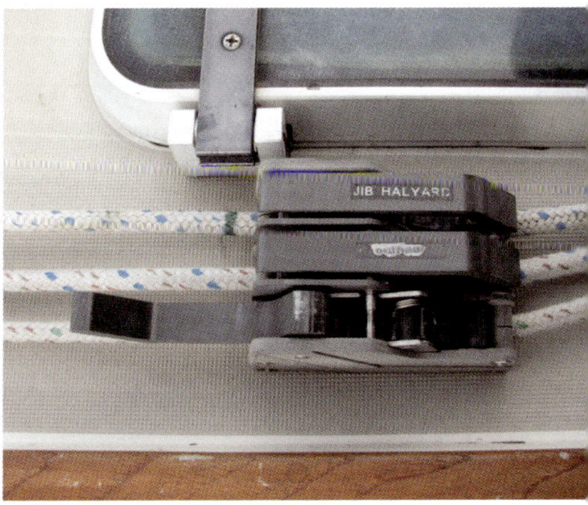

Three line stoppers for control lines led back to the cockpit. The bottom stopper is open (handle to the left). Different color ropes are used to make it easier to identify the lines.

list, listing – the angle a vessel leans to one side is a list, usually caused by uneven loading or cargo shifting. HEELING is caused by the wind.

liters to gallons – One liter is equal to 0.26 U.S. gallons, and 0.22 British (Imperial) gallons. One U.S. gallon is equal to 3.79 liters. One British (Imperial) gallon equals 1.2 U.S. gallons or 4.55 liters.

Lloyd's Register of Shipping, LR – a marine CLASSIFICATION SOCIETY.

LNB – abbreviation for LARGE NAVIGATIONAL BUOY.

LNM – abbreviation for the U.S. Coast Guard's LOCAL NOTICE TO MARINERS.

LOA – abbreviation for LENGTH OVER ALL.

load – (1) in electrical terms, the load refers to the AMPERAGE drawn by the equipment connected to a circuit. (2) the amount of weight pulling on a rope or chain; the strain.

load waterline, LWL – the WATERLINE when a vessel is loaded with provisions, cargo, supplies, fuel, and water. It may be different from the designed waterline.

local conditions – COAST PILOTS and CRUISING GUIDES have important information about wind, wave, and weather conditions in specific areas. Study these guides to plan your route and avoid or be prepared for hazardous areas.

local knowledge – information about an area from people who know the area. CRUISING GUIDES include information based on local knowledge, and people from an area may offer advice. Harbormasters and port captains usually have the most up-to-date information. Where critical navigation is concerned use local knowledge with care. Also, unless you know the DRAFT of a vessel don't blindly follow her into shallow areas; a large sail or powerboat may have a shallow draft.

local magnetic anomaly – *see* MAGNETIC ANOMALY.

Local Notice to Mariners, LNM – *see* NOTICE TO MARINERS, LOCAL.

locker – nautical name for any cupboard or storage area on a vessel. Some locker names include hanging locker (where clothing is hung), dish locker (in the galley), PROPANE locker (for a propane bottle), wet locker (for storing FOUL WEATHER GEAR), tool locker, liquor locker, COCKPIT lockers (under the cockpit seats), etc.

locks – two types: (1) in canals, to raise and lower vessels between bodies of water of differing heights. (2) for a tidal area marina or BASIN, to retain water within an area. The most up-to-date information about canal and marina locks is on their websites. They have depths, changes affecting navigation, operating hours, and WORKING CHANNELS, as well as other important and useful information. There are guides for small vessels ("skippers' guides") on some canal websites. See the bibliography under "Publications" for some examples. General information, including suggestions for transiting locks, may be included in CRUISING GUIDES and

The lock into the Shotley Marina, near Harwich, England.

The lock into the Royal Quays Marina, River Tyne, on the east coast of England.

A lock on the Crinan Canal in Scotland. All but two of the 15 locks are hand-operated by the crews of the yachts. The nine-mile canal was completed in 1809.

The mechanism for a lock on the Caledonian Canal in Scotland. The 29 locks all have lock keepers to operate the gates. The 60-mile canal was opened in 1822.

NAUTICAL ALMANACS. Some canals with locks used by yachts include the Panama Canal, the Caledonian Canal and the Crinan Canal in Scotland, the Göta Canal in Sweden, the Keil Canal in Germany, and the St. Lawrence Seaway and the Welland Canal in Canada. There are harbor and marina locks at some locations in the UK, France, Ireland, and elsewhere where there's a significant tide RANGE.

lock, sea – the first or last lock sea level lock in a series of locks. A sea lock may be left open all the time, tidal conditions permitting, so that vessels can enter and wait to proceed through the other locks.

lock-to-lock – phrase applied to turning a steering wheel from hard over to PORT to hard over to STARBOARD. Count the number of turns lock to lock, and turn the wheel back half the number of turns to center the rudder.

LOD – abbreviation for LENGTH ON DECK.

log, log book, ship's log – (1) a written record of the vessel's daily operations (courses, speeds, positions, FIXES, navigation information, weather, engine hours, etc.). Note clock times in a ship's log in 24-hour time. A vessel's log is considered a legal document and, as such, entries should be written in ink. A skipper may be asked by a port official to see the ship's log. Some skippers may choose to keep a log in electronic form, but a paper record should also be maintained, in case the electronics fail. (2) an instrument for measuring the speed and/or distance through the water; a speed log, a distance log.

long ends – long overhangs at the BOW and STERN. Older designs may have long ends, while modern designers seem to favor short ends, with plumb (straight) or almost-plumb bows and REVERSE TRANSOMS.

This full-keeled, engineless classic racing sailboat has long ends.

longitude – the distance in degrees, minutes, and seconds east or west of the GREENWICH MERIDIAN. Longitude lines (meridians) pass through the north and south poles, and thus are not parallel lines. Longitude is measured on the top or bottom chart scales. *See* LATITUDE.

longitudinal – same as FORE-AND AFT. Refers to BULKHEADS or structural features that run fore-and-aft. (this term isn't related to geographic LONGITUDE). See the next entry.

longitudinals or stringers – structural frames that run FORE-AND-AFT.

"long legs" – slang for a DEEP KEEL or a deep DRAFT. "Sue's boat has long legs; she won't be able to get into this anchorage."

long splice – *see* SPLICES, TYPES OF.

lookout – Rule 5 of the NAVIGATION RULES specifies that "a proper look-out by sight and hearing shall be maintained at all times by all available means." A lookout is required even if the vessel's radar is operating. A lookout must have good visibility all around the vessel in order to do this job properly, and the person shouldn't have other things to do that interfere with keeping a proper WATCH.

"look out the window" – with the AUTOMATION OF NAVIGATION FUNCTIONS on a ship's bridge, it appears that some marine accidents have occurred because the officers relied completely on electronics, and didn't use traditional PILOTING techniques to fix the ship's position. Some marine professionals have observed that, when faced with a navigational uncertainty, navigators who have not practiced traditional visual piloting skills try to find out what's wrong with the electronics, while navigators skilled in traditional piloting look out the window to check the ship's position.

loom – (1) the distant glow from a lighthouse or city lights, seen well before the actual lights are visible. (2) the part of an oar between the handle and the blade. (3) wire loom is a strong, flexible plastic, hose-like material that fits over groups of wires or cables to protect them and route them between electrical panels and equipment. It comes in various diameters, it's split lengthwise so it fits easily around wires, and it's re-usable. Also called split conduit. Buy some loom, CABLE TIES, and SPIRAL WRAP, and DRESS those dangling wires.

loose-footed – a sail not attached to a BOOM along its FOOT, but only at its TACK and CLEW. Many in-mast furled mainsails are loose-footed. See the photo with MOTORSAILER.

lop, loppy – same as CHOP, CHOPPY.

Loran, Loran-C – electronic position-fixing signals, used before GPS was developed. The U.S. Coast Guard permanently terminated transmission of all U.S. Loran-C signals in 2010. At the present time, there's no backup for a GPS system failure or outage. That's only one reason why knowing visual navigation and PILOTING is very important. *See* eLORAN.

loud hailer – it's more than for making your voice heard at a distance. Newer FIXED-MOUNT loud hailers amplify incoming sounds for better audibility, function as the vessel's horn, and serve as an intercom with additional speakers. Some models have pre-programmed SOUND SIGNALS for navigating in REDUCED VISIBILITY. For full functionality, consider having two speaker/horns, one facing forward and one AFT.

low – the usual name for a LOW PRESSURE SYSTEM. There are different types of lows, such as a closed low, cold low, cutoff low, tropical low, extra-tropical low, and warm low. These are discussed in weather books. See the bibliography under "Weather."

low, lower – a direction away from the wind; further away from the wind. "We're too low on this heading." "Let's sail lower on this HEADING." The opposite is, logically, HIGH, HIGHER.

low-cut – a HEADSAIL that has a deep or low, curving FOOT. A low-cut sail can make it difficult to see forward, and it may scoop waves when it's rough. Another name is deck-sweeper.

low, deep – non-specific term applied to a LOW PRESSURE SYSTEM that has pressure significantly lower than surrounding areas. "Keep an eye on that deep low to the south of us."

lowers – the SHROUDS on a MAST that don't extend to the MASTHEAD.

low power (radiotelephone) – *see* HIGH POWER, LOW POWER.

low pressure system, low, cyclone – an area where the barometric pressure is lower than the surrounding areas. The air circulation around a low pressure system is counterclockwise (anticlockwise) in the Northern Hemisphere, and clockwise in the Southern Hemisphere. The rotation of lows and high pressure systems is caused by the CORIOLIS EFFECT. In a low pressure system the air is moving upward (convection). Low pressure systems generally have poor or stormy weather. The movement of surface lows and HIGHS is driven by the wind flow at the 500mb level – that's why 500MB CHARTS are important for forecasting surface weather. To determine where a low is in relation to you, use BUYS BALLOT'S LAW.

low pressure systems, semi-permanent – the Aleutian Low and the Icelandic Low are two examples in the Northern Hemisphere.

low, rapidly-intensifying, RIL, bomb – a maritime CYCLONE whose central pressure is dropping, or is expected to drop, at a rate of 1MB (or more) per hour for 24 hours. As the LATITUDE decreases, lesser pressure drops qualify a low as a RIL. The rapid drop in pressure indicates that the low is rapidly intensifying, hence the name. A NOR-EASTER is frequently a bomb, as are a number of notorious storms around the world, such as the 1979 Fastnet yacht race storm and the 1994 Queen's Birthday yacht race storm near New Zealand.

LPG – abbreviation for liquid PROPANE gas.

lph – abbreviation for liters per hour. *See* FUEL CONSUMPTION and GALLONS OR LITERS PER HOUR.

LR – abbreviation for LLOYD'S REGISTER OF SHIPPING, a marine CLASSIFICATION SOCIETY.

lubber line, lubber's line – the central line or pointer inside a compass that indicates the HEADING of the boat. It's yellow on some compasses. A compass may have two other lubber lines, each at a 45° degree to the central line, to allow the heading to be viewed from the side, or to estimate a TACKING ANGLE. If there's ALIGNMENT ERROR, the lubber line reading will be inaccurate.

luff, luffing – (1) the forward part or leading edge of a sail. When the luff flaps because the sail isn't properly trimmed or there's very little wind it luffs or is luffing. *See* SAIL, PARTS OF. (2) to head up toward the wind (to luff up). May be done when sailing in gusty conditions. See the next entry.

"luff in a puff; keep her full in a lull" – good old-time advice for BEATING to WINDWARD. When you head up (luff) in a puff of wind, the boat moves HIGHER on the course for a short time, thus gaining ground to windward. In the lull that follows the puff, BEAR OFF a bit and keep the sails full, thus maintaining speed.

luff rope – a rope or thin line sewn into the LUFF of a sail that slides into a groove or slot in a ROLLER FURLER or the MAST. Also called a BOLT ROPE.

lull – a temporary or abrupt decrease in the wind. A lull can occur in light or heavy airs.

"lunch hook" – *see* "HOOK, LUNCH."

LW, LWN, LWS – abbreviations for low water, low water NEAPS, low water SPRINGS.

LWL – abbreviation for LENGTH ON THE WATERLINE or LOAD WATERLINE.

lying a-hull – *see* A-HULL.

M

m – abbreviation for meter or meters.

macerator – a pump in a marine sanitation system that macerates solid waste from a MARINE TOILET before treating it (with chlorine or other chemicals). After treatment the waste is sent to a HOLDING TANK or discharged overboard (where it's legal).

mackerel sky – the name given to cirrocumulus CLOUDS containing ice crystals; these clouds have a rippled appearance like fish scales. In temperate or tropical regions this sky may indicate the approach of a storm or HURRICANE. In the winter it's a fair weather sky. *See* WEATHER RHYMES.

macroburst – a strong downdraft with an area at least 2.5 miles wide, and peak winds lasting between five and 20 minutes. Intense macrobursts can cause damage like a tornado. *See* MICROBURST.

maelstrom (pronounced **male** strum) – a very strong whirlpool, created by the change of tides in constricted areas. A TIDE RACE may also be called a maelstrom. Three notable European maelstroms are the Saltstraumen (near Bodø, Norway), the Moskestraumen (in the Lofoten Islands, Norway), and Corryvreckan (on the west coast of Scotland).

magnet – carry a small one when you visit a marine supply or hardware store to test for FERROUS metals. Some STAINLESS STEEL is magnetic, but less so than plain steel. Plain steel "jumps" onto a magnet; magnetic stainless steel has a weak attraction or none at all. A magnetic retrieving tool on a flexible spring-like rod is useful for trying to capture steel items lost in the bilge.

magnetic anomaly, local magnetic anomaly – an area where a magnetic compass may give unreliable readings because of a disturbance to the earth's magnetic field. The presence of a known magnetic anomaly is indicated on the chart in the area where it occurs. Magnetic disturbances may occur in the vicinity of large metal structures or electric power lines above or below the water, or in areas where magnetic geological features affect surface navigation.

magnetic bearing – the direction in degrees with reference to MAGNETIC NORTH measured *from* one location *to* another location. A TRUE BEARING to which VARIATION has been applied is a magnetic bearing. The label for a magnetic direction is a capital M (197°M), which is used when writing in a log.

magnetic course, direction, heading – a COURSE, direction, or HEADING made with reference to MAGNETIC NORTH, which is indicated on the inner COMPASS ROSE on a chart, or is determined by applying VARIATION to a TRUE direction. If a compass has no DEVIATION, it indicates magnetic courses. The label for a magnetic direction is a capital M (110°M), which is used when writing in a log.

magnetic compass – *see* COMPASS MAGNETIC.

magnetic disturbance – a MAGNETIC ANOMALY.

magnetic north – magnetic north is indicated on the inner COMPASS ROSE on a chart. The difference between TRUE NORTH and magnetic north is expressed in degrees east or west. This difference is called VARIATION. The direction of magnetic north varies by geographic location on earth. Use the compass rose on the chart nearest the area where the vessel is navigating to determine the variation. *See* CONVERSION OF DIRECTIONS.

main, mainsail (pronounced **main**'s'l) – the sail hoisted on the AFT side of the MAIN MAST. Some mains are conventional (stowed folded on the BOOM and SET by hauling it up the mast on the main HALYARD). Others roll up and stow in or near the aft side of the mast or in the boom (in-mast furling or in-boom furling).

main, battenless – a mainsail can be constructed with no ROACH, so it doesn't need battens to hold the shape of the LEECH. Some sailboat owners specify a battenless main because the extra sail area in the roach is less important to them than having the sail catch on the TOPPING LIFT or BACKSTAY, or having BATTEN POCKETS to wear out. *See also* MAIN, FULLY-BATTENED.

main boom – the BOOM that's attached to the MAIN MAST, which is the tallest mast on a vessel with more than one mast.

main, fully-battened – a MAINSAIL that has full-length BATTENS extending from the LUFF to the LEECH. Each batten rides on a special CAR in or on the mast track.

main halyard – the HALYARD used to hoist the MAINSAIL.

main mast, mainmast – on a sailboat with more than one MAST, the main mast is the tallest one.

mainsheet – the line(s) that control the lateral angle of the BOOM and the MAINSAIL.

make way, making way – a vessel moving through the water under sail or engine power is making way (UNDERWAY), and not drifting.

make fast, made fast – the action of tying a rope securely to a fixed point or object; to secure; tied securely.

make sail – to hoist or SET the sails.

making colors – according to FLAG ETIQUETTE, colors are made (hoisted) each morning at 0800 (morning colors), and lowered each evening at sunset (evening colors). A yacht club may signal the time with a morning and evening gun.

At 0800 hoist the yacht's national ENSIGN or the U.S. YACHT ENSIGN, or put the flagstaff in place.

When in home waters, hoist your yacht club, organization, or squadron BURGEE, or the yacht's PRIVATE SIGNAL after the national ensign is in place.

When visiting a foreign country, hoist the COURTESY FLAG after the vessel's ensign, and before any other special flags or burgees.

At sunset, lower any flags that are not properly flown during the night, in reverse order, with the vessel's ensign last.

The proper display of flags is considered very important in many countries. In a foreign country follow the practice for making colors observed on local vessels or at a yacht club. When a vessel is underway colors are not made, as the flags fly all the time while underway.

maneuvering board, radar transfer plotting sheet – these pre-printed paper sheets (or a plastic device on which you can plot directly) are used for solving relative motion problems, without electronics. A navigator can plot radar TARGETS, graphically calculate the CLOSEST POINT OF APPROACH and the course to steer to avoid a collision, determine the course to steer in a current, and solve other relative motion problems. Although electronics have replaced the maneuvering board and radar plotting sheets for many navigators, learning to use the paper-and-pencil method could be important if the electronics fail. It takes practice, but it's not difficult. Some sailors actually find it interesting.

maneuvering sound signals – *see* SOUND SIGNALS, MANEUVERING.

manifold – a device with one or more inlets and several outlets. Examples include the EXHAUST MANIFOLD and the intake manifold on an engine, a FUEL FILTER MANIFOLD and a SEA CHEST.

manifold, exhaust – internal combustion engines with more than one cylinder have an exhaust manifold, which captures the exhaust gas from each cylinder and directs it to a single outlet (the exhaust elbow or pipe). In the case of a water-cooled engine, seawater is injected into the exhaust elbow along with the exhaust, and the seawater and exhaust gases are discharged together out the boat's exhaust outlet (at the STERN or on the side of the hull). *See also* ENGINE, AIR-COOLED.

manifold, fuel filter – *see* FUEL FILTER MANIFOLD.

manifold, seawater – *see* SEA CHEST.

manila rope – *see* ROPE, MANILA.

man overboard, MOB – two words you never want to hear aboard a vessel, except when you're practicing MAN OVERBOARD RECOVERY TECHNIQUES. The words "crew overboard" are sometimes used; however, it's easier to yell "maaaaan overboard," and there's no mistaking its meaning. "Crew" could mean several people overboard – a really serious situation.

man overboard alarm system – a specialized electronic device that assists in recovering a crewmember who falls overboard. It has a receiver for the boat (or for a specially-adapted RADAR or CHART PLOTTER) and battery-operated individual transmitters for each crewmember. Several types are available. A range trigger device activates the alarm when the crewmember wearing the transmitter moves a pre-set distance from the boat. *See also* PERSONAL LOCATOR BEACON.

man overboard button – a GPS or CHART PLOTTER may have a man overboard "button" that instantly records the LATITUDE and LONGITUDE when it's pushed, creating a WAYPOINT so you can navigate back to the position where you hope the victim still is. Having access to this button in the COCKPIT is an important safety feature. If the GPS or chart plotter is below decks, install a remote button in the cockpit; check the equipment manual to see if it's possible. If not, have a handheld GPS with a MOB button in the cockpit. Practice using it during man overboard drills. See previous entry.

man overboard drill – *see* EMERGENCY DRILL, MAN-OVERBOARD, and MAN OVERBOARD RECOVERY TECHNIQUES.

man overboard equipment – includes such things as a LIFESLING® or MOM® MODULE, HORSESHOE BUOY, LIFE RING, FLOATING STROBE LIGHT, MAN-OVERBOARD POLE, electronic equipment, or other devices for use in a man overboard situation. Practice using all items that are aboard.

man-overboard pole, dan buoy – a tall floating pole with a flag on top (CODE FLAG "Oscar") that sits upright in the water; it's thrown overboard to mark the location of a MOB incident. The pole usually has a flotation aid, such as a HORSE SHOE BUOY, and a floating waterproof light attached to it, so the victim can swim to it (if conscious), and you can locate the victim. Throwable, self-inflating MOB poles are available.

man overboard recovery techniques – much has been written about various man overboard recovery techniques, and research is on-going. Study everything you can find, attend a SAFETY AT SEA SEMINAR or other on-the-water learning experience, and practice the techniques appropriate to the vessel and crew.

- Don't let it happen! Make personal safety the first rule aboard the boat at all times.
- No single recovery technique is right for all circumstances, every condition of sea and weather, or all types of boats and crew.
- Seamanship skills under sail and power are essential, especially close-quarters maneuvering when approaching the victim.
- With a multi-person crew, the most capable person should direct the recovery. In some cases, the most capable person may not be the helmsman or the skipper.
- With a short-handed crew or a crew of two, all persons must be skilled in boat handling under sail and power.

- Practice, practice, practice in all conditions, in daylight and at night. To simulate a person in the water use a floating cushion or a fender. Add a floating strobe light for night practice.

The summary for any MAN OVERBOARD incident is **shout, throw, spot, steer, recover**.

- *Shout* is self-explanatory. Yell more than once if no one notices. If you're now alone on the boat you may be yelling other words.
- *Throw* anything that floats: a lifejacket if one's lying around, float cushions, FENDERS, LIFE RING. Don't waste time with man-overboard gear unless it's *immediately* deployable. The victim needs something to hang onto, and several floating objects help guide you back to the person. Deploy special man-overboard gear next. Push the MAN OVERBOARD BUTTON, (if there is one) as soon as possible when someone goes over.
- *Spot*: one person should immediately locate the victim and point to the person all the time as the helmsman maneuvers. If you're the only one aboard, it will be a challenge to keep an eye on the victim and steer at the same time.
- *Steer*: see MAN OVERBOARD RECOVERY TECHNIQUES below.
- *Recover*: before an emergency arises determine how to get a person back aboard once the victim is alongside the boat. If you're single-handing this will be a personal challenge IF you can get back to the boat. Don't let it happen!

The basic techniques (research the specific details) for recovering a man overboard include:

- Lifesling® or similar towed device – can be used with all sail recovery techniques or under power; this technique may be the best choice for a short-handed crew or crew of two (which will be a crew of one if the other person goes over).
- Power recovery – under many conditions a power rescue may be the best choice, no matter what the crew size. Two basic recoveries under power are an ordinary circle turn back to the victim, and the WILLIAMSON TURN. Use a Lifesling® (or similar towed device) with a circle or Williamson Turn. Check for lines in the water, start the engine, approach the victim, put engine in neutral when near the person, turn engine off when person is secured to the boat.
- Quick stop – done under sail (requires a JIBE); very good for a fully-crewed boat, when the crew reacts quickly and the victim's still near the boat. Not good for high boat speeds, and possibly not for heavy weather because of the jibe. See the OFFSHORE SAFETY entry for more information about the quick stop.
- Figure eight – very easy to do under sail (requires only a TACK); very good with skilled full crew. The boat sails about five boat lengths away and returns, going HEAD-TO-WIND alongside the victim.
- Fast return (variation of the figure eight) – done under sail (requires only a tack); very good with skilled full crew; requires a fast response from crew to avoid getting too far from victim. The

boat sails about two or three boat lengths away from the victim and returns, going head-to-wind alongside the victim. Not for strong winds and rough seas.

• Deep BEAM REACH (variation of the figure eight) – easily done under sail (requires only a tack). Good with a shorthanded crew. The boat sails about two boat lengths away and returns, going head-to-wind alongside the victim. Not for strong winds and rough seas.

Determine how to get an unconscious person or a conscious but exhausted victim back aboard. Articles and books describe several methods. Rescue gear must be quickly available and immediately deployable. If the crew is usually two people, choosing and practicing an appropriate technique is especially important. It's unlikely that anyone, even a strong and fit individual, will be able to climb up a boarding ladder at sea when cold, wet, and scared, or if it's rough. The victim should not try to help in his/her own rescue, to prevent injury or stressing the heart. If you can safely practice getting a real person aboard (perhaps while at anchor in warm tropical waters) it's a good learning experience.

If there is any chance that the victim may have HYPOTHERMIA bring the person aboard horizontally (rather than lifting him/her vertically with legs dangling). Lifting vertically taxes the heart and post-rescue collapse or death may occur. Rig a full body sling from a sail or net, put ropes under his armpits and behind his knees, put him flat in a dinghy and lift the dinghy, etc. to keep the victim as horizontal as possible while he is lifted aboard. Handle a hypothermic victim slowly and gently at all times. Speed is not important in this phase of a rescue. If a crewmember must go in the water to assist a victim, that person must wear a lifejacket and be tied to the boat – it's hard enough to recover one man overboard.

manuals – you know what these are, but do you read them? If you don't have a book for something, check the manufacturer's website; there may be manuals available for download.

manuals, electronic equipment – "if all else fails, read the manual." While some people resist reading, the complexity and features of modern electronic equipment requires that you read the book, even if you've operated similar equipment. Some "malfunctions" turn out to be operator error. There are many things electronics can do beyond basic functions, and these may not be evident just by following intuition and the menus. There isn't time to check the manual in a stressful or emergency situation. If the manual is poorly-written or unclear, write your own instructions, once you figure out how to do something.

manuals, engine – *see* ENGINE MANUALS.

manuals, owner-operator – information about the boat and all its equipment compiled by the boat manufacturer. Manuals that come with new boats may be better than those prepared for older vessels (if any). ABYC report T-24 deals with owner/operator's manuals. If the boat's manual is poor, incomplete, or nonexistent, prepare your own BOAT MANUAL.

Marconi rig, Bermudan, Bermuda rig – the triangular MAINSAIL used on modern sailboats. See SAIL, PARTS OF for a drawing.

Marelon® – a non-metallic, non-conductive, non-corroding glass-reinforced composite material used for SEACOCKS and other plumbing fittings. Marelon® fittings meet UL and ABYC standards.

mares' tails – thin, streaky cirrus CLOUDS with wispy ends that look like horses' tails. They indicate high altitude winds. *See* WEATHER RHYMES.

marine, marine environment – normally used to indicate saltwater but may be applied to fresh water, as in the general term "marine equipment."

marine architect, naval architect – a person trained in the design of recreational or commercial vessels and marine structures, such as offshore oil platforms. Architects may specialize in certain types of vessels, such as yachts, powerboats, racing sailboats, luxury yachts, ships, etc. You may employ the services of a marine architect for a custom design or to design major modifications for a vessel. *See also* WESTLAWN.

marine electrical wire – *see* WIRE, ELECTRICAL, MARINE USE.

marine-grade, for marine use – *implies* suitability for use in the MARINE ENVIRONMENT. Higher construction standards and better materials are used in good quality equipment designed for saltwater use. Vibration, corrosion, heavy strains, harmful effects of UV rays and ozone, saltwater spray, etc. all take their toll on boat gear. Marine electronics may have corrosion-resistant contacts and components. MARINE METALS and synthetic materials are used in fittings, SPARS, and other items exposed to saltwater.

marine hoist – a large, square machine with four legs on large rubber tires with a pair of boat slings between the legs. The hoist rides out on a special hoisting area over the water or down a ramp into the water. One end of the hoist is open so a boat can enter the hoist. The vessel floats in, and the slings are lowered and positioned under the hull. Large winches raise the slings, and the hoist can be driven to a storage area. New yachts have labels near the deck edge to show where the slings should be placed; older yachts should add these labels. Marine Travelift, Inc. and Wise are two makers of marine hoists, which are available in sizes from 20 to 1,000 tons.

A small marine hoist.

One of the four wheels on a very large marine hoist.

marine insurance – protecting your boat from losses and protecting you from liability on the water is the job of marine insurance. It's different from auto and homeowner's insurance in several ways: first, in the U.S. the marine insurance industry is *not* regulated by the states or the federal government, which means you must deal with reputable companies, brokers, and agents. Secondly, the details of marine insurance policies differ from other insurance you may be familiar with. Following are some things to consider when you seek insurance for your boat.

Price: looking mainly at the cost of different policies is not the way to compare and choose coverage. You must understand what is covered and excluded with each policy.

Choose a marine insurance agent or broker who specializes in recreational boats (unless you're insuring a COMMERCIAL VESSEL). A marine agency has staff who know MARITIME LAW. Look for an agency that has the flexibility to get you several quotes from different companies. Your homeowner's or auto insurance company may insure boats, but do their agents know maritime law, and do their policies offer what you need?

Marine insurance has two basic parts: hull coverage (insures the vessel and anything aboard for the use and maintenance of the boat), and liability coverage.

An "all risk" policy is usually the best choice for hull coverage. It includes everything except for the specified exclusions. Such things as normal wear and tear, deterioration, damage from CORROSION, and other things will be listed in writing as not covered. Read this carefully.

Some policies offer coverage for "named perils," in which case there will be a list of what these perils are, and a lot of things will be excluded. Therefore "all-risk" coverage is a better choice.

An "agreed value" policy pays the agreed value of your vessel in the event of a total loss.

An "actual cash value" policy pays the value of the boat at the time of a total loss, which will include depreciation and other factors. This type of policy is not desirable.

For a partial loss check whether the policy pays the replacement costs or the actual cash value of the lost or damaged equipment. The actual cash value will be lower than the replacement costs.

Liability coverage (also called protection and indemnity, or P&I). This part of the policy covers both the liability of the vessel and personal liability. Under maritime law a vessel is considered to be an entity, and she can be sued. Maritime law limits the liability award in many cases to the value of the vessel, so discuss the level of additional coverage you may need with your insurance agent. The majority of marinas in the U.S. and many foreign countries require proof of liability insurance to stay at the marina or store on land.

Deductibles: read carefully about the deductibles for the hull coverage and for the liability portion of the policy.

Extra coverage: some policies offer things that you may not need, such as towing insurance and uninsured boater coverage. If you select towing coverage, when you get towed you have an insurance claim on your record. This becomes part of your insurance history and may affect future coverage. If you want towing insurance look for separate coverage from commercial towing services. "Uninsured boaters" coverage is not the same as your auto insurance "uninsured motorist" coverage. This type of insurance applies only to bodily injury caused by an uninsured boater, which, believe it or not, is not a frequent occurrence.

Seaworthiness: there is a seaworthiness clause somewhere in the policy. "Seaworthiness" includes both the vessel and the crew. When you sign the insurance contract, you are agreeing to maintain and operate your boat in a SEAWORTHY manner. If a claim is made, seaworthiness may be an issue.

Crew: in the quote, insurance companies may specify the minimum number of crew required when operating the boat. Read carefully.

Area of navigation: the cost of insurance varies with the area of operation of the vessel. The policy will specify the area you select. If you want to take the boat out of her area of operation, contact your agent for a trip endorsement. You're not covered out of your area without an endorsement.

Full-time liveaboards who don't have a land home are a special case for marine insurance. Several companies offer coverage for liveaboards. If you don't have a house (with homeowner's insurance) you need personal liability insurance to cover you while you're ashore, and personal property coverage to cover your property when it's not aboard the boat. It's also desirable to have a "loss of use" clause in a marine policy. For example, if you have to stay in a hotel while your boat is being repaired after a covered loss, a policy may pay for this loss of use.

The application: when you fill out the application form answer all questions with complete accuracy and honesty. Do you want a six month navigation period and a six month lay up, or 12 months navigation? Have you had a previous insurance claim within the time period specified on the application? If you're unsure of anything ask the agent as you fill out the application.

You'll be dealing with either a marine insurance broker or a marine insurance agent. A broker represents the insured (you), and an agent acts for the company or companies he/she represents. Their responsibilities are essentially the same, and they work to get you the policy that meets your needs. Although there's no significant difference in the vast majority of routine cases, it can matter a great deal when the agent is a "captive agent" (a person who sells policies exclusively for a single company). The opposite of a captive agent is an independent agent, a person who represents several insurance companies.

marine metals – metal suited for use in the MARINE ENVIRONMENT, such as STAINLESS STEEL, BRASS, BRONZE, ALUMINUM, TITANIUM, and other non-FERROUS metals and ALLOYS.

marine railway – equipment for hauling boats out of the water. Railroad tracks extend out into the water, and an adjustable boat cradle rides on the rails. At a suitable state of the tide a vessel is floated onto the cradle and the cradle is winched out of the water. When work is being done on the vessel it usually stays on the railway in the cradle, unless the shipyard has a method of moving the cradle off onto side tracks. Shipyards and some boatyards have marine railways. *See also* the photo with KEEL, FULL.

This 40.6ft/12.4m fin-keeled racing yacht is ready for launch on the marine railway. She's *Opposition*, ex-*Morning Cloud*, built for then-Prime Minister Edward Heath in 1971.

marine supply catalog – some are very good and others are mostly lists with prices and little information. West Marine has a large, informative catalog (in paper and on line), as do some other companies. Get paper copies or check websites and browse; there's a lot to learn from a good catalog.

marine survey – an examination of a vessel by one or more qualified MARINE SURVEYORS. There are several types of surveys, depending on the purpose of the examination. In general, a survey assesses the vessel's condition, its value, and the compliance with legal and other marine standards, practices, and requirements. The total cost of a survey varies with the size and complexity of the vessel, the surveyor's fees and travel expenses, plus the additional costs for a haul-out, mast removal, and/or a SEA TRIAL (if needed). Ask the surveyor if you may observe (quietly) while he/she works. See the next three entries and CORROSION SURVEY.

marine survey types – there are three basic types of marine surveys:

Insurance and/or financing survey: for obtaining and renewing MARINE INSURANCE and/or for obtaining a marine mortgage. This is known as a condition and valuation (C &V) survey. The surveyor does a *visual* inspection of the vessel. He/she does *not* start the engine or generator or observe operations underway or during a SEA TRIAL. Usually the boat is examined in the water, although an insurance company or a surveyor may require that the vessel be hauled. An insurance survey is *not* intended for use in making a purchasing decision. The surveyor will tell you how to prepare for the survey.

Pre-purchase survey: this survey is more detailed than an insurance survey, and two (or more) surveyors may be involved. Its purpose is to provide sufficient information about the condition and value of the boat and its machinery and equipment so that the prospective purchaser can make an informed decision, and use the information in negotiations with the seller/ broker. The surveyor(s) will advise about the requirements for preparing for the survey. The boat be should be hauled out for a proper inspection. Prior to the survey, a prospective buyer should request full disclosure from all parties to the sale, to include, but not be limited to, the boat's title status, service history, damage experience, records of maintenance and repairs, engine logs, owner's manuals, etc. A test run of the boat (a sea trial) is strongly recommended. If a test run is requested, the owner or the owner's authorized agent must operate the boat so the surveyor can concentrate on the inspection process. If a test run is not requested, the owner or the owner's authorized agent must be available to start and operate propulsion and auxiliary machinery, which is then observed in static operating mode only. A qualified marine engine surveyor is recommended, in addition to the other surveyor(s).

Damage or loss survey: after an accident involving another vessel or structure, a grounding, lightning strike, fire, storm damage, etc. a survey will be necessary for insurance and repair purposes, or to determine if the vessel is a "total constructive loss" (the cost of repair exceeds the value of the vessel). The insurance company will advise you about the procedures, and the company will arrange for their surveyor to examine the vessel. In some cases it is advisable for the vessel owner to have his/her own independent surveyor conduct a separate survey to protect his/her interests in negotiations with the insurance company.

marine surveyor – a professional who conducts a MARINE SURVEY. Surveyors may be generalists, or specialize in certain types/sizes of vessels or vessel systems (such as engines, electrical, rigging, or complex systems). Surveyors should know the legal requirements as well as the recommended standards in force for the area and country where they work. Surveyors are not regulated or licensed in the U.S. or in some other countries. Anyone can print up business cards and call himself/herself a marine surveyor. Many surveyors are members of one or more professional surveyors' certification organizations, and subscribe to codes of ethics and professional conduct. However, membership alone does not prove competence. See the next entry, NAMSLOBAL®, and SAMS.

marine surveyor selection – the *reputation* of the surveyor, as confirmed by independent sources, (e.g., people other than the seller, the broker or anyone else with a vested interest in the outcome of the survey), is the most important factor in selecting an individual.

Consult surveyors' websites for resumes or request one from each person you're considering. What are their areas of expertise and experience?

Ask each surveyor you're considering for references and a sample survey. Contact the references.

Don't use comparisons of the surveyors' fees as a guide: you do get what you pay for, and if someone's fee seems very low compared with quotes from other surveyors there may be a good reason.

A surveyor works for the person or company who pays his/her fees, but the surveyor's professional opinions should be unbiased to any interests except the condition and value of the boat. The survey should not be slanted to the interests of the fee-paying entity, whether the buyer or the seller.

Find out what the scope of the survey is. What does the surveyor do? Just as important is what he/she does not do.

Take time to research and select a surveyor who will meet your needs and expectations. Don't let pressure from a seller/broker rush your decision.

After you've selected a surveyor, understand that a comprehensive survey report will take time to prepare and deliver. Sometimes the surveyor must do additional research to make the report complete; sometimes you'll be waiting for reports from more than one surveyor.

marine toilet, MSD – in the U.S. marine toilets (MSDs) must meet Coast Guard regulations for the treatment of waste before it's discharged overboard (where permitted). There are two types of marine toilets that discharge overboard: Type I and Type II. Type II treats waste to a higher standard (a lower bacterial count). Both types meet current U.S. ENVIRONMENTAL PROTECTION AGENCY (EPA) standards. Type III devices don't discharge overboard; these are legal everywhere. There are electric toilets that incinerate waste, leaving a small residue of sterile ash or sludge. Some areas are designated NO-DISCHARGE AREAS, and only a Type III or a HOLDING TANK system are permitted. Marinas everywhere are no-discharge areas. Boat operators must be aware of the regulations in force in a particular area or country; fines can be levied for violations of discharge regulations. How do the authorities know? They may supply a dye to be placed in the toilet system (if there's no holding tank), or ask to check the plumbing from the toilet. If there's a DIVERTER VALVE, it must be locked in the holding tank position, with the key kept in the skipper's pocket. *See also* HEAD RULES.

mariner – general term for someone who operates a boat or serves as crew on a recreational or commercial vessel.

maritime law – another name for ADMIRALTY LAW.

Maritime and Coastguard Agency, MCA, UK – the MCA mission statement includes the phrase "Safer Lives, Safer Ships, Cleaner Seas." The website has information and links relevant to recreational and commercial mariners. www.mcga.gov.uk.

Maritime Mobile Service, MMS – *see* MMS.

Maritime Safety Information, MSI – *see* MSI.

mark, navigation mark – general term for a floating or fixed aid to navigation. Marks are LATERAL or CARDINAL. "Our next mark is buoy number 12."

"mark" – when spoken it means "now," or "at this exact time." For example, the skipper may ask a crewmember to write down the position and time that the boat passes a navigation aid, or the exact time of a celestial observation when he/she says "mark."

marline (pronounced **mar** lin) – light line or cord used to for SEIZING or WHIPPING (not as scary as it sounds). See the photo with SEIZE.

marlinspike – a tapered metal FID for splicing rope or wire. A folding marlinspike may be included as part of a sailor's knife. *See* SPLICES, TYPES OF.

marlinspike seamanship – working with CORDAGE, tying knots, splicing, and repairing rope.

mast – a vertical SPAR that supports the sails. It's held in place by SHROUDS and STAYS. A sailboat with a particularly tall mast has a "tall rig." A mast that does not have shrouds and stays is an UNSTAYED MAST.

mast boot – a protective covering of cloth or rubber material at the deck level on a KEEL-STEPPED MAST to prevent water from entering the mast hole and going below decks.

mast climbing – climbing the mast is sometimes a routine chore and sometimes a necessity, but it's always dangerous, even at the dock. It's the responsibility of the skipper to make sure that all safety precautions are observed when a person goes aloft. On a boat with MAST STEPS there's a temptation for someone to say "I'll just climb up." No one should go aloft without a bosun's chair or proper climbing harness, even if they use the mast steps. Some basic precautions include:

- Attach two HALYARDS to the bosun's chair or climbing harness, one for safety. The halyard on the chair/harness should go through a masthead SHEAVE (not an external BLOCK at the masthead). The crew on deck will have to tend two halyards, but one has the weight of the person, and the other is a safety line.

In addition to sitting in a bosun's chair, this rigger has his safety belt around the mast.

• Tie the bosun's chair or climbing harness onto the main halyard and the safety halyard with a BOWLINE; don't use a SHACKLE unless it's a screw-pin shackle.

• Use two crewmembers on deck, if available. If a halyard WINCH is not SELF-TAILING, a second person is essential.

• Winch the person carefully up the mast. Have enough wraps around the winch so there's not much pull on the tail of the halyard. Avoid a RIDING TURN on the winch. If the halyard winch is self-tailing keep a hand on the tail of the halyard in case it slips out of the tailer jaws or have a second person hold the tail. If the halyard runs through a LINE STOPPER keep the stopper closed as you take in the slack. Use extreme caution if the winch is electric. If a person is using mast steps, keep the bosun's chair/harness tight under his/her butt as he/she climbs.

• When the person is at the proper height, keep the wraps on the winch, and secure the halyard to a CLEAT. Don't rely on the self-tailer jaws, a cleat, or a line stopper alone to hold the weight of the person.

• While the person is working aloft, crew on the deck should stand away from the mast, in case tools or other items fall. Raise and lower items in a canvas bag on a light line attached to the bosun's chair or a spare halyard, if there is one. For safety, all tools used aloft should have LANYARDS on them. Even if they don't hit someone, they can put a hole in a hatch or the deck falling from a height.

• When the person is ready to come down, carefully uncleat the line (and open the line stopper, if there is one), and EASE the halyard on the winch, under control, as the person descends. Avoid the temptation to give an elevator ride down to the deck. Control the halyard so it doesn't jump off the winch or get a riding turn.

• There are several mast climbing devices intended for use by one person – research unbiased evaluations before purchasing this equipment. Climbing solo has additional and considerable hazards.

Someone may need to go aloft at sea, which this poses a major safety risk, and certainly should be avoided, if at all possible. Is it really necessary to go up, or can it wait until the boat is in port or in very calm water? Only fearless, 'round the world ocean racing sailors seem to be able to get away with going aloft at sea.

mast, deck-stepped – a mast with its HEEL resting in a special fitting on the deck or the cabin top. A deck-stepped mast usually has a COMPRESSION POST under it, unless it's a very small boat. For a photo see BOW RAIL and ENDS.

masthead, mast truck, truck – the very top of the MAST.

masthead light, steaming light – a white NAVIGATION LIGHT mounted on the CENTERLINE of the vessel or on the MAST (but not necessarily at the MASTHEAD), which is visible from forward to 22.5° ABAFT the BEAM on either side of the vessel. It must be at least one meter (40 inches) higher than the SIDELIGHTS. Display this light, along with the other required navigation lights, when

UNDERWAY *under power* at night or in RESTRICTED VISIBILITY. Masthead light is the term used in Rule 21(a) of the NAVIGATION RULES. Two lights are required on a vessel over 50m/164 ft. in length. If there are two masthead lights on a large vessel the forward light is lower than the AFT light, and they are called RANGE LIGHTS.

masthead rig – a rig where the FORESTAY goes to the top of the MAST. *See* FRACTIONAL RIG.

mast, keel-stepped – the MAST goes through the deck or cabin top, and the HEEL of the mast rests in a special fitting on the keel in the bilge. See the next entry.

mast partners, partners – the hole where a KEEL-STEPPED MAST goes through the deck into the cabin. The term comes from structural members (the partners) used on a wooden boat to support the area around the mast hole. *See also* MAST BOOT, MAST WEDGES and SPARTITE®.

mast pumping – under certain wind conditions a MAST may vibrate back and forth repeatedly, with enough force to shake the boat. It can happen under sail, at anchor or at a dock. Pumping seems to occur more often with a DECK-STEPPED, single-SPREADER mast that has only one set of lower SHROUDS. If the mast base isn't perfectly square with the MAST STEP, or the step is not firmly affixed to the deck, this can allow the mast to pump, among other causes. To try and stop the pumping: (1) If the boat has an INNER FORESTAY, try tightening it more. (2) If there's no inner forestay, rig a temporary wire one, and attach it to the mast just above the spreaders. Secure a TACKLE or a TURNBUCKLE to the lower end of the temporary stay, and attach that to a strong fitting at the STEM. Tension the stay as much as possible. If that stops the pumping, then a more permanent fix may have to be considered. This could involve installing forward and AFT lower shrouds, additional TANGS on the mast, and new CHAINPLATES and hull reinforcing for the lower ends of the shrouds. Consult a qualified rigger and a marine engineer. This is a big job, but if the pumping is bad it might be worth the effort.

mast rake – *see* RAKE.

mast safety rails – rails mounted on either side of the MAST or around three sides of the mast, where a crew member can stand securely or attach a HARNESS TETHER while working at the mast. Otherwise known as "granny rails." For a photo see CHAINPLATES.

mast step – the base that the MAST rests on. The step may have a pin to go through the bottom of the mast. Steps are used on deck (DECK-STEPPED MAST), on the keel (KEEL-STEPPED MAST) or in a MAST TABERNACLE.

mast steps – metal steps going up the mast, either part way or to the top. Various kinds are available. Folding steps offer less WINDAGE, but feet can slip off. Enclosed steps may be safer. Make sure an enclosed step is wide enough to accommodate a wide foot; some have a very narrow opening. Even if the mast has steps, anyone going aloft should also use a BOSUN'S CHAIR or climbing harness. *See* MAST CLIMBING.

mast tabernacle, tabernacle – a special MAST STEP mounted on deck, with a hinged mechanism near the base of the mast, to allow it to be pivoted and lowered. Boats that frequently go under fixed bridges may have a tabernacle as a design feature. For safety, the tabernacle and the raising and lowering mechanism must be carefully engineered. For a photo see **CHARLIE NOBLE**.

mast, unstayed – a free-standing mast that doesn't have **SHROUDS** and **STAYS**. This rig is used on Nonsuch and Freedom yachts, some custom designs, and on some small sailboats.

An unstayed mast on a fractional rig Freedom sloop. The crew is in the process of reefing the sails in the strong winds.

mast wedges – used at the MAST PARTNERS to support a KEEL-STEPPED mast in the deck hole. Wedges may be made of wood, hard rubber, or SPARTITE®, a permanent plastic material.

Mayday – a *distress* call sent over a radiotelephone. A Mayday situation is one in which a vessel, person, or aircraft is in *grave and imminent danger*, and requires immediate assistance. If the situation is serious but not life-threatening issue a PAN PAN CALL.

Mayday situations include a serious fire aboard, imminent danger of sinking, an explosion, pirate attack, a severe grounding in dangerous conditions where the vessel and crew are in peril, a life-threatening medical emergency, a man-overboard situation in conditions where rescue of the victim will be difficult, and other grave dangers to life or the vessel.

A Mayday *is the highest priority radio traffic*, and all other communication not directly involved in the distress must cease until the Mayday is resolved.

If there's unnecessary radio traffic, a station can say "SEELONCE MAYDAY" to tell everyone to maintain radio silence. *See also* "PRUDONCE."

When a Mayday situation has been resolved, either you or the Coast Guard *must* cancel the Mayday on the radio, using a specific radio procedure. *See* MAYDAY CANCELLATION.

Log all Mayday calls and cancellations you make or hear in the ship's log.

Have a pre-printed reference card near the radio so that the crew can make the call or a cancellation using the proper procedure. See the next entry.

Mayday call – use VHF Channel 16 and/or the assigned SINGLE-SIDEBAND DISTRESS FREQUNCIES. To issue a Mayday say the following:

- **MAYDAY** three times.
- **This Is** [name of your vessel three times].
- Say your CALL SIGN, or MMSI number, or boat registration number once.
- Repeat **MAYDAY** and your vessel's name one more time.
- **My Position Is** [give your position by LATITUDE and LONGITUDE, or by BEARING and distance to a well-know landmark, an aid to navigation, land feature, or in any terms that will help a responding station locate you].
- Give the size of your vessel and her identifying features or colors. Give information about course, speed, and destination, if applicable.
- Describe the nature of your distress (sinking, fire, medical emergency, etc.).
- **There Are** [number of persons] **Persons Aboard**.
- **I Require** [describe the assistance you need].
- **This Is** [your vessel's name once].
- **Over.** – wait for a response. If no response after one minute, repeat the call.

When a Mayday situation has been resolved, either you or the Coast Guard *must* cancel the Mayday on the radio, using a specific radio procedure; see the next entry. Log all Mayday calls and cancellations in the ship's log. See the next entry.

Mayday cancellation, Pan Pan cancellation – when a Mayday or PAN PAN situation is resolved either you or the Coast Guard *must* make a cancellation call on the same channel(s) that were used for the distress or Pan Pan call. To make a Mayday or Pan Pan cancellation say the following:

- **All Stations** three times.
- **This Is** [name of your vessel three times].
- Say your radio CALL SIGN, MMSI number, or boat registration number once.
- **Time Is** [give the time in 24 hour time (UTC time preferable), or identify if local time is used].
- **Cancel My Mayday** (or **Pan Pan**) **Distress Alert.**
- **This Is** [name of your vessel] once.
- Say your call sign, MMSI number or boat registration number once.

Out. to end the transmission.

Maintain a listening watch on Channel 16 or the other distress frequency you used to see if there's any communication about the cancellation.

Mayday DSC call – one of the great advantages of a DSC RADIOTELEPHONE is that it makes an automatic Mayday call with the touch of the emergency button.

Mayday, false or accidental – in most countries there are civil and/or criminal penalties for issuing a false or accidental distress alert. If a voice MAYDAY, DSC MAYDAY, a PAN PAN, an EPIRB, or a PERSONAL LOCATOR BEACON alert is made *accidentally* you *must* cancel it by immediately calling the Coast Guard, and then following the MAYDAY CANCELLATION procedure.

Mayday, hearing a call – if you hear a Mayday call, note the position of the distressed vessel and stand by on the channel. Wait to hear if the coast guard or another vessel near the distressed vessel replies. If no one replies you should answer the Mayday by calling the distressed vessel, saying "Mayday Received," give your vessel's name, and offer to assist. *See* MAYDAY RELAY, and ASSISTANCE AT SEA.

Mayday Relay – if you hear a Mayday call and a response from a receiving station, but it's evident that the vessel calling Mayday can't hear the response, you can relay communications between the vessel and the Coast Guard or other station. A Mayday Relay may also be used for distress communication on behalf of a vessel that doesn't have a radio or it's inoperative. To do a Mayday Relay, *say the following*:

- **Mayday Relay** twice.
- **This Is** [the name of *your vessel* once]. Give *your vessel's* CALL SIGN, MMSI number, or boat registration number once.
- **Mayday Vessel** [name of distressed vessel].
- **At Position** [give position of distressed vessel].
- Describe nature of distress.

• Describe assistance required.
• **Over. –** wait for a response.

Use the words **Mayday Relay** and *your vessel's name* at the start of subsequent transmissions in a relay, and use **Mayday Vessel** and the distressed vessel's name when you're talking about that vessel. You can also use Mayday Relay for a DSC distress call you hear, if it's evident that the Coast Guard has not responded in five or more minutes.

mb – abbreviation for MILLIBAR or millibars.

MCA – abbreviation for the UK MARITIME AND COAST GUARD AGENCY.

meat hooks – short pieces of broken wire strands that stick out from rigging or steering system wire. Meat hooks indicate that the wire has been over-stressed or worn and should be replaced. Even one meat hook is a warning. Meat hooks may be hard to see until you cut yourself, or snag a sail or clothing. Wearing a cloth glove, run your fingers gently along wires to check for meat hooks.

mean – the arithmetical average of a number of observations, as in mean high water, mean low water, mean RANGE of the tide, mean wind speed.

mechanical advantage, purchase – a method of multiplying the force needed to move or lift a weight. A TACKLE (a purchase) provides a mechanical advantage, depending on how many SHEAVES and lines are used in the tackle. For example: a tackle with a 4:1 advantage would be able to move a 100lb/45kg weight with 25lb/11kg of force (disregarding the effects of friction).

mechanical terminals – *see* TERMINALS, MECHANICAL.

medevac – medical evacuation of an ill or injured person by a rescue vessel or helicopter. Issue either a MAYDAY (life-threatening condition) or a PAN PAN call (serious but not life-threatening condition) to contact the Coast Guard. Before calling have the following information *written down* to tell the Coast Guard:

Patient's gender, age, and name.

Nature of the illness or injury.

Vital signs (pulse, respiration; temperature, and blood pressure, if you can check it).

History of the illness or injury.

Assistance given to the patient.

Level of medical care available aboard the vessel.

If the patient can move or walk.

Prepare the patient for evacuation:

Put the above medical information sheet in the patient's clothing.

Include list of medications, if any, patient's ID cards, emergency contact information.

Put a lifejacket on the patient, warm clothes and a blanket (if possible).

Put hearing and eye protection on the patient (for a helicopter rescue).

Have the patient on deck before the rescue craft arrives, if it's safe, to minimize rescuers' time on-scene.

Rescue personnel may be deployed to the boat to help.

If the patient's condition changes for better or worse, notify the Coast Guard while the rescue service is en route.

medical assistance offshore – a number of telemedicine organizations are available to assist commercial and recreational offshore voyagers. Satellite communication facilitates this service. See the bibliography under "Crew and Health" for resources.

Med moor – a method of mooring one end of a boat to the shore, named after the common practice in the Mediterranean. Two ways: (1) STERN to the QUAY (shore), BOW out to an anchor. Fairly easy to get off the boat over the stern; less privacy in the COCKPIT. (2) bow to quay, stern to an anchor. Must climb over the bow rail; more privacy in cockpit. Both methods require practice and good FENDERS PORT and STARBOARD. Some boats are difficult to steer in reverse; in this case a BOW THRUSTER is very helpful. Read about the techniques, and ask other sailors that know how to do it. Boats that frequently Med moor can make or buy a PASSERELLE to use as a gangplank off the bow or stern. Med mooring allows a large number of boats to have access to the quay, without the problems associated with RAFTING.

medical information, crew – *see* CREW MEDICAL INFORMATION.

medium-frequency, MF – frequencies between 300kHz and 3MHz, just below the high frequency SPECTRUM. NAVTEX uses 518kHz and 490kHz; the U.S. AM radio broadcast band is 530 to 1700kHz.

meeting situation – same as a HEAD-ON SITUATION.

mega – prefix for one million (1,000,000).

megahertz, MHZ – one million HERTZ. Marine VHF radio, AIS transmitters, and SINGLE-SIDEBAND radios use frequencies in the MHz range.

Mercator projection, Mercator chart – the CHART PROJECTION most frequently used in marine navigation. The general characteristics of this projection are: (1) a RHUMB LINE is a straight line. (2) a rhumb line crosses each MERIDIAN at the same angle. (3) distances can be measured accurately on the chart. (4) lines of LATITUDE and LONGITUDE are parallel. The Mercator projection is named after Gerardus Mercator, a century Flemish cartographer who produced a world map with this projection in 1569.

mercury barometer – *see* BAROMETER, MERCURY.

meridian – name for a line of LONGITUDE. Meridians pass through the north and south poles, and thus are not parallel lines. *See* LATITUDE and PARALLEL.

meridian sailing – if you sail north or south along or parallel to a meridian of LONGITUDE, you can estimate the DEAD RECKONING LATITUDE at one minute of latitude for each nautical mile traveled. Before mariners learned how to determine longitude, they used meridian sailing.

mesoscale (pronounced **meezo** scale) – term referring to the size of a weather system that's smaller than a SYNOPTIC-SCALE system but larger than a STORM-SCALE system. A mesoscale system ranges in size from approximately 50 miles to hundreds of miles across. Individual thunderstorm systems, a group of multiple thunderstorms, squall lines, and a small TROPICAL STORM are examples of mesoscale systems.

messenger – (1) a light line used temporarily in place of a heavier line. For example, a messenger can be used to replace a HALYARD while the halyard is brought down to the deck for repair or replacement. Use the messenger to pull the halyard back up the mast. *See also* MOUSE(2). (2) another name for a HEAVING LINE.

Met, Met office – term for meteorological office. Met offices issue land and marine weather forecasts; check websites for the text versions and the definitions of terms used in the forecasts. Note that most Met office forecasts are *not* part of the GMDSS system (this will be stated on the websites), but the office may provide the forecasts disseminated by the Coast Guard or other government agency. *See also* GMDSS WEATHER FORECASTS.

metal, active – an active metal doesn't have a protective natural oxide or an oxide produced by a PASSIVATION process on its surface. In the MARINE ENVIRONMENT active metals corrode more rapidly than the same metals that are PASSIVE. *See* GALVANIC SERIES.

metal, ferrous – metals containing steel or iron, which rust. They're magnetic, and will affect the accuracy of a compass if placed near it.

metal, marine – *see* MARINE METAL.

metal, passive – *see* PASSIVE.

meteorological tide – a tide, such as a SEICHE or a STORM SURGE, that's influenced by meteorological conditions rather than astronomical factors.

meter – one meter is equal to approximately 3.3 feet. Meters are used on some charts and in the NAVIGATION RULES.

MF – abbreviation for MEDIUM-FREQUENCY.

microburst – a strong downdraft with an area on the ground of less than 2.5 miles in width, and with strong winds lasting less than approximately five minutes. Microbursts may create dangerous wind shears, which can cause damage and affect aircraft in flight. *See* MACROBURST.

micron – a micron is one thousandth (1/1000) of a millimeter or 40-millionth of an inch.

micron rating – applied to filters, such as fuel and water filters. The lower the number, the finer the filtration. Use the fuel filter specified by engine manufacturer for the on-engine (secondary) fuel filter. Check the engine manufacturer's recommendations for a PRIMARY FUEL FILTER: using a too-fine filter may not be advisable.

mid-channel buoy – another name for a SAFE WATER MARK.

middle latitudes, mid-latitudes, or the temperate region – LATITUDES between approximately 35°- 60° north and south.

midnight sun – a period when there is 24-hours of daylight, in the summer above the ANTARCTIC and ARCTIC CIRCLES. It lasts for a few days to months depending on the LATITUDE.

The midnight sun near the Arctic circle lends a rich glow to these traditional Norwegian vessels. The time is near 2300.

midship – adjective form of AMIDSHIPS.

midship spring – a SPRING line led from AMIDSHIPS either forward or AFT to a dock or another vessel. A midships spring helps control the FORE-AND-AFT movement of the boat. When coming alongside the midships spring is usually the first line to secure or give to a person on the dock; then deploy the BOW and STERN lines as needed. If the boat lacks a midships CLEAT you may be able to tie one end of the spring line to a CHAINPLATE near amidships. *See* SPRING, TO.

mild steel – *see* STEEL, MILD.

military operations at sea – under some conditions WARSHIPS may conduct exercises or operate at night without lights, or with special lights in addition to their NAVIGATION LIGHTS.

military time – same as 24-HOUR TIME.

millibar, mb – a unit of measurement of atmospheric pressure. BAROMETERS have scales calibrated in inches or millibars or both. An electronic barometer can be set to either unit. Millibars are used by some weather services and on SYNOPTIC CHARTS. One mb is equal to one hectopascal (hPa), which is used by some weather services. *See* ISOBAR.

minutes – divisions within a degree of LATITUDE or LONGITUDE. One minute of *latitude* is equal to one nautical mile. There are 60 minutes in one degree.

minutes and seconds, decimal – *see* DECIMAL MINUTES AND SECONDS.

"miss stays, to" – being IN IRONS.

mixed tide – *see* TIDE, MIXED.

mizzen – the sail set on a MIZZEN MAST or the mast itself.

mizzen mast – on a two-masted sailboat the AFT MAST is the mizzen. On a KETCH or a YAWL it's shorter than the MAIN MAST.

MLW, MLLW – abbreviations for mean low water and mean lower low water. See CHART DATUM.

MMS – abbreviation for Maritime Mobile Service, an internationally-allocated radio service for commercial and recreational mariners on oceans and inland waterways. Communication involving the safety of life and property at sea has first priority. Marine radio stations aboard vessels and on land are the two primary parts of this system. In the U.S. the FEDERAL COMMUNICATIONS COMMISSION (FCC) regulates ship and land services for all marine activities in U.S. waters, and for U.S.-registered vessels that sail in international waters and to foreign countries. FCC rules affecting ship and land stations distinguish between COMPULSORY users of marine radio for safety at sea, and VOLUNTARY users. FCC rules for the Maritime Mobile Service meet the requirements of the Coast Guard, which is responsible for monitoring the marine distress frequencies.

MMSI – abbreviation for Maritime Mobile Service Identity, used domestically and internationally with DSC radiotelephones and AIS *transmitters* for distress and non-distress calling of other vessels and shore stations. See the following four entries.

MMSI, Canada – TRANSPORT CANADA regulates marine radio communications for Canadian vessels. For information about obtaining a Canadian MMSI number for DSC ship's radio see the bibliography under "Radio." The U.S. and Canadian government agencies and boating industry groups are working to harmonize regulations for MMSI numbers between the two countries, so that MMSIs obtained in both countries will be recognized across the borders.

MMSI, international – the ITU maintains an international database which contains the MMSI numbers of every vessel, including recreational boats, that travels internationally.

MMSI, UK – Ofcom regulates marine radio licensing in the UK. MMSI numbers are only issued to vessels with DSC radio or satellite communication equipment. See the bibliography under "Radio" for the Ofcom website.

MMSI, U.S. – if your vessel is VOLUNTARY-EQUIPPED, (which includes most U.S. recreational vessels that operate *solely* in U.S. waters), you can get an MMSI number by contacting BoatU.S. (www.boatus.com), Sea Tow (www.seatow.com), or the UNITED STATES POWER SQUADRONS ® (www.usps.org). A U.S.-registered vessel needs only one MMSI number, no matter how many DSC radios are on the boat. All DSC devices aboard the same vessel must be programmed with the same number: these include VHF/DSC radios, SINGLE-SIDEBAND DSC radios, an AIS TRANSMITTER, and an INMARSAT telephone. When applying for an MMSI number you'll be asked for information about your boat, which the Coast Guard uses to respond to a distress call. If you sell your DSC radio or DSC-equipped boat, the new owner will have to update the information; the number cannot be erased from the radio's memory. If you operate a COMPULSORY-EQUIPPED vessel or a vessel that will travel to FOREIGN WATERS you'll be assigned an MMSI number during the radio licensing process. Check the www.boatus.com/MMSI/faq.htm before taking a U.S.-registered vessel to Canada. *See* LICENSE, SHIP STATION.

MOB – abbreviation for MAN OVERBOARD.

MOB button – abbreviation for a MAN OVERBOARD BUTTON.

mole – a large breakwater, which may also serve as a pier for vessels.

MOM® Man-Overboard Rescue Module – trademarked equipment for use in a man-overboard incident.

Monel® – a non-magnetic, corrosion-resistant metal, used for propeller shafts, fasteners, tanks, and other marine applications. Monel wire is available in small spools, and it's excellent for wiring SHACKLE pins and other SEIZINGS. STAINLESS STEEL seizing wire may be used, but it's slightly magnetic, which may be a consideration if it's to be used near a compass.

monkey's fist – a heavy knot, usually with a small weight inside, formed at the end of a HEAVING LINE. The monkey's fist helps the line travel farther when thrown.

monohull – a vessel with a single hull. A MULTIHULL has more than one hull.

moor, moored – to tie up (make fast) to a dock or mooring buoy.

mooring – (1) a shore-based tie-up location such as a pier, dock or slip. (2) a floating buoy with a permanent anchor system to which a vessel may tie up. When using a mooring, especially a rental, visitor's, or borrowed mooring, don't put your absolute trust in it. The weight limit (in tons) may be marked on it, but you don't know the inspection schedule or maintenance of the chain and anchor. A harbormaster (if there is one) usually has information about the moorings. The websites of some mooring authorities (such as municipalities, harbormasters, or yacht clubs) may give information about the locations and maintenance schedules for buoys under their control. Use your own line or lines on the buoy; don't trust the line provided, unless it's obviously very strong and in good condition. *See* MOORING, PICKING UP.

mooring compensator – another name for a SNUBBER.

mooring eye, hurricane eye – a very strong attachment point or fitting at the BOW located low on the STEM, near the waterline, to which a CHAIN SPRING can be attached. Small craft frequently have a mooring eye, but it can be used on larger yachts. The purpose of the eye at the waterline is to lower the angle of pull on a chain RODE, thus helping the anchor to hold better, and eliminating chafe at the deck level. It's not just for strong winds; a low angle of pull is also useful in crowded harbors so other boats are less-likely to run over your anchor rode. On a metal boat a strong plate can be welded to the stem at the waterline; on a boat with a BOBSTAY, the bobstay fitting may have an extra hole in it, or room for one to be drilled. For a fiberglass vessel that doesn't have a fitting for an eye, consult a marine engineer for ways to fabricate one. The term hurricane eye came from wooden boats, some of which had a strong eye bolt installed in the stem near the waterline for the purpose of anchoring in strong winds. See the inset drawing with CHAIN SPRING.

mooring line, dock line, mooring WARP – (1) interchangeable terms for a line used to tie a vessel to a dock or another boat. (2) the rope attached to a mooring buoy is a mooring line. Some mooring buoys have a length of chain for its mooring "line." Attach your own rope or ropes to one or more links of the chain and lead them to the CLEATS on the deck.

mooring lines – the diagram shows the names and arrangement of various lines used to moor a boat alongside a dock or another vessel. Depending upon the circumstances, fewer lines may be used. If conditions are calm, a bow line, a stern line, and one midships spring line may be sufficient. If the middle of the boat is located near a dock cleat, a short line can be led to the boat's midship clear to serve as both a spring and a breast line. If strong winds and/or waves affect a mooring location, lines should be doubled up and good chafe protection added. In tidal areas if the dock is not floating, an allowance for the range of the tide must be made in the mooring lines. See the photo of the SLOOP with DRY OUT.

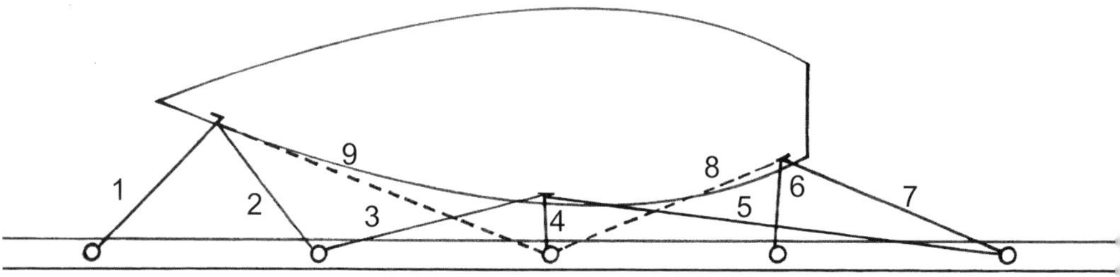

1. Bow line. 2. Forward breast line. 3. Forward spring. 4. Midship breast line. 5. After spring. 6.Stern breast line 7.Stern line. If the boat does not have a midship cleat, a forward spring (8) and an aft spring (9) from the bow and stern cleats would be used. In a typical mooring situation lines 1, 3, 5, and 7 are sufficient, with 4 if the wind is blowing the boat away from the dock.

mooring, picking up – learn how to pick up a mooring under power and sail. If the mooring has a rope attached to it, usually a BOATHOOK can catch it. Some moorings have a convenient PICK-UP BUOY on the mooring line or chain.

Have a long boathook: buy the longest, strongest telescoping boathook available. If the BOW is the highest part of the boat it may be easier to come alongside the mooring, pick it up AMIDSHIPS, and then carry the mooring line to the bow.

If the boat has a **REVERSE TRANSOM** or a boarding or swim platform, and if conditions are right, pick up the mooring at the **STERN** where it's easily reached. Attach a long line at the bow, bring it back to the stern, put it through the ring on the mooring, and carry the line back up to the bow.

If the mooring has a pick up buoy with a small-diameter rope on it, don't use this line to tie the vessel to the mooring, except temporarily in very light winds. Attach the heavier mooring line or chain securely to the boat. If it's too large to fit around the boat's **CLEATS**, pass one or two of your own lines through the eye of the large rope or chain links, and secure the smaller lines to the cleats. Alternatively, it may be possible to remove an anchor from its **ANCHOR ROLLER** (if there is one), and lead a large rope or chain over the roller, securing it on deck with your own smaller lines.

A mooring with a convenient pick-up float and a crewmember with a nice long boathook.

If there's no line on the mooring, then you'll have some fun, especially single-handed. Some techniques for snagging a buoy that doesn't have a rope on it:

Use a special hook attached to a boathook or another pole that grabs the buoy ring or its **SHACKLE**. One type is a strong metal hook that will hold the boat temporarily to the mooring; remove the hook after you've put your own ropes through the ring. Another type of hook (usually made of plastic) threads a light rope, to which you've attached your stronger mooring line, through the ring. This plastic hook isn't strong enough to hold the boat, even temporarily, so something stronger is required to first catch and hold the buoy.

Use a special buoy lasso, made of two lengths of rope with a length of about 3ft/1m of ¼ in/6mm chain between the ropes; overall length about 15ft/5m. The weight of the chain makes the line sink around the buoy. Tie one end of the lasso to the boat, hold the other end and throw the chain part over the buoy so it catches on the mooring's anchor chain. Once the buoy is captured attach your mooring lines and remove the lasso.

"motorboating" – the rapid fluttering sound made by the **LEECH** of a **MAINSAIL** or **HEADSAIL** that's either stretched out of shape or that should have the **LEECH LINE** tightened. The sound is like the putt-putt-putt of a motorboat.

motorsailer – a sailboat with a large, powerful engine, designed to move well under power, and perhaps not as well under sail alone. A motorsailer is usually a heavy **DISPLACEMENT** vessel and may have a **PILOTHOUSE**. For other photos see **BULWARK** and **CHARLIE NOBLE**.

A motorsailer with a large genoa and a loose-footed roller-furling mainsail.

motorsailing – a sailing vessel proceeding under sail *and* with the engine providing motive power is motor-sailing. She's a power-driven vessel under the NAVIGATION RULES. Check the engine manual for the permissible maximum angle of HEEL while motorsailing. See the next entry.

motorsailing cone – the black cone DAYSHAPE required for a sailing vessel proceeding under engine power with the sails set. Rule 25(e) of the NAVIGATION RULES specifies that when motorsailing the boat shall display the dayshape of a cone with the apex pointing down. Under the INLAND RULES a sailing vessel less than 12m/39.4ft is not required to display the cone, but may do so. Cones are available in solid black plastic or cloth. Usually the cone is hoisted on a SPREADER HALYARD, but if a JIB isn't being used it should be hoisted in the FORETRIANGLE where it's more visible, How often have you seen a motorsailing sailboat displaying this cone? See previous entry.

Morse code – a system for communicating with sound signals or a flashing light. The code consists of the letters of the alphabet, numbers, and special combinations of letters to speed communication. Short (dot) and long (dash) signals are used. The light on a MID-CHANNEL (FAIRWAY) buoy flashes Morse code "A," which is short, long . A RACON's signal is a Morse code letter displayed on a radar screen. NAUTICAL ALMANACS and some CRUISING GUIDES have a table of the code. The code was developed by Samuel Morse in the 1830s and '40s for telegraph communication.

mouse – (1) a technique for closing the opening of a hook with several turns of light line (a SEIZING), to prevent something from slipping out of an open hook. "I'm going to mouse that hook when we lift the dinghy aboard." (2) Mouse may also refer to a small weight on the end of a long, light line (a MESSENGER), used for fishing wires or ropes through an upright MAST.

A moused hook. The tip of the hook must have a curve so the seizing stays in place.

MSD – abbreviation used in the U.S. for marine sanitation device, i.e. a MARINE TOILET.

MSI – abbreviation for Maritime Safety Information, an international designation by the IMO and IHO for navigation warnings that immediately affect the safety of life or property at sea. GMDSS services and NAVTEX transmit MSI bulletins.

mud berth – a boat that can safely take the ground (such as a BILGE KEELER) may sit on the bottom when the tide goes out, resting comfortably in her mud berth. For a photo see DRY OUT.

muffler, exhaust – a vessel with the engine mounted near or below the waterline may have a waterlift muffler, which helps quiet the exhaust noise, and collects the exhaust cooling water for discharge overboard. Waterlift mufflers are available in metal, fire-retardant fiberglass, or plastic materials, and in stock or custom designs. Some plastic mufflers can melt from high exhaust heat if the cooling water flow becomes blocked. If the boat has a plastic muffler, carry a spare or fit an exhaust temperature alarm. The relevant ABYC Standard is P-1 Installation of Exhaust Systems for Propulsion and Auxiliary Engines.

multifunction display, MFD – a single display screen that shows data from a variety of instruments, either from other electronics networked to the display or from integral electronics within the unit. The trend in marine electronics is toward powerful processors and interconnected or networked equipment. On a ship it's called an INTEGRATED BRIDGE SYSTEM. *See also* NMEA 0183 and 2000.

multihull – a sail or power vessel with more than one hull, such as a CATAMARAN or TRIMARAN. A multihull's speed is usually higher than similar monohull vessel, and there is more room in the ACCOMMODATION than in a monohull of a similar length.

multimeter – an electrical test meter that reads VOLTS, AMPERES, and OHMS. It may have an analog scale or, preferably, a digital read-out. Some multimeters are only for AC or DC (not both), and some work with both types of current. It's an easy-to-use instrument for testing circuits and diagnosing electrical problems. Meters have two wires with probes on one end that are connected to the test points. Some have clamps that go around wires (clamp-on meter), which read the current in the wires while equipment is operating. Many different multimeter brands and types are available; some good digital, AC/DC clamp-on meters are under $70. Have one aboard your boat and learn how to use it. Electrical troubleshooting articles and books explain how to use the meter.

multiple vessels – the NAVIGATION RULES don't address situations that involve multiple vessels. They are for *two* vessels meeting HEAD ON, CROSSING, or OVERTAKING. That's why situational awareness is so important: be alert to situations where the Rules will be difficult to apply, and try to avoid maneuvering in a way that creates a CLOSE-QUARTERS SITUATION with other vessels.

Murphy's Law – "whatever can go wrong will go wrong, and at the worst possible time." Murphy loves to go out on boats. Beware. *See also* **BLACK BOX THEORY.**

M/V – prefix for motor vessel, which implies a **COMMERCIAL** vessel rather than a yacht. *M/V Arctic Explorer*.

M/Y – prefix for motor yacht, to distinguish the vessel from a commercial vessel. *M/Y Seven Seas*.

N

NAD83 – abbreviation for North American Datum of 1983, which is a modern **CHART DATUM** equivalent to **WGS84.**

NAMSGlobal® – abbreviation for the **NATIONAL ASSOCIATION OF MARINE SURVEYORS, INC.**

NASBLA – abbreviation for the **NATIONAL ASSOCIATION OF STATE BOATING LAW ADMINISTRATORS.**

National Association of Marine Surveyors, NAMSGlobal® – a professional organization that certifies **MARINE SURVEYORS** worldwide. NAMS members perform a variety survey activities for recreational and commercial vessels. The website has open-access information, including a technical and reference bibliography of interest to small vessel owners, operators, and marine trades personnel. www.namsglobal.org. *See also* **SAMS®**.

National Association of State Boating Law Administrators, NASBLA – a U.S. organization that sets standards for national boating education programs, as well as performing other functions related to recreational boating safety, education, and law enforcement. The "Public Policy," "Education," and "Law Enforcement" tabs are of interest to recreational mariners. NASBLA's voluntary Boat Operations and Training (BOAT) Program establishes national standards for the training, qualification, and credentialing of maritime law enforcement and rescue personnel. The organization works with the U.S. Coast Guard and other government agencies. http://nasbla.org.

National Fire Protection Association, NFPA® – a U.S. organization that develops standards for all aspects of fire prevention and protection, including extinguishers and extinguishing systems. U.S. Coast Guard requirements for vessels embody some NFPA standards.

National Geospatial Intelligence Agency, NGA – a U.S. government agency with a maritime unit that supports navigation safety and international maritime obligations. The U.S. **NOTICE TO MARINERS** and other electronic publications of interest to mariners are available to the general public at: http://msi.nga.mil/NGAPortal/MSI.portal; click on "Publications." The NGA issued paper charts (formerly **NIMA** or **DMA** charts), but after April 2010 the Agency ceased to publish paper charts or to make certain electronic publications available to civilian customers. They now issue only electronic charts for waters outside the U.S., which are currently available only to federal vessels. However, authorized reproductions of these products may still be purchased from some commercial vendors, which are listed on the website. NGA charts are generally old and it's difficult to bring them up-to-date. However, they are good for reference and general passage planning. Note: the NGA Notice to Mariners (which has NGA and NOS chart corrections of interest to ocean-going vessels) is *not* the same as the Coast Guard **LOCAL NOTICES TO MARINERS**.

National Hurricane Center, NHC – one of three branches of **NOAA**'s Tropical Prediction Center (TPC). The Center maintains a continuous watch on **TROPICAL CYCLONES** over the Atlantic, Caribbean, Gulf of Mexico, the Central Pacific basin (June 1 to November 30), and the Eastern Pacific basin (May 15 to November 30). The NHC prepares and distributes the hurricane watches and warnings.

National Imagery and Mapping Agency, NIMA – the nautical chart functions of NIMA are currently performed by the **NATIONAL GEOSPATIAL INTELLIGENCE AGENCY (NGA)**. To further confuse things, NIMA took over the chart functions from the Defense Mapping Agency **(DMA)**. Some older charts for waters outside the U.S. may have NIMA or DMA designations or numbers.

National Institute of Standards and Technology, NIST – formerly known as the National Bureau of Standards, NIST develops and promotes technical and scientific standards in a variety of fields. NIST broadcasts accurate time signals from **WWV** and **WWVH** in Fort Collins, Colorado. www.nist.gov.

National Marine Electronics Association, NMEA® – a trade organization. The NMEA's mission is to support the marine electronics industry and to educate the boating public about the "safe and proper" use of marine electronics. NMEA conducts a variety of technical education programs for industry professionals, and provides publications and seminars for the general boating public. The website has a variety of articles and links to topics of interest for the recreational and professional mariner. www.nmea.org.

National Marine Manufacturers Association, NMMA® – a U.S. marine industry trade association that disseminates and monitors engineering and safety standards for non-commercial vessel construction and equipment. NMMA certification standards incorporate federal regulations and **ABYC** standards. NMMA also conducts educational seminars for marine professionals. www.nmma.org. Click on the "Certification" link and explore the site. Also see www.discoverboating.com for a list of NMMA Certified boat manufacturers.

National Marine Manufacturers Association, Canada, NMMA Canada – an industry trade association that develops and monitors engineering and safety standards for the Canadian recreational marine industry. www.cmma.ca.

National Oceanic and Atmospheric Administration, NOAA – among many responsibilities, NOAA issues U.S. land and marine weather forecasts and warnings, and, with the Office of Coast Survey (OCS), issues a wide range of navigational publications and charts for the coastal waters of the U.S. and its territories. These are available in a variety of formats, including paper charts, PRINT-ON-DEMAND CHARTS, RASTER Navigational Charts® (NOAA RNCs), and Electronic Navigational Charts® (NOAA ENCs), which are VECTOR charts that conform to international standards. NOAA also produces several nautical publications: the United States Coast Pilot® series, CHART NO. 1, *Distances Between U.S. Ports*, and chart catalogues. The website has useful information about charts and chart products: www.nauticalcharts.noaa.gov/staff/chartspubs.html.

National Telecommunications and Information Administration, NTIA – a U.S. government agency that has a role in regulating marine radiotelephone communications. The website has nothing specific for the mariner, but it's the reference resource for U.S. radio frequency spectrum management and international advocacy for U.S. telecommunications interests. www.ntia.doc.gov.

National Weather Service, NWS – a unit of NOAA that provides land and marine weather forecasts and other weather-related services. In the U.S. marine forecasts are broadcast on VHF WEATHER CHANNELS, and disseminated on the Internet at www.nws.noaa.gov/om/marine/home.htm#text.

nautical almanac – (1) a reference book of information for PILOTING a vessel in a particular geographical area. It contains navigation information, tide and current tables and diagrams, details about harbors and ports, communication, and a great deal of necessary and useful information. Many almanacs are issued annually, and others at longer intervals. Examples include *Reed's Nautical Almanac* (individual annual editions for the U.S. east coast, west coast, Caribbean, and Europe), *Eldridge Tide and Pilot Book* (annual edition for the north American east coast from Florida to Nova Scotia), and *The Cruising Almanac* (biennial editions covering the Faeroes to Gibraltar), published by the CRUISING ASSOCIATION. See the bibliography under "Publications" for complete citations. (2) an annual almanac of astronomical tables used in CELESTIAL NAVIGATION (navigating by the sun, moon, and stars) when sailing offshore.

nautical mile, NM, M (on a chart) – unit of measurement of 6076ft/1852m/1.15 statute miles, used on coastal and ocean waters. In marine navigation one minute of LATITUDE (*not* LONGITUDE) equals one nautical mile. The nautical mile is used in most marine navigation situations. STATUTE MILES are used on lakes, rivers, and on the INTRACOASTAL WATERWAY.

nautical slide rule – not really a slide rule, but a handy plastic device that graphically solves TIME, SPEED AND DISTANCE problems. Weems & Plath® product #105 is an example of a commonly-used nautical slide rule.

naval architect – another name for a MARINE ARCHITECT.

navigable semicircle – *see* SEMICIRCLE, NAVIGABLE.

navigation – general term for the art and science of determining a vessel's position and moving the vessel safely from one location to another. PILOTING is navigation in sight of land.

navigation aids, electronic – electronic navigation aids aboard a vessel include GPS, CHART PLOTTER, RADAR, AIS, DEPTH SOUNDER, SPEED AND DISTANCE LOGS. New navigational electronics are constantly developed, as ship electronics technology trickles down to yachts.

navigation at night – *see* NIGHT NAVIGATION.

navigation buoys – *see* BUOYS, NAVIGATION.

navigation calculator – a type of scientific calculator programmed to do navigation calculations of all types: SIGHT REDUCTION, FIXES using horizontal and vertical angles and special BEARINGS, SPEED, TIME AND DISTANCE problems, SET and DRIFT calculations, GREAT CIRCLE and RHUMB LINE calculations, and much more. The Tamaya NC 2100-E and Starpilot T86, 89, 92-Plus and V200 are examples. These calculators are relatively easy to use, and greatly help the navigator with traditional PILOTING and celestial navigation.

navigation courses – a number of organizations and maritime training schools offer classroom and online courses for traditional navigation (paper and pencil) and electronic navigation. The quality, time requirements, and cost of the instruction varies; if possible, check with students who have taken the courses. Some excellent courses are not expensive. To become a competent and safe mariner sign up for instruction in traditional PILOTING and navigation. It's the foundation for electronic navigation.

navigation, electronic – *see* ELECTRONIC NAVIGATION.

navigation, head of – *see* HEAD OF NAVIGATION.

navigation lights, running lights – the NAVIGATION RULES require that power and sailing vessels display their running lights when UNDERWAY at night and in RESTRICTED VISIBILITY. The lights may also be shown during the day. The basic navigation lights are red (PORT) and green (STARBOARD) SIDELIGHTS and a white STERN LIGHT. A POWER-DRIVEN vessel also shows a white MASTHEAD LIGHT when underway. There are additional specific lighting requirements; these are contained in Rules 20-31 of the Navigation Rules. Navigation lights indicate the vessel's course, type and size of vessel, and its NAVIGATION STATUS. The vessel operator must make certain that nothing on the boat obscures her lights, such as a DINGHY on the stern or a SELF-STEERING vane that completely blocks the stern light. Under some conditions military vessels may conduct exercises or operate at night without lights, or display other lights in addition to navigation lights. See the next entry.

navigation lights, special – Rules 23-31 of the NAVIGATION RULES require some vessels to display special, ALL-AROUND lights in addition to their prescribed NAVIGATION LIGHTS. These lights indicate the type of vessel (fishing, trawling, sailing, pilot vessel, towing vessel, mine sweeper), and/or HER NAVIGATION STATUS. The vessels listed below display these all-around lights in a vertical line; this memory aid is in the RIGHT OF WAY PRIORITY order, highest priority first:

- Red over red – "the captain's dead" (NOT UNDER COMMAND).
- Red, white, red – "restricted ability ahead" (RESTRICTED IN ABILITY TO MANEUVER).
- Three reds in a row – "no room below" (CONSTRAINED BY DRAFT); INTERNATIONAL Rules only.
- Red over white – "FISHING at night."
- Green over white – "TRAWLING at night."
- Red over green – "sailing machine."

• White over red – "pilot ahead" (a PILOT VESSEL).

• Yellow over yellow – "pushing or HIP-TOWING fellow" (tug with barge(s); INLAND Rules only.

• Yellow over white – "my towline is tight" (tug towing barges ASTERN).

• Three greens in a cross – "mine-clearing boss."

The Annex to the Rules contains other special lights for fishing vessels, dredges, vessels conducting underwater operations, law enforcement vessels, and for moored barges. All mariners should know these lights. See Rule 3 and the individual entries for NAVIGATION STATUS and types of vessels.

Navigation Rules – common name for the International Regulations for Preventing Collisions at Sea (also known as the COLREGS or the Rules of the Road). The operators of all power and sail vessels, no matter the size of the vessel, are legally obligated to know and follow these rules. The Navigation Rules contain the Steering and Sailing rules, rules for lights and DAYSHAPES, sound and light signals, and distress signals, as well as other important and essential information. Some of the rules for lights and dayshapes are slightly different for vessels under 7m/22ft in length. The coastal waters of the U.S. fall under both INLAND and INTERNATIONAL Rules; where the changes occur are indicated by DEMARCATION LINES printed on charts. In other countries the International Rules apply to all coastal and ocean waters, except where small modifications have been made by a government, harbor, port, or river authority. Consult a NAUTICAL ALMANAC for the particular country or area. The Steering and Sailing Rules apply to situations involving only *two* vessels; they don't cover situations involving multiple vessels. Sailing vessels and power-driven vessels have different rules. In addition to the Rules, read the Annexes at the back of the book, which contain rules for fishing vessels, dredges, vessels conducting underwater operations, law enforcement vessels, and for moored barges. A mariner must know the rules for all types of vessels.

The U.S. Coast Guard publication, *Navigation Rules – International and Inland*, has the Inland and International Rules on facing pages. A copy if the Rules is required aboard all U.S. vessels over 12m/39.4ft in length. For smaller vessels and for quick reference, buy a plastic-laminated chart of the Navigation Rules and lights. Download and print a copy of the Rules from www.navcen.uscg.gov/mwv/navrules/navrules.htm, or buy the inexpensive book. *See also* GENERAL PRUDENTIAL RULE and RULE OF GOOD SEAMANSHIP.

Navigation Rules, Steering Rules memory aid – here's a rhyme to help mariners remember the basic Steering Rules. It's not a substitute for learning the complete rules; it was created to help 19th century sailors remember the general rules for two vessels MEETING or CROSSING. Thomas Gray (head of the Marine Department of the British Board of Trade from 1869 to 1893) wrote it in 1867.

When all three lights I see ahead,
I turn to Starboard and show my Red:
Green to Green, Red to Red,
Perfect Safety -- Go Ahead.

But if to Starboard Red appear,
'Tis my duty to keep clear –
To act as judgment says is proper:
To Port or Starboard, Back or Stop her.

And if upon my Port is seen
A Steamer's Starboard light of Green,
I hold my course and watch to see
That Green to Port keeps Clear of me.

Both in safety and in doubt
Always keep a good look out.
In Danger, with no room to turn,
Ease her, Stop her, Go Astern.

navigation software – computer software to use with ELECTRONIC CHARTS and to perform other navigation functions. A number of different programs are available, but most are not compatible with each other. The industry is working to address compatibility issues.

navigation status – the phrase refers to whether a vessel UNDERWAY is NOT UNDER COMMAND, RESTRICTED IN ABILITY TO MANEUVER, FISHING, MOTORSAILING, CONSTRAINED BY DRAFT, or TOWING or mine clearing. There are special NAVIGATION LIGHTS and DAYSHAPES for these vessels.

navigation warnings – urgent marine information broadcast (MSI) issued between the regular dissemination interval of a NOTICE TO MARINERS. Warnings include such things as a danger to navigation, a light being extinguished or showing improper CHARACTERISTICS, the establishment of a danger zone around a wreck or diving operations, the approach of severe weather, etc. Navigation warnings are broadcast by the Coast Guard and on NAVTEX.

navigational aid – a magnetic compass, PLOTTING TOOLS, charts, electronics or anything aboard the vessel that assists the navigator. An *aid to navigation* is a light, buoy, or other object located off the boat.

NAVTEX – acronym for navigational telex, which is an international, automated electronic system that provides text information about safety, weather, navigation warnings, and search-and-rescue. The information is sent by MEDIUM-FREQUENCY radio signals to a small, inexpensive NAVTEX receiver that displays the information on a screen, and/or prints it out either on the device itself, on a CHART PLOTTER, or on an attached computer. Two frequencies are used: 518kHz (the main channel, text in English), and 490 kHz (a secondary channel, in local languages). NAVTEX units are available as single or dual-channel models. 4290.5 kHz is being developed for tropical regions. The range of NAVTEX stations is generally 100-500NM. The system works automatically; turn it on and leave it on as long as it's needed. The receiver draws very little power. It can be set to receive the nearest NAVTEX stations automatically, if it's interfaced with a GPS, or stations can be manually selected. NAVTEX stations are listed in NAUTICAL ALMANACS, and the NAVTEX manual may have a list. The stations in a particular area are sequenced so they don't interfere with each other. NAVTEX is part of GMDSS. Because it's receive-only equipment, no license is required.

"neaped" – caught aground on a neap tide. *See* TIDE, NEAP.

neap tide, neaps – *see* TIDE, NEAP.

neck lanyard – *see* LANYARD, NECK.

nettles- another name for REEF PENDANTS.

NFPA® – abbreviation for the NATIONAL FIRE PROTECTION ASSOCIATION.

NGA – abbreviation for the NATIONAL GEOSPATIAL INTELLIGENCE AGENCY.

NHC – abbreviation for the NATIONAL HURRICANE CENTER.

night navigation – sometimes it's easier than navigating in daylight, if there are lighted aids to navigation, and little or no interference from shore lights. Prepare a PASSAGE PLAN with the lights, their CHARACTERISTICS, and range of visibility. See next two entries.

night vision devices – special binoculars, goggles, and cameras that enhance the received light or detect temperature differences (FLIR, forward-looking infrared) to significantly improve night vision. Military technology comes to the consumer market. This gear is expensive, but if you do a lot of night navigation it may be worth it if your budget allows. If possible, test a night vision device in actual use before purchase; it may not meet your expectations on a moving vessel.

night vision, human – night vision takes 15-20 minutes in a dark environment to develop. Once the crew's eyes have adjusted to the dark it's important to preserve night vision. Install red lights below decks at the chart table and for a few cabin lights, such as those in the galley and HEAD, and have small flashlights or headlamps with red lenses for the crew. A useful trick when trying to see something at a distance in the dark is to look about 10° to the side of the object – you'll see it better than when trying to look directly at it. The skipper should ask any crew member who's assigned to a night watch if he/she is color blind; not being able to distinguish the colors of NAVIGATION LIGHTS and lighted aids to navigation could be deadly.

nine – the numeral "9" is spoken on the radio as "**nine**-er" so it's clearly distinguished from other numbers.

NIMA – abbreviation for the NATIONAL IMAGERY AND MAPPING AGENCY.

nip, "freshen the nip" – the nip is a bend in a rope where it goes around a CLEAT, or through a BLOCK, FAIRLEAD or CHOCK. Chafe can occur at this point if the line is in place for a long time under a strain. EASE or haul-in on the line slightly to freshen the nip.

nipped, beset – caught in the ice. "Shackleton's *Endurance* was nipped in the ice near the South Pole."

NIST – abbreviation for the NATIONAL INSTITUTE of STANDARDS. *See* WWV.

NMEA® – abbreviation for the NATIONAL MARINE ELECTRONICS ASSOCIATION.

NMEA 0183 and NMEA 2000 – two electronic interface standards for electronic and data communication between marine electronic devices. These two protocols allow the interconnection of electronics, such as GPS, CHART PLOTTER, DEPTH SOUNDER, electronic engine monitoring systems, tank gauges, and other electronic devices. The data from each instrument can be sent to a MULTIFUNCTION DISPLAY or other screens. 0183 is the older standard.

NMEA 2000 makes interconnecting electronics easier than with 0183. You'll encounter these terms in equipment manuals and if you talk to an electronics technician. Research the topic for the technical details.

NMMA® – abbreviation for the NATIONAL MARINE MANUFACTURERS ASSOCIATION.

NOAA – abbreviation for the NATIONAL OCEANIC AND ATMOSPHERIC ADMINISTRATION.

NOAA weather alert – in the U.S. in the event of an extreme weather disturbance, such as a storm or hurricane warning, NOAA sends a weather alert to VHF radios equipped for reception of the alert (check the radio manual). The alert is preceded by an attention-getting 1050 HZ tone, and then the weather alert is broadcast on the WEATHER CHANNELS.

noble – noble metals are those with more resistance to GALVANIC CORROSION in saltwater. Noble metals are more CATHODIC, and corrode less. Less-noble metals are more ANODIC, and they corrode more readily. *See* GALVANIC SERIES.

no-discharge area or zone, NDA, NDZ – a designated body of water or area where the discharge of treated and untreated boat sewage is prohibited. U.S. Federal law prohibits the discharge of *untreated* sewage from all vessels within three miles of shore on all navigable waters of the U. S., including the TERRITORIAL SEAS. In some areas "no discharge" may include GRAY as well as BLACK WATER. Check the environmental protection agencies in the states, provinces or particular country for specific regulations. The U.S. Environmental Protection Agency (EPA) website has links to some regional regulations. All vessels, no matter the country of registry, must comply with no-discharge regulations, and fines or civil penalties may be imposed for violations. It's your responsibility to know where these areas are. Most marinas worldwide are no-discharge areas. *See* MARINE TOILET.

nominal range – the nominal range of a light is the theoretical maximum distance the light can be seen in clear weather (visibility defined as 10NM). It's based on the intensity of the light, and does *not* consider the height of the light or the observer's eye or the curvature of the earth. U.S. LIGHT LISTS give the nominal range for lighted aids; other light lists or charts may indicate the GEOGRAPHIC RANGE.

non-commercial vessel – a recreational vessel or pleasure craft.

non-tidal basin – a BASIN where the water level remains relatively constant through the use of gates or a lock. *See* TIDAL BASIN.

noon sight – *see* SIGHT.

Nor'easter– a rapidly intensifying LOW PRESSURE SYSTEM that occurs on the Atlantic coast of North America from Georgia to the Canadian Maritimes, primarily in winter, but it can form in spring and fall. A Nor'easter may begin as a low pressure system in the Gulf of Mexico, and then travel up the east coast, intensifying as it goes, particularly around Cape Hatteras, North Carolina. It's called a Nor'easter because of the predominantly northeast winds. It can bring storm winds and waves to the coast, along with coastal damage, blizzards, or heavy rains. Because the cold Labrador current meets the warm GULF STREAM in the north Atlantic, the U.S. east coast is a prime area for the formation of Nor'easters. *See* LOW, RAPIDLY INTENSIFYING.

North American Datum of 1983, NAD83 – a modern CHART DATUM equivalent to WGS84.

Northern Lights – common name for Aurora Borealis, a spectacular display of shifting lights and colors in the middle and high latitude winter sky. The comparable phenomenon in the Southern Hemisphere is the AURORA AUSTRALIS.

northing – to make good a distance in a northerly direction. "It would be good to make as much northing as we can in the next two days." Easting, southing, and westing can also be used in this sense.

North Pacific High – a semi-permanent, subtropical area of HIGH PRESSURE in the North Pacific Ocean. It's strongest in the Northern Hemisphere's summer; in the winter it's forced toward the equator when the Aleutian Low becomes dominant. The BERMUDA HIGH and the AZORES HIGH are comparable systems in the Atlantic.

north-up display – some electronic instruments (radar, AIS or a CHART PLOTTER) may be set (using the menu) to display north (either TRUE or MAGNETIC) at the top of the screen. The screen display is like looking at a chart that's printed with north up. It does not display what you're seeing in front of the boat (unless you're heading north). When the heading of the vessel changes, the display doesn't change as it does on a HEAD-UP DISPLAY. To have a north-up display the electronic equipment must have an input from an electronic compass or a GYROCOMPASS. Switching between head-up or north-up can be a source of dangerous confusion, even on a ship's bridge.

North Wall – the north side boundary of the GULF STREAM, generally extending northeast from Cape Hatteras. The WEST WALL is the boundary that's toward the U.S. east coast, typically south of Cape Hatteras.

notices to mariners, chart corrections – information disseminated at intervals by government sources or private chart publishers about changes in aids to navigation, hazards, safety zones, or anything important to safe navigation that have taken place since a chart or COAST PILOT was published. Even though private chart publishers issue periodic chart corrections for their products, a mariner should also consult government chart publishers' websites for weekly corrections. Notices to mariners apply to a specific edition of a chart or COAST PILOT; when a new edition is published it may be difficult or impossible to find corrections for older editions. If a marine accident takes place investigators may check to see if the vessels involved have up-to-date charts and pilots aboard. Canadian Notices to Mariners are available at www.notmar.gc.ca. The UK Hydrographic Office (www.ukho.gov.uk) issues weekly Notices to Mariners for their worldwide paper and electronic charts, and for the Admiralty Leisure chart series. See the following two entries for the U.S. forms of notices to mariners.

Notices to Mariners, NtM – in the U.S. the NGA's Notices to Mariners is for ocean-going vessels sailing in U.S. waters or making a port call from overseas. Because the NGA no longer publisher paper charts and their electronic charts are available only to military vessels, recreational mariners have little reason to check the NtM, unless they have some old NGA/NIMA/DMA charts. Notices to Mariners are available at the NGA website: http://

msi.nga.mil/NGAPortal/MSI.portal; click on "Notice to Mariners." See the next entry.

Notice to Mariners, Local, LNM – issued weekly, the U.S. Local Notice to Mariners is for all vessels using U.S. waters, including the INTRACOASTAL WATERWAY. The LNM lists the changes to aids to navigation and other important information that have occurred since the last LNM. These notices have the most up-to-date information for correcting charts or COAST PILOTS. Each Coast Guard District publishes the LNM for a particular district; click on the map at www.navcen.uscg.gov for the USCG district applicable to a particular area. See previous entry.

not under command, NUC – Rule 3(f) of the NAVIGATION RULES defines a vessel not under command as "a vessel which through some exceptional circumstance is unable to maneuver as required by these Rules and is therefore unable to keep out of the way of another vessel." This rule applies to any vessel that's UNDERWAY, not just power-driven vessels. An exceptional circumstance might include such things as loss of steering, an inoperative engine or loss of engine power so the vessel cannot maintain steerage, entanglement with nets or other obstructions that prevent maneuvering, a becalmed sailboat that can't operate her engine to get out of the way, or a vessel dragging anchor. The problem must be one that makes the vessel *unable* to be maneuvered to keep out of the way of another vessel. If you're drift fishing with your engine shut down you are *not* a NUC vessel. Rule 27(a) prescribes the lights and DAYSHAPE for a NUC vessel:

- If the vessel is underway and making way she displays two ALL-AROUND red lights in a vertical line ("red over red, the captain's dead").
- When underway she displays SIDELIGHTS and a STERN LIGHT. She does not display MASTHEAD LIGHTS.
- If she's underway but not making way, she displays only the two red lights in a vertical line.
- The dayshape is two black balls in a vertical line.

ASI-A indicates NUC vessel status. Rule 35 prescribes the SOUND SIGNALS for these vessels in RESTRICTED VISIBILITY.

NTIA – abbreviation for NATIONAL TELECOMMUNICATIONS AND INFORMATION ADMINISTRATION.

NUC – abbreviation for a vessel NOT UNDER COMMAND.

NWS – abbreviation for the NATIONAL WEATHER SERVICE.

O

oarlock, rowlock – the round or U-shaped hardware that holds an oar when rowing. The oar may be loose in the oarlock, or it may have a pin through it to secure it to the rowlock. A THOLE PIN is a type of oarlock.

occluded front, occlusion – *see* FRONT, OCCLUDED.

ocean-crossing rally, offshore cruising rally – mariners planning to cross an ocean may choose to participate in an organized group event, such as the Atlantic Rally for Cruisers (ARC), the CARIBBEAN 1500, or a number of events sponsored by cruising rally organizations or CRUISING CLUBS. These events may appeal for a first offshore trip or to enjoy the organizational assistance and camaraderie of a group event. Events are scheduled for sailing vessels and long-range power yachts. Advantages of participation in an offshore rally include: vessel and crew preparation guides, organization of special departure and arrival events and services, fleet weather routing, communication and tracking of participating yachts, skipper's handbooks and port guides, and other benefits, depending upon the rally organizer. The main disadvantage of signing up for an offshore rally is being caught up in the HERD MENTALITY and the constraints of SCHEDULES. A skipper may feel pressure to depart with the fleet when the weather seems unfavorable to him/her. Everyone aboard has planned for the trip, money has been spent, and the there may be a reluctance to delay departure and sail on your own later, or cancel the trip altogether. Experienced cruisers know that to be safe, sailors should make well-informed, independent decisions based on the capabilities of the boat and the particular crew. Be honest in your self-assessment. If your gut feeling says "don't go," heed the inner warning. Also, if the yacht is not up to offshore standards it may involve additional expense to meet the rally's safety requirements. If the yacht's not up to offshore sailing, are you?

Ocean Cruising Club, OCC – qualification, nomination, and approval are required for membership. The OCC has publications, harbor information, port representatives, and activities for members worldwide. The club is administered from the UK. www.oceancruisingclub.org.

ocean current – *see* CURRENT, OCEAN.

offing, in the offing – a distance offshore away from navigation hazards, but still in sight of land. To make or keep a good offing is to LAY a course well clear of dangers.

offshore, offshore waters – waters of oceans, gulfs, and seas located beyond coastal waters, usually implying out of sight of land. Depending on the definition used in a particular country, offshore waters extend out a specified distance from the coastline, to a specified depth contour, or to an area defined by specific LATITUDE and LONGITUDE coordinates.

offshore breeze, land breeze – a breeze that blows from the land towards the sea. An offshore breeze generally occurs at night when the land cools and the sea is warmer than the land.

offshore cruising rally – another name for an OCEAN-CROSSING RALLY.

offshore medical assistance – *see* MEDICAL ASSISTANCE OFFSHORE.

offshore safety – safety standards have been developed for offshore racing, and the standards are definitely applicable to offshore cruising sailboats. There are standards for MONOHULLS and MULTIHULLS, structural standards, specifications for yacht equipment and safety gear, and crew training standards. The INTERNATIONAL SAILING FEDERATION (ISAF) website has information relevant to offshore yachts and crews: see www.sailing.org.

Click on "Documents and Rules" and "Offshore Special Regulations" and "Equipment Rules." ISAF also sponsors the SAFETY AT SEA SEMINARS. See the bibliography under "Safety" and "offshore" for additional resources.

off soundings, on soundings – *see* SOUNDINGS, ON OR OFF.

off station – applied to a floating aid to navigation that is not in its correct position. Off station information is communicated in NOTICES TO MARINERS and on VHF broadcasts.

off the wind – applied to POINTS OF SAIL from a BROAD REACH to a RUN.

ohm – a measure of resistance (the opposition to the flow of current) in an electric circuit or equipment. A MULTIMETER measures ohms.

oil, engine – always use oil of the correct specification for the engine, as indicated in the ENGINE MANUAL. Some engines require mineral oil, while others may be able to use synthetic engine oil. Diesel engine oil turns black very quickly; that's normal. If the oil is gray, brown, or appears to have water in it, don't run engine, and call a mechanic. Check the oil level daily – if the level *increases* on the dipstick, then water or fuel is getting into the oil, another reason to call a mechanic. Avoid overfilling the engine when changing the oil; too much oil is harmful. If someone else changes the oil, check the level yourself.

oil filter, engine – observe the oil change interval as specified in the engine or generator manual, and change the filter at every oil change. A new filter is cheap insurance; carry spares. Many engines have the oil filter mounted horizontally on the engine, so it's impossible to avoid spilling oil when replacing it. Consider installing a remote (off-engine) oil filter, which has the filter mounted upright so it doesn't spill (as much) when it's removed. If someone else changes the oil always check the level afterwards before running the engine. More than one yacht has had trouble because the person who changed the oil forgot to refill it or didn't put enough in.

oil pressure, engine – one of the ENGINE INSTRUMENTS.

oil pressure sender – a small device mounted in the engine block that senses the engine oil pressure and electrically sends it to the oil pressure gauge on the instrument panel. If the gauge isn't working check the sender first. A wire may have come off, or it needs to be replaced, a fairly easy task.

oilskins, oilies – wet-weather clothing. Old-time sailors' clothing was made of oil or grease-impregnated cloth.

"old salt" – a mariner who has a good deal of experience at sea. Sometimes a salty-looking sailor is just wearing a costume and the non-descript individual has 200,000 sea miles.

"one hand for yourself and one hand for the ship" – an adage from the days of sailing ships that's still true today aboard any vessel. Hold on to something solid, rather than a rope or LIFELINES, and don't rely on a safety HARNESS to hold you while you use two hands. When it's rough you'll need two (or three) hands for yourself.

"on her ear" – slang for sailing when heeled far over. "Camille likes to sail *Temptress* on her ear."

on her lines – said of a boat that floats as designed, resting evenly along her designed waterline.

onshore wind, sea breeze – a wind that blows from the cool ocean onto warmer land. The breeze is caused by the unequal rates of heating and cooling of water and land.

on soundings, off soundings – *see* SOUNDINGS, ON OR OFF.

on the beam – same as ABEAM.

on the hard – on land, applied to a vessel stored ashore. "I stored my boat on the hard this winter."

"on the nose" – directly on the BOW; dead ahead, usually applied to the direction of the wind.

on the wind – sailing CLOSE-HAULED

open, opens – applied to the separation between RANGE (transit) objects when the vessel moves off to one side of the range line. "Keep the lighthouse open to the right of the church spire when you enter the channel."

open array – *see* ARRAY.

open roadstead – *see* ROADS, ROADSTEAD.

open water – non-specific term that implies being in unprotected waters or waters some distance from land.

outboard – (1) a direction away from the CENTERLINE of the boat. "Lead the SHEETS outboard of the SHROUDS." INBOARD is toward the centerline. (2) a portable or removable propulsion engine used on the STERN of some boats. ABYC has a number of standards for various components of outboard engine-driven boats.

outboard rudder – *see* RUDDER, OUTBOARD.

outfall – drainage from a sewer or street drain through a pipe that extends into the water. An outfall may be marked on a chart. It may have a buoy or DAYMARK if it's a hazard to navigation, or to indicate where the pipe is, so a vessel doesn't anchor over it.

"outfoot" – to sail faster than another yacht. "With our new SPINNAKER we'll outfoot the whole fleet on the last LEG."

outhaul – a line or TACKLE that pulls a sail out into the correct shape along its FOOT. A MAINSAIL usually has an outhaul that runs from the CLEW to the AFT end of the BOOM.

outpoint – to sail closer to the wind than another sailboat, especially when racing. "Mary Ann's boat can outpoint us, so she's going to get there first." *See* POINT (1).

out of sight, out of mind – a poor maxim on a boat. Hidden and inaccessible things can and do develop problems, so delve into those small spaces, make inaccessible areas accessible with hatches, doors, and inspection ports, and keep ahead of silent surprises. An INSPECTION MIRROR, a HEADLAMP, and a small, bright flashlight are good aids.

"over and out" – how NOT to end a radio transmission. You'll hear it quite frequently, but not from professional mariners. It's a Hollywood war movie phrase. Just say "out" when you're finished talking with the other station and you don't expect a reply. *See* PROWORDS.

overfalls – steep, short seas created by the action of WIND AGAINST TIDE. Under some conditions breaking overfalls can be dangerous to small and large vessels. Sometimes called TIDE RIPS. CRUISING GUIDES and notations on some charts warn of overfall areas.

The waves in these overfalls are about 3ft/0.9m high.

overhang or ends – the amount the BOW and/or STERN projects out from the waterline. If it projects out some distance from the waterline it's called a long overhang or a long end. Long overhangs or long ends are features of older sailing yacht design. For photos see CLASSIC VESSEL and LONG ENDS.

overhead – the nautical term for the "ceiling" over your head when below decks. "There's dirt on the overhead in the GALLEY." The word CEILING has a different meaning aboard a boat.

override – another name for a RIDING TURN.

over-rigged, under-rigged – an over-rigged boat has rigging that's heavier and stronger than typically recommended. Over-rigging adds weight above the waterline, but it's sometimes done, especially on a long-distance cruising boat. Pure racing sailboats may be under-rigged, with rigging slightly smaller than the recommended minimum to save weight.

overtaking – overtaking rules apply to both power-driven and sailing vessels. Rule 13 of the NAVIGATION RULES discusses the basic overtaking situation in open water. The vessel that's being overtaken has the highest RIGHT OF WAY PRIORITY of all vessels. If a sailing vessel overtakes a power boat, the power boat has the right of way. An overtaking situation is one in which you see the STERN of the vessel, or at night only her STERN LIGHT. If you can see the side of a vessel or either the red or the green NAVIGATION LIGHT it's a CROSSING SITUATION.

- If in doubt as to whether you're overtaking, assume that you *are* overtaking, and act accordingly.
- A vessel being overtaken should maintain her course and speed until the other vessel is past and clear. However, the vessel being overtaken may adjust her course to stay in a channel, slow down to allow the other vessel to pass, or take any other action necessary to avoid collision if the overtaking vessel gets too close.
- The overtaking vessel must stay clear and pass safely.
- If in doubt as to the actions of the other vessel, the vessel to be overtaken shall sound the DANGER SIGNAL (at least five short and rapid blasts on the whistle).

See SOUND SIGNALS, MANEUVERING and SOUND SIGNALS, OVERTAKING IN A NARROW CHANNEL.

overtaking sound signals – *see* SOUND SIGNALS, MANEUVERING.

overtaking in a narrow channel, sound signals – *see* SOUND SIGNALS, OVERTAKING IN A NARROW CHANNEl.

owners' associations – a good source for information and discussion forums related to specific brands and models of production sail and power boats. Check out an owner's association website before purchasing a new or used boat. Use a search engine to find relevant groups. See *Good Old Boat* in the bibliography, under "Maintenance," for one source of links to sailboat owners' associations.

oxide, oxidation – exposure to oxygen in the atmosphere causes metal to oxidize; rust on FERROUS metals is a common type of oxidation. Oxides on ALUMINUM and STAINLESS STEEL are actually protective. *See* PASSIVATE.

P

pack ice, sea ice – ice too thick for most vessels to navigate through, except for some icebreakers. If you're navigating near ice in the fog and the waves are smaller than you expect, pack ice may be nearby. If the water temperature is below 32°F/0°C the edge of the pack ice is probably within 50 miles.

packing – a grease-impregnated rope-like material that's inserted in a STUFFING BOX to keep it from leaking. Tighten the packing nut to compress the packing until the leak almost stops. It should be loose enough to allow two or three drops a minute when the prop shaft is turning. The drip ensures that the packing isn't too tight around the shaft to cause undue wear. As the packing wears, tighten the nut a little. When the drip becomes too frequent and the nut can't be tightened any more, replace the packing. *See* STUFFING BOX, DRIPLESS.

packing gland – another name for a STUFFING BOX.

Pactor – a modem for use with SINGLE-SIDEBAND RADIO and a computer to allow the sending and receiving of email, weather fax charts, GRIB files, and other data via SAILMAIL, WINLINK, or other services.

pad eye – a piece of metal hardware that consists of a flat plate with holes for fasteners and a metal loop standing up on it. Some have a loop that folds down. Pad eyes are used on SPARS, on the deck, or anywhere a strong attachment point is needed. BLOCKS, JACKLINES, a safety HARNESS TETHER, a VANG or other items can be attached to pad eyes.

A pad eye on the toe rail.

paint – when a radar beam hits a TARGET, it "paints it" and makes it show up on the screen. "My radar won't paint a target that small at this distance."

painter – the line attached to the BOW of a DINGHY or other small boat, used to tie it up.

Pan Pan (pronounced pahn pahn) – an *urgency* call on a radiotelephone for situations *other than* grave and imminent danger to human life or the vessel. It is *not* a distress call.

Use a Pan Pan call for incidents such as a non-life threatening medical emergency, a man-overboard incident in conditions where the victim is likely to be recovered without difficulty, a vessel in difficulty due to severe weather, a vessel aground or dragging anchor (but *not* with immediate danger to human life or loss of the vessel), loss of engine power (and no wind) in a shipping channel, etc.

The purpose of a Pan Pan is to alert the Coast Guard or other listening stations that you are in difficulty and require or may require assistance. It's better to issue a Pan Pan, and then cancel it if you resolve the problem, rather than wait until you've got a MAYDAY situation.

If a Pan Pan situation becomes life-threatening, broadcast a Mayday.

When a Pan Pan situation has been resolved, either you or the Coast Guard *must* cancel the Pan Pan on the radio, using a specific radio procedure. *See* MAYDAY CANCELLATION.

Have a pre-printed reference card near the radio so the crew can make the call or a cancellation using the proper procedure.

Pan Pan call – the procedure for making a Pan Pan call on VHF Channel 16 or on SINGLE-SIDEBAND DISTRESS FREQUENCIES is to say:

- **Pan Pan** three times.
- **All Stations** three times.
- **This is** [the name of your vessel three times].
- Your CALL SIGN or MMSI number, or boat registration number once.
- **My Position Is** [give your position by LATITUDE and LONGITUDE, or by BEARING and distance to a well-know landmark, an aid to navigation, land feature, or in any terms that will help a responding station locate you].
- **There Are** [number of people] **Aboard**.
- Describe the nature of your problem.
- **I Require** [describe the assistance you need].
- **This Is** [your vessel's name once].
- **Over**. – wait for a response.

If no response after one or two minutes, repeat the call. If the Coast Guard responds on the radio they may ask you to call them back at specific intervals to tell them how you are getting along controlling the situation, or they may choose to send assistance. A PAN PAN call *must* be cancelled using the proper radio procedure when the situation has been resolved. *See* MAYDAY CANCELLATION. *See also* MAYDAY and SECURITÉ calls.

Pan Pan cancellation – *see* MAYDAY CANCELLATION.

parallel – a line of LATITUDE.

parallel rulers, parallels – a plastic or metal device used by a navigator for PLOTTING on a chart. It consists of two straight rulers connected together so they can be moved in parallel across the chart to a COMCPASS ROSE, to measure a COURSE or BEARING. Some parallel rulers have a protractor scale printed on one edge. Designed for use on a ship's large chart table, they aren't as easy to use as a COURSE PLOTTER.

parcel, parceling – to cover a rope with strips of canvas or leather when making permanent CHAFING GEAR. *See* WORM for the procedure.

partners – short name for MAST PARTNERS.

parts of a line – *see* LINE, PARTS OF.

parts manual, engine – *see* ENGINE MANUALS.

pass – another name for an INLET (1).

passage – (1) a trip at sea; one leg of a voyage. May imply being offshore, and it's not specific as to the length of the trip. "We were on passage from New York to Boston when we saw the whales." (2) a channel or pass between obstacles; a navigable channel leading to a harbor or lagoon. "There is a rock-strewn passage leading to that anchorage."

passage plan, pre-trip plan – a plan for a trip or passage made before departing. It's for use aboard the boat, in contrast to a FLOAT PLAN, which is for persons at home. Take the time to prepare it carefully. If you encounter difficult conditions along the way that's no time to make sure the plan is accurate. It's a good idea to review the passage plan with the crew. If it's written down they can look at it during the trip. Someone may notice information that should be corrected, or see the need for additional information. A basic passage plan includes:

> Departure information: a weather forecast, tide and current information, aids to navigation, hazards on the way out of the harbor.
>
> Passage information: courses, distances, tides and currents, ETAs, navigation aids, danger areas, WAYPOINTS or routes (if used), alternate harbors along the way.
>
> Arrival information: hazards on or near the approach, aids to navigation for the approach and entering harbor, tide and current details, harbor information, specific VHF channels for marina, harbormaster, port officials, bridges, etc.

Electronic devices can be used to prepare a general passage plan, but a paper plan with specific notes is important in case the electronics fail.

passenger vessel – considered a COMMERCIAL vessel in most countries.

passengers for hire – *see* COMMERCIAL VESSEL.

passerelle – a gangplank deployed off the BOW or STERN, used when MED MOORING. Commercial models are available, but some people make their own. A gangway is a plank or ramp on the side of a vessel used for boarding and disembarking.

passive, passivate – (1) a passive metal has developed a natural protective oxide on its surface, or the oxide has been created by a passivation process. A metal that hasn't been passivated is considered an active metal in the GALVANIC SERIES. Active metals corrode more easily than passive metals of the same type. (2) to passivate is to make a metal more resistant to corrosion. STAINLESS STEEL is frequently passivated. An acid bath or ELECTROPOLISHING removes iron embedded in the stainless steel by the manufacturing or machining process, thus helping to prevent rust spots from forming.

pawl – a part of a WINCH, WINDLASS, or CAPSTAN that engages the gear teeth to prevent it from turning backwards. A pawl is operated by the action of a spring or by gravity. A winch service kit includes spare pawls and springs.

pay off – to allow the BOW to turn away from the wind, especially when TACKING. "When you tack, let her pay off onto the new HEADING."

pay out, veer – to release a line in a controlled manner, as when paying out the anchor RODE. Pay out implies letting out more line than when EASING.

pecking order – commonly-used term for the RIGHT OF WAY PRIORITY under the NAVIGATION RULES.

pedestal, steering pedestal – a vertical structure in the COCKPIT on which the steering wheel and (usually) the compass are mounted. The pedestal may have a pedestal guard or handgrip of curved metal or wood, with navigation electronics attached to it.

pedestal guard – a curved metal rail attached to the pedestal. It's a handhold and a place to mount electronics.

pedestal winch, coffee grinder – a tall WINCH used on some racing sailboats, designed to be cranked by two crew members who stand facing each other.

pelican hook – an elongated hook with a metal "keeper" that slips over the hook, or another locking mechanism, to prevent it from accidentally opening. Pelican hooks are commonly used on LIFELINE GATES.

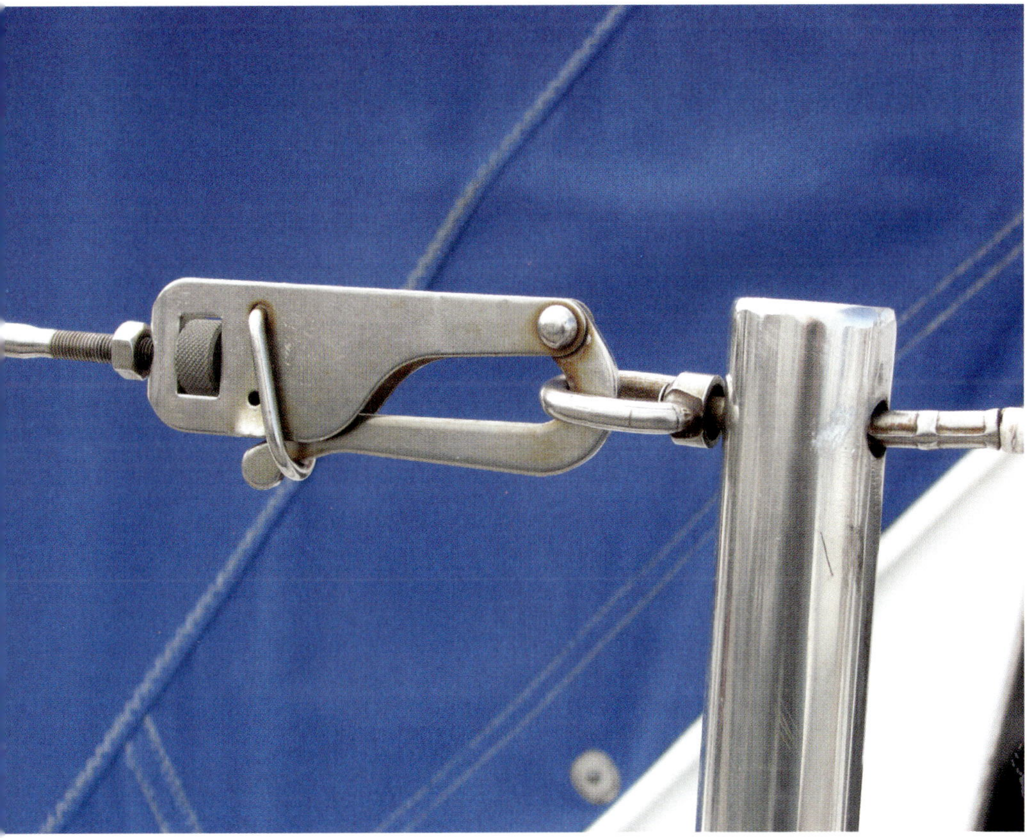

A pelican hook on a lifeline gate.

pelorus – a simple navigation instrument for taking RELATIVE BEARINGS. It's a circular device with two vertical sighting vanes located at 180° to each other, and a degree scale on a circular card (like a COMPASS CARD). Sight across the vanes at an object, and read the bearing on the card scale. Bearings taken with a pelorus are computed by reference to the steering compass. The HAND-BEARING COMPASS and COMPASS BINOCULARS have replaced the pelorus for taking visual bearings, but a pelorus works, and it's simple.

pendant, pennant – (1) interchangeable names for special purpose short lines, such as REEF PENDANTS (reef points) or a pennant on the TACK of a sail (to allow the sail to be raised higher off the deck). (2) a small flag, frequently triangular, used as a BURGEE for a yacht club or other organization.

performance cruiser, performance yacht – a marketing term implying that the sailboat has been designed for good speed under sail and power, as well as cruising comforts. This type of boat usually has a modern hull form and KEEL, a tall, powerful rig, and a large engine. *See* CRUISER-RACER.

period of waves – *see* WAVE PERIOD.

"permission to come aboard?" – it's customary and polite to ask the skipper or a crewmember on another boat for permission before boarding the vessel.

permit, cruising – *see* CRUISING PERMIT.

personal locator beacon, PLB – a small EPIRB designed to be carried by crewmembers. PLBs operate on 406 MHz, with a 121.5MHz homing signal (the same as the larger units). They're available with or without an integral GPS. The battery life of a PLB is 30-35 hours at -4°F/-20°C (in contrast to 48-72 hours for a large EPIRB). A PLB isn't as robustly-built as a large EPIRB, and *it is not* a substitute for a full-size EPIRB. It's registered to a person, not the vessel. Each PLB has a unique number that identifies the beacon. It's *required by law* that it be registered with the appropriate government agency, and the registration renewed every two years. Registration informs search-and-rescue about the person sending the signal, which helps in the rescue effort. See the bibliography under "Emergencies" for beacon registration information. Some brands of PLB can be set up to transmit brief, custom, non-distress text/email messages to people back home. This service requires a subscription fee/service plan. *See also* SPOT II .

personal watercraft, PWC – a fast and highly-maneuverable small vessel, such as a jet-ski, designed for one or two persons. Operators of these craft are required to observe the NAVIGATION RULES, but operators of larger vessels should be vigilant when PWCs are operating nearby.

pets – if you have a seagoing pet and you're "going foreign," check the regulations for pets in other countries. If rabies is not in a country, the laws are especially strict. In some countries a pet is not allowed off the boat or on deck under any circumstances (even to visit a veterinarian), and you may not be permitted to tie up at a shore location. Fees may be charged to have an officer make regular visits to the vessel to check if the pet is still aboard. Penalties for violating animal control laws can be severe, including loss of the animal. Taking a pet to a country that permits pets may involve getting a veterinarian's certificate for health and vaccinations, sometimes within a rather short time period before arriving in a country. Check CRUISING INFORMATION WEBSITES, government websites, and articles in magazines for pet regulations.

PFD – U.S. Coast Guard abbreviation for personal flotation device, commonly called a lifejacket.

phonetic alphabet – internationally-understood ENGLISH LANGUAGE words used on a radiotelephone to indicate the letters of the alphabet, as when spelling out the name of a vessel or other words, giving the letters in a CALL SIGN, or communicating using the INTERNATIONAL CODE OF SIGNALS.

The letters are Alpha, Bravo, Charlie, Delta, Echo, Foxtrot, Golf, Hotel (hoh **tell**), India, Juliet, Kilo (**kee** low), Lima (**lee** mah), Mike, November, Oscar, Papa (Pah **pah**), Quebec (kay **beck**), Romeo, Sierra, Tango, Uniform (**you** nee form), Victor, Whiskey, X-Ray, Yankee, Zulu.

Speak all numbers: one, three, six, **nine**-er for nine, and zero (not "oh."). For numbers from nine upward, speak all numbers, e.g. "one zero" for ten, "six eight" for 68, or "one-eight-five" for 185.

A decimal is said as *decimal* (not "point"). "My position is five eight degrees, five six *decimal* seven zero north."

pick-up buoy, pick-up float – a small buoy or float with a small-diameter rope attached to the larger rope or chain on a mooring buoy, to make it easier to pick it up with a BOATHOOK. A pick-up float may also have a vertical stick to grab. Don't use the pick-up buoy's small rope to tie the vessel to the mooring, except temporarily in light winds. Always attach the heavier mooring line or chain securely to the boat. *See* MOORING, PICKING UP.

pier – (1) a structure on wood, metal or concrete pilings that projects out from the shore; a jetty. A pier may have berths alongside for vessels. The seaward end is the pierhead. (2) the vertical supports for a bridge.

"pig stick" – slang term for the short flagstaff at the top of a mast from which the vessel's PRIVATE SIGNAL or a BURGEE is flown. The stick is raised on a light HALYARD dedicated to that purpose.

pilot – (1) a COAST PILOT. (2) a professional mariner who guides ships into and out of ports.

pilot boat – same as PILOT VESSEL.

pilot chart – *see* CHART, PILOT.

piloting or inshore navigation – specific terms applied to navigating in coastal waters, using visual and/or electronic means to determine the vessel's position and move her safely from point-to-point. The phrase "traditional piloting" implies PLOTTING on paper or electronic charts, using DEAD RECKONING, taking BEARINGS, etc. to determine the vessel's position.

piloting, blind – navigating only with instruments, in very poor visibility or at night with no lighted aids to navigation or shore lights. Practice blind piloting in clear weather to gain experience with the electronics for when they are really needed.

pilothouse – a raised, enclosed structure with visibility forward and to the sides that has a HELM, a chart table, and possibly other accommodations in it. Some yachts have a pilothouse with a wheel (an inside steering station), as well as a helm on deck. For photos see BULWARK (*Sleipner*), CHARLIE NOBLE, CHINE (the orange sloop), MOTORSAILER, and RIDING SAIL.

pilot station – see the next entry.

pilot vessel, pilot boat – a vessel that takes PILOTS (2) to and from ships. Pilot boats use specific areas (a pilot station), which are usually marked on a chart. In this area they meet ships to deliver and remove pilots. They are power-driven vessels under the NAVIGATION RULES. Rule 29 specifies the lights for a pilot vessel:

- When the pilot boat is on duty she displays red and green SIDELIGHTS, a STERN LIGHT, and two ALL-AROUND lights in a vertical row, red over white ("pilot at night").
- When she's on duty at anchor, she displays an ANCHOR LIGHT or the anchor ball DAYSHAPE.
- When a pilot boat is not on duty she displays the lights for a power-driven vessel of her size.

pinch, pinching – to sail very close to the wind, closer than the boat's optimum wind angle (TACKING ANGLE). Pinching slows down a sailboat. "We'll have to pinch to LAY that course." "I'm pinching too much."

pintle, gudgeon – a pintle is a fitting on an OUTBOARD RUDDER that fits into a gudgeon on the hull to attach the rudder to the boat and allow it to pivot. Two or three pairs are used.

The pintle is on the rudder and the gudgeon is on the hull.

pitch – (1) the up and down motion of a boat's BOW as she proceeds through HEAD SEAS. (2) the theoretical distance advanced by a boat's propeller in one revolution.

pitchpole – a pitchpole occurs when a huge wave lifts the STERN of a vessel and causes her to flip end-over-end, stern over BOW. Pitchpoling is a *very* rare occurrence because of the extreme conditions necessary to produce waves of a size and steepness to cause it. Perhaps the most well-known pitchpole incident is the one survived by Miles and Beryl Smeeton and friend John Guzzwell in 1956. They were sailing around Cape Horn in their 46ft/14m yacht, *Tzu Hang*, when the vessel was pitchpoled. Miles tells their gripping story in *Once is Enough*, an all-time sea classic. For another hair-raising term, see KNOCKDOWN.

pivot point – the point somewhere along the CENTERLINE of a vessel around which she turns when the RUDDER is put over. A FIN KEEL sailboat pivots around the keel. The pivot point when going ahead is approximately one-third of the vessel's length back from the BOW; it's near the STERN when moving in reverse. The loading or trim of a vessel affects the location of the pivot point. Experiment with a boat to determine the location of the pivot point in forward and reverse.

pivot wear – *see* COMPASS, PIVOT WEAR.

plain sail – inclusive term for the WORKING SAILS. "It's time to set all plain sail and get going again."

plait, plaited – *see* ROPE, PLAITED.

plane, planing hull – a boat planes when most of her hull lifts out of the water. The most common example is a fast powerboat, where a small area at the STERN is in the water at the boat's higher speeds. However, advances in racing yacht design and technology produce large sailboats that can attain planing speeds under sail. MONOHULL yachts that plane have a narrow BOW and a flat hull form all the way to the stern. A DISPLACEMENT HULL can't go faster than the wave length created by the hull as it moves through the water. (*see* SPEED/LENGTH RATIO). Although a displacement hull can surf down waves and reach speeds higher than hull speed, this type of hull can't sustain those speeds like a planing hull. Open 50, 60, and 70 Class ocean racing sailboats, custom racers, and some small sailboats are designed to reach planing speeds.

Coxswains and boatcrews from U.S. Coast Guard Station Monterey operate a 47-foot motor lifeboat in heavy weather. *U.S. Coast Guard photo by Petty Officer 3rd Class Erik Swanson.*

pleasure craft – another term for a RECREATIONAL VESSEL.

plot, plotting – (1) the plot is the lines drawn on a chart indicating the intended or actual course(s) of a vessel. (2) plotting is the process of drawing course lines and bearings on a chart. A CHART PLOTTER does this electronically, but a mariner should know how to plot on a paper chart.

plotting, importance of – even with GPS or other electronics, CHART PLOTTERS, and automatic logging it's very important to maintain a written record on a chart and in a log of positions, FIXES, courses, times, and distances. Take the data from the electronics and write them down. In critical navigation situations, such as RESTRICTED VISIBILITY and PILOTING in hazard-filled waters, update the chart and log with position, course, speed, time, and other notes every 15-30 minutes. Electronics can and do fail, even on ships, and a fail-safe written record is essential. If there's a marine accident you may be asked to show the written log and plot.

plotting sheet, small area plotting sheet, universal plotting sheet – a blank chart pre-printed with a circle marked in degrees in the center that allows MERIDIANS of LONGITUDE to be constructed for any LATITUDE, so you can make a custom chart for any geographical position. Set it up for the appropriate latitudes and scale. Plotting sheets are used for plotting CELESTIAL NAVIGATION FIXES, for PILOTING, as a MANEUVERING BOARD, or for solving wind or current navigation problems. A sheet can be used to calculate angles for TACKING DOWNWIND, or for courses in an ocean race. You can construct a rough LARGE SCALE chart for an area you don't have a detailed chart for, by plotting positions and land features taken from a LIGHT LIST and a COAST PILOT, and drawing a CHARTLET. A plotting sheet is easy to use, and they're sold in pads of 50 sheets.

plotting tools, plotting instruments – hand tools used by a navigator to plot courses and positions on a paper chart. Typical plotting tools include a COURSE PLOTTER or PARALLEL RULERS, DIVIDERS, a NAUTICAL SLIDE RULE, a small calculator, magnifying glass, pencils, pencil sharpener, and a large eraser.

point – (1) the angle of the boat to the wind, as in point of sail or POINTS OF SAIL. Also may refer to the TACKING ANGLE in a non-specific way: "This boat points well" (she can sail very close to the wind). (2) on a compass, one point is 11-1/4°. Points are used in the NAVIGATION RULES. A very old compass may be marked in points rather than degrees. (3) Points are used to indicate an approximate RELATIVE BEARING: "The tanker is two points off our STARBOARD BOW," i.e. about 22°. When using points in this sense, ignore the quarter-degrees. (4) REEF PENDANTS (reef points) are short lines attached to a sail used to tie up the excess when it's reefed.

point(s) of sail – indicate the relationship of the wind to the HEADING of the sailboat. Starting at the BOW and going toward the STERN the points of sail are HEAD TO WIND, CLOSE-HAULED, CLOSE REACH, BEAM REACH, BROAD REACH, RUN.

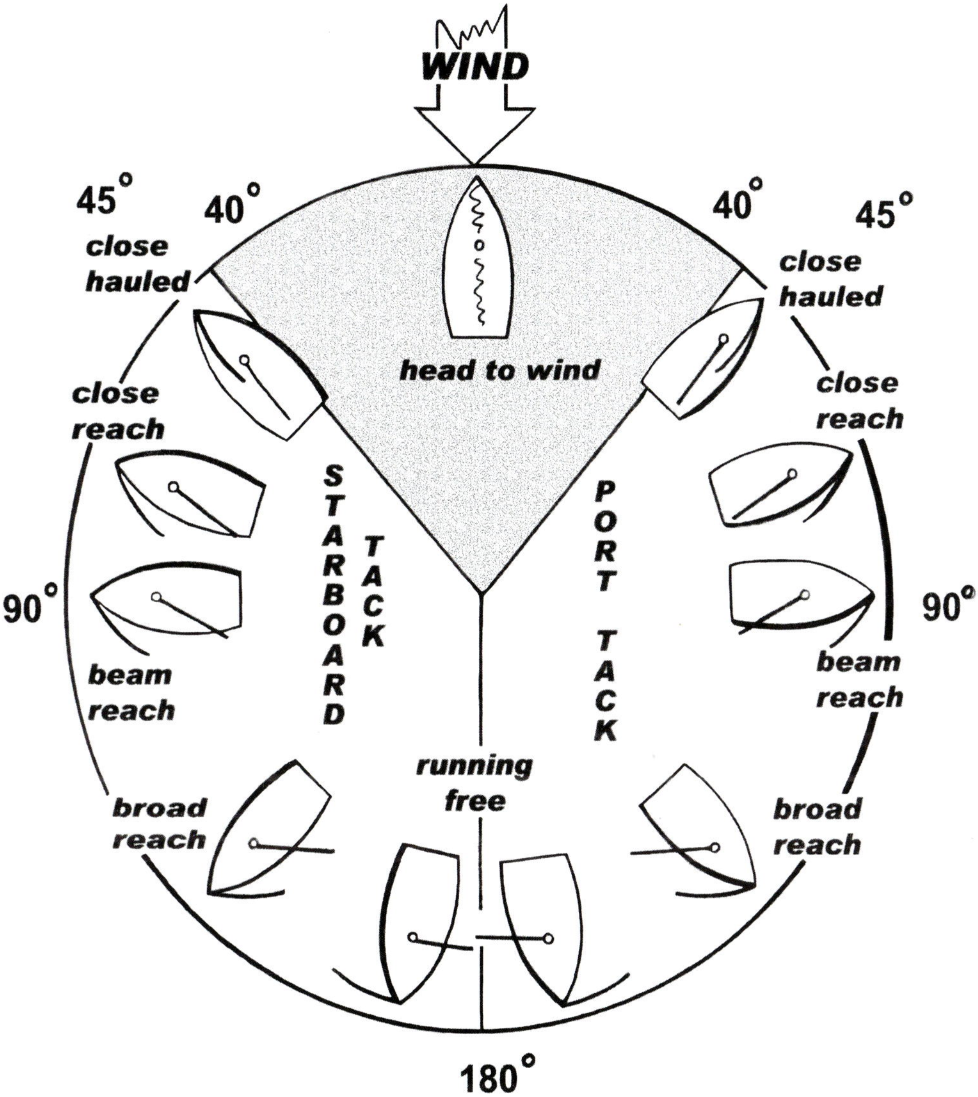

Points of Sail

The wind is coming from the top of the circle. The shaded area between 40° to port and 40° to starboard is the "dead zone" or the "no-go zone." Typical cruising sailboats can't sail closer to the wind than 40° or 45°.

pointy end – the BOW. (I said this book was for complete beginners.)

polarity – DC and AC currents have polarity. With DC, positive (+) and negative (-) current flows in separate wires from the respective TERMINALS of the battery to the boat's DC panel and/or directly to equipment. Wires from the panel distribute power to various locations around the boat. It's essential to observe polarity when connecting equipment. The positive and negative wires and terminals on the equipment are usually labeled, color-coded, and identified in the equipment manual. Usually, but not always, the positive wire is red and the negative is black. Color codes for non-North American boats and equipment may differ. Not all equipment is sensitive to reverse polarity, but if you don't know, assume that it is. Read instructions very carefully, and check the polarity of the power source wires with a MULTIMETER before hooking something up. If a device is connected incorrectly the least serious thing that could happen is that a fuse blows or a circuit breaker trips. The worst case is that the equipment is seriously damaged. Read the manual, check wire colors, and test the polarity. See the next two entries.

polarity indicator – a portable or permanently-installed device that checks the POLARITY of AC or DC wiring. See the next entry.

polarity, reverse – DC reverse polarity occurs if the positive and negative wires are reversed. AC reverse polarity occurs when the hot and the neutral wires are reversed. Reverse polarity can be caused by an error in wiring a circuit or an electrical connector, or a fault in electrical equipment on or off the boat. DC polarity can be checked with a MULTIMETER. AC polarity can be tested (carefully) in energized wires with a multimeter, or with an safe, inexpensive AC polarity indicator/tester, available at hardware stores. For North American power, this device looks like a small three-pronged household plug. When the tester is plugged into a live AC outlet or electric extension cord, small lights on it illuminate, showing if the circuit is OK, or if there's reverse polarity or other electrical fault, such as an open ground. Some boats have an integral polarity indicator/test and protection device on the AC electrical panel. This device automatically tests the polarity when the boat is plugged into shore power. If the shore power has a fault the device shuts off the power at the panel. Some fixed-mount polarity indicators may be a source of STRAY-CURRENT CORROSION.

"pollywog" – a participant in a CROSSING THE LINE CEREMONY.

polynya (pronounced pah **lin** yah or **pal** in yah) – an open area of water enclosed by ice.

pontoon – a floating dock where vessels may be moored, or a float tied along a vessel to work on the hull near the water.

pooped – (1) taking a big wave over the STERN of the vessel. (2) (we all know this one) very tired, exhausted.

port – (1) the left side of a vessel when facing the BOW, or a direction to the left ("turn to port"). Port replaced the old term "larboard" in the 1840s. (2) a window in the hull of a boat. The relevant ABYC Standard is H-3 Exterior Windows, Windshields, Hatches, Doors, Port Lights and Glazing Materials. (3) a harbor that has facilities for vessels. (4) an inlet or outlet in a pump or other mechanical equipment.

port fees – *see* HARBOR DUES.

"port fever" or "harbor fever" – not a disease, but a slang term applied to the desire to get into a port no matter what. You're tired, it's rough, everyone wants to go ashore, friends are waiting, you're so happy to have arrived at your first landfall. These are just some of the things that can make one contract port fever. Suffering from this condition may cause a skipper to try and run a tricky INLET or negotiate a difficult entrance at night when it would be safer to stay at sea or wait for daylight. Even in ideal conditions the fever may distract the skipper from concentrating fully on the immediate PILOTING tasks approaching the harbor. Recognizing that port fever can affect the crew's judgment is usually enough to overcome it.

port hand – on the PORT side or to be kept on the port side of the vessel. When returning from sea, green buoys are port hand buoys in North America.

porthole, port – a window on a vessel that's permanently closed or can be opened.

port of entry – a port or harbor that has Customs officers to CLEAR foreign vessels. NAUTICAL ALMANACS, CRUISING GUIDES, and SAILING DIRECTIONS list ports of entry. Yachts usually have more choices of ports of entry than ships.

port of refuge – general term for a harbor that's safe (relatively) in bad weather or a storm. COAST PILOTS, NAUTICAL ALMANACS, and CRUISING GUIDES usually indicate these locations.

port tack – the wind is on the PORT side of the sailboat and the MAIN BOOM is out toward the STARBOARD side. A boat on the port tack generally does *not* have right of way when meeting a sailboat that's on the STARBOARD TACK.

port traffic signals, international – some ports and harbors have red, green, white, and yellow traffic lights, in a vertical line, which are visible when approaching the harbor. The combination of lights indicates the status of the port, such as open, closed, one-way traffic, two-way traffic, proceed only when given permission, and special messages. A NAUTICAL ALMANAC for areas where these signals are used has explanations of the lights.

Port traffic signals: three greens indicate "vessels may proceed, one-way traffic."

position – the location of a vessel or navigation aid. A position may be precise (a FIX), an ESTIMATED POSITION (EP), or a DEAD RECKONING (DR) position. Use both visual PILOTING techniques and electronics to determine positions. Knowing the vessel's position at all times is essential to safe navigation. **A prudent mariner doesn't rely on a single source of navigational information; always use a second method to determine the position of the vessel.**

position approximate, PA – a notation on a chart that means the position is not accurate or it changes. It's not the same as POSITION DOUBTFUL.

position doubtful, PD – *see* DOUBTFUL.

position, estimated – *see* ESTIMATED POSITION.

position, line of, or LOP – *see* LINE OF POSITION.

"pot metal" – slang for ZAMAK.

pound, pounding – repetitive slamming of the BOW as the boat PITCHES into short, steep head seas. It's hard on the boat, her gear, and the crew. A boat with flat hull sections near the bow pounds more than a boat with a FINE ENTRY.

powder-coat – a protective or decorative coating of special powder applied by an electrostatic process or a spray gun to ALUMINUM or other metals. Powder coatings come in a variety of colors. Black or dark gray is frequently used on marine fittings and equipment. UV exposure may break down these coatings in five to ten years.

power-driven vessel – "any vessel propelled by machinery;" Rule 3(b) of the NAVIGATION RULES. A sailing vessel operating the engine with the sails up (MOTORSAILING) is a power-driven vessel under the Rules.

power inlet – same as SHORE POWER INLET.

pram – a small DINGHY with a squared-off BOW. Used as a sailing dinghy for teaching children, as well as a yacht TENDER. For a photo see CANOE STERN.

pratique, free pratique – the permission granted by government authorities for a vessel to enter the country; Customs CLEARANCE for the vessel. Flying the yellow Q-FLAG when entering a foreign country says to the authorities "My vessel is healthy and I request free pratique." Pratique is "permission to conduct business at the port." The phrase applies to both RECREATIONAL and COMMERCIAL VESSELS.

pre-departure checklist – *see* CHECKLIST, PRE-DEPARTURE.

preheat – (1) to energize the GLOW PLUGS on some diesel engines to aid starting. (2) a button or switch on the instrument panel of some diesel engines that sends DC current to the glow plugs. The ENGINE MANUAL explains how to use the preheat control.

pressure gradient – the difference in pressure between two points related to the distance between the points. On a SYNOPTIC CHART the spacing of the ISOBARS indicates the pressure gradient. A steep gradient has closely-spaced isobars, indicating strong winds. *See also* WIND, GEOSTROPHIC.

pre-tinned electrical wire – this type of wire is tinned in the manufacturing process to increase resistance to corrosion. Bare pre-tinned wires have a silver appearance (rather than a copper color). High quality marine electrical wire is pre-tinned AWG wire. In wires that aren't pre-tinned, moisture travels up the wire under the plastic outer covering over time, increasing the RESISTANCE of the wire, and decreasing the amount of electrical power available for use by equipment. Some equipment is sensitive to the VOLTAGE-DROP that occurs in corroded wires. Severe corrosion in wires or on terminals can create enough heat in an energized circuit to completely block the flow of current or cause a fire.

preventer – a preventer keeps the BOOM from swinging over in an accidental JIBE, and improves the shape of the mainsail by holding the boom down. It's an important safety device, helping to prevent injury to the crew or damage caused by an accidental jibe, which may occur when sailing BY THE LEE. There are two basic types of preventers: (1) a line attached to the end of the BOOM (end-boom preventer) and led forward to a strong point or to a TURNING BLOCK near the BOW. A turning block at the bow should have twice the breaking strength of the preventer line because the 180° turn imposes twice the strain on the block than a straight pull on the line. (2) a line or TACKLE attached to the mid-point of the boom (mid-boom preventer), led to a strong point on the deck or TOE RAIL near AMIDSHIPS.

primary fuel filter – a filter installed between the fuel tank(s) and the engine.

prime meridian – the GREENWICH MERIDIAN.

priority scan – a feature on some VHF radios that allows scanning of more than two channels. For example, when navigating in crowded waters with large vessels, priority scan Channels 6, 13, and, 16 to monitor their movements. In priority scan mode the radio automatically defaults to Channel 16 when a message is sent on that channel. Use DUAL WATCH to scan only two channels.

private aid to navigation – an AID TO NAVIGATION not established or maintained by the government or an official agency. "Priv" is noted on the chart by the aid. Use them with caution, as they may be less reliable than government established and maintained aids.

private signal – *see* FLAG, PRIVATE.

privileged vessel – older term for STAND-ON VESSEL.

procedure, radio – *see* PROWORDS and RADIO PROCEDURE.

procedure words, radio – *see* PROWORDS.

projection – usually means a CHART PROJECTION.

proof coil – common chain; *see* CHAIN, PROOF COIL.

propagation – refers to how radio waves travel, as ground waves or sky waves. (1) with ground-wave propagation the radio waves travel along the surface of the earth. Low frequencies and frequencies at the high end of the MEDIUM-FREQUENCY band (around 1600kHz) use ground waves. They generally travel less than 100 miles in the daytime, but farther at night. (2) with sky wave propagation the radio waves are refracted by the ionosphere (the upper atmosphere of the earth) and returned to earth to achieve long-distance communication. SINGLE-SIDEBAND communication relies on sky-wave propagation. This propagation changes throughout a 24-hour period. In general, frequencies below approximately10MHz propagate most efficiently at night, and frequencies above 10MHz propagate better in the daytime. Sunspot cycles and other factors influence sky wave propagation. A rule of thumb for estimating the minimum propagation distance is the frequency in MHz x 100. The maximum distance is approximately twice the minimum distance. A SSB manual and ham radio books may have general charts of distances and times of day for various frequencies; use propagation software, or research propagation on the Internet.

propane, LPG – a fuel used in galley stoves and cabin heaters. It's stored in a gas bottle (tank) located in a dedicated, ventilated locker above decks and delivered to the stove or heating appliance through special propane hose or rigid piping. ABYC Standard A-1 recommends a pressure gauge in the system. A REGULATOR with a gauge is available. The flow of gas to the stove can be controlled in two ways: (1) by opening the valve on the bottle when the stove or heater is to be used, and closing it when the appliance is no longer needed. (2) by the action of an electrically-operated solenoid valve at the tank that's opened and closed by a switch in the galley or at a heating appliance. Propane is heavier than air, and if a leak develops gas can accumulate dangerously below decks or in the bilge, creating an explosion hazard. Install a FUME DETECTOR. Follow ABYC standards for the installation of propane systems and equipment. The relevant ABYC Standards are A-1 Marine Liquefied Petroleum Gas (LPG) Systems, A-3 Galley Stoves, A-14 Gasoline and Propane Gas Detection Systems, A-22 Marine Compressed Natural Gas (CNG) Systems, A-26 LPG and CNG Fueled Appliances, and A-30 Cooking Appliances with Integral LPG Cylinders. In some countries work on a propane system may only be done by a certified or licensed professional.

propane hose – flexible hose for use in a propane system must be designed for use with propane. The hose will be marked "LP Gas, 350 psi," (or similar) with UL or other approval abbreviation. Inspect propane hoses for cracks or damage, and immediately replace the entire hose from the propane tank to the appliance. Do not use anything other than certified propane hose with any propane appliance. In some countries rigid piping is required for propane systems. All connections should be LEAK-TESTED regularly. To improve safety aboard, install a FUME DETECTOR.

propane, refilling – in North America it's relatively easy to get propane bottles refilled or exchanged when cruising. In other countries it may be more difficult. Refilling a North American propane tank overseas or a foreign tank in North America may be impossible (because of the mismatch between screw fittings), or not permitted by law. It may be necessary to switch to the propane bottle and regulator used in the particular country. If you discover a creative way to refill your propane bottle in a foreign country, be sure to follow all safety practices for working with propane, including using propane-rated hose.

propane regulator – a device that reduces the high pressure from the propane tank into useable pressure for the galley stove or a propane heater. When changing a regulator from one tank to another *don't* use Teflon tape or lubricant on the threads. These may cause an improper seal and a propane leak. Leak test connections in a propane system with soapy water or a commercial leak-check solution. Screw threads on propane bottles and regulators are right-hand (turn to the right to loosen). A regulator should be

UL-listed, and have a pressure gauge to meet the ABYC standard A-1 Marine Liquefied Petroleum Gas (LPG) Systems.

propeller, adjustable pitch – a prop that has a mechanism for changing the pitch (the angle) of the blades when the boat is out of the water, rather than underway. *See* PROPELLER, VARIABLE PITCH.

propeller, feathering – a prop with blades that turn and feather (lie parallel to the flow of the water) to reduce drag when sailing. Feathering props are as efficient in reverse as in forward. They are available in two, three, and four blade models. Some brand names are Gori®, Kiwi-Prop™, Max-Prop, Seahawk Autostream®, and Variprop.

propeller, fixed – a propeller with blades that are permanently fixed in one position. See the other propeller types.

propeller, folding – a prop with blades that fold into a compact, streamlined shape to reduce underwater drag. Some folding props may not be as efficient in reverse as in forward. They're favored by sailboat racers, and are available in two, three, and four blade models. Some brand names are Flexofold, Gori®, Varifold, and Seahawk Slipstream®. For a photo see SAILDRIVE.

propeller names – prop, screw (single-screw vessel, twin-screw vessel), wheel. "When I hit those rocks I damaged both wheels."

propeller pitch – the theoretical distance advanced by the propeller in one complete revolution. The pitch calculation doesn't consider any side slip as the prop rotates. Pitch is determined by the angle of the blades. The pitch is usually stamped on the hub of a fixed-blade prop. If the boat has an ADJUSTABLE PITCH prop, the pitch setting should be indicated the boat's notebook or in the prop's manual.

propeller rotation – props are either left-hand or right-hand, which indicates the direction of rotation when looking at the prop from ASTERN, with the engine in forward gear. Of course, it's not easy to check with a boat in the water. Knowing which rotation a prop has indicates the PROP WALK to expect when going astern. In reverse gear, a right-handed prop kicks the stern to PORT; a left-handed prop kicks it to STARBOARD. To determine whether the prop is left- or right-handed: from a stationary position, put the engine into reverse, increase the rpms slightly, and see which way the STERN moves. Or, when moored to a dock, look at the engine from the front when it's running in forward gear. If the flywheel rotation is to the right (to port) it's a right-hand prop. If the flywheel rotates to the left (to starboard) it's a left-hand prop. This method applies to an engine that faces forward in the boat. Knowing the prop rotation helps the helmsman make a STANDING TURN and come alongside more easily. *See* PROP WALK.

propeller shaft, prop shaft – the metal shaft that runs through the STERN TUBE from the SHAFT COUPLING at the engine to the CUTLESS BEARING at the STERN. A shaft may run through the keel to the prop, or go to a SKEG or STRUT at the stern, which holds the cutless bearing. A SAILDRIVE unit doesn't have a prop shaft. The relevant ABYC Standard is P-6 Propeller Shafting Systems.

propeller, variable-pitch – a propeller with a mechanism that allows the blade angles to be changed underway, either automatically or with an on-board control. Changing the pitch makes the propeller more efficient for the sea conditions. Bruntons Varifold and Autoprop, and one type of Max Prop are examples of variable pitch props.

propeller walk, prop walk – the tendency of a propeller to push the STERN either to PORT or to STARBOARD when a short burst of reverse power is applied. It's caused by the direction of PROPELLER ROTATION. Prop walk is important to understand when going ASTERN, maneuvering at slow speeds, or perform a STANDING TURN in a tight space. In *reverse*, a right-hand prop kicks the stern to port, and a left-hand prop kicks the stern to starboard. When possible, the helmsman on a boat with a right-hand prop usually prefers to come alongside a dock port side to, so the stern will kick toward the dock when the engine is put into reverse to slow down. On a boat with a left-hand prop the helmsman usually prefers to go starboard side to. The amount of kick varies with the boat and the RPMS applied when first putting the engine in reverse. Prop walk is influenced by the shaft angle where it exits the hull, or if the shaft is offset to one side of the keel. A steep shaft angle produces less prop walk because the prop is less efficient when it points downward. A folding prop usually does not produce much prop walk because it's not especially efficient in reverse. In contrast, a feathering prop or a variable pitch prop is designed to be efficient in forward and reverse; thus, the prop walk is likely to be noticeable. Backing into the wind may minimize the effect of prop walk. A SAILDRIVE unit has almost no prop walk.

propeller wrap, prop wrap – something you definitely do not want to experience. Fishing nets, plastic tarps, plastic bags and construction material, buoy lines from lobster and crab traps, discarded rope and other junk is lurking beneath the surface, just waiting to snag a passing prop. When a long line is used on a fishing gear buoy to accommodate a large tide range, at low tide a wide arc of floating rope can be very difficult to detect. By the time it's noticed, it may be too late to avoid snagging it.

In a tidal area with lobster or crab trap buoys, pass DOWN TIDE or DOWNWIND of them, especially at low tide when extra rope may be near the surface.

If the wrap pulls up a lobster or crab trap or other solid object it can damage the prop or hit the hull.

A prop wrap can stop an engine abruptly, perhaps breaking one or more motor mounts.

This iron-hard propeller wrap is displayed on the wall near a Norwegian lifeboat's berth. It must have been a challenge to remove it.

A wrap can bend the shaft or tear a prop STRUT from the hull.

A rope wrap that doesn't stop the engine may cut off the flow of water to the CUTLESS BEARING, causing the shaft to overheat and damage the bearing.

Despite eternal vigilance you can still get a prop wrap. Install a LINE CUTTER to help prevent or clear a wrap. Yachts, life boats, rescue vessels, and fishing vessels use these devices. See next entry.

propeller wrap, clearing – several techniques, short of going swimming, can be tried to clear a prop wrap. (1) Try putting the engine gently into forward and reverse a few times, at the lowest RPMS. (2) If it's a rope or piece of plastic, try pulling or untangling it with a BOATHOOK, or cutting it away with a sharp knife on a boat hook. If it's a fishing net, it will be difficult to clear.

(3) Going over the side is a last resort; carefully evaluate all the risks involved. A wrapped rope can be twisted into a mass as hard as metal, and it can't be cut by a knife; some swimmers have had luck with a hacksaw or large pruning shears (on a boat?). It may be safer to call for towing assistance, if available. A LINE CUTTER may help prevent a prop wrap.

protected waters – an area that's not exposed to the full force of wind and waves because of the proximity of land or constructed features, such as a BREAKWATER. In some cases, if the wind changes the area will no longer be protected.

provisioning – nautical term for stocking the boat with food and supplies. A provisioning list is a shopping list.

prowords, procedure words – internationally-recognized, ENGLISH-LANGUAGE words and phrases used when communicating via radiotelephone. They're used by coast guards, rescue services, professional mariners, the military, and air traffic controllers (with some differences specific to ATC). Everyone who uses a radiotelephone should use prowords. Speak all letters and numbers using the PHONETIC ALPHABET. You may be asked to spell the name of your boat, so if it's a long name, write the spelling in phonetics and post it by the radio, along with a copy of the phonetic alphabet. Three prowords have very specific meanings and radio procedures: MAYDAY, PAN PAN, and SECURITÉ. General prowords and phrases to learn and use:

This is [followed by the name and/or CALL SIGN of the calling station]

Affirmative or **Roger** = yes.

Negative = no.

Station calling – initial response when the calling station's name or call sign is unknown or unclear. "Station calling, this is Norfolk Coast Guard." The unidentified station should respond with **This is** and identify itself.

How do you read? = can you hear me? Said after a transmission when it's uncertain if the other station has heard the initial call.

I read you – [followed by adjectives or numbers indicating how well the station's signal is heard.] "Loud and clear" or "I read you five by five" = "I hear you perfectly and your signal is strong." See radio check responses, below.

Stand by on (switch to) channel "X" = change to the channel I said and wait for me.

Stand by = wait and I will get back to you.

Go ahead or **Send your traffic** = send your message.

Correction = an error has been made. Then say the correct word or words.

Over = this part of my message is over, and I am waiting for your response.

How copy? = did you hear and understand my message? Asks the responder to repeat the sender's message, word-for-word, if possible.

I copy = I understand your message. Then repeat the information in the sender's message to tell the sender that the message has been understood. "I copy, your intention is to alter course three-zero degrees to starboard."

Good copy or **Correct** = you have correctly understood my message. Response from a station when a message is read back correctly by the responder.

I Repeat – used to reinforce an important part of a message. "Do not turn to port, I repeat, do not turn to port." It is not the same as "say again."

Say again = I didn't understand your message (or part of it).

Say again all before or **all after** – used with a long message when requesting that a specific part of the message be repeated.

I say again – used by the responder when answering a **say again** request. **All before** or **All after** is used in the response, if that was specified in the request. "I say again all before."

I spell = I will spell the word(s) in the phonetic alphabet. Used when requested or if you think the recipient will not understand the first time. "This is *Nomad*. I spell November, Oscar, Mike, Alpha, Delta."

What is your intention? – request for a vessel to reply with information about how she is maneuvering or intends to maneuver. It's used in CROSSING and HEAD ON SITUATIONS, when OVERTAKING, and other circumstances when there's uncertainty about the actions of a nearby vessel. Sample responses: "I intend to turn to starboard." "I cannot deviate from my course." "I intend to overtake you on your port side."

All Received = I have received and understood your message.

Out. = my transmission is complete and I do not expect a response. Speak the name and/or call sign of your station before **out**. "**This is** *Ocean Voyager*, **out**." Don't use "over and out."

Radio check = a request for a station to respond with a signal report.

Loud and clear = a response to a radio check. The location of the responder is spoken after loud and clear. "Loud and clear at Duck Island Roads."

Weak but readable = a response to a radio check if the signal is not very clear. The location of the responder is spoken after weak but readable. "Weak but readable in Halifax harbor."

Weak and unreadable = a response when a request for a radio check has been made, but the responding station can't understand anything. The location is spoken after weak and unreadable. "Weak and unreadable at the Golden Gate bridge."

"prudonce" = "prudence" or "caution," spoken on the radio by the Coast Guard to indicate that while a distress situation is still ongoing, normal WORKING CHANNELS may now be used for limited communication not related to the distress. "SEELONCE MAYDAY" and "SEELONCE FEE NEE" are also used with distress and urgent communications.

PTT – abbreviation for "push to talk," which refers to the button or KEY on a radio microphone. While it may seem obvious, remember to release it to listen. Sometimes it gets stuck.

puff – a sudden, temporary increase in wind speed; a little gust. When working to WINDWARD the helmsman may LUFF IN A PUFF.

pulpit – applied to BOW RAIL(S) and STERN RAILS.

pump – some general types of pumps are DIAPHRAGM, PISTON, IMPELLER, and vane (centrifugal).

Pumps are usually self-priming, except for centrifugal pumps, which must be primed.

Any pump can develop an air lock or lose prime and not be able to pump. Bleed the pump intake line or otherwise eliminate air from the system, or re-prime the pump.

A diaphragm pump can be operated without water in the system; all other types of pumps must have liquid in them to prevent damage to impellers or seals.

Most pumps can't handle solid materials, and thus are fitted with strainers.

The efficiency of a pump is affected by the length of its suction and discharge hoses, and the height to which the liquid must be pumped (the HEAD (4). BILGE PUMP INSTALLATION should be planned for maximum efficiency.

A pump may be designed only for water. Pumps and hoses for oil and fuels must be designated for these types of liquids. For an oil change pump or a fuel transfer pump, check the pump manual or catalog description.

Many electric pumps are designed for intermittent duty. Check the catalog or manual if you require a pump that is able to run continually to move large amounts of liquid.

pump, foot – foot-operated pumps in the galley and HEAD save water, make little noise (good at night), and are a backup for a failed pressure water system. To conserve fresh water install foot pumps for sea or lake water to use for rinsing the sinks and dishes before washing.

pump, piston – a mechanical pump that works by moving a handle up and down to create suction and discharge pressure. Piston pumps include small hand-operated bilge pumps, hand-operated oil change pumps, and the pump on some marine toilets. Piston seals may be replaceable; check the instructions.

pumping mast – *see* MAST PUMPING.

pump-out station – a shore location where the waste in a boat's HOLDING TANK can be pumped out through the "waste" DECK PLATE, using the facility's commercial pump. In some locations there may be a pump-out boat (affectionately known as a honey-wagon) that will come to the boat to perform this service. Some boats have a manual pump that can be fitted to the waste deck plate so that the holding tank can be emptied where permissible, usually outside the three-mile coastal limit, unless this is within a designated NO-DISCHARGE AREA.

purchase – another name for a TACKLE.

pushpit – same as STERN RAIL.

push to talk – refers to the button or KEY on a radio microphone. The abbreviation PTT is usually used.

- Q -

Q flag, quarantine flag – the Q CODE FLAG, a yellow rectangle, has the meaning "My vessel is healthy and I request free PRATIQUE" i.e. Customs CLEARANCE.

quadrant – may refer to a RUDDER QUADRANT. In historic usage, a quadrant was a simple navigation instrument used to determine position at sea.

quadrantal correctors, quadrantal spheres (pronounced kwa **dran** tul) – a pair of iron balls placed ATHWARTSHIPS on either side of a magnetic compass on some steel vessels. The correctors help minimize compass DEVIATION.

Quadrantal correctors on a tall ship's binnacle, red on port and green on starboard.

quadrilateral sail – a sail with four sides. A GAFF MAINSAIL and many of the sails on a SQUARE-RIGGER are quadrilateral. See SAIL, PARTS OF for a drawing.

quarter – the sides of a vessel located between AMIDSHIPS and the STERN are called the PORT quarter and STARBOARD quarter.

quartering seas – seas that approach the boat from either the PORT or STARBOARD QUARTER. Some quartering seas may cause the boat to ROLL and/or PITCH.

quay, quayside (pronounced key, keyside) – a wall, usually of concrete or stone, along the shore. Some quays have mooring space for vessels.

R

race – another name for a TIDE RACE.

racon, RACON (pronounced **ray** con) – also known as a radar responder or a radar transponder beacon, a racon is a TRANSPONDER used as a navigation aid for vessels equipped with radar. Racons are placed on land-based and floating structures. When pulses from a vessel's radar hit the racon, the transponder sends back an identifying signal, displayed on the screen as a single Morse Code letter preceded by a dash (a long line). It's a large, dramatic target on the screen radiating out from the racon's location. There's a slight delay in the racon's response that causes the Morse code letter to appear behind the radar echo from the structure that the racon is mounted on. Charts indicate racons and their characteristics. In the U.S. racons are used to:

Identify aids to navigation.

Identify landfalls or positions on low coastlines.

Indicate the navigable span(s) under bridges.

Identify offshore oil platforms and similar structures.

Identify and indicate environmentally-sensitive areas such as coral reefs.

Outside the U.S. racons have additional uses, which may include (1) to mark new and uncharted hazards (Morse code "D"), (2) to identify the center and turning points in a channel or fairway, and (3) to identify a RANGE or LEADING LINE.

racon visibility – why can't I see a racon when it should be within the range of my radar? The range of a racon is approximately line-of-sight. Range depends on the height of the radar, the height of the racon, atmospheric conditions, and the sensitivity of the racon's receiver.

Racons are only active for some period of seconds, for example, 20 seconds on, then off for the next 20 seconds. Racons installed on shore usually operate 75% of the time, because battery life isn't a consideration. Battery-operated racons installed on buoys operate approximately 50% of the time. A racon doesn't show up on every sweep of the radar beam, so check the screen frequently until you see the identifier.

The rain clutter or sea clutter control on the radar could mask the racon's return signal, and it may need to be adjusted or turned off.

Automatic clutter-rejection features on some radars can suppress a racon.

The range at which the radar detects a racon may be reduced if it isn't tuned properly. Try tweaking the radar's tuning controls.

When you're close to a racon its signal can temporarily block out some other **TARGETS** on the screen. Eventually, **AIS** will replace racons on navigation aids (or the racons will be modified) because continuous wave **BROADBAND RADAR** doesn't activate a racon.

radar – an electronic instrument that transmits a beam of electronic energy and displays an image of solid objects "reflected" by the radar beam. Radar signals are microwaves in the **MEGAHERTZ** and **GIGAHERTZ** frequency range, depending on the type of radar. The beam may be a pulsed (intermittent) beam or a continuous wave (**BROADBAND RADAR**). Radar displays the position of objects such as land, other vessels, or aids to navigation, and it measures distances and **BEARINGS**. Radar can detect rainstorms, weather cells, and waterspouts. A radar can only see what is within its range; the height of the **TARGET**, the height of the **SCANNER** on the vessel, and the vertical area of the target are three of several factors that determine how well and at what distance a radar sees a target. Use radar for **PILOTING** and collision avoidance, by day or night, or in poor visibility. Display types include **CATHODE-RAY TUBE**, LCD (liquid-crystal display), and digital LCD, in monochrome or color. Target-tracking information (**ARPA**, **AIS**) and electronic charts can be combined with a radar display. However, information overlays may mask targets. No license is required for radar in U.S.waters. To learn to use radar effectively study the manual, read a radar textbook, try radar training software, take a training course, and practice in good visibility. Radar is an acronym for RAdio Detection And Ranging. *See also* **RADAR SAFETY**.

radar and visual lookout – using radar *does not* eliminate the requirement under **NAVIGATION RULE** 5 that a lookout by sight and hearing be maintained at all times.

radar bearing – a **BEARING** obtained by radar. Radar can accurately determine the distance from a target, but it's not able to give a perfectly accurate bearing because of the beam width (a few degrees). Because of this, it may not be easy to identify a narrow harbor entrance or a passage between two islands, or to distinguish between two buoys or objects that are close together.

radar, broadband or FM continuous wave radar – advantages of broadband radar include an instant-on feature that eliminates warm-up time, it requires much less power than non-broadband radar (important for boats with limited battery power), and the screen shows better detail close to **TARGETS** (the advertised close range is 1/32NM rather than the 1/8NM of regular radar). Broadband radar emits much less radiation than traditional radar (because of its low power), so being near an operating **ARRAY** is not hazardous to humans. Disadvantages of broadband radar include: detail further than six to 10 miles away may be less good than with regular radar, and the CLUTTER rejection capabilities of broadband is good for solid targets, but this feature may degrade the ability to see rain, thunderstorms, and squalls. RACONS respond to radar pulses, and until they are modified or replaced by AIS, they may not respond to continuous wave broadband radar. See the next entry.

radar, digital – digital technology applied to broadband radar to improve automatic signal processing and display capabilities.

radar display modes – some radars have more than one display mode. The default is usually HEAD-UP, but when the radar is interfaced with other electronics it may have NORTH-UP and/or COURSE-UP display capabilities.

radar fix, RaFix – a FIX established by radar. It can be from multiple BEARINGS or from a bearing and distance off.

radar, LCD – a monochrome or color radar with an LCD (liquid-crystal) display screen.

radar range, radar horizon – how far can my radar see? The range of a radar is determined by the height of the RADAR SCANNER above the water, the power of the radar, and the height and size of the TARGET. The sea state also affects the range. Radar is essentially line-of-sight, so the curvature of the earth affects its horizon. Experiment with the radar in good visibility to see how far away an object or vessel is when it is first visible on the screen. Some approximate distances for mast-mounted radar at a height of approximately 16 feet/5.5m above the water:

Small buoy, around 1NM or less. A buoy with a good radar reflector shows up sooner.

Small yacht with RADAR REFLECTOR, 1-3NM.

Large buoy, 2-6NM.

Large yacht or fishing vessel, with a good radar reflector or metal hull, 3-7NM.

Ships, 6-12NM.

If a vessel doesn't have a good radar reflector or is approaching head-on or nearly so, she will not show up as soon. Metal vessels show up better than wood or fiberglass, unless these vessels have a good radar reflector. A non-metal vessel without a radar reflector may not show up at all, even at close range. A metal MAST is not a good radar reflector.

radar range or distance off – radar is quite accurate for determining the RANGE (distance from) an object that provides a good RADAR RETURN. This makes it a very useful PILOTING aid.

radar reflector – a device or design feature on a vessel or aid to navigation that enhances a received radar signal so that it shows up more clearly as a large TARGET on a radar screen. A vessel should have a reflector permanently mounted as high as possible. There are many types available, including passive and active reflectors (which require DC power). Research the types, and follow the instructions for mounting it. Without a radar reflector, even fairly large, non-metallic vessels sometimes don't show up well on radar. Radar reflectors are required in Canadian waters. One type of passive radar reflector is visible in the photo with the FISHING VESSEL entry.

radar return, target, "blip" – the signal returned from an object PAINTED (hit) by a radar beam. Some targets show up large and clearly on the radar screen, others are small and may not be evident all the time or be lost in rain or sea CLUTTER. AIS and CHART PLOTTER overlays, or a RACON's signal may hide a blip on the radar screen.

radar safety – the beam transmitted by traditional (non-BROADBAND) RADAR is hazardous to humans. Read the safety warnings in the radar manual. Don't stand or work near an operating RADAR SCANNER. On some small vessels the scanner has been (inexplicably) mounted so low that a person may easily stand in line with its beam. BROADBAND RADAR has low power, so it's not hazardous.

radar scanner – the rotating part of the radar (a horizontal bar) that sends out the radar beam. It may be an open ARRAY or be covered by a RADOME.

radar separation of targets – as a rule of thumb, to show up as individual targets on a radar screen the objects must be approximately 300yds/100m apart. The type, size, and aspect of the targets, and the capabilities of the radar unit influence these distances. A radar with a narrow horizontal beam provides greater target separation. Large commercial radars have better target discrimination than smaller radars.

radar target – same as a RADAR RETURN.

radar transfer plotting sheets – same as a MANEUVERING BOARD.

radio check – a call made on a radiotelephone to check that the radio is transmitting. In the U.S. radio checks must made on VHF *Channel 9*, or directly to another boat or shore station on a WORKING CHANNEL. Say the name of your vessel and "requesting radio check," or reply to a request and test your radio. The U.S. Coast Guard does not normally respond to radio checks, while coast guards in some other countries may respond if called. Use PROWORDS for radio communication.

radio direction finder, RDF – a sensitive radio receiver that can receive one or more frequencies broadcast by an EPIRB, PERSONAL LOCATOR BEACON, or an RDF station. RDF equipment is mainly used for search-and-rescue activities for homing in on the 121.5MHz signals transmitted by an EPIRB or a personal locator beacon. The ACR Vecta3™ is a hand-held RDF that receives 121.5 MHz signals. With widespread use of GPS and radar, RDF shore stations that broadcast direction-finding signals have been eliminated; the U.S. doesn't have any, but a few other countries do.

radiofacsimile, radiofax – a graphic image, such as a WEATHERFAX sent using a SINGLE-SIDEBAND RADIO or other means of transmission by radio frequencies.

radio frequency – *see* FREQUENCY, RADIO.

radio ground – *see* RF GROUND.

radio license – *see* LICENSE, SHIP STATION.

radio operator license – *see* LICENSE, RADIOTELEPHONE OPERATOR.

radio procedure, basic – use PROWORDS (standard words, phrases, and procedures) when communicating by radio with other vessels and shore stations. The basic procedure for a routine call is:

• Select the proper calling VHF channel: either 16 (or 9 in the U.S.). If you know the channel monitored by another boat or shore station call on that channel.

• Use low power if you are near the other station.

• Say the name of the station you're calling three times, followed by

• **This is** [the name of your vessel three times]. Wait for the other station to reply. If the other station doesn't reply wait at least one minute before repeating the call. If contact can't be made after three tries, give up and try later.

• When contact is established, switch to a WORKING CHANNEL: say **switching to Channel X** [the number agreed upon].

• Say the word **Over** when you've finished each transmission with the other station and expect a reply from the other station.

• At the end of all communication, say **This is** and the name of your vessel once, **out**.

Don't use "Over and out" at the end. Keep radio communications as brief as possible. MAYDAY, PAN PAN, and SECURITÉ calls have different, specific procedures.

radiosonde – an instrument used with a WEATHER BALLOON.

radio station, ship – a ship radio station includes all the transmitting radio equipment installed aboard a vessel of any size. See LICENSE, SHIP STATION.

radiotelephone – a VHF or SINGLE-SIDEBAND TRANSCEIVER. Usually just called a radio.

radio watch – *see* WATCH, RADIO.

radome (pronounced ray-dome) – the covering over a RADAR SCANNER that prevents lines or sails from entangling the rotating scanner.

raft, rafting – (1) tying vessels alongside each other at a dock, at anchor or on a mooring. Rafting should only be done when the weather is relatively calm and wind and wave action is minimal. Rafting on rental moorings is usually prohibited, and it's not a good idea on any mooring. Use SPRING LINES, in addition to BOW and STERN lines, between the rafted vessels to prevent excessive motion. (2) a life raft or a group of boats rafted together. See the next entry.

rafting etiquette – even though you may prefer not to raft to another vessel, in some areas it's a necessity. Follow these basic tips for being a good neighbor:

Ask permission before coming alongside. If no one's aboard, ask permission as soon as they return or in the morning. If they don't want you there, move.

If you raft silently late at night, be aware that the boat next to you may be planning to move early in the morning. Don't fall asleep too soundly.

Make sure your SPREADERS can't touch the other boat's spreaders or rigging.

Use lots of fenders and tie your boat properly, so she doesn't move around.

Ask for and follow the advice of the other skipper or crew about where you should tie your lines on his/her vessel (unless it seems to be bad advice). Make sure the lines don't chafe on the other boat.

Run a BOW and STERN line from your boat to the dock.

If you're the outer boat in a raft, check with the other crews about when they're going to depart. Be ready to move before the other crew has to call you, no matter what hour they're leaving.

If you're an inner boat, tell the other skippers when you plan to leave. When departing, try to stick to the time you said; if a crew woke up at 0500 just so you could leave at 0515 and you decide not to leave until 0630, it's bad manners.

Walk quietly across the other vessel's FOREDECK, not through or near the COCKPIT.

Take your shoes off when walking on someone's deck.

Keep the noise down in your cockpit.

Invite the neighbors over, if they seem congenial.

Don't run a generator or the engine at night, if your neighbors are aboard. Even if the engine/generator is quiet the exhaust fumes may blow onto the other boat.

Be careful about smoking on deck. Go ashore or smoke belowdecks with the hatches closed.

rail, safety rails – (1) "the rail" refers to the outermost edge of the deck. It may be the top of a BULWARK, a low TOE RAIL or a flat deck edge. The crew of a racing sailboat perched along the rail on the WINDWARD side are sometimes called "railbirds." (2) a protective bar of metal or wood along the deck edge or at the BOW or STERN to protect crew from falling overboard. LIFELINES are safety rails.

"railbirds" – crew seated on the WINDWARD RAIL of a sailboat, using their weight to counteract HEELING.

"rail down" – sailing HEELED over so far that the LEE rail is in the water. The sensation when sailing rail down is that you're going very fast, when, in fact, having so much of the boat's TOPSIDES in the water slows the boat down. REEF, sail more upright, and go faster.

RAINWAT – countries that have implemented the ATIS system.

rake – the angle or tilt of the MAST or other SPAR from the vertical. Mast and flagstaff rake is usually slightly AFT. See the photo of the blue boat with LEEBOARDS.

RAM – abbreviation for RESTRICTED IN ABILITY TO MANEUVER.

range – four basic definitions for mariners:

1. The distance to another vessel, the shore, an aid to navigation, or a WAYPOINT.

2. The distance in feet or meters between high and low tide; the tide range.

3. The theoretical distance at which a light is visible. Charts and LIGHT LISTS indicate the range of most lights, which is either the GEOGRAPHIC RANGE or the NOMINAL RANGE.

4. Two fixed, vertical objects in line from front to back form a range (TRANSIT or LEADING LIGHTS). When the two objects are in line (in transit) the boat's located somewhere along a line drawn between them. A range may be a specific installation of fixed structures placed to guide vessels navigating a channel or entering a harbor. The object that forms the front of the range is lower than the object at the back. Ranges have colored DAYBOARDS, and may also be lighted, and/or have a SECTOR LIGHT. If there is no constructed range, create a natural range by lining up existing charted objects, such as a church steeple and a radio tower, the end of a pier and a fixed aid to navigation, etc., to guide you into a harbor or safely past a danger.

range lights – (1) the lights on a RANGE. (2) the two MASTHEAD LIGHTS required on a power-driven vessel over 50m/164ft in length, under Rule 23 of the NAVIGATION RULES. The forward light is lower than the AFT light. Range lights on a large vessel indicate her direction of travel. If you see the range lights in a line directly over each other the ship is heading toward you.

range, natural – a RANGE (transit) formed between two charted objects, natural or man-made, that aren't designed specifically as a range, but which can be used by a navigator.

range, tide – *see* TIDE RANGE.

raster chart – *see* CHART, RASTER.

ratlines (pronounced **rat** lins) – a series of permanent rope, wood, or metal steps, like a ladder, attached between two SHROUDS. The steps usually run FORE-AND-AFT, but may be installed ATHWARTSHIPS between the forward lower shrouds. Ratlines are usually used PORT and STARBOARD. They allow a crewmember to climb up for a better view, particularly when directing the helmsman through coral, ice, or other obstructions visible in clear water. The vessel in the BOWSPRIT photo has rope ratlines.

Rope ratlines.

Wood ratlines.

raw water – the water that the boat is operating in; salt, BRACKISH, or fresh.

raw water cooled engine – *see* ENGINE, RAW WATER COOLED.

raw water strainer – a strainer installed between the engine water intake SEACOCK and the engine to filter debris from the water before it can get into the engine. Marine grass, small pieces of trash, mud, and even jellyfish can get sucked up into a strainer. Strainers come in various sizes and configurations; they should be inspected regularly. If the engine overheats and there is little or no water coming out of the exhaust this is the first thing to check. Some mariners install dual strainers so a clogged one can be closed to clear it, and the other one opened while underway.

RCC – (1)commonly-used abbreviation for Rescue Coordination Center, a center operated by a coast guard or COSPAS/SARSAT. *See also* AMVER. (2) acronym for the ROYAL CRUISING CLUB.

RCD – abbreviation for the European RECREATIONAL CRAFT DIRECTIVE.

RDF – abbreviation for RADIO DIRECTION FINDER.

reach, reaching – (1) a reach is a straight stretch in a winding channel or river. (2) general terms applied to sailing OFF THE WIND. Three POINTS OF SAIL are called a reach: close reach, beam reach, and broad reach.

reaching strut – a pole that attaches to the MAST and extends out beyond the SHROUDS, to hold out an AFTERGUY when using a SPINNAKER.

"ready about" – the command before TACKING. It tells the crew to prepare to tack. When the crew is ready they say "Ready." When all are ready the helmsman says "hard alee" or "lee-ho," and then steers the BOW through the wind.

"ready to jibe" – command used before executing a JIBE.

reciprocal – a direction that is exactly 180° in the opposite direction. The reciprocal of 90° is 270° and vice-versa. Used in the phrase reciprocal course.

reciprocal privileges – some yacht clubs have an arrangement with other clubs so their members may enjoy privileges at another club, such as use of the dining room, a mooring, dock space, or other benefits that would normally be unavailable to non-members.

Recreational Craft Directive, RCD – this document promulgates the technical, safety, and environmental standards for recreational vessels built or sold in the EU. These standards apply to non-commercial vessels 2.5m to 24m in length. The INTERNATIONAL MARINE CERTIFICATION INSTITUTE assists European marine product manufacturers with compliance. See the bibliography under "Design" for sources for the RCD text.

recreational vessel, pleasure craft – a vessel that's operated for recreational rather than commercial purposes. Some counties may have a more specific and detailed definition. The standards for construction, safety, equipping, and licensing of operators of pleasure craft vary from those applied to COMMERCIAL VESSELS.

recreational vessel construction standards – see STANDARDS FOR RECREATIONAL VESSEL CONSTRUCTION.

"red right returning"– phrase to help to remember the direction of buoyage in IALA REGION B, which includes North America. Red buoys should be kept on the right (starboard) side of the vessel when returning from sea.

reduced visibility – *see* VISIBILITY, RESTRICTED.

reduction gear – another term for the engine TRANSMISSION.

reef – (1) to make a sail smaller as the wind increases by partially rolling it in or partially lowering it. Types of reefing and reefing techniques vary with boats; see the reefing entries below. Some boats will need to reef sooner than others in the same winds. A properly reefed vessel sails faster and more upright than one that carries too much sail, HEELING excessively, and dragging the TOPSIDES through the water. A general guideline is to reef when you first think about it, rather than wait to see if the wind will go down. If it gets windier, it will be more difficult to reef. It's easy to shake out the reef (un-reef) if the wind lessens. (2) a submerged or partially-submerged obstruction such as rocks or coral that may be a hazard to navigation or anchoring.

reef cringle(s) – large GROMMETS on the LUFF and LEECH of a sail, used with reefing lines on a conventionally-reefed sail. *See* REEFING, SLAB and SAIL, PARTS OF for a drawing.

reef, deep or deeply-reefed – a deep reef is one that takes in a lot of sail, perhaps to the third or fourth row of REEF PENDANTS (reef points), or rolls in a lot of sail. *See* ROLLER REEFING. A deeply-reefed sail is very small in comparison to the unreefed sail.

reef patches – extra layers of sail cloth sewn on as reinforcements at the places on a sail where the REEF PENDANTS (reef points) are attached, and to reinforce the LUFF and LEECH where the reefs are located. Not all sails have these. *See* the next entry.

reef pendants, reef points, nettles – some slab-reefed MAINSAILS (and some JIBS) have short lines tied through GROMMETS on the sail, which extend from LUFF to LEECH in two, three or four rows. The pendants are used to tie up the excess sail (the BUNT) when the sail is reefed. The drawing with SAIL, PARTS OF shows lines of reef pendants. *See also* REEFING, SLAB and other reefing entries, below.

reef points – another name for REEF PENDANTS.

reefing, conventional – a reefing system that uses REEF PENDANTS (reef points), rather than ROLLER REEFING. *See* SAIL, PARTS OF for a drawing.

reefing hooks – hooks at the forward end of the BOOM mounted PORT and STARBOARD or tied to a short lanyard at the GOOSENECK. They are used with a SLAB-REEFED mainsail.

reefing, in-mast or in-boom – a reefing system where the sail is rolled into the MAST or BOOM to REEF it.

reefing, jiffy – another name for slab reefing. See below.

reefing lines – inclusive term for all the lines used to reef a sail. Some sails are reefed with a single line, while others may have two or more reefing lines.

reefing, roller – *see* ROLLER REEFING.

reefing, slab, or jiffy reefing – reefing a conventional MAIN by lowering it to a line of REEF PENDANTS (reef points) and tying up the excess. Slab reefed sails have two, three, and occasionally four lines of pendants. The first reef is the row nearest the BOOM, and the next reefs are identified by the numbers two, three, or four. The third or fourth reef makes the sail much smaller. The basic sequence for slab reefing is: (1) EASE the MAIN HALYARD and hook the LUFF reef CRINGLE into the REEFING HOOK. If the boat has a BOOM GALLOWS or BOOM CRUTCH, lower the boom into the gallows when you ease the halyard. It's much easier to tie in the reef if the boom isn't swinging around in rough seas. (2) Pull the CLEW reef cringle down to the boom with the appropriate reefing control line. Some sailors tie a strong separate line through the clew cringle and around the boom, so the reefing line doesn't chafe. (3) tie up the BUNT of the sail with the reef pendants, using SQUARE KNOTS. Some sails don't have pendants, so the bunt is left loose. (4) raise the reefed sail to its proper height to tighten the luff.

reeve, rove – to lead a line through a BLOCK or FAIRLEAD. "Please reeve the JIB SHEETS." Rove is the past tense of reeve. "Bob rove the new mainsheet before they set out."

reference station – a main port on a TIDE or CURRENT TABLE to which information is referenced.

reflective tape, retro-reflective tape – an adhesive-backed tape with a highly-reflective surface on one side. It's designed for use on equipment such as lifejackets, foul-weather clothing, life rafts, man-overboard gear, or anything that would benefit from enhanced visibility at night. SOLAS tape is the best choice for the marine environment.

refrigeration – is considered a necessity by many cruisers who stay out longer than a weekend at a time. Ice, particularly block ice, is not easy to find in many locations, and refrigeration systems are available in a range of types and prices. Some systems are suitable for DIY installation. No matter which type of refrigeration you choose or already have aboard, the following are basic considerations. The more insulation around the box, the better. The system will run less-frequently, saving power or engine running time. It may be possible to add more insulation to an existing system. Top opening refrigerator and freezer compartments are preferable to front opening, because the cold stays inside better. ABYC Standard A-6 deals with marine refrigeration. See the next two entries.

refrigeration, 12-volt – a refrigeration system that relies on battery power to operate the compressor. This system is suitable for boats with a large BATTERY BANK and a good charging capacity. The box must be very well insulated to minimize engine or generator running time. A well-designed 12-volt system can make ice in a freezer compartment. They are available in air-cooled and water-cooled systems. Some units are suitable for DIY installation by a skilled individual; other systems may require professional installation.

refrigeration, engine-driven – this system relies on a refrigeration compressor mounted on or near an engine or generator, driven by a V-BELT or a direct drive. The compressed refrigerant gas circulates through cold plates (holding plates) in the refrigerator and/or freezer compartments. An engine-driven system can freeze food and make ice. It's suitable for large compartments with good insulation. An engine-drive system may be seawater-cooled. Systems are also available for 120 or 220V AC power, either from the boat's generator or SHORE POWER. At least one marine refrigeration manufacturer offers an engine-driven system with an integral shore power unit. The relatively complex system must be carefully-designed and installed, preferably by a professional.

Region A, Region B – refers to the IALA A and IALA B systems of buoyage.

Registro Italiano Navale (RINA) – abbreviation for a marine CLASSIFICATION SOCIETY. (An unrelated group, the Royal Institution of Naval Architects, has the same identifying abbreviation).

regulator, electrical – a device that monitors the flow of charging current to the batteries as delivered by an ALTERNATOR, SOLAR PANELS, or a WIND or WATER GENERATOR. The regulator prevents overcharging. Regulators are single and multi-stage, adjustable and non-adjustable. Some alternators have an internal regulator. New models of regulators can be set for different types of batteries and different charging programs; however, the same type of batteries should be used in a BATTERY BANK connected to a regulator. Consult technical articles, a qualified marine electrician, and a good marine supply catalog before buying a new regulator.

regulator, propane – *see* PROPANE REGULATOR.

relative bearing – *see* BEARING, RELATIVE.

relieving the watch – *see* WATCH, CHANGE OF.

remote oil filter – *see* OIL FILTER, ENGINE.

renovating a boat – *see* BUILDING OR RENOVATING A BOAT.

Rescue 21 – a new U.S. Coast Guard *distress* system based on the use of VHF DSC radio and Coast Guard position-locating equipment. The system is effective up to 25 miles from the receiving stations. It's part of the National Distress and Response System (NRDS). See the bibliography under "Safety."

rescue knife, safety knife – a knife with features, including a very sharp blade, that make it suitable for emergency as well as everyday use. There are several types available. Some can be easily opened with one hand, some float, some have a rounded tip to help prevent puncturing inflatable equipment, and most have a pocket clip. It's a very useful item for all crew members to carry.

rescue line – *see* THROWING LINE.

resistance, electrical – opposition to the flow of the current in an AC or DC circuit; it's measured in OHMS. Resistance is an inherent feature of electrical circuits, but unwanted resistance can be caused by corrosion in wires, connectors, on terminals and switches, and by undersized wires. If there's too much resistance in a circuit a VOLTAGE DROP may result or the equipment may not work at all. Low voltage can affect the operation of voltage-sensitive equipment. Electric lights don't care (they may get dim), but some motors and other equipment may run improperly, overheat, or cease to work. In some cases excessive resistance in a circuit or at connections can cause enough heat to melt insulation or start a fire. If wires or connectors are warm when equipment is operating, there's too much resistance. Determine and correct the cause.

restricted in ability to maneuver, RAM – Rule 3(g) of the NAVIGATION RULES defines a vessel restricted in her ability to maneuver as "a vessel which from the nature of her work is restricted in her ability to maneuver as required by these Rules and is therefore unable to keep out of the way of another vessel." The definition applies to both power-driven and sailing vessels. A RAM vessel may be able to maneuver (in contrast to a vessel NOT UNDER COMMAND), but her *work* prevents her from following the Rules. Examples of RAM vessels include, but are not limited to, vessels that are:

- Working with navigation aids, submarine cables and pipelines.
- Dredging, surveying, or conducting underwater operations.
- Transferring cargo or persons while underway.
- Launching or recovering aircraft.
- Engaged in a towing operation that severely restricts them and their tow from deviating from their course.
- Involved in mine clearing.

Rule 27(b-f) specifies the lights and DAYSHAPES for RAM vessels.

- A RAM vessel UNDERWAY and making way displays three ALL-AROUND lights in a vertical line: two red lights with a white light in the middle ("R-W-R, restricted ability ahead").
- Underway and making way she displays SIDELIGHTS, a STERN LIGHT, and MASTHEAD lights appropriate to her size.
- At anchor she displays the R-W-R lights, and an ANCHOR LIGHT.
- The black DAYSHAPES for a RAM vessel are two balls with a diamond in the middle, in a vertical line (ball-diamond-ball).
- A RAM towing vessel displays the lights prescribed for a towing vessel in Rule 24 *and* the lights for a RAM vessel. She looks like a Christmas tree, and it's important to learn these lights.
- A RAM dredge or vessel engaged in underwater operations has complex lights and shapes. She doesn't display an anchor light; Rule 27(d). If it's impractical for a vessel conducting underwater operations to display the prescribed lights and shapes, she displays the red-white-red lights in a vertical line *and* a rigid replica of **CODE FLAG** "A," which should be visible all around the vessel.
- A mine clearing vessel displays the navigation lights prescribed for a power-driven vessel of her size, plus three all-around green lights in a cross ("mine clearing boss"). Her dayshape is three black balls in a cross. You may see naval ships on maneuvers displaying these lights and shapes.
- A vessel less than 12m/39.4ft in length is not required to display RAM lights and shapes, unless she is engaged in underwater operations; Rule 27 (g).

Rule 35 prescribes the SOUND SIGNALS for these vessels in RESTRICTED VISIBILITY.

restricted radiotelephone operator's permit – *see* LICENSING, RADIO OPERATOR.

restricted visibility – *see* VISIBILITY, RESTRICTED.

restricted visibility sound signals – *see* SOUND SIGNALS, RESTRICTED VISIBILITY.

reverse osmosis – a process used by some WATERMAKERS.

reverse sheer – *see* SHEER.

reverse transom – *see* TRANSOM, REVERSE.

RF – abbreviation for radio frequency. *See* FREQUENCY, RADIO.

RF ground – a ground connection to the seawater for a SINGLE-SIDEBAND radio. There are several ways to achieve an RF ground; consult technical references. A VHF radio doesn't need an RF ground.

rhumb line, rhumb line course – a straight line drawn on a MERCATOR chart is a rhumb line. A rhumb line course is used in coastal navigation. East-to-west and west-to-east courses, routes of over approximately 600 miles, and routes that go closer to the poles (rather than nearer the equator) may be shorter if the vessel takes a GREAT CIRCLE COURSE rather than a rhumb line. A GPS or NAVIGATION COMPUTER can calculate the difference in distance for a great circle course or a rhumb line course between two WAYPOINTS. To choose between the two, in addition to the distance, consider the prevailing winds, ocean currents, and weather systems on both routes. A PILOT CHART helps make routing decisions.

RIB – abbreviation for rigid INFLATABLE boat. The abbreviation is usually used. It's has a solid lower hull and inflatable tubes above the hull. The military, rescue services, law enforcement agencies, and private companies use large, seaworthy RIBs.

A 20ft/6m inboard-powered RIB.

A 36ft/11m RIB, powered by large twin outboard engines. This RIB makes offshore trips.

ridge – (1) on a weather map or SYNOPTIC, a ridge is an elongated area of relatively high atmospheric pressure. The pressure is higher on the inside of the ridge curve. A TROUGH is the opposite of a ridge. (2) a long, narrow raised area with steep sides on the bottom of the sea; such as the mid-Atlantic Ridge. (3) broken ice forced upward in a ridge line; an ice ridge.

riding light – another name for an ANCHOR LIGHT.

riding sail – a small triangular sail used on the BACKSTAY of a sailboat to hold her steady into the wind while at anchor or on a mooring. The sail HANKS onto the backstay and is pulled up with a HALYARD. It's mounted backward, with one edge (the LUFF) on the backstay and the CLEW pulled forward toward the MAST with a line. The riding sail helps stop sheering from side to side or SAILING AT ANCHOR. A KETCH or YAWL may leave the MIZZEN up at anchor as a riding sail. A riding sail isn't the same as a STEADYING SAIL, although the terms are used interchangeably.

A riding sail on the backstay of a cutter with a tall rig. An anchor ball is displayed aloft. The white cylinder on the mast above the radar is a radar reflector and the hanked-on staysail is in the blue bag on the foredeck.

riding turn, override – a riding turn occurs on a WINCH when the line coming to the winch rides up over the turns already on the winch. This makes it difficult or impossible to release the line or to continue winching it in. A ROLLING HITCH can be used to correct an override. If a line leads downward to a winch overrides may be a continuing problem: the line should lead upward from slightly below the winch drum.

rig, rigged – (1) the basic arrangement of the MAST and sails on a boat, such as SLOOP rig, SCHOONER rig or -rigged. (2) to set up a line, TACKLE or other boat gear ready for use. "Please rig the VANG on the PORT side."

rig dimensions – used when comparing similar boats and sailplans and for ordering sails. Don't measure existing sails for these dimensions; take measurements on the boat (or the sailmaker will do it). The basic dimensions are:

I = the measurement along the front of MAST from the highest HALYARD point to the main deck. The main deck is the level of the deck, not including a DECKHOUSE.

J = the base of the FORETRIANGLE measured along the deck from the HEADSTAY to the mast.

P = the length of the MAINSAIL'S LUFF, measured along the AFT side of the mast from the top of the BOOM to the highest point to which the main can be hoisted.

E = the length of the FOOT of the mainsail, measured along the boom from the aft side of the mast to the outermost point on the boom to which the main can be pulled.

rig, fractional – *see* FRACTIONAL RIG.

rig, masthead – *see* MASTHEAD RIG.

rigger – a person who specializes in the repair, maintenance, and installation of rigging.

rigging – inclusive term for all the SHROUDS, STAYS, lines, and other hardware used to support the SPARS and control the sails. STANDING RIGGING includes SHROUDS, STAYS, and semi-permanent rigging which is infrequently adjusted. RUNNING RIGGING includes SHEETS, HALYARDS, CONTROL LINES, and other lines that are frequently adjusted when sailing.

rigging cutter, cable cutter – a tool specifically designed for cutting rigging wire and rod. This tool makes a neat, square cut, which is necessary for properly installing MECHANICAL TERMINALS. An easy-to-operate cutter is essential in an emergency, such as a dismasting. Manual cutters cut wire up to 5/8"/16mm; hydraulic cutters handle larger wire and rod than the manual models; and an explosive cartridge tool ("Toolva Shootit") cuts wire up to ½"/14mm). Hydraulic and cartridge cutters take little strength to operate, and some will also cut rod rigging. Check with the tool supplier to see if an explosive cartridge cutter makes a proper square cut for installing mechanical terminals; it is marketed as an emergency cutter. A sharp hacksaw (have lots of new blades) or a cold chisel can cut rigging, but in an emergency it will be difficult (more likely impossible) and slow. Bolt cutters won't cut typical rigging wire or rod. See the bibliography under "Rigging" for sources of rigging cutters.

rigging inspection – it can spoil your day if you lose the rig. Do a general inspection at least once a season or twice a year if the boat is in service all year, and a comprehensive inspection no less than every three years. Sailboats that receive hard use or high-tech racing boats require more frequent and detailed rigging checks. Tropical saltwater environments are hard on rigging. After a heavy weather experience, a severe grounding, lightning strike, or a collision conduct a thorough rigging examination, in addition to other inspections. Check with your MARINE INSURANCE AGENT for any mandated rigging inspection or replacement intervals. A comprehensive rig check should be done with the MAST on the ground, rather than in the boat. You can do a basic inspection yourself, or you may wish to hire a professional rigger; an insurance company may require a professional rig check. A general inspection includes examination for:

Broken rigging strands, MEATHOOKS, kinks in wire, or bent rod. Replace the wire/rod if any defects are found.

Misalignment between wire/rod and its terminals or attachment points (CHAINPLATES, TANGS, HOUNDS). Correct misalignment and replace wire/rod if it's bent.

Bends, deformation, cracks, or elongated holes on or near attachment points, CLEVIS PINS, TURNBUCKLES, and the mast cap. Clean off surface rust or corrosion, use a magnifying glass, and/or A DYE PENETRANT TEST. Most problems occur at the terminals, attachment points, or other fittings, particularly at deck level.

Rust on or near SWAGED or MECHANICAL TERMINALS or other fittings. Rust may indicate a crack. Open mechanical terminals to inspect inside, and replace the cones or other internal parts when reassembling (check the instructions). Dye penetrant test swaged terminals. The lower terminals are especially vulnerable.

Corrosion or cracks on or near fittings on the mast or spars.

Bent SPREADERS, cracked mast attachment sockets, corroded inboard or outboard spreader ends.

Damage to masthead SHEAVES, and signs of chafe on the mast.

Damage or chafe on ROLLER FURLING gear.

Cracks or damage on T-HOOK fittings, which have a shorter life than the wire/rod rigging itself.

Damage to rope rigging.

rigging life expectancy – the life expectancy for wire, rod, and synthetic rigging varies with the size of the rigging (oversized or undersized), years of service, type of service (lake, coastwise, ocean, tropical waters, racing), how the rigging has been stored (indoors or outside), the frequency and quality of maintenance, and whether it's been subjected to unusual stresses, such as a storm or a severe grounding. Some MARINE INSURANCE companies specify a rigging replacement interval. In general, the life expectancy of well-cared for STAINLESS STEEL rigging in a tropical or semi-tropical saltwater environment may be 5-10 years, in a temperate or colder saltwater environment 10-15 years, and in a freshwater environment 15-20 years. *See also* RIGGING, SYNTHETIC.

rigging, rod – *see* ROD RIGGING.

rigging, running – *see* RUNNING RIGGING.

rigging screw – another name for a TURNBUCKLE.

rigging, synthetic – high-tech, very high strength synthetic rope is being developed that can replace wire rigging. It's much lighter than wire, significantly reducing weight aloft. End terminals and fittings are available that are similar to those used on wire rope. It is easily spliced, using simple hand tools, so it's ideal for DIY installation. This new technology hasn't been around enough years to fully evaluate it's longevity, but the life of synthetic rigging seems to be eight years or possibly longer. UV rays weaken the fibers over time, and manufacturers will address this issue as the technology develops. Dyneema® and Spectra® single braid line is approved for use as LIFELINES; see the bibliography under "Rigging" for an article about these lines.

rigging tension gauge – a tool used to adjust the tension of the STANDING RIGGING. Gauges come in various sizes and models for wire or rod rigging. A rigging gauge is easy to use, and ensures that the rigging is properly tuned (tensioned) on both sides of the boat. See the bibliography under "Rigging" (Loos & Co. Inc.) for a source of tension gauges.

rigging wire – another name for WIRE ROPE.

righting moment – a measure of the stability of a vessel. It's determined by the distance between the center of gravity and the center of buoyancy and the total weight of the boat. The MARINE ARCHITECT calculates the righting moment of his/her designs.

rigid dodger – a DODGER made of solid materials.

right of way priority, pecking order – under Rule 3 of the NAVIGATION RULES certain vessels have right of way over other vessels. It's essential to memorize the priority. A memory aid is "**O**h, **N**ever **R**equest **C**redit **F**or **S**omething **P**retty **S**mall." Each type of vessel is defined elsewhere in this book. The list is from highest priority to lowest; vessels lower on the list stay out of the way of vessels higher on the list.

Overtaken (all overtaking vessels keep out of the way)
Not under command, NUC
Restricted in ability to maneuver, RAM
Constrained by DRAFT, CBD
Fishing vessel
Sailing vessel
Power-driven vessel
Seaplane

RINA – abbreviation for the ROYAL INSTITUTION OF NAVAL ARCHITECTS, and the unrelated REGISTRO ITALIANO NAVALE, a marine CLASSIFICATION SOCIETY.

ring buoy, life ring – a circular flotation device to throw to a person in the water. It should have the name of the vessel on it. Look for Coast Guard or other approval on its label.

riprap – large stones or chunks of concrete piled along a shore, a breakwater, or around navigation aids to protect them from erosion and damage from wave action. Give a wide berth to riprap, as it may extend out under the water.

rip-stop nylon – a lightweight cloth used for SPINNAKERS and other light wind sails. As the name implies, it doesn't tear easily. Adhesive backed rip-stop cloth is available in rolls for temporary repairs and chafe protection on sails and other cloth items.

risk of collision – *see* COLLISION, RISK OF.

RNC – abbreviation for RASTER navigational charts produced by NOAA.

RNLI – abbreviation for the ROYAL NATIONAL LIFEBOAT INSTITUTION.

roach – not the creepy-crawly, but the outward curve along the LEECH of a MAINSAIL that extends past a straight line drawn from HEAD to CLEW. BATTENS hold the shape of the roach. The roach gives more sail area. A **BATTENLESS** main has no roach.

roads, roadstead – an open anchorage area. A roadstead has limited protection from the seas; it's less secure than a harbor.

rode – (1) the **ANCHOR** line or chain. (2) held by or captive. Used with the word tide or wind, as in **TIDE-RODE** or **WIND-RODE**, it indicates that a vessel is lying to the tide or the wind.

rode, chain – secure the **BITTER END** of an all-chain **RODE** in a belowdecks **CHAIN LOCKER** with a length of rope that comes up on deck, where it can be cut if necessary to free the chain in an emergency. Cut the rope, tie a **FENDER** to the rope to buoy the chain, and throw the fender over, so you can get away from a dangerous situation. Return later and retrieve your anchor. See chain entries for more information.

rod rigging – **STANDING RIGGING** made from **STAINLESS STEEL** rod rather than wire rope. Rod stretches less than wire, which is mostly a concern for racers and performance sailors.

rogue wave – see **WAVE, ROGUE**.

roll – the motion of a vessel as it rocks from side-to-side. Beam seas or sailing downwind under poled out **HEADSAILS** may make a vessel roll. A fast, snappy roll is very uncomfortable.

rollover – something no sailor wants to experience. The vessel completely rolls over, through 360°, and with luck comes upright again, but usually minus important things like the **MAST**, deck gear, and possibly a crewmember. A rollover is *very* rare because of the extreme conditions of waves and wind necessary to cause it. It may seem to be more frequent because the event makes headlines and a good story for articles and books. If you're not scared already, see **PITCHPOLE**.

roller furling, roller furler – the process of rolling a sail around a **STAY**, into the **MAST** or into (or around) the **BOOM** to furl it (put it away). The device used for roller furling is a roller furler. Roller furling is used on **HEADSAILS**, **MAINSAILS**, and other sails. The practice of leaving a small portion of the **CLEW** of a headsail sticking out when the sail is furled invites a strong wind to unfurl the sail, even if the furling line is tight. Roll two or three wraps of the **SHEETS** around the furled **JIB** to secure it. This can't be done with a headsail that has a sheet **BLOCK** at the clew. A roller furling mainsail must leave a portion of the clew out of the mast or a bit of the **HEAD** sticking up from the boom. For more photos see **BOW, PLUMB**; **BOW RAIL**; **CHINE**; **CLASSIC VESSEL**; **DOUBLE-ENDED**; **ENDS**; **JIB, YANKEE**; **MOORING, PICKING UP**; **RIDING SAIL**; **TIDE RIPS**; and **TRANSOM, TRADITIONAL**.

A Passport 52 cruising sailboat with twin roller furling headsails, an in-mast roller furling mainsail, a rigid boom vang, and an anchor roller on a short projection.

roller reefing – the process of rolling a sail around a STAY, into the MAST, or into (or around) a BOOM to make it smaller (reef it) as the wind increases. Some HEADSAILS are designed to be used in strong winds with part of the sail rolled in; others are not. The furling line must be strong enough to take the strain. A partially furled headsail is less effective than a smaller headsail in strong winds because some of the area of the furled sail is high up, which doesn't reduce heeling as much as a smaller headsail. The same is true of in-mast roller reefing for a mainsail. See the photo with TIDE RIPS for a yacht sailing with a roller-reefed genoa.

rolling hitch – a non-slip knot made around a round object like a rope or a pole; it's used to pull lengthwise on the object. A common use for a rolling hitch is to clear a RIDING TURN on a WINCH. Make the hitch on the line ahead of the winch, lead the end of the line from the rolling hitch to another winch or otherwise pull it tight, and tie it off it so it holds the strain. Remove the tangled line from the winch and clear the override. A rolling hitch is also used to attach a CHAIN SPRING to the anchor chain. See KNOTS, BASIC for a photo.

rope – cordage used aboard a boat is called "line" or another name when it's been put to a specific use, such as dock line, anchor RODE, SHEET or HALYARD. However, there are eight ropes used on a vessel that are called "ropes:" bell rope (attached to the clapper of a bell); bucket rope (attached to a bucket or pail); bolt rope (a rope sewn along the LUFF of a sail); head rope (the part of a bolt rope that is attached to the HEAD of a sail); tiller rope (wire rope attached to a TILLER above or below decks); man ropes (ropes used as handrails aboard a ship or along a GANGWAY); foot ropes (the ropes sailors stand on while working aloft on the horizontal spars of a SQUARE-RIGGER); becket rope (a short rope used for a variety of special purposes). The language police will overlook it if you call a line a rope once in a while. See entries for ROPE CONSTRUCTION and individual rope types.

rope, braided – types include: (1) single braid with a hollow core or a braid core. (2) double braid or braid-on-braid. (3) 6-, 8- or 12-strand braid (may also be called PLAITED rope). Braided ropes are not as elastic as THREE-STRAND rope; for this reason braid isn't ideal for an anchor RODE. Braid is frequently chosen for SHEETS, HALYARDS, and CONTROL LINES because it doesn't stretch. Consult marine supply catalogs or manufacturers' literature for selection. It can be spliced with simple tools; instructions are on rope manufacturers' websites and in MARLINSPIKE SEAMANSHIP books. See the bibliography under "Lines."

rope, breaking strength – the load at which new rope breaks in a laboratory test. *See* ROPE, SAFE WORKING LOAD.

rope, care of – for safety and long-life rope should be cared for and used properly. Regularly inspect all lines for signs of aging, wear, and damage. Rope with broken strands or HOCKLES should be discarded or cut into shorter, undamaged ropes. Discolored rope may have been damaged by chemicals, oil, diesel fuel, or other harmful liquids. UV damage from long exposure to sunlight hardens and weakens rope. It can be damaged, with no outward signs, by heat from excessive strain (loads exceeding the rope's working load), heat resulting from friction over a surface, or high heat in a rope storage area. Consult rope manufacturers' literature or websites for recommendations about care of particular types of rope. All ropes, including an anchor **RODE**, benefit from a freshwater wash with mild detergent to remove salt and dirt. *See* **ROPE, SAFE WORKING LOAD** and **ROPE SAFETY**.

rope clutch – another name for a **LINE STOPPER**.

rope construction – types include **LAID** rope (made of twisted strands), **PLAITED** rope (made of multiple strands plaited or braided together), and **BRAIDED** (various construction methods). Different construction methods and materials are used for specific purposes. Select rope for elasticity (mooring and anchoring), low-stretch properties (**HALYARDS, SHEETS**, and **CONTROL LINES**), high strength, resistance to wear and UV damage, ease of handling and stowage, floating characteristics, etc. Rope manufacturers' websites and marine supply catalogs have selection guides. See individual rope entries.

rope cutter – another name for a **LINE CUTTER**.

rope, laid or twisted rope – rope constructed of stands twisted together. Nylon three-strand is a common type of laid rope. *See* **ROPE, THREE STRAND**.

rope locker – a locker or location at the **BOW** on or under the deck where a rope anchor **RODE** is stowed.

rope, manila – **THREE-STRAND** rope made from brown, natural fiber. It's used on some **TRADITIONAL** vessels and for decorative uses ashore. Modern, stronger synthetic rope that looks like manila has replaced it where real manila was once used.

rope, plaited – a type of rope constructed by a special braiding technique (plaiting). 8-plait and 12-plait are ropes made of eight strands and 12 strands. Plaited rope is easy to handle and stows compactly. It's not as elastic as **THREE-STRAND** rope and it may snag on rough surfaces. It's not especially easy for an amateur to splice. *See* **ROPE, BRAIDED** and **ROPE, THREE-STRAND**.

rope safety – there can be hundreds or thousands of pounds of pull on a **SHEET**, or any other rope under tension.

Don't allow anyone to stand behind or within 45° on either side of a line under tension. If it breaks, the recoil force can cause serious injury. **HEADSAIL** sheets, towing lines, and **KEDGE** lines are particularly dangerous.

If you use bare hands to grab a line under strain and the line pulls out of your hand, you'll get a rope burn or worse.

Wrapping a line around your hand to get extra pulling power isn't a good idea. If a sudden pull occurs your hand can be yanked into a **WINCH** or otherwise damaged.

Sharp bends, exceeding approximately 90° (as with **TURNING BLOCKS**), greatly reduce the strength of a line.

Rope loses strength from age, UV exposure, knots, and splices. An old rope under tension can be dangerous.

Regularly inspect all rope for signs of damage such as broken or worn strands, a damaged outer core on braided line, stiffness, excessive dirt or oil. Replace suspect lines, or put them to uses where lower loads occur.

The Cordage Institute, which sets standards for the rope industry, has a technical, but readable, one-page guide to rope safety, at www.ropecord.com/CI1401.PDF. *See* **WINCH SAFETY; ROPE, CARE OF** and the next entry.

rope safe working load, SWL – the working load limits for various rope diameters are listed in tables in marine supply catalogs and on rope manufacturers' websites. If only the breaking strength is given, estimate the safe (a relative term) working load by applying a safety factor to the breaking strength (see below).

Use information specific to the rope brand (if possible), the type of fiber used in the rope, and the construction (BRAID, THREE-STRAND or other construction).

The strengths of the same diameter rope varies between manufacturers, and with the fibers used in the rope's construction.

Tables of working loads or breaking loads indicate the load that should not be exceeded with various sizes of *new* rope. The tables are for guidance in non-critical, normal use. Actual loads on a rope can greatly exceed a working load, because of conditions that produce dynamic, rather than static, forces. Examples of dynamic loading include the jerking of a boat on her mooring lines, the jerking of SHEETS in strong winds when TACKING, and sheering and jerking forces on a tow line.

A minimum safety factor of 5:1 (20% of the breaking strength) is commonly used for ordinary uses of rope. Rope loses strength from age, knots and splices, from excessive stretching, damage from continual stress (as with sheets, mooring lines, and anchor RODES), shock loads, high loads over the recommended safe working load, from heat (friction and stress create heat), and UV damage.

For critical operations where the safety of life may be at risk, seek the advice of a qualified engineer or other expert. In some cases, selecting a rope with a large safety factor (as high as 12:1) may be appropriate. Going up the MAST on a HALYARD of unknown condition or strength is an invitation to trouble; that's why two halyards should be used when going ALOFT. Of course, two old halyards could break, so there's always danger.

rope selection – marine equipment catalogues have general guides for selecting rope, but for comprehensive guides go to the manufacturers' websites, such as New England Ropes, Samson Ropes, and Yale Cordage. See the bibliography under "Lines."

rope splicing – basic rope splices are not difficult to learn, and the few tools needed are inexpensive. Consult a MARLINSPIKE SEAMANSHIP book or check rope manufacturers' websites. If it looks too difficult, hire a professional. *See* SPLICES, TYPES OF.

rope, three-strand – rope made up of individual yarns wound together into a single strand, and then three strands are laid into a single rope. Three-strand is either right-hand lay or left hand lay, which indicates the direction in which the three strands are twisted together. All the laid rope in the photos in this book is right-hand lay. There are two types of lay: hard and soft; hard-laid rope is firm to the touch, and it resists snagging and holds knots and splices better than soft-laid rope. Three-strand is commonly used for MOORING LINES and ANCHOR RODES because of its elasticity, resistance to abrasion, and ease of splicing. *See* ROPE, BRAIDED.

rope-to-wire splice – *see* SPLICES, TYPES OF.

rope, wire – *see* WIRE ROPE.

RORC – abbreviation for the ROYAL OCEAN RACING CLUB.

round turn and two half-hitches – an easily-tied, secure basic hitch for tying a line around a spar, a piling, or any round or square object. See KNOTS, BASIC for a photo.

round up – turning toward the wind, either by the action of the helmsman or by the action of WEATHER HELM in gusty winds.

rove – (1) past tense of REEVE. "We rove this TACKLE last week so we could use it on our trip." (2) copper roves are circular washers used at the end of copper nails to form a rivet, used in the construction of some wooden boats.

rowlock, oarlock – the round or U-shaped hardware that holds an oar when rowing. The oar maybe loose in the oarlock or it may have a pin through it to secure it to the rowlock. A THOLE PIN is a type of rowlock.

Royal Cruising Club, RCC – a member organization based in England and dedicated to furthering cruising under sail. Membership is by invitation only, and is limited to 400 members. The RCC Pilotage Foundation (www.rccpf.org.uk) produces PILOT BOOKS and other publications for worldwide cruising. These are available to the general public through booksellers. Logs of members' worldwide cruises and adventures are available to non members in the form of the RCC's annual journal, *Roving Commissions*, which may be ordered on the Pilotage Foundation website.

Royal Institution of Naval Architects, RINA – an international professional organization based in London. The Institution sponsors technical education events, publishes professional papers, and represents its members worldwide. The RINA has cooperative agreements with other naval architect societies around the world. (An unrelated group, the Registro Italiano Navale, a marine CLASSIFICATION SOCIETY, has the same identifying abbreviation).

Royal National Lifeboat Institution, RNLI – "the charity that saves lives at sea." Founded in 1824, the RNLI is the lifeboat service for the waters of the UK, the Channel Islands, the Isle of Man, and the Republic of Ireland. Supported entirely by voluntary donations and staffed by trained volunteers, the RNLI performs search-and-rescue duties for commercial and recreational mariners at sea and on the beaches. RNLI lifeboats are designed for their duties in particular waters, and the crews are highly-trained for their mission. There are a number of ways to support the organization, including through personal memberships. The RNLI administrative and training facilities are at Poole, England. The organization works cooperatively with lifesaving organizations around the world. www.rnli.org.uk.

A 17m/55.7ft. RNLI Severn Class lifeboat. She is decorated for a special event.

A motto of the RNLI.

Royal Ocean Racing Club, RORC – a UK organization that sponsors and co-sponsors a variety of ocean yacht races. The website has links to a number of sailing websites for racers and cruisers, including training facilities. www.rorc.org.

Royal Yachting Association, RYA – based in England, the RYA is the national body for all forms of boating, on the sea and inland waterways of the UK. It promotes racing and cruising under sail and power, offers high-quality training and certification programs, and publishes excellent instructional books. Educational programs include classroom and on-the-water courses for recreational and professional mariners, including the rigorous YACHTMASTER certification examinations. RYA courses are offered in a number of worldwide locations. www.rya.org.uk.

rpm(s) – abbreviation for revolutions per minute; the speed the engine (or other mechanical equipment) is turning. Engine rpms are displayed on an instrument called a tachometer (rhymes with thermometer), the same instrument found on some vehicles. There's a high rpm that shouldn't be exceeded under normal operating conditions; look for that information in the engine operator's manual or the boat's notebook.

RTFM – acronym for "read the fine manual." Some readers may know another meaning. Marine electronics and equipment are complicated and have features not immediately obvious from playing around with the menus. Read the manual, even if you're generally familiar with the equipment or have used an earlier model of the same device. There's usually something to learn in a manual or instruction sheet. If the manual's not "fine" write your own instructions once you figure out how to do something.

rub rail, rubbing strake – a strong strip of wood or metal along the sides of the hull parallel to the deck, either at the deck level or below it, designed to prevent hull damage when a boat rubs against a piling or a pier. Not all boats have a rub rail.

rudder – the vertical underwater part of the boat at or near the STERN attached to a TILLER (directly to the rudder head or via a RUDDER STOCK), or to a steering wheel with cables, gears, or hydraulics. The rudder steers the boat, and water must be moving past the rudder for the boat to have steerage. Rudders have many different shapes, attachment methods, and STEERING SYSTEMS. Some boats have twin rudders. See the individual RUDDER entries, below.

rudder, balanced – a portion of the rudder is forward of the RUDDER STOCK and a portion is ABAFT the stock. See the photos with APERTURE and RUDDER, SKEG-HUNG.

rudder, centering – before starting to maneuver a boat, it's a good idea to have the rudder centered (unless you're planning a specific maneuver that begins with the rudder off to one side or the other). Centering is easy with a TILLER. With a wheel (if the KING SPOKE is not marked) determine the center position for the rudder by turning the wheel all the way over to one side, and then by turning it all the way back to the other side, while counting the number of turns "lock-to-lock." Half the number of turns means the rudder is centered. Counting turns works for any type of wheel steering system, cable, direct drive, or hydraulic. Check it on an unfamiliar boat; it takes less than 30 seconds, unless you turn the wheel really slowly. Some boats have a RUDDER POSITION INDICATOR, which makes it too easy.

rudder, keel-hung – a rudder attached to the AFT end of the KEEL. It's an UNBALANCED rudder. The photos with APERTURE; KEEL, FULL; and MARINE RAILWAY show this type of rudder.

rudder, kick-up – a rudder with a hinge that allows it to pivot upward for shallow water, beaching or trailering, or to get the WINDWARD rudder on a twin rudder boat out of the water.

A kick-up outboard rudder on a small daysailer.

rudder, outboard – a rudder mounted on a TRANSOM or CANOE STERN (and occasionally on a SKEG located well AFT). GUDGEONS and PINTLES attach the rudder to the boat. An outboard rudder may have a TILLER or be connected to a wheel steering system. It's easy to inspect it without hauling out, and because the lower edge of the rudder is (usually) higher than the bottom of the KEEL it is somewhat protected from damage in a grounding. However, an outboard rudder is exposed to attacks from ASTERN. For another photo see DOUBLE-ENDED; KEEL, FULL; and KETCH.

An outboard rudder on a double-ended ketch. The metal frame around the rudder supports the windvane self-steering gear.

rudder position indicator – this device has a dial with a needle that indicates if the rudder's centered or the number of degrees it's off to PORT or to STARBOARD. On a vessel with hydraulic wheel steering you can't tell by the position of the wheel where the rudder is because there's no consistent KING SPOKE (it changes a little over time). Count the turns lock-to-lock (half the number of turns means the rudder is centered), or install a rudder position indicator.

rudder post – another term for RUDDER STOCK.

rudder quadrant, quadrant – a cast bronze or aluminum fitting (covering a 90° arc) that fits over the RUDDER STOCK inside the boat, to which steering cables are attached. It's an important inspection and maintenance item, usually hidden away in the STERN of the boat.

rudder, skeg-hung – a rudder attached to a SKEG; it may be BALANCED or UNBALANCED. The skeg protects the rudder and improves directional stability (in comparison to a SPADE rudder).

A skeg-hung unbalanced rudder on a long skeg. Note the three anodes on the propeller shaft forward of the shaft strut.

A skeg-hung balanced rudder on a short skeg.

rudder, spade – a free-standing rudder, attached to the hull only by the RUDDER STOCK. On some boats it may be attached to a short SKEG. It's either BALANCED or UNBALANCED. A spade is used on FIN KEELED racing sailboats and many cruising boats. This rudder maneuvers the boat quickly and easily, in both forward and reverse, but in rough seas the helmsman must be attentive or the AUTOPILOT very active to stay on course. Because it's free-standing, a spade rudder is vulnerable to damage in a grounding, and to snagging hazards floating beneath the surface. For other photos see **KEEL, FIN** and **RUDDERS, TWIN.**

A free-standing spade rudder, attached only by the rudder stock.

rudder stock, rudder post – the metal rod or tube that attaches the rudder to the boat. The stock enters the boat through one or more STUFFING BOXES (rudder gland), which is a maintenance item. A TILLER ARM, RUDDER QUADRANT, or control devices for a steering wheel and an AUTOPILOT (if fitted) are attached near the top of the rudder stock.

rudders, twin – some sailing yachts have twin rudders, so that one rudder will have maximum effect when the boat is heeled. A powerboat with twin engines may also have two rudders.

Twin canted rudders on *Pindar*, an Open 60 ocean racer.

rudder, unbalanced – the RUDDER STOCK is at the forward edge of the rudder and the rest of the rudder is ABAFT the stock. KEEL-HUNG and OUTBOARD rudders, many SKEG-hung, and some SPADE rudders are unbalanced rudders. See the photos with RUDDER, SKEG-HUNG.

Rule of Good Seamanship – Rule 2(a) of the NAVIGATION RULES is also known as the Rule of Good Seamanship. "Nothing in these Rules shall exonerate any vessel, or the owner, master or crew thereof, from the consequences of any neglect to comply with these Rules or of the neglect of any precaution which may be required by the ordinary practice of seamen, or by the special circumstances of the case." What this means is that there's nothing in the Rules that *excuses* a mariner who:

Doesn't comply with the Rules.

Doesn't take precautions that a prudent seaman would take under the circumstances.

Doesn't take into account any special circumstances of the situation which may require special precautions.

Of course, there are a lot of vague words in this rule that engage lawyers and judges in legal debates. Seamanship evolves along with technology, so in addition to basic seamanship skills, a mariner is expected to know how to use the all navigational aids on the vessel. The seamanship skills of a licensed mariner are judged by a higher standard. The GENERAL PRUDENTIAL RULE is related to this rule.

Rule of Twelfths – a method of *estimating* the height of a SEMI-DIURNAL TIDE at any hour in a six hour cycle of the FLOOD or EBB. The rule says that in the first hour after low, the water will rise one-twelfth of the tide RANGE, in the second hour two-twelfths, in the third hour three-twelfths, etc. The sequence is 1,2,3,3,2,1. To apply the Rule of Twelfths you need a TIDE TABLE with the times and heights of high and low water at your location. Determine the RANGE (the difference in height between high and low water). Divide the range by 12. The resulting number is the estimate of how much the tide will rise or fall in each of the six hours, according to the sequence. The assumption is that the tide rises and falls in equal steps during a six hour period, which, in reality, it doesn't, so that's why the rule is an estimate. One-half the total rise or fall happens during the third and fourth hours of the six-hour cycle. If the tide range is large, the current will be strongest in these two hours. This information may be helpful to estimate when there will be enough water for the vessel's DRAFT. When can I enter the channel to the marina? How long will I be stuck here? Should I take a nap?

Rules of the Road – the NAVIGATION RULES.

run, running – (1) a run or running is sailing before the wind; sailing with the wind ASTERN; sailing downwind. See POINTS OF SAIL. (2) applied to a line it means to run free, without tangles or obstruction. "Make sure the HALYARD can run." Run is not the same as EASE, PAY OUT, and SLIP. (3) being underway. "If we run this course for another hour we should see the island."

runaway diesel – fortunately a rare occurrence, a runaway diesel goes out of control, unable to be stopped because it's feeding on its own lubrication oil. The RPMS increase until the engine destroys itself, and scares the crew to death. The only way to stop a runaway is to completely block the air intake, with a plug or other solid object (*not your hand)*, or by discharging a CO_2 fire extinguisher into the intake. Consult a diesel engine book for the causes.

runners – short name for RUNNING BACKSTAYS.

running backstays, runners, "running backs" – *see* BACKSTAYS, RUNNING.

running lights – another name for NAVIGATION LIGHTS.

running rigging – running rigging includes SHEETS, HALYARDS, CONTROL LINES, and other lines that are frequently adjusted when sailing.

RYA – abbreviation for the ROYAL YACHTING ASSOCIATION.

S

SAE – abbreviation for SAE International, formerly known as the Society of Automotive Engineers. What's this doing in a nautical book? SAE International promulgates standards for the automotive and aerospace industries, some of which are applicable to the marine industry, particularly in relation to engines, fuel, and electrical systems. *See* WIRE, ELECTRICAL, SAE.

safe boating classes – education in basic boating, offered to the public all over the U.S. and Canada. Many courses meet the requirements for boater licensing or certification in various states or Canadian provinces. Instruction is in a classroom setting and/or online. Individual states may offer classes, and national organizations offering instruction include the U.S. COAST GUARD AUXILIARY (www.cgaux.org), the U.S. POWER SQUADRON (www.usps.org), BoatU.S. (www.boatus.org), and Nautical Know-How, Inc. (http://boatsafe.com). *See also* LICENSE, BOATING.

safe distance – the NAVIGATION RULES don't define a specific safe distance between vessels when observing the Rules. Safe distance is interpreted in court decisions. In general, these decisions indicate that safe distance is determined by many factors, including good SEAMANSHIP practices, and the:

- State of the visibility.
- Necessity to reduce speed to give time to assess a CLOSE-QUARTERS SITUATION.
- Amount of maneuvering room in an area.
- Effects of current and wind.
- Vessel traffic in the area.
- Maneuvering characteristics of your vessel and other vessels.
- Potential for necessary or unexpected maneuvers.
- Appearance of a third vessel in a two-vessel situation.

safe speed – Rule 6 of the NAVIGATION RULES defines safe speed: "Every vessel shall at all times proceed at a safe speed so that she can take proper and effective action to avoid collision and be stopped within a distance appropriate to the prevailing circumstances and conditions." There are a lot of indefinite adjectives in the sentence. Maritime courts debate their precise meaning. The Rule lists the factors to consider and the use of radar in determining a safe speed:

- State of visibility.
- Density of traffic in your area (including concentrations of fishing vessels or other vessels).
- State of the wind, sea , and current.
- Proximity of navigational hazards.
- Maneuverability of your vessel and her DRAFT.
- At night, the effect of lights on the shore that may obscure lights of other vessels or navigation aids.

If you have operational radar the Navigation Rules say that you're expected to use it. When using radar, consider the following factors:

- The characteristics and limitations of the radar equipment.
- The limitations of the radar scales in use.
- The effect of the sea state, weather, and other sources of interference on radar detection.
- The possibility that small vessels or floating objects may not be detected by radar at all or at an adequate range in order to take action.
- The number, location, and movement of vessels detected by radar.

Safety at Sea Seminars – educational seminars for the public, conducted by US SAILING at various U.S. locations; see the website for information and a calendar. http://offshore.ussailing.org/SAS.htm.US Sailing says "Before you head offshore to cruise or race, join us for the most authoritative daylong seminar on safe seamanship, heavy weather tactics, weather forecasting, communications and boat preparation. See safety equipment demos and crew-overboard recovery techniques. Pose questions to our expert bluewater sailors. Tuition fees vary and seating is often limited so call or go on-line now for reservations. This could be the most important day of your sailing life." There's an optional second day with practical, hands-on training in the water and ashore.

safety carabiner – *see* CARABINER, SAFETY.

safety check, vessel – *see* VESSEL SAFETY CHECK.

safety checkout – always do a safety checkout with the crew, including children old enough to understand, and review it periodically, even if you sail with the same people. It takes less than 30 minutes, and your lives may depend upon it. If the trip is short, in protected waters and good weather, simplify the checkout to the lifejackets, fire extinguishers, VHF radio emergency procedure, and the MOB button (if any) on the GPS or CHART PLOTTER. A complete checkout includes:

The location of lifejackets, safety HARNESSES, fire extinguishers, first aid kit, flares and other distress signals, man-overboard equipment, THROUGH-HULL DIAGRAM, location of the DAMAGE CONTROL KIT, EPIRB, ABANDON SHIP KIT, and the LIFE RAFT (and how to deploy it).

How to use the MAN OVERBOARD BUTTON (if any).

Demonstrate how to use safety gear; don't assume crew know how to use it.

How to operate the VHF, make a DSC MAYDAY call, and give the vessel's position.

Review the EMERGENCY PROCEDURE CARDS with the crew and assign tasks. Choose the people most suited to do each task. Give children something to do within their capabilities.

Once they know where everything is and what their "jobs" are, surprise them with an EMERGENCY DRILL every so often. If you sail with only one other person, decide who's going to do what in an emergency, and spring a surprise drill on each other.

safety drill – another name for an EMERGENCY DRILL.

safety equipment, boat – typical items include:

jacklines
Lifesling® or similar towed device
MOM® man-overboard rescue module
man-overboard pole
electronic man-overboard alarms
strobe light
horseshoe buoy
life ring
rescue throwing rope
EPIRB
signaling mirror
automated SOS signal light
flashlights
SOLAS reflective tape
flares
smoke signals
dye markers
life raft
horn
safety/rescue knife
radar reflector
dayshapes (anchor ball, motorsailing cone)
fire extinguishers
fire blanket
first aid kit
emergency boarding ladder
abandon ship kit
emergency water and food
survival blankets
hand-operated watermaker
wooden through-hull plugs
damage control kit
rigging cutter
sea anchor
drogue
hand-held VHF radio
SART

Most of these items are discussed elsewhere in this book.

safety equipment, personal – general term that includes such items as lifejacket, exposure suit, flotation clothing, immersion suit, safety harness and tether, personal locator beacon, personal man overboard alarm, reflective tape on clothing, personal strobe, personal flares, rescue whistle, rescue/ safety knife. Most of these items are discussed elsewhere in this book.

safety equipment, U.S. Coast Guard required – the *minimum* equipment required on U.S. recreational vessels varies with the size of the boat. This equipment includes lifejackets and other flotation devices; fire extinguishers; whistle, horn or other sound signaling device; a bell; visual DISTRESS SIGNALS; NAVIGATION LIGHTS; engine compartment ventilation, and a backfire flame arrestor (on inboard gasoline engines). Lifejackets, flotation devices, fire extinguishers, and visual distress signals must be Coast Guard-approved. Navigation lights must meet the requirements of the NAVIGATION RULES. Schedule a VESSEL SAFETY CHECK to make sure your boat has what is required. The requirements are *minimum*, but a prudent skipper carries more than required. The list doesn't include essential items such as an anchor and RODE, a compass, charts, mooring lines, first aid kit, and other important safety items. See the Coast Guard website or CHAPMAN for the requirements. States may require additional equipment. The requirements do not apply to non-U.S.-registered vessels.

safety harness – *see* HARNESS, SAFETY.

safety knife – same as RESCUE KNIFE.

safety standards and regulations – governments issue safety regulations and many organizations worldwide work to develop safety standards for recreational and commercial vessels and equipment. So many variables affect safety afloat that just having all the required and recommended equipment does not ensure safety. If you're a DIY person safety is important in many types of repair, upgrade, and renovation activities. Standards and regulations don't prevent accidents; they're guidelines, not guarantees. The ultimate responsibility rests with the vessel operator and crew. A good way to check if your boat meets applicable safety regulations is to have a VESSEL SAFETY CHECK.

safety zone, exclusion zone, controlled-access area – the Coast Guard, captain of the port or other authority may establish a safety or exclusion zone at any time for a special purpose. All vessels (except those designated to operate in the area) are prohibited from entering the zone. When a zone is established it's published in the NOTICES TO MARINERS and announced on the VHF at regular intervals. Exclusion zones may be established around naval vessels, ships carrying hazardous materials, salvage and diving operations, power plants, oil terminals, or for an event, such as a vessel race, naval review, or head-of-state visit. Safety zones are patrolled by vessels and/or aircraft, and there may be criminal penalties for violating the zone. If you must enter a zone in an emergency immediately contact the Coast Guard.

safe water mark, fairway buoy, mid-channel buoy – this buoy marks a landfall approach point, a harbor approach or the middle of a channel. It can be passed on all sides. It's red-and-white vertically striped, and if lighted may flash either Morse Code "A" (short, long), or another CHARACTERISTIC that can't be confused with other lighted aids to navigation. The topmark (if any) is a red sphere. It may have a letter, number, name or be unmarked. This type of buoy is similar in both IALA REGION A and REGION B.

The top of a safe water mark, with a spherical topmark and solar panels. This buoy can be passed on all sides.

safe working load for chain – *see* CHAIN, SAFE WORKING LOAD.

safe working load for rope – *see* ROPE, SAFE WORKING LOAD.

Saffir-Simpson Hurricane Wind Scale – a HURRICANE CATEGORY scale from 1 to 5 used to describe the winds in a hurricane.

sag, sag off – when BEATING TO WINDWARD, if a boat can't hold her course and is pushed to LEEWARD she sags or sags off.

sail area/displacement ratio, SA/D – this ratio gives an idea of how well a boat sails in light winds. It can be used to compare sailboats. Some specifications give the ratio or it can be calculated. The formula is the sail area in square feet divided by the displacement in cubic feet, to the 2/3 power; ($SA/D^{.667}$) Some approximate ratios:

cruising yacht or motorsailer	10-15
ocean cruiser/cruiser-racer	14-17
coastal cruiser	16-18
inshore or ocean racer	18-20
high performance race	above 20
"extreme" racer	above 25

sail at anchor, to – *see* ANCHOR, TO SAIL AT.

Saildocs – an email-based document-retrieval system for text Internet documents (including text weather forecasts) or GRIB weather data, on request or by subscription. It's designed for reception by receivers with limited bandwidth, such as SINGLE-SIDEBAND RADIO. Saildocs works cooperatively with SAILMAIL. WINLINK is a similar system for use by licensed ham radio operators.

saildrive, SD – a propulsion system for a sailboat that consists of an inboard engine directly connected to a lower unit under the hull which has the gears and propeller. There's no STERN TUBE or propeller shaft. Saildrives may be used on engines up to approximately 80HP.

A saildrive with a two-blade folding propeller.

sailing directions – another name for a COAST PILOT.

sailing vessel – a vessel using only sails for propulsion. If the engine is operating she's a power-driven vessel according to the NAVIGATION RULES.

sailing vessels, rules for – Rule 12 of the NAVIGATION RULES gives the rules for two sailing vessels approaching each other where the RISK OF COLLISION exists. These rules apply when the vessels are IN SIGHT of each other, not in RESTRICTED VISIBILITY. Under this rule the WINDWARD side is defined as the side of the vessel *opposite* to the side on which the MAINSAIL is carried. For example, if the main is out to PORT, the boat is on the STARBOARD tack. If it's a SQUARE RIGGER, her windward side is opposite to the side on which the largest FORE-AND-AFT sail is carried (you may meet one of these vessels).

- When the two sailing vessels are on a different TACK, the vessel on the PORT tack keeps out of the way of the vessel on the STARBOARD tack. Starboard tack has the right of way.
- When the two sailboats are on the same tack, the vessel to WINDWARD keeps out of the way of the LEEWARD vessel.
- If a vessel on the port tack can't determine what tack the other vessel is on, the sailboat on the port tack keeps out of the way.

Sailmail® – a non-profit association of yacht owners that operates and maintains an email communication system for use by its members; anyone can join. SailMail email can be sent to a vessel via SailMail's own world-wide network of SINGLE-SIDEBAND, PACTOR radio stations, via satellite (IRIDIUM, INMARSAT, or GLOBALSTAR), or any other method of Internet access. If using single-sideband radio you also need a computer and a PACTOR modem to use Sailmail®. WINLINK (for use by licensed ham radio operators) and SAILDOCS.COM are two other similar communication systems.

sailmaker's palm – a leather strap with a metal fitting on it used for pushing a sail needle through heavy materials. Palms are available for lefties or righties.

A sailmaker's palm. The base of the needle rests in a bronze cup, so the sailmaker can push the needle through thick materials.

sail measurements – RIG DIMENSIONS are used to measure for sails.

sail, parts of – the basic parts of a sail are the same on gaff mainsails and triangular sails.

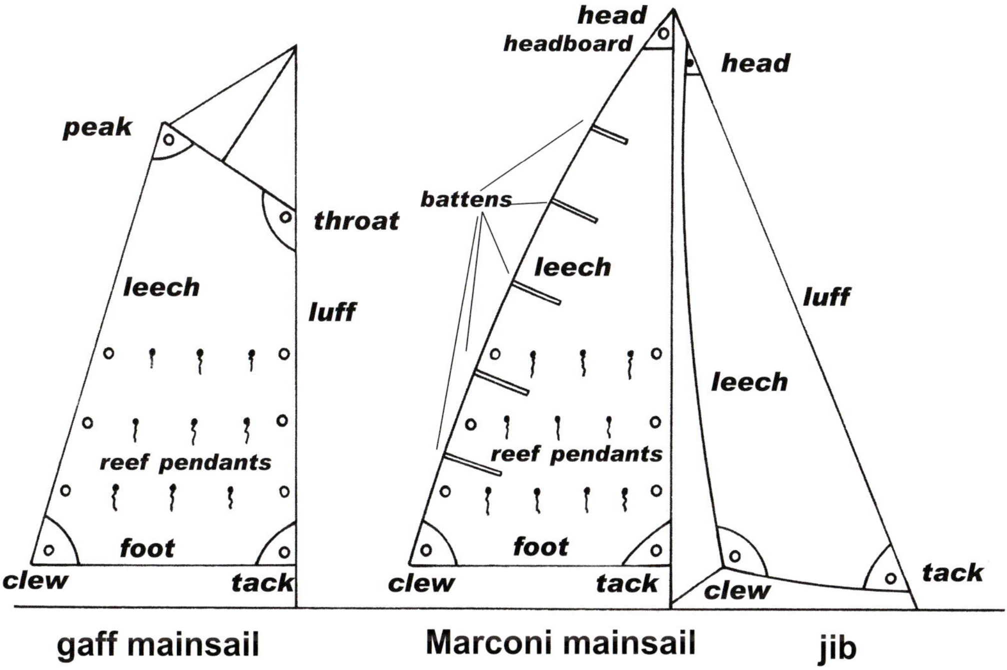

Two conventional mainsails. The small circles are the tack cringles, the clew cringles, and the reefing cringles (by each row of reef pendants at the luff and leech). Cringles are used for halyards, jib sheets, control lines, and attachment hardware. The pendants are also called reef points.

sail plan – (1) the arrangement of sails on a vessel. (2) a drawing of the sails and rigging for a boat. Basic sail plan types are sloop, cutter, ketch, yawl, schooner, and catboat. See individual entries.

sail repair kit – typical items include:

piece of Dacron® (polyester) sail cloth (4in/10cm x 15ft/4m)

roll of sticky-back Dacron® tape (4in/10cm wide)

sticky-back rip-stop nylon tape (4in/10cm wide)

roll of seam-stick basting tape (0.5in/12.5mm)

several sizes of sailmaker's needles
SAILMAKER'S PALM
waxed hand sewing thread
beeswax cake (for unwaxed thread)
HOT KNIFE and wind-proof lighter
needle-nose pliers
regular pliers
good cloth shears
awl
rope splicing kit
spare hardware specific to the sails
webbing 0.5in/12.5mm" and 1in/25mm
(8ft/2.5m each)
large stainless steel rings
sail slides for FOOT and LUFF (if used)
various SHACKLES specific to the sails
LEECH line cleat (if used)
one or more extra battens

sail, riding – *see* RIDING SAIL.

sail, shorten – to REEF a sail.

sail slide, sail slug – small plastic or metal hardware attached at intervals along the LUFF and/or FOOT of a mainsail. Sail slides are either internal (fit into a groove) or external (fit over a metal track). They come in several sizes; have some spares aboard. Not all sails have sail slides; some have a LUFF ROPE.

sail, steadying – *see* STEADYING SAIL.

sail trim – adjusting the sails for most efficient operation and best speed. There's a lot to learn. Sail trim varies with wind strength, POINT OF SAIL, type of boat, the sails used, and many other factors. Practice and observe the effects of small and large adjustments to the SHEETS, TRAVELER position, and other control lines. Read sail trim books and articles, and offer to crew for racing sailors. A good racing sailor can teach you a lot.

sail twine – heavy thread, usually waxed, used for WHIPPING the end of a rope or hand-sewing heavy materials.

St. Elmo's Fire, corposant – no, not the song or the 1985 movie, but the bluish glow around a MASTHEAD, high lightning rod, or tall pointed structure produced by an extreme buildup of electricity in the atmosphere. It's a coronal discharge. It can last for several minutes, and a lightning strike may follow. Named after St. Elmo (St. Erasmus, Bishop of Formiae), one of the patron saints of sailors. This phenomenon may also occur on aircraft wings.

sallying ship – rocking a boat by having the crew move quickly together from side to side. Sallying can be tried to free a boat when she's run gently aground on a soft bottom, if the crew's weight is enough to rock the boat. Sallying is one time when it's good to rock the boat.

saloon – the nautical name for the main cabin on a vessel. The "dining table" is the saloon table.

salvage – salvage is the voluntary and successful rescue of a vessel, her cargo, and/or persons aboard from *peril* at sea, and the successful avoidance of environmental damage. Whether you need an ordinary tow or a salvage effort may not always be clear: the difference between towing and salvage is determined by the potential for *peril* to the distressed vessel and/or to the salvor (rescuer). The legal aspects of salvage are governed by ADMIRALTY LAW.

Salvage includes, but is not limited to, rescuing a vessel hard aground or on the rocks, taking on water, involved in a collision, sinking or sunk, on fire, drifting with no one aboard, and other conditions of danger.

If equipment, other than towing gear, is needed, such as pumps, divers, air bags, pollution containment booms, repair materials, and tools, it's salvage.

A successful salvage effort usually is rewarded with a monetary award based upon the length of the vessel or a percentage of the vessel's value (as determined after the accident), and compensation for the amount of risk to the salvor and the rescue vessel(s).

Salvage is usually covered by a good marine insurance policy. Check with your agent.

A reputable commercial towing company will have a standard towing and salvage contract when the towboat arrives on scene. You will be required to sign it before services are attempted. There are a number of legal aspects involved in a salvage process. BOATU.S. advises boaters to

> "review their marine insurance coverage with their agent to make sure the policy provides for salvage up to the full value of the boat, not a percentage of its value, and that there is no deductible for salvage cost.
>
> If you do have an incident, ask questions first, not later, to confirm whether the job is towing or salvage.
>
> Have your insurance claims department phone number aboard. If it's salvage, you'll want to try to contact them to help negotiate a fixed price.
>
> When all else fails, have a copy of BoatU.S. Open Form Yacht Salvage Contract aboard. You can get one for free at http://www.BoatUS.com/salvage."

SAMS® – abbreviation for the SOCIETY OF ACCREDITED MARINE SURVEYORS, INC.®

Samson post – a strong vertical post on the BOW used to secure the the anchor RODE or mooring lines. For a photo see BULWARK.

SAR – abbreviation for SEARCH-AND-RESCUE.

SART – acronym for Search-and-Rescue Transponder or Transmitter. It's activated in a DISTRESS situation. There are two types: radar SART and AIS SART. The radar SART TRANSPONDER enhances radar returns with a sequence of 12 bright BLIPS (TARGETS). The SART works when it's hit by 9GHz radar, which is standard on search-and-rescue craft. The range is about 8NM. The AIS SART transmitter sends out an AIS CLASS A signal to all AIS receiver-equipped vessels. Both types are battery-operated, and have a standby and an operational mode. A SART is required on GMDSS-compliant vessels, but may be used on any vessel.

scan, priority – *see* PRIORITY SCAN.

scanner, radar – *see* RADAR SCANNER.

scantlings – the construction and materials dimensions for a vessel, which includes structural specifications such as the size of frames and the thickness for fiberglass or metal plate. The MARINE ARCHITECT specifies the scantlings.

scend (pronounced send) – the vertical movement of water, in repeated cycles, in a harbor or anchorage. A scend will cause a boat to rise and fall repeatedly.

schedules – we're certainly bound by schedules on land, but on the water schedules can be inconvenient or even dangerous. Having to depart on a passage when the weather is likely to be unfavorable just to get a crewmember home at a particular time is an invitation to a nasty time at sea, unless you're lucky. Emphasize flexibility in time planning for yourself and the crew. It may be safer to pay extra to change a flight or a stay in a hotel than endure discomfort or worse.

schooner – a sailing vessel that has two MASTS of equal or almost equal height. The foremast is usually shorter than the the main mast (the AFT mast). For another photo see YARDARM.

A Maine schooner and a small sloop ghost into a calm anchorage.

scope – the ratio of the length of the anchor RODE to the depth of the water. For example, in calm conditions (winds under 10kn) and a protected anchorage, a ratio of 5:1 is commonly selected as a *minimum* scope for anchoring with a rope rode. If the boat has a heavy anchor and an all-chain rode 3:1 is sometimes used in calm conditions. In tidal areas check the tide range and the state of the tide when first anchoring, so there will be enough scope for high water. Also include the height of the BOW from the water in the calculation: if the water is 20ft/6m deep and the bow is 6ft/2m above the water, the calculation should be based on 26ft/8m, which means 130ft/40m of rode at 5:1. Mark anchor chain and line to determine the proper scope; don't guess. Use more scope (for example, 7:1 or more for rope and 5:1 or more for chain) if it's windy, if the holding ground is poor or the anchorage is exposed. If there's not enough scope the anchor can drag or pull out because the rode pulls on the anchor from too high an angle, thus lifting it out of the bottom. A SENTINEL can be used on the rode to increase the CATENARY, helping to keep the pull low on the anchor. If the amount of swinging room in an anchorage is limited, this may suggest the need to use short scope (less than the minimum or ideal), but this isn't a good idea for safety reasons. *See also* ANCHOR SETTING.

scope, short – anchoring with a length of anchor RODE less than recommended or ideal. See the previous entry.

scrubbing grid – an arrangement of timbers or a concrete pad along a wall in a DRYING HARBOR where the boat can be positioned so the crew can work on the bottom when the tide goes out. Secure the yacht to the wall and the MAST to a strong point ashore so she leans a little toward the wall. Adjust the mooring lines as the tide goes out to keep her upright on the grid. It may be difficult to settle a vessel with a narrow FIN or BULB keel safely on a grid.

scud – (1) to sail before a strong wind, perhaps with STORM SAILS. (2) low, ragged and broken clouds moving rapidly.

scull – (1) a rowing technique using a single oar at the STERN of a small boat. (2) a sleek, narrow rowing boat; a rowing shell.

scuppers – (1) the outboard edge of the deck along the TOE RAIL, where deck drains may be located. (2) the deck drains themselves, or drain holes (freeing ports) in BULWARKS.

A scuttle over the forward companionway on a large traditional ketch. The lifelines are rope.

scuttle – (1) to sink a vessel intentionally by opening all the SEACOCKS with the hoses removed, or by cutting holes in the bottom of the vessel. A severely damaged vessel is sometimes scuttled at sea if she will be a hazard to navigation. (2) the name for a type of curved hatch over a deck hatch or a COMPANIONWAY.

scuttlebutt – gossip. The term comes from the scuttlebutt (a water container) on old ships where the crew would gather to talk.

sea, seas – a general term that includes WIND WAVES and SWELLS.

sea anchor – a fabric or webbing parachute-like DRAG DEVICE that limits the drift of a vessel, or holds the BOW of a vessel toward the seas. It may be deployed from the bow of a yacht on a very long, strong line in HEAVY WEATHER or storm conditions. The sea anchor floats near the surface and grabs the water, helping keep the bow of the vessel headed toward the seas. The engine or sails aren't used with a sea anchor. A sea anchor is supplied with a LIFE RAFT to limit drift, and to help prevent the raft from capsizing. A drag device deployed from the STERN is a DROGUE. Read about deploying and retrieving a sea anchor; don't just toss it in the water and hope it works.

sea areas – (1) inshore or offshore weather forecast areas. Marine weather services in each country have specific definitions for the areas. Some sea areas are offshore areas (for example Malin, Fastnet, Fitzroy in the UK), and some are inshore areas, which may be named, numbered, delineated by geographical coordinates, or by offshore hydrographic features (for example, to the Continental Shelf). Check a NAUTICAL ALMANAC, CRUISING GUIDE, or the weather service website. (2) GMDSS SEA AREAS.

sea breeze – same as ONSHORE WIND.

sea buoy – the outermost seaward buoy that marks the start of a channel, FAIRWAY, or harbor entrance. It may be a SAFE WATER MARK or a lateral buoy indicating the PORT or STARBOARD side of the channel. Sea buoys may be large, in comparison with buoys closer to shore.

sea chest – (1) a seawater MANIFOLD. It has a single inlet from a THROUGH-HULL SEACOCK and a number of outlets that have individual seacocks. Hoses for equipment that require seawater, such as the engine, marine HEAD, seawater-cooled refrigeration, WATERMAKER, seawater service to sinks, etc. are connected to the seacocks. A sea chest limits the number of holes below the waterline, as a safety measure. (2) a chest for a sailor's personal effects, on a ship or on a yacht with a lot of room.

sea clutter – numerous small TARGETS created on a radar screen by the waves. Sea clutter obscures small targets. Radars have a control to reduce sea clutter, but using it may also suppress other targets, such as small vessels or buoys.

seacock, sea cock, sea valve – a valve on a THROUGH-HULL fitting, with a hose or pipe attached to the inboard end. A seacock controls the flow of water into the boat. For safety, all through-hull fittings below the waterline (at rest or when HEELED) must have a seacock. The boat should have a diagram in the boat's notebook showing the location of all them. In addition, THROUGH HULL PLUGS should be tied near each seacock. The valve has a quarter-turn handle that closes it when the handle is at right angles, and opens it when the handle is in line with the seacock. Modern seacocks are BALL VALVES, but some older ones use a tapered plug as the internal mechanism. They're available in BRONZE, STAINLESS STEEL, and MARELON® (a non-metallic composite material). Look for compliance with ABYC, UL, or ISO standards when purchasing a seacock. In the U.S. non-metallic seacocks cannot be used on INSPECTED VESSELS or COMMERCIAL passenger vessels. Some quarter-turn valves are ordinary BRASS ball valves (brass looks like bronze), which are not approved for use as seacocks. ABYC Standard H-27 discusses seacocks, through hull fittings, and drain plugs. A GATE VALVE should never be used as a substitute for a seacock.

seacock, safety, or service seacock – a seacock with an extra port (opening) in its side. If a safety seacock is used for the engine water intake, a hose can be easily attached to the service port for emergency bilge pumping or for winterizing the engine. Close the seacock handle and liquid will be drawn through the hose attached to the service port.

sea fog – *see* FOG, ADVECTION.

sea ice – any kind of frozen seawater.

sea kindly – adjective applied to a vessel that has a comfortable motion and is relatively easy to steer in rough seas.

sea legs – being relatively immune to SEASICKNESS and having good balance while the boat is moving in the waves. "It takes me two days offshore to get my sea legs."

seamanlike *(adj.)* – doing something according to good seamanship practices or techniques; in a seamanlike manner.

seamanship – all the knowledge and skills necessary to operate a vessel: navigation, boat handling, line handling, sailing, anchoring, engine operation, maintenance, etc. "Good seamanship" refers to the commonly-accepted good practices for safely and efficiently operating a vessel. See RULE OF GOOD SEAMANSHIP.

seamanship, marlinspike – *see* MARLINSPIKE SEAMANSHIP.

sea mark – another name for a TIDE MARK.

seamount – a mountain under the sea that rises abruptly, 4,000 ft/1,000m or more, above the sea floor. Most seamounts aren't a danger to surface navigation, as their tops are hundreds of feet/ meters or more below the surface. However, they are a danger to submarine navigation, and in some areas a seamount may cause changes in waves and SWELLS.

search-and-rescue, SAR – search activities conducted in response to MAYDAY calls, which may involve not only the Coast Guard but other vessels and aircraft. When an EPIRB or PERSONAL LOCATOR BEACON is activated, SAR activities are initiated. Anyone who makes a false or accidental distress communication, especially one that launches SAR activities, may be prosecuted and/or fined. In some countries, governments have decided to charge persons for the cost of their rescue. A SAR operation launched to assist someone who gets in trouble because of an obviously unsafe vessel or due to blatant disregard of weather and safety advice may be charged for rescue services. *See* MAYDAY, FALSE.

Search-and-Rescue Radar Transponder or Transmitter – *see* SART.

sea room – not too close to the shore, other vessels, or obstructions. "We have enough sea room to practice sailing in this bay."

seas, heavy – a general term describing large, breaking waves.

seas, high – *see* HIGH SEAS

seasickness – of course, this doesn't have to be defined, unless you've never felt even a bit queasy (be honest). Being able to see the horizon is important to getting used to the motion at sea, so keep crew on deck or where they can see the horizon. Having a task to do above decks, such as steering, helps divert a person's mind. Some of the factors that contribute to making crew turn green are:

a trip longer than a few hours the first time out
heading offshore on the first day of a cruise
eating and drinking too much the day before
becoming dehydrated (drink water, not caffeine or alcohol)
beating to windward
diesel fumes on deck when motoring downwind
going below (cooking, navigating, using the **HEAD**)
seeing someone be sick or cleaning up
talking about food when someone feels ill
close eye work above or below decks
rolling in a beam sea or downwind
rough seas or a change in the seas
working on the foredeck
eating too much or not enough
diesel or other smells below decks
a large, slow, oily swell and no wind
alcohol or spicy food
stress, anxiety, or fear
getting too warm or too cold
reading this list

Be kind to the crew and yourself and make a **PASSAGE PLAN** that will minimize discomfort until all get their sea legs. Research available natural remedies (ginger, Coke syrup, wrist bands, etc.) and motion-sickness medications (try them first on land to see if there are side-effects; discuss with a doctor). Queasy crew resist eating and drinking and become dehydrated. Make sure everyone regularly drinks sips of water or a non-caffeine sports drink and eats small amounts of bland food. A person in any stage of mal de mer may not be mentally alert and should be watched to avoid an accident. If someone's sick over the side, hold on to his or her clothing or lifejacket/ **HARNESS**. Anyone can become seasick with the right conditions; there's always a first time. For more advice see Charles Mazel's helpful book, in the bibliography under "Crew."

sea smoke, arctic sea smoke – *see* **FOG, ARCTIC**.

seas, short – waves with a short distance between crests; close together. See **SWELL** and **SQUARE WAVES**.

sea state – description of **WIND WAVE** heights used in wind speed and sea state tables (**BEAUFORT WIND FORCE SCALE**) and marine forecasts. Sea state refers to waves in *deep water*. Actual wave heights closer to shore and in some areas (such as an area with **WIND AGAINST TIDE** or a protected area) may be significantly different from sea state forecasts, either higher or lower.

sea, territorial – *see* **TERRITORIAL SEA**.

seat locker – a storage compartment located under cabin or **COCKPIT** seats.

sea trials – the initial tests of a vessel after launch or as part of a MARINE SURVEY, to make sure everything's operating correctly. It's better to discover problems during sea trials than after setting off on a trip.

sea valve – another name for a SEACOCK.

seawater, weight of – a cubic foot /0.03 cubic meter of seawater weights 64 lbs./29kg. Imagine the force of a wave crashing on deck multiplied by the speed of the wave. Ouch!

seaway – (1) general term applied to an area with irregular, moderate to rough wave action. "We were stuck wallowing in that seaway until we could get into the LEE of the island." (2) a passage from inland out to the sea, such as the St. Lawrence Seaway. (3) a shipping lane.

seaworthy or well-found – adjective applied to a vessel that's strong, well-maintained, well-equipped with gear in good condition, and is ready for travel in her intended area of operation. A boat that's seaworthy for lake, river, or near-coastal operation may not be seaworthy for a passage in open or offshore waters. It's an owner's legal obligation to maintain and operate the vessel in a seaworthy manner. If an accident occurs and it's determined that the vessel or its operation was unseaworthy, legal or insurance claims may be affected.

seconds – chart scales are marked in divisions of tenths of a minute or in 15, 30, and 45-second divisions. A LARGE-SCALE chart may have smaller divisions of seconds. Check the scale before entering LATITUDE and LONGITUDE from a chart into a GPS or CHARTPLOTTER. The chart's minutes and seconds may have to be converted to DECIMAL MINUTES AND SECONDS for the electronics.

secondary fuel filter – a filter installed on the engine.

secondary port – another name for a SUBORDINATE STATION in a TIDE or CURRENT TABLE.

sector light – a light on a navigation aid that has one or more sectors (segments of the arc of visibility) with different colors. Sector lights are marked on charts. For some lights a white sector indicates "safe water;" and a red sector covers an unsafe area. For a channel, red and green sectors indicate which side of the channel the boat's on, with the white light visible when the boat is centered in the channel. The sectors may not have clear cutoffs when you're very close to the light.

secure – to MAKE FAST or to tie in a manner that something can't become loose; "Secure that SPRING line, please."

Securité (pronounced say-**cure**-ee-tay) – an informational call of a non-distress or non-urgency nature, made on VHF channel 16 to *alert* vessels to a hazard to navigation, important weather conditions, the establishment of a SAFETY ZONE, a large vessel getting underway in a harbor or navigating a narrow channel, or other immediate navigation information. Securité calls are issued by shore stations to warn mariners of dangers to navigation or severe weather, and vessels make securité calls about their operations and movements. Make the initial call on Channel 16 and switch to a working channel to broadcast the information, unless it's *brief and urgent*. To make a Securité call on Channel 16, say:

- **Securité** three times.
- **All Ships** three times.
- **This is** [give your vessel's name once or twice].
- **For Information About** [describe the nature of the information in a few words].
- **Switch to Channel X** [*if the information is urgent, transmit on 16*].
- Change to the channel specified and give the information.
- **This Is** [name of station], **Out.**

You do *not* have to cancel a Securité call (unlike MAYDAY and PAN PAN calls which *must* be cancelled).

"seelonce fee nee" – "radio silence is ended." Spoken on the radio (usually by the Coast Guard) when it's no longer necessary to maintain radio silence during a distress operation. See the next entry.

"seelonce Mayday" – "silence, Mayday in progress." Spoken instruction to all stations to maintain radio silence because a MAYDAY is in progress. Only communication related to the distress is permitted. See previous entry and "PRUDONCE."

seiche (pronounced **say** sh) – a STANDING WAVE in an enclosed or partially-enclosed body of water, such as a lake, harbor or bay. The wave goes back and forth in a relatively regular oscillation between the land boundaries. It has a long WAVE LENGTH, perhaps with its crest at one end of the body of water and the trough at the other end. The WAVE PERIOD can be from a few minutes to more than an hour. Strong winds, changes in BAROMETRIC PRESSURE, or an earthquake can cause a seiche. If it occurs underwater, the effects may be hardly noticeable, but if the seiche is on the surface you can see or feel a visible rise and fall of the water level. A seiche can have a large, dangerous wave. Long, narrow Lake Erie is prone to wind-caused seiches; Lakes Superior, Huron, and Michigan can experience strong seiches. In Europe, the Adriatic and Baltic Seas feel the effects of seiches, which can greatly affect water depths.

seize, seized, seizing – (1) stuck together because of corrosion or GALLING, particularly with threaded parts. "Those fasteners will seize if we don't use ANTI-SEIZING COMPOUND." (2) a seizing is a wrapping of light line or wire to tie something together, or the act of tying things together with light line or wire. Seizing is an aspect of MARLINSPIKE SEAMANSHIP. Seize the end of a rope around a THIMBLE, put a seizing over a splice to protect it or MOUSE a hook with a seizing. The screw pin of a SHACKLE should be seized to the body of the shackle with STAINLESS STEEL or MONEL® wire, so the pin can't come loose.

There is a lashing on the left round thimble and a black marline seizing on the right thimble. The marline in the lay of the rope on the right is called worming.

selective availability, SA – prior to May, 2000 the U.S. government degraded **GPS** signals so that the accuracy of GPS positions was not as precise as today. If selective availability is being applied, the speed displayed on a GPS may indicate approximately 0.1 or 0.3 kn of boat speed when the vessel is stationary. SA is not in use at the present time.

self-bailing – an adjective applied to a **COCKPIT** or a small boat in which accumulated water drains out by itself.

self-steering – may refer either to an **AUTOPILOT** or to other forms of steering that don't rely on a person at the **HELM**. See the next entry.

self-steering, vane steering, wind vane – a piece of equipment with a wind vane extending above the **STERN** rail that's used to steer a sailboat when under sail, without the need for a person at the **HELM**. The action of the wind on the wind vane moves some sort of underwater apparatus that steers the boat, either directly or via a mechanism attached to the boat's steering system. Electrical power isn't required, and thus wind vane self-steering is often chosen for long-distance cruising sailboats. A wind vane doesn't work in very light winds, so a sailboat may also have an electric **AUTOPILOT**. There are many types of self-steering gear available. Scanmar Marine at www.selfsteer.com has an informative discussion of wind vane self-steering equipment. Some brands are Aries, auto-helm, Beaufort®, CapeHorn, Hydrovane, Monitor™, Navik (out of production), Saye's Rig, and Windpilot. See the bibliography under "Systems" for manufacturers' websites.

A self-steering vane lower unit. The auxiliary rudder is lowered into the water and a windvane on top (not in place in the photo) actuates the rudder to steer the boat.

self-tacking – a sail that can be TACKED without doing anything other than adjusting the SHEETS on the new tack. A sail attached to a BOOM is self-tacking.

self-tailing, self tailer – a type of WINCH that can be operated by one person. Special jaws grip the line as it's winched in, eliminating the need for a person to tail (pull) the line.

semaphore – general name for a visual signaling method that uses flags or shapes to communicate. See the next entry.

semaphore signaling – a system of communicating by hand with flags. The arm positions of the signalman indicates letters, numbers, or a code. Scouts and some military signalmen may learn semaphore, but it's rarely used today. For an illustrated guide see www.anbg.gov.au/flags/semaphore.html.

semicircle, dangerous – the half of a CYCLONIC storm or hurricane in which the storm's forward motion and its rotary motion reinforce each other, pushing a vessel into the path of the storm. In the Northern Hemisphere the side to the right of the storm center is the dangerous semicircle; in the Southern Hemisphere it's the side to the left of the storm center. The side opposite the dangerous semicircle is the navigable semicircle, or perhaps the less-dangerous semicircle, as both sides will have extreme conditions. See the next entry.

semicircle, navigable or less-dangerous semicircle – the half of a CYCLONIC storm or hurricane in which the storm's forward motion and its rotary motion counteract each other, and the winds tend to push the vessel away from the path of the storm. In the Northern Hemisphere the navigable semicircle is to the left of the storm center; in the Southern Hemisphere it's to the right. You don't want to be in either semicircle of a storm or hurricane. See previous entry.

semidiurnal – a period or cycle of approximately one-half day. *See* DIURNAL and TIDE, SEMIDIURNAL.

sentinel, kellet, chum, Anchor Buddy™ – a weight attached to an anchor RODE partway down the rode to increase the CATENARY, creating a lower angle of pull on the anchor to help it stay dug into the bottom. Attach the weight as the anchor chain is paid out, or slide it down along a rope rode using a separate line. Buy a sentinel or make your own, using a weight of 25-30 lbs/11-14kg. Use a length of chain in a canvas bag or make one from cement with a metal loop (for a SHACKLE) embedded in the cement on top. There is also a Sentinel® brand of anchor, made by Dutton-Lainson.

Separation Zone – the zone separating inbound and outbound lanes or inshore routes in a TRAFFIC SEPARATION SCHEME. Rule 10(e) of the NAVIGATION RULES specifies that "a vessel other than a crossing vessel or a vessel joining or leaving a lane shall not normally enter a separation zone or cross a separation line except: in cases of emergency to avoid immediate danger, or to engage in fishing within a separation zone." Separation zones and lanes are indicated on charts.

series drogue – a type of STERN DROGUE.

serve, serving – to wrap MARLINE or sail twine around a splice or other part of a rope to protect it. A serving at the end of a rope to keep it from fraying is called a WHIPPING A serving may be applied over canvas or leather on a rope to make permanent chafing gear. *See* WORM.

set – (1) the direction *toward* which a current flows is its set. (2) to hoist or unfurl a sail. (3) to dig an anchor into the bottom, using reverse engine power, sail power, the weight of the boat itself, or all three methods. *See* ANCHOR SETTING. (4) to establish a COURSE. "Set a course for Tortola."

set flying – a sail not on a SPAR or STAY; it's just attached at the TACK, HEAD, and CLEW.

set sail – to depart under sail or power.

seven seas, the – by tradition, the world's main oceans: the Arctic, Antarctic, North and South Atlantic, North and South Pacific, and Indian Ocean.

Seven Seas Cruising Association, SSCA – a member organization for cruising sailors, but you don't have to have a boat to belong. It's a good resource for people considering taking up cruising, as well as those actively enjoying the cruising lifestyle. Associate Membership is open to all applicants. Qualification, nomination, and approval are required for Commodore (voting member) status. All members have access to worldwide information, monthly *Bulletins*, special publications, member activities, Cruising Station hosts worldwide, discounts on goods and services at selected vendors. Headquarters in Florida. www.ssca.org.

sextant (pronounced **sex** tnt) – a precision optical device used to take observations (SIGHTS) of the sun, moon, planets, and stars for CELESTIAL NAVIGATION, and to measure horizontal and vertical angles in PILOTING. An inexpensive plastic sextant is an excellent instrument for piloting. See the following two entries and SIGHT REDUCTION.

sextant angle, horizontal – measuring the angle between two charted objects with a SEXTANT gives a LINE OF POSITION or establishes a DANGER BEARING. Taking two measurements on two different pairs of objects, and crossing the two position lines gives a FIX. CHAPMAN and navigation books discuss these techniques.

sextant angle, vertical – *see* DISTANCE BY VERTICAL ANGLE.

shackle – a U-shaped metal fitting, with a round pin across the open end of the U. The pin can be a screw pin or a CLEVIS PIN. To keep a screw pin from coming unscrewed, SEIZE a screw pin to the body of the shackle with a few wraps of MONEL® or STAINLESS STEEL wire. Shackles are used for a number of purposes aboard a boat, such as attaching BLOCKS to a SPAR or PAD EYE, or to attach chain or rope to an anchor.

shackle, snap – a hinged hook with one side that opens by pulling a ring or LANYARD; it snaps securely closed. It's a quick and safe fastener. Snap shackles are used on BLOCKS, the chest end of a HARNESS TETHER, and for many other uses. However, using a snap shackle to attach SHEETS to a HEADSAIL is an invitation to a nasty whack on the head if crew goes forward and the sail's flogging. Tie sheets onto headsails with a BOWLINE (it hurts less when it hits you). See BLOCK, SNATCH for a photo.

shaft alignment – for the propulsion system to work efficiently the TRANSMISSION COUPLING and the SHAFT COUPLING should be properly aligned. Misalignment causes vibration and can damage the shaft and the CUTLESS BEARING. Technical references describe in detail how to check and correct misalignment. In general, the distance between the coupling flanges should be the same all around, approximately .003-inch/0.08mm, as measured with a feeler gauge. If the distances are uneven, the shaft is misaligned. A FLEXIBLE COUPLING or a CONSTANT-VELOCITY JOINT can accept some amount of misalignment; check the instructions with the coupling. A SAILDRIVE unit does not require shaft alignment.

shaft coupling – *see* COUPLING, SHAFT.

shaft log, shaft seal – another name for a STUFFING BOX.

shaft strut – *see* STRUT (2).

shaft tube – another name for a STERN TUBE.

"shake out the reef" – to "un-reef," making the sail larger.

shallow draft, shoal draft – *see* DRAFT, SHALLOW.

shallow water – (1) for ocean waters it's a relative term: when ocean depths decrease from 1,000ft/300m to 200ft/60m the water may be called shallow. When the depth is within a few feet/half-meter of your DRAFT (or less, depending upon how "brave" you are) it's shallow. (2) In waves terms, shallow water is when the depth of the water is less than one-half of the WAVE'S LENGTH. The depth of the water affects the size and pattern of waves; if the size or pattern changes noticeably, look at the DEPTH SOUNDER or the chart.

shank – *see* ANCHOR, PARTS OF.

shape – same as DAYSHAPE.

shape, to – to plan a course. "I'll shape a course to stay well clear of Sow and Pigs Reef."

she, her – traditional pronouns used to refer to a vessel, instead of "it" or "its," with many speculations about how this term came to be used. One explanation is that a good boat takes care of us like a good mother, and we should treat her with respect.

sheave (pronounced shiv) – the metal or plastic wheel in a BLOCK over which a rope passes. Some blocks have multiple sheaves (shivs). Sheaves are mounted in the MASTHEAD for HALYARDS. Sheaves should be large enough for the diameter of the lines that run over them. A too-small sheave chafes a rope and makes it harder to pull.

sheer, sheering – (1) the vertical curve of the deck from BOW to STERN. A traditional sheer is higher at the bow and stern and lower in the middle (concave). A reverse sheer (HOGGED sheer) is higher in the middle (convex). Some boats have a straight sheer line. (2) sheering is SAILING AT ANCHOR, by moving to PORT and STARBOARD to the extent of the RODE. "That boat sheered all over and got really close to us." A vessel being towed may sheer on the towline.

sheet – a line used to control the lateral movement of a sail, a BOOM or other SPAR. Sheets take their names from the sails they control: JIB sheets (a jib has two sheets; one for use on each TACK), STAYSAIL sheets, SPINNAKER sheets, mainsheet (for the MAINSAIL).

sheet bend – a knot used to tie two ropes together. It's a more secure variation of a SQUARE KNOT, and it also works well with two ropes of unequal size. See KNOTS, BASIC for photos.

"sheet in" – command to pull or WINCH a SHEET tighter.

sheet loads – there are formulas to estimate the loads on SHEETS, depending on sail size and wind strength. For a good discussion of how to calculate loads on sheets and BLOCKS see Ian Nicolson's *Boat Data Book* (full citation in bibliography under "Design"). The formula isn't difficult, and you may want to do actual calculations for the boat, rather than relying on general information in a marine supply catalogue or article. Sheets and blocks are subjected to strains higher than might be expected because of shock loading in strong winds and rough conditions The load exerted by a sheet, HALYARD or other line also varies with the angle the line makes going through the block. The sharper the angle, the higher the load on a block. Choose blocks and rope with an appropriate safety factor. *See* BLOCKS, LOAD ON and ROPE, SAFE WORKING LOAD.

shelf, continental – *see* CONTINENTAL SHELF.

shell – (1) the outside casing of a BLOCK; the CHEEKS. (2) a narrow, sleek rowing boat (also called a SCULL) used for recreation and for individual and rowing team competition.

"shellback" – a participant in a CROSSING THE LINE CEREMONY.

shingle – an area with stones of various sizes; a shingle beach or bottom.

ship – (1) a large vessel, bigger than a boat. *See* BOAT, SHIP, YACHT. (2) to bring aboard or to come aboard. To ship the oars is to bring the oars into the boat; to ship provisions is to bring them aboard; to ship a sea is to take a wave aboard.

ship, dressing – *see* DRESSING SHIP.

shipping a yacht – to maximize cruising time in distant lands some people have their yachts shipped across land or sea to a new destination, instead of sailing there or CHARTERING a vessel. Of course, it's an expensive option, but it eliminates one or more ocean passages, and places the yacht in the desired cruising grounds. A number of companies provide land transport on specially-equipped yacht trailers, and there are a few companies that transport yachts as cargo on ships. Research the options and speak to people who have used the companies.

shipping lane – an established ocean route for ships. If you need assistance it may be useful to go near a shipping lane, but in RESTRICTED VISIBILITY you don't want to be there.

ship's agent – a person who takes care of the needs of a vessel in a port. Ship's agents normally serve large vessels, but in some countries the CLEARANCE procedures or bringing in spare parts is so complicated or difficult, that a yacht may hire a ship's agent to negotiate the bureaucracy and deal with language barriers.

ship's ground – the common GROUND point where all elements of the BONDING SYSTEM are connected. Not the same as the ENGINE GROUND or a radio ground (RF GROUND).

shipshape – a place for everything and everything in its place on deck and below. "Shipshape and Bristol fashion" is a phrase used to denote a very well-maintained vessel, from the days when Bristol, England was known for its fine, strong ships.

ship's log – another name for the LOG.

ship's papers – the official documents related to the vessel and her crew. May include some or all of the following:

Proof of ownership (boat registration or DOCUMENTATION papers).

Marine insurance certificate.

SHIP STATION LICENSE.

RADIO OPERATOR LICENSE(S)).

CREW LIST (names, nationality, and passport numbers).

Passports for all crew.

Visas.

Health certificates and vaccination records.

CRUISING PERMIT and/or ZARPE.

Customs CLEARANCE.

Any other country-specific documents.

Papers for a pet.

Store the ship's papers together in a waterproof envelope, ready to show upon request to a law-enforcement officer, Coast Guard officer, or Customs and Immigration officials. If you must ABANDON SHIP, take the ship's papers.

ship station license – *see* LICENSE, SHIP STATION.

ship, tall – *see* TALL SHIP.

shoal – (1) shallow water; a shoal area. (2) an obstruction, BAR, reef, or other feature on the bottom that makes the water shallower than surrounding areas. (3) to become less deep. (4) a large group of fish swimming close together, such as a shoal of herring.

shoal draft – same as shallow draft. *See* DRAFT, SHALLOW.

shore power – AC power at a dock.

shore power inlet – a fitting on a boat where the shore power cord is plugged in. It should be an marine electrical receptacle with a weatherproof or waterproof cover (if there's any chance it can be submerged even for a moment). It may be located somewhere on deck, on the STERN, or in a COCKPIT LOCKER. Check the connections on the inlet and the shore power cable for corrosion, and spray them from time to time with a corrosion preventative spray.

short scope – *see* SCOPE, SHORT.

shorten sail – to REEF the sail.

shorthanded sailing – *see* CREW, TWO-PERSON.

short sea(s) – *see* SEAS, SHORT.

shot – one shot of chain is 90ft/28m/15 fathoms. The term is used for chain on ships.

shore lead (ice) – see the first LEAD entry.

"shout, throw, spot, steer, recover" – a memory aid for a MAN-OVERBOARD situation.

shrouds – the STANDING RIGGING at the sides of a MAST that provide lateral support. Shrouds that extend from the deck to the MASTHEAD over the SPREADERS are the upper shrouds, "uppers," or cap shrouds. Shrouds that extend from the deck part way up the mast (but not over the spreaders) are the lower shrouds or "lowers." Lower shrouds that extend forward are the forward lowers; lower shrouds that extend AFT are the aft lowers. Shrouds on the mast that don't reach the deck are called intermediates. The STAYS are FORE-AND-AFT rigging that supports the mast.

sidelights, side lights – the red (PORT) and green (STARBOARD) NAVIGATION LIGHTS on a vessel, visible from forward to 22.5° ABAFT the BEAM on either side of the boat. Sidelights are displayed by a vessel UNDERWAY at night or in RESTRICTED VISIBILITY; Rule 21(b) of the NAVIGATION RULES. Sidelights on a vessel under 20m/65.6ft may be combined in a single light with red and green lenses. A TRICOLOR light combines the red and green sidelights with the white STERN LIGHT in one unit at the top of the MAST.

side to – words used with PORT or STARBOARD to indicate which side of the boat is next to a dock or another vessel. "When we go to the fuel dock, we'll go port side to."

sight – an observation by SEXTANT of the angle between horizon and the sun, moon, a planet, or star. Sights are used in CELESTIAL NAVIGATION. The most basic and easy sight is a NOON SIGHT, where the angle of the sun is observed exactly at 1200 local time, and a simple calculation gives the vessel's LATITUDE. Determining the vessel's position from a sight is called SIGHT REDUCTION.

sight, in sight – Rule 3(k) of the NAVIGATION RULES says "vessels shall be deemed to be in sight of one another only when one can be observed *visually* from the other." If the other vessel is visible only on radar or AIS, she's not in sight under the Rules.

sight reduction – the process of taking the information from SEXTANT observations and calculating the position of a vessel. Sights can be reduced using a NAVIGATION CALCULATOR, computer software, or even on a paper form, the old-fashioned way. See the next entry.

sight reduction tables – tables of information used when computing (reducing) a celestial observation to find your position at sea. Tables are available in book form or for download on the NGA website at http://msi.nga.mil/NGAPortal/MSI.portal; click on "Publications." A NAVIGATION COMPUTER has the tables in its memory, eliminating the need for a book.

signal flags, signaling flags – another name for CODE FLAGS.

signal halyard – same as FLAG HALYARD.

signaling mirror – a small hand-held mirror used to flash the sun's rays to attract attention. Use a CD or DVD as a substitute.

signals to attract attention (not distress signals) – Rule 36 of the NAVIGATION RULES says that any kind of light or sound signals or other visual signals may be made to attract the attention of another vessel, as long as they cannot be mistaken for a signal authorized elsewhere in the Rules, or for an aid to navigation. This may include shining a searchlight in the direction of a danger to warn another vessel, shining a searchlight on your sails to warn a vessel of your presence, waving a shirt or jacket up and down, etc. In INLAND waters a strobe light may *not* be used to attract attention; it's a DISTRESS SIGNAL.

signal-to-noise ratio, SNR or S/N – a measure of the strength of an electronic signal compared to electrical noise in the circuit (not audible noise). The ratio is usually measured in DECIBELS (dB), and indicated in equipment specifications. The SNR can be used to compare similar electronic equipment. A high SNR is desirable (a much stronger signal than the noise).

significant wave height – *see* WAVE HEIGHT, SIGNIFICANT.

sill, cill – a horizontal structure across the entrance to a LOCK or TIDAL BASIN that keeps some water inside when the gates are open. There may be a gauge to indicate the depth of water over the top of the sill.

This is low tide from outside the harbor. The flap gate is up, forming a sill to keep water in the harbor at Peel, Isle of Man.

This is a view of the gate from inside the harbor. The gate will open soon, as the water outside is almost the same level as inside. The pedestrian bridge above the gate swings opens to allow vessels to pass. Note the traffic lights and tide gauge (in meters) at the left of the sill.

simplex channel – *see* CHANNEL, SIMPLEX.

single-handed sailing, single-handing – operating anything other than a small boat on your own can be easy, challenging, exhilarating, scary, or all of these at the same time. If you already single-hand you probably worked up to it over time by reading and practicing. You know the sense of accomplishment you feel when you meet new challenges and overcome anxiety. If you've never single-handed, you may be thrust into the situation by an unforeseen circumstance. It's a good idea to learn to operate a boat solo, because you may have to do it one day, or perhaps you'll like it. Practice with one or more crew aboard who stand by as you learn. When you single-hand you'll figure out different ways of doing things, and quickly learn that some tasks take longer than with a crew. Usually speed doesn't matter. It's essential to have some form of SELF-STEERING for a trip longer than a few hours. An AUTOPILOT, a wind vane, or balancing the boat under sail (not always possible) will free you from the HELM. Determine how you can get back aboard if the worst happens, and you're close enough to reach the boat if you fall overboard. There are engine stop devices available for a solo sailor—they work with a small transmitter worn by the skipper that triggers a signal to stop the engine if the person goes overboard. Of course if you're under sail that's a big problem. It's better to stay aboard! If single-handing interests you, read as much as you can, talk to other solo sailors, and gradually increase your skills. DOCKING single-handed is almost always "interesting." Picking up a mooring or anchoring is easier. Check your marine insurance policy to see if solo sailing is permitted.

single-screw – a vessel with one propeller. A vessel with two props is a twin-screw vessel. The techniques for maneuvering each type of vessel under power are different.

single-sideband, SSB, MF or HF radio – a radio used for communication beyond the normal range of VHF radio. For marine communications, SSB radio normally operates between 2-26MHz. By international agreement SSB channel numbers have been assigned to specific frequencies (see www.navcen.uscg.gov/marcomms/high_frequency/default.htm or a SSB manual.) A vessel with a SSB radio TRANSCEIVER must have a ship station license and a CALL SIGN issued by the FCC. A SSB receiver only (cannot transmit) doesn't require a license. SSB can also be used to receive high seas weather broadcasts, and, with a computer and modem, it can receive SYNOPTIC CHARTS, email and Internet from coast station providers such as SAILMAIL, SAILDOCS, or WINLINK (ham license required). Select SSB frequencies for the best PROPAGATION, based on the time of day and approximate distance between stations. *See* LICENSE, SHIP STATION and the LICENSE, RADIO OPERATOR entries.

single-sideband distress frequencies – by international agreement the following ITU channels, with their corresponding frequencies are designated as *distress* frequencies:

ITU Chan. 450 – 4125 kHz
ITU Chan. 650 – 6215 kHz
ITU Chan. 850 – 8291 kHz
ITU Chan. 1250 – 12290 kHz
ITU Chan. 1650 – 16420 kHz

Regarding the former distress frequency of 2182kHz: in 1999 the IMO allowed GMDSS-regulated ships to discontinue watch-keeping on 2182kHz. The U.S. Coast Guard, other coast guards, and some ships may still monitor it. A SSB may have a 2182 "distress button" on it, but be aware that this frequency may not have the necessary range if receiving stations aren't nearby, and no one may be monitoring 2182.

"single up lines" – an instruction to the crew to remove any double mooring lines or unneeded lines, and be ready to cast off the remaining lines, as directed by the skipper. Singling up is done immediately before departing a dock.

siphon break – another name for an ANTI-SIPHON VALVE.

"Six Pack" – no, not well-defined abs or a quantity of beer. "Six Pack" is the informal name for the U.S. Coast Guard captain's license required for the skipper of a vessel authorized by the USCG to carry six or fewer PASSENGERS FOR HIRE. *See* LICENSE, U.S. COAST GUARD MERCHANT MARINER.

skeg – a vertical underwater part of a boat's hull near the STERN to which the rudder is attached. There are different types of skegs: some are deep and narrow, others are short and wide. Not all boats have a skeg. *See* RUDDER, SKEG-HUNG for photos.

skeg-hung rudder – *see* RUDDER, SKEG-HUNG.

skipper – casual name for the captain. When speaking on the radio to a large vessel use captain.

skywave – a radio wave that is PROPAGATED by the ionosphere (the upper atmosphere of the earth). Skywaves are used for SINGLE-SIDEBAND radio communication.

slab reefing – *see* REEFING, SLAB OR JIFFY.

slack – (1) loose (applied to rigging or a line); not moving (as in slack water). (2) a gradual curve of the hull at the waterline, as in SLACK BILGES. (3) to loosen or EASE. "Slack the HALYARD before you REEF the MAIN."

slack, slack water, slack tide – the time between the FLOOD and EBB when the TIDAL CURRENT isn't moving (the STAND), or moving very little. Slack may last only a few minutes or much longer, and it doesn't necessarily correspond to the exact time of high or low tide. The time and duration of slack can vary quite a bit, depending on a number of factors, including wind, the RANGE of the tide, and the moon phase. TIDAL CURRENT TABLES or diagrams usually have a prediction for the time of slack.

slick – (1) an area of smooth water that forms on the WEATHER side of a boat sliding off to LEEWARD in the waves. (2) a smooth area on the water caused by oil on the surface; an oil slick.

slide, sail – *see* SAIL SLIDE.

slip – (1) a berth for a vessel between pilings, or between two piers or docks. The boat enters the slip either BOW first or STERN first. (2) to free a mooring line by pulling it off the dock: "Slip the SPRING LINE now."

sloop, sloop-rigged – a sailboat with one MAST and one HEADSAIL forward of the mast.

slot effect – the slot is the space between the HEADSAIL and the MAINSAIL. When the JIB and main are properly trimmed, the slot effect improves the boat's performance ON THE WIND. With a proper slot, the two sails work together to produce more power. There are many methods of achieving a proper slot. One general method is:

When sailing CLOSE-HAULED, trim the slot so the curve of the jib's LEECH matches the curve of the LEECH of the main. Make the slot as small as possible, but not so tight that the jib backwinds the main. If the main LUFFS from backwinding, EASE the jib sheet to open the slot a little.

On a REACH, trim the jib first, and then ease the main until it luffs, but isn't backwinded. Then adjust the MAINSHEET so the leech of the main matches the leech of the jib.

For a detailed discussion of how and why the slot effect works, and methods of trimming for slot effect see the bibliography under "Sailing" for sail trim resources. Sailing with a good racing sailor can teach you a lot about sail trim.

slough (pronounced slew) – a shallow passage or INLET, particularly in southern U.S. waters. Slough implies slow-moving, swampy waters, but some sloughs are navigable.

small area plotting sheet – same as PLOTTING SHEET.

small craft – generally considered to be vessels under approximately 65ft/20m in length, but there's no precise or legal definition. In addition to the size of a vessel, other factors relevant to determining the applicability of the term to a boat or to a weather forecast are the experience of the skipper and crew and the SEAWORTHINESS of the vessel. See the next entry.

small craft advisory, small craft warning – the issuance threshold varies with geographical region, but, in general, small craft advisories are issued by government weather services when sustained surface winds or frequent gusts of approximately 18–22 knots to 33 knots (BEAUFORT FORCE F 6-7) are forecast or occurring in a particular area. Over 33 knots it will be a GALE WARNING, STORM WARNING, or HURRICANE WARNING.

small craft chart – charts intended for recreational mariners. See CHART, SMALL CRAFT.

small-scale chart – a chart that shows a large area in less detail. *See* CHART SCALE.

small stuff – cordage in small diameters, such as sail twine or light lines used for LANYARDS and SEIZINGS.

smell the bottom– same as FEEL THE BOTTOM.

smoke flare, smoke signal – a DISTRESS SIGNAL for daytime use, usually with orange smoke.

SNAME – abbreviation for the SOCIETY OF NAVAL ARCHITECTS AND MARINE ENGINEERS.

snap shackle – *see* SHACKLE, SNAP.

snatch block – *see* BLOCK, SNATCH.

snub a line – to stop the movement of a running line quickly by holding it firmly around a CLEAT, BITT, or other strong point, but not actually tying it off. For example, snub and EASE a SPRING LINE several times to slow the forward motion of the boat when she comes alongside, to avoid jerking her to a stop.

snubber, dock line snubber, mooring compensator – in some situations at a dock the mooring lines may pull and snatch at the CLEATS on the boat and the dock. There are several types of strong, stretchy rubber or metal spring-like devices available to attach to the mooring lines to lessen the jerking.

snug down – to employ HEAVY WEATHER PREPARATION tactics, such as REEFING sails, adding extra LASHINGS to deck gear, and securely stowing everything on deck and in the cabin.

Society of Accredited Marine Surveyors, Inc., SAMS® – a professional and certification organization for MARINE SURVEYORS. Its membership includes surveyors in the U.S. and 18 other countries. Affiliate memberships include non-surveyors who are professionals in a variety of maritime-related fields.

See the webpage for frequently asked questions about marine surveyors and surveying, and useful links for boaters and surveyors. *See* www.marinesurvey.org.

Society of Naval Architects and Marine Engineers, SNAME – an international professional organization for practitioners in the maritime industry. The Society sponsors research, supports education and represents its members worldwide.

sock, spinnaker – *see* SPINNAKER SOCK.

soft lay – a type of rope construction. The other type is hard lay. *See* LAY(4).

SOG – abbreviation for SPEED OVER THE GROUND.

solar activity, sunspot cycle – periods of high solar activity can damage or disrupt satellite systems (such as GPS), and it affects the PROPAGATION of SINGLE-SIDEBAND radio signals. A cycle is 11 years. Scientists use various methods of predicting the minimum and maximum intensity of solar activity: a maximum is predicted for May, 2013.

solar panels – provide DC charging current for the boat's batteries. There are many types and mounting styles. Some solar panels have a REGULATOR and others don't, in which case they must be monitored so they don't overcharge the batteries. In addition to the amount of sun, the angle of the sun is important to the output of the panel, but newer panels are more tolerant of wide angles. Solar panels still work in daylight if there's not direct, bright sun, although their output is diminished. The output of a panel is reduced significantly by a sharp shadow line cast on the panel by rigging, a SPAR or other object between the sun and the panel.

SOLAS – acronym for the International Convention for the Safety of Life at Sea. SOLAS promulgates safety standards for merchant shipping worldwide. SOLAS-certified safety equipment meets high standards, and it's available for the recreational boating market.

soldering – aboard a boat it's not advisable to solder electrical wire TERMINAL fittings or other connections. Soldered areas are more likely to FATIGUE, crack, or corrode than properly crimped connections and terminals. Use ratchet CRIMPERS and add heat-shrink protection for a secure, strong connection.

sole – the "floor" of the cabin or COCKPIT (the cabin sole, cockpit sole).

sonar – used as a synonym for DEPTH SOUNDER, a true sonar measures both the depth and the direction of underwater objects.

sonar, forward-looking – *see* DEPTH SOUNDER, FORWARD-LOOKING.

sound – (1) to take depth measurements. (2) a body of water between an island and the mainland, a strait, or an arm of the sea. (3) to dive deeply, as a whale dives.

sounding, soundings – (1) the water depths indicated on a chart. A sounding is a single depth notation. (2) sounding or taking soundings is the process of taking depth readings with an electronic instrument or a LEADLINE.

sounding lead (pronounced led) – the weight at the end of a LEADLINE.

soundings, on or off – on soundings refers to being in water under 100 FATHOMS. Off soundings indicates water over 100 fathoms (600ft/183m) deep.

sound signals – signals made on a vessel's horn or whistle for maneuvering and in RESTRICTED VISIBILIY. Rule 34 and 35 of the NAVIGATION RULES prescribe the signals. Two definitions are important: a "short blast" has a duration of about one second; a "prolonged blast" is four to six seconds in duration. If there's any chance of poor visibility or fog, make sure the horn works, and have an extra air canister if it's a portable air horn. ABYC Standard A-23 Sound Signal Appliances gives the technical specifications; these are the same as in the Navigation Rules. Sound signals may also be used for alerting a bridge tender that you desire an opening. See the next four entries.

sound signals, maneuvering – Rules 34 of the NAVIGATION RULES prescribes the maneuvering and warning sound signals for *power-driven* vessels. These signals are used in HEAD-ON, CROSSING, and OVERTAKING SITUATIONS in open water (not in a narrow channel). The meaning of the maneuvering signals are different in the INTERNATIONAL and INLAND RULES. The signals under International Rules mean "I *am* maneuvering." Under Inland Rules they mean "I *intend* to maneuver." Because of this difference, Inland signals require the other vessel to *acknowledge with the same signal* on her whistle if she agrees. Under International Rules the other vessel is not required to acknowledge. A short blast is one second; a prolonged blast is four to six seconds.

- Under International Rules the maneuvering vessel sounds either one short blast ("I am altering my course to starboard"), or two short blasts ("I am altering my course to port"). The other vessel *does not respond* with a whistle signal.
- Under Inland Rules the maneuvering vessel sounds either one short blast ("I intend to leave you on my starboard side"), or two short blasts ("I intend to leave you on my port side"). If in agreement, the other vessel *responds with the same whistle* signal.
- Under both International and Inland Rules five short and rapid blasts is the DANGER SIGNAL: "I don't understand what you are doing" or "I doubt that what you are doing is sufficient to avoid collision."
- Under Inland Rules a vessel leaving a dock or berth sounds one prolonged blast.

Under International Rules the whistle signals should be sounded when the vessels are IN SIGHT of each other. Under Inland Rules, the signals are given when the "vessels are underway in sight of one another and meeting or crossing at a distance within half a mile of each other." Flashing lights timed to the whistle signals may also be used. Under the Inland Rules vessels may reach agreement on VHF CHANNEL 13, and whistle signals don't have to be exchanged, but may be used as well. The International and Inland signals for OVERTAKING IN A NARROW CHANNEL are different from the above. A mariner must know all the sound signals applicable to the waters the vessel navigates.

sound signals, overtaking – these are the same as the maneuvering signals, above.

sound signals, overtaking in narrow channel – Rule 34(c) and Rule 9(e)(i) of the NAVIGATION RULES prescribe the sound signals when overtaking in a NARROW CHANNEL or FAIRWAY. There are several important differences between the INTERNATIONAL and INLAND Rules for these signals:

- Under International Rules, the vessel intending to overtake signals her intention with either two prolonged and one short blast ("I intend to overtake you on your starboard side"), or two prolonged and two short blasts ("I intend to overtake you on your port side"). The vessel to be overtaken *indicates agreement* with one prolonged, one short, one prolonged , and one short blast, in that order.
- Under Inland Rules, the vessel intending to overtake signals her intention with either one short blast ("I intend to overtake you on your starboard side"), or two short blasts ("I intend to overtake you on your port side"). The vessel to be overtaken *indicates agreement by answering with the same whistle signal*, either one short or two short blasts.
- Under both International and Inland Rules if the vessel to be overtaken is in doubt or *disagrees* she sounds the danger signal of at least five short and rapid blasts on the whistle.

A short blast is approximately one second; a prolonged blast is four to six seconds in duration.

sound signals, restricted visibility – Rule 35 of the NAVIGATION RULES prescribes the sound signals for power-driven and sailing vessels *in or near* an area of RESTRICTED VISIBILITY, day or night. The signals are essentially the same under the INTERNAIONAL and INLAND Rules. All mariners must know the signals for all types of vessels. A short blast is one second; a prolonged blast is four to six seconds.

- A power-driven vessel making way sounds one prolonged blast at intervals of not more than two minutes.
- A power-driven vessel UNDERWAY but stopped and making no way sounds two prolonged blasts in succession at intervals of not more than two minutes.
- A vessel NOT UNDER COMMAND, RESTRICTED IN ABILITY TO MANEUVER (whether underway or at anchor), CONSTRAINED BY DRAFT, a vessel towing or pushing, a FISHING VESSEL (underway or at anchor), and a SAILING VESSEL sound one prolonged and two short blasts in succession at intervals of not more than two minutes.
- A vessel being towed or the last vessel in a multiple-vessel tow sounds a prolonged blast with three short blasts in succession at intervals of not more than two minutes. This signal should be sounded immediately after the signal made by the towing vessel.
- A vessel at anchor rings a bell rapidly for about five seconds at intervals of not more than one minute. A vessel over 100m/328ft rings a bell at the BOW and immediately after the bell strikes a gong near the STERN for about five seconds each. In addition, a vessel at anchor may sound a warning signal of a short, a prolonged, and a

short blast in succession to warn an approaching vessel of the risk of collision. Under International Rules vessels less than 20m/65.6ft in length don't have to make the bell signals, but shall make an "efficient sound signal" at intervals of not more than two minutes. Under Inland Rules vessels less than 12m/39.4ft in length do not have to make the bell signals, but shall make an "efficient sound signal" at intervals of not more than two minutes. Also under Inland Rules a vessel less than 20m/65.6ft and a barge, canal boat, or "non-descript craft" at anchor in a designated SPECIAL ANCHORAGE AREA isn't required to make sound signals at anchor.

• A vessel aground sounds the bell (and gong, if required), and immediately *before and after* the bell (and gong) sounds three separate and distinct strokes on the bell.

• A pilot vessel, when on duty, makes the sound signals for a power-driven vessel of her length when underway or at anchor, and may also sound an identity signal of four short blasts.

See also FOG SIGNALS, AUTOMATIC.

southing – to make good a distance in a southerly direction. "We ran down our southing and then turned toward Barbados." Easting, northing, and westing may also be used in this sense.

South Pacific Convergence Zone, SPCZ – an area in the western Pacific from approximately 140°E near the equator to approximately 120°W at 30°S. In the Southern Hemisphere warm season it's located just south of the equator. It's a 110NM to 220NM wide zone stretching from the ITCZ near the Solomon Islands to Fiji, Samoa, Tonga, and farther southeast.

sou'wester – (1) a strong wind or storm from the southwest. (2) a traditional fisherman's waterproof coat or a hat with a long brim at the back and a short, flip-up brim in front.

spade rudder – *see* RUDDER, SPADE.

spar – a pole of any size or shape on a boat. Spars include MASTS, BOOMS, REACHING STRUTS, SPINNAKER POLES, WHISKER POLES, and other poles (except boathooks). They're made of aluminum, wood, fiberglass, carbon fiber, or other high-tech materials.

spar buoy – a buoy in the shape of a pole that floats vertically. It may have colors and a radar reflector; it's usually unlighted.

Spartite® – a tough, two-part liquid plastic used with a KEEL-STEPPED mast, to replace MAST WEDGES. It lasts many years. The material is installed with the mast in place, and when the liquid hardens it forms a collar around the mast that conforms to the mast hole. Spartite® eliminates the need for mast wedges. The collar stays on the mast when it's removed, and it slides back into the hole when the mast is re-stepped. Put a coating of petroleum jelly on the plastic so it slides in easily.

special anchorage area – an area designated for small or large vessels. There may be special regulations for anchoring in these areas. They're indicated on charts and described in COAST PILOTS.

special lights, navigation – *see* NAVIGATION LIGHTS, SPECIAL.

Special Marine Warning – issued by weather services when a local severe storm or sudden strong winds are forecast for a coastal area. In the U.S. and Canada VHF WEATHER CHANNELS carry these warnings, and the Coast Guard may also broadcast them.

special purpose buoy – *see* BUOY, SPECIAL PURPOSE.

spectrum, radio frequency – a continuum of electromagnetic frequencies from low frequencies to high frequencies. The radio spectrum is from approximately 10kHz to 300GHz.

speed/length ratio formula – a rule of thumb formula used to calculate the approximate theoretical speed of a DISPLACEMENT or semi-displacement HULL. It's useful for a general comparison of boats. The theoretical speed in knots = 1.34 times the square root of the waterline length in feet. For example, a boat with a 25ft. waterline has a theoretical hull speed of 1.34 times 5, which equals 6.7 knots. A displacement hull can't go faster than the length of the wave created by the hull as it moves through the water. Although a displacement hull can surf down waves and reach speeds much higher than hull speed, this type of hull can't sustain those speeds like a PLANING hull.

speed log, knotmeter – nautical name for a speedometer that measures the speed of the boat through the water, which isn't necessarily the SPEED OVER THE GROUND. It may be combined with a DISTANCE LOG in one instrument. A common type of speed log uses a small paddlewheel in the water to measure the speed. Some speed logs have no moving parts. The log can be calibrated to be fairly accurate, but when calibrating choose an area with calm water and no current to affect its reading. For a paddlewheel log, paint the wheel lightly with ANTIFOULING paint each season.

speed of approach – when two vessels are meeting HEAD ON or in a CROSSING SITUATION, the combined speed of the vessels must be considered when calculating the risk of collision. If the distance is close, the combined approach speeds may be high, requiring quick and timely action.

speed of advance, SOA – (1) the speed you intend to make over a course. (2) the average speed that must be maintained to arrive at the destination at a particular time. It's used to calculate the ETA.

speed over the ground, SOG – the speed the vessel is actually making over the bottom, taking into account the effects of current, wind, and LEEWAY acting on the boat. Calculate the SOG by using the time and distance between two FIXES, or refer to a GPS. A SPEED LOG indicates the speed through the water. Make an estimate of a FAIR or FOUL current by comparing the speed log's reading to the SOG displayed on a GPS. *See* the next entry.

speed through the water – measured by a SPEED LOG, this is the speed of the boat through the water, not necessarily the speed over the ground. *See* previous entry.

speed, safe – *see* SAFE SPEED.

Speedseal™ – a replacement cover for an engine or generator's RAW WATER pump that can be removed with bare hands – no tools required, no gasket or small screws to lose. Covers are available for a variety of pumps commonly found on marine engines. If you've ever had to replace an IMPELLER in a hurry or lost one of the small impeller cover screws in the bilge, never to return, this cover solves the problem. See www.speedseal.com.

spinnaker, "chute" – a large triangular HEADSAIL made of lightweight cloth, and usually brightly colored. It's used on POINTS OF SAIL from approximately a BEAM REACH to DOWNWIND. There are two general types of spinnakers: ASYMMETRIC and SYMMETRIC. They are available in cloth weights for light to heavy winds. A SPINNAKER SOCK may be used to control the sail when hoisting and furling it, and on downwind points of sail a SPINNAKER POLE may be used. See the following entries for photos.

spinnaker, asymmetric – a SPINNAKER that has one corner (the TACK) affixed to the BOW (or to a short pole projecting from the bow) and the other corner (the CLEW) controlled by two SHEETS, like a JIB. The head of the sail is hoisted on a HALYARD. A spinnaker pole may not always be necessary with this sail, except when sailing between a BROAD REACH and DEAD DOWNWIND. A cruising spinnaker is an asymmetric spinnaker.

An asymmetric spinnaker. The tack is attached at the bow and the clew is controlled by the sheet, which is led to a block at the port quarter. The spinnaker sock is rolled up near the top of the mast.

spinnaker, cruising – an asymmetric spinnaker. See previous entry.

spinnaker halyard – the HALYARD used to hoist a spinnaker.

spinnaker pole – holds out the CLEW of a spinnaker when sailing DOWNWIND.

spinnaker sock, spinnaker snuffer, chutescoop, Chutescoop® – a long tube of strong, lightweight material such as RIPSTOP nylon that's used to enclose a spinnaker to control it when hoisting and furling. It's particularly useful on short-handed sailboats. The details and sequence of steps for using a sock vary with the type of spinnaker and the configuration of the boat. Instructions come with a sock or a sailmaker can explain how to use it. The general procedure is:

While it's in the sock, attach the SHEETS to the spinnaker and prepare the other control lines, as needed.

With the spinnaker **HALYARD** hoist the sock with the spinnaker inside to the proper height.

Using the control line in the sock, pull the sock upward off the spinnaker, thus deploying the sail. Trim the sheets. While the spinnaker is flying, the sock stays rolled up at the masthead.

To furl the sail, spill the air out of the spinnaker by **EASING** the sheets.

Pull the sock down over the sail with the control line.

Stow the spinnaker in its sock in a sailbag. Sailmakers make socks, and several proprietary brands are available. A sailmaker can also make a furling spinnaker. See **SPINNAKER, ASYMMETRIC** for a photo showing the sock at the masthead.

spinnaker, symmetric – a spinnaker with two corners that fly free (compared to an **ASYMMETRIC** spinnaker, which has the **TACK** attached to the boat). The **WINDWARD** corner of the sail becomes the tack, which is controlled by an **AFTERGUY** and the **SPINNAKER POLE**. The **LEEWARD** corner is the **CLEW**, controlled by a **SHEET**.

A symmetric spinnaker. The spinnaker pole holds out the starboard (windward) clew and a sheet controls the port clew.

spiral wrap – flexible, tough plastic wrap used around wires to keep them neat and to protect them from damage. It can be used and reused above and below decks. Use spiral wrap along with CABLE TIES and LOOM (3) to DRESS the wires on a boat.

splice – (1) to join two ropes permanently together by interweaving the strands (stranded rope) or other parts of the ropes (braided rope). (2) the joint created by splicing. See the next entry.

splices, types of – the basic splices for THREE-STRAND or BRAIDED ROPE:

A short splice joins two ropes. It increases the diameter of the ropes at the splice, and thus it may not be able to pass through BLOCKS or FAIRLEADS. A short splice is stronger than a long splice, and stronger than any knot used to join two ropes. It's a good way to save a damaged mooring line (not an anchor line): cut out the damaged part and join the ends with a short splice.

A long splice joins two ropes so that the diameter of the splice is only slightly larger than the ropes, and thus it will pass through most blocks and fairleads.

An eye splice creates a permanent loop in the end of a rope or around a THIMBLE.

A back splice prevents the end of a rope from unlaying (fraying). This splice creates a larger diameter at the end of a rope, which may not go through a block or fairlead.

A rope-to-wire splice is used on wire HALYARDS or other running rigging to provide a rope tail that can be used on a WINCH.

A rope-to-chain splice is sometimes used to join a rope ANCHOR RODE to the anchor chain. It is stronger than a knot.

Splices can be tapered for appearance. A FID, MARLINSPIKE, or other simple, inexpensive hand tools are used for splicing. Mechanical devices are sometimes used with braided ropes instead of hand-splicing techniques. For splicing instructions consult a MARLINSPIKE SEAMANSHIP book or check rope manufacturers' websites. Basic splices aren't difficult to learn, but if it looks too difficult, hire a professional.

split conduit – another name for LOOM (3).

split ring – performs the same function as a COTTER PIN, but it has no sharp ends. Split rings are also used on SNAP SHACKLES to attach a pull LANYARD to the shackle pin.

spoils, spoil ground – (1) waste materials such as dredged bottom material, construction or demolition waste, or non-buoyant materials. (2) a spoil ground is a designated area where spoils can be dumped legally by barges. These areas are marked "spoils," "dumping ground," or similar on a chart.

SPOT II – a GPS-based personal tracker and "satellite messenger" device that tracks your location and sends short "I'm OK" messages to family and friends. It's *definitely not* a marine distress signal device. It's small and inexpensive; there's a nominal basic subscription fee, with additional add-on services. Coverage is all of North America, Europe, Australia, and some of South America, northern Africa, and northeast Asia. Spot is not a substitute for an EPIRB, a PERSONAL LOCATOR BEACON, or satellite telephone, but it may be a useful way to stay in contact with home when traveling on land or sea out of normal communication range. The equipment and service is not part of any marine safety system, and its reliability cannot be guaranteed. See **PERSONAL LOCATOR BEACON** for this type of non-distress notification function with some PLBs.

spray hood – another name for a **DODGER.**

spreaders, crosstrees – the pair of short, horizontal **SPARS** projecting laterally **ATHWARTSHIPS** from both sides of a **MAST** to hold the **SHROUDS** out toward the side of the boat, creating a better angle to support the mast. There may be more than one set of spreaders. The number of spreader pairs identifies a mast: single-spreader, double-spreader, triple-spreader, and so on. The taller the mast, the more pairs. Some spreaders are angled **AFT**, while others project at right angles to the mast. An **UNSTAYED MAST** doesn't have spreaders.

spreader lights, deck lights – lights mounted on the **SPREADERS** or the sides or front of a mast that shine downward to illuminate the deck.

spring, spring line – a basic mooring line used to control the **FORE-AND-AFT** movement of a boat at a dock or next to another boat. Usually a forward and an **AFT** spring are used at the same time. The name of the spring line indicates the direction it goes *from* the boat *to* the dock. A forward spring leads toward the **BOW** and keeps the boat from moving aft; an aft spring leads toward the **STERN** and prevents the boat from moving forward. **MIDSHIPS SPRINGS** are attached amidships and lead forward and/or aft to the dock. See **MOORING LINE** for a diagram and the photo of the sloop with **DRY OUT.**

spring, to – to use a **SPRING LINE** to move the boat at a dock or pier with gentle application of engine or **WINCH** power. Lines used for springing under power must be strong; undersized or weak ropes can break and cause an injury if they recoil. Three basic spring line techniques:

The tanker is using a spring from the port bow led to a bollard on the shore to assist maneuvering in tiny Galway harbor. She powers ahead very slowly and uses the bow thruster (note the white symbol on the hull under her name). The deck crew adjusts the spring line. When there's enough room for her stern to clear the harbor wall she will back down to the fuel depot tanks.

To bring the middle of the boat close to the dock, power gently ahead on a MIDSHIPS spring that's attached AMIDSHIPS on the boat and led AFT to a piling or a strong point on the dock, where it's tied off by a person on the dock. Turn the wheel away from the dock (push a TILLER toward the dock) and apply forward power at low RPMS. This technique is especially useful when the wind is blowing the boat away from the dock or the boat is too far out to step off easily.

To spring the BOW away from the dock, back down slowly on a spring that's tied at or near the STERN on the boat and led forward to the dock or a piling forward of amidships. A person on the dock holds it firmly around the piling or strong point on the dock. If you're single-handing double the line from the strong point back to near the helm where you can control it. Put a fender between the stern QUARTER and the dock before backing down at low rpms. To depart the dock when the bow is out far enough, the person on the dock releases the spring, or the helmsman slips it from the helm position.

To spring the stern away from the dock, drive ahead gently and carefully on a short spring that's tied at the bow and led aft a short distance to a strong point on the dock. Put a fender between the bow and the dock. As the vessel moves ahead on the spring, ease the line slightly to allow the stern to move out away from the dock. When you back away someone on the dock must release the spring, or double the bow line back to the boat and the crew can slip it as the boat moves away. If there are pilings or other obstructions on a dock or pier, it may not be possible to do this technique on a boat with a bowsprit or other bow projection.

With all spring line maneuvers, start slowly with low rpms at first, increasing them gently until the desired effect is achieved. Current or wind conditions may prevent a spring line maneuver from working. Ships use spring lines for maneuvering in tight quarters.

springs, spring tide – *see* TIDE, SPRING.

squall, squall line – a sudden increase in wind speed, usually associated with a thunderstorm or other unsettled weather. The duration of a squall is relatively short, but it can still be dangerous. A squall line is a group of severe thunderstorms that form along or ahead of a COLD FRONT. Squall lines are frequently dangerous because of high winds, heavy rain, reduced visibility, and perhaps lightning. A white squall is a strong squall that has WHITECAPS and driving rain and spray.

square end – the STERN, unless the boat is a DOUBLE-ENDER. (I said this book was for complete beginners.)

square knot, square reef knot – a knot used for joining two ropes. It works best when the lines are of equal diameter. A slipped square knot (with a loop to pull it open) is sometimes used for tying up REEF PENDANTS (reef points). See KNOTS, BASIC for photos.

square-rigger, square-rigged – a sailing vessel with sails and SPARS that are mounted ATHWARTSHIPS on one or more MASTS. Large sailing vessels of the 19th century and earlier were square-rigged, and there are modern replicas afloat. TALL SHIP is used as a synonym.

A three-masted sail-training square-rigger.

HMS Warrior, a 435ft/133m steam-and-sail warship of the British navy, commissioned in 1860. Her berth is at the Royal Naval Museum at Portsmouth Historic Dockyard on the south coast of England.

"square waves" – short, steep waves where the height of the waves and the distance between them is almost the same. Square waves make a vessel PITCH and can be dangerous in some cases. Strong winds against a current can create square waves.

squeaking lines – *see* LINES, SQUEAKING.

squelch, squelch control – a control on a radiotelephone that eliminates the normal "white noise" (static) heard when the radio isn't receiving a signal while in standby. To adjust the control, turn it down until white noise is heard, and then turn it up until the noise just disappears. Some radios have a button or menu squelch control. If the squelch is turned up too high, weak stations are suppressed.

SSB – abbreviation for SINGLE-SIDEBAND radio.

SSCA – abbreviation for the SEVEN SEAS CRUISING ASSOCIATION.

stability, directional – the ability of a vessel to resist the sideways force of the seas and hold a steady course. Directional stability depends, in general, on the underwater form of the yacht. A sailboat with a narrow FIN KEEL and a SPADE RUDDER doesn't have much lateral plane (area) underwater to resist sideways forces, so she requires an attentive helmsman or a busy AUTOPILOT or SELF-STEERING. A yacht with a LONG KEEL or with a rudder on a large SKEG has good directional stability because of her underwater lateral plane.

stability, lateral – the resistance to HEELING; a measure of sail-carrying ability. Hull form, DRAFT, and DISPLACEMENT are just some of the factors that go into determining lateral stability. The basic principles are important for a sailor to understand, even though it's a little technical. Understanding the basics helps you to compare boat designs and evaluate their performance capabilities and limitations. As naval architect Ted Brewer explains, lateral stability depends on

> "the displacement of the vessel and the length of the righting arm. The length of the righting arm depends on the location of the center of gravity and the location of the heeled center of buoyancy. The lower the center of gravity, the longer the righting arm. The farther to leeward the heeled center of buoyancy, the longer the righting arm."

A yacht can carry more sail or heeling will be reduced if weight is low in the keel; thus some yachts are designed with a DEEP keel and/or a BALLAST BULB. A beamy yacht with the BEAM carried well AFT heels less than a narrower, deep-bilge hull. A hull with reasonably high FREEBOARD (and ballast located low) is relatively stable at high angles of heel, because the buoyancy of the TOPSIDES resists the downward pressure of the wind on the sails.

The lateral stability of a MULTIHULL depends on the same principles, but these designs have inherent stability limitations. Although the wide beam of a multihull creates high lateral stability, the weight of the ballast is limited and isn't carried low in the hulls. A multihull has high initial stability, but if she overturns (eek!), she's as stable inverted as upright. Of course, multihull designers take this into account and design for very high initial stability.

stability in rough water – the loading of a vessel is important to maintain stability in rough water. Uneven loading at the BOW or STERN or on one side will adversely affect stability in the waves. When you load a boat, add weight above the waterline, or make a structural change you may change her stability. Consult a MARINE ARCHITECT before attempting any major changes that could affect stability.

stability test – a scientifically-conducted test that measures the resistance of a vessel to capsize, by HEELING her to a pre-determined angle. A stability test is required for U.S. Coast Guard INSPECTED VESSELS, but not for private yachts. In the U.S. if you're thinking about getting your boat certified to carry more than six PASSENGERS FOR HIRE, you need to understand what's involved. See www.uscg.mil/pvs/SPV.asp for a full discussion of small passenger vessel stability testing. Some other countries have specific requirements for stability testing small COMMERCIAL VESSELS. An ocean-racing organization may require stability tests for a yacht of new or unfamiliar design before the vessel can participate in a race.

stable atmosphere – warm air over cold air produces a stable atmosphere. Cold air over warm air or water produces an UNSTABLE atmosphere.

stainless steel – *see* STEEL, STAINLESS.

stanchion (pronounced **stan**-shun) – a vertical metal post near the TOE RAIL. Stanchions hold the LIFELINES. Many stanchions are quite short, and low lifelines are not very effective in preventing someone from falling overboard. Stanchion bases may not be strong enough to take the weight of someone falling against them or using the lifelines to help climb aboard, and the base may pull out of the deck. Use caution when relying on stanchions and lifelines. Don't attach a safety HARNESS TETHER to a stanchion or the lifelines.

stand – the period of time when the tide has stopped rising or falling. The stand may or may not coincide with SLACK WATER.

standards for recreational vessel construction and equipment installation – in the U.S. the ABYC and other organizations promulgate standards for construction and installation of equipment on non-commercial vessels, and the NMMA® certifies compliance with relevant standards. In the EU the RECREATIONAL CRAFT DIRECTIVE contains the safety standards for RECREATIONAL VESSELS built or sold in EU countries. The INTERNATIONAL MARINE CERTIFICATION INSTITUTE (IMCI) certifies the compliance of manufacturers who engage IMCI services. The ABYC and NMMA participate in cooperative efforts to harmonize international standards for recreational vessels. The U.S. Coast Guard and the Canadian Department of Transport use safety standards from ABYC and other standards organizations. COMMERCIAL VESSELS and INSPECTED VESSELS must follow additional mandated standards, and government organizations or approved representatives inspect certain classes of small commercial vessels for compliance.

stand a watch, to – *see* STANDING ORDERS and WATCH.

standby light – an EMERGENCY LIGHT on an aid to navigation.

standing orders – procedures for the WATCH crew to follow in the absence of the skipper. On a long passage, written standing orders remind the watch of what should be done, and allow the skipper to rest without having to worry (too much). Standing orders have a place on recreational vessels as well as ships. The person on watch must know the NAVIGATION RULES, visual navigation techniques, and the operation of the vessel, including the engine and all electronics. Typical standing orders:

Call the skipper if you're in doubt about anything.

In an emergency take necessary action; then call the skipper.

Display the proper **NAVIGATION LIGHTS** or DAYSHAPES.

Use all electronic and visual navigation aids; don't rely only on **GPS** or **CHART PLOTTER.**

Plot and record the boat's position in the log hourly offshore and at shorter intervals inshore or in **RESTRICTED VISIBILITY** (captain specify the interval).

Maintain radio watch on Channel 16 offshore, and **DUAL WATCH** on 16 and 13 in shipping areas.

Don't leave the **COCKPIT** at night or in rough conditions without another *alert* person on deck.

Use your **HARNESS** and **TETHER** at night and in rough weather.

Check the bilges hourly.

Log the **BAROMETER** readings hourly, monitor local weather conditions, and update the weather forecast.

Under power, monitor the engine instruments.

At night call the next watch 20 minutes early to allow that person's eyes to become accustomed to the dark.

Don't change a watch in a **CLOSE QUARTERS SITUATION.**

Tell the oncoming watch about the course, position, weather status, operational activities, and the presence of nearby vessels.

If you feel ill or have trouble staying alert or awake, call the skipper or another crewmember.

Notify the skipper the event of:

Any mechanical failure of gear, sails, engine, etc.

Visibility falling below 3NM (skipper specify distance).

CPA to radar or **AIS** target less than 4NM (skipper specify distance).

Sustained winds increasing by five knots or more.

If you believe a major sail change is necessary.

If you believe we should make a significant course alteration (other than in an emergency).

If weather deteriorates, or a forecast warns of significant change within six hours or less.

See **WATCH, CHANGE OF.**

standing part – the part of a rope that's *not* used to make the knot, or the part of the rope around which a knot is constructed. The **WORKING END** makes the knot. The phrase is used in knot-tying instructions.

standing rigging – includes the **SHROUDS** and **STAYS** that support the mast, as well as other semi-permanent rigging. Standing rigging is infrequently adjusted, while **RUNNING RIGGING** is frequently adjusted. Standing rigging is made of wire rope, metal rod, or high-tech synthetic fiber that's as strong as metal and much lighter, saving weight aloft.

standing turn – a term applied to turning a vessel in her own length. A SINGLE-SCREW boat is turned using engine power, alternating forward and reverse with the rudder HARD OVER. In a twin-screw vessel a standing turn is done with the engine controls rather than the rudder. This technique is essential to learn for successful close-quarters maneuvering. Depending on the direction of PROPELLER ROTATION it will be easier to make the turn in one direction than the other. Learn how to use the wind, if any, to assist a standing turn.

standing wave – *see* WAVE, STANDING.

standing wave ratio, SWR – the SWR (as indicated on a meter) gives an indication of how well a radio antenna system is working. In an antenna system some of the power from the radio transmitter travels to the antenna (the forward power) and some of it travels back from the antenna to the transmitter (the reflected power). When the forward and reflected power pass each other on the antenna cable (the feed line) this causes VOLTAGE standing waves on the line. A low SWR is desirable, because it indicates that the feed line and the antenna are well-matched. An antenna tuner in the system matches the line and the antenna. Consult a ham radio book or a radio technical manual for a thorough discussion of SWR.

stand off – (1) to stay away from the coast. "We'll stand off until dawn." (2) to stand by; to wait nearby. Said to another vessel, "We'll stand off until help arrives."

stand on, to – to continue on course. "Let's stand on for another hour."

stand-on vessel, privileged vessel – in a right of way situation, under Rule 17 of the NAVIGATION RULES, the stand-on vessel has the right of way. The stand-on vessel "shall maintain course and speed (unless forced to maneuver or to avoid collision) and shall not alter course to port for a vessel on her own port side (if the circumstances permit)." The GIVE-WAY vessel must keep out of her way. Privileged vessel is an older term, still in use.

starboard – (1) the right side of a vessel when facing the BOW. (2) When spoken (or yelled) from a sailboat on the STARBOARD TACK to a nearby sailboat on the PORT TACK "Starboard!" means "I have right of way – you're getting too close to me."

starboard hand – to be kept on the STARBOARD side of the vessel. "In Europe the starboard hand buoys are green when returning from sea."

starboard tack – the wind is on the STARBOARD side of the vessel and the main BOOM is out toward the PORT side. A sailboat on a starboard tack has the right of way when meeting a sailboat that's on the PORT TACK, unless the starboard tack boat is OVERTAKING.

"start" – to EASE a line a little; "Start the SHEET."

static dissipater, air terminal – a metal rod with a brush-like top made of small metal wires, which is supposed to reduce the chance of a lightning strike when mounted on the top of a MAST. Experts disagree on the effectiveness of this device, possibly because it's very difficult to gather test data from actual lightning strikes.

station – (1) a vessel or shore facility with a radiotelephone. (2) a specific location on a vessel, such as a steering station (the HELM), or the geographical position of a buoy or other aid to navigation. (3) to place crew in a specific location. "Station Linda on the FOREDECK." (4) one of a series of evenly-spaced, numbered TRANSVERSE sections of a hull, as shown on a MARINE ARCHITECT's lines drawing or a construction drawing.

station bill – a list of emergency procedure tasks and the crew assigned to each, as for ABANDONING SHIP, firefighting, MAN-OVERBOARD procedure, etc. Used on large vessels, a station bill has a place on small craft, even if there are only two aboard. EMERGENCY PROCEDURE CARDS are station bills.

station-keeping, to keep station – staying in one position at sea. Describes a vessel UNDERWAY that's maneuvering with sail and/or engine techniques to stay relatively in the same place, as when waiting for a bridge to open or a space to become available at a fuel dock or marina. HEAVING-TO under sail is a form of keeping station, although in some conditions a hove-to sailboat may move some distance from its original position and cannot keep station.

station, on or off – on or off station refers to whether a floating navigation aid is at its charted position. This information is announced on a VHF NOTICE TO MARINERS, and may be printed in local notices to mariners.

station pointer – a THREE-ARM PROTRACTOR.

stationary front – *see* FRONT, STATIONARY.

statute mile – unit of measurement of 5,280ft/1.6km, used on land and most U.S. inland waters and lakes. The INTRACOASTAL WATERWAY on the U.S. east coast uses statute miles.

state of the tide – *see* TIDE, STATE OF.

state registration – if a U.S. vessel "equipped with propulsion machinery" is not DOCUMENTED, she must be registered and numbered in the state or U.S. territory of principal use. The rules of the FEDERAL BOAT SAFETY ACT OF 1971 apply to all undocumented vessels, with the exception of foreign, military, or governmentally-owned vessels and ship's lifeboats.

stay(s) – (1) the FORE-AND-AFT STANDING RIGGING that supports the MAST; such as the FORESTAY, HEADSTAY, BACKSTAY, INNER FORESTAY, etc. (2) the term is also used in a general sense to refer to all the standing rigging. "The stays are loose." SHROUDS are the lateral standing rigging.

staysail (pronounced **stay** s'l), **forestaysail** – a JIB set on a STAY between the HEADSTAY and the MAST. A SLOOP with a jib and a staysail is called a cutter.

staysail halyard – the HALYARD that hoists a STAYSAIL.

staysail stay – another name for an INNER FORESTAY.

steadying sail – a small triangular sail used on a short mast near the STERN of a powerboat to steady the motion. Small fishing vessels and trawler yachts may use a steadying sail. It's not the same as a RIDING SAIL, although the two terms are used interchangeably.

A gaff steadying sail on a small inshore fishing vessel.
A small dayshapeis displayed in the rigging.

steaming light – another name for a MASTHEAD LIGHT.

steel, galvanized – steel coated with zinc to protect it from corrosion.

steel, mild – carbon steel, the most common type of steel.

steel, stainless – a steel ALLOY with chromium or other metals added to increase corrosion and rust resistance. A protective layer of oxide forms on stainless steel which prevents most rust. The oxide self-repairs if it's scratched. Stainless steel can be PASSIVATED to increase corrosion resistance. Common types of stainless used in marine applications include stainless steels in the 300 Series (AUSTENITIC), which are alloys of iron, chromium, and nickel:

Type 301 - ductile, used for formed products such as tubes.

Type 303 - easily machined.

Type 304 - the most common stainless, also called 18/8. It's stronger than 316.

Type 316 - more corrosion-resistant than 304 but slightly less-strong.

steep-to – an area where the water depths increase rapidly as you move away from the shore or an underwater feature, such as a reef. "That shore is steep-to, so there's no place to anchor."

steerage, steerageway – the motion of the boat through the water sufficient to allow her to be steered. Water must be flowing past the RUDDER (from forward to astern) to steer. If a boat loses forward momentum she can't be steered. Also, a boat proceeding with a strong current from astern may not have enough water flowing past the rudder to have steerage. For this reason the NAVIGATION RULES specify that a vessel proceeding with the current has right-of-way over a vessel proceeding against a current.

steering pedestal – another name for PEDESTAL.

steering station – another term for the HELM.

steering systems – the basic types of steering systems are (1) mechanical or cable. (2) hydraulic. (3) electric/electronic. All systems require maintenance; if steering fails it's usually at a most inopportune time. The relevant ABYC Standards are P-17 Mechanical Steering Systems, P-21 Manual Hydraulic Steering Systems, P-22 Steering Wheels, P-27 Electric/Electronic Steering Control Systems, and H-30 Hydraulic Systems.

stem – (1) the very front of the BOW, running vertically from the deck level to the front of the keel. It's a main structural feature. "From stem to STERN" is a general phrase that means all over the boat: "We've cleaned this boat from stem to stern."(2) to make headway against a current; to stem the tide.

stem fitting, stemhead fitting – a metal fitting on the BOW of a boat at the STEM, to which the HEADSTAY is attached. An ANCHOR ROLLER may be part of the stem fitting.

step – (1) the place on deck or below deck where the foot (heel) of the MAST rests. Logically, a mast that rests on the deck or cabin top is called a deck-stepped mast, and a mast that rests on the keel is a keel-stepped mast. (2) to step the mast is to raise it and put it in place. To remove a mast is to un-step it.

stern – the back end of a boat or the area near the back; the square end, unless the boat has CANOE STERN.

stern arch – frequently seen on powerboats, the stern arch is becoming more common on sailboats. It provides a convenient location for antennas, radar, a wind generator, solar panels, a flag staff, the stern light, etc. A stern arch may have DAVITS incorporated into the design. See the photo of the Ovni sailboat with the CHINE entry.

stern, down by the – *see* DOWN BY THE STERN.

sternboard, make a sternboard – to go backward when intending to go forward, but the seas or wind make the boat move backward. "When we tried to TACK it was so rough we made a sternboard."

stern drogue – *see* DROGUE, STERN.

stern gland – another name for a STUFFING BOX.

stern line – the line that leads from the STERN to the dock. See MOORING LINE for a diagram.

stern light, sternlight – a white NAVIGATION LIGHT at the STERN, visible from ASTERN through an arc of 135°, displayed when the vessel is UNDERWAY at night or in RESTRICTED VISIBILITY; Rule 21(c) of the NAVIGATION RULES.

stern rail, stern pulpit, pushpit – a metal or wood safety rail around the STERN area, to which the LIFELINES attach. Some stern rails have an open section, closed with a LIFELINE, to allow access to a boarding platform. For photos see DAVITS.

stern tube, shaft tube – the propeller shaft goes from the SHAFT COUPLING on the TRANSMISSION to the propeller through a stern tube (larger than the diameter of the shaft) for part of the distance. The stern tube is a structural feature of the boat.

sternway – going ASTERN or to make a STERNBOARD. The opposite of HEADWAY.

stiff – resistant to HEELING. A sailboat that doesn't heel easily is stiff. Hull form and the amount and location of BALLAST affect the stiffness of a boat. *See* STABILITY, LATERAL.

stock, anchor – *see* ANCHOR, PARTS OF.

stock, rudder – *see* RUDDER STOCK.

stopper – same as LINE STOPPER.

stopper knot – a knot in the end of a rope that prevents it from escaping through a BLOCK, FAIRLEAD, or LINE STOPPER. A FIGURE -EIGHT KNOT and a BLOOD KNOT are two easily-tied stopper knots. See KNOTS, BASIC for photos.

stopping distance – it's important to know the stopping distance for a boat under power or sail at various speeds. Experiment to see how long it takes to come to a complete stop from the moment you put the engine in reverse or let the SHEETS fly. Be aware that a folding propeller may not open quickly or at all, which could create a problem when approaching a dock too fast. The emergency stopping distance for a ship, from the time the engines are put full ASTERN to when she comes to a stop, may be measured in miles.

storm force winds – winds from 48 to 63 knots (BEAUFORT FORCE 10-11). In some forecasts "storm" is used for F10 (48-55 knots) and "violent storm" for F11 (56-63 knots). A STORM WARNING is issued at the approach of these winds.

storm jib – *see* JIB, STORM.

storm sails – a STORM JIB and STORM TRYSAIL.

storm scale system – a weather system approximately the size of a thunderstorm.

storm shutter – another name for a DEADLIGHT.

storm surge – an abnormal rise in the sea level caused primarily by the winds of a HURRICANE, or other very intense storm. The storm pushes the water ahead of it, especially on the right side of the storm's track (on the left side of the track in the Southern Hemisphere). The height of the surge depends on the topography of the coastline, the angle at which the storm strikes the coast, the wind speed, the BAROMETRIC PRESSURE, and the speed of the storm center itself.

storm tactics – actions taken by a vessel in HEAVY WEATHER or a storm. Some of the tactics for power and sailing vessels are different. The basic tactics for a sailing vessel include:

REEF the sails or change to smaller sails (STORM TRYSAIL, STORM JIB)

HEAVE-TO.

Lie A-HULL.

Run off before the wind with small sails or under BARE POLES.

Use a SEA ANCHOR.

Use a STERN DROGUE.

Not all techniques are appropriate for all types of boats and all conditions. No one tactic is "the best," and experimentation may be necessary to find what works for a boat in a particular situation. A number of books and articles discuss these and other tactics. See the bibliography under "Sailing," "heavy weather sailing."

storm tide – the actual level of the sea that results from the combination of the astronomical tide and the STORM SURGE.

storm, tropical – *see* TROPICAL STORM.

storm trysail – *see* TRYSAIL, STORM.

storm warning – issued by government weather services when sustained surface winds or frequent gusts from 48 to 63 knots (BEAUFORT FORCE F10-11) are either predicted or occurring. In some forecasts "storm" is used for F10 (48-55 knots) and "violent storm" for F11 (56-63 knots).

stow – to put away.

stowage plan – logically, a list of where things are stowed. There are so many stowage locations and items on a cruising boat that using a simple computer database program for a stowage plan is a great help to finding things. A 42ft/12.8m long-distance cruising sailboat can easily have over 1,000 different items. The database can also be used as a checklist for ordering parts and supplies as they're used up (if you remember to check things off).

strainer – usually refers to a RAW WATER STRAINER.

strait – a narrow waterway connecting two bodies of water, such as the Straits of Florida, Straits of Gibraltar, Straits of Magellan.

strand, stranding – (1) the strand is the shore or the beach. (2) a stranding is a serious grounding, usually where it will be difficult to re-float the vessel. Going aground on an EQUINOCTIAL TIDE, or waves pushing a grounded vessel up onto the shore can leave a her stranded high and dry. Freeing a stranded vessel is a SALVAGE situation.

strand, to – to suffer a serious grounding; to run hard aground; to be pushed up on a beach by the waves.

stray current corrosion – *see* CORROSION, STRAY CURRENT.

stream – (1) to put something in the water and tow it, such as a SEA ANCHOR, WARPS, or a WATER GENERATOR. "Let's stream the water generator now." (2) to fly something aloft. (3) a small river.

streaming warps – a HEAVY WEATHER or STORM TACTIC used to slow a vessel down so she doesn't surf out of control. A DROGUE is a form of streaming warps.

strength of chain and rope – *see* CHAIN, SAFE WORKING LOAD, and ROPE, SAFE WORKING LOAD.

stringers – another term for LONGITUDINALS or longitudinal frames.

strobe light – a high intensity white ALL-AROUND light that flashes 50 to 70 times per minute. It is permitted as a *distress* signal under the INLAND NAVIGATION RULES. Small strobe lights are available as safety gear to be attached to a HORSESHOE BUOY or to be worn by crew members. Buy SOLAS-approved personal strobes.

strut – (1) a short SPAR or structural component. Struts are used on a MAST to spread the load of the rigging (JUMPER STRUTS), with an AFTERGUY as a REACHING STRUT, and larger structural struts connect the hulls of a MULTIHULL vessel. (2) a shaft strut is a fixture projecting downward from the hull that supports the propeller shaft and the prop after it exits the boat from the STERN TUBE. There is a CUTLESS BEARING in the strut. It is used on boats that have SPADE RUDDERS, and on some powerboats.

A shaft strut. The cutless bearing is in the strut. Look closely to see the scissors-type line cutter in front of the propeller.

stud – (1) a threaded pin or bolt to which electric wires or other parts can be attached. (2) a screw post on a battery. (3) the screw-thread part of a TURNBUCKLE.

stud-link chain – *see* CHAIN, STUD LINK.

stuffing box, packing gland – a fitting inside the boat at the forward end of the STERN TUBE that prevents water from entering the boat around the propeller shaft. A regular stuffing box has PACKING in it to keep water out. It may also have a grease cup to add grease to the fitting. See the next entry.

stuffing box, dripless – A STUFFING BOX that has a flexible rubber bellows with a graphite plate on it, which compresses against a matching STAINLESS STEEL collar mounted on the prop shaft. Water comes into the rubber bellows to lubricate the shaft as it turns, but the water is contained inside the bellows. It's a maintenance-free stuffing box. The PSS Shaft Seal and Duramax® are two brands, available for a wide range of shaft and STERN TUBE sizes.

subordinate station, secondary port – a port in a TIDE or CURRENT TABLE that isn't the main reference port for the table. Tide and current tables may have a list of secondary ports with the corrections to apply to the main port to calculate the tide or current at secondary ports.

sump – a BILGE SUMP.

sunspot cycle – a period of SOLAR ACTIVITY.

superstitions, sailors' – many persist to this day. The basic superstitions involve days of the week to start a voyage (many of these relate to events in Christian history), specific actions, or words to use or avoid, colors, flora and fauna.

Days of the week: an almost universal superstition, still observed today by some mariners, is that it's unlucky to start a voyage on a Friday (the day Christ was crucified). Other unlucky days to depart on a cruise or voyage are the first Monday in April, the second Monday in August, and December 31.

Lucky actions: throw coins or pour wine on the sea or on the deck (messy) when beginning a voyage as an offering to the sea gods, especially Neptune, for a safe voyage. Tattoos and piercings ward off evil spirits (oh, so that's why people get tats and piercings?). Put a silver coin under the MAST STEP (still done today by some sailors).

Unlucky actions: don't step on or off the boat with your left foot first. Don't throw stones into the sea or you'll cause a storm with great waves, or your vessel will never return home. Avoid cutting your hair or nails at sea (better not be a long cruise). Don't bring flowers, plants, or bananas aboard. On the boat never utter the word "pig" or "drowned." A woman aboard makes the sea angry, but if she's naked she will calm the seas (that's the reason for naked figureheads on old ships). Don't look back once your ship leaves port. Avoid losing a bucket overboard. No whistling aboard, because "whistling up a wind" gets you more wind than you want. Don't hand a flag through a ladder. Avoid coiling a rope "against the sun" (counter-clockwise/ anticlockwise).

Superstitions involving animals: lucky animals are black cats aboard or a pod of dolphins following or leading the boat. Unlucky: seeing a cormorant at sea (it's OK to see one near shore). Sharks following the vessel. Killing an albatross or a seagull (those birds contain the souls of sailors lost at sea). Killing a dolphin (dolphins are a good omen).

Miscellaneous superstitions: hearing church bells at sea means someone aboard will die. Redheads bring bad luck, but if you speak to them before they speak to you this makes it OK. Black duffel bags or sea bags bring bad luck. Painting a boat green is bad luck (but lots of green boats seem to be lucky). ST. ELMO'S FIRE around the head of a sailor means he or she will die within a day (if not immediately from fright). If you're becalmed, stick a knife in a wooden mast to get a breeze.

superstructure – general term for the structural parts of a vessel above the deck level.

surface analysis – a SYNOPTIC CHART of surface weather at a particular time.

surfing, yacht – same idea as on a surfboard, a boat surfs when sailing DOWNWIND and wave after wave propels her along. Moderate-size waves can cause surfing. It can be fun (some say exhilarating), but steering may require attention at helm if the AUTOPILOT or SELF-STEERING gear can't cope. When waves get really large, surfing can be dangerous because of the possibility of BROACHING, so it's time to slow the boat down (unless you're on racing boats in an ocean race – they rarely slow down). Deploying a DROGUE is one method to slow the boat's speed.

surge, surging – (1) to control a line using friction around a CLEAT, BOLLARD, or WINCH. To surge a dock line, EASE and SNUB it several times, slowing down the vessel until she's in position along the dock. This prevents jerking the boat to a stop. (2) a surge is the forward and backward movement of water in repeated cycles. When a vessel repeatedly moves FORE-AND-AFT at a dock due to the action of moving water or wind she is surging. Use tight forward and aft SPRING LINES to control surging.

surveyor, marine – *see* MARINE SURVEYOR.

survival blanket – a lightweight blanket made of very thin plastic material, designed to cover a person to help prevent HYPOTHERMIA. Put a few of these small, inexpensive safety items in the ABANDON SHIP KIT and with the first aid kit.

survival in cold water – many people believe that a person will die from HYPOTHERMIA when immersed in cold water unless they are rescued very quickly. However, without a lifejacket or other flotation aid a person will drown before hypothermia sets in. Wearing a lifejacket gives time for a victim to be rescued. It is difficult to put on a lifejacket when you are already in cold water. Understanding the basics about cold water survival can save your life. There's no firm definition of cold water, but water below about 60°F/16°C is cold for survival purposes.

F°	C°	Exhaustion/ Unconsciousness	Expected Survival Time
+ 80	+27	may not occur	indefinite
70-80	21-27	3 to 12 hours	3 hours - indefinitely
60-70	16-21	2 to 7 hours	2 – 40 hours
50-60	10-16	1 to 2 hours	1-6 hours
40-50	4-10	30-60 minutes	1-3 hours
32.5-40	0-4	15-30 minutes	30-90 minutes
under 32	under 0	under 15 minutes	under 15-45 minutes

Survival depends primarily on wearing a lifejacket and understanding what to do if you fall into cold water. Research shows that you can stay alive for at least one hour in very cold water IF you can stay afloat; this is only possible with a flotation aid.

There are three physiological reactions that occur when someone is immersed in cold water; understanding these reactions is a key to survival:

1. *immersion shock*: uncontrolled gasping, increased heart rate, sometimes uncontrolled movement. This phase lasts from approximately one to three minutes immediately following immersion. If you're not wearing a lifejacket your mouth may be under water when involuntary gasping occurs.

2. *cold incapacitation leading to swimming failure*: the blood flow to the arms and legs shuts off and the person can't swim. Even a very fit swimmer will drown without some form of flotation.

3. *hypothermia*: without a flotation aid the victim will drown before becoming hypothermic. However, a lifejacket gives time to attempt a rescue before this stage occurs.

Dr. Gordon Giesbrecht (a leading authority on thermal physiology) explains a simple "1-10-1" survival principle in the excellent video *Cold Water Boot Camp USA* (see the bibliography under "Safety, cold water survival"). The numbers mean one minute – ten minutes – one hour. To survive these minutes you must be wearing a lifejacket or have an immediately available flotation aid. In the first minute try to get calm and control your breathing. The next ten minutes are the approximate time for "meaningful movement" to rescue yourself or have someone reach you and get you out of the water. If you can't get out of the water, stop swimming and curl up into the HELP position to conserve body heat while awaiting rescue. One hour is the approximate time before you may become unconscious from hypothermia if you can't get out of the water.

The time to hypothermia depends on many factors: age, health status, body size and build, body fat, tolerance of cold, shivering response, psychological factors (will to live, positive attitude), amount of clothing, activity in the water, or having alcohol in one's system. An EXPOSURE SUIT and an IMMERSION SUIT increase survival time in cold water. If you operate in cool or cold water, wear proper clothing to stay dry and prevent HYPOTHERMIA, and take all precautions to stay aboard. See www.mariovittone.com for more details about cold water survival.

survival suit – another name for an IMMERSION SUIT.

swage, swaging (pronounced **sway** juh or to rhyme with hedge) – a mechanical process used to attach end fittings to rigging wire or rod. See the next entry.

swage or swaged terminals – the end fittings attached by a mechanical swaging process. *See* TERMINALS, MACHINE SWAGE.

"swallow the anchor" – slang for sailing to an area that captures your life and you decide to stay there "forever." "When we got to Niue we swallowed the anchor."

swamp – to fill with water, but not necessarily FOUNDER.

swan neck – another name for a GOOSENECK (2).

swash – (1) a narrow passage of open water between sandbanks or between a sandbank and the shore. Some of these are named "Swash Channel," as in New York harbor; Sarasota, Florida; and at Poole and the Thames estuary in England. (2) a bar over which the sea washes.

sweating or swigging – a technique for manually tightening a line that is made fast at one end (such as a dock line or HALYARD). It's performed by keeping the free end of the line SNUBBED around a CLEAT (or other strong point) and pulling the line up or out to create slack. Release the line, and at the same time quickly take up the slack and snub it again. Repeat until the line is tightened. Maintaining friction by snubbing keeps the line from slipping back until it can be tied off. Sweating can be done by one person or two, if extra strength is needed to pull the line. Swigging is an old term, still used by some sailors.

sweep – (1) to drag a wire or other device across the bottom to locate or clear obstructions, or to determine the depths in an area. Also applied to mine clearing operations. (2) a sweep is one complete rotation of a radar SCANNER.

swell – ocean waves created by distant strong winds or storms. The direction of swells is the direction from which they're coming. The crests of swells are far apart, and the direction is relatively constant, in contrast to WIND WAVES, which change more readily when local winds change. The length of a swell (distance from crest to crest) is proportional to the FETCH; the longer the fetch, the longer the swells. The PERIOD of swells is from five to 30 seconds. The arrival of a large swell may indicate an approaching storm.

SWL – abbreviation for safe working load. *See* CHAIN, SAFE WORKING LOAD and ROPE, SAFE WORKING LOAD.

swigging – old term for SWEATING.

swinging room – the area covered by a boat lying to her anchor. It's an arc of some degrees or perhaps a circle if the wind or current changes. In a small anchorage there may not be enough swinging room for more than a few boats. *See* SAIL AT ANCHOR and SCOPE, SHORT.

swinging ship – a process used to prepare a DEVIATION TABLE by running the vessel on different HEADINGS across a RANGE. CHAPMAN discusses this relatively simple technique, which gives precise results if carefully done.

swing keel – *see* KEEL, LIFTING.

S/V – prefix for sailing vessel. *S/V Magic*. Sometimes used to mean Survey Vessel.

SWR – abbreviation for STANDING WAVE RATIO.

S/Y – prefix for sailing yacht. *S/Y Falcon*.

symmetric spinnaker – *see* SPINNAKER, SYMMETRIC.

synoptic chart, synoptic (pronounced sih **nop** tick) – a weather map, such as those seen on TV, the Internet, in newspapers, or on a WEATHERFAX. A synoptic shows the state of the atmosphere over a particular geographic area at a specific time, or a forecast for future weather developments. The synoptic is produced by meteorologists who interpret computer data and models in light of their professional experience. In the U.S. a forecaster puts his or her name on the synoptic. A surface analysis is a chart of surface weather observations at a particular time. Using standardized symbols, it depicts HIGHS and LOWS, FRONTS, TROPICAL CYCLONES, squall lines, and other significant weather features. The VALID TIME (in UTC) and date are indicated on the chart. Synoptics are based on worldwide observations taken every day at 0000 and 1200 UTC. Through international agreements, data is exchanged between countries. The main synoptic times are 0000, 0600, 1200, and 1800 UTC. Various synoptics and forecasts are issued for 12, 24, 36, 48, 72, 96, and 120 hour time periods. Two types of synoptics particularly useful for mariners are surface pressure charts and 500-MB CHARTS.

synoptic scale or large-scale weather system – refers to the size of a weather system, as in the phrase "synoptic-scale CYCLONE." HIGH and LOW PRESSURE SYSTEMS are synoptic scale features. The area covered by synoptic scale weather is several hundred miles or more. *See also* MESOSCALE and STORM SCALE SYSTEM.

- T -

tabling (rhymes with enabling) – extra strips of sailcloth sewn along the edges of a sail as reinforcement or as a cover for a LEECH line.

tabernacle – *see* MAST TABERNACLE.

tachometer, tach (rhymes with thermometer, tack) – an ENGINE INSTRUMENT that indicates the RPMS of the engine.

tack – (1) the forward lower corner of a triangular sail. (2) each leg of a zig-zag course is a tack. (3) to change the heading of the boat by steering the BOW through the wind so that the wind comes on the other side of the sails.

tack, favored – when BEATING to WINDWARD, one TACK usually brings you closer to your destination; this is the favored tack. Maximize the time on this tack. Wind and sea conditions affect which tack gives the better TACKING ANGLE. *See* the next entry.

tacking angle – how close to the wind a boat can sail, expressed in degrees. Knowing the tacking angle (it varies with boats and the wind and sea conditions) allows you to estimate the new heading after a tack. If the tacking angle is 45° to the wind, in theory, when you change TACKS you go through 90° to achieve a new CLOSE-HAULED heading. *See* previous entry.

tacking downwind – when the wind is DEAD AFT it's usually more comfortable and faster to sail on a BEAM REACH on one tack for a while, and then JIBE onto a beam reach on the other tack. Changing course approximately 20° to either side of dead ASTERN helps stop rolling, and the faster boat speed makes up for the extra miles sailed. There are mathematical formulas and tables to help analyze tacking angles and speed gained vs. the extra distance sailed. A general example: if the straight-line course is 100 miles and you tack downwind with the wind 20° away from dead aft, this adds approximately six more miles to the trip. If your speed increases just a quarter to a third of a knot more than the speed when sailing dead downwind, you'll cover the extra distance in the same time as the shorter distance, and it will be more comfortable.

tackle (the old pronunciation **tay** cul is occasionally heard), **block and tackle, purchase** – one or more BLOCKS and a line used together to increase the mechanical advantage (the pulling or lifting power). A VANG with blocks and lines is a tackle, and a lifting tackle is used with a LIFESLING® to hoist a person aboard. For a photo *see* HORSE.

tackle, vang – *see* VANG.

taffrail – the STERN deck area or the rail at the stern.

taffrail log – a device for measuring distance traveled through the water. It consists of a dial instrument, with a long line attached to it, and a spinner or rotator at the other end. In the water the spinner turns the line which moves a needle on the instrument dial to indicate the miles through the water. Electronic speed and distance logs have replaced taffrail logs, except for a few traditionalists.

tag line – a line attached to something, such as a canvas bucket, when it's hoisted up the MAST. The tag line controls the swing of the item and guides it back down to the deck. In a HELICOPTER ASSIST it may be called a trail line.

tail, to – on a WINCH that is not SELF-TAILING, a crew member has to pull the end of the line as it's winched in. That person is called the tailer. "Karen, please tail the winch for Don."

take a turn – to loop a line partially around a CLEAT, BOLLARD, or other strong point in order to SNUB it or take the strain off, without tying the line off. If a rope is pulling too hard and slipping out of your hands, take a turn around something strong to hold it until you can control it.

take departure – *see* DEPARTURE, TO TAKE.

take the ground – to go aground, either intentionally or by accident. A sailboat with a fairly long, flat keel or BILGE KEELS can take the ground in a DRYING HARBOR.

taken aback – *see* ABACK.

take way off – *see* WAY.

tall rig – a sailboat with a tall mast, and therefore more sail area. Some models of yachts are available with a choice of a standard rig or a tall rig. See the photo with RIDING SAIL.

tall ship – a large, traditionally-rigged sailing vessel, frequently a SQUARE RIGGER of some type. Some are old and some are modern replicas. Governments own tall ships as national representative vessels, and private organizations may have a tall ship for sail training or luxury CHARTERS. Tall ship races and port visits are held all over the world, and are popular events for sailors and spectators. The U.S. Coast Guard's tall ship, *Eagle*, dates from 1936, and the *USS Constitution* (the oldest warship in COMMISSION) dates from 1797.

tang – pieces of metal mounted on the MAST to which the upper ends of STANDING RIGGING are attached. Instead of tangs, mast slots for T-HOOKS are used on some boats.

tank, flexible or flex tank – a tank for liquid made from strong, flexible plastic or rubberized material. Flexible tanks are available in a number of capacities for potable water, diesel fuel, and waste. They're useful for carrying extra liquids on a long trip or as a permanent installation.

target – a RADAR RETURN.

TCPA – abbreviation for TIME TO CLOSEST POINT OF APPROACH.

technical resources – in addition to books, articles, magazines, and technical experts a number of websites have information about selection, installation, and maintenance of all kinds of boat equipment. Use Internet resources with care; some are disguised marketing tools and make exaggerated claims for a particular product. See the bibliography under "Maintenance" and "Publications" for some technical resources.

telltale compass – *see* COMPASS, TELLTALE.

telltales – light pieces of yarn or very thin strips of lightweight material attached to the AFT lower SHROUDS, in pairs on both sides of the LUFF of a HEADSAIL, and on the LEECH of a mainsail. Telltales on sails indicate the APPARENT WIND flow over the sails to help you TRIM for maximum efficiency. For example, when the telltales on a jib are streaming equally on both sides of the sail, the jib is properly trimmed.

temperate region – another name for the MIDDLE LATITUDES.

tend – (1) to adjust a line as needed, or to be ready to adjust the line. "Tend the STERN line." (2) to lead in a specific direction. "The coast tends eastward from the HEADLAND."

tender – (1) a DINGHY or small vessel that ferries crew and supplies to a larger vessel; a ship's boat. (2) easily tipped or made to HEEL; the opposite of STIFF.

terminals for electrical wire – (1) the posts on a battery where the battery cables are attached. (2) screw terminals on an electrical panel or other equipment where wires are attached. (3) fittings attached to the ends of electrical wires and cables to connect the wires to an electrical panel or the battery terminals. Wire terminals are sized for both the wire and the STUD. Use captive spade or ring terminals, which are unlikely to be loosened or dislodged by vibration. Electrical wire terminals are normally CRIMPED on, rather than SOLDERED.

terminals, hand-crimp, hand-swage/swaged (pronounced **sway** juh or to rhyme with hedge) – fittings used to form an eye or to attach end fittings to wire rigging or LIFELINES. Hand-swaged fittings are designed to be applied with a hand tool; they aren't the same as machine-swaged terminals. Special tools crimp the fittings onto the wire; these are either like a large bolt cutter with long handles, or a simple bolt-together tool that clamps over the fitting and compresses it onto the wire. Read about the recommended uses for the two tools. Hand-swaged fittings may not hold the rated strength of the wire, as do properly installed MECHANICAL or MACHINE-SWAGED terminals. For this reason hand-crimping may not be suitable for high-load applications. *See* next two entries.

terminals, machine swaged (pronounced **sway** zh'd or to rhyme with hedged) – terminals for rigging wire or rod applied with an industrial machine that uses pressure to bond the terminals to the wire/rod. See the next entry.

terminals, mechanical – end fittings for wire rigging and LIFELINES applied with simple hand tools (wrenches, screwdriver, pliers). Mechanical terminals for metric or Imperial wire come in a variety of configurations, such as TURNBUCKLE STUD, fork, eye, TOGGLE, and insulators (for BACKSTAY antennas). When properly installed according to the directions, these terminals hold the rated strength of the wire. They can be opened for inspection, or to re-use on new wire. When re-using mechanical terminals read the instructions about replacing internal parts, such as the cone, wedge, or former. Brand names are Castlok, Sta-Lok®, Norseman®, and Suncor Quick-Attach™ fittings. If the boat has SWAGED wire rigging, carry a few mechanical terminals for use in an emergency. *See* the bibliography under "Rigging" for websites.

territorial sea – the waters extending out 12NM from the shore that are under the jurisdiction of a state that has a seacoast. This definition is expressed in the United Nations Convention on the LAW OF THE SEA:

> "every State has the right to establish the breadth of its territorial sea up to a limit not exceeding 12 nautical miles." All vessels are guaranteed the right to pass through territorial seas: "Subject to this Convention, ships of all States, whether coastal or land-locked, enjoy the right of innocent passage through the territorial sea."

Most countries use the 12-mile definition. *See also* **CONTIGUOUS ZONE, HIGH SEAS**, and **200-MILE LIMIT**.

tether – a **HARNESS TETHER.**

Thames measurement, TM (pronounced Tems) – a system for the measurement of yachts and small vessels used in the UK. It uses length and beam for the calculations. Other measurements for yachts and ships use some form of TONS.

thick, thick weather – implies conditions of very RESTRICTED VISIBILITY. "It's so thick out there I think we'll stay in harbor today."

thimble – a round, oval, or teardrop-shaped metal fitting with a groove around the edge into which a rope or wire is fitted with an EYE SPLICE or a SEIZING. The thimble protects the rope or wire eye from chafe. Use thimbles on a rope anchor RODE and anywhere a strong, chafe-proof eye is needed at the end of a rope. The strongest thimbles are cast metal rather than stamped out of lighter metal. Plastic thimbles are available, but they're only for very light duty. For round thimbles *see* SEIZE.

A heavy-duty cast stainless steel thimble, shown here on the port leg of a stern bridle for a series drogue. The bridle thimbles are shackled to welded tabs port and starboard on this metal vessel. The line is 1-1/8"/28mm braid. The shackle pin hasn't been wired yet.

thole pin – a vertical wooden or metal pin on the GUNWALE of a boat that's used to hold an oar when rowing. The pin can be single or used in a pair with each oar. The oar isn't attached to the boat or pin, but rests against the pin on the pulling stroke. Thole pins are the earliest form of an OARLOCK.

T-hook, T-ball – a fitting SWAGED to STANDING RIGGING to attach the rigging to a slot in the MAST. These hooks have a shorter life than other types of wire terminals. Examining them carefully should be part of a RIGGING INSPECTION.

three-arm protractor, station pointer – a PLOTTING instrument with a graduated circle, a fixed arm and two moveable arms. The arms can be pivoted around the circle and set to the horizontal SEXTANT ANGLES observed between three objects. A three-point FIX can be plotted on the chart. Weems and Plath® NP 116 is a plastic model.

three-strand – *see* ROPE, THREE STRAND.

three-way valve – a valve that connects two tanks to a single outlet, allowing selection of one tank or the other. They may be used with water or fuel tanks; for fuel use, use valves that meet ABYC or UL standards. A DIVERTER VALVE is also a three-way valve.

through-hull – an opening in the hull, above or below the waterline, for water intakes (engine, galley, HEAD, and others), or for water outlets (bilge pump, engine exhaust, drains). Through-hulls below the waterline must be fitted with SEACOCKS so the opening can be closed as a routine practice or in an emergency. There should be a diagram in the vessel's notebook that shows the locations of all the through-hulls. See the next entry.

through-hull plug – tapered soft wood plugs for emergency use to stop water from coming into a broken through-hull fitting or SEACOCK. A plug of the proper size should be tied near each through-hull. These tapered plugs have non-emergency uses as well, such as temporarily closing the open end of a hose or pipe. Buy them at a marine supply store.

throwing line, rescue line – a type of HEAVING LINE designed to be thrown to a person in the water. Rescue lines usually have a weight at the end to make the line go farther when it's thrown. One throwing device (the Mustang Rescue Stick) sends a self-inflating horseshoe collar to the person in the water; range approximately 100ft/30m. There's also a model of self-inflating, throwable LIFESLING®, range approximately 50ft/15m. Research the available devices and have more than one type aboard.

tidal – logically, waters that have a tide. "Tide" is frequently used as a synonym for tidal.

tidal atlas, tidal stream atlas – a series of CHARTLETS or diagrams for the TIDAL CURRENTS in a specific area. There are usually 13 diagrams, one for high water (HW), and for each of the six hours before and after HW. They show the direction and speed of the tidal current at SPRINGS and NEAPS. One or two main ports are used as the REFERENCE STATION for determining the time; for example "on Boston" or "on Dover." Find tidal current diagrams in COAST PILOTS, NAUTICAL ALMANACS, CRUISING GUIDES, and in separate booklets for specific areas. CURRENT TABLES that show daily times for the changing of currents at various locations are also available.

tidal basin – a harbor or basin that doesn't have a gate or a lock to prevent water from flowing out as the tide EBBS. A non-tidal basin has a gate or a SILL that retains a level of water in the basin. *See* TIDAL GATE (2).

tidal bore – this phenomenon occurs when the incoming tide meets the outflow current of a river, creating a STANDING WAVE where the tide and the current meet. The outgoing current must be stronger than the incoming tide for this to happen, and there must be a large tide RANGE. The shape of the river's estuary and the tide range influence the formation and height of a tidal bore. The wave becomes stronger as the river narrows and shallows. The effect is most dramatic at SPRING tides, when a bore can reach speeds over 20 mph. The wave may stay in an area of a few hundred yards/meters or travel some distance up a river. In the Amazon Basin, the bore on the Rio Guajara travels over 180 miles inland. According to the *Guinness Book of Records,* the largest the tidal bore is on the Qiantang River in China. It can reach a height of 29.2ft/8.9m and a speed of 25 mph. The Severn River in England has over 250 bores a year, which are enjoyed by surfers who ride up the river for as much as six miles. In Atlantic Canada there's a bore at the mouth of the Shubenacadie River near the upper Bay of Fundy in Nova Scotia, and another at the head of the Bay of Fundy at St. John, New Brunswick, named the Reversing Falls. In Europe bores are found on the Gironde, Orne, and Seine Rivers in France, and in the Straits of Messina. There are about 100 tidal bores worldwide.

tidal constants, tidal differences – correction factors applied to tide predictions at a main tide reference station to determine the time and height of the tide at a SUBORDINATE STATION.

tidal current, tidal stream – the horizontal movement of water that's caused by the rise and fall of the tide. "The tidal stream is strongest here three hours before high tide." The word tide is often used to refer to current. "The tide's weaker over by the shore."

tidal current tables – usually called CURRENT TABLES, these have daily predictions for the time of the change of the tidal currents at various locations.

tidal gate, tide gate – (1) an area where the tidal current runs very strongly; it's usually a constricted area. A TIDE RACE is one form of tidal gate. (2) a mechanical gate at a harbor or basin that's opened and closed according to the level of the tide; a flap gate.

The tidal gate at Padstow, England is opening, as you can see from the tilted walkway. The gate rotates and submerges to allow access to the harbor.

tidal stream – same as TIDAL CURRENT.

tidal wave – usually refers to a TSUNAMI or STORM SURGE.

tide – the vertical rise and fall of the ocean caused by the gravitational effects of the moon and sun. The number of daily tide changes and the amount of rise and fall varies from area to area around the world. Tides are DIURNAL, SEMI-DIURNAL, or MIXED. The Great Lakes experience a tiny tide (approximately 0.4in. to 1.5in/10.7mm to 35.6mm). The word tide is often used to refer to the TIDAL CURRENT. "The tide's strong here." TIDE TABLES give daily information about tides in an area.

tide-bound – unable to depart a harbor or proceed further because of insufficient water depth at a particular STATE OF THE TIDE.

tide, diurnal – one high and one low water per day. Areas of the U.S. Gulf Coast, including the western part of the Florida Panhandle, eastern Mexico, and some Caribbean islands have a diurnal tide. These tides often have weak currents with long periods of slack and little tidal range. Most tides are SEMI-DIURNAL.

tide, down – *see* DOWN TIDE.

tide, equinoctial – *see* EQUINOCTIAL TIDE.

tide, fair – *see* FAIR CURRENT.

tide gate – same as a TIDAL GATE.

tide gauge – (1) a painted vertical board at a tidal lock, BASIN, or harbor, which indicates the height of water at the entrance or in a part of the harbor. (2) an instrument, such as a special buoy, for measuring the height of the tide. For other photos see DRY OUT, SILL, and TIDAL GATE.

Low tide on this tide gauge. The range is approximately 12ft/4m.

tide, head – *see* HEAD TIDE.

tide, height at a given time – *see* RULE OF TWELFTHS.

tide mark, sea mark – (1) the water mark left by high water, seen on seawalls, rocks, pilings, and other structures in the water. By noting the tide mark you can tell if it's high water.

tide, mixed – a SEMI-DIURNAL tide where the heights of the two high tides and the two low tides are significantly different, with more than the small differences normally seen in a semi-diurnal tide. The U.S. west coast has mixed tides.

tide, neap or neaps – when the moon is at first quarter or third quarter neap tides (neaps) occur. Moon phases are frequently included on TIDE TABLES. The TIDE RANGE is at its minimum. The high water is lower than average, and the low water is higher than average; *lower highs/higher lows.* Two neap tides occur in a 29-day period. The time between neaps and SPRINGS is about seven days. The abbreviation for low water neaps is LWN. If you go really hard aground at high water neaps (HWN) you may have to wait until the next spring tide to re-float; the boat is "neaped." Looking at a tide table you can see neaps and springs approach by noting the tide levels each day. *See* TIDE, SPRING.

tide race, race – a localized condition where the tide change causes strong currents and turbulent water, sometimes with STANDING WAVES and whirlpools (sometimes called a MAELSTROM). Under some conditions, such as with WIND AGAINST TIDE, a race can be dangerous to small vessels as well as ships. Races occur in areas with a relatively large tide RANGE, around HEADLANDS, and where the water passes through a constricted passage. The contours of the bottom also influence the formation of a race. TIDAL CURRENT TABLES and diagrams, COAST PILOTS, and CRUISING GUIDES identify races in an area, and give information about navigating them. Some well-known tide races include Hell Gate in New York city's East River, The Race at the eastern end of Long Island Sound on the U.S. east coast, Corryvreckan on the west coast of Scotland, the "Merry Men of Mey" at the eastern end of the Pentland Firth in northern Scotland, the race off Portland Bill on the south coast of England, the Alderney Race in the Channel Islands, and the Saltstraumen near Bodø, Norway.

tide range – the difference in feet or meters between the height of high water and low water is the range. TIDE TABLES give the heights of high and low water for every day in a particular year.

tide rips – small or medium-sized STANDING WAVES formed when two opposing currents meet, or when the current flows over a relatively shallow, irregular bottom. CRUISING GUIDES and notations on some charts warn of tide rip areas. Sometimes called OVERFALLS.

A sloop with a roller-reefed genoa is working her way through tide rips in 23 knots.

tide-rode – describes a vessel at anchor when she lies to the current rather than to the wind. Being tide-rode may be uncomfortable, especially if the boat lies beam-on to the waves or SWELL. It may be possible to rig a BRIDLE between the BOW and STERN and attach it to the anchor RODE to adjust the position of the boat so her bow points more toward the waves. A vessel that lies to the wind, rather than the current is WIND-RODE.

tide, semi-diurnal – two high tides and two low tides per day. The heights of the two highs and the two lows may not be the same; TIDE TABLES indicate the differences, which are usually small. If the differences are large, the tide is a MIXED TIDE. Some tide tables may specifically indicate higher high water (HHW), lower high water (LHW), higher low water (HLW), and lower low water (LLW). The U.S. east coast and the Atlantic coast of Europe (among many other areas) have semi-diurnal tides.

tide, spring or springs – spring tides occur around the time of the new moon and the full moon. Moon phases are frequently included on TIDE TABLES. At springs, the tide RANGE is at its maximum. High water is higher and low water is lower; *higher highs/lower lows*. The duration of SLACK water is shorter than average, and the tidal currents are stronger than average. Note that lower lows may produce depths below CHART DATUM (marked with a minus sign in a tide table). The abbreviation for low water springs is LWS. Two spring tides occur in a 29-day period. The time between NEAPS and springs is about seven days. Looking at a tide table you can see neaps and springs approach by looking at the tide levels each day. If you're unfortunate enough to go hard aground at high water springs (HWS), you may have to wait two weeks to re-float or be pulled off. The highest spring tides of the year occur at or near the time of the equinoxes. You *really* don't want to go hard aground or STRAND on an EQUINOCTIAL TIDE.

tide, state of – refers to whether the tide is flooding (water level rising) or ebbing (water level falling). Obviously, it's important to know the state of the tide when checking depths for anchoring, before passing through a shallow area, before passing under a fixed structure such as a bridge or power lines, or if you've gone aground.

tide tables – predictions of the times and heights of high and low water for every day in a particular year at specific locations. Actual tide levels and times can vary from the predictions due to the effects of wind and other meteorological conditions. Tide tables are issued annually. The table doesn't cover all locations in an area; there are one or more main ports (REFERENCE STATIONS) to which SUBORDINATE STATIONS (secondary ports) are referenced. A table for secondary ports gives correction factors for the difference in the times and heights of high and low water. Find tide tables in an annual NAUTICAL ALMANAC, as a separate book or folder, with navigation software, and on the Internet.

tide, turn of – when the tide changes from FLOOD to EBB or vice-versa. The SLACK and STAND may or may not occur with the turn of the tide. The phrase is also used to refer to a change in the direction of a current.

tide, up – up tide is the same as UPSTREAM.

tiller – a piece of wood or metal connected directly or indirectly to the rudder or RUDDER POST to move the rudder. A tiller does the same thing as a wheel, although it's used differently. To turn the boat, push the tiller in the opposite direction to which you want to go: to turn to PORT, push the tiller to STARBOARD. Carry a spare tiller in case one breaks. A wheel steers the boat like a vehicle.

tiller arm – a short STRUT, usually made of cast BRONZE or ALUMINUM, attached near the top of the RUDDER STOCK to facilitate the attachment of steering mechanisms, such as a hydraulic steering ram or an AUTOPILOT. The tiller arm is usually below decks near the STERN. Because it's an essential part of the STEERING SYSTEM, it should be regularly checked.

tiller, emergency – a boat with a wheel should have an emergency TILLER in case the steering system fails. The tiller usually connects directly to the top of the RUDDER POST, through an access plate in the COCKPIT SOLE. Test it in actual use; it may be poorly-designed, difficult to use, or not fit properly. If it's hard to use in calm conditions, imagine what it'll be like if it's rough.

tiller ropes – wire rope that leads from a TILLER ARM or RUDDER QUADRANT through a series of BLOCKS to the mechanism that attaches to the steering wheel.

time signal, time tick – a signal from WWV, CHU, or other accurate time signal broadcasting source, used to set the precise time on a ship's clock or CHRONOMETER. BBC radio broadcasts an accurate time tick on the hour: it's preceded by five "pips" and a long beep exactly on the hour. Accurate time is required for CELESTIAL NAVIGATION.

time, speed, and distance formula – the basic calculation used in DEAD RECKONING. The formula is D = ST (distance equals speed multiplied by time). See DEAD RECKONING for an easy visual way to solve the equation for any of the factors. There are flat, plastic time, speed, and distance calculators (called nautical slide rules) available to do the calculations quickly and visually, without math or a calculator. Weems & Plath® product #105 is a commonly-used nautical slide rule.

time to closest point of approach, TCPA – the time (in minutes or seconds) to the closest point at which two vessels will pass if they both maintain their present courses and speeds. AIS and modern radars with ARPA can calculate the TCPA, if the radar is properly interfaced with other instruments on the boat. The vessels can also be plotted on a MANEUVERING BOARD or RADAR TRANSFER PLOTTING SHEET. You have to be skilled to do this calculation quickly on paper. The abbreviation TCPA is usually used.

time zones – the globe is divided into 24 time zones, one for each 15° of LONGITUDE. There's an hour difference between each zone. The zones are measured east and west of the PRIME MERIDIAN (0°00.00′, the longitude of Greenwich, England). The zone lines may vary to accommodate geographic and political boundaries. The zone centered on Greenwich is zero (it is UTC time), and the numbers increase sequentially to +12 (east of Greenwich) or -12 (west of Greenwich). The zone to the east of the International Date Line (180° longitude) is a -12 zone, and the zone to the west of it is a +12 zone: the time is the same in these two zones. The U.S. east coast is -5; the west coast is -8. Knowing the time zone number and if it's a plus or minus zone tells you how to calculate the local time from UTC or UTC from the local time. Add or subtract the zone number to UTC to get the local time. Apply the opposite sign and number to the local time to find UTC time. For example, when it's 2000 in London (the zero or UTC zone) it's 1500 in New York (a -5 zone).When it's 1200 in New York it's 1700 in London. If you use both local time and UTC aboard, have two clocks or a dual time zone wristwatch.

tip clearance – the distance between a propeller blade and the hull or SKEG at its closest point. Adequate tip clearance is necessary for the proper operation of the prop. If it's too close, vibration will result, and the propeller will be less efficient. The tip clearance is part of the marine architect's calculations. However, if you plan to install a slightly larger prop, tip clearance may be a factor. A rule of thumb for tip clearance is that it should be more than approximately 10% of the diameter of the prop. If the tip clearance is too great this may mean that the angle of the shaft is fairly steep, and a prop isn't efficient when it points downward too much. Consult a professional before changing a prop, or if you think there may be a problem with an existing prop.

titanium – a metal with high strength-to-weight properties and excellent corrosion resistance. It's among the most NOBLE metals on the GALVANIC SERIES. It has many uses afloat and ashore.

to-do list, work list – Fact: on a boat this list never gets shorter. Cross off one item, and there are two (five, ten?) more jobs to add. Prioritize the list, with safety items first.

toe rail, bulwark – a low or high rail at the outboard edge of the deck or the outboard edge of the deck itself. A bulwark is a high toe rail.

toggle – a piece of marine hardware that's used on STANDING RIGGING to allow side-to-side and FORE-AND-AFT movement, so that the RIGGING TERMINALS aren't stressed. Use two toggles on a HEADSTAY, one at the top and one at the deck end, so the stay can move laterally with the force of the wind on the HEADSAIL.

ton (T) – a measure of weight that has three basic definitions: (1) short ton (2,000lbs/907.2 kg), used in the U.S. (2) long ton (2,240lbs/1016kg), used in the UK and other European countries, and for indicating the DISPLACEMENT of ships. (3) metric ton (1,000kg/2,204.6lbs). The metric ton may be indicated by "tonne." It's close to the long ton and the terms are sometimes used interchangeably.

tons, gross, GT, and gross register tons, GRT – a standardized measurement of all the enclosed spaces on a vessel; a measurement of the total interior *volume*. It gives the layman an idea of the size of a ship, and marine authorities use GT for applying ship regulations, harbor dues and fees, officer and crew licensing and manning regulations. Gross register tons is an older term still in use. The measurement is applied to DOCUMENTED yachts as well as ships.

tons, net , NT – the volume of the *cargo-carrying* spaces in the hull. Ship regulations, harbor dues and other fees may be calculated based on net tons. The measurement is applied to DOCUMENTED yachts (even though non-commercial vessels don't carry cargo) as well as ships.

tons, Thames measurement, TM (pronounced Tems) – *see* THAMES MEASUREMENT.

"tonnage yields to tonnage"– a phrase to remind us that, in general, small vessels should keep out of the way of larger vessels. Of course, the NAVIGATION RULES always apply.

Should the sailboat insist on right-of-way?

tool kits – many articles and books discuss the recommended tools to have aboard. Outfit the boat with an appropriate selection of tools for the type of cruising you do. The further away from home you travel, the more comprehensive a tool kit should be. Have a basic kit easily accessible. One "multi-tool" isn't enough. A selection of separate tools should be part of a DAMAGE CONTROL KIT.

top hamper – inclusive term for everything above the deck level, such as the cabin, WHEELHOUSE or other structures, SPARS, and gear. Top hamper increases WINDAGE and decreases stability. "All that top hamper on Tom's fishing boat makes her really TENDER."

topmark – a shape on top of a buoy that identifies it or indicates its purpose. Topmarks are round, square, triangular, octagonal, or X-shaped (with some variations). For a photo see SAFE WATER MARK.

topographic features – unfortunately some modern paper and electronic charts don't have topographic contours for land near the water. Looking at the topography helps you predict what the effects of the land may be on the winds near the coast, in an anchorage, or in a harbor. Are there features that might produce GAP WINDS or CORNERING WINDS? Will winds be CHANNELED in the area? Could there be ANABATIC or KATABATIC winds? Will winds accelerate over nearby high terrain? CRUISING GUIDES and COAST GUIDES may not have this information for all the places you sail. Look for old charts of an area if you value having topographic information.

topping lift – (1) a line running from the top of the mast to the AFT end of the BOOM, used to hold up the end of the boom, especially when furling or REEFING the sail. A sailboat with a rigid BOOM VANG doesn't need a topping lift, but may have one. (2) a line that supports a SPINNAKER POLE.

topsides, "topside" – (1) the part of the hull from the waterline to the deck level. "John waxed the topsides, and they look like new." (2) on deck as opposed to being below decks. "I left the tools topside."

towing astern – power-driven vessels that are towing barges, vessels, or objects ASTERN display special lights, as prescribed in Rule 24(a) of the NAVIGATION RULES. Rule 24(e) specifies that the vessel or object being towed shall display SIDELIGHTS and a STERN LIGHT. Note that a tow may exceed 200m/650ft in length, and the lights on the vessel or object being towed may not be especially visible. During the day a long tow line isn't always easy to see, as it may sag to the surface of the water. Take all precautions to not pass astern of a vessel that's towing, until you are absolutely certain that the towed object is well past your location. At sea a tug may have a barge a quarter-mile or more astern, and the towline can be submerged. Terrible accidents occur when a vessel goes between a tug and its tow. Learn the lights for towing vessels and be vigilant day and night, and especially in RESTRICTED VISIBILITY.

towing light – Rule 21(d) of the NAVIGATION RULES defines a towing light as a "yellow light having the same characteristics as the STERN LIGHT."

towing warps – a STERN DROGUE, used to slow a vessel down in storm conditions.

track – (1) the actual course of the vessel over the ground; the COURSE MADE GOOD. (2) to follow the movement of a vessel or a radar TARGET. ARPA is an automatic radar target tracking system.

trade winds, trades – tropical winds in waters between approximately 5° and 30° north and south that blow from a consistent direction, depending on the time of year. The trades blow from subtropical HIGH PRESSURE centers towards the equatorial LOW. In the Northern Hemisphere the northeast trades blow from the northeast toward the southwest. In the Southern Hemisphere the southeast trades blow from southeast toward northwest.

traditional, traditionally-rigged – non-specific terms applied to older vessels or modern replicas, sail, power, or rowing boats. TALL SHIPS, GAFF-RIGGED sailboats, SCHOONERS, and pre-20th century vessels fall into this category.

traditions, nautical – some nautical traditions come and go with the ages, but basic traditions persist among mariners: respect for the sea and good SEAMANSHIP, and pride in a PASSAGE well-accomplished. Naval vessels and some merchant vessels observe traditions such as DIPPING THE COLORS, the CROSSING THE LINE CEREMONY, DRESSING SHIP, gun salutes, and manning the rails or YARDARMS on TALL SHIPS. Yachts may choose to observe a tradition or adapt a tradition to their own use.

Traffic Separation Scheme, TSS – in some crowded, busy waters, the IMO has established lanes for ship traffic to help prevent collisions. The lanes are marked on charts. A VESSEL TRAFFIC SERVICE (VTS) control office monitors the TSS by electronic means (TV, radar, AIS), and aircraft or vessels may also patrol the areas. All mariners operating in these areas must know where the lanes are, and observe the rules for operating in or near a TSS. Fines may be levied for not observing the rules. If you can safely navigate outside the scheme, do so, and leave the lanes for large vessels. Use the Inshore Traffic Lanes or stay completely out of all lanes. Rule 10 of the NAVIGATION RULES specifies the conduct of vessels operating in or near a TSS. The basic rules are:

- When using a traffic lane, travel in the proper lane with the flow of traffic.
- If you aren't using a TSS, stay away from the lanes and SEPARATION ZONES.
- When entering or departing a lane try to do it at the *end* of a lane, but if you join a lane in the middle, merge into the lane in the direction of travel at a small angle.
- When crossing a lane, cross at a right angle, or as close to a right angle as possible, to minimize the time it takes to cross.
- Vessels under 20m/65.6ft in length, sailing vessels, and FISHING VESSELS may use an inshore traffic zone.
- Vessels under 20m/65.6ft in length or a sailing vessel shall not impede a power-driven vessel following a traffic lane.
- A fishing vessel shall not impede the progress of *any* vessel following a traffic lane.
- Navigate with caution in the areas near the terminations of a TSS.
- Avoid anchoring in a TSS or in areas near its terminations.

The traffic lanes are separated by Separation Zones (marked on the chart): Rule 10(e) of the Navigation Rules specifies that "a vessel other than a crossing vessel or a vessel joining or leaving a lane shall not normally enter a separation zone or cross a separation line except in cases of emergency to avoid immediate danger, or to engage in fishing within a separation zone."

trail line – a line dropped from a helicopter to deliver equipment to a vessel. See HELICOPTER ASSIST and TAG LINE.

transceiver – a radio that can both transmit and receive. A VHF radio is a transceiver.

transducer – an electronic device used to measure speed through the water (speed transducer, SPEED LOG), or depth (DEPTH SOUNDER transducer), and send the information to a display unit.

transfer – *see* ADVANCE AND TRANSFER.

transformer – an electrical device that changes incoming AC voltage from one voltage to another. It can be a step-up (120V to 240V), step-down (240V to 120V) or a dual conversion transformer. A typical transformer doesn't change the FREQUENCY of the current.

transformer, isolation – a specialized transformer that separates the AC system of the boat from the AC shore power, by transferring the current from shore power to the boat via electromagnetic induction between the transformer's primary and secondary windings. An marine isolation transformer reduces AC shock hazard and the potential for GALVANIC CORROSION. They may be used on all vessels, but they're especially important on a metal boat. Some isolation transformers may also be used to change incoming voltage to another voltage, such as 240V to 120V. Isolation transformers should meet ABYC Standard E-11 AC and DC Electrical Systems on Boats; a transformer can be UL-listed, but it must be tested by an independent laboratory to prove compliance. Consult a marine electrician and technical references.

transit – (1) another name for a RANGE (4). (2) in celestial parlance a transit is the passage of a celestial body across a celestial meridian or the face of another heavenly body. A well-known and rare transit is the Transit of Venus, in which Venus passes between the sun and the earth, and can be seen against the sun. The dates of upcoming transits are December 2117 and December 2125. Get your sun-viewing devices ready.

transmission coupling – *see* COUPLING, SHAFT.

transmission or gearbox – the part of the engine, usually at the AFT end, that has the forward and reverse gears in it. There's a reduction gear in the gearbox that reduces the engine RPMS to a speed appropriate for the propeller. For example, a 2:1 gearbox reduces 2000 engine rpms to 1000 rpms at the propeller. A propeller shaft COUPLING is attached to the output end of the transmission (except on a SAILDRIVE unit). The relevant ABYC Standard is P-4 Marine Inboard Engines and Transmissions.

transmission (radio) – general term for a radio broadcast, such as weather broadcast, emergency message, or a communication between stations.

transmission fluid – the transmission on some engines uses transmission fluid (ATF), and some use other oils. Consult the engine manual, change the fluid at the specified interval, and use only the recommended fluid. Carry spare fluid. Clean transmission fluid is red and clear: if there are red stains under the engine, check the level of fluid in the transmission and look for leaks. If fluid is very dark or milky the cause must be determined and corrected before refilling with clean, new fluid.

transom – the ATHWARTSHIPS part of the STERN. There are different styles of transoms: see the following entries.

transom, canoe stern – a transom that's pointed, like a canoe. A boat with a canoe stern and a pointed BOW is DOUBLE-ENDED or a double-ender. See CANOE STERN for a photo.

transom, reverse – a transom that slopes outward from the deck level to the waterline. This type of transom gives a longer waterline, which increases hull speed, and provides a boarding and swim platform at the STERN.

transom, sugar scoop – a REVERSE TRANSOM.

This racing sloop has a reverse transom and a fast-draining open cockpit.

The reverse transom on *Hot Toddy II* has a nice boarding platform and ladder. The yachts are transiting a lock in Scotland's Crinan Canal.

transom, traditional – a transom that is vertical or slopes forward from the deck level toward the waterline; the lower part of the transom is further forward at the bottom than at the top.

A traditional transom, with folded self-steering gear, on a sturdy Tradewinds 39 twin headsail cruiser. The mainsail has lazyjacks and there's a wind generator on the stern.

transponder – a device that receives a signal, such as a radar beam, and responds with its own signal. A RACON and a SART are two examples of transponders.

Transport Canada – the government agency responsible for regulating Canadian-registered recreational and commercial small vessels. The website has important information for recreational mariners and links to useful websites. The portal is www.tc.gc.ca/eng/marine-menu.htm.

transverse – at right angles to the CENTERLINE; ATHWARTSHIPS, as in "transverse frames."

traveler – a device (usually a track or bar mounted ATHWARTSHIPS) to which the MAINSHEET is attached, allowing the angle of the BOOM to be changed on different POINTS OF SAIL. A HORSE is a type of traveler. Not all sailboats have a traveler.

Travelift® – brand name for a MARINE HOIST, frequently used as a generic term.

trawling – a vessel fishing with nets or trawls that restrict maneuverability is a fishing vessel under the NAVIGATION RULES 3(c). A vessel TROLLING is not a fishing vessel under the Rules.

triatic, triatic stay – a STAY that runs between the two mastheads on a SCHOONER, KETCH, or YAWL. The triatic provides mutual support to both masts. Not all two-masted vessels have a triatic.

tricolor – a red, green, and white NAVIGATION LIGHT combined into one unit at the top of the mast on sailing vessels less than 20m/65.6ft when sailing (not when MOTORSAILING). If you are sailing with a tricolor and then turn on the engine, even if the sails are set, you must turn off the tricolor and use only the prescribed lights for a power-driven vessel, which are red and green SIDELIGHTS, a white MASTHEAD LIGHT above the sidelights, and a white STERN LIGHT.

"trick," "trick at the helm" – the time spent at the helm. "You've had such a long trick, you must be tired." "Wake up, it's your trick."

trim – (1) adjusting the sails with the SHEETS or other control lines. Proper sail trim is a complex and interesting subject. Good racing sailors understand SAIL TRIM, and a cruising sailor benefits from crewing on a racing boat. (2) adjusting the way the boat floats (the trim) by moving people or gear.

trimaran – a vessel with three hulls, constructed with two smaller hulls (outriggers or amas) connected to the larger center hull by STRUTS. Trimarans can be sail or power vessels.

The 75ft/22.9m ocean-racing trimaran ex-*B&Q Castorama*, in which Ellen MacArthur (now Dame Ellen) sailed around the world solo in 71 days in 2005.

A Zefyr 43/13.1m trimaran with airfoil Wingsails. Designed by John Walker, four of these ocean-going yachts were built.

trip line, tripping line, buoy rope – a line fastened to the CROWN of an anchor before lowering it, to enable the anchor to be retrieved if it fouls (gets stuck) on the bottom. The upper end of the line is attached to a small buoy or float. Have enough line on the buoy to account for high tide. A trip line isn't always used, but if there's a possibility that the anchor might become caught, use a trip line.

trip, to – to retrieve an anchor with a tripping line. See previous entry.

trip plan –another name for a FLOAT PLAN.

trolling – fishing with lines over the side of the boat. A vessel fishing with lines that do not restrict maneuverability is *not* a fishing vessel under the NAVIGATION RULES, 3(c). A vessel TRAWLING is a fishing vessel according to the Rules.

tropical cyclone – an organized LOW PRESSURE SYSTEM that develops over tropical or subtropical waters.

tropical depression – a TROPICAL CYCLONE that has maximum sustained surface winds of 33 knots. It's the stage of development between a TROPOCAL DISTURBANCE and a TROPICAL STORM.

tropical disturbance – a weather system of organized thunderstorms over tropical or subtropical waters, with a diameter of approximately 100-300NM. It's the stage of development before a TROPICAL DEPRESSION.

tropical storm – a TROPICAL CYCLONE that has maximum sustained surface winds from 34 to 63 knots. At this stage the NATIONAL HURRICANE CENTER gives the storm a name, a tradition that began in the 1940s. The practice of alternating male and female names began in 1979. Tropical storms in the Northeast and Northwest Pacific BASIN are also named.

tropical waters – the ocean waters between approximately 23°N and 23°S. LOW PRESSURE SYSTEMS in these waters gain strength traveling over the warm waters, and may develop into HURRICANES.

trough, TROF (on a SYNOPTIC) – (1) An elongated area of relatively low pressure, usually not associated with a closed circulation, and this distinguishes it from a LOW PRESSURE SYSTEM. However, a large trough may have one or more LOWS in it. A trough is typically associated with a VEERING wind shift. It's the opposite of a ridge. (2) a deep trench in the ocean. (3) the lowest part of a wave between two crests.

truck, mast truck – the top of the mast.

true, true course, true direction – the direction in degrees with reference to TRUE NORTH. Lines plotted on a chart using the outer COPASS ROSE indicate true directions. The abbreviation for a true direction is a capital T (285°T), which is used when writing in a log. *See also* MAGNETIC NORTH, MAGNETIC COURSE, COMPASS COURSE.

true bearing – the direction in degrees measured with reference to TRUE NORTH *from* one location *to* another location. BEARING lines plotted on a chart using the outer COMPASS ROSE are true bearings. The label for a true direction is a capital T (309°T), which is used when writing in a log.

true north – the north indicated on a CHART on the outer COMPASS ROSE, and the direction of the geographical north pole.

true wind – the wind direction and speed that you feel when the boat isn't moving or when you're stationary on land. The APPARENT WIND is what you feel when the boat's moving.

trunk – *see* CENTERBOARD TRUNK.

trysail, storm trysail (pronounced **try** s'l), **storm try** – a small triangular sail used on the MAST in place of the MAINSAIL in very strong winds. The LUFF attaches to the mast, but not to the BOOM. The trysail SHEET(s) (one or two sheets like on a JIB) are tied to the CLEW and led back to the COCKPIT WINCHES. When a trysail is used the mainsail must be removed, and the boom lowered and lashed down. Because it isn't easy to remove the mainsail in rough seas, some boats have a second track on the mast for the trysail. If the boat has in-mast roller furling, a second track is necessary. With a second track the trysail can be attached to it and stowed in its bag at the base of the mast, with sheet(s) attached, ready for use. Furl the main, secure the boom, and hoist the trysail.

TSS – abbreviation for TRAFFIC SEPARATION SCHEME.

tsunami (pronounced tsoo **na** mee or soo **na** mee) – a series of very long ocean waves, often over 50NM in length or more, with a WAVE PERIOD of tens of minutes. Tsunami may be created by an earthquake on or near the sea floor, an underwater volcano, or an underwater landslide. In the open ocean the height of a tsunami wave is very small (under a foot/30cm), and the wave may not be noticed by a vessel. The waves travel at very high speeds, sometimes over 400 knots, and in the open ocean they don't lose much energy. When tsunami reach shallower water as they approach land, they slow down and become steeper, growing to great heights, from 30ft/10m to as much as 100ft/30m. If a tsunami is funneled toward land through a bay or harbor, the size of the wave can be further increased. Because of the amount of water and great energy of tsunami they can devastate coastal areas, as we've seen on TV and in disaster movies.

tumblehome – the inward curve of a vessel's TOPSIDES toward the deck at or near the SHEER line.

tune, tuning – (1) the process of setting up the rigging to its optimal tension, so that it's not too loose or too tight. Use a RIGGING TENSION GAUGE to achieve the desired tension. (2) adjusting a SINGLE-SIDEBAND radio or radar to maximize the reception and transmission of signals.

Turk's Head knot – a decorative and practical knot worked around a round object, such as a steering wheel, handrail, or a person's wrist as a bracelet.

turnbuckle, rigging screw – a metal fitting (with two screw studs) used at the lower end of the SHROUDS and STAYS, other STANDING RIGGING, or LIFELINES. It adjusts the tension of the wire or rod. Rigging turnbuckles are attached to CHAINPLATES at the deck; they may also be used ALOFT on INTERMEDIATE SHROUDS. Use COTTER PINS or an alternative in the holes in the threaded parts to prevent them from turning. An ANTI-SEIZING compound on the turnbuckle studs will help prevent GALLING. *See* the next entry.

turnbuckle body – the body is the center part of the turnbuckle, into which the two threaded studs screw. There are two types: open-body turnbuckles are usually (but not always) used on rigging, and closed-body on LIFELINES or small diameter wires. It's easy to inspect the threads of an open-body turnbuckle. Closed-body turnbuckles are more streamlined, and they don't need COTTER PINS (they have a securing nut). Closed-body turnbuckles are available for rigging sizes up to quarter-inch/6mm, and open-body turnbuckles for small and large diameter rigging.

turnbuckle boot – a metal or plastic tube, or a cloth or leather covering placed over turnbuckles to cover the COTTER PINS and prevent things from snagging on the turnbuckles. Boots may be a better choice than using tape to cover cotter pins on turnbuckles, because CREVICE CORROSION can occur under tape.

turn of the bilge – *see* BILGE, TURN OF.

turn of the tide – *see* TIDE, TURN OF.

turning basin – a dredged area in a harbor where a large vessel can turn.

turtle or hood – a cover forward of the COMPANIONWAY into which the companionway hatch slides when it's open. "My sunglasses got stuck under the turtle when Richard opened the hatch."

twin-screw vessel – a vessel with two propellers. A vessel with one prop is a single-screw vessel. A twin screw vessel is usually easily able to perform a STANDING TURN.

two-block, two-blocked – (1) to pull a TACKLE together so its blocks touch. "Please two-block the VANG before you put it away." (2) describes a tackle with the blocks touching. "The tackle's two-blocked and I can't pull any further."

two-stage cooling system – a type of engine COOLING SYSTEM.

typhoon – a hurricane in the Pacific that occurs north of the equator and west of the INTERNATIONAL DATELINE. A typhoon is a TROPICAL CYCLONE with sustained surface winds of 64 knots or greater. Typhoons are named, as are hurricanes.

typhoon season – logically, the part of the year that has a relatively high incidence of TROPICAL CYCLONES. In the western North Pacific, the typhoon season is from July 1 to December 15. Tropical cyclones can occur year-round in any basin.

typhoon, super – a typhoon with winds of at least 130 kn/150mph, equal to a Category 4 or 5 hurricane (on the SAFFIR-SIMPSON HURRICANE WIND SCALE).

Typhoon "Tip" – a huge typhoon in the Western Pacific in October, 1979. Tip holds the record for the largest CYCLONE in diameter, 1350NM wide, and, on October 12, the lowest BAROMETRIC PRESSURE ever recorded on earth, 869mb. Maximum winds were clocked by reconnaissance aircraft at 190 mph.

U

UHF – abbreviation for Ultra High Frequency radio waves between 300MHz and 3GHz.

UL – abbreviation for UNDERWRITER'S LABORATORIES.

uncertainty, area of – an area around a DEAD-RECKONING (DR) position or ESTIMATED POSITION (EP) where the boat *may* be located, lacking precise positioning. If two or more LINES OF POSITION cross at angles of less than about

60°, there will be doubt as to the exact position. If three or more lines of position are crossed, a small triangle results, which is the area of uncertainty. When using a DR or EP, draw a circle around the position, with a radius that estimates the possible error. As a rule of thumb, in calm conditions with no current or LEEWAY, make the radius of the circle 5% of the distance you traveled from the last FIX. In conditions where there is current and/or leeway affecting the boat, make the radius of the circle 10% of the distance since the last fix. In rough conditions or when you've been TACKING a lot make the radius 15% of the distance since the last fix. Draw the circle around the DR or EP, and note if there are any hazards in or near the circle. Always leave a margin for safety.

uncorrecting – the process of converting a TRUE direction to a MAGNETIC or COMPASS direction. To go from true to magnetic or compass, *add* westerly VARIATION and/or DEVIATION (subtract easterly variation or deviation) to the true direction. The algebraic sum of variation and deviation may be used when converting directly from true to compass. The process of converting from compass to magnetic or true is called CORECTING. In casual use "correcting" is used to mean both uncorrecting or correcting. For an easy method, see CONVERSION OF DIRECTIONS.

underbody – all of the hull below the waterline.

underway – (1) Rule 3(i) of the NAVIGATION RULES defines underway as not anchored, aground, or made fast to the shore. This is a very important definition. As soon as you cast off the last mooring line or raise the anchor off the bottom you are underway. A vessel dragging anchor or drifting is underway. Underway but not making way (i.e. stopped in the water) is an important distinction for the SOUND SIGNALS IN RESTRICTED VISIBILITY; see Rule 35(a,b). (2) in motion. "We were underway for an hour when we realized we forgot Tom."

underwater epoxy – an epoxy patching material that sets in damp or wet conditions, as well as when it's dry. It should be a part of a DAMAGE CONTROL KIT. It's available in a paste form and in epoxy-impregnated tape or cloth.

Underwriter's Laboratories, UL – specific UL fire standards for flammability and smoke toxicity apply to marine products used in vessel construction and furnishing. Compliance with UL regulations is assured by regular inspections at manufacturing sites. See the bibliography under "Safety" for a link to the UL marine page.

unfurl – to set a sail, applied to unrolling a ROLLER-FURLING sail. The opposite is FURL.

Union Jack – a special maritime flag of the United States, which consists of the blue canton with 50 stars (as on the American flag). U.S. Navy, Coast Guard, and other government vessels fly the Jack from a BOW staff when anchored or moored (not UNDERWAY). Private U.S. vessels may fly the Union Jack on a bow staff when anchored or moored.

United Nations Convention on the Law of the Sea – the formal name for the LAW OF THE SEA.

United States Power Squadrons® – a non-profit educational, public service, and social organization for power and sail boaters. Local Squadrons regularly offer basic boating safety courses, which may meet state requirements for boater certification or licensing. The basic course is open to the general public. Anyone may join a local Squadron, and take advantage of their more advanced educational offerings, which include seamanship, piloting, celestial navigation, cruise planning, engine maintenance, marine electronics, sailing and more. Experienced member instructors teach the courses, using good textbooks and instructional materials. Local Squadrons work with the U.S. COAST GUARD AUXILIARY to conduct free VESSEL SAFETY CHECKS, and they participate in many community service activities. *See* www.usps.org.

unlay, unlayed – (1) to separate the strands of a rope for SPLICING. (2) when a rope is twisted against its LAY or when the end is not heat-sealed or WHIPPED it can become unlayed into loose strands.

unsettled weather – weather that can change at any time; implies a change to worse weather. See the next entry.

unstable, unstable atmosphere – used to describe weather conditions which can change rapidly, such as when cold air moves in over warm air or water. When the atmosphere is unstable, CONVECTION begins, creating cumulus and cumulonimbus CLOUDS, which can lead to thunderstorms. The opposite is a STABLE ATMOSPHERE.

unstayed mast, unstayed rig – see MAST, UNSTAYED.

unstep – to remove the mast from the boat. Putting it in the boat is to step it.

up – a direction toward the wind. HEAD UP and HARDEN UP are also used to mean toward the wind. Away from the wind is down.

"up and down" – when the anchor is free of the bottom, the RODE is straight up and down. When weighing anchor the crew on the BOW should tell the helmsman that the anchor is "up and down." When the anchor's off the bottom the vessel is UNDERWAY, according to the NAVIGATION RULES.

upbound – a vessel traveling against the current. A vessel traveling with the current is downbound. The terms are used in the NAVIGATION RULES.

uppers – SHROUDS that extend from the deck to the top of the mast.

upslope winds – *see* WINDS, ANABATIC.

upstream – against the current; UPBOUND, or UP TIDE. The opposite is DOWNSTREAM.

up tide – the direction where the current is coming from. Heading into a current is working up tide or the boat is UPBOUND. "With this much current we should stay up tide of the dock so we won't get swept past it." DOWN TIDE or DOWNBOUND is the direction away from where the current is coming from; traveling in the same direction as the current.

upwelling – water rising from the depths toward the surface. Upwelling can be caused by ocean currents, persistent winds, and/or by changes in the topography of the bottom. Upwelling brings food for fish to the surface. Upwelling occurs near BANKS, which makes them good fishing grounds.

upwind – toward the wind, to WINDWARD. BEATING is sailing upwind. The opposite is downwind.

urgency or urgent communication – non-DISTRESS communication; a PAN PAN call.

U.S.C. – abbreviation for the U.S. Code, the general and permanent laws of the United States. Sections of the Code apply to vessels, and are embodied in the U.S. Coast Guard NAVIGATION RULES. Some sections of the CFR also apply to vessels.

USCG – abbreviation for U.S. COAST GUARD.

U.S. Coast Pilot® – *see* COAST PILOT, U.S.

U.S. Coast Guard, USCG – a branch of the U.S. Armed Forces, founded in 1790, with multiple modern missions. The Coast Guard is responsible for maritime security, law enforcement, search and rescue, marine environmental protection, and the maintenance of river, coastal, and offshore AIDS TO NAVIGATION. Its jurisdiction covers U.S. as well as INTERNATIONAL WATERS. The Coast Guard motto is "Semper Paratus," (Always Prepared). The USCG maintains a number of useful and well-done websites with information of interest to small craft as well as ships. For recreational vessels, see the Boating Safety Resource Center at www.uscgboating.org, and the next entry.

U.S. Coast Guard Auxiliary – a volunteer organization of over 30,000 members, dedicated to supporting the U.S. Coast Guard through safety patrols, safe boating courses, VESSEL SAFETY CHECKS, and environmental protection activities. "The Auxiliary has members in all 50 states, Puerto Rico, the Virgin Islands, American Samoa, and Guam. Membership is open to men and women, 17 years or older, U.S. citizens of all states and territories, civilians or active duty or former members of any of the uniformed services and their Reserve components, including the Coast Guard. Facility (radio station, boat or aircraft) ownership is desirable but not mandatory." *See* www.cgaux.org. The CANADIAN COAST GUARD AUXILIARY performs similar functions.

U.S. Coast Guard required safety equipment – *See* SAFEY, EQUIPMENT, U.S. COAST GUARD.

U.S. Coast Guard standards – many USCG safety standards and regulations are based on ABYC, UL, NFPA®, international maritime organization standards, and other certifying agencies' marine standards.

U.S. Code – *see* U.S.C.

U.S. Code of Federal Regulations – *see* CFR.

U.S. Power Squadrons – *see* UNITED STATES POWER SQUADRONS®.

USS – abbreviation for United States Ship, used with the name of a U.S. naval vessel. *USS George H.W. Bush*.

US Sailing – the national governing body for U.S. sailing activities from junior sailing to the Olympics and offshore racing. The website at www.ussailing.org has links to training and certification courses for sail and power. One of US Sailing's most important service activities is its SAFETY AT SEA seminars. See the bibliography under "Safety" for links to safety studies on the US Sailing website.

UTC – the usual way of referring to COORDINATED UNIVERSAL TIME.

V

V-belt – this important item on the engine or generator is essential; carry spares of the proper length and type. Some equipment, such as a large ALTERNATOR or high capacity pump, requires two belts. General V-belt specifications include overall length, cross-section (the angle of the V), and the duty rating (heavy or light duty). Some belts are ribbed on the outside or inside. Keep the belt adjusted to the proper tension; it stretches as it's used. If a belt squeals when the engine is first started the belt is slipping (too loose or glazed and worn). A belt dressing spray product can help correct slipping, but only up to a point. Measure belt tension with a gauge, or push down lightly on the belt: it should deflect no more than about 3/4in/20mm. If there's black dust on the engine or associated equipment the V-belt is too loose, the wrong size (belt angle), or it's wearing out from age or misalignment.

vacuum gauge – a gauge that indicates how easily the fuel is flowing through the fuel system, by reading the vacuum in a fuel line. As a FUEL FILTER becomes clogged, the vacuum increases, and the needle on the gauge moves toward a "red zone" or a higher number. Use a vacuum gauge to monitor the condition of fuel filters, because it warns before a filter becomes so clogged that the engine stops. Vacuum gauges are available for mounting directly on top of a particular brand of diesel fuel filter, or for remote mounting where it's more visible than on top of a filter. A vacuum gauge is relatively easy to install, and it's a good safety feature.

Valid Time, VT – the period of time during which a weather forecast or warning is valid, until it's updated or superseded by a new forecast. The VT is expressed in UTC or Z time. The abbreviation is used on SYNOPTIC charts.

valve, ball – *see* BALL VALVE.

valve, check – *see* CHECK VALVE.

vane steering, vane gear – a type of SELF-STEERING that doesn't require electric power.

vang, boom vang – a TACKLE or other piece of equipment that pulls the BOOM downwards, helping to control the shape of the sail, particularly when the boom is out to the side when REACHING or RUNNING. The vang is attached to the boom, usually near the mid-point, and the other end of the vang goes to near the bottom of the MAST (rigid boom vang),

A rigid boom vang.

or to a strong point AMIDSHIPS on the deck or RAIL (tackle vang). A vang is sometimes used as a PREVENTER, but it's not as effective as a real preventer. For another photo see ROLLER FURLING.

variable pitch propeller – *see* PROPELLER, VARIABLE PITCH.

variation – the difference between TRUE NORTH and MAGNETIC NORTH, expressed in degrees east or west. Variation changes with geographic location. The inner COMPASS ROSE near the area where a vessel operates indicates the variation for the area. The process of applying variation to a true direction to determine a magnetic course or BEARING is called UNCORRECTING. See CONVERSION OF DIRECTIONS for an easy method of applying variation and DEVIATION.

vector chart – *see* CHART, VECTOR.

vector diagram, vector triangle – a graphic solution for calculations when navigating in a current. Use a vector diagram to calculate the SET and DRIFT of a current, to determine a course to steer when set and drift are known, or to analyze the effect of a current on the boat's SPEED OVER THE GROUND (and your ETA to a location). It's not difficult to learn to do vector diagrams, and they're important PILOTING tools that don't rely on electronics. CHAPMAN and navigation books discuss vector diagrams.

veer – (1) a clockwise wind shift in the Northern Hemisphere; counter-clockwise (anticlockwise) in the Southern Hemisphere. The opposite of veer is BACK. "When the cold front passes the wind will veer to the northwest." "The wind has been veering all day." (2) when the wind shifts AFT in relation to the boat it veers. (3) to let out more rope or chain in a controlled manner, as with an anchor RODE. "I'm going to veer another 25 feet of chain."

vented loop – another name for an ANTI-SIPHON VALVE.

Venturi effect – when air or liquid passes through a constriction it accelerates, because of higher pressure on the UPWIND or UPSTREAM side of the constriction and lower pressure on the downstream side as the air or liquid exits. The Venturi effect is used to explain (without getting too technical) how an aircraft wing or a sail gets its lift: the air moves faster across the curved portion of the airfoil (high speed, low pressure), and slower on the straight side (slow speed, high pressure), thus creating lift on the curved side. The Venturi effect is sometimes used to explain the SLOT EFFECT, but it's a topic of debate among sailors. GAP WINDS are the result of the Venturi effect.

vertical sextant angle – *see* SEXTANT ANGLE, VERTICAL.

vertical danger angle – *see* DANGER ANGLE, VERTICAL.

vessel – in the NAVIGATION RULES (3,a) "the word 'vessel' includes every description of water craft, including nondisplacement craft, WIG CRAFT and seaplanes used or capable of being used as a means of transportation on the water."

vessel safety check – the U.S. COAST GUARD AUXILIARY, the U.S. POWER SQUADRON, the CANADIAN POWER AND SAIL SQUADRONS, and boating organizations in other countries offer a free vessel safety check (courtesy exam) upon request. The examiner goes over the boat with a list of required equipment. In the U.S. and Canada the examiner is a trained specialist and a member of the Coast Guard Auxiliary or the Power Squadron. In other countries the examiners are members of organizations authorized to conduct the safety checks. During the vessel checkout, the examiner also makes recommendations and discusses safety issues that will help to make you safer on the water. There are *no* government reports involved. It's an excellent way to be sure your vessel complies with Coast Guard and local boating safety requirements. In the U.S. see www.safetyseal.net for information about this important, free safety check.

Vessel Traffic Service, VTS – a system of active monitoring and communication for vessels operating in a TRAFFIC SEPARATION SCHEME (TSS) area. Rule 10 of the NAVIGATION RULES prescribes the rules for *all* vessels operating in or near a Traffic Separation Scheme. These areas are established in busy, confined waterways. A VTS is designed to prevent collisions and groundings, facilitate the smooth flow of shipping, and assist safe navigation in all weather. There are two types of VTS: (1) a surveilled system with land-based sensors, such as radar, AIS and/or closed-circuit TV, that send data to the VTS control office. (2) a non-surveilled system, which has one or more reporting points where ships are required to radio their identity, course, speed, and other information to VTS control. Some VTS control centers require or request that small vessels identify themselves when operating in a VTS, so that they can warn shipping of the presence of small craft. Call VTS Control and announce your presence; this is especially important in RESTRICTED VISIBILITY. The appropriate VHF channels are indicated on charts and in COAST PILOTS and NAUTICAL ALMANACS.

The U.S. Coast Guard operates 12 Vessel Traffic Centers (VTC): Prince William Sound (Valdez), Puget Sound (Seattle), San Francisco, Los Angeles/ Long Beach, Houston-Galveston, Port Arthur, Berwick Bay (LA), New Orleans, Louisville, Saint Mary's River (Sault-Ste. Marie), Tampa, and New York. The areas and the VHF contact channels are listed in the back of the U.S. *Navigation Rules* book and in the relevant U.S.COAST PILOTS. There are several VTS services for Bermuda. In Canada, the VTS areas are Vancouver, Tofino, Prince Rupert, Halifax, the Straits of Canso, Port aux Basques, Placentia Bay, St. John's, Northumberland Strait, and the St. Lawrence Waterway, plus some local VTS zones. In the UK VTS operates at the Severn River, Southampton, Dover Strait, Port of London, and the Humber Estuary. VTS areas in France are at Le Havre, Marseille, and Rouen. For worldwide VTS information see www.worldvtsguide.org.

VHF – (1) abbreviation for very high frequency radio signals; 30-300MHz. (2) a type of marine radiotelephone.

VHF channels – *see* CHANNELS, VHF RADIOTELEPHONE.

VHF radiotelephone – it transmits and receives signals in line-of-sight, over distances of approximately 20-30 miles. If the radio antenna is low and/ or there are high obstructions between you and the other radio antenna you may not be able to communicate. A handheld VHF doesn't have as great a range as a FIXED-MOUNT VHF because the handheld's antenna is low, and a handheld doesn't have as much power as a fixed-mount VHF.

virtual aid to navigation – to put an AIS signal electronically in a specific place to warn of a new hazard to navigation, a boundary area, or to replace a missing aid to navigation. The coast guard can "ghost in" an AIS signal (a virtual aid to navigation) where necessary, a great safety feature.

visibility, restricted – an indefinite term describing visibility which is impaired to some degree by fog, rain, snow, dust, smog, haze, smoke, sandstorm, or other cause. Night itself is *not* restricted visibility. Rule 19 of the NAVIGATION RULES has the rules for the conduct of vessels in restricted visibility, and Rule 35 specifies the SOUND SIGNALS for RESTRICTED VISIBILITY. If you are *near* an area of restricted visibility, you are considered to be *in* restricted visibility, even if you can see around you. Something may be lurking in the fog and headed your way.

visibility, restricted, sound signals – *see* SOUND SIGNALS, RESTRICTED VISIBILITY.

visibility, arc of – *see* ARC OF VISIBILITY.

visual navigation – navigating or PILOTING without the aid of electronics; using your eyes, the compass, and a HAND-BEARING COMPASS or COMPASS BINOCULARS. No matter how sophisticated the electronics are on a vessel, problems can occur with the electrical system on the boat, or with electronic navigation system itself. GPS or AIS can suffer an outage or fail altogether, and the user can make a mistake using the electronics or when entering COORDINATES or other data into the electronics. Learn piloting and "LOOK OUT THE WINDOW."

volt, V – the basic unit of "pressure" in an AC or DC electrical circuit. Volts are used in simple calculations (such as the WATTAGE FORMULA) to determine wire size and the size of CIRCUIT BEAKERS or FUSES. See the next three entries.

voltage drop – the amount of voltage lost in a circuit due to the wire size (AWG) and length, and the presence of corrosion in circuit components that increase the RESISTANCE. Technical resources have tables of voltage drop for particular wire sizes and lengths. For equipment related to safety (such as NAVIGATION LIGHTS and bilge pumps) wires should be sized to meet a 3% voltage drop standard. For non-safety related equipment a 10% drop may be acceptable.

voltage, dual – some equipment is designed to operate on more than one voltage. The information is on the equipment itself, in its instruction manual, or in a marine supply catalog.

voltmeter – a digital or analog meter that measures VOLTS in a circuit. A voltmeter that also measures OHMS (resistance) is called a volt-ohm meter or VOM. A MULTIMETER is a voltmeter.

voluntary-equipped – a term used to identify a vessel that is *not* required by Coast Guard, GMDSS, SOLAS, or IMO regulations to have certain radio or other equipment aboard. Most recreational vessels fall into this category. A COMPULSORY-EQUIPPED vessel must comply with specific regulations.

VOM – abbreviation for volt-ohm meter; a VOLTMETER.

voyage – a complete trip composed of several parts (legs) or PASSAGES; a trip at sea.

VT – abbreviation for VALID TIME, used on SYNOPTICS and in some weather forecasts.

VTS – abbreviation for VESSEL TRAFFIC SERVICE.

W

WAAS – abbreviation for Wide Area Augmentation System. This new electronic navigation system consists of satellites and ground stations that provide GPS signal "corrections" to a WAAS receiver, to improve the accuracy of positions. The repeatable accuracy (return to the same position 95% of the time) for a WAAS receiver is advertised to be better than 10ft/3m. The U.S. Federal Aviation Administration (FAA) and the Department of Transportation (DOT) are developing this system. As of 2010 WAAS was only available in North America, but governments in other countries are developing compatible systems that offer similar accuracy.

wake – the turbulent water behind a vessel as it moves ahead. This water becomes the WASH after the vessel passes by a location. Sailboats create less wake than power vessels. Wake is frequently used as a synonym for wash.

warm front – *see* FRONT, WARM.

warp, to warp – (1) a rope used as a mooring line; a mooring warp. (2) to move a vessel using lines. "We can warp the boat to the other side of the dock."

warships – under Rule 1(c) of the NAVIGATION RULES warships, vessels under convoy, and fishing vessels fishing as a fleet may display additional lights, DAYSHAPES, or use additional whistle signals which, so far as possible, do not conflict with those authorized elsewhere in the Rules.

wash – the waves created by a vessel. The wash from a ship can be dangerous to smaller vessels. A vessel is legally responsible for any damage done by its WAKE or wash. Wake is frequently used as a synonym for wash.

washboards – removable boards used to close the COMPANIONWAY.

watch, watchstander – (1) the crew (one or more persons) on lookout duty. Rule 5 of the NAVIGATION RULES specifies that "a proper look-out by sight and hearing shall be maintained at all times by all available means." A watchstander must be knowledgeable enough to perform the duties required. Assigning someone who isn't qualified is an invitation to trouble. The skipper should ask any crew member who is assigned to a night watch if he/she is color blind; not being able to distinguish the colors of NAVIGATION LIGHTS or aids to navigation could be deadly. A person on watch shouldn't have other duties that distract from maintaining a proper lookout. Having written STANDING ORDERS are a good way to help the crew perform their necessary duties while on watch. (2) a watch is the period of time designated for a person to be on lookout duty. The watch schedule lists the times and crewmembers assigned to each period. "You're on watch from 0400 to 0600." (3) a listening watch maintained on a radio; a RADIO WATCH.

watch, change of, or relieving the watch – when the watch changes and another person takes over, communicate clearly the following information to the oncoming watch:

- Where we are on the chart or CHART PLOTTER.
- Course to steer.
- Our last positive position FIX.
- Upcoming course changes and navigation aids expected.
- Essential tide or current information.
- Weather information now and expected.
- Other vessels in the area, visible or on radar and/or AIS.
- Problems or concerns the watch should be aware of.

Make sure the person understands by repeating what you said, not just nodding or grunting - he or she may be sleepy! It's up to the skipper or the person going off watch to determine if the oncoming crew is fit to stand a watch. If a person seems ill, sleepy, confused or otherwise not competent, an alert crewmember must take over.

watching properly – a lighted aid to navigation that's operating and exhibiting its correct CHARACTERISTIC. The phrase is used in VHF NOTICES TO MARINERS, to indicate that a malfunctioning aid has been restored to its proper operational status.

watch-on-watch – being on watch one period after the other without time off. It's exhausting, but sometimes necessary if a member of a shorthanded crew is unable to stand his or her watch. "I had to stand watch-on-watch when Jack became ill."

watch, radio or radio watch keeping – the NAVIGATION RULES specify that any vessel equipped with a VHF radio (whether VOLUNTARY or COMPULSORY-EQUIPPED) must maintain a listening watch on Channel 16 whenever the radio is not being used to communicate. In addition, the BRIDGE-TO-BRIDGE RADIOTELEPHONE REGULATIONS require certain vessels to maintain a watch on **CHANNEL 13** (and Channel 16) while navigating on U.S. INLAND WATERS. When operating in a VESSEL TRAFFIC SERVICE (VTS) area, vessels required to monitor Channel 13 must also maintain watch on the designated VTS frequency, instead of Channel 16. Small vessels should understand what channels these vessels use, in case they need to communicate with them, and to hear communications between large vessels that may be nearby.

water ballast – *see* BALLAST, WATER.

water, emergency – *see* EMERGENCY WATER SUPPLY.

watercraft, personal – *see* PERSONAL WATERCRAFT.

water generator – *see* GENERATOR, WATER.

waterlift muffler – *see* MUFFLER, EXHAUST.

waterline – (1) where the water lies along the hull when the boat is at rest. It may be the designed waterline (DWL) or a different one, based on the loading of the vessel or other factors. (2) where the land and the water meet.

watermaker, desalinator – equipment designed to produce fresh, potable water from seawater. Desalination may be accomplished by a membrane process or reverse-osmosis. Permanently-mounted watermakers are available, and a small, hand-operated watermaker should be part of an ABANDON SHIP KIT.

water separator – a type FUEL FILTER that removes water from the fuel.

waterspout – a tornado over the water, most common over tropical or sub-tropical waters. It shows up on radar. Fortunately, it's a rare event.

water system, potable – this can be a pressurized system, a foot-pump system, or a combination system. The relevant ABYC Standard is H-23 Installation of Potable Water Systems for Use on Boats.

water temperature, engine – *see* ENGINE INSTRUMENTS.

water temperature sender – a small device mounted on the engine that senses the engine cooling water temperature and sends it to a gauge on the instrument panel. If the water temperature gauge is not working, check the sender first; a wire may have come off or the sender needs to be replaced, a fairly easy task.

waterway – a general term for navigable water. A FAIRWAY is the part of a waterway that's used by many vessels entering and leaving harbors and ports.

waters, coastal or inshore waters – an indefinite term that includes the waters from the shore of a mainland or an island, including bays, harbors, and sounds, extending perhaps as far out as 60NM. Coast guards and weather services define what they consider to be coastal or inshore waters. Inshore waters are not the same as INLAND WATERS, which is a specific distinction in the NAVIGATION RULES.

waters, inland – see INLAND WATERS.

waters, offshore – an indefinite term that includes the waters of oceans, gulfs, and seas beyond coastal waters. Offshore waters extend out to a specified distance from the coast, to a specified DEPTH CONTOUR, or cover an area defined by LATITUDE and LONGITUDE coordinates. Coast guards and weather services define what they consider to be offshore waters.

watt – a unit of electrical power that describes how "fast" AC or DC electrical equipment uses electrical energy. For example, a VHF radio transmitter may use 25 watts when transmitting; an AC electric heater may use 1500 watts when operating. Wattage is indicated on equipment labels and in manuals. See the next two entries.

wattage – the number of AC or DC WATTS used by an operating piece of electrical equipment. Find wattage information in an equipment manual, on a label, in a marine supply catalog, or marked on a light bulb or its packaging. Knowing the wattage is important to determine if the wiring in a circuit and the CIRCUIT BREAKER/FUSE has the capacity to carry the load of multiple items or one piece equipment without overheating, tripping the circuit breaker, or causing the equipment to malfunction (because of VOLTAGE DROP). Use the WATTAGE FORMULA to make these calculations.

wattage formula – a simple formula used to calculate WATTS, AMPS, and VOLTS in an AC or DC circuit when two of the three factors are known. It is W = VA. (Watts equal volts times amps. "West Virginia" is a memory aid.) Use it to calculate the total amperage draw of equipment and light bulbs when estimating how long electrical equipment can be operated before the boat's battery drains too much. Or it may be used to calculate the size of the CIRCUIT BREAKER/FUSE needed when adding or installing electrical equipment.

For example: what size (the amp rating) circuit breaker should be used for a 100-watt spotlight, and the boat has 12 VDC power? Divide 100 watts by 12 volts, which gives 8.3. The nearest size larger circuit breaker is probably 10 amps, so you need a 10A circuit breaker. It's handy if the instructions or the label on the equipment specifies the amps, so you don't have to calculate.

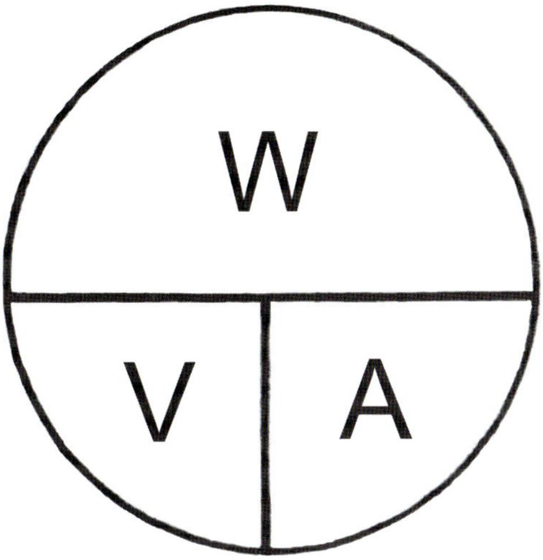

wattage formula

To determine one of the numbers, put your finger over the one you want, and do the mathematical operation indicated by the position of the other two factors.

wattmeter – a device that measures WATTS. One use for a wattmeter is to measure the output power of a radio transmitter.

wave basin, wave trap – an area outside an inner harbor that has constructions, seawalls, or BREAKWATERS to reduce the effect of waves as they approach the harbor.

wave, breaking – when a wave reaches a certain height, the top of the wave breaks into foam and the wave collapses. We see breaking waves at a beach, where they can be small or large enough to surf. As a wave encounters shallow water, it becomes steeper and breaks. Wind strength, current, and depth influence when waves will begin to break. Shallow water is a relative term in the ocean: certain bottom features such as SEAMOUNTS, BANKS, or obstructions near the surface can create conditions that foster breaking waves, whereas, in nearby deeper water the waves may be less likely to break. Some of these areas are indicated on charts with the notation "breaks" or "breaking waves." Wave theory is complex, but a basic understanding of the factors that create breaking waves is important for mariners to understand. **WHITECAPS** are various-sized breaking waves, which can be used to estimate wind strength.

wave energy – the energy or force with which a wave hits something is directly proportional to the square of its height. A 3ft/1m wave has nine times more energy than a 1ft/0.5m wave. Cold air gives more energy to the waves than warm air. In cold winds, seas build up more quickly.

wave height – is measured from **TROUGH** to crest. The height is determined by the wind speed, the **FETCH**, and the length of time it's been blowing. Wave heights in waters near the coast, in shallow water relative to surrounding depths, or with **WIND AGAINST TIDE** can be higher than in open water. Tables of theoretical wave heights, such as those on the **BEAUFORT SCALE**, on weather broadcasts, and in the table below are *estimates* for waves in the open ocean.

FETCH, TIME, and WAVE HEIGHT

	F 4 11-16 kn.			F 5 17-21 kn.			F 6 22-27 kn.			F 7 28-33 kn.		
Fetch	Time	Ht.	Per.	Time	Ht.	Per.	Time	Ht.	Per.	Time	Ht.	Per.
10	3.7	2.6	2.4	3.2	3.5	2.8	2.7	5.0	3.1	2.5	6.0	3.4
20	6.2	3.2	2.9	5.4	4.9	3.3	4.7	7.0	3.8	4.2	8.6	4.3
40	10.3	3.9	3.6	8.9	6.2	4.1	7.8	9.0	4.6	7.1	11.2	4.9
60	14.0	4.0	4.0	12.0	6.8	4.6	10.2	10.3	5.1	9.6	13.2	5.5
80	17.0	4.0	4.1	15.0	7.2	4.9	13.0	11.0	5.6	12.0	14.5	6.0
100	20.0	4.0	4.4	17.5	7.3	5.3	15.1	11.4	6.0	14.0	15.5	6.5
200	33.5	4.3	5.6	29.0	8.0	6.4	25.4	12.2	7.1	23.1	17.5	7.7
300	47.0	4.4	6.3	38.5	8.0	7.1	34.1	13.1	8.0	31.5	18.0	8.7
400				48.0	8.0	7.7	42.2	13.5	8.6	38.8	18.4	9.5
500				58.0	8.0	8.2	49.2	13.8	9.1	45.5	19.1	10.1
600							56.3	13.8	9.5	51.8	19.7	10.5
700										58.5	19.8	11.0
800												
900												
1000												

Fetch = nautical miles. Time = hours. Ht. = wave height in feet. Per. = wave period in seconds.

	F 8 34-40 kn.			F 9 41-47 kn.			F 10 48-55 kn.			F 11 56-63 kn.		
Fetch	Time	Ht.	Per.	Time	Ht.	Per.	Time	Ht.	Per.	Time	Ht.	Per.
10	2.3	7.3	3.9	2.0	8.0	4.1	1.9	10.0	4.2	1.8	10.0	5.0
20	3.9	10.0	4.4	3.5	12.0	5.0	3.2	14.0	5.2	3.0	16.0	5.9
40	6.5	14.0	5.4	5.8	17.7	5.9	5.4	21.0	6.2	5.4	25.0	6.7
60	8.7	17.0	6.0	8.0	21.0	7.9	7.4	25.0	7.0	7.0	27.5	7.5
80	11.0	18.9	6.6	10.0	24.0	7.1	9.3	28.0	7.7	8.6	31.5	7.9
100	12.8	20.5	6.9	11.9	26.5	7.6	11.0	32.0	8.1	10.3	35.0	8.5
200	21.5	23.5	8.5	19.3	32.5	9.2	18.1	40.0	9.5	17.1	46.0	10.3
300	29.0	25.0	9.5	26.2	35.0	10.4	24.3	45.0	11.1	23.2	53.0	11.6
400	35.6	26.0	10.2	32.5	37.0	11.2	30.2	47.5	12.0	28.9	56.0	12.6
500	42.1	27.5	10.9	38.3	38.0	11.9	35.5	49.0	12.7	33.9	58.0	13.4
600	47.7	27.5	11.3	43.6	39.0	12.5	40.3	50.0	13.3	38.7	60.0	14.0
700	53.2	27.5	11.8	49.0	40.0	13.1	45.4	50.5	14.0	43.5	60.5	14.5
800	59.2	27.5	12.3	53.8	40.0	13.5	50.6	51.5	14.5	47.8	61.5	15.0
900				58.2	40.0	14.0	54.6	52.0	14.9	52.0	62.0	15.5
1000							59.3	52.0	15.3	56.3	63.0	16.0

Fetch = nautical miles. Time = hours. Ht. = wave height in feet. Per. = wave period in seconds.

wave height, average – the average wave height is 64% of the SIGNIFICANT WAVE HEIGHT.

wave height, highest – 187% of the SIGNIFICANT WAVE HEIGHT.

wave height, highest 10% – 129% of the SIGNIFICANT WAVE HEIGHT.

wave height, significant (sig wave) – as used in forecasts, observation reports, and wave tables, significant wave height is the average height, from TROUGH to crest, of the *one-third highest* waves in the open ocean. Individual waves and waves near shore can be substantially higher than the significant wave height. Wave theory and observations indicate that the highest individual waves in a typical storm may be approximately two times the significant wave height. A wave higher than twice the significant wave height is an extreme or ROGUE WAVE.

wave length – the distance from crest to crest; approximately equal to five times the WAVE PERIOD squared. A wave with a four second period has a length of 5 x 4 x 4 = 80ft/24m.

wavelength – the physical length of a radio wave. High frequency waves have a short wavelength; low frequency waves have a long wavelength.

wave, parts of – the four parts of an ocean wave are height, length, period, and speed. See the individual wave entries.

wave period – the time, in seconds, between the passage of consecutive wave crests past a fixed point.

wave, rogue – a wave that is much higher and/or steeper than other waves in the prevailing sea or SWELL system; an extreme wave higher than twice the significant wave height. A rogue wave may come from another direction than the main waves in an area, and it can cause damage to large ships. The movie *The Perfect Storm* featured a monster rogue wave. *See* WAVE HEIGHT, SIGNIFICANT.

waves, largest ocean – the Southern Ocean between approximately 40°S and 60°S is home to the largest waves in the world. Here the winds blow unobstructed by land, with a FETCH of thousands of miles. The strong winds and high waves in this part of the world have given special names to high southern latitudes: the "Roaring Forties," "Furious Fifties," and the "Screaming Sixties." Read books by round-the-world racing sailors to see what goes on in these areas.

wave speed – the speed of a wave is three times its PERIOD: for a wave with a four second period the speed is 12 knots. The speed of a WAVE TRAIN is approximately half the speed of the individual waves.

wave, standing – (1) a wave on the surface that doesn't travel any distance, or a wave that goes back and forth between two boundaries, above or under the water. WIND AGAINST TIDE and a TIDAL BORE can create standing waves, which may be surfed or ridden by small boats or surfers for sport. Some standing waves are large and dangerous, as may occur in a TIDE RACE or a SEICHE. (2) a standing wave in a radio transmitter antenna system is caused by a mismatch between the antenna and the antenna cable (the feed line). Using an antenna tuner is one way to correct the mismatch. Consult a radio technician or an amateur (ham) radio book for an explanation of standing waves. Some SINGLE-SIDEBAND or VHF radio manuals discuss measuring the STANDING WAVE RATIO to determine if the system is operating to its full capabilities.

wave steepness – the ratio of WAVE HEIGHT to WAVE LENGTH. It's an indicator of the stability of the wave (resistance to breaking). In the open ocean when wave steepness exceeds a 1:7 ratio; the wave typically becomes unstable and breaks. If there's WIND AGAINST TIDE or the depth decreases waves will break sooner.

waves, wind – the most common type of waves, created by the wind. Wind waves change direction when the wind changes, creating CROSS-SEAS. The direction of wind waves changes more quickly than the direction of SWELLS. The WAVE HEIGHT is determined by the wind speed, the FETCH, and the length of time it's been blowing. See the table with WAVE HEIGHT.

wave train – a series of waves moving in the same direction. When the direction of the wind changes it creates a new wave train, which is overlaid on the previous one, creating confused seas. The speed of a wave train is approximately half the speed of the individual WAVE SPEED.

way – (1) "making way" or "to have way on" are phrases applied to a vessel moving through the water. Both phrases indicate that the vessel is under sail or engine power and is UNDERWAY, according to the NAVIGATION RULES. (2) the inertia of a moving vessel that keeps it moving when the engine or sails are no longer providing motive power. A vessel may be said to "carry a lot of way" which means that she'll drift some distance before coming to a natural stop. Putting the engine in reverse "takes way off," as when approaching a dock or a mooring. "Take all way off before starting the turn." The STOPPING DISTANCE of a vessel is influenced by the amount of way the vessel carries.

waypoint – a location specified by LATITUDE and LONGITUDE, and entered into a GPS or CHART PLOTTER for navigation guidance. The GPS indicates the BEARING and RANGE (distance) to the waypoint as the boat travels. While it may seem obvious, the waypoint coordinates for an object in navigable water should not be the exact position of the navigation aid, but should be offset by approximately 0.1NM (or more) so that the boat won't hit it – yes, it happens more often than you might think. When navigating in RESTRICTED VISIBILITY be aware that the waypoints you choose may also have been chosen by a number of other vessels, who may all converge on the same spot out of the fog. Keep a good lookout when approaching waypoints based on navigation aids, especially in restricted visibility. Take care to enter waypoint COORDINATES carefully into the GPS. Keeping a written log of waypoint coordinates will allow you to check that they are correctly entered, and to cross-check them with the chart, if something seems wrong as you navigate toward a waypoint.

WD-40®– as indispensable as DUCT TAPE on a boat or at home. Use it for freeing frozen fasteners, loosening rusted parts, drying out electrical connections, preventing corrosion, removing sticky residue from tape or product labels, protecting tools from rust, light lubrication, stopping things from squeaking, and many more uses. See the website for more than 2,000 uses for this product afloat and ashore; www.wd40.com.

wear – interchangeable term with JIBE (if the crew knows the words). "We'll have to wear ship in a few minutes."

weather, to weather – (1) a direction toward the wind (to WINDWARD), or toward where the wind is coming from. The wind blows from a WEATHER SHORE out to the water. "It's not going to be easy to get to weather in this wind." A direction away from the wind is to LEEWARD, and the wind blows out from a LEE SHORE. (2) to survive or to weather a storm.

weather alert, NOAA – *see* NOAA WEATHER ALERT

weather balloon – a six ft/1.5m wide helium or hydrogen-filled balloon that takes a radiosonde aloft to provide data for forecasters. A radiosonde is a small, expendable instrument package. It measures pressure, temperature, and relative humidity. By tracking the position of the radiosonde as it flies, information on wind speed and direction aloft is also obtained. A very small battery-powered radio transmitter sends the readings to a ground receiver. Worldwide, there are nearly 900 upper-air observation stations. Most are located in the Northern Hemisphere. All observations are usually taken at the same UTC time, at 0000 and 1200, every day of the year. Through international agreements data are exchanged between countries and used by meteorologists worldwide.

weather channels – in the U.S and Canada VHF Channels WX 1-10 are for NOAA and Canadian marine weather broadcasts. Select the channel with the best reception in your area. NOAA WEATHER ALERTS are also broadcast as severe weather approaches an area. In other countries, the Coast Guard usually broadcasts the weather forecasts on VHF WORKING CHANNELS, announcing the particular channels on Channel 16 before the broadcast. A NAUTICAL ALMANAC or CRUISING GUIDE gives the channels for different areas.

weather cloths, dodgers – pieces of fabric tied to a vessel's LIFELINES along the QUARTERS or around the STERN, to help prevent spray and waves from coming aboard in rough weather. Weather cloths also provide protection from the wind. Tie weather cloths to the top lifelines with light lashings that will break if a heavy sea comes aboard, so the impact doesn't bend or break the STANCHIONS. For other photos see DAVITS and TRANSOM, TRADITIONAL.

A memorable name.

Racing yachts display their numbers on their weather cloths.

weather deck, weather side – the vessel's deck area or side exposed to the wind, the side the wind is blowing onto, the WINDWARD side.

weather event, short-term – weather of short or relatively short duration, such as a MACROBURST, MICROBURST, WATERSPOUT, tornado, hailstorm, or a SQUALL. Despite its short duration, this kind of weather event can arise with little or no warning and be violent. Learn to read your local weather.

weatherfax, WEFAX, radiofacsimile, radiofax – a weather map (SYNOPTIC) sent over various methods of radio or satellite communication. Use a special weatherfax receiver or a SINGLE-SIDEBAND receiver with computer software and a simple modem. A TRANSCEIVER is not necessary. There are other technologies for receiving weatherfax; research what's appropriate for your vessel. Governments vary in their budget support for radiofacsimile transmissions, and the basic technology is old, but being modernized in some countries. Do an Internet search for "marine radiofacsimile schedules" or see www.nws.noaa.gov/om/marine/rfax.pdf for a worldwide schedule and other links to radiofax products. Read a good weather textbook, take a marine weather course, and try weather training software to learn how to use weatherfaxes. They give the "big picture" to supplement other weather information and forecasts.

weather forecast – the usefulness of marine weather forecasts depends on how long you'll be at sea and the areas you'll travel through. Do you have a short WEATHER WINDOW, or can the trip be made easily in good weather, even if you're delayed? Here are some tips to help make the forecasts you hear, receive by weatherfax or NAVTEX, or read on the Internet more useful.

What is the current weather at your location?

What does the current SYNOPTIC surface analysis show?

Where is the weather coming from in relation to your trip, and what is heading your way?

Are there any marine warnings in effect or forecast for your area or where you're going?

Are there weather observations or buoy reports for your area and for areas you'll pass through?

What's the *trend* of the forecasts or synoptics? Is it getting better, worse, or staying the same?

Will the trip be offshore, near the shore, or through areas where conditions might be particularly affected by the expected weather? Conditions near the shore can vary from offshore weather forecasts. Wind and wave predictions are for the open sea.

Are there safe harbors available if the weather deteriorates while en route? Can you get into these harbors with the expected winds and sea conditions?

weather forecast accuracy – of course, there are varying degrees of accuracy for many reasons. Weather forecasts may be given hourly, but they're based on data gathered at six or twelve hour intervals. Local weather conditions can vary greatly from a forecast. Are there unusual CLOUDS? Do you feel cold air on your skin on a hot day? Are there reports of wind and sea conditions from buoys, reporting stations, or other vessels near or far from your area? Have the SWELLS begun to get bigger? Are you in an area where there are no forecasts available or they don't meet your needs? Learn to read local weather signs and SYNOPTIC weather charts. Study a good weather book for mariners, buy weather training software, or take a marine weather class. It's a fascinating subject.

weather forecast terms – weather services use words in forecasts that have specific meanings. What do words such as "poor, soon, rough, imminent, later, or moderate" mean? Check the marine weather service or meteorological office website for the precise definitions and the format used in marine weather voice broadcasts or text forecasts.

weather forecasts on the Internet – *see* WEATHER WEBSITES.

weather helm – the tendency of a sailboat to turn toward the wind (round up) when the wind is gusty or when the HELM is released for a moment. Weather helm can be corrected to some extent by adjusting the trim of the sails. Weather helm is less of a problem than LEE HELM, because when the boat turns into the wind in a strong gust some wind is spilled from the sails; with lee helm, the boat may heel more strongly.

weather, hemispheric – weather systems behave differently in the Northern and Southern Hemispheres. When the earth is viewed looking down from the North Pole, the earth's rotation is clockwise; when viewed from the South Pole the rotation is counter-clockwise (anticlockwise). This rotation produces a force called the CORIOLIS EFFECT, which influences the movement and rotation of weather systems and ocean currents. In the Northern Hemisphere the rotation around a LOW PRESSURE SYSTEM is counter-clockwise and clockwise around HIGHS. In the Southern Hemisphere the rotation is the opposite: clockwise around lows and counter-clockwise around highs.

weatherly – a sailboat that goes well sailing to WINDWARD. "Janet's new boat is really weatherly."

weather reports, buoy reports – it's good to know the location of observation stations. Do the reports come from protected or exposed locations? Are the weather buoys in open waters or shielded from the full force of the wind and waves? Marine weather websites and some NAUTICAL ALMANACS have maps of the locations of buoys and reporting stations.

weather rhymes and proverbs – sailors, fishermen, and farmers are keen observers of the weather, and over the centuries they've created various rhymes to forecast the weather. The doggerel is based on observations of CLOUDS, wind, BAROMETRIC PRESSURE, and humidity, data still important in modern forecasts. These informal predictions generally cover a time period of 12 to 24 or 48 hours. Some rhymes are relatively accurate, and some are quite inaccurate; use them with caution, along with your local forecasting abilities. Here's a selection of some of the better-known rhymes that relate to marine weather.

Red sky at night, sailor's delight,
Red sky in the morning, sailors, take warning.

Poor or stormy weather usually approaches from the west in MID-LATITUDE regions. When there's a lot of water vapor in the atmosphere around sunrise, a red sky may appear in the morning cirrus clouds, which precede a WARM

FRONT. Air pollution can affect the colors, and a red sky at night can't forecast a distant but fast-moving storm system. The prediction is true 50-60% of the time.

Pale moon rains, red moon blows,
White moon neither rains nor snows.

When the air is very clear the moon appears white; when dust is in the atmosphere the moon takes on a different color. Tiny particulates in the atmosphere are required for rain to form.

Morning dew means weather fair,
When dew is gone a change beware.

Morning dew occurs with a **STABLE ATMOSPHERE**. If there's no dew it was either evaporated by wind, or the sky is cloudy, both signs of possible rainy weather.

Thunder in the morning, all day storming.

This describes an UNSTABLE ATMOSPHERE where the earth is already warm in the morning, with an upward motion to the atmosphere. This sets the stage for afternoon thunderstorms *if* cooler air arrives later in the day. If cold air moves in over warm water or land during the night, cumulonimbus clouds may appear in the morning, and the thunderstorms arrive before the afternoon.

Rain before wind, topsails lower and halyards mind,
Wind before rain, you may soon make sail again.

This rhyme describes an approaching **COLD FRONT** or **LOW PRESSURE** center. If rain arrives first it may mean that the storm is strong enough to force the rain ahead of it, indicating strong winds to follow. If the wind comes before the rain, the front or low is moving quickly, and it may pass your location in a relatively short time, with less intensity than when rain precedes the wind. The rhyme is true about 70% of the time.

Long notice, long last,
Short notice, soon past.

This relates to the previous rhyme in that a slow-moving weather system will announce its presence well before it arrives, and it stays longer because it's moving slowly. Conversely a fast-moving weather system gives a short warning, but moves through quickly. This rhyme is true probably 70% of the time.

Rain before seven, dry by eleven.

During the night and at sunrise there may be warm air coming down to the cooler earth and water. If the ground is very cool then a rain cloud may have formed overnight, causing morning drizzle. If the land or water heats up, the rain may stop by the afternoon. This rhyme isn't very accurate.

Mackerel skies and mares' tails
Make lofty ships carry lower sails.

The altocumulus or cirrocumulus clouds of a mackerel sky looks like the stripes on a fish. The stripes indicate a high-altitude wind rippling high layers of ice crystals. Mares' tails are wispy cirrus clouds. Cirrus clouds indicate the approach of a frontal system. Together these forecast the approach of strong winds or a storm front, usually within 24-48 hours. If you see these skies, keep an eye on the direction of the wind and check the forecast.

If a circle forms 'round the moon [or the sun, but it doesn't rhyme]
'Twill rain soon.

Halos around the moon or sun are caused by ice crystals in high cirrus or cirrostratus clouds. Halos may predict the approach of a **LOW PRESSURE SYSTEM**, bringing poor weather in 18-24 hours. Add a halo to wind shifts with a falling **BAROMETER** for a more accurate prediction. In **MID-LATITUDES** the rhyme is true about 60% of the time.

When clouds descend, good weather ends.

Warm air over cold water or land produces stratus (low) clouds and/or fog, which may be accompanied by drizzle or rain.

At sea with a low and falling glass, soundly sleeps the careless ass.
Only when it's high and rising truly rests a careful wise one.

A basic guide to interpreting the barometer (the "glass").

First rise after low
Soon foretells a stronger blow.

The first rise of the barometer after the passage of a **LOW** may have stronger winds than when the low approached. You can see this on a **SYNOPTIC CHART** where a low has more closely-spaced **ISOBARS** on the left side of the low than the right or leading side (in the Northern Hemisphere.) If the rise is fast, there will usually be strong winds.

When the wind is blowing in the north
No fisherman should set forth,
When the wind is blowing in the east,
'Tis not fit for man nor beast,
When the wind is blowing in the south
It brings the food over the fish's mouth,
When the wind is blowing in the west,
That is when the fishing's best!

This rhyme works fairly well for **LOW PRESSURE SYSTEM** weather in the Northern Hemisphere. Northerly winds occur after a low passes; they can be cold and blustery. As a low approaches, easterly winds increase. Southerly winds are warm and westerly winds usually bring fair, clear weather.

When the winds back and the glass falls,
Prepare the ship for gales and squalls.

In the Northern Hemisphere, a wind that backs (changes in a counter-clockwise direction) indicates the approach of a **LOW PRESSURE SYSTEM** from the southwest.

When the wind shifts against the sun,
Trust it not for back it will run.
When the wind follows the sun,
Fine weather will never be done.

When the wind shifts against the sun, it **BACKS**, indicating the approach of a **LOW PRESSURE SYSTEM**. The rhyme is sometimes true in the Northern Hemisphere; the reverse applies to the Southern Hemisphere.

Seagull, seagull, sit on the sand,
It's never good weather when you're on the land.

This rhyme relates to LOW PRESSURE, which makes the air heavier or gusty, and it's harder for birds to fly. However, seagulls walking on the sand may be foraging for food; when they sit, they may be predicting the weather or just resting. Don't trust their forecasting abilities.

weather routing services – commercial services available for ships and yachts that provide overall weather advice as well as day-to-day weather forecasts and routing information for vessels on offshore voyages. Weather routers communicate with vessels at sea with a variety of equipment, from SINGLE-SIDEBAND radio to GLOBALSTAR, IRIDIUM, and INMARSAT. With a custom forecast, a weather router provides advice tailored to the capabilities of the vessel. Whether you're doing a long coastal passage, crossing the GULF STREAM or an ocean, a weather routing service may be a good choice. However, using a routing service does not mean that you don't have to know anything about forecasting your own weather. If you understand weather forecasting you'll use a router's forecasts more effectively. Weather routers make erroneous predictions, just like any other meteorologists. Weather systems don't pay attention to forecasts. If the communications are disrupted you're on your own, and reading your on-scene weather may be more accurate or helpful than the weather router's information.

weather shore – the shore to WINDWARD or to WEATHER; the upwind shore. The wind blows from a weather shore out to the water. When a vessel is near a weather shore, she's in the LEE of the shore, and receives some protection from wind and waves.

weather side – same as WEATHER DECK; the side of the boat the wind is blowing on.

weather websites – in addition to marine weather broadcasts by coast guards, many resources are available on the Internet, by telephone, and from private WEATHER ROUTING SERVICES. In the U.S., check the websites of NOAA, the Ocean Prediction Center (Tropical Analysis and Forecast Bureau), the National Hurricane Center, and the Central Pacific Hurricane Center. Outside the U.S. see websites of Environment Canada, the European Center for Medium-Range Weather Forecasts, the UK Met Office, Met Éireann (Republic of Ireland, Northern Ireland), Meteo France (French only), the Norwegian Met Office (text forecasts in English), and meteorological office websites in other countries.

Websites offer many types of text forecasts, graphic charts, GRIB files, and other useful weather products for the mariner. See the bibliography under "Weather." Marine weather forecasts disseminated on the Internet are usually *not* part of the GMDSS Maritime Safety Information (MSI) system, and shouldn't be relied upon as the only means to obtain the latest marine forecasts and warnings. Access to the service and updates can be interrupted or delayed, and updates may not be posted in a timely manner. If you use web pages, use the "refresh" or "reload" button on your browser. NAVTEX, GMDSS WEATHER FORECASTS, or INMARSAT-C SAFETYNET provide the latest information. Official met office and government forecasts are not necessarily more accurate than unofficial forecasts; use all with caution, and compare them with your own forecasts and observations.

weather window – a time to sail in between unfavorable weather systems. Waiting for a weather window can be a good time to make new friends among the boats stuck in harbor. If you've been stuck waiting for the right window, don't fall victim to the HERD MENTALITY.

websites, cruising information – *see* CRUISING INFORMATION WEBSITES.

wedges, mast – *see* MAST WEDGES and SPARTITE®.

weep – a slow leak, which may result in dripping or just trails of moisture. Weeps can occur around fittings, hatches, metal tank seams, and many other places on a boat. A weep over the skipper's bunk is a catastrophe.

WEFAX – acronym for WEATHERFAX, a radio-based system for transmitting SYNOPTICS (weather charts) and imagery.

weigh anchor, weighing anchor – *see* ANCHOR, WEIGHING.

well-found – adjective applied to a boat that is well-equipped and SEAWORTHY. "The boat I'm thinking of buying is really well-found."

Westlawn Institute of Marine Technology – the only U.S. accredited distance-learning school of small vessel design and marine technology. Students worldwide study with Westlawn programs, and enter careers in recreational and small commercial vessel design, as well as other industry careers. A number of well-known designers and marine professionals have Westlawn degrees, to name just a few: Ted Brewer, Britton Chance, John Cherubini, Bill Crealock, Dudley Dix, Dave Gerr, Jack Hargrave, Rod Johnston, Royal Lowell, Charlie Morgan, Gary Mull, Dave Napier, Bill Shaw. The Institute was founded in 1930. www.westlawn.edu.

West Wall – the boundary side of the GULF STREAM that's toward the U.S. east coast, typically south of Cape Hatteras. The NORTH WALL is the other boundary, extending northeast from Cape Hatteras.

westing – to make good a distance in a westerly direction. "We ran down our westing to Hawaii in nine days." Easting, northing, and southing may also be used in this sense.

wet locker – a locker dedicated to the storage of foul weather gear (waterproof clothing).

wetted surface – the amount of the vessel's hull (and TOPSIDES when heeled) that's under the water. When a boat HEELS, wetted surface increases. Up to a point, this doesn't have much effect on speed. When a boat heels excessively it slows down because of the increase in wetted surface beyond optimal. That's why REEFING early is a good idea.

WGS84 – abbreviation for World Geodetic Survey of 1984. WGS84 is a modern, worldwide horizontal CHART DATUM. Charts using a different datum will state if it is equivalent to WGS84.

wharf – another name for a pier or QUAY; it may be constructed on pilings or along the shore.

"what if?" – on long, quiet WATCHES at sea ask yourself (or a crewmember, if it doesn't scare the person) "what if such and such happens?" Doing what-ifs keeps your mind occupied, and helps you review alternatives and emergency procedures if something unforeseen happens.

wheel – (1) the steering wheel or HELM. (2) a propeller.

whelps – the vertical ridges on the drum of a WINCH or CAPSTAN that help the rope get a grip. Andersen brand winches and capstans have whelps, which Andersen calls the Power Rib™.

whip, whipping – (1) to apply many turns of light line or sail twine around the end of a rope to prevent it from unraveling and fraying. A sailmaker's whipping uses a needle with the sail twine to make the whipping more secure. MARLINSPIKE SEAMANSHIP books show how to do this simple technique. See also SERVE and WORM. (2) a whip TACKLE is a line that runs through a single BLOCK to lift or pull a load.

whisker pole – a metal, wood, or carbon fiber pole, lighter in construction than a SPINNAKER POLE, that's used to hold out the CLEW of a HEADSAIL when sailing DOWNWIND or WING-AND-WING.

whistle – (1) a vessel's horn or ship's whistle used to make the prescribed SOUND SIGNALS under Rules 32-35 of the NAVIGATION RULES. (2) a small signaling whistle that can be worn by a crew member or be attached to man-overboard gear. Buy whistles that work when wet; a referee's whistle doesn't work with water in it. Attach one to each crewmember's lifejacket or safety HARNESS.

whistle signals – same as SOUND SIGNALS.

whitecaps, white horses – the white, breaking tops of waves. Small whitecaps begin to form on the wavelets in winds of approximately seven to ten knots (BEAUFORT WIND FORCE 3). They become more numerous and larger as the wind increases. Over about 25 knots (F6), the whitecaps will be everywhere and there'll be spray. Learn to gauge the approximate wind strength by how many and how big the whitecaps are. If there are whitecaps in an area where the water is otherwise relatively calm, avoid the area or be cautious if you must go through it – it may be a shoal, a rock or other obstruction, or a WIND AGAINST TIDE condition.

white metal – another name for ZAMAK.

white squall – a type of SQUALL with driving rain and spray.

wide berth – a safe distance away from something. "Give that shoal a wide berth."

WIG craft – *see* WING-IN-GROUND EFFECT.

wildcat – a GYPSY for use with chain; a chainwheel.

Williamson Turn, buttonhook turn – a technique for recovering a man overboard under power. To do a Williamson turn, steer 60° toward the side that the person went overboard (if known), and then turn 180° and steer back onto the RECIPROCAL of the original course. A Williamson turn brings the boat back on her original course, which is helpful if the visibility is poor or if you don't know the time the person went overboard. A disadvantage is that the turn takes you some distance from the victim, and you have to remember how to do it. Practice solves the remembering.

williwaw – a sudden, unpredictable gust of wind that can occur in mountainous coastal areas, especially in HIGH LATITUDES. It's a KATABATIC wind. The winds can be very strong, approaching 100 kn or more. Strong williwaws are frequent in the Aleutians in Alaska and the Straits of Magellan at the southern tip of South America.

winch – (1) to use a winch. "Winch the MAINSHEET in another foot." (2) a mechanical device with a vertical rotating drum, used in or near the COCKPIT, on the MAST of a sailboat and in other locations. A winch increases the pulling force on a line, such as a SHEET or HALYARD. Winch basics:

- Wrap lines clockwise around all winches; if you forget the direction of rotation turn the winch with the palm of your hand on the drum before wrapping the line.
- Use at least three wraps on the winch so the line doesn't slip.
- Winches are single-speed, two-speed, or three-speed. On a two-speed winch the handle turns in both directions to change the speed. High speed pulls the line in fast; low speed is slower but gives more power (and makes it easier to turn the handle). Three-speed winches have a mechanism (such as a button or lever) for the third speed. Some winches are electrically or hydraulically-powered, and don't need a handle.
- Winch handles are available in different lengths, and with a single grip or double grip, which allows you to use two hands for more power. Some handles float. The expensive metal ones don't.
- Winch handles are locking or non-locking; a locking handle doesn't fall out of a winch.
- A winch that doesn't need a second person to pull on the tail of the line is called a self-tailing winch or a self-tailer.
- Some older sailboats may have a wire HALYARD winch, which is designed specifically for use with wire. On modern sailboats if wire halyards are used, there's a wire-to-rope SPLICE so that the rope tail can be used on a regular winch.

For safety learn how to use a winch properly because a line on a winch is under great strain, even in moderate winds. See the next entry.

winch safety – in addition to following ROPE SAFETY guidelines, the following cautions apply when using a winch:

- Make sure all crew know how to operate the winches (don't assume).
- Keep long hair, loose clothing, and NECK LANYARDS away from a winch.
- Position your body over a winch so you can use your shoulders, upper body, and legs to assist your arms. Grinding a winch with just your arms can be tiring. Maintain a safe and balanced position, which may not be easy when it's rough.
- Learn how to wrap a line around a winch without getting your fingers between the line and the winch. Keep your hands as far away from a winch as possible when you wrap.
- Remove the handle before you wrap the winch or take line off.
- Learn how to prevent and clear a winch OVERRIDE using a ROLLING HITCH.

• If you're going to release a line quickly (when TACKING or lowering a sail), FLAKE the tail of the line so it can run freely.

• Watch what you're pulling or easing; don't look at the winch. Electric winches can be especially dangerous because they're so powerful.

• When EASING a line, if the line's stuck on the winch, use the palm of your hand, with your fingers together, to coax the coils counter-clockwise (anti-clockwise). Or carefully remove one turn from the winch, while keeping a firm hold on the tail of the line.

• Don't sit or stand in front of a winch that has a loaded line on it.

• If there's a LINE STOPPER ahead of a winch and a strain on the line, ease the load on the stopper by winching the line in a little before opening the stopper.

• When not in use turn off electric winches so they can't accidentally start and catch a person's clothing or body parts.

• Maintain winches regularly and check internal parts for damage.

wind against tide, wind over tide – when the wind blows in opposition to the direction that a current is flowing, under some conditions steep, short seas (OVERFALLS) may be created. Wind against tide decreases the WAVE LENGTH and increases the WAVE HEIGHT. It doesn't have to be very windy for short, steep seas to develop. In extreme conditions, such as with strong or storm winds against a current, these seas can be dangerous, even to large vessels. A TIDE RACE may have very dangerous conditions with wind against tide. *Wind with tide* increases the wave length and decreases the wave height, so it's not as dangerous.

windage – the amount of a boat's TOPSIDES, SUPERSTRUCTURE, and RIGGING exposed to the wind. A boat with a lot of TOP HAMPER has more windage than a boat with less surface area above the waterline. Windage hinders progress when powering into the wind, and it makes a boat difficult to maneuver under power in a breeze, particularly at slow speeds. It also creates higher forces on an anchor RODE and mooring lines. On most boats the BOW has more windage, and it blows off before the STERN. It's important to control the bow. A BOW THRUSTER helps, but it's not an essential item to have if the helmsman learns to anticipate the action of the wind on the bow and maneuvers accordingly.

wind, anabatic or upslope wind – in mountainous areas, during the day the sides of the mountains become warmer than the sea, and winds blow up the mountains. These localized winds can be strong and different in direction from other winds near the area. *See* WINDS, KATABATIC.

wind and wave analysis and forecast – NOAA and meteorological offices in various countries, produce ocean wind and wave charts, and some met offices also have buoy reports (SIGNIFICANT WAVE HEIGHT AND PERIOD). Charts are available by SINGLE-SIDEBAND RADIOFACSIMILE, satellite communications, or on WEATHER WEBSITES. Buoy reports are on the Internet, some are available by telephone from a met office, and some coast guards broadcast buoy reports with their marine weather forecasts. Learn how to acquire and interpret charts and reports for planning your trip.

wind, channeled, funneled and gap – (1) winds blowing in areas between land masses or in fjords are channeled along the axis of the passage. (2) winds blowing through narrow areas are funneled by the land, creating higher wind speeds than elsewhere. Sometimes the local wind speed can be double that of the prevailing wind. (3) gap winds are localized strong winds caused by the wind being funneled through a gap between high terrain. The wind on the LEE side of the gap is stronger than the wind on the WINDWARD side of the gap, perhaps double the wind on the windward side. Observing the contours of the coastal land as shown on the chart may also help you predict where channeled, funneled, and gap winds are likely to occur. COAST PILOTS or CRUISING GUIDES may warn of these areas. See the next entry.

wind, cornering – when winds blow around a steep HEADLAND, cliff, or island the speed of the wind is accelerated and bent toward the shore on the LEE side, sometimes dramatically, with a resultant increase in the waves around the corner. The contours of a high headland may be on the chart, if it has topographical information, or COAST PILOTS and CRUISING GUIDES may warn of these areas.

wind direction – the direction of the wind is identified by where it *comes from*; a northerly wind blows from the north. Observations and forecasts use TRUE directions.

wind, eye of the – the exact direction where the wind comes from. When you TACK, the BOW passes through the eye of the wind.

wind generator – *see* GENERATOR, WIND.

wind, geostrophic (pronounced gee oh **stro** fick) – the theoretical wind at a specific height above the earth that results from the PRESSURE GRADIENT force being directed by the CORIOLIS FORCE. The wind is parallel to the ISOBARS on a SYNOPTIC, with LOW PRESSURE on the left (looking downward on the synoptic chart). The strength of the geostrophic wind is related to the spacing of the isobars on a synoptic (the spacing is the pressure gradient). The more-closely spaced the isobars, the stronger the wind. Learning how to interpret the geostrophic wind is essential for estimating surface wind speeds from a synoptic chart. A rule of thumb: count the number of isobars within five degrees of latitude and multiply by ten. This gives the geostrophic wind speed over the area in knots. When you know this speed use a table or a correction factor to get the surface wind. You can also use the geostrophic wind scale in the corner of a weather chart by measuring the spacing between isobars at a particular LATITUDE. However, this scale may not be easy to read on a synoptic, so the rule of thumb is useful. It's not difficult to learn how to use the geostrophic wind; study a good marine weather book.

wind indicator – a mechanical or electronic instrument that reads the direction of the wind by means of pivoting wind vane. When the boat's in motion the vane shows the APPARENT WIND. It's usually used at the MASTHEAD of a sailboat. A Windex® is a common brand of mechanical wind indicator;

many yachts use both a mechanical and an electronic indicator, because the sensitive mechanical vane reacts instantly to the wind.

wind, katabatic – a wind created by air moving downhill, especially in mountainous areas. The air cools at night and flows downhill toward the water; katabatic winds can be gusty and extend a mile or two out to sea. The Strait of Belle Isle (between Newfoundland and Labrador) experiences FUNNELED and katabatic winds, which can be three times stronger than the winds outside the Strait. The Santa Ana winds in California, the Mistral in the Mediterranean, and the Bora in the Adriatic are other examples. WILLIWAWS are a type of strong katabatic wind that occur where there are high mountains near the sea; for example, in the Aleutians in Alaska and Tierra del Fuego at the tip of South America, as well as other HIGH LATITUDE mountainous areas. *See* WINDS, ANABATIC.

windlass – a horizontal WINCH on the BOW that's used to raise or lower the anchor or to adjust mooring lines. It can be manual, electric, or hydraulic. A vertical windlass is a CAPSTAN, but the terms are often used interchangeably. A windlass designed to handle an all-chain RODE has a wheel with indentations (pockets) for each link of the chain to fit into; it's called the chain gypsy or chainwheel. Chain shouldn't be used on a windlass or capstan that doesn't have a chain gypsy because it will damage the windlass drum. If there's a short section of chain attached to a rope rode bring the chain aboard by hand. Some gypsies are designed for both chain and line or a windlass may have two gypsies. A windlass isn't designed to hold the weight of a boat at anchor: a CHAIN SPRING and a CHAIN STOPPER (if fitted) should be used on a chain rode, or a rope rode should be secured to strong bow fittings.

A windlass with a chain gypsy on the left and a rope gypsy on the right. Each gypsy can be operated independently.

wind over tide – same as WIND AGAINST TIDE.

wind radii (pronounced **raid** ee eye) – a term used in U.S. TROPICAL CYCLONE forecasts and advisories. Wind radii are the longest radii of a wind speed found in a particular quadrant around the compass. The quadrants are northeast (000°-090°), southeast (090°-180°), southwest (180°-270°), and northwest (270°-000°). For example, with a maximum 34 knot wind that extends out to 150NM at 045°, 90NM at 120°, 40NM at 260°, and 150NM at 300° the following line would be printed or spoken in the forecast or advisory: "150NE 90SE 40SW 150NW." When you hear these words spoken on a HIGH-SEAS weather broadcast it's confusing at first; it's easier to understand in print.

wind-rode – when a vessel at anchor swings to the wind and not to the current she is wind rode. A vessel swinging to the current is TIDE RODE.

wind rose – wind roses are printed on **PILOT CHARTS** in various areas of the ocean, to show the average speed, direction, and the percentage of winds in a particular area. The data are derived from observations taken over many years.

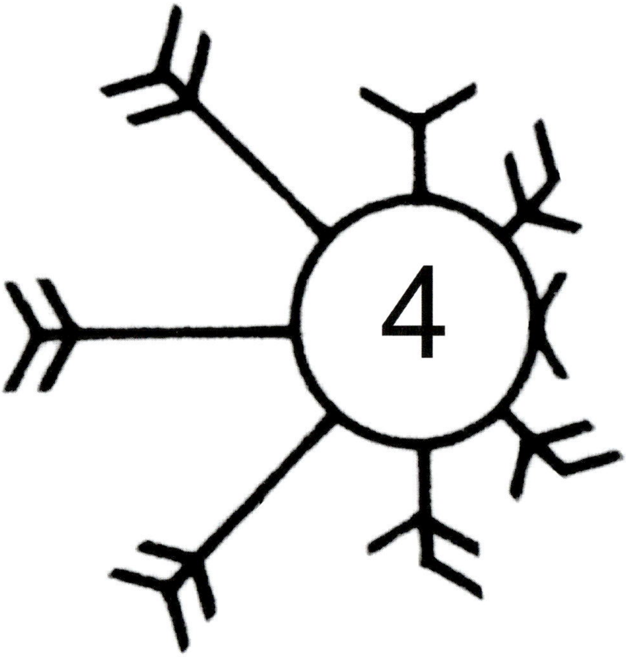

wind rose

Wind roses are printed in blue on pilot charts in each 5° square area. The number in the circle is the percentage of calms in the area. The arrows fly with the wind and show the wind directions. The length of the arrow (measured against a scale on the chart) is the percentage of winds from that direction. The number of feathers at the end of the arrow is the Beaufort Force number for each wind direction.

windscoop – a lightweight cloth ventilator inserted into a hatch to catch the breeze.

wind shadow – the area DOWNWIND (in the LEE) of a large ship, a high mountain, or other high terrain, that doesn't receive the full force of the wind. Winds in the shadow area may be different from the prevailing wind, be FLUKY, or have DOWNDRAFTS. When the wind blows over high terrain towards the sea, the wind shadow can extend out for some distance, perhaps many miles. The wind shadow can be helpful to a vessel, as the wind waves will be smaller in this area. *See also* WINDS, KATABATIC.

wind sock – like those used at small airports, wind socks may also be placed at harbor or canal entrances or other locations where it's helpful to have a wind indicator to assist vessels.

windward – toward the direction from which the wind is blowing. *See* WEATHER, TO.

windward side –the side the wind is blowing on; the WEATHER SIDE. In the NAVIGATION RULES the windward side of a sailboat is defined as "the side opposite to that on which the mainsail is carried or, in the case of a square-rigged vessel, the side opposite to that on which the largest fore-and-aft sail is carried."

wind with tide – Wind with tide increases the wave length and decreases the wave height, so it's not as dangerous as an area where there's WIND AGAINST TIDE.

wind vane, wind vane steering – the same as SELF-STEERING.

wind waves – *see* WAVES, WIND.

wing-and-wing or wing-on-wing – when sailing DOWNWIND you can put the CLEW of a HEADSAIL out on one side of the boat with a WHISKER or SPINNAKER POLE, while the MAINSAIL is out on the other side of the boat. Both sails will catch the wind (draw), increasing your speed. It may be possible to sail wing-and-wing without a pole, depending on the wind direction and how the headsail is trimmed.

wing-in-ground effect (WIG) craft – a vessel that operates completely above the surface of the water on a cushion of air. A WIG craft is not a HOVERCRAFT. It rises above the water because of aerodynamic lift resulting from the ground effect between the vessel and the water surface. WIG craft are capable of operating at speeds over 100 knots. When a WIG craft is above the water (for take-off, landing, and in flight) it's operating in the non-DISPLACEMENT MODE and must keep out of the way of all other vessels. When it settles onto the water, it's operating in the displacement mode, and is subject to the same rules as a power-driven vessel. See Rule 18(f) (i,ii) of the NAVIGATION RULES (INTERNATIONAL). Rule 23(c) specifies the lights for this craft.

Winlink – Winlink 2000 (WL2K*)* is a "worldwide system of volunteer resources supporting e-mail by radio, with non-commercial links to Internet e-mail. These resources come from Amateur Radio, the Military Auxiliary Radio System (MARS) and other volunteer organizations. The system provides valuable service to emergency communicators, and to licensed radio operators without access to the internet. To use the Winlink 2000 system, you must hold an Amateur Radio license or be a member of a supported organization or agency. Use of the system and all software is free of charge for those who qualify." A SINGLE-SIDEBAND radio, a computer, and a PACTOR modem are required to use this service, in addition to a ham radio operator's license. SAILDOCS and SAILMAIL offer similar services for everyone, no ham license required.

winter buoy, winter stick – a temporary buoy, usually a short SPAR, that replaces a regular buoy in the winter, where ice may be a problem. It can be used to replace aids to navigation or mooring buoys.

wire, current-carrying capacity – the current-carrying capacity of an electrical wire depends, in general, upon (1) the diameter of the wire; (2) for DC, the length of the wire calculated *to and from* the power source to the device being powered; (3) for AC, the number of wires bundled together; (4) the condition of the wire and TERMINALS (new or corroded). Other factors may also apply. Large gauge wire can carry more current than small gauge wire. Select the WIRE GAUGE for the minimum amount of acceptable VOLTAGE DROP in a circuit, as well as other factors. Technical reference books, some marine supply catalogues, and technical websites discuss the selection of wire for marine use. ABYC Standard E-11 AC and DC Electrical Systems on Boats covers all aspects of AC and DC electrical wires. The complete E-11 Standard is available with a free trial of ABYC Standards at www.abycinc.org. A summary of wire capacity and voltage drop is at www.marinco.com/page/wire-tech-data. Before attempting a DIY electrical project, consult authoritative reference sources. You may decide to employ the services of a qualified marine electrician.

wire, electrical, marine color code – ABYC Standard E-11 AC and DC Electrical Systems on Boats specifies the colors for wires so that circuits, functions, and POLARITY can be easily identified. There are some differences between color codes for AC and DC. Most manufacturers observe the code, but a boat that has had electrical work done over the years may have all sorts of wires that don't conform to any code. This is both dangerous and frustrating when working on an electrical system. Wire color codes may be different on equipment or vessels from non-U.S. suppliers. The complete E-11 Standard is available with a free trial of ABYC Standards at www.abycinc.org. A summary of the U.S. color code is at www.marinco.com/page/marinecolorcodes.

wire, electrical, marine use – ABYC standard E-11 AC and DC Electrical Systems on Boats covers all aspects of boat wiring. Although not required by standards, pre-tinned wire resists corrosion better than ordinary wire. UL-approved marine wire is marked on the outer jacket of the wires. "Boat Cable" meets UL1426 standard: it has extra-flexible strands, and abrasion, moisture, UV, and chemical-resistant and flame-retardant PVC insulation. The U.S. Coast Guard accepts UL and ABYC standards. The complete E-11 Standard is available with a free trial of ABYC Standards at www.abycinc.org. A summary of ABYC E-11 is available at www.marinco.com/page/abyc-standards. Some older vessels modified improperly or manufactured outside the U.S. may have solid wire, but ABYC, USCG and ISO standards do not allow it on a vessel. Consult a qualified marine electrician if your boat has solid wire. Have a VESSEL SAFETY CHECK to make sure the electrical system meets the requirements.

wire, electrical, SAE – SAE wire is ordinary wire sold in hardware and auto supply stores. It has different diameters than AWG (it's about 12% smaller), so larger SAE wire must be used to achieve the current-carrying capacity of AWG wire. SAE wire is only for DC voltages. SAE wire types acceptable for use on a boat are J378 (marine engine wiring), J1127 (battery cable), and J1128 (low tension primary cable). Use only wire that is marked on the outer jacket. See the previous entry.

wire gauge, AWG – abbreviation for American Wire Gauge. The abbreviation is usually used. The gauge number indicates the diameter of the wire. AWG wires are the type used in marine wire reference tables. The lower the number, the larger the wire diameter; the higher the number, the smaller the diameter of the wire. Examples: AWG 16, 18 and 22 are small diameter wires; AWG 10, 12, 14 are "medium" diameter; AWG 6, 2, 1/0, 4/0 are large diameter battery cables. (the "0" is pronounced as "ought"). Some marine wire is PRE-TINNED, which helps prevent corrosion in the wire. Other countries may use different gauge systems. Wire gauges in Europe may be expressed in square millimeters; consult reference tables when selecting these wires. See WIRE, CURRENT-CARRYING CAPACITY.

wire rigging – also called WIRE ROPE. See the next entry.

wire rope, wire cable – used for STANDING RIGGING, some RUNNING RIGGING, LIFELINES, and steering system cables. Wire rope is made of strands of wire twisted into a rope. For the marine environment, wire rope for yachts is made of type 302/304 or 316 STAINLESS STEEL. Wire types commonly used on boats include:

> 1x19 wire has a central core wire with 19 wire strands around it. Because it's not very flexible, 1x19 is used primarily for standing rigging. It's available in Type 302/304 and 316. Use SWAGED or MECHANICAL TERMINALS with this wire.
>
> Dyform® wire is a high-tech, low-stretch wire used for standing rigging. Its breaking strength is 30% higher than regular 1x19 wire. Use swaged or mechanical terminals designed for Dyform.
>
> 7x7 wire is constructed of six strands of seven wires in each strand arranged around a core of seven wires. White, vinyl-coated 7x7 wire is commonly used for lifelines, although some people prefer bare 7x7. Use swaged or mechanical terminals with this wire.
>
> 7x19 wire is constructed of seven bundles of 19 smaller strands, with six bundles arranged around a central core of the same construction. It's used in steering systems and for HALYARDS because of its flexibility. However, because the individual strands are small, and the wires usually make a number of bends around BLOCKS in a steering system or on the mast, this wire is less durable than other flexible wires. For this reason, regularly inspect wire steering system cables and halyards.

New high-tech, very high strength synthetic rope is being developed that can replace wire rigging. It's much lighter than wire, significantly reducing weight aloft. End terminals and fittings are available that are similar to those used on wire rope. *See* RIGGING, SYNTHETIC.

wire rope, galvanized – some TRADITIONAL vessels and vessels used in fresh water have GALVANIZED steel wire rope rigging. When properly maintained, this wire lasts reasonably well. It's less-expensive than stainless steel wire rope.

wire ties – another name for CABLE TIES.

wishbone boom, wishbone rig – a BOOM with two sides that are connected together at the ends and open in the middle, shaped somewhat like a wishbone. A basket of lines below the boom (similar to LAZYJACKS above a boom) control the sail when it is lowered. The wishbone is used on some sailboats, such as Freedom and Nonsuch yachts.

A wishbone boom on a Nonsuch 30 cruising catboat. The mast is unstayed.

work, working – (1) in moderate or rough seas, parts of a boat's hull move around or "work." The terms are usually applied to a wooden vessel, but metal and fiberglass hulls also work in a SEAWAY. Some of the creaking and groaning below decks in moderate or rough seas is the hull and BULKHEADS working. (2) in ice navigation a vessel works when she makes headway through ice. Mostly applicable to icebreakers or ice-reinforced ships.

work list, to do list – Fact: on a boat this list never gets shorter. Prioritize the tasks. Anything related to the safety of the vessel or the crew should be first on the list.

working channel, working frequency – *see* CHANNEL, WORKING.

working end, working part – the part of a line that's used to make the knot, bend or hitch. The phrase is used in knot-tying instructions. *See* LINE, PARTS OF.

working jib – *see* JIB, WORKING.

working load, safe, SWL for chain – *see* CHAIN, SAFE WORKING LOAD.

working load, safe, SWL for rope – *see* ROPE, SAFE WORKING LOAD.

working sails – the sails used in normal sailing conditions; the basic suit of sails. A CRUISING SPINNAKER, SPINNAKER, and STORM SAILS are not working sails.

World Cruising Club – an organization that sponsors OCEAN CROSSING RALLIES. www.worldcruising.com.

World Geodetic Survey, WGS – The World Geodetic Survey of 1984 (WGS84) is a modern, worldwide horizontal CHART DATUM.

worm, worming – to wind MARLINE in the space between the strands of a THREE-STRAND ROPE. This makes the diameter of the rope more even. After worming the rope can be parceled (covered with canvas or leather strips), and then SERVED with more marline the length of the wormed and parcelled area. This makes strong, permanent CHAFING GEAR. The old time memory aid for how to do the whole procedure is "Worm and parcel with the lay; turn and serve the other way." MARLINSPIKE SEAMANSHIP books show how to do this easy technique. See LAY (4) and SEIZE for a photo of worming.

wrap, propeller – *see* PROPELLER WRAP.

"Wreckhouse winds" – localized very strong winds on the southwest coast of Newfoundland, between Cape Ray and St. Andrews. They are caused by mountain winds coming off Table Mountain. These winds can reach 50-60 knots up to 20 miles out from the coast near Wreckhouse (thus the name).

WWV and WWVH – radio stations operated by the U.S. NATIONAL INSTITUTE OF STANDARDS (NIST). WWV broadcasts on 2.5, 5, 10, 15 and 20MHz from Fort Collins, Colorado, using a male voice. WWVH broadcasts on 2.5, 5, 10, and 15 MHz from Kauai, Hawaii, using a female voice. The variety of frequencies makes it likely that at least one frequency will be usable at all times. Both stations continuously broadcast a timing signal (a series of tones and beeps), 24/7. The voice information includes time announcements, geophysical alerts, marine storm warnings, and GPS status reports. See www.nist.gov/pml/div688/grp40/wwv.cfm. Click on "Broadcast Formats" for details about WWV and WWVH broadcasts. Mariners who require a precise time signal to set their clocks or to check radio wave PROPAGATION listen to these stations. CHU in Canada also broadcasts accurate time signals.

WX – abbreviation for "weather."

X

XTE – abbreviation for CROSS-TRACK ERROR.

Y

Y-valve – a THREE-WAY VALVE used on fuel, water, or waste systems, connecting either of two inlets to a single outlet. A DIVERTER VALVE is a three-way valve.

yacht – a power or sail RECREATIONAL VESSEL, not a COMMERCIAL VESSEL. Yacht is sometimes used to mean a sailing vessel. *See* BOAT, SHIP, YACHT.

yacht designer – a MARINE ARCHITECT who specializes specifically in yacht design. Yacht designers may concentrate on a particular type of yacht, such as cruising or racing sailboats, fast powerboats, trawler yachts, luxury yachts, metal yachts, or innovative designs.

yacht ensign – the U.S. yacht ensign has the red and white stripes of the American flag, but a white fouled anchor replaces the stars in the blue field. This ensign may be flown instead of the American flag on a U.S-registered recreational vessel in U.S. waters. In FOREIGN WATERS, a U.S. vessel flies the American flag. FLAG ETIQUETTE provides guidelines for correctly flying flags aboard vessels.

Yachtmaster – a high-level certification program of practical examinations for sail and powerboat skippers, administered by the RYA. The three certificates are Yachtmaster Coastal, Yachtmaster Offshore, and Yachtmaster Oceans. Applicants must possess the required sea time and experience to take the exams. Formal courses are not part of the certification process. The RYA website (www.rya.org.uk) has the requirements and details. Approved Yachtmaster examinations are offered at various locations worldwide.

Yankee, Yankee jib – *see* JIB, YANKEE.

yardarm – a SPAR mounted ATHWARTSHIPS on a MAST. Do you know what happens when the sun is over the yardarm?

Two yardarms on the foremast of this schooner. The high bulwarks are raised to create freeing ports all along the deck.

yaw, yawing – side-to-side movement of the vessel at the BOW and/or STERN, created by QUARTERING or following seas or combinations of wave systems. "Those waves were so jumbled we were yawing all over the place." In rough, confused seas a yacht may also PITCH and ROLL, along with yawing, challenging the helmsman, the AUTOPILOT, or the SELF-STEERING to hold a course, and the crew to avoid seasickness.

yawl – a yacht with two masts, with the AFT mast (the MIZZEN mast) shorter than the MAIN MAST. The mizzen mast on a yawl is located ABAFT the RUDDER POST. A KETCH has a mizzen, but it is forward of the rudder post. It's not always easy to tell where the rudder post is when looking at a boat; the definition reflects a technical distinction.

A classic yawl in New York harbor.

Z

zarpe – outward CLEARANCE papers issued by authorities in Spanish-speaking countries. When visiting some countries the authorities may request the zarpe from your last port.

zero – the numeral "0" is spoken as "zero," on the radio and when speaking a compass direction.

Zamak, Zamac, white metal, pot metal – an ALLOY of zinc, aluminum, magnesium, and copper. (Zamak is an acronym). It is suited for non-saltwater applications, but is also found in some items marketed for saltwater use. It's primarily used for die-cast fittings, and it's frequently chrome-plated. A Zamak fitting is not as strong as a fitting made of other MARINE METALS. Over time in the marine environment, a Zamak item can become pitted or eventually break due to corrosion. You can tell if an unknown, unlabeled fitting is Zamak by comparing its weight to that of a similar STAINLESS STEEL or chromed BRASS or BRONZE fitting: Zamak is lighter in weight.

zinc, sacrificial zinc – another name for an ANODE.

zinc pencil – a thin, tubular zinc ANODE attached to a screw-in cap, used in engines, generators, refrigeration condensers, and other equipment that uses RAW WATER cooling. The anode helps prevent internal GALVANIC CORROSION. Equipment manuals show the location of zinc pencils, and the manual may indicate a service interval. Check pencils regularly for deterioration. When the pencil is about half gone, replace it. If you wait too long, pieces of zinc flake off and can get pulled into the cooling system. Using pliers, carefully unscrew the old zinc from its cap. If the zinc breaks off (it usually does), melt the remaining zinc out of the cap with a propane torch (off the boat!), so that a new one can be threaded in. Don't use any thread sealer or Teflon tape on the threads of the screw-in cap. Carry a number of spare pencils and a few spare caps – they're cheap insurance.

zone balancing – *see* COMPASS, ZONE BALANCING.

zone description – the number that is added to or subtracted from ZONE TIME to obtain UTC. See TIME ZONES for an example.

zone time, ZT – the local time within a TIME ZONE, in contrast to UTC.

zulu (time), Z – the same as UTC. "We send the WEATHER BALLOON up at 1200 zulu."

BASIC BOATING LIBRARY

The following books are recommended for a mariner's reference library. For complete information on these titles see the bibliography under the topic headings indicated in parentheses.

Foundation books for all sailors:
Calder, Nigel. *How to Read a Nautical Chart*. (Charts)

Colgate, Doris. *Woman's Guide to Sailing*. (Sailing)

Maloney, Elbert S. *Chapman Piloting and Seamanship*, 66th ed. (or newer). This is a complete reference to all aspects of boating under power and sail, suitable for beginners to advanced mariners. Highly-recommended as the first book in a nautical library. (Sailing)

Rousmaniere, John. *The Annapolis Book of Seamanship*, 3rd ed. (Sailing)

U.S. Coast Guard. *Navigation Rules: International and Inland*. If you navigate solely outside U.S. waters you need only the International Rules. (Navigation Rules)

Wing, Charlie. *The One-Minute Guide to the Nautical Rules of the Road*, 2nd ed. (Navigation Rules)

Books to build the library:
Brewer, Ted. *Understanding Boat Design*, 4th ed. (Design)

Burch, David. *The Barometer Handbook*. (Weather)

——— *Modern Marine Weather*. (Weather)

Gibson, Rob. *RYA Boat Handling for Sail and Power*. (Sailing)

Hinz, Earl. *The Complete Book of Anchoring and Moorin*g, 2nd rev. ed. (Anchoring)

Hiscock, Eric. *Cruising Under Sail: Incorporating Voyaging Under Sail.* (Sailing)

Leonard, Beth. *The Voyager's Handbook*, 2nd ed. (Sailing)

Meisel, Tony. *On-board Emergency Handbook.* (Emergencies)

Pardey, Lin with Larry Pardey. *The Care and Feeding of Sailing Crew*, 3rd ed. (Crew)

Poiraud, Alain, Achim Ginsberg-Klemmt, and Erika Ginsberg-Klemmt. *The Complete Anchoring Handbook*. (Anchoring)

Roth, Hal. *Handling Storms at Sea*. (Sailing)

——— *How to Sail Around the World*. (Sailing)

Smith, Hervey Garett: *The Arts of the Sailor*. (Lines)

Watts, Alan. *Instant Weather Forecasting*, 2nd ed. (Weather)

——— *Instant Wind Forecasting*. (Wind)

——— *Instant Storm Forecasting*. (Weather)

For boat owners:

Brotherton, Miner and Edwin Sherman. *The 12-Volt Bible for Boats*, 2nd ed. (Electrical)

Calder, Nigel. *Boatowner's Mechanical and Electrical Manual*, 3rd ed. (Systems)

——— *Marine Diesel Engines*, 3rd ed. (Engines)

Marino, Emiliano. *The Sailmaker's Apprentice*. (Sailing)

Pallas, Jean-Luc. *Marine Diesel Engines*. (Engines)

Payne, John C. *The Marine Electrical and Electronics Bible*, 3rd ed. **or**

Wing, Charlie. *Boatowner's Illustrated Electrical Handbook*, 2nd ed.

ANNOTATED BIBLIOGRAPHY

Following is a personal selection of publications and websites taken from my own library and research. Perhaps you'll see some of your favorites here, as well as find some new resources to engage your interest. If you're new to boating and sailing see the *Basic Boating Library* before the bibliography for an extracted list of publications that create a foundation for a mariner's reference library. Not everything is on the Internet, and certainly not in a single reference. Some publications go out-of-date, while others offer timeless advice; therefore, some worthwhile out-of-print titles are included here. It may be relatively easy to find them with an Internet search. There are also websites of coast guards, government authorities, boating organizations, and marine companies in the U.S., Canada, Ireland, and the UK, which provide useful information no matter where you sail. Governments (in particular) frequently change URLs as they modernize their websites; it may take some resourcefulness to find the correct site, if you're not automatically redirected to the new link.

When doing an Internet search, especially for topics related to navigation and safety at sea, consider the credibility of the information sources. Open forums, for example, present a wide variety of opinions, some of which may be valid, while others may be unsafe or incorrect. Of course, the same is true for print publications and websites. Where safety is concerned, seek a variety of opinions from recognized experts, rather than relying on a single source.

Publications and websites are arranged alphabetically in categories under the same main headings as the *Topic Index*. A descriptive phrase precedes some of the website information. A number of resources would fit under more than one topic heading, but to avoid repetition, a resource was placed in a category that seems most appropriate for the general content, and in some instances a short title is listed more than once.

ANCHORING and MOORING (*see also* Chain; Lines)

anchors and anchoring:

Gerr, Dave: *Boat Mechanical Systems Handbook*. See complete citation under "Systems." This book has a good section on anchors and anchoring systems.

Hinz, Earl. *The Complete Book of Anchoring and Mooring*, 2nd rev. ed. Centreville, Maryland: Cornell Maritime Press, 2001.

Poiraud, Alain, Achim Ginsberg-Klemmt, and Erika Ginsberg-Klemmt. *The Complete Anchoring Handbook*. Camden, Maine: International Marine, 2008.

www.imtra.com/product/anchoring_systems/anchor_chain_line_and_rodes.htm.

www.sailingissues.com/yachting-guide/anchors.html.

careening and drying out: www.sailnet.com/forums/gear-maintenance-articles/20121-delicate-art-careening.html.

sentinel: www.anchorbuddy.co.nz. Anchor Buddy™.

windlasses, technical advice: www.boatus.com/boattech. Click on "BoatTech Guides."

CHAIN and ROPE (*see also* Anchoring; Lines)
chain:
www.wachain.com/Marine_hardware_from_Washington_Chain.htm.

New England Ropes: www.neropes.com.

Samson Ropes: www.samsonrope.com.

Yale Ropes: www.yalecordage.com.

rope safety, Cordage Institute: www.ropecord.com/CI1401.PDF.

CHARTS (*see also* Navigation and Piloting)
Bellingham Chart Printers, Ltd.: www.tidesend.com. A mail-order publication supplier that offers worldwide U.S. government paper and electronic charts, economical U.S. government chart reprints, worldwide cruising guides, navigation publications, software, courtesy flags, and more. Bellingham is also an official Canadian Hydrographic Service chart agent.

Calder, Nigel. *How to Read a Nautical Chart: A Complete Guide to the Symbols, Abbreviations, and Data Displayed on a Nautical Chart*. Camden, Maine: International Marine, 2003. Detailed explanations of everything on a nautical chart, with many illustrations. Everyone who uses paper or electronic charts should study this book and keep it aboard for reference. The book includes Chart No. 1.

charts and GPS: see the brochure *Using Nautical Charts with GPS* at http://msi.nga.mil/NGAPortal/MSI.portal; click on "miscellaneous products."

charts and publications, U.S.: www.nauticalcharts.noaa.gov. The main portal for NOAA's Office of Coast Survey, "The Nation's Chartmaker." Browse the links on this page for related NOAA websites.

www.nauticalcharts.noaa.gov/staff/chartspubs.html. Portal to U.S. charts and publications, including links to informative articles about charts and navigation.

chart datum, horizontal: www.tc.gc.ca/marinesafety/bulletins/2002/02-eng.htm. Canadian Coast Guard advisory regarding horizontal chart datums.

charts, electronic:

Doyle, Mark and Diana: *Get Onboard with E-Charting: the Complete Reference Guide to Electronic Charting and PC-based Marine Navigation*. Bloomington, Minnesota: semi-local publications, 2009. www.semi-local.com.

www.navcen.uscg.gov/enav/ecs/ElectronicChartingRNB.htm.

charts, online viewer: www.nauticalcharts.noaa.gov/mcd/OnLineViewer.html. View all NOAA charts for U.S. waters, including Alaska and the Great Lakes. These charts are up-to-date with corrections from the most recent Notice to Mariners.

charts, paper and electronic: www.allianceforsafenavigation.org. In addition to important resources about paper and electronic charts, there's a link that allows you to check if your NOAA charts are up to date. *See also* "charts, online viewer," above.

charts, print-on-demand: www.oceangrafix.com. Oceangrafix is NOAA's commercial partner, with retail locations across the U.S., and in Canada, Mexico, Japan, and Panama.

charts, raster: www.nauticalcharts.noaa.gov/mcd/Raster/index.htm.

charts, raster and vector comparison: www.landfallnavigation.com/electroniccharts.html.

charts, vector: www.nauticalcharts.noaa.gov/mcd/enc/index.htm.

ECDIS: www.nauticalcharts.noaa.gov/staff/docs/nRNC_EDISperformstandards.pdf.

pilot charts, download: http://msi.nga.mil/NGAPortal/MSI.portal. Click on "Publications." Downloads cover all oceans of the world, one chart for each month. Pilot charts are also available in paper form from chart agents.

COMPASS
compass, general: www.danforthcompass.com *and* www.ritchienavigation.com.

compass pivot wear: www.oceanireland.com.

CORROSION (*see also* Electrical)
Collier, Everett. *Boatowner's Guide to Corrosion*. Camden, Maine: International Marine, 2001. Excellent coverage of all aspects of corrosion for the layman and marine professional.

corrosion control meter: www.sterling-power.com/products-system-test.htm.

corrosion control meter, how to make: www.oceannavigator.com. *Ocean Navigator* #119, Jan/Feb 2002.

CREW and HEALTH (*see also* Safety; Sailing)
Medications and treatments described in first aid and medical books and articles should be considered carefully, because significant changes in recommendations may occur over the years. Review specific recommendations with a medical professional, particularly when stocking an on-board first aid kit.
crew:
Burke, Katy. *The Handbook for Non-Macho Sailors.* Newport, Rhode Island: Seven Seas Press, 1985. How to tackle the strength jobs aboard by learning effective techniques for multiplying muscle power. Out-of-print, available used.

Giesemann, Suzanne. *It's Your Boat Too: A Woman's Guide to Greater Enjoyment on the Water*. Arcata, California: Paradise Cay Publications, 2006. Good advice for women who want to be more than passengers aboard a sail or power yacht.

Greenwald, Michael. *The Cruising Chef Cookbook*, 2nd ed. Ancata, California: Paradise Cay Publications, 2000. A classic galley cookbook, over 20 years in print, with great recipes and many useful tips. The chef will enjoy Greenwald's humorous style, and the crew will enjoy the meals.

Groene, Janet. *Cooking On the Go*, rev. ed. New York: William Morrow, 1987. Simple cooking and provisioning for sailors and campers, with many helpful ideas.

Hayden-Miller, Lisa. *The Galley Guru: Effortless Gourmet Cooking Afloat*. Ancata, California: Paradise Cay Publications, 2008. Wonderful recipes and ideas, all suitable for the limitations of a galley.

Henderson, Richard. *Singlehanded Sailing: The Experiences and Techniques of the Lone Voyagers.* Camden, Maine: International Marine, 1988, 1992. A good basic reference for solo sailors and two-person crews.

Jacobson, Don and John Roberts. *The One-Pot Galley Gourmet: Simple Cooking on Boats*. Camden, Maine: International Marine, 2004. Meat, fish, and vegetarian recipes, menu planning for short cruises. Spiral-bound.

Mazel, Charles. *Heave Ho: My Little Green Book of Seasickness*. Larchmont, New York: Bernel Books, 1995. Written with humor, but full of good advice; read this book before you go out on the water.

Pardey, Lin with Larry Pardey. *The Care and Feeding of Sailing* Crew, 3rd ed. Arcata, California: Pardey Books, 2006. Almost everything you need to know to keep your crew happy, well-fed, and entertained aboard. An excellent, practical reference for cruising and voyaging sailors.

Silver, Jan. *Heavy Weather Cooking*. Camden, Maine: International Marine, 1980. Simple, nutritious meals for rough weather sailing that don't require the cook to spend a lot of time in the galley. If you sail offshore look for this good book. Out of print, but available used.

medical:

Beilan, Michael. *Your Offshore Doctor: A Manual for Medical Self-Sufficiency at Sea*, 2nd ed. Dobbs Ferry, New York: Sheridan House, 1996. Although out-of-date in some respects, this is a useful reference.

Briggs, Spike and Campbell Mackenzie. *On-board Medical Emergency Handbook: First Aid at Sea*. Camden, Maine: International Marine, 2008. Includes quick reference charts.

Brookside Associates™: www.brooksidepress.org/products.htm. Medical education information, with articles, DVDs, and other resources for medical professionals and serious laymen.

Eastman, Peter F. and John M. Levinson. *Advanced First Aid at Sea*, 4th ed. Atglen, Pennsylvania: Schiffer Publishing, 2000. Written by two doctors, this book covers more serious injuries than basic first aid books.

Gill, Paul G. *The On-Board Medical Guide: First Aid and Emergency Medicine Afloat*. Camden, Maine: International Marine, 1996. Although an older book, much of Dr. Gill's advice is still valid. The book has quick-reference cross listings and covers material not found in typical cruising medical books (including childbirth at sea!).

Justins, Douglas and Colin Berry. *First Aid at Sea*. Ancata, California: Paradise Cay Publications, 2010. A sturdy spiral-bound guide to emergency first aid. Recommended by the Royal Ocean Racing Council.

U.S. Public Health Service. *The Ship's Medicine Chest and Medical Aid at Sea.* Fredonia Books: Amsterdam, The Netherlands, 2001. Comprehensive diagnosis and treatment of injuries and illnesses, described in non-technical language. Contains the medical signal code of the International Code of Signals. Designed for merchant mariners and recommended for anyone on land or sea who is away from medical care.

offshore emergency medicine seminars: various organizations host seminars for offshore sailors, conducted by medical professionals. Look for advertisements in cruising magazines.

offshore medical assistance: organizations offer telemedicine services for offshore voyagers, and some also offer emergency medical training for offshore crews. Three examples of companies providing these services are:

Maritime Medical Access at the George Washington University Department of Emergency Medicine: www.gwemed.edu/telemedicine_solutions/maritime_medical_access.aspx.

MedAire (Tempe, Arizona): www.medaire.com/maritime_yacht.asp.

WorldClinic (New London, New Hampshire): www.worldclinic.com.

DESIGN and CONSTRUCTION (*see also* Maintenance; Sailing; Systems)
boatbuilding, maintenance, marine surveying: www.customyachtbuilder.com/links.html. Categorized links to Canadian, UK, and U.S. marine resources.

books and websites:
Brewer, Ted. *Ted Brewer Explains Sailboat Design*. Camden, Maine: International Marine, 1985.

———*Understanding Boat Design*, 4th ed. Camden, Maine: International Marine, 1993. Covers sail and power boat design with clear explanations of the technical aspects, providing a good foundation for understanding boat design and for making a purchase decision. Recommended for people new to the world of boats, as well as more experienced boaters.

———www.tedbrewer.com/yachtdesign.html. His website has information and technical discussions.

Desirable and Undesirable Characteristics of Offshore Yachts. by the Technical Committee of the Cruising Club of America, ed. John Rousmaniere. New York and London: W.W. Norton, 1987. Although the book was written more than 20 years ago, the theories and advice are still valid. The analyses are based on the 750,000 combined offshore miles sailed by the authors, who include engineers and four highly-respected yacht designers. Just because marketing literature says "offshore cruiser" doesn't mean that it's true. Study this book and evaluate yachts for yourself.

Doane, Charles. *The Modern Cruising Sailboat*. See complete citation under "Sailing."

Gerr, Dave. *The Elements of Boat Strength for Builders, Designers, and Owners*. Camden, Maine: International Marine, 1999. Technical and engineering data and information.

———*The Nature of Boats: Insights and Esoterica for the Nautically Obsessed.* Camden, Maine: International Marine, 1995. Aspects of boat design for many types of recreational vessels explained in clear, non-technical language.

Larsson, Lars and Rolf E. Eliasson. *Principles of Yacht Design*, 3rd ed. Camden, Maine: International Marine, 2007.

Nicolson, Ian. *The Boat Data Book*, 6th ed. London: Adlard Coles, 2009. An excellent reference for boat owners and marine professionals. *See also* Vigor's *Boatowner's Handbook*, below.

Sponberg Yacht Design, Inc.: www.sponbergyachtdesign.com. Click on "Articles" for yacht design and engineering articles.

Vigor, John. *Boatowner's Handbook*. See the complete citation under "Maintenance." This book has different information than Nicolson's *Boat Data* Book, above.

———*The Practical Encyclopedia of Boating*. See complete citation under "Sailing."

———*Seaworthy Offshore Sailboat: A Guide to Essential Features, Handling and Gear.* Camden, Maine: International Marine, 2001.

British Waterways Boat Safety Scheme: www.boatsafetyscheme.com/site/Home_1.asp.

Canadian small vessel regulations portal: www.tc.gc.ca/eng/marine-menu.htm. Commercial and non-commercial vessels.

NMMA Certified boat manufacturers: www.discoverboating.com.

passenger-carrying vessels, U.S.: www.access-board.gov/pvaac/commrept/report-summary.htm. Although the report's main emphasis is access for passengers (under the Americans with Disabilities Act), the beginning of the report has a summary of the classification and types of U.S. passenger vessels, with definitions and explanations.

Recreational Craft Directive, application of: www.rya.org.uk/infoadvice/regssafety/Pages/recreationalcraftdirective.aspx.

Recreational Craft Directive text: www.britishmarine.co.uk/upload_pub/RCD_Boatbuilders_Guide_Apr06.pdf, and www.imci.org, click on "Boats and Components."

Spartite®: http://spartite.com.

UK MCA Code of Practise for small commercial vessels: www.bms.com.tr/registration-&-coding/mca-coding.html.

UK MCA regulations for small commercial vessels: www.mcga.gov.uk/c4mca/mcga07-home. Click on "Ships and Cargos" and "Vessel Information."

U.S. Coast Guard boatbuilder regulations: www.uscgboating.org/regulations/boat_builders_handbook_and_regulations.aspx.

U.S. Coast Guard small vessel stability: www.uscg.mil/pvs/SPV.asp.

wing-in-ground craft: www.se-technology.com/wig/index.php.

EDUCATION, TRAINING, LICENSING (*see also* Radio; Safety)

There are many classroom and online sources for formal education and training in a variety of marine fields such as sailing, navigation, celestial navigation, diesel engines, captain licensing, powerboat operation, and many other areas. A few of the many are listed below. Use a search engine, read school advertisements in sailing magazines, and talk to people who have taken a course at the school you may be considering. Some courses are expensive and others are inexpensive or free. Cost is not always an indicator of quality, although courses for professionals and hands-on courses are more expensive than online and basic classroom courses.

American Boat and Yacht Council, ABYC: www.abycinc.org. Professional technical courses.

The ABYC Standards are available for a free trial at the website. A good resource for the serious DIY person.

American Sailing Association, ASA: www.asa.com. Many sailing schools across the U.S. and in a number of other countries offer ASA courses.

basic boating courses and exams, U.S. and Canada:
www.boat-ed.com.

www.boaterexam.com.

Canadian pleasure craft operator card (PCOC):

www.cps-ecp.ca.

www.boaterexam.com/canada.

www.tc.gc.ca/eng/marinesafety/debs-obs-paperwork-paperwork_operatorfaq-2233.htm.

Canadian Power and Sail Squadron: www.cps-ecp.ca. Click on "Courses." More than 18 courses are offered to members.

***Cruising World* seminars**: www.crusingworld.com. The magazine hosts a variety of seminars and presentations at boat shows and other boating events around the U.S. Check the *CW* and boat show websites.

Safety at Sea Seminars: http://offshore.ussailing.org/SAS.htm. Sponsored by ISAF, these day-long seminars include practical demonstrations of safety equipment. There's an optional second day with practical, hands-on training in the water and ashore. Recommended for sailors venturing offshore.

Sailtrain online education: www.sailtrain.co.uk.. Self-study of many topics for sailors and cruisers, including the International Navigation Rules, navigation and piloting, anchoring, safety, and other subjects. The website is designed to assist candidates for the RYA Day Skipper, Coastal Skipper or Yachtmaster practical and theory courses and exams, and the information is excellent for beginning to advanced sailors. *The section on "Tips" is worth browsing*. Although aimed at UK sailors, almost all the information is relevant no matter where you sail.

Seven Seas Cruising Association: SSCA "webinars" are online seminars for members on a variety of nautical topics. The organization also hosts seminars and presentations for cruisers at SSCA gams.

Starpath School of Navigation: www.starpath.com. Starpath offers online courses, books, and software for learning coastal piloting, celestial navigation, Navigation Rules, radar, marine weather, and emergency navigation. The website also has links to other nautical resources.

U.S. boater licensing: www.boaterexam.com.

U.S. Coast Guard merchant mariner licensing: www.uscg.mil/nmc.

U.S. Power Squadrons: www.usps.org. Seamanship, piloting, engine maintenance, celestial navigation, cruise planning, and other courses for members.

Westlawn Institute of Marine Technology: www.westlawn.edu. Professional courses for yacht designers, marine surveyors, and other marine industry professionals.

ELECTRICAL (*see also* Engines)
ABYC standards for electrical installation, summary: www.marinco.com/page/abyc-standards.

AC electrical standards worldwide: www.kropla.com/electric2.htm.

battery basics: www.autoshop101.com/forms/hweb3.pdf. An introduction to basic battery technology.
books:
Brotherton, Miner and Edwin Sherman. *The 12-Volt Bible for Boats*, 2nd ed. Camden, Maine: International Marine, 2003. This book is appropriate for the beginner; it provides a foundation for understanding more complex marine electrical books and articles.

Payne, John C. *The Marine Electrical and Electronics Bible*, 3rd ed. Dobbs Ferry, New York: Sheridan House, 2007. Comprehensive, with practical troubleshooting guides; emphasis on sailboat systems.

Sherman, Edwin. *Electronics Troubleshooting: A Manual for Boatowners and Marine Technicians.* Camden, Maine: International Marine, 2007. Edwin Sherman is an ABYC senior instructor and writer. This excellent book is suitable for people with some experience in marine electrical systems and equipment.

Wing, Charlie. *Boatowner's Illustrated Electrical Handbook*, 2nd ed. Camden, Maine: International Marine, 2006. Maintaining, repairing, and upgrading a boat's AC and DC electrical systems to ABYC standards. Suitable for novice or experienced DIY persons, and a good guide to understanding the electrical system, even if you don't do the work yourself.

Ferris Power Products: http://ferrispowerproducts.com/professional.html. Alternators, wind and water generators, and solar power for boats, home, and travel vehicles.

marine electrical wire: Ancor marine grade™ electrical wire and cable: www.marinco.com.

www.marinco.com/page/marinecolorcodes.

www.marinco.com/page/wire-tech-data.

ELECTRONICS and ELECTRONIC NAVIGATION (*see also* Navigation and Piloting; Radio)

AIS Class B Static Data form: www.sea-tech.com/ClassB.pdf.

AIS live ship tracking*:* www.marinetraffic.com. A fascinating website.

AIS technology*:*
Militech Marine: www.milltechmarine.com. A company that specializes in AIS equipment and accessories. See the FAQ for questions and answers about AIS.

www.navcen.uscg.gov/enav/AIS.

electronic charts: Doyle, Mark and Diana. *Get Onboard with E-Charting*. See complete citation under "Charts."

electronics, general

Ellison, Ben. "Where Are We Headed? Marine Electronics Finally Seem to Have the User in Mind." *Yachting Magazine* online, Jan. 4, 2010. www.yachtingmagazine.com/article/Where-Are-We-Headed.

Wood, Jason Y. "The Electronics of Long-Range Cruising." *Yachting Magazine* online, Mar. 24, 2009. www.yachtingmagazine.com/article/The-Long-View.

www.powerandmotoryacht.com/boat-electronics. Search the site for marine electronics articles and reviews.

electronics quick reference card: see Davis Instruments under "Navigation and Piloting."

forward-looking sonar:
www.echopilot.com.

www.farsounder.com.

www.interphase-tech.com.

www.powerandmotoryacht.com/electronics/0702sonar.

www.pilotmarine.com.

LORAN-C discontinuation: www.navcen.uscg.gov/Loran/default.htm.

Racon: www.navcen.uscg.gov/enav/racon.htm.

radar:
Bartlett, Tim. *Radar Afloat*, 3rd ed. Chichester: Wiley Nautical, 2006. This basic book is recommended for the RYA radar course.

Burch, David. *Radar for Mariners*. Camden, Maine: International Marine, 2005. The book includes a CD with an interactive radar simulator, sample radar manuals, radar plotting aids, and a complete copy of the *Navigation Rules*.

Ellison, Ben. "Small Radar Systems Explained." *Yachting Magazine* online, Sept. 15, 2009. www.yachtingmagazine.com/article/Value-Added.

EMERGENCIES (*see also* Safety)
book:
Meisel, Tony. *On-board Emergency Handbook*. Camden, Maine: International Marine, 2006. The cover says the book is "your indispensable guide for handling any challenge at sea." Very clear process diagrams for fast reference. Keep this book aboard and study it before you need it.

Emergency drills: Alaska Marine Safety Association (AMSEA) video, *Beating the Odds: Onboard Emergency Drills*, 2002.

EPIRB batteries replacement and disposal: www.suite101.com/content/improper-epirb-battery-replacement-a175566.

EPIRB registration, Canadian beacons: www.canadianbeaconregistry.forces.gc.ca.

EPIRB registration, UK beacons: www.mcga.gov.uk. Click on "Search and Rescue" and scroll down to EPIRB registration.

EPIRB registration, U.S. beacons: https://beaconregistration.noaa.gov. Registration is free. Beacon registry can be transferred to a new owner, who must re-register it.

helicopter rescue: http://amsea.org. (Alaska Marine Safety Association) DVD *Rescue at Sea: A Guide to Helicopter Rescue and Dewatering Pumps*, 2003.

helicopter rescue articles: www.sailingmagazine.net/news/features/1009-helicopter-rescue-procedure.

www.sailtrain.co.uk/seamanship/helicopter.htm

helicopter rescue video:
www.youtube.com/watch?v=-wc7mY4wy7o&feature=player_embedded. A U.S. Coast Guard video in two parts.

single-sideband distress frequencies and watchkeeping schedules, U.S. Coast Guard:

www.navcen.uscg.gov/marcomms/cgcomms/call.htm.

ENGINES and PROPULSION (*see also* Electrical; Maintenance)

Baja fuel filters: www.bajafilters.com.

biodiesel:

www.biodieselathome.net.

www.biodiesel.org.

www.biodiesel.org/resources/faqs.

books:
Calder, Nigel. *Marine Diesel Engines: Maintenance, Troubleshooting and Repair*, 3rd ed. Camden, Maine: International Marine, 2006. A comprehensive reference for understanding and maintaining diesel engines. Calder writes very clearly, and the many photos and diagrams will guide you through engine tasks, or help you understand the process when a mechanic will do the work.

Gerr, Dave. *The Propeller Handbook: The Complete Reference for Choosing, Installing and Understanding Boat Propellers*. Camden, Maine: International Marine, 2001. Written for the layman but with enough engineering talk to explain the "whys," this book has all you need to know about propellers.

Pallas, Jean-Luc. *Marine Diesel Engines: Maintenance and Repair Manual*. Dobbs Ferry, New York: Sheridan House, 2006. Excellent book with many color photographs, diagrams, and clear explanations. Tasks are categorized by degree of difficulty.

CV joints and propeller tip clearance: http://aquadriveusa.com/articles/novibes_goodvibes.htm.

diesel-electric propulsion systems:
Calder. *Marine Diesel Engines*, pp. 261-263.

www.ossapowerlite.com.

www.technipowersystems.com/marine-products.

diesel fuel lubricity tests: www.johnfjensen.com/Diesel_fuel_additive_test.pdf. This study was done in 2007; further studies will be carried out as ultra-low sulfur diesel becomes the only type available.

fuel polishing: www.engineeringtalk.com/news/par/par541.html.

propeller manufacturers:
Autoprop and Varifold Propellers: Bruntons Propellers: www.bruntons-propellers.com.

Flexofold Propellers:www.flexofold.com.

Gori® Propellers: http://ab-marine.com/node/3 and www.gori-propeller.dk.

Kiwiprops™: www.kiwiprops.co.nz.

Max Prop:www.max-prop.com and www.pyiinc.com.

Seahawk Propellers: www.seahawk.com.au. Stainless steel propellers.

Variprop: http://eng.variprop.de.

propellers, general:
www.northcoastproptech.com/problems.htm.

propeller shaft line cutters:
www.propprotect.com. Gators.

www.quickwater.com.au. The quicKutter™.

www.spursmarine.com. Spurs®.

www.wardmarine.com/proprotec.html. The Prop Protector.

saildrives:
Calder. Marine Diesel Engines, pp. 205-08.

www.saildrive.us/index.html.

www.yanmar.com.

shaft seal, PSS brand: www.shaftseal.com.

Speedseal™ pump covers: www.speedseal.com.

waterlift muffler operation and installation: www.practical-sailor.com/marine/waterliftmuffler.pdf.

GEOGRAPHICAL and GEOPHYSICAL
physical geography: www.physicalgeography.net/physgeoglos/.html.

territorial sea: www.un.org/Depts/los/convention_agreements/texts/unclos/part2.htm.

LINES and KNOTS (*see also* Rigging)
baggywrinkle, instructions for making:
www.schoonerman.com/sailingterms/baggywrinkle.htm.

knot tying instruction:
There are probably 30 knot tying books. Because learning to tie knots is a visual experience, the drawings and instructions must be clear and easy-to-follow. Not all people learn the same way. Therefore, don't buy a knot book without looking at it to see if it makes sense to you. Below are three basic resources that many sailors have used to teach themselves:

www.animatedknots.com. In my opinion, this is the best resource. The website is comprehensive, has animations that show how to tie the knots, and offers downloads and a CD. There are knots for all sorts of non-nautical applications as well. There's even a phone app.

Blandford, Percy. *Practical Knots and Ropework*. n.p.: Dover Publications, 2007. The previous Tab Books edition (1980) may be available used, but the Dover edition covers synthetic ropes. www.doverpublications.com. Not a fancy book, but the line drawings are clear and relatively easy to follow. Lots of knots for many uses.

Smith, Hervey Garett. *The Arts of the Sailor*: *Knotting, Splicing and Ropework*. n.p.:Dover Publications, 1990. Older editions of this classic may be available used.

———*The Marlinspike Sailor*. Camden, Maine: International Marine, 1993. In addition to teaching some basic knots and splices, the book has decorative and functional rope and canvas projects, illustrated with excellent drawings.

Ashley, Clifford W. *The Ashley Book of Knots*. Garden City, NY: Doubleday, 1944. Still in print, this is the bible of knots. It has 7,000 excellent drawings of over 3,900 knots. One of the more basic knots and ropework books will suffice for most of us, but if you become smitten by knots, this book is for you. It's great for browsing.

sheet loads: www.harken.com/pdf/loads.pdf.

MAINTENANCE (*see also* Design; Engines; Rigging; Sailing)

boatbuilding, maintenance, marine surveying: www.customyachtbuilder.com/links.html. Categorized links to Canadian, UK, and U.S. marine resources.

books, magazines, websites:

BoatU.S.: www.boatus.com/boattech. A website with technical advice for buying, installing, maintaining, and using a variety of marine products.

Calder, Nigel: *Boatowner's Mechanical and Electrical Manual*. See complete citation under "Systems."

Casey, Don. *Canvaswork and Sail Repair*. Camden, Maine: International Marine, 1996. Basic sail repair and useful fabric projects, illustrated with clear drawings.

———*Don Casey's Complete Illustrated Sailboat Maintenance Manual*. Camden, Maine: International Marine, 2005. A comprehensive book for the DIY sailboat owner.

———*Inspecting the Aging Sailboat*. Camden, Maine: International Marine, 2004. If you own an aging sailboat or are thinking of buying one, read this book.

———*This Old Boat*, 2nd ed. Camden, Maine: International Marine, 2009. An excellent resource for the committed DIY person.

DIY Boatowner: www.diy-boat.com. A monthly magazine devoted to maintaining and upgrading power and sailboats. Articles are written by a variety of marine professionals and skilled DIY mariners. Also available are CDs and other electronic publications that cover specific topic areas.

Good Old Boat: www.goodoldboat.com. A magazine with articles written by boat owners about maintenance and upgrades to cruising sailboats of the 1950s to the 1990s. Articles and a number of links related to older boats, including a comprehensive list of owners' associations.

Marino, Emiliano. *The Sailmaker's Apprentice: A Guide for the Self-reliant Sailor*. Camden, Maine: International Marine, 2001. The book includes a discussion of sail theory and instructions for constructing, repairing, and maintaining traditional sails (i.e. not high-tech racing sails). There are a number of useful tables and excellent illustrations.

Mustin, Henry. *Surveying Fiberglass Sailboats: A Step-by Step Guide for Buyers and Owners*. Camden, Maine: International Marine, 1994. Although the book was written some years ago, it's a basic guide for an owner or prospective buyer. Using this book may help you determine if a vessel is worth considering for purchase or major renovation, before having a professional marine survey.

Practical Boat Owner: www.pbo.co.uk. An online and print magazine for the DIY sailor. The website has a link to Yacht and Boating World (www.ybw.com), which has articles on all aspects of recreational boating, including boat and product reviews. Although aimed at the UK reader, both websites provide useful information for all sailors.

Practical Sailor: www.practical-sailor.com. A monthly magazine that presents tests results and reviews of boats, marine equipment, maintenance products, books, safety gear, and more. *PS* accepts no advertising, so there's a degree of impartiality in the opinions. The website has open-access links to a number of nautical websites. A subscription is required to access complete articles.

Vigor, John. *Boatowner's Handbook: Reference Data for Maintenance, Repair, Navigation, and Seamanship.* Camden, Maine: International Marine, 2001. A comprehensive reference. *See also* Nicholson. *The Boat Data Book* (under "Design"), which has different useful information.

———*The Practical Encyclopedia of Boating*: see complete citation under "Sailing."

Yacht and Boating World: www.ybw.com. See *Practical Boat Owner*, above.

marine products:

AWAB stainless steel hose clamps: www.awabllc.com. AWAB manufactures high quality stainless steel hose clamps, "Tail Tips," and two types of flexible drivers that fit AWAB clamp screws. The website has a list of distributors for AWAB products.

Duck Tape®: www.duckbrand.com.

Jamestown Distributors: www.jamestowndistributors.com. Marine products of all kinds: hardware, boatbuilding and maintenance products, tools, safety gear, electronics, boating supplies, and more. *Click on "How To" for more than 1,000 categorized articles*. An excellent resource.

Jubilee® clips (hose clamps): www.jubileeclips.co.uk.

Sailrite: www.sailrite.com. Online supplier of everything for sailmaking and boat fabric projects: sewing machines, tools, sewing supplies, fabrics, books, videos, instruction sheets, and downloadable resources.

WD-40®: www.wd40.com. 2000 uses afloat and ashore for this product.

METALS (*see also* Corrosion; Rigging)
chrome plating: www.finishing.com/faqs/chrome.html.

electropolishing and passivation: www.ableelectropolishing.com/electrop.htm.

stainless steel: www.corrosionist.com/Materials_Stainless_Steel_Properties.htm.

www.delstar.com/passivating.html.

MISCELLANEOUS
flag etiquette and dressing ship: www.usps.org/f_stuff/etiquett.html#dressing-ship.

flags and meanings: www.boatsafe.com/nauticalknowhow/flags.htm.

marine equipment manufacturers and suppliers: (a small sampling)
The Binnacle, online marine chandlery: http://ca.binnacle.com. Based in Halifax, Nova Scotia, the company offers a variety of marine products, including Canadian charts and publications. The website has links to websites of interest to boaters in Canadian waters.

Defender® Marine Outfitters: www.defender.com. A U.S. mail-order marine supply company that ships internationally.

Edson® Marine:www.edsonmarine.com. Steering systems and marine accessories.

Forespar® Marine Products: www.forespar.com. Equipment for power and sail vessels, including Marelon® marine plumbing products.

Harken® : www.harken.com. Equipment for sailboats.

Imtra® Marine Products: www.imtra.com. Equipment for power and sail vessels, including windlasses, anchoring system components, bow thrusters, and more.

Jamestown Distributors: www.jamestowndistributors.com. Marine products of all kinds: hardware, boatbuilding and maintenance products, tools, safety gear, electronics, boating supplies, and more.

Landfall Navigation™: www.landfallnavigation.com. The company's slogan is "Where Safe Voyages Begin." Safety gear, navigation products (paper and electronic charts, electronics, navigation tools), nautical books, clothing, marine training courses, and more. On line store and chandlery in Stamford, Connecticut.

Lewmar: www.lewmar.com. Equipment for sail and power vessels.

Navimo USA: www.plastimousa.com. Wholesale importers of a wide variety of marine equipment, including products from Plastimo, Max Power, Goiot, Nuova Rade, XM Yachting, Andersen winches, and Manson anchors. See the website for products and distributors.

Schaefer Marine: www.schaefermarine.com. Equipment for sail and power vessels.

Soverel 33: www.soverel33.com/Quicklinks/Index.html. Sponsored by the Soverel 33 class association, but for all sailors. The categorized "Quick Links" to hundreds of marine equipment manufacturers speeds up your research.

Ronstan: www.ronstan.com. Sailboat hardware.

Torresen Marine, Inc.: http://shop.torresen.com/ships_store. Comprehensive on line ship's store with all types of marine products for sailing vessels, including engine parts, reference articles, and discussion forums for Universal, Volvo, Westerbeke, and Yanmar marine engines. The company ships internationally.

Tylaska: www.tylaska.com. American manufacturer of hardware for small and large sailboats, including many types of shackles, shackle fids, spar fittings, and more.

Vetus®: www.vetus.nl. Marine equipment manufacturer of engines, windlasses, bow thrusters, engine controls, tanks, hatches, ventilators, and more. Distributors in many countries.

West Marine: www.westmarine.com. A U.S. marine supply company (online and retail stores) that ships internationally. The West Marine catalogue (paper and online) has articles about the selection, installation, and use of marine products. Click on "West Advisor®."

Wichard®: www.wichard.com. Hardware for sailboats, including blocks, pad eyes, snap hooks, shackles, swivels, and safety products (jacklines, tethers, safety hooks, boom brake).

metric conversions: www.sciencemadesimple.com/conversions.html. A convenient site for fast calculation of metric and other unit conversions for all kinds of measurements.

no-discharge areas, U.S. general information:

www.epa.gov/owow/oceans/regulatory/vessel_sewage.

semaphore signaling: www.anbg.gov.au/flags/semaphore.html.

superstitions, sailors':
http://boatingsailing.suite101.com/article.cfm/traditional_nautical_superstitions.

www.dockwalk.com/Essentials/HotTopics.aspx?id=23170.

http://madmariner.com/tip/031508.

http://pacificoffshorerigging.com/nautical_superstitions.htm.

www.superstitious-minds.info/Nautical-Superstitions.html.

time signals, CHU Canada:
www.nrc-cnrc.gc.ca/eng/services/inms/time-services/short-wave.html.

time signals, WWV and WWVH: www.nist.gov/pml/div688/grp40/wwv.cfm.

U.S. Coast Guard recreational boating website: www.uscgboating.org.

weather instruments and nautical instruments: www.robertwhite.com.

websites:

Explorersweb™: www.explorersweb.com/oceans. Explorersweb is devoted to expeditions and adventures on land and sea. The website has links to information of interest to offshore and adventurous sailors.

The Mother of All Maritime Links (John's Nautical links): www.boat-links.com/boatlink.html. A fascinating website with categorized links to almost everything nautical. Great browsing.

Ocean Ireland: www.oceanireland.com. Marine surveyors and charter agents based in Kinsale, Republic of Ireland. Click on "Yacht and Small Craft Surveys" and "Services" for informative general information.

Panama Canal live lock cameras: www.pancanal.com/eng/photo/camera-java.html.

world time zones: www.worldtimezone.com.

NAUTICAL TERMS, GENERAL (*see also* Design; Sailing)

Desouter, Denny. *The Adlard Coles Book of Boatwords: A Dictionary of Nautical Terms*. London: Adlard Coles, 1991 and 2010 (reissue). A dictionary of "over 1,500" historical and modern nautical terms for sail and power. Brief explanations and line drawings. If you're not familiar with British usage, this book will be helpful when reading UK publications or when speaking with UK sailors.

NAVIGATION and PILOTING (*see also* Charts; Electronics; Navigation Rules, Publications)

binoculars and goggles, marine:

www.captainsnautical.com.

www.opticsplanet.net/binmarine.html.

www.westmarine.com. Click on "West Advisor®," "West Advisor Articles," and scroll to "binoculars."

thermal (IR and FLIR) technology: www.infrared1.com *and* www.flir.com.

books and websites:

Bowditch or *The American Practical Navigator*. Bethesda, Maryland: National Imagery and Mapping Agency, 2002. A standard reference for professional and dedicated recreational mariners. All topics in marine navigation are covered, including navigational astronomy, oceanography, and weather. It has an extensive glossary of marine navigation terms. Recommended for mariners who are ready to progress toward a professional understanding of navigation and piloting. It also has a number of useful tables for navigation and meteorological calculations. Paper copies and a searchable CD-ROM are available from a variety of sources, or download (individual chapters or the complete book) at http://msi.nga.mil/NGAPortal/MSI.portal. Click on "Publications."

Cutler, Thomas J. *Dutton's Nautical Navigation*, 15th ed. Annapolis, Maryland: The Naval Institute Press, 2003. Written for dedicated recreational mariners and professional navigators, this book covers all topics in modern navigation. Learn navigation from Maloney's *Chapman*, and then consider this more advanced book.

Eyges, Leonard. *The Practical Pilot: Coastal Navigation by Eye, Intuition and Common Sense*. Camden, Maine: International Marine, 1989. Out-of-print, but it's well-worth seeking a used copy. This book covers a number of interesting and effective techniques for navigating without electronics.

Goode, John and Dick Everitt: *Navigation Made Simple.* Poole, England: E.G. Publications, 1992.

Maloney, Elbert S. *Chapman Piloting and Seamanship*. See complete citation under "Sailing."

Trimmer, John W. *How to Avoid Huge Ships*, 2nd ed. Centreville, Maryland: Cornell Maritime Press, 1993. Out-of-print, but worth seeking a used copy. Ship captain Trimmer wrote this book to help small vessel operators understand how ships operate so that they can avoid close encounters, or worse.

U.S. Coast Pilots®: www.nauticalcharts.noaa.gov. Click on "Nautical Charts & Pubs." and "United States Coast Pilots." Coast Pilots are available in paper and PDF form.

U.S. Light Lists: www.navcen.uscg.gov. Scroll down to "Maritime Information," click on "Nav Pubs and Documents" and follow the links. Light Lists are available in paper and for download in PDF form.

Canadian navigation resources:
Canadian Coast Guard portal: www.ccg-gcc.gc.ca.

Canadian Coast Guard Aids to Navigation and Notices to Mariners portal: www.notmar.gc.ca.

Canadian Coast Guard aids to navigation system: www.ccg-gcc.gc.ca/eng/Ccg/atn_Aids_To_Navigation_System.

Canadian Hydrographic Service: www.charts.gc.ca.

St. Lawrence Seaway: www.greatlakes-seaway.com/en/index.html. Click on "Recreational Boating."

Welland Canal: www.wellandcanal.com.

charts and GPS: See the brochure *Using Nautical Charts with GPS* at http://msi.nga.mil/NGAPortal/MSI.portal; click on "miscellaneous products."

cruising guides and pilots: see "Publications."

IALA buoyage system: www.nauticalissues.com/en/iala.html.

ice navigation: *Bowditch* chapter 33 Ice Navigation, and download at http://msi.nga.mil/NGAPortal/MSI.portal. Click on "Publications."

lighthouses:
Ireland and Northern Ireland: www.commissionersofirishlights.com.

Scotland and Isle of Man: www.nlb.org.uk.

UK (including Wales and the Channel Islands): www.trinityhouse.co.uk.

U.S.: www.uscg.mil/history/h_lhindex.asp.

navigation instruments and navigational aids:
Captain's Nautical Supplies: www.captainsnautical.com. Worldwide charts, navigational tools, books, software, optical products, compasses, weather instruments, and more.

Celestaire: www.celestaire.com. According to the website, Celestaire has the "world's largest selection of marine sextants, navigation computers, compasses, books, videos and software for traditional navigation." An excellent resource.

Davis Marine Instruments: www.davisnet.com/marine/index.asp. Navigation and other marine products, including a series of useful plastic quick reference cards: basic boating guide, coastwise piloting, a set of pocket cards (pre-departure check, fuelling, U.S. buoyage, Rules of the Road, radio, navigation lights, emergencies), marine electronics, International Navigation Rules and buoyage, U.S. navigation rules and buoyage, celestial navigation, and weather. Available at chandleries and from nautical booksellers. Highly-recommended.

Weems & Plath®: www.weems-plath.com. Navigation tools, clocks, barometers.

UK chart and navigation publication updating:
Admiralty charts weekly notices to mariners: www.ukho.gov.uk/ProductsandServices/MartimeSafety/Pages/NMPublic.aspx.

Imray charts and publications: www.imray.com. All Imray products may be updated by consulting this website. The Admiralty weekly notices to mariners should also be checked when updating Imray charts.

UK light lists: www.ukho.gov.uk. UK and worldwide light lists in paper form.

U.S. chart and navigation publication updating:

NOAA charts: www.nauticalcharts.noaa.gov/mcd/OnLineViewer.html. View all NOAA charts for U.S. waters, including Alaska and the Great Lakes. These charts are up-to-date with corrections from the most recent Notice to Mariners.

U.S. Coast Pilots®: www.nauticalcharts.noaa.gov. Click on "Nautical Charts & Pubs." and "United States Coast Pilots." Links to the corrections are with each Coast Pilot volume.

U.S. Local Notice to Mariners and U.S. Light List corrections: www.navcen.uscg.gov. Scroll down to "Maritime Information," click on "Nav Pubs and Documents," and follow the links to the publications and corrections.

U.S. Coast Guard aids to navigation system: www.uscg.mil/d13/dpw/docs/usaidstonavigationsystembooklet23dec03.pdf. Complete information, including color charts.

U.S. Coast Guard Navigation Center: this is the first place to look for U.S. navigation information, including the Local Notice to Mariners, Light Lists and corrections, navigation rules and regulations, the electronic copy of the Navigation Rules, AIS information, radio communications, GPS/DGPS information, and more.

Vessel Traffic Services worldwide: www.worldvtsguide.org.

NAVIGATION RULES

books:

Allen, Craig H. *Farwell's Rules of the Nautical Road*, 8th ed. Annapolis, Maryland: Naval Institute Press, 2005. A comprehensive reference for anyone who attempts understand what the terse and sometimes cryptic Navigation Rules really mean. You'll also get a sense of why the interpretation of the Rules is so difficult for mariners and the courts alike. Read this book after you've mastered the Rules.

Navigation Rules: International and Inland. U.S. Coast Guard. Ancata, California: Paradise Cay Publications, n.d. Buy the latest edition. An up-to-date copy of this book (or the electronic version) is required on all vessels over 12m/39.4ft in length operating in U.S. waters. *See also* "Navigation Rules updating," below.

Navigation Rules download: www.navcen.uscg.gov/mwv/navrules/navrules.htm. (International and Inland Rules).

Wing, Charlie. *The One-Minute Guide to the Nautical Rules of the Road: A United States Power Squadrons' Guide*, 2nd ed. Camden, Maine: International Marine, 2006. The book includes a complete copy of the Navigation Rules, with interpretations and decision-making guidance.

Navigation Rules online study:

www.boatus.com/foundation/guide/navigation_1.htm.

www.starpath.com/navrules/navrules_title.htm.

www.seasources.net.

www.sailtrain.co.uk/lrpcs. (International Rules only).

Navigation Rules poem (public domain): cited in www.boatsafe.com/nauticalknowhow/pneumonics.htm, *ELDRIDGE Tide and Pilot Book*, and *The Oxford Companion to Ships and the Sea*.

Navigation Rules quick reference cards: recommended for all boats. See Davis Marine Instruments, under "Navigation and Piloting," "navigation instruments."

Navigation Rules, updating: www.navcen.uscg.gov. Click on "Navigation Rules." This website has changes to the Rules before they appear in printed copies; check to see if any corrections apply to a paper copy.

ORGANIZATIONS

American Boat and Yacht Council, ABYC®: www.abyc.com.

American Bureau of Shipping, ABS: www.eagle.org.

American Sailing Association, ASA: www.asa.com.

AMVER system: www.amver.com.

British Marine Electronics Association, BMEA: www.bmea.org.

British Waterways Marinas, Ltd., BWML: www.bwml.co.uk.

Boat Owners Association of The United States, BoatU.S.: www.boatus.com.

BoatU.S. Foundation: www.boatus.org.

Canadian Coast Guard: www.ccg-gcc.gc.ca.

Canadian Coast Guard Auxiliary: www.ccga-gcac.com.

Canadian Power and Sail Squadron: www.cps-ecp.ca.

Canadian Safe Boating Council, CSBC: www.csbc.ca.

Canadian Standards Association, CSA: www.csa.ca/cm/ca/en/home.

Cruising Association, CA: www.cruising.org.uk.

Cruising Club of America, CCA: www.cruisingclub.org.

Canadian Yachting Association™ ,CYA: www.sailing.ca.

COSPAS-SARSAT: www.cospas-sarsat.org.

Cruising Association, CA: www.cruising.org.uk.

Cruising Rally Association: www.carib1500.com.

Den Norske Veritas, DNV: www.dnv.com.

Environment Canada: www.weatheroffice.gc.ca/canada_e.html.

European Union: http://europa.eu/abc/european_countries/index_en.htm.

Federal Communications Commission, FCC: www.fcc.gov.

Germanischer Lloyds, GL: www.gl-group.com.

Globalstar: www.globalstar.com/en.

IALA/IASM: www.iala-aism.org.

Inmarsat: www.inmarsat.com.

International Association for Marine Electronics, CIRM: www.cirm.org.

International Hydrographic Organization, IHO: www.iho-ohi.net/english/home.

International Marine Certification Institute, IMCI: www.imci.org.

International Maritime Organization, IMO: www.imo.org.

International Organization for Standardization, ISO: www.iso.org/iso/home.htm.

International Sailing Federation, ISAF: www.sailing.org.

International Telecommunications Union, ITU: www.itu.int.

Iridium Communications: www.iridium.com.

Irish Sailing Association, ISA: www.sailing.ie.

Lloyd's Register, LR: www.lr.org.

Maritime and Coast Guard Agency, MCA: www.mcga.gov.uk.

National Association of Marine Surveyors, NAMSGlobal®: www.namsglobal.org.

National Association of Safe Boating Administrators, NASBLA: http://nasbla.org.

National Fire Protection Association, NFPA®: www.nfpa.org.

National Geospatial and Intelligence Agency, NGA: www1.nga.mil.

National Institute of Standards and Technology, NIST:www.nist.gov.

National Marine Electronics Association, NMEA®: www.nmea.org.

National Marine Manufacturers Association, NMMA®: www.nmma.org.

National Marine Manufacturers Association, Canada, NMMA Canada: www.cmma.ca.

National Oceanic and Atmospheric Administration, NOAA: www.noaa.gov.

National Telecommunications and Information Administration, NTIA: www.ntia.doc.gov.

National Weather Service, NWS: www.nws.noaa.gov.

Ocean Cruising Club, OCC: www.oceancruisingclub.org.

Registro Italiano Navale, RNLI: www.rina.org.

Royal National Lifeboat Institution, RNLI: www.rnli.org.uk.

Royal Ocean Racing Club, RORC: www.rorc.org.

Royal Yachting Association, RYA: www.rya.org.uk.

SAE International, SAE: www.sae.org.

Sea Tow®: www.seatow.com.

Seven Seas Cruising Association, SSCA: www.ssca.org.

Society of Accredited Marine Surveyors, Inc., SAMS®: www.marinesurvey.org.

The Society of Naval Architects and Marine Engineers, SNAME: www.sname.org/SNAME/SNAME/Home.

Transport Canada: www.tc.gc.ca.

Transport Canada marine: www.tc.gc.ca/eng/marine-menu.htm.

Underwriters Laboratories: www.ul.com.

United States Coast Guard, USCG: www.uscg.mil.

United States Coast Guard Auxiliary: www.cgaux.org.

United States Power Squadrons®: www.usps.org.

U.S. Sailing: www.ussailing.org.

World Cruising Club: www.worldcruising.com.

PUBLICATIONS, GENERAL and WEBSITES

cruising guides and pilots: available from nautical booksellers and chandleries. A small selection follows.

Canada: The Cruising Club of America, CCA: www.cruisingclub.org. Click on "Publications." CCA cruising guides to the Canadian Maritimes (individual books for Nova Scotia, Newfoundland, and Labrador).

See also The Binnacle and The Nautical Mind under "nautical booksellers," below.

Europe, general guides:

The Cruising Almanac (biennial editions covering the Faeroes to Gibraltar, including the UK and Ireland), published by the Cruising Association. Available from the Cruising Association and nautical booksellers.

Cruising Club of America, CCA: www.cruisingclub.org. Click on "Publications." A PDF planning guide for yachts intending to sail in European waters may be downloaded from the website.

Reed's Nautical Almanac: www.reedsnauticalalmanac.co.uk. Annual editions for European waters. Available from chandleries, nautical booksellers, and in digital editions

Royal Cruising Club (RCC) Pilotage Foundation: www.rccpf.org.uk; click on "Publications." The RCC produces pilots and cruising guides for European waters.

Ireland: Irish Cruising Club at www.irishcruisingclub.com. Click on "Publications." The ICC publishes two definitive cruising guides for all Irish waters: *East and North Coasts* and *South and West Coasts*.

Scotland:
Caledonian Canal Skipper's Guide at www.waterscape.com/media/documents/20714.pdf.

Clyde Cruising Club at www.clyde.org. Click on "Sailing Directions." The CCC publishes six definitive cruising guides to Scottish waters.

Crinan Canal skipper's guide at www.waterscape.com/media/documents/21281.

U.S., the Caribbean, and other waters:
Consult the websites of "nautical booksellers" for areas of interest. Extensive selection.

Eldridge Tide and Pilot Book. Boston, Massachusetts: Marion Jewett White, Robert Eldridge White, Jr., and Linda Foster White Publishers. Annual edition for the north American east coast from Florida to Nova Scotia, with online supplements. Since 1875 east coast mariners have relied on this excellent pilot. Look for the yellow cover.

Reed's Nautical Almanac: Individual annual editions for the U.S. east coast, west coast, and the Caribbean. Available at chandleries and nautical booksellers.

Royal Cruising Club (RCC) Pilotage Foundation: www.rccpf.org.uk; click on "Publications." The RCC produces pilots and cruising guides for the north and south Atlantic, the Southern Islands, and the Antarctic Peninsula.

magazines and websites:
Bluewater Sailing: www.bwsailing.com. A monthly magazine for cruising

sailors, covering a wide range of topics. Subscribers may choose to receive an informative weekly email newsletter.

Cruising World: www.cruisingworld.com. A monthly magazine that covers all aspects of cruising under sail. The website has open-access information, as well as special features for subscribers. Different coverage from *Sail* and *Sailing Magazine*.

MyBoatsGear: www.myboatsgear.com. A website with reviews of all types of marine products. This is a good site for learning about new products and doing comparison shopping. It has direct links to manufacturers. Easy to navigate and recommended for browsing.

Mad Mariner: www.madmariner.com. A *daily* electronic magazine for subscribers, by the publishers of *DIY Boatowner* (see "Maintenance"). Articles and links with a broad appeal for power and sail boaters. Also available in Spanish: www.marineroloco.com.

Ocean Navigator: www.oceannavigator.com. A magazine for offshore sailors, covering a wide range of topics. It's available by print or electronic subscription. Subscribers may sign up for email notifications of new articles in topic areas of interest.

Professional Mariner: www.professionalmariner.com. A monthly journal of the maritime industry. Serious recreational mariners will find interesting articles to make them more aware of the nautical world that small craft shares with ships. Legislation updates and the casualty news and analyses are very instructive.

Sail: http://sailmagazine.com. A monthly magazine devoted to subjects of interest to racing and cruising sailors. Articles and information on the website. Different coverage from *Cruising World* and *Sailing Magazine*.

Sailing Magazine: www.sailingmagazine.net/home. Monthly large-format paper publication and online magazine. The website has articles on a variety of topics, how-to articles and tips, boat design reviews by naval architect Bob Perry, comprehensive used boat evaluations, and more. Different approach from *Cruising World* and *Sail* magazine.

Yachting Magazine: www.yachtingmagazine.com. Articles, equipment reviews, and features for power and sail mariners.

Yachting Monthly: www.yachtingmonthly.com. A magazine for boaters in European waters, but with information for all sailors. The website has articles on all aspects of sail cruising.

miscellaneous:

Distance Between Ports, Pub. 151 – a reference book from the NGA of tabulated distances between worldwide departure ports, junction points, and arrival ports. Although designed for ships, the information is useful for voyaging yachts and as a general reference. The NGA issues new editions approximately every two years. Download it from http://msi.nga.mil/NGAPortal/MSI.portal; click on "Publications."

International Code of Signals, H.O. 102, United States Edition, 1969. Washington, D.C.: U.S. Government Printing Office, 1968. Available in paper form or for free download at http://msi.nga.mil/NGAPortal/MSI.portal. Click on "Publications."

The Oxford Companion to Ships and the Sea, 2nd ed. edited by I.C.B Dear and Peter Kemp. Oxford University Press, 2005. Encyclopedic coverage of historical and modern nautical topics.

Vigor, John. "Black Box Theory:" www.johnvigor.com/Black_Box_Theory.html. Mr. Vigor's essay may make you think more seriously about seamanship.

nautical booksellers' websites: (a small sample)

Armchair Sailor: www.armchairsailorseattle.com. Books, worldwide charts, nautical software, miscellaneous products.

The Binnacle: http://ca.binnacle.com. Based in Halifax, Nova Scotia, the company offers a variety of marine products, including Canadian charts and publications.

Bluewater Books and Charts: www.bluewaterweb.com. Books and worldwide charts from many government and private publishers.

Bookharbour: www.bookharbour.com. Books and charts from many publishers.

Landfall Navigation: www.landfallnavigation.com Books and charts from many publishers.

The Nautical Mind: www.nauticalmind.com. This Canadian company offers a wide variety of nautical books, paper and electronic charts (North America and Europe from the Mediterranean to northern Norway), worldwide cruising guides, and software.

Publishers, U.K.: (publications available from nautical booksellers and chandleries)

Adlard Coles Nautical (A&C Black: London) www.acblack.com/nautical. Publisher of cruising guides, *Reed's Nautical Almanac*, and many other titles.

Imray, Laurie, Norie and Wilson, Ltd. (Imray), St. Ives, England. www.imray.com. Publisher of charts, pilots, and cruising guides for the Atlantic and Caribbean, the Mediterranean, and northwest Europe.

Kelvin Hughes (UK): www.kelvinhughes.com/leisure. The retail website is www.bookharbour.com. This website is good for researching nautical books and charts from many publishers.

Royal Cruising Club (RCC) Pilotage Foundation: www.rccpf.org.uk; click on "Publications." The RCC produces pilots and cruising guides for European waters, the north and south Atlantic, the Southern Islands, and Antarctic Peninsula, the journal of the RCC, *Roving Commissions*, (available to non-members), and has links to other websites of interest to sailors.

Wiley Nautical: www.wileynautical.com. Based in Chichester, England, Wiley publishes a wide variety of nautical books for sail and power boating, including sail racing.

RADIO and SATELLITE COMMUNICATION

ATIS equipment and requirements, explanation: http://licensing.ofcom.org.uk/radiocommunication-licences/ships-radio/faq/atis-faq.

ATIS information for pleasure craft: www.rya.org.uk/infoadvice/boatingabroad/Pages/atis.aspx. This RYA website is the starting place to investigate the radio requirements for traveling where ATIS is required.

Bridge-to-Bridge Radio Act: www.navcen.uscg.gov/mwv/regulations/33CFR026/33CFR26.htm.

Canadian marine radio: www.tc.gc.ca/eng/marinesafety/tp-tp14070-2915.htm.

Canadian MMSI: www.tc.gc.ca/eng/marinesafety/debs-obs-equipment-radio-mmsi-1607.htm.

FCC portal for the Maritime Mobile Service: http://wireless.fcc.gov/services/index.htm?job=service_home&id=maritime.

FCC ship's radio and operator licensing, U.S.: http://wireless.fcc.gov/services/index.htm?job=wtb_services_home.

Globalstar Satellite communications: www.globalstar.com/en.

Inmarsat-C SafetyNet: www.nws.noaa.gov/om/marine/inmarsat.htm.

Iridium satellite phones: www.iridium.com.

marine radio and frequencies, U.S.: www.navcen.uscg.gov/marcomms/boater.htm.

MMSI numbers for U.S. recreational vessels:
www.boatus.com/MMSI/faq.htm. This website will answer most of your questions about MMSI numbers in the U.S.

www.seatow.com/boating_safety/mmsi.asp.

www.usps.org/php/mmsi/home.php.

radio ground, Dynaplate: http://dynaplate.com.

radio watchkeeping: http://navcen.uscg.gov/marcomms/watch.htm.

RAINWAT: www.rainwat.bipt.be/rainboat.html. The official site with contact points for authorities in each RAINWAT country. No information applicable to small vessels.

satellite communication for small vessels: www.oceannavigator.com/content/pocket-satellite-communicator.

single-sideband distress frequencies and watchkeeping schedules, U.S. Coast Guard:
www.navcen.uscg.gov/marcomms/cgcomms/call.htm.

single sideband email:

Saildocs: http://saildocs.com. Email service for yachts. Works cooperatively with Sailmail.

Sailmail: http://sailmail.com. Email service for yachts via SSB, Iridium, and Inmarsat.

Winlink: www.winlink.org. Email service for licensed ham radio operators.

single-sideband frequencies, general: www.naval.com/hf-freq.htm.

www.navcen.uscg.gov/marcomms/high_frequency/default.htm.

single-sideband radio and PACTOR: www.docksideradio.com. Dockside Radio is a resource for information about marine SSB radio, FCC licensing, email, and weatherfax reception. The website says "Dockside Radio is committed to making sure your SSB and e-mail system is working properly, and that you understand how to set up and use your SSB and modem."

UK ship's radio licensing: http://licensing.ofcom.org.uk/radiocommunication-licences/ships-radio/faq.

UK radio and operator licensing guide: http://licensing.ofcom.org.uk/binaries/spectrum/ships-radio/of168a.pdf.

VHF radio, U.S.:
www.navcen.uscg.gov/marcomms/othrcoms/fcc.htm.

http://navcen.uscg.gov/marcomms/vhf.htm.

http://wireless.fcc.gov.

RIGGING, SPARS, FITTINGS (*see also* Miscellaneous; Sailing)
book:
Toss, Brion. *The Rigger's Apprentice: Tools and Techniques for Modern Traditional Rigging.* Camden, Maine: International Marine, 1997. This book combines Toss's earlier books, *The Rigger's Apprentice* and *The Rigger's Locker*. See Toss's website for more books and resources: www.briontoss.com/catalog/books.html.

dye penetrant testing:
Magnaflux testing: www.magnaflux.com.

www.promtechaerosol.com/dyepenetrant.html.

www.welding-technology-machines.info/inspection-and-testing-of-welds/liquid-dye-penetrant-test.htm.

Dyform rigging: www.navtec.net: Click on "Rigging."

hand-crimp lifeline terminals: C. Sherman Johnson Company at http://csjohnson.com.

mechanical terminals articles:
www.practical-sailor.com/marine/swaged-terminals-vs-screw-on-terminals.htm. A comparison of swaged vs. mechanical terminals.

www.practical-sailor.com/marine/terminals.pdf. Discussion of mechanical terminals.

mechanical terminal manufacturers:
Cast-Lok fittings: www.loosco.com.

Norseman® fittings: www.navtec.net. Click on "Rigging" and "Wire Rigging."

Sta-Lok® fittings: www.stalok.com.

Suncor Quick-Attach™ swageless fittings: www.suncorstainless.com/quickattach.html.

rigging and related products:
American Rigging Supply:www.americanriggingsupply.com. The company offers rigging supplies, products, and product support for the following manufacturers: Antal, CDI, Charleston Spars, Edson®, Forespar®, Furlex, Harken®, Hayn, Johnson, Navtec®, New England Ropes, Ronstan, Samson Ropes, Schaefer, Selden, Spinlock, Sta-Lok®, Tylaska, U.S. Spars, and Wichard. Links to the companies and specific catalog pages make this an excellent place to check when doing rigging research. Highly-recommended.

Landfall Navigation: www.landfallnavigation.com. Manual, hydraulic, and explosive cartridge rigging cutters.

Loos & Co. Inc.: www.loosco.com. Loos rigging wire and accessories. Click on "Product Catalogues" to download the "Cableware Catalog," which has rigging tension gauges, cable cutters, and more. The website has a glossary of wire rope terms.

Navtec®: www.navtec.net: Click on "Rigging." Wire, rod, fiber rigging and related products, Norseman mechanical terminals, and other hardware.

Rope Inc.:www.ropeinc.com/cat-wire-rope.html. Wire and synthetic rope.

Soverel 33:www.soverel33.com/Quicklinks/Fittings/Links.html. Links to manufacturers of rigging products.

U.S. Rigging Supply:www.usrigging.com. Wire rope, fittings, cable cutters, and hand swaging tools.

rigging inspection: www.lewmar.com/cms/assets/1/literature/navtecriggingservice.pdf.

synthetic rigging:
Guide to the use of Dyneema® and Spectra® for lifelines: http://offshore.ussailing.org/Assets/Offshore/SAS/PDF/Dyneema+Article.pdf.

Navtec®: www.navtec.net: Click on "Rigging" and "fiber rigging."

Rope Inc.: *see above* under "rigging and related products."
SAFETY (*see also* Emergencies; Navigation Rules; Radio)
accident reporting, U.S.: www.uscgboating.org/safety/accident_reporting.aspx. Blank forms.

ACR marine safety electronics: www.acrelectronics.com/default.aspx.

Canadian ship safety: Transport Canada Ship Safety Bulletins: www.tc.gc.ca/marinesafety/menu.htm. The bulletins have information relevant to recreational mariners. Search by alphabetical keywords.

Canadian waters, safety equipment requirements for foreign vessels: www.tc.gc.ca/eng/marinesafety/debs-obs-quick-quick_visitor-1610.htm.

CG66: see UK Maritime and Coastguard Agency, below.

cold water survival: *Cold Water Boot Camp USA* video: short version at http://vimeo.com/3838573. 30-minute version at http://vimeo.com/4534662. Explains the "1-10-1" principle, which could save your life. Video was produced by the National Water Safety Congress.
http://gcaptain.com/cold_water/?11198.

www.mariovittone.com. Click on "Boating Safety" and "Water Safety."

www.seagrant.umn.edu/coastal_communities/hypothermia.

www.ussartf.org/cold_water_survival.htm.

hydrostatic releases: www.cmhammar.com.

Ireland Code of Practice for the Safe Operation of Recreational Craft: www.transport.ie/upload/general/9650-0.pdf. The document includes statutory requirements and recommended guidelines for pleasure craft of all types. A comprehensive guide for small craft, no matter their country of operation.

lifesaving equipment: www.datrex.com.

man overboard, general: Loughlin, Clive."M.O.B. Could Your Crew Cope?" taken from a series of articles in *Sailing Today* magazine, Dec.2008 to Feb. 2009. Download the excellent 12 page PDF of the article at www.oceancruisingclub.org/images/stories/Publications/Seamanship/sailingtodaymob.pdf.

man overboard techniques analysis: *Practical Sailor*, Vol. 36, No. 1 (January 2010) pp.7-11.

NFPA codes: www.nfpa.org/aboutthecodes/AboutTheCodes.asp?DocNum=302.

offshore safety:

International Sailing Federation: www.sailing.org. Click on "Documents and Rules" and then "Offshore Special Regulations." In addition to the rules read the various Appendices for other important safety information. "Equipment Rules" has technical details for all yacht equipment. Offshore racing standards are relevant to all yachts sailing offshore. *See also* "Safety at Sea Seminars," below.

Offshore Racing Congress, ORC: www.orc.org. Click on "Rules and Regulations." Standards for racing yachts are also relevant to cruising sailboats.

US Sailing:http://offshore.ussailing.org/Offshore_Home.htm. Click on "General Information" and "Safety at Sea" and for a variety of useful links.

rescue devices:

Lifesling® owner's preparation guide, 2010 update: download from the Cruising Club of America's website at www. cruisingclub.org.

www.myboatsgear.com/newsletter/2009225.asp. Evaluation of rescue devices.

Safety at Sea Seminars: http://offshore.ussailing.org/SAS.htm. Sponsored by ISAF (International Sailing Federation), these day-long seminars include practical demonstrations of safety equipment. Highly-recommended for sailors venturing offshore.

safety equipment and techniques, links to studies: http://offshore.ussailing.org/SAS/General_Information/Safety_Studies.htm

safety, general:
www.mariovittone.com. Mario Vittone is a U.S. Coast Guard marine safety specialist who writes extensively on all aspects of boating and water safety. The website is updated regularly and it has a number of useful links.

Seatow®:www.seatow.com: Click on "Boating Safety."

Trimmer, John W. *How to Avoid Huge Ships*, see complete citation under "Navigation and Piloting."

U.S. Coast Guard Boating Safety Resource Center: www.uscgboating.org. Links to boating safety, regulations, safety defects and recalls, and other websites of interest to recreational mariners.

www.watersafetycongress.org. Website of the National Water Safety Congress. Safety resources and links.

SAILING and CRUISING (*see also* Design; Navigation and Piloting; Publications)
beginners new to sailing: www.newtosailing.com.

heavy weather sailing:
Bruce, Peter. *Adlard Coles' Heavy Weather Sailing*, 6th ed. Camden, Maine: International Marine, 2008. An all-time classic, this seamanship book recounts real-life storm experiences, and gives sound advice for managing a monohull or multihull sailing yacht in heavy weather. Everyone who ventures offshore to race or cruise should study this book.

Cunliffe, Tom. *Heavy Weather Cruising*, 2nd ed. Chichester: Wiley Nautical, 2006.

Dashew. *Surviving the Storm*. See complete citation under "sailing and cruising, general" above.

Pardey, Lin and Larry: *Storm Tactics Handbook: Modern Methods for Heaving-to for Survival in Extreme Conditions*, 3rd ed. Arcata, California: Pardey Books, 2008.

Roth, Hal. *Handling Storms at Sea: The 5 Secrets of Heavy Weather Sailing.* Camden, Maine: International Marine, 2009. This is a definitive book on managing a yacht in heavy weather, based on Roth's more than 200,000 miles at sea, his in-depth research, and his analysis of the pros and cons of the five basic techniques. This book will help you evaluate what you may read or hear about storm management from other sailors. A useful resource at the end of the book is a reprint of Fitzroy's 1858 *Barometer and Weather Guide*, which is still applicable to forecasting marine weather today. Highly-recommended.

Silver, Jan. *Heavy Weather Cooking*. See complete citation under "Crew."

high latitude sailing: see "offshore voyaging," below.

lee bowing: www.j105.org/docs/noleebow.pdf. This short essay by noted racing sailor and writer Dave Perry explains why he believes that this technique has no effect.

ocean-crossing rallies:

Atlantic Race for Cruisers: www.worldcruising.com/arc.

Caribbean 1500: www.carib1500.com.

World Cruising Club: www.worldcruising.com. Sponsors various worldwide ocean-crossing rallies.

offshore voyaging and high latitude sailing: (see also "sailing and cruising, general," below)

Atlantic crossing guides: there are a variety of guides available. Look inside each before you buy to see if it meets your needs.

Attainable Adventure Cruising: www.morganscloud.com. "The Offshore Voyaging Reference Site." The website has categorized information for offshore sailors, written by voyagers Phyllis Nickel and John Harries, with contributions from other experienced sailors. Good coverage of high latitude sailing. Sailors can ask questions and post comments on the website. The excellent and regularly-updated *Norwegian Cruising Guide* (in e-book and paper form) is also available here.

Beth and Evans:www.bethandevans.com: the website of circumnavigators and high-latitude sailors Beth Leonard and Evans Starzinger. In addition to many resources for offshore sailing, click on "Favorite Places" for high latitude destinations.

Cornell, Jimmy. *World Cruising Destinations*. Camden, Maine: International Marine, 2010.

———*World Cruising Essentials: The Boats, Gear, and Practices That Work Best at Sea.* Camden, Maine: International Marine, 2003. Excellent information for offshore sailors.

———*World Cruising Routes*, 6th ed. Camden, Maine: International Marine, 2008. Emphasis on yacht routes. *See also* Heikell, below.

Dashew. *Offshore Cruising Encyclopedia*. See complete citation under "sailing and cruising, general" above.

Desirable and Undesirable Characteristics of Offshore Yachts. See complete citation under "Design."

Heikell, Rod and Andy O'Grady. *Ocean Passages and Landfalls: Cruising Routes of the World*, 2nd ed. St. Ives: Imray, Laurie, Norie and Wilson, 2006. *See also* Cornell, above.

Howard, Jim. *Handbook of Offshore Cruising: The Dream and Reality of Modern Ocean Sailing*, 2nd ed. revised and updated by Charles J. Doane. Dobbs Ferry, New York: Sheridan House, 2009. Good advice for sailors planning to go offshore in boats of approximately 30 to 40ft.

Mapes, Ed. *Further Offshore: A Practical Guide for Sailors*. Dobbs Ferry, New York: Sheridan House, 2008. A clearly-written guide for the sailor who plans to begin sailing offshore. Captain Mapes's *Ready to Sail* is an excellent companion volume.

———*Ready to Sail: A Captain's Guide to Boat Inspection and Repairs: Preparation of Boat and Crew for Offshore Passagemaking*, 2nd ed. Dobbs Ferry, New York: Sheridan House, 2008. A practical guide to checking a yacht and its systems before heading offshore; it includes a number of good checklists.

Ocean Passages for the World (NP136), United Kingdom Hydrographic Office, 4th ed. 2004. Used by ships and some yachts planning voyages across oceans, it has information about ocean waters and routes not normally covered in sailing directions. See Cornell and Heikell, above, which are specifically written for cruising sailors.

Seiffert, Bill with Daniel Spurr: *Offshore Sailing: 200 Essential Passagemaking Tips*. Camden, Maine: International Marine, 2001. Sailors planning to go offshore should read this book and incorporate the knowledge in their preparations and during the passage. Highly-recommended.

Van Dorn, William G. *Oceanography and Seamanship*, 2nd ed. Atglen, Pennsylvania: Schiffer Publications, 1993. Technical analysis of the oceans, wave theory, and how vessels react to various conditions. Mathematical formulas for the scientifically-inclined, but the reader doesn't have to understand the technical details to find the book rewarding. Many excellent illustrations and diagrams explain the theories. Recommended for offshore sailors.

Vigor, John. *Seaworthy Offshore Sailboat*: see complete citation under "Design."

offshore yacht guidelines: see "offshore safety" under "Safety," above.

online study of cruising techniques, www.sailtrain.co.uk. Seamanship, navigation and piloting, anchoring, and other skills. A good introduction to the basics, with diagrams, photos, and links. Aimed at UK sailors, but relevant to all.

sailing and cruising, general:
Burke, Rory and Sandra. *Bluewater Trilogy: Managing Your Bluewater Cruise, Greenwich to the Dateline,* and *Bluewater Checklist.* www.burkepublishing.com; click on Bluewater. Each book is available separately. *Managing Your Bluewater* Cruise is a preparation guide; *Greenwich* is a travelogue of the Burke's cruise, with useful appendices; *Bluewater Checklist* has a number of checklists, covering subject areas from provisioning to safety, appropriate for a 40 to 50 ft. sail cruiser.

Colgate, Doris. *Woman's Guide to Sailing*. Camden, Maine: International Marine,1999. An excellent introduction to sailing for beginning and intermediate sailors. Clearly-written, with many photos and drawings. Includes basic navigation rules and tips for comfort and safety. Highly-recommended.

Cooper, Bill and Laurel. *Sell Up and Sail: Pursue the Dream*, 5th ed. Dobbs Ferry, New York: Sheridan House, 2006. A guide for sailors contemplating making a boat their home and cruising far and near. Written in an enjoyable style, the book covers all logistics

Dashew, Steve and Linda. http://setsail.com. This website has many resources for offshore sailors. The Dashews are circumnavigators and yacht designers, with extensive world voyaging under sail and power. The website describes their four comprehensive books and a video series: *Offshore Cruising Encyclopedia* (1232 pages); *Mariners Weather Handbook: A Guide to Forecasting and Tactics* (594 pages); *Practical Seamanship: Essential Skills for the Modern Sailor* (644 pages); *Surviving the Storm: Coastal & Offshore Tactics* (672 pages); *Offshore Voyaging DVD Series* (3 DVDs with over 5 hours of cruising video from all over the world). The books contain a wealth of knowledge and many practical ideas from the Dashew's experience and research. For the intermediate and advanced sailor, they are excellent additions to a nautical library, and the DVDs are good for all sailors. In my opinion, the books are somewhat overwhelming for a beginning cruising sailor, who may not have the experience to completely understand and evaluate some of the more complex information.

Doane, Charles. *The Modern Cruising Sailboat:* See complete citation under "Design."

Gibson, Rob. *RYA Boat Handling for Sail and Power*. Southampton, England: The Royal Yachting Association, 2008. An excellent book, with fine illustrations by Andrew Simpson, for learning the theory of boat handling. The book covers many different maneuvering, mooring, and anchoring situations.

Henderson, Richard: *Singlehanded Sailing*. See complete citation under "Crew."

Hiscock, Eric. *Cruising Under Sail: Incorporating Voyaging Under Sail*, 3rd. ed. Oxford: Oxford University Press, 1981. *and* London: Adlard Coles, 2008. (paperback re-issue). This is a classic reference for cruising sailors of all levels of experience. Although the book does not cover new developments in yacht design or electronic navigation, Hiscock discusses all the necessary skills and attitudes for coastal and offshore sailing and seamanship. His advice is detailed, conservative, and sound. Many world voyagers learned from this book, and it's still an excellent, resource, whether you sail a new yacht or a traditional sailing vessel. Highly-recommended.

Leonard, Beth. *The Voyager's Handbook: The Essential Guide to Bluewater Cruising*, 2nd ed. Camden, Maine: International Marine, 2006. Comprehensive discussions of everything you need to go cruising, from the vessel to the logistics of being away from home for an extended period of time. This book and Hal Roth's *How to Sail Around the World* are different enough in content and approach that both books have a place in a cruiser's library. Leonard and Evans Starzinger maintain an informative website for cruisers, with excellent resources and links: www.bethandevans.com. *See also* Hiscock's *Cruising Under Sail*, above.

Maloney, Elbert S. *Chapman Piloting and Seamanship*, 66th ed. New York: Hearst Books, 2009. Considered by many mariners to be the bible of boating, *Chapman* is the first book to have in your boating library. Millions of copies sold attest to its importance as the standard boating reference. Highly-recommended.

Nicholas, Mark. *The Essentials of Living Aboard a Boat*. Arcata, California. Paradise Cay Publications, 2005.

Pardey, Lin and Larry: *Capable Cruiser*, 3rd ed. Arcata, California: Pardey Books, 2010. Expanded from previous editions with new chapters, the Pardeys offer good advice on many topics based on their more than 200,000 sea miles much of it in engineless sailboats.

———*The Cost Conscious Cruiser: Champagne Cruising on a Beer Budget*. Arcata, California: Paradise Cay Publications, 1998.

———*The Self Sufficient Cruiser*, 2nd ed. Arcata, California: Pardey Books, 1997.

Parsons, Kathy. *French for Cruisers*: *The Boater's Complete Language Guide for French Waters.* Hallettsville, Texas: Aventuras Publishing, 2004. Spiral bound guide for everything a mariner needs to communicate in French, including basic conversational French. Arranged for fast reference, the book has illustrations of many items, including an engine and its internal parts. If you can't pronounce something you can point. This is the best French book for sailors. Highly-recommended. See next entry and Webb. *Yachtsman's Ten Language Dictionary*, below.

Parsons, Kathy. *Spanish for Cruisers: Boat Repairs and Maintenance Phrase Book*. Hallettsville, Texas: Aventuras Publishing, 2000. Includes basic conversation plus many words and phrases for everything technical on a boat. Arranged for fast reference, the book has illustrations of many items, including an engine and its internal parts. If you can't pronounce something you can point. This is the best Spanish book for sailors. Highly-recommended. See previous entry. *See also* Webb. *Yachtsman's Ten Language Dictionary*, below.

Roth, Hal. *How to Sail Around the World: Advice and Ideas for Voyaging Under Sail.* Camden, Maine: International Marine, 2004. Whether you're cruising close to home or have your eyes set on far horizons, this book should be part of your library. Hal Roth's more than 200,000 sea miles and his excellent writing and research skills make this, and his other books, a foundation for a good nautical library. Highly-recommended. *See also* Leonard's *Voyager's Handbook* and Hiscock's *Cruising Under Sail*, above.

Rousmaniere, John: *The Annapolis Book of Seamanship*, 3rd ed. New York: Simon and Schuster, 1999. This book, by an expert sailor and writer, will take you from beginning sailor to advanced mariner. It's used as a textbook in a number of teaching programs. Highly-recommended.

RYA books: www. rya.org. Click on "RYA Shop" and "Books." The Royal Yachting Association produces a number of excellent, well-illustrated, and reasonably-priced instructional books for beginners to advanced sailors and powerboaters. No matter what other books you have in your boating library, RYA publications will add to your knowledge and enjoyment on the water. The books are available in North America through online booksellers.

Stadler, Michael. *The Psychology of Sailing: The Sea's Effects on Mind and Body.* Camden, Maine: International Marine, 1988. This interesting out-of print book is worth seeking on the used book market.

Vigor, John. *Boatowner's Handbook*: see complete citation under "Maintenance."

———*The Practical Encyclopedia of Boating: An A-Z Compendium of Seamanship, Boat Maintenance, Navigation, and Nautical Wisdom.* Camden, Maine: International Marine, 2004, 2008. Alphabetically-arranged; covers some of the same topics as this book, as well as different topics. Clear explanations and good diagrams.

Webb, Barbara, Cruising Association, and Jeanine Simon, editor. *Yachtsman's Ten Language Dictionary*, 3rd ed. Dobbs Ferry, New York: Sheridan House, 2008. Helpful illustrations, nautical terms, names for boat parts, and many other words and phrases important to cruising sailors, in English, French, German, Dutch, Danish, Italian, Spanish, Portuguese, Turkish, and Greek. Recommended. *See also* Parsons: *French for Cruisers* and *Spanish for Cruisers*, above.

sailing and cruising websites:
www.bestboating.org/boatsail.htm. Links to sailing websites.

www.boatus.net/sailing.html. Links to worldwide sailing websites. (not affiliated with BoatU.S.)

www.noonsite.com: Up-to-date worldwide cruising information and links. An excellent resource.

www.onpassage.com. Worldwide cruising information, links to marine weather websites.

www.sailamerica.com/home.asp. A sailing industry website, with links to U.S. boat shows.

www.sailinglinks.com. Links to over 1,600 websites.

www.sailnet.com. Articles, sailors' forum, links.

sails and sail trim:
Bainbridge sailcloth: www.sailcloth.com. Glossary of sailcloth terms.

Chutescoop®: www.chutescoop.com. Spinnaker furling sock. Chutescoop® is a registered trade mark of the V.F. Shaw Co., Inc.

Dutchman sail flaking system: www.doylesails.com/cruising/dutchman.

Hancock, Brian and Sir Robin Knox-Johnson: *Maximum Sail Power: The Complete Guide to Sails, Sail Technology, and Performance.* n.p. Nomad Press, 2003. A good book for cruising or racing sailors.

Nielsen, Peter: *Sailpower: Trim and Techniques for Cruising Sailors*, Dobb's Ferry, New York: Sheridan House, 2004.

Ross, Wallace. *Sail Power: The Complete Guide to Sails and Sail Handling*. New York: Knopf. 1985. A classic. Some sail types and materials have changed, but the basics are still the same. Out-of-print, available used.

UK Halsey Sailmakers: www.ukhalsey.com/learningcenter/encyclopedia/encyclopedia4b.asp. A 56 page sail encyclopedia.

SYSTEMS and COMPONENTS (*see also* Electrical; Engines)

bilge pump ratings: www.boatus.com/boattech/bilgp.htm.

general systems:
Calder, Nigel: *Boatowner's Mechanical and Electrical Manual: How to Maintain, Repair, and Improve Your Boat's Essential Systems*, 3rd ed. Camden, Maine: International Marine, 2005. This book should be aboard every boat. It's a basic reference for understanding all the systems, whether you or a technician will do the work. Calder's writing is very clear and non-technical, and the photographs and diagrams are excellent. *See also* Gerr. *Boat Mechanical Systems Handbook*, below.

———*Boatowner's Practical and Technical Manual*. London: Adlard Coles. 2007. For beginners to advanced mariners this book covers topics from boat selection to equipping and sailing it.

Ferris Power Products: see complete citation under "Electrical."

Gerr, Dave: *Boat Mechanical Systems Handbook: How to Design, Install and Recognize Proper Systems in Boats.* Camden, Maine: International Marine, 2008. The engineering aspects of design and installation are emphasized, with many tables and drawings. In addition to mechanical systems, there is a good section on anchors, anchor handling, and anchoring. This book is recommended reading for designers, builders, and owners of power or sail vessels.

Vigor, John. *The Practical Encyclopedia of Boating*: see complete citation under "Sailing."

marine refrigeration:
Calder's *Boatowner's Mechanical and Electrical Manual* has newer information on specific refrigeration equipment than his refrigeration book; see next entry.

Calder, Nigel. *Refrigeration for Pleasure Boats: Installation, Maintenance, and Repair.* Camden, Maine: International Marine, 1990. A basic, general systems guide, somewhat out-of-date.

Frigibar Industries, Inc. marine refrigeration: www.frigibar.com.

Frigoboat Marine Refrigeration: www.frigoboat.com.

Kollmann Marine Refrigeration Specialists: www.kollmann-marine.com.
Sea Frost® marine refrigeration: www.seafrost.com.

Technautics, Inc. marine refrigeration: www.technauticsinc.com.

Thermal Dynamics Sales marine refrigeration: www.thermaldynamicssales.com.

Windvane self-steering:
Aires: www.selfsteer.dk.

auto-helm, Monitor™, Saye's Rig: www.selfsteer.com.

Beaufort®: www.beau-fort.com.

Cape Horn windvane: www.capehorn.com.

Hydrovane: www.hydrovane.com.

Navik: no longer in production; do an Internet search for a used one or parts. Suitable for light-weight boats to about 30ft/9m.

Windpilot: www.windpilot.com.

WATER and WAVES (*see also* Navigation and Piloting; Weather; Wind)
tidal bores: http://hyperphysics.phy-astr.gsu.edu/HBASE/waves/tidbore.html.

http://news.nationalgeographic.com/news/2005/02/0222_050222_tidalbore.html.

www.tidalbore.info.

wind and wave forecasts: see "worldwide weather" under "Weather," for websites.

wind speed, fetch, time, and wave height: *Bowditch*, Chapter 32, p. 442 *and* NOAA Mariners Weather Log, Dec. 2000: www.vos.noaa.gov/MWL/dec2000.pdf.

WEATHER (*see also* Water and Waves; Wind).
Weather websites outside your home country often have informative articles and links of general interest.

500mb charts: Sienkiewicz, Joe and Lee Chesneau, "500 Millibar Charts" at www.vos.noaa.gov/MWL/dec_08/milibar_chart.shtml.

Burch's *Modern Marine Weather*. See below for complete citation.

Chen and Chesneau. *Heavy Weather Avoidance and Route Design*. See below for complete citation.

books and websites:
Burch, David. *The Barometer Handbook*. Seattle, Washington: Starpath Publications, 2009. A full discussion of aneroid and electronic barometers and their use.

———*Modern Marine Weather*. Seattle, Washington: Starpath Publications, 2008. Excellent book for studying marine weather. *See also* Carr's *Weather Predicting Simplified*, below.

———*Modern Marine Weather Workbook*. Seattle, WA: Starpath Publications, 2008. Companion volume to Burch's *Modern Marine Weather.*

Carr, Michael William. *Weather Predicting Simplified: How to Read Weather Charts and Satellite Images*. Camden, Maine: International Marine, 1999. A clear explanation of weather charts and images, with charts and illustrations. *See also* Burch's *Modern Marine Weather*, above.

Chesneau, Lee: www.marineweatherbylee.com. U.S. professional meteorologist's informative website with links.

Chesneau, Lee S. and Ma-li Chen. *Heavy Weather Avoidance and Route Design*. Arcata, CA: Paradise Cay Publications, 2008. A book for the serious student of marine weather.

Dashew, Steve and Linda: *Mariner's Weather Handbook.* See complete citation under "sailing and cruising, general" in "Sailing," above.

Singleton, Frank: see citation under "European Weather," below.

Watts, Alan. *Instant Weather Forecasting*, 2nd. ed. Dobbs Ferry, New York: Sheridan House, 2001. A small-format book for land and sea weather.

———*Instant Storm Forecasting*. Dobbs Ferry, New York: Sheridan House, 2009.

———*Instant Wind Forecasting*. Dobbs Ferry, NY: Sheridan House, 2002 (first paperback edition).

Canadian weather:
Bowyer, Peter and John M. Gray. *Where the Wind Blows: Marine Weather in Atlantic Canada*. St. John's: Breakwater Books, 1995. The first half of the book is an excellent illustrated guide to general marine weather; the second half applies to local weather in Atlantic Canada. If you're going to cruise Nova Scotia, the Gulf of St. Lawrence, Newfoundland or Labrador have this book aboard. Available from the publishers at www.breakwaterbooks.com. Highly-recommended.

Environment Canada: www.weatheroffice.gc.ca/canada_e.html *and* www.weatheroffice.gc.ca/marine/index_e.html. In addition to selecting regional marine areas, click on "Educational Resources, Publications" and scroll down to the "Weather and Meteorology" link.

Caribbean weather: http://weather.mailasail.com/Chris-Tibbs/home. Caribbean weather and custom weather routing services from a professional meteorologist and sailor.

custom forecasts: www.commandersweather.com. Custom, specialized forecasts, and weather routing for racing and cruising yachts.

European weather:
See also the "worldwide weather" websites, below.

European Center for Medium-Range Weather Forecasts: www.ecmwf.int.

www.eurometeo.com/english.

France: Meteo France: http://france.meteofrance.com.

Singleton, Frank, weather website: http://weather.mailasail.com/Franks-Weather/Home. British meteorologist and sailor Frank Singleton's extremely comprehensive site: almost everything you need to know about forecasts, GRIBs, weather information resources, details for the North Atlantic, the Mediterranean, Adriatic, Baltic, Icelandic waters, and the Bay of Biscay. This is a must-read website, even if you're not sailing in those areas, because of the wealth of educational information about marine weather.

forecast links, including GMDSS: www.users.zetnet.co.uk/tempusfugit/marine/gmdss.htm. *See also* Frank Singleton's website, immediately above.

GRIBs:

GRIB and weatherfax article: Lee Chesneau, SSCA *Bulletin*, Feb 2010, pp. 24-27.

GRIB files, worldwide: www.grib.us. Select your geographical area of interest.

Gulf Stream:
Gulf Stream location: http://polar.ncep.noaa.gov/gsf.
Gulf Stream public websites: www.nws.noaa.gov/om/marine/faq.htm#6.

Gulf Stream weather: http://users.erols.com/gulfstrm. Jenifer and Dane Clark's Gulf Stream forecast website. These professional meteorologists provide custom weather routing for Gulf Stream passages. The U.S. government currently does not provide Gulf Stream forecasts.

hurricane records: http://earthobservatory.nasa.gov/Features/Hurricanes.

www.hurricane.com/hurricane-records.php.

www.hurricaneville.com/historic.html.

www.nhc.noaa.gov/aboutsshs.shtml.

hurricanes:
hurricane preparation guide, BoatU.S.: www.boatus.com/hurricanes/hurr_prep_guide.pdf.

Mariners Guide to Hurricane Awareness in the Atlantic Basin download at www.nhc.noaa.gov/marinersguide.pdf. An excellent book for mariners going offshore in the Atlantic.

National Hurricane Center: www.nhc.noaa.gov *and* a glossary at www.nhc.noaa.gov/aboutgloss.shtm. Resources about hurricanes, including forecasts for land and sea.

Saffir-Simpson hurricane wind scale: www.nhc.noaa.gov/sshws.shtml.

Ireland meteorological office: www.met.ie.

NOAA websites:
general: www.noaa.gov.

land and marine weather portal: www.noaa.gov/wx.html.

marine forecast, National Weather Service (NWS): www.nws.noaa.gov/om/marine/home.htm#text.

marine forecasts and weather links: www.nws.noaa.gov/om/marine/pub.htm. Informative NOAA publication downloads.

Mariners Weather Log: www.vos.noaa.gov/mwl.shtml. Also available in hard copy. "The Mariners Weather Log (MWL), a publication of the National Weather Service (NWS), contains articles, news and information about marine weather events and phenomena, storms at sea, weather forecasting, the NWS Voluntary Observing Ship Program, Port Meteorological Officers, cooperating ships officers, and their vessels." Very interesting reading.

offshore weather, NOAA Ocean Prediction Center (OPC): www.opc.ncep.noaa.gov.

offshore weather terms and symbols: www.opc.ncep.noaa.gov/product_description/keyterm.shtml.

weather glossaries:
http://forecast.weather.gov/glossary.php.

http://www.srh.noaa.gov/mrx/glossary.php.

North Atlantic and Pacific weather: www.marineweatherbylee.com. U.S. meteorologist Lee Chesneau's website, with links to synoptics and forecasts for the North Atlantic and Pacific, and educational information.

Northern & Southern Hemisphere weather: http://joseph-bartlo.net/articles/061097.htm.

radiosonde information: www.erh.noaa.gov/gyx/weather_balloons.htm.

Typhoon "Tip":
http://flhurricane.com/cyclone/showflat.php.

www.islandnet.com/~see/weather/almanac/arc2009/alm09oct.htm.

UK meteorological office marine forecasts: www.metoffice.gov.uk/weather/marine.

weatherfax, worldwide schedules: www.nws.noaa.gov/om/marine/rfax.pdf.

weather glossaries, general:

www.weather.com/glossary.

www.weather.gov/glossary.

weather phenomena and rhymes*:*
www.docweather.com/2/show/118.

www.islandnet.com/~see/weather/almanac/arc2006/alm06nov.htm.

www.oceannavigator.com/ July/August 2003.

http://wilstar.com/skywatch.htm

worldwide weather:
Buoyweather®: www.buoyweather.com. Free and paid access information.

Magicseaweed: http://magicseaweed.com. A surfing website with easy-to-read, animated coastal wind and wave maps and forecasts.

Noonsite: www.noonsite.com: links to worldwide weather websites.

Onpassage: www.onpassage.com: links to worldwide weather websites.

Windfinder: www.windfinder.com: A surfing website with a variety of useful information for mariners.

Windguru: www.windguru.com: Free and paid-access information for Europe, the Mediterranean, the Canary Islands area, Red Sea north, Egypt, Israel, Lebanon, Argentina, Chile, and Uruguay.

Weather Underground®: www.wunderground.com/MAR/?MR=1. Links to other marine weather sites.

WIND (*see also* Water and Waves; Weather)

wind speed, fetch, time, and wave height: *Bowditch*, Chapter 32, p. 442 *and* NOAA Mariners Weather Log, Dec. 2000: www.vos.noaa.gov/MWL/dec2000.pdf.

Watts, Alan. *Instant Wind Forecasting*. Dobbs Ferry, NY: Sheridan House, 2002 (first paperback edition). A small-format classic. See other Alan Watts titles under "Weather."

worldwide weather: see "worldwide weather" under "Weather," above, for websites with wind and wave forecasts.

TOPIC INDEX

[quotation marks denote spoken language]

Alfa
Kilo
Uniform
India
Sierra
3rd Substitute